Understanding Actuarial Practice

Stuart A. Klugman
Editor

Jeffrey A. Beckley
Patricia L. Scahill
Matthew C. Varitek
Toby A. White

SOCIETY OF ACTUARIES

Library of Congress Cataloging-in-Publication Data

Understanding actuarial practice / Stuart A. Klugman, editor.
p. cm.
ISBN 978-0-9759337-5-6 (alk. paper)
1. Actuarial science. I. Klugman, Stuart A., 1949–
HG8781.U495 2013
368'.01—dc23

2011050636

ISBN 978-0-9759337-5-6

First Edition

Printed in the United States of America

19 18 17 3 4 5

Contents

Preface

A critical point in an actuary's education is the transition from understanding the mathematical underpinnings of actuarial science to putting them into practice. The problems become less well-defined and the solutions less clear-cut. This is not only a challenge for candidates who are making the transition but also a challenge for those who are guiding their learning and assessing their performance. In 2003 the Society of Actuaries Board of Governors took the inspired step of moving a candidate's education in this transition from a self-study reading of textbooks followed by a proctored exam to delivery of the candidate's education through a supported e-Learning environment. Starting in 2006, candidates for the ASA designation began taking the Fundamentals of Actuarial Practice Course (FAP).

The FAP Course brought several new features to the education and assessment process. Among them were:

- Self-paced learning through online modules. The modules were designed to guide candidates through the material. This would be done through readings (both online and offline), review questions, case studies, activities, and exercises.
- Rather than organize the course by function or practice area, the course was organized around the control cycle. This is a framework for problem solving and decision making that begins with defining the problem, continues with designing the solution and concludes with monitoring the results. Candidates are made aware that external forces affect the process and that the work must be completed in a professional manner.
- Formal assessments evolved to become take-home open book problems that often required making judgments and recommendations to be communicated to the intended audiences, usually in the form of memos.

Fortunately, a suitable text was available (Bellis, et. al., 2003) covering the application of the control cycle to solving actuarial problems. In order to supplement the overview provided by this text, course candidates were asked to purchase several additional texts covering risk management, property and casualty insurance, investments, retirement benefits, health insurance, and life insurance and annuities. Because these texts were written for other purposes, disjoint sections of each text were used for FAP. This was both inconvenient and expensive for candidates. In 2010 a project was undertaken to create a text that would be purpose-written for FAP candidates with coverage of finance, life insurance and annuities, retirement benefits and health insurance.

Four authors with extensive experience were recruited to write the sections. Biographical information about each appears elsewhere in this book. They were asked to ensure that all the information on their subject that is covered in FAP appears in their section. However, while the FAP Course makes reference to readings in this text, the text itself does not reference other aspects of the FAP Course. Thus, this text also provides a stand-alone introduction to actuarial practice in each area.

The text begins with an introductory section that has a brief review of the actuarial profession, some comments on what it means to be a professional and a discussion of the Actuarial Control Cycle. It is designed to provide context for FAP candidates and for the rest of this book. Each of the four practice area sections of this book are self-contained and can be studied in any order. FAP candidates will skip from some parts of this book to others as their study in FAP is organized by the Actuarial Control Cycle and not by practice area.

As you read this book there will be references to "online resources." There is a dedicated webpage for this text. At it, you can download additional readings, spreadsheets that support various examples and exercises, and solutions to the book's exercises. These resources can be found at www.soa.org/FAP.

To both FAP candidates and those who want an introduction to how actuarial science is practiced in the four areas covered, I hope this book is both illuminating and enjoyable.

Stuart Klugman, FSA, CERA

January 2012

Acknowledgments

Many people contributed to the production of this book. Guidance throughout was provided by the Society of Actuaries' (SOA) e-Learning leaders, in particular, Steve Eadie, the e-Learning Chair and Jill Carpenter, the Fundamentals of Actuarial Practice (FAP) Curriculum General Officer. Several people reviewed drafts of the various sections, including Jill Carpenter, Kathy Eadie, Steve Eadie, Andrew Gillies, Juan Herrera, Warren Luckner, Kory Olsen, Marcus Robertson, Brett Roush, and Heather Waldron. Jules Gribble contributed a version of the control cycle that appears in Chapter 3. Ken Westover and Sheldon Selby assisted with the material on the Canadian Asset Liability Method in Chapter 18. Karen Perry, the SOA's Publications Manager coordinated all the work of turning our manuscript into a published text. She ensured that everything kept to schedule so that we would have this book ready in time for the January 2012 roll out of the revised FAP Course. I also want to thank the four authors who wrote most of the content. Producing high-quality work on tight deadlines is not easy, but they rose to the challenge. —*Stuart Klugman*

My thanks go to my wife Jean for her patience during the writing of the Life and Annuity Section. Also, I want to thank James Christou, Michael Kavanagh, and Chris Fievoli for help with the Canadian material. Finally, Stuart Klugman was a tireless reviewer which greatly improved my section. —*Jeffrey Beckley*

I am grateful for the encouragement and understanding I received from my husband, Gary Larreategui, and Nyhart's CEO, Tom Totten, as I juggled priorities while working on the Retirement Plans section. Stuart Klugman was an excellent reviewer of the material and I am glad he asked me to participate in this wonderful endeavor. —*Pat Scahill*

I am forever grateful to my wife Joy for supporting me through the exams, cheering my successes and helping me through difficult times. I am grateful to Sara Teppema for inviting me to participate in this project, and am honored to work with Stuart Klugman to complete the Group and Health section. I thank the many actuaries and other thought leaders who have valued my work over the years—and I thank you, the readers of this book, for seeking actuarial education and for using this book as part of your education. May you continue to grow and prosper in this rewarding profession. —*Matt Varitek*

I would like to thank my wife Ruth, and my daughters Aleah and Callie, for allowing me additional time away from home in the process of completing the Investments Section. Also, I owe much gratitude to Stuart Klugman for giving me the opportunity to write this material, and for working with me at each step along the way to continually improve the quality of the final product. Finally, thanks to the Finance and Actuarial Science departments at Drake University for granting me the time to spend on this project. —*Toby White*

About the Authors

Editor

Stuart A. Klugman, FSA, CERA, PhD

Stuart is Staff Fellow, Education at the Society of Actuaries (SOA), a position he has held since 2009. Prior to that he was Professor of Actuarial Science at The University of Iowa (1974–1988) and Drake University (1988–2009). He earned a B.S. in actuarial science from Drake University in 1970 and a Ph.D. in statistics from the University of Minnesota in 1975. He served on the SOA Board as both member and as Vice-President. He co-chaired the committee that redesigned the SOA's education system in 2005 and has been extensively involved in the creation and maintenance of the e-Learning modules. He is a co-author of *Loss Models: From Data to Decisions*, a required text for Exam C. In 2007 he received the SOA President's Award.

Authors

Jeffrey A. Beckley, FSA

Jeff is the Co-Director and Professional Actuary in Residence for the Actuarial Science Program at Purdue University. Prior to joining Purdue in 2003, he spent 18 years as a consulting actuary for life and health insurance companies and seven years working for life insurance companies. Jeff is a 1978 graduate of Ball State University. He has been a consistent volunteer for the Society of Actuaries since earning his Fellowship in 1980. Among other roles, he has served as the Examination Chairperson, the Chair of the Committee on Life Insurance Research, and has been on the Board of Directors for the Society of Actuaries.

Patricia L. Scahill, FSA, EA, JD

Pat is General Counsel for Nyhart, a leading independent actuarial and employee benefits consulting firm located in Indianapolis, Indiana. She has a BA degree in Mathematics from Indiana University and a Juris Doctor degree from the University of Maryland School of Law. Pat worked as an actuary, including more than 25 years specializing in retirement plans, before focusing on her legal expertise. Pat served on the Society of Actuaries Board of Directors, including two years as Vice President. Pat has been involved in the Education and Examination Committee for many years, and she helped launch the Fellowship Admissions Course.

Matt Varitek, FSA, MAAA

Matt is an actuary for the Arizona Health Care Cost Containment System (AHCCCS), which is Arizona's version of Medicaid. His primary responsibilities include rate setting for various programs offered by AHCCCS, risk adjustment modeling, and other efforts to prepare for the 2014 implementation of Affordable Care Act provisions. He has 14 years of actuarial experience in the commercial health insurance industry, performing individual and small-group pricing, reserving, forecasting, rating factor analysis, and support for provider negotiations. His previous employers include Blue Cross/Blue Shield plans in Arizona and Wisconsin, Fortis Health (now known as Assurant) and John Alden Life. He is active in SOA volunteer efforts and in leadership of the Arizona Actuarial Club. His essay "Beautiful Minds, Healthy Bodies" was published by the SOA in a 2009 e-book of actuaries' visions for the future of the U.S. healthcare system. Matt has a B.S. in mathematics from Illinois State University.

Toby A. White, FSA, PhD, CFA

Toby is an Assistant Professor of Finance and Actuarial Science at Drake University. After graduating from Kalamazoo College and The University of Iowa, Toby worked for four years at The Lincoln Financial Group in the mid-to-late 1990s. Thereafter, Toby was a consultant for Tillinghast-Towers Perrin in Chicago, and a visiting lecturer at The University of Illinois in Champaign-Urbana. Toby became a Fellow of the Society of Actuaries in 2000 and became a Chartered Financial Analyst (CFA) in 2003. In 2008 he earned a Ph.D. in Statistics from the University of Washington. He currently writes questions for Exams P, FM, and MFE, and has served in the past on committees for Course 5, Course 6, Course 7, and FAP. Before joining the MFE exam committee, Toby also authored a study manual for Exam MFE.

INTRODUCTION

Stuart A. Klugman

CHAPTER 1
Introduction

1.1 Purpose of This Textbook

The purpose of this textbook is to introduce you to four areas of actuarial practice. You have likely studied the mathematics that support actuarial science but have had less exposure to the financial security systems and products with which actuaries work and the considerations involved in their work. This textbook will help you make the transition from abstract, mathematical concepts to some of the common practical issues encountered in actuarial work.

The four practice areas covered each have a part of the textbook.

The first area of actuarial practice introduced in this textbook, investments, has relatively recently become recognized as an area of practice for actuaries. While most actuaries who practice in investments work in the insurance industry, actuaries have branched out into the broader financial services market. Actuaries now apply their skills to investment problems for mutual fund companies, asset management firms, commercial and investment banking firms and other financial services enterprises, as well as for traditional employers of actuaries.

The other three of the four practice areas introduced in this textbook—life insurance and annuities, retirement benefits, and health insurance—have been considered traditional areas of practice for actuaries for many years. Most practicing actuaries continue to work for providers of financial security systems or consult to such providers in the life insurance, retirement benefits, or health fields.

Actuaries also provide their services in casualty insurance, but that area of practice is not covered in this textbook.

All four areas of practice covered in this textbook are briefly described in the following sections.

1.1.1 Investments—Part 2

Most financial security systems consist of significant financial assets that must be managed in an advantageous manner. For example, a life insurance company may hold a life insurance policyholder's premiums for decades before a death benefit is paid.

The investment of assets is critical to a financial security system's success for a variety of reasons. Among them are:

- A higher rate of investment return may result in more profits or lower premiums for a life insurance company product. However, this must be managed in accordance with the amount of risk the life insurance company wishes to bear.
- A higher rate of investment return can provide larger pensions in a defined benefit pension plan and so the success of the pension plan is directly tied to investment performance.

- The investments must produce cash (such as from maturing bonds or stock sales) when needed to pay benefits in a health insurance program or for a casualty insurance company product (e.g., a car insurance pool). Ensuring that such cash is available to pay benefits is important in reducing risk for a financial security system.

1.1.2 Life Insurance and Annuities—Part 3

These were the first traditional products for actuaries. They are somewhat complementary in that life insurance provides protection against the risk of dying early while annuities provide protection against the risk of living too long. In either case, in return for paying money to the insurance company, the insured receives payment(s) that are tied to the length of life of a designated individual.

In recent times, the variety of insurance and annuity products has increased dramatically. In this textbook, we will explore the reasons for this evolution in insurance products and review representative insurance products.

This part will be devoted to two major functions that actuaries perform when managing these products. The first is setting prices, or pricing. Determining how much to charge for an insurance product is challenging due to the variety of factors (such as future expenses, investment earnings, and mortality rates) that must be modeled. An important aspect of pricing is recommending how a product's potential to produce profit should be measured.

The second function is setting reserves or reserving. Several entities (e.g., government regulators and taxing authorities) are interested in determining how much money the company should set aside at a particular point in time to ensure that future obligations can be met.

A third function is funding. Insurance companies must plan for the financial needs of the company over time. Actuaries in the finance area of practice work on problems associated with ensuring the insurance company's financial health over time. This work is analogous to funding problems encountered in other types of financial security systems. Funding problems will not be emphasized in the life insurance and annuities part of this textbook.

1.1.3 Retirement Benefits—Part 4

As noted, the primary life insurance actuarial functions are related to pricing and reserving problems. Managing pension plans primarily involves the third major actuarial function—managing funding problems. The key task in funding for pension plans is to determine the amount and timing of contributions to be made to the pension plan fund to allow the fund to pay the promised pension benefits when they become due.

This part will focus on methods of providing income to those who have retired from work. There is an extensive discussion of why this is necessary and the different ways in which retirement income may be provided. Examples include government programs, employer-sponsored pension plans, and personal savings.

While actuaries work in all aspects of managing retirement benefits, this section's primary focus is employer-sponsored pension plans. Employees have come to depend on this source of retirement income; thus, it is important that actuarial expertise be used to manage the long-term viability of the underlying pension plan. In many countries, the government mandates actuarial oversight of both government and private pension plans.

1.1.4 Health Insurance—Part 5

Similar to retirement benefits, health insurance is provided through a variety of mechanisms, including government, employer, and personal programs. However, two major differences exist between typical retirement benefits programs and health benefit programs. The first major difference is the nature of the health benefit. Rather than formulaic amounts of money provided under retirement benefits programs, the health insurance program provides either direct health care or reimbursement for health care-related expenses. As a result, a health insurance program involves an additional party—the entity providing the health care.

The second major difference between retirement benefits programs and health benefit programs is that most health insurance is provided through a short-term contract. The health insurance premium covers health-related incidents that occur in the next six months or one year. A new contract is formed to cover the next time period. This typically means that there is much less need to invest the health insurance premiums, and adjustments can be made quickly with regard to premiums if they are not sufficient to cover the health benefits. Unlike long-term insurance products, there tends to be far more short-term variability in claims costs resulting in risk and uncertainty.

As with life insurance and annuity products, the main actuarial tasks required to manage health insurance products are pricing and reserving. These tasks, along with a description of the great variety of health insurance products, are the subject of Part 5.

1.2 Prerequisites

While most of this textbook is self-contained, the one key prerequisite is knowledge of basic life contingencies. This is needed for the parts on life insurance and annuities and retirement benefits. The skill needed is the ability to determine the expected present value of life-contingent events. In particular, the concept of net (or benefit) premiums and reserves are assumed to have been previously covered.

1.3 How to Use This Textbook

As noted, this textbook is designed to introduce four areas of actuarial practice. Each part can be read separately without reference to the other part. This text was also written to be used in conjunction with the Society of Actuaries' Fundamentals of Practice (FAP) course. Candidates taking the FAP course will be directed to various pages in this textbook as appropriate as they work their way through the FAP online course materials.

The Actuarial Control Cycle is introduced in Chapter 3. The Actuarial Control Cycle is a process used by actuaries to manage their work and is generally described as a three-stage process—define the problem, design the solution, and monitor the results. In this textbook, we review the evolution of the Actuarial Control Cycle and illustrate the differences in the application of the Actuarial Control Cycle around the world.

1.4 Actuarial Work and the Actuarial Profession

Chapter 2 provides an introduction to actuarial work and the actuarial profession. It begins with a brief history of the actuarial profession and then describes what actuaries do.

Actuaries tend to work with financial security systems. This concept is explained in Section 2.3. It is followed by an expanded discussion of actuarial practice areas. The last part of Chapter 2 provides a discussion of the key competencies required to be a successful actuary.

Chapter 3 provides an introduction to and a description of the Actuarial Control Cycle. It is a general framework for how actuarial work is done, and it is the organizing principle used in the education programs of several actuarial organizations.

Chapter 4 closes the introductory part of this book with a discussion of actuarial principles.

CHAPTER 2

Actuarial Science and the Actuarial Profession

2.1 A Brief History of Actuarial Science and the Actuarial Profession

While the actuarial profession dates only to the 18th century, the business of insurance dates back almost 4,000 years. In 1800 B.C., the Code of Hammurabi discussed *bottomry*. "Bottomry was a loan or mortgage taken out by the owner of a ship to finance the ship's voyage."[1] If the ship was lost, the loan did not have to be repaid. This early version of marine insurance continued until the Roman era.

This section does not provide a complete history of the development of the actuarial profession. It highlights only a few of the major advancements.

2.1.1 Early Actuarial Applications

The material in this section is excerpted from *A History of Probability & Statistics and Their Applications before 1750* by Anders Hald (1990). The first person to bring an actuarial treatment to probability and statistics is John Graunt. In the 1530s, London parish clerks were obligated to submit weekly reports, called bills of mortality, on the total number of deaths and the number of those due to plague. The purpose was to provide an early warning for the next outbreak. While the data was readily available, Graunt was the first to publish an analysis of this data (*Natural and Political Observations Made Upon the Bills of Mortality*, 1662). Among his observations was that the ratio of male to female births is fairly stable over time and location. He also used the data to estimate the size of the population. Most significantly, he constructed a mortality table. It did not include all ages, and the two most reliable values he determined were the probability of surviving from birth to age 6 (0.64) and to age 76 (0.01). It appears he used geometric interpolation to fill in values at ages 16, 26, 36, 46, 56, and 66.

The next major advancement was in 1669 when Lodewijk Huygens used Graunt's table to determine the life expectancy for an individual who was alive at each of the ages in the table. The gaps in the table were filled in by assuming a uniform distribution of deaths in each interval—a practice that remains in use today.

Shortly thereafter, the new concept of a life table and of a probabilistic interpretation was applied to life annuities. Such annuities were commonplace, often being used as a device for governments to raise funds. An individual would give money to the government and in return receive a life annuity. At that time, the annuity payment was not dependent on age, so it was common to put the annuity on the life of a child. Hald (1990, p. 118) quotes rates that imply $a_x = 9$ regardless of age.

An interesting variant of the life annuity was the tontine (named for its inventor, Lorenzo Tonti). In a typical tontine, each member of a group of n_0 people, who are all about the same

---

1 Bernstein (1996), p. 92.

age, provides an amount b to the state. In return, each year, the state provides interest at a guaranteed rate, i, on the total fund, to be divided among the survivors. Thus, at time t in years, if there are n_t surviving participants, each receives $n_0 bi/n_t$ from the state. When the last person has died, the state keeps the fund. There are many variations on the basic concept of the tontine. The concept of a tontine has been outlawed for many years in some jurisdictions. See Jennings and Trout (1982) for a thorough treatment of the tontine.

A major step forward occurred around 1694 with the publication of "An Estimate of the Degrees of the Mortality of Mankind, Drawn from Curious Tables of the Births and Funerals at the City of Breslau, with an Attempt to Ascertain the Price of Annuities upon Lives" by Edmond Halley.[2] This was the first time reliable data was available on births and deaths. Unlike previous tables, he prepared values for each age and did some smoothing to make the results align with expected patterns. With his table, he was able to determine the value at any age of both single- and two-life annuities.

In 1725,[3] Abraham de Moivre attacked the problem of pricing annuities from a different direction. Using a function rather than a table, he calculated (using modern notation)

$$a_x = \frac{1}{i} - \frac{(1+i)a_{\overline{86-x}|}}{i(86-x)}, 10 \le x < 86.$$

This was done assuming $l_x = 86 - x, 10 \le x \le 86$, which today is commonly referred to as de Moivre's law. Having seen Halley's mortality table, de Moivre knew his approximation was too crude; however, performing calculations with Halley's table was laborious. As a compromise, he proposed that a piecewise linear function be used. So although today we tend to characterize de Moivre as an advocate for an overly simple model (a uniform distribution from birth to death), that is not so.

De Moivre remained a believer in using mathematical laws rather than empirical mortality tables. Although many other mathematical laws have been proposed to represent mortality since his time, the vast majority of actuarial work has been done using experience-based mortality tables.

By the middle of the 1700s, all the formulas (without modern-day notation) for obtaining net premiums for insurances and annuities on single and joint lives had been developed by de Moivre and others.

2.1.2 Development of the Actuarial Profession

In 1974, as part of its 25th anniversary celebration, the Society of Actuaries commissioned Robert Mitchell to write a history of the profession.[4] An excerpt from the book is available as part of the online resources for this textbook.

---

2 While famous in actuarial circles for his mortality table, he is more well-known for discovering the comet that bears his name.

3 His textbook was titled *Annuities on Lives or, The Valuation of Annuities upon any Number of Lives, as also of Reversions. To which is added, An Appendix Concerning the Expectations of Life and Probabilities of Survivorship.* Over the following 250 years, there has been a trend toward shorter titles for texts.

4 Mitchell (1974).

As society's attitude toward risk changed over time, there was more need for actuarial expertise. New financial security systems developed requiring actuarial expertise. Examples of these new financial security systems include workers compensation early in the 20th century and funded defined benefit pension plans in the mid-20th century. Today, the public demands sophisticated financial security systems to manage products such as modern universal life insurance and variable annuity products. Actuaries have had to continually improve their skills, models, and techniques to manage these sophisticated innovations.

In addition to managing financial security system products, actuaries are also responsible for helping ensure the success of the financial security system as a whole. Actuaries are also often involved in managing the risks that the underlying sponsor of the financial security system takes on through sponsorship of the financial security system, for example, managing the risks to a company sponsor of a defined benefit pension plan sponsored on behalf of the company's employees.

The additional responsibilities account for the view of actuaries as professionals, with responsibilities to entities (those who use financial security system products) beyond those who pay for their services (usually the financial security system or its sponsor).

A more recent history of the actuarial profession was written in 2004 by James Hickman.[5] It includes a description of some of the changes that have occurred in the 30 years since the Mitchell history was written.

2.2 What Actuaries Do and What Sets Them Apart

When you tell someone you are an actuary, you may get one of these responses:

- That's nice. I hear it is really hard. Don't you have to take some tests? I have a relative/friend/neighbor who is an actuary. Maybe you know him or her? What's that? I wanted to be an actuary, but the math was too hard.
- So, you use training in mathematics, probability, statistics, finance, and economics to measure and manage risk, usually in the context of services provided through a financial security system.

You aren't likely to get the one-sentence description provided in the last response. This response is a good description of what an actuary typically does. It is likely that if you are reading this book, you have a good idea of what defines an actuary and may already have some experience doing actuarial work. In this section, you will be provided with some definitions and a discussion of what sets an actuary apart from others who work in related areas.

Most professional actuarial organizations have a definition for an actuary. Here are four of them:

The Society of Actuaries (2010):

> An actuary is a business professional who analyzes the financial consequences of risk. Actuaries use mathematics, statistics, and financial theory to study uncertain future events, especially those of concern to insurance and pension programs. They evaluate the likelihood of those events and design creative ways to reduce the likelihood and decrease the impact of adverse events that actually do occur.

---

5 Hickman (2004), pp. 831–838.

> Actuaries are an important part of the management team of the companies that employ them. Their work requires a combination of strong analytical skills, business knowledge and understanding of human behavior to design and manage programs that control risk.

The Actuarial Profession (2010) in the United Kingdom:

> Actuaries apply financial and statistical theories to solve real business problems. In effect, they use their skills in maths and statistics to create theoretical models of the world around them.
>
> A typical business problem might involve analysing future financial events, especially when the amount or timing of a payment is uncertain. But it could also involve understanding something like the weather: assessing when and where devastating storms may hit can help predict risks, and their associated costs, for investments or insurance. So a lot of the work an actuary does might be thought of as risk management.

The Institute of Actuaries of Australia (2010):

> Actuaries are among the brightest people in the business world. They apply their mathematical expertise, statistical knowledge, economic and financial analyses and problem solving skills to a wide range of practical business problems. Actuaries help organizations to understand the long-term financial implications of their decisions, many of which can affect individuals as well as the wider community.
>
> Actuaries apply their skills in a variety of areas including:
>
> - Measuring and managing risk and uncertainty
> - Designing financial contracts
> - Advising on investments
> - Measuring demographic influences on financial arrangements
> - Advising on a wide range of financial and statistical problems.

The Casualty Actuarial Society (2010):

> Actuaries evaluate the financial impact of current economic, legal, and social trends on future events. The accurate and responsible matching of risk to price is the foundation upon which the financial integrity of the actuary's company or client rests. For these reasons, actuaries are known for their scientific approach and demanding standards.
>
> Because human events and their financial implications occur over long periods of time, an actuary is a researcher, a planner, and a decision maker. He or she is a specialist in the business world, and may be knowledgeable as well in a number of other disciplines, such as economics, law, health, and finance.

2.2.1 An Actuary Is a Professional

A thorough discussion of professionalism in general and actuaries in particular can be found in Chapter 3 of *Understanding Actuarial Management, 2nd ed.*[6] A few of the key points are:

- The profession has a specialized body of knowledge and skills necessary to perform some specific work. Significant education and experience is necessary to master that knowledge and skills.
- The profession provides value to society and does so with a high standard of ethical behavior.
- The profession is organized in a way that supports the two previous items.

The second point is especially important. Professionals, and actuaries in particular, serve not only their employers and clients, but the public as well. By having a code of conduct and a discipline process, high standards of behavior can be expected and maintained.

Besides the three components that apply to all professions noted previously, there are a few more that apply to actuaries (and some other professions):

- The profession has a continuing education requirement. For actuaries, this may be implicit through continuing qualification requirements throughout their career or explicit through a formal professional development requirement mandated by the profession.
- The profession has standards of practice. Many national actuarial organizations have developed standards of practice for various aspects of actuarial work. An actuary must follow the standards of practice to continue as a member of the organization.

2.2.2 An Actuary Has a Broad Knowledge of Financial Services

Many professionals work alongside actuaries in the general financial services industry. However, most of them (e.g., accountants, portfolio managers, and IT staff) tend to specialize in one part of a financial security system or organization that relies on their specific expertise. An actuary is expected to have some familiarity with all of these areas and many other areas of a financial security system. In some specific roles, an actuary is expected to have significant expertise in the specific area of the financial security system.

One way to view this breadth of knowledge required of an actuary is to examine the International Actuarial Association's (IAA) education syllabus. All member associations must include these topics in the prequalification education system as part of their membership requirements. The topics are listed here. All actuaries must be educated and appropriately examined on every one of these topics.

1. Financial Mathematics
2. Probability and Mathematical Statistics
3. Economics
4. Accounting
5. Modeling
6. Statistical Methods

6 Bellis, et. al. (2010)

7. Actuarial Mathematics
8. Investment and Asset Analysis
9. Actuarial Risk Management
10. Professionalism

Detailed information about each topic is available at the IAA website.[7]

2.2.3 An Actuary Has a Deep Knowledge of at Least One Area of Practice

Most actuarial associations require that members at their highest level have extensive knowledge of at least one subject area and familiarity with the others. The Society of Actuaries requires completion of all of the prequalification requirements for one area, with choices of:[8]

- Individual Life and Annuities
- Group and Health Insurance
- Retirement Benefits
- Investments
- Finance and Enterprise Risk Management

The Institute of Actuaries of Australia has a similar requirement, with these choices:

- Life Insurance
- General Insurance (also referred to as Property and Casualty Insurance)
- Global Retirement Income Systems
- Investment Management and Finance

The United Kingdom Actuarial Profession takes a slightly different approach. Two subjects are required at the specialist technical level and one subject at the higher specialist applications level. The subject areas are similar to those previously mentioned.

2.2.4 An Actuary Is a Creative Problem Solver

In the movie, *The Paper Chase*, Professor Kingsfield told his class of first-year law students "You come in here with a skull full of mush and you leave thinking like a lawyer."[9] What does it mean to "think like an actuary?" One view is that actuaries are creative problem solvers. In this context, being a creative problem solver means finding reasonable solutions to unstructured problems with limited resources and information.

Key points about actuarial thinking are:

- The result of your work is often not the only possible acceptable solution.
- The acceptable solution is rarely found in the back of the book.
- The information or data you wish you could have is rarely all available.

---

7 Full descriptions of these topics are available at http://www.actuaries.org/ABOUT/Documents/Education_Syllabus_EN.pdf, accessed March 7, 2011.

8 In 2013 the last two areas will be renamed Quantitative Finance and Investments and Corporate Finance and Enterprise Risk Management respectively.

9 www.imdb.com, accessed December 15, 2010.

- The time or resources required to build and run the best model is often not available.
- The results of your work will be affected by subsequent decisions made by people (such as policyholders) who react to the design of the product in unexpected ways.
- The future will be unlike the past due to known events with unknown outcomes.
- The future will be unlike the past due to unknown events.

The last two items may require some clarification. Sometimes, we know the future might be different. For example, when the United States reduced maximum speed limits to 55 miles per hour, automobile insurers knew it would have an effect on accident rates, but the magnitude of the effect was unknown when they developed new insurance premiums. In other problems, there may be changes that likely could not have been anticipated. Examples include extreme stock market movements and pandemics. The difference is that in the first problem, the unknown is the magnitude of the effect of a known change; in the second problem, it is the effect of an event that was not anticipated and may not happen at all.

By having a wide and deep understanding of the problem and by considering a variety of solutions, actuaries are able to bring appropriate solutions to difficult problems.

2.3 Financial Security Systems

Most actuaries work with financial security systems and generally in the financial services industry. This section provides an introduction to financial security systems. It is adapted from Carpenter (2000).

2.3.1 What Is a Financial Security System?

The term *financial security system* is used in a very broad context. A financial security system is an entity that provides financial security products to its members to reduce or eliminate the financial insecurity related to one or more of the economic losses that could cause financial insecurity to the entity's members. Financial security systems provide products that encompass life insurance, health care financing, retirement plans, property and casualty insurance, and nontraditional forms such as warranties or other coverage that provide for a member's economic well-being.

These various financial security systems often need to be considered together with each system proving coverage for a certain risk, thereby providing layers of protection. In the following descriptions of financial security systems, we review the layers of protection provided to users of financial security systems from the bottom up in the sense that we review the financial security systems that provide the most widespread coverage to users of financial security systems first.

Financial insecurity may be experienced if there is uncertainty regarding the continuation of future income. Financial insecurity is caused by an economic loss. The following is a partial list of the types of contingencies that could cause an economic loss.

- Death of the primary wage earner in the family causing loss of future income or significant funeral/final expenses.
- Disability of primary wage earner causing a loss of future income over a disability period ranging from a few weeks to permanently.

- Personal illness or injury causing unexpected medical expenses and loss of income.
- Living beyond an age with future income needs to maintain a standard of living but with no remaining sources of income.
- Living to an extended age with increased costs for medical coverage or for long-term care.
- Automobile accident with an unexpected need to repair or replace the vehicle or to pay for medical care and other expenses.
- Damage to property caused by fire, earthquake, wind, and so on.
- Other risks of equipment failure or product malfunction causing an economic loss.
- Environmental damage resulting in significant costs to restore property.

2.3.2 Examples of Financial Security Systems

2.3.2.1 Social insurance

The base level of protection against financial insecurity is often provided by social insurance. This is coverage established by the government. Typically, the plans provide income benefits at retirement, death and disability, medical expense payments, and workers compensation. In the United States, social insurance programs include old-age, survivors, disability and health insurance, workers compensation, and unemployment insurance programs. In Canada, social insurance programs include the Canada/Quebec pension plan, old age security and guaranteed income supplement, and provincial medical plans.

2.3.2.2 Group insurance and retirement plans

Employer-provided benefits make up the second layer of coverage or protection. Group benefits are generally provided to active employees and can include group life insurance, medical and dental expense plans, and disability benefits. These plans supplement benefits payable by social insurance programs.

Many employers also have pension and retirement plans that provide income for employees after retirement. Other post-retirement plans cover medical expense, death, and disability. These plans are often designed to supplement social insurance benefits.

Individuals who are self-employed or employed by an employer that provides limited benefit plans may be eligible to participate in a financial security system through a labor union or a professional or trade association.

2.3.2.3 Individual insurance

The final layer of protection comes from individual insurance sources. In this discussion, the term *individual insurance* encompasses all types of policies that provide coverage for an individual, as opposed to a group of individuals. Individual insurance programs include life, disability, health, automobile, and homeowners insurance. In addition, an individual annuity or personal savings account provides insurance in the form of retirement income.

In addition to the individual person, the business owner also needs protection in the event of the death of a key person as well as property and liability protection.

2.3.3 Financial Security System Model

A financial security system is an arrangement for financing unknown future benefits in which an entity (one person or institution) assumes an obligation to provide the future benefits to offset undesirable economic consequences that may be experienced by a second entity (person or institution). This is done in return for payments, by or on behalf of a second person.

Any financial security system can be described by answering the following questions.

- Who is responsible for paying the benefit?
- What is the benefit provided?
- Who receives the benefit?
- Who pays for the coverage?
- How much is paid?

Before answering these questions for the various types of financial security systems, there is one further distinction. A financial security system is defined as mandatory if all persons in a group or in society are required to participate; otherwise, it is described as voluntary.

2.3.3.1 Social insurance

Social insurance is a mandatory financial security system. There is a range of benefits provided by social insurance, including retirement, medical care, and workers compensation. Here is how social insurance relates to the descriptors of a financial security system.

- Who is responsible for paying the benefit? Government.
- What is the benefit provided? Generally, payments upon death, disability, rehabilitation costs, medical needs, and retirement income.
- Who receives the benefit? Plan participants or dependents.
- Who pays for the coverage? Employers and/or employees, retirees, and perhaps other taxpayers.
- How much is paid? The government sets the rates.

2.3.3.2 Group insurance

With group insurance, there is a contractual relationship between the group policyholder and the insurer. The insured persons and their dependents are third-party beneficiaries. The institutions (often called *providers*) assuming the obligation to provide benefits include insurance companies, health care service corporations, health maintenance organizations, preferred provider organizations, and others. In medical insurance, many providers contract to provide medical services directly, rather than reimbursement for the cost of medical services.

To acquire and retain employees, an employer must provide not only a fair wage but also a package of benefits that offsets the expense and economic loss resulting from medical treatment, disability, or death. Employers purchasing group insurance on behalf of their employees usually are characterized as single employers. Unions and multiple-employer groups also are policyholders of group insurance for their members. Single employer contracts make up by far the largest share of the group market, accounting for about 90 percent of all group policies in force.

Here is how group insurance relates to the descriptors of a financial security system.

- Who is responsible for paying the benefit? The provider.
- What is the benefit provided? Includes death benefits, disability income payments, medical and other health care expenses, and post-retirement medical coverage.
- Who receives the benefit? Employees or members of a group association (both while working and perhaps in retirement) and dependents.
- Who pays for the coverage? Premiums can be paid by any subset of the employer, employee, labor union, and professional or trade association.
- How much is paid? Usually set by the employer, perhaps in negotiation with the employees.

2.3.3.3 Retirement plans

Employers (or other plan sponsors) establish private pension plans to provide post-retirement income to their employees. The plan sponsor agrees to provide the covered employees with incomes during their retirement. The plan sponsor establishes a separate fund to hold the assets that are set aside to provide the future benefits. The plan sponsor is ultimately responsible to provide the promised benefits.

- Who is responsible for paying the benefit? The employer.
- What is the benefit provided? A lump sum or income stream at retirement and possibly disability and death benefits.
- Who receives the benefit? Employees and dependents.
- Who pays for the coverage? May be shared between the employer and employee.
- How much is paid? Usually set by the employer, perhaps in negotiation with the employees.

2.3.3.4 Individual insurance

There is a contractual relationship between the policy owner or policyholder and the insurance company to pay a benefit or claim to offset an economic loss. The insurance policy or contract describes what is covered and under what circumstances the benefits will be paid and to whom the benefits will be paid. For example, with life insurance a death benefit is paid to the beneficiary when the insured dies. An automobile insurance policy typically covers liability, medical, uninsured or underinsured motorist, collision, and other than collision.

Here is how individual insurance relates to the descriptors of a financial security system:

- Who is responsible for paying the benefit? The insurance company.
- What is the benefit provided? Benefits can include death, disability, annuity income, medical expenses, automobile, homeowners, and renters.
- Who receives the benefit? Policyholders and beneficiaries.
- Who pays for the coverage? Policy owner (who need not be the party insured or the beneficiary).
- How much is paid? The premium is specified in the contract.

2.3.3.5 Manufacturer's warranty

A service contract or a warranty is a form of a financial security system. Here is how warranties relate to the descriptors of a financial security system:

- Who is responsible for paying the benefit? The manufacturer.
- What is the benefit provided? Repair or replacement of the product.
- Who receives the benefit? The purchaser of the product.
- Who pays for the coverage? The purchaser of the product.
- How much is paid? The fee is set in the contract.

2.3.4 Providers of Financial Security Systems

In this section, the term *provider* is used to describe the institution assuming the obligation to provide benefits. The provider varies, depending on who pays for the coverage and the types of benefits provided. We will start with the most straightforward scenario—individual insurance.

2.3.4.1 Individual insurance

The provider of most individual insurance coverage is an insurance company. There is a contract between the insurance company and the individual policyholder to provide benefits to or on behalf of the insured in return for the premium payments. The insurance company assumes the risk and is the provider of benefits as specified in the contract. This contractual relationship exists for individual life and some individual health insurance, automobile and homeowners insurance, and annuities.

In the capital accumulation marketplace, there are more products and players. The variable accumulation annuity is a product used for retirement funding in which the policyholder invests in stock funds and shares in the stock market's performance. Accumulation annuities and other accumulation plans such as Individual Retirement Accounts and mutual funds are offered by other financial institutions such as stockbrokerages and banks, in addition to insurance companies.

2.3.4.2 Group insurance

In the group marketplace, it is generally the employer that sponsors the coverage, usually specified in a plan document or contract. There are a number of providers of coverage in this marketplace. In the case of medical coverage, the provider sometimes provides medical care directly, rather than offsetting the cost of those services. The following description of health care providers is from the perspective of U.S. private health care.

2.3.4.2.1 Insurance companies

Insurance companies offer a range of life and medical coverages. These products are typically indemnity-type benefits. Insurance companies also offer managed care products such as Health Maintenance Organizations (HMOs) and Preferred Provider Organizations (PPOs). HMOs generally provide service benefits, in that they provide direct medical services, rather than reimbursement for those services.

2.3.4.2.2 Health care service corporations

Health care service corporations write medical and dental coverage. In the United States, they cannot provide life and disability coverage, although they sometimes have affiliated companies that provide these products. They are not-for-profit entities. The majority of the Blue Cross/Blue Shield plans are health care service corporations, although many have converted to mutual or stock insurance companies.

2.3.4.2.3 Health maintenance organizations

HMOs typically offer comprehensive medical service benefits. They have direct contact with the health care providers. Some HMOs provide care directly through their own hospitals and physician employees. HMOs usually cover a local service area. They provide managed care and their coverages are usually service benefits, although most offer an "out of plan" option. The benefits are very comprehensive with co-payments per visit rather than coinsurance and deductibles. Some HMOs offer dental and vision care. They cannot offer life and disability coverage. Not-for-profit or for-profit companies can own HMOs. Examples of owners include insurance companies, health care providers, and Blue Cross/Blue Shield Plans. Some HMOs are free standing.

2.3.4.2.4 Preferred provider organizations

PPOs differ from insurance companies, health care service organizations, and HMOs in that they do not take the insurance risk. PPOs enter into a contract with health care providers and perform utilization review services. PPOs lease their provider contracts to insurance companies and employers. The insurance risk stays with the insurance company or employer.

PPO coverages are usually defined by what the employer or insurance carrier wants. The coverages range from comprehensive major medical benefits with coinsurance and deductibles to in-network benefits with co-payments per visit. Often, two levels of benefits are offered with a higher level applied to services from the contracted providers. PPOs offer health benefits, sometimes including vision and dental benefits.

Like HMOs, PPOs are sponsored by health care providers or owned by insurance companies. Claim processing is not done by the PPO but by the insurance company or employer's administrator.

2.3.4.2.5 Self-insured employers

Employers self-insure primarily to save money. Another reason for self-insuring is to avoid having to provide mandated benefits. It gives the employer greater flexibility. They can offer medical, dental, life, and disability benefits. The employer takes the insurance risk when it self-insures. Many self-insured employers use an insurance carrier or a third-party administrator to administer claims and to contract with a managed care network.

2.3.4.3 Retirement plans

In the private pension marketplace, the employer sponsors the plan and can be considered the provider of the benefit. There are two major categories of pension plans: defined benefit plans and defined contribution plans.

2.3.4.3.1 Defined benefit plan

Under a defined benefit plan, the plan document specifies the benefit that will be paid to the participant at retirement, termination, or death. Employer and sometimes employee contributions fund it. Various funding vehicles can be used. A third-party administrator may handle the administration of benefit payments. It is the employer, however, that assumes the investment risk and contributes whatever is necessary to fund the promised benefit.

In the United States and Canada, defined benefit plans are highly regulated, and there is generally some form of mandatory insurance that provides some relief in the event of a plan termination.

2.3.4.3.2 Defined contribution plan

In a defined contribution plan, funds are set aside, invested using various options, and made available to the participant at retirement. Throughout the accumulation stage, the investment risk is borne by the participant. There is no guarantee that a certain level of benefits can be provided.

At retirement, the accumulated funds are applied to provide income. This can be accomplished through the purchase of an individual annuity contract or through systematic withdrawals from the accumulated capital. If the participant elects to use the funds to purchase a fixed annuity, the investment and mortality risk is transferred to the insurance company issuing the contract.

2.3.4.4 Social insurance

The government is the sponsor of social insurance programs. The benefits are financed by general tax revenue and/or payroll tax revenue (i.e., an earnings tax, paid by employers, employees, and self-employed persons). The administrative functions can be handled by the government or contracted with another entity such as an insurance company or an administrative service organization. These functions include claim processing, disbursing of funds for benefits, determining compliance, and utilization review.

2.3.4.4.1 Medical

In the United States, the three largest government medical programs are Medicare, Medicaid, and CHAMPUS (Civilian Health and Medical Program of the Uniformed Services).

Medicare is provided for eligible elderly and disabled persons. It includes both service benefits and indemnity benefits. HMOs can contract with Medicare to provide benefits directly.

Medicaid provides coverage for lower income individuals. It is administered by the states and funded by both the state and federal governments. Many Medicaid programs have contracted with HMOs and are developing managed care programs.

CHAMPUS provides health coverage for dependents of active military personnel and retired military personnel and dependents.

Insurance companies and HMOs can interact with government programs as an administrator to process claims or they can contract with the government to provide benefits directly (e.g., HMOs).

National health care in Canada is defined under the Canada Health Act. A complete range of medical services, including hospital care and physician services, is provided. Health care is the responsibility of the provincial government and is financed by both the provincial and federal government.

2.3.4.4.2 Workers compensation

Workers compensation benefits include medical care, disability income, death benefits, and rehabilitation services. In Canada, workers compensation is normally administered by a Workers Compensation Board controlled by the provincial government. In the United States, an employer can satisfy the compulsory workers compensation law by obtaining private insurance (the most common method), by self-insurance, or by use of the state workers compensation fund.

2.3.4.4.3 Retirement benefits

In the United States, retirement benefits are provided by the Old Age Survivors Disability Insurance (OASDI) system, commonly called Social Security. Benefits are provided upon retirement, death, or disability. Benefits are progressive—benefits in relation to pay are larger for low-income recipients than for high-income recipients. The program is funded through payroll taxes paid by employers and employees.

In Canada, the Canada/Quebec pension plan, old age security, and guaranteed income supplement programs provide retirement benefits, disability benefits, and some death benefits.

2.3.5 Distributors of Financial Security Systems

In this section, we will discuss how the various financial security system product and plans are marketed and sold. We will see that how a product or plan is marketed depends on both the financial security system provider (the seller) and the financial security system consumer or sponsor (the buyer). We will look at the individual insurance market first and then employee benefits market second (group benefit plans and retirement plans). Distribution of social insurance is an extension of group insurance and retirement plans.

2.3.5.1 Individual insurance

Individual insurance is sold through a variety of channels. We will discuss the channels currently used for individual life insurance and for property casualty insurance.

2.3.5.1.1 Individual life insurance

The majority of individual life insurance is sold through agents who are licensed by life insurance companies to sell their products. Following is a brief description of the ways in which individual life insurance is sold.

- Captive agents or career agents—These individuals sell primarily one company's products.
- Independent agents or brokers—These agents are free to choose the insurance companies they represent and can present to the buyer the most competitive products or products from the highest rated company.
- Banks—In most countries, banks are not allowed to issue life insurance policies and take insurance risks; however, many countries allow banks and insurance companies to own one another or be owned by a common parent. Banks are often allowed to act as an agent for an insurance company.

- Direct marketing—This term is used to describe insurance companies selling directly to customers without the use of agents. Approaches include direct mail, telemarketing, direct response using a call center, and online.
- Fee-for-Service—Financial advisors, including attorneys and accountants, may provide expert advice such as assistance with wills, trusts, estate planning and investment tax, financing, and insurance. Payment is often based on an hourly rate or consulting fee for an assignment.
- Debit agents—These agents sell to the low-income market in amounts to cover funerals, collecting premiums at the insured's home or workplace on a frequent (such as weekly) basis.
- Employer-sponsored—Insurance companies work directly with employers to sell individual life insurance to their employees. Payroll deduction is often used.

2.3.5.1.2 Property and casualty insurance

Property and casualty insurers use distribution channels similar to those used by life insurance companies.

- Captive agents or career agents—These individuals sell primarily one company's products.
- Independent agents or brokers—These agents are free to choose the companies they represent and can present to the buyer the most competitive products or highest-rated company.
- Direct marketing—This term is used to describe insurance companies selling directly to customers without the use of agents. Approaches include direct mail, telemarketing, direct response using a call center, and online.

2.3.5.2 Group insurance

The marketing techniques for group insurance products are best described by separating the different product segments by size of policyholder, type of policyholder, and line of coverage sold. Our focus will be initially on single employer groups. The marketplace can be segmented by policyholder size, as follows:

- Small groups (2 to 50 employees);
- Pooled groups (51 to 200 employees);
- Experience-rated groups (201 to 1,000 employees); and
- Large groups (over 1,000 employees).

2.3.5.2.1 Single employer groups

2.3.5.2.1.1 Small groups

The following methods are used to market to small groups:

- Group sales representatives, selling business directly to clients or through agents and brokers;
- Directly by agents and brokers (without a home office representative);
- Exclusive broker arrangements or general agents; and
- Direct mass-marketing or telemarketing by home office marketing departments.

2.3.5.2.1.2 *Pooled groups*

Sales to pooled groups are generally made through group sales representatives working with life insurance agents, through brokers specializing in group insurance and/or through property casualty brokers.

2.3.5.2.1.3 *Experience-rated groups*

The marketing of experienced-rated groups is generally through group sales representatives. Brokers and consultants may also be involved with the marketing.

2.3.5.2.1.4 *Large groups*

For the most part, group insurance representatives working with employee benefit consultants market to large employer groups. The consultants are usually compensated on a fee basis paid by the client rather than the insurance company. Brokers are compensated on a commission basis, paid by the insurance carrier.

2.3.5.2.2 *Other types of groups*

Other types of groups include association programs, multi-employer welfare association trusts, and Taft-Hartley multi-employer trusts. Specialized brokers in a specific industry generally market association programs. Brokers and consultants that specialize in union-negotiated benefit programs usually market Taft-Hartley multi-employer trust plans.

2.3.5.2.3 *Marketing of products*

Insurance carriers market their various products in different ways. Some insurance carriers have their group insurance representatives market all of their product lines (e.g., group life, medical/dental, long-term care, and short- and long-term disability). Other insurance carriers use a segmented or specialized approach. As the marketplace becomes more complicated, there has been a trend toward specialization on the part of group representatives. Specialization may be a more prevalent approach to marketing in the large cities; in the smaller cities, the group representative may be more of a generalist.

2.3.5.3 Retirement plans

There are distinctions in the marketing of retirement plans based on the size of the employer group. For the smallest groups (2 to 50 employees), the employer would likely work with a financial planner who is often an insurance agent or broker. Insurance products and investment vehicles, offering tax advantages, would often be used to meet the retirement needs of the small employer.

Larger groups usually design their plans with the assistance of an employee benefit consultant who is knowledgeable of the regulatory environment, plan design alternatives, and providers of investment and administrative services.

The products used for funding retirement plans depend on the plan design.

2.3.5.4 Social insurance

Because social insurance is a mandatory program, no marketing is needed to assure participation. Employers in the United States and Canada collect the employees' portion of the tax and remit the employee and employer tax to the federal government. There are penalties if the employer does not comply with their requirements.

2.4 Insurance Industry Overview

The previous section provided a thorough discussion of financial security systems and their products, providers, and distributors. This section takes a closer look at the insurance industry itself.

2.4.1 Insurance Industry Introduction

As you learned previously, two of the several financial security system models are the group insurance model and the individual insurance model. Both of these models are used in the insurance industry, which encompasses a variety of organizations that provide insurance products to individuals, businesses, or groups.

Individuals and organizations use insurance products to reduce their financial risk, substituting a smaller, known premium for a larger, unpredictable expense. Some insurance products are designed to incorporate elements supporting wealth management to attract purchasers. Examples are universal life insurance and variable universal life insurance.

Generally, an insurer must have an amount of available assets that, together with expected investment income and expected future premium payments, is sufficient to pay future claims and expenses. Estimating the amount of assets required (i.e., the reserves) is a role for actuaries. Both actuaries and non-actuaries may participate in investing the insurer's assets to achieve the desired investment returns and profitability.

Insurance industries exist in most countries, but the industry structure, its products, and the system of regulation vary from country to country.

2.4.2 U.S. Insurance Industry Overview

The U.S. Bureau of Labor Statistics summarizes the basic characteristics of the U.S. insurance industry in the following excerpts taken from its website.[10]

> The insurance industry provides protection against financial losses resulting from a variety of hazards. By purchasing insurance policies, individuals and businesses can receive reimbursement for losses due to car accidents, theft of property, and fire and storm damage; medical expenses; and loss of income due to disability or death.
>
> The insurance industry consists mainly of insurance carriers and insurance agencies and brokerages. In general, insurance carriers are large companies that provide insurance and assume the risks covered by the policy. Insurance agencies and brokerages sell insurance policies for the carriers. While some of agencies and brokerages are directly affiliated with a particular carrier and sell only that carrier's policies, many are independent and are thus free to market the policies of a variety of insurance carriers.

10 U.S. Department of Labor (2011).

In addition to these two primary components, the insurance industry includes establishments that provide other insurance-related services, such as claims adjustment or third-party administration of insurance and pension funds. These other insurance industry establishments also include a number of independent organizations that provide a wide array of insurance-related services to carriers and their clients. One such service is the processing of claims forms for medical practitioners. Other services include loss prevention and risk management. Also, insurance companies sometimes hire independent claims adjusters to investigate accidents and claims for property damage and to assign a dollar estimate to the claim.

Insurance carriers assume the risk associated with annuities and insurance policies and assign premiums to be paid for the policies. In the policy, the carrier states the length and conditions of the agreement, exactly which losses it will provide compensation for, and how much will be awarded. The premium charged for the policy is based primarily on the amount to be awarded in case of loss and the likelihood that the insurance carrier will actually have to pay. In order to be able to compensate policyholders for their losses, insurance companies invest the money they receive in premiums, building up a portfolio of financial assets and income-producing real estate which can then be used to pay off any future claims that may be brought. There are two basic types of insurance carriers: *primary* and *reinsurance*. Primary carriers are responsible for the initial underwriting of insurance policies and annuities, while reinsurance carriers assume all or part of the risk associated with the existing insurance policies originally underwritten by other insurance carriers.

Primary insurance carriers offer a variety of insurance policies. *Life insurance* provides financial protection to beneficiaries—usually spouses and dependent children—upon the death of the insured. *Disability insurance* supplies a preset income to an insured person who is unable to work due to injury or illness, and *health insurance* pays the expenses resulting from accidents and illness. *An annuity* (a contract or a group of contracts that furnishes a periodic income at regular intervals for a specified period) provides a steady income during retirement for the remainder of one's life. *Property-casualty insurance* protects against loss or damage to property resulting from hazards such as fire, theft, and natural disasters. *Liability insurance* protects policyholders from financial responsibility for injuries to others or for damage to other people's property. Most policies, such as automobile and homeowner's insurance, combine both property-casualty and liability coverage. Companies that underwrite this kind of insurance are called property-casualty carriers.

2.4.3 Size of the U.S. Insurance Industry

According to the Insurance Information Institute (2011), in 2009 there were 1,106 life and health insurance companies and 2,737 property and casualty insurance companies in the United States. The companies collected \$934 billion in premiums and had \$4.4 trillion in assets. The industry as a whole employed 2.2 million people (which, in addition to those working for insurance companies, includes employees in reinsurance, agencies, brokers, and other insurance-related enterprises).

2.4.4 U.S. Insurance Industry Regulation

U.S. insurance companies are chartered and regulated primarily by individual states, each having its own set of statutes and rules. The McCarran-Ferguson Act, passed by Congress in 1945, ceded regulation of the insurance industry to the states as being in the public interest. There have been and continue to be challenges to state regulation, including proposals for a federal role in creating a more uniform system and allowing insurers the choice of a federal or state charter similar to banks.

Each state has its own requirements for chartering an insurance company. One of the most significant requirements is that the company maintains at least minimum levels of capital to support the business. An insurance company chartered in a state is called a domestic company; one chartered in another state is a foreign company.

State insurance departments oversee insurer solvency and market conduct. To varying degrees, they also review and rule on requests for rate increases for coverage. Personal lines of the property/casualty insurance business—such as auto and homeowners insurance and workers compensation in commercial lines—are the most highly regulated, largely because these types of insurance are generally mandated by state law or required by banks and other lenders. The National Association of Insurance Commissioners develops model rules and regulations for the industry, many of which must be approved by state legislatures before they can be implemented.

Primary responsibility for overseeing solvency rests with the state of domicile, the state in which the company is chartered. Special accounting rules are used to measure solvency. These rules, called statutory accounting principles, are intended to be conservative measures of an insurer's ability to pay future claims. The rules include restrictions on investments by the company as well as rules for minimum reserves on some products. Annual statutory financial statements must be submitted using a required form, called a statement blank. All of these forms require an actuarial opinion regarding the reserves. Companies with low levels of surplus assets, assets minus reserves, are scrutinized especially closely. Insurers with inadequate surplus may be declared insolvent and taken over by the state's insurance department.

2.4.5 Canadian Insurance Industry Overview

The Canadian insurance industry is similar to the U.S. industry with respect to the types of insurance companies and their products. However, there are significantly fewer companies, and the regulatory environment differs.

A 2009 report[11] indicates about 230 Canadian property and casualty companies with premiums of $37.9 billion and assets of $116 billion. This part of the industry employs 110,135 people. A 2010 report[12] indicates 96 life and health insurance companies held $474.9 billion in assets, collected $79.1 billion in premiums, and paid $58.6 billion in benefits. This part of the industry employed 131,900 individuals.

---

11 Insurance Bureau of Canada (2009).

12 Canadian Life and Health Insurance Association (2010).

The federal and provincial governments jointly regulate Canadian insurers. The federal government oversees the solvency and stability of companies chartered by the federal government. The federal Office of the Superintendent of Financial Institutions (OSFI) provides this oversight. The provincial governments oversee the solvency of the insurers with provincial charters. To put the relative responsibilities regarding solvency in perspective, OSFI reported that federally chartered life insurance companies received 90 percent of the Canadian life insurance premiums. Property/casualty companies overseen by OSFI represent 80 percent of that industry.

Canadian policyholders are protected from the effects of insurer insolvency through two not-for-profit insurance companies: the Property and Casualty Insurance Compensation Corporation and the Canadian Life and Health Insurance Compensation Corporation.

The primary role of provincial regulation involves the terms and conditions of insurance contracts and the licensing of agents and brokers. This includes product design, pricing, and marketing. Regulation is particularly strong with respect to mandated automobile insurance.

2.4.6 The Insurance Industry in Other Countries

2.4.6.1 United Kingdom

The U.K. insurance industry is somewhat larger than Canada's. It is closely tied to the insurance industry in the rest of Europe. The Financial Services Authority (FSA) primarily regulates U.K. insurance companies. The FSA is a regulatory body created in December 2001 to regulate the entire financial services sector, including insurance.

2.4.6.2 Mexico

Insurance is not as widespread in Mexico as in many other developed nations. The Mexican industry is small, with fewer than 100 companies. A very small number of these control more than half of the market.

2.4.6.3 China

Until very recently, the Chinese insurance industry was underdeveloped. Today, it is growing rapidly and is directly affecting economic development in the country. The industry faces challenges following its entry into the World Trade Organization (WTO). A wide range of external forces have an effect on China's insurance industry.

2.5 Actuarial Areas of Practice

You have just read an overview of financial security systems, including an overview of the typical providers and distributors of financial security system products and plans. Where do actuaries fit in?

Actuaries typically align themselves with one area of practice. Each of the areas of practice are generally based on the risks that a particular financial security system is designed to address. Some areas of practice are more specialized and provide support for a particular function within a financial security system. For example, actuaries practicing in the investment practice area often provide their services to manage investment problems found in a life insurance company or other financial security system.

Actuaries work to manage the risks inherent in the products and plans provided through financial security systems. They also help to manage the risks associated with the financial security system. For example, actuaries manage the accident claims related to automobile insurance (product risk management) and help manage the investment strategies of a life insurance company (financial security system risk management). Finally, actuaries also help manage the risks related to a sponsor of a financial security system. For example, consulting actuaries often help private employers manage the effect of sponsoring a defined benefit pension plan on the finances of the underlying sponsor.

2.5.1 Investments

2.5.1.1 Risks

Actuaries in these areas manage financial risks (financial effect from financial transactions) associated with the investment function: returns on investments, defaults, and asset-liability management. The well-being of an enterprise is also affected by operational risks (financial effect from nonfinancial matters) as well as issues of capital measurement, allocation, and management. Therefore, the entire risk "package" is increasingly becoming an area of focus for the actuary, with enterprise risk management a prime example. Once the operations of an enterprise are financed, decisions must be made regarding how to invest what the enterprise has while balancing risk and return.

2.5.1.2 Financial security systems

A wide variety of financial security systems (life insurance companies, health insurance companies, casualty insurance companies, annuity providers, pension plan funds, etc.) involve the investment of premiums or contributions to accumulate benefits to be paid later. Therefore, the risks associated with the investment area appear, and must be managed, in all of these financial security systems.

2.5.1.3 The actuary's contribution

The actuary practicing in the finance and investment area understands the investment needs of the relevant financial security system. For instance, are the needs short term or long term? What are the risk tolerances? What are the liability cash flow patterns? These actuaries also manage risks associated with financing new investments. Asset liability management (ALM) is central to the actuary's understanding of the business and the inherent risks that contribute to a company's profitability and solvency. Finance and investment actuaries understand operations of financial markets, available instruments, and embedded options. They understand a company's assets in relation to its liabilities. Finance and investment actuaries solve problems related to the risk of mismatch between assets and liabilities, credit risk, liquidity risk and equity risk, as well as market risks in general.

2.5.2 Life Insurance and Annuities

2.5.2.1 Risks

Life actuaries are concerned with financial risks associated with the variability of life spans. One risk is that an individual will die prematurely and thereby leave unfulfilled financial commitments. For example, dependents may be left without an adequate source of income. Life insurance (individual or group) is the primary product offered to manage this risk.

A second risk that must be managed is that a client may outlive their financial resources. This is often referred to as longevity risk. Products to manage this type of risk include annuities and long-term care insurance. Factors that include an aging population and longer expected lifetimes have resulted in an increased demand for longevity products while reducing the demand for life insurance.

While insurance protects the individual against premature death and longevity risks, insurance companies must manage their own risks to both make a return from premiums and investments and fulfill the promises made to policyholders. Accordingly, the life actuary takes into consideration not only the underlying risks of premature death or longevity, but also the interrelationships of:

- Insurance product benefits and guarantees;
- Target customers and risk pools;
- Anti-selection;
- Interest rates and the economic environment;
- Strategies and third-party contracts to manage risks;
- Tax and regulatory requirements;
- Legal restrictions;
- Various insurance product distribution channels; and
- Competitors.

2.5.2.2 Financial security systems

Providers of life insurance and annuities include traditional insurance companies, marketing organizations that serve insurance companies, and government entities.

2.5.2.3 The actuary's contribution

Life actuaries identify, model, and manage life and annuity insurance risks. They work in different areas and address a range of issues, product lines, and customer groups, including:

- Life product development (e.g., individual or group life term insurance, whole life insurance, and universal life insurance);
- Annuity product development (e.g., immediate or deferred annuities, fixed and variable annuities);
- Regulatory filing;
- Mortality and other experience studies;
- Reinsurance; and
- Products sold by captive agents, independent agents or brokers, banks, direct marketing, fee-for-service or debit agents, and employer-sponsored sales.

Actuaries working in this practice area are involved with the design, pricing, valuation, and risk management associated with life insurance and annuities. They design products, both short and long term, that are equitable to the consumer while also being competitive and profitable enough to sustain the company. Design considerations include benefit and premium patterns, how policies are underwritten, and options and guarantees for the consumers. Pricing is influenced by assumptions involving such things as mortality, lapses, expenses, profit targets, and the state of competition. Key considerations for valuations include methods of calculation, conservatism, and standards of practice. Risk management activities include actuaries' work on investment strategies, modeling, and ongoing monitoring of experience.

2.5.3 Retirement Benefits

2.5.3.1 Risks

The retirement actuary manages the risk that an individual may not have sufficient income when employment ends. These include the risk of outliving retirement income, losing retirement income due to a career change, and insufficiently funding retirement benefits. The time at which an individual leaves the workforce is determined by physical or cognitive soundness, energy, desire or interest, and/or the age at which it is socially acceptable to retire. Post-retirement risks include longevity, increasing health care needs, long-term care needs, inflation, and investment performance.

Beyond the post-retirement risks to individuals, risks from the plan sponsor perspective need to be managed. For example, there might be an unexpected increase or decrease in pension plan liabilities. Assets might increase or decrease with market movements.

2.5.3.2 Financial security systems

There is, of course, an interrelationship between the retirement area of practice and each of the other areas of practice—health and life, in particular. Financial security systems that address the risk of insufficient income at retirement include public and private pension plans. Public plans typically involve contributions based on salary while the individual is working and a salary-related income after retirement. Formal retirement programs are designed to address risks while balancing the needs of the plan participant and plan sponsor. Pension plans offered by employers are defined benefit plans, defined contribution plans, or a combination of defined benefit and defined contribution plans.

2.5.3.3 The actuary's contribution

A retirement actuary has expertise in the design, funding, and regulatory aspects of public and private retirement plans. The retirement actuary generally consults with private pension plan sponsors, typically employers on behalf of plan participants, which typically are employees.

A retirement actuary must understand plan objectives such as cost savings, employee retention, visibility of program, cash flow and cost volatility management, and the tradeoffs involved with certain decisions. For example:

- Cost savings with respect to benefit reductions;
- Lower long-term costs at the expense of added cost volatility;
- Facilitating retirement while encouraging employee responsibility; and
- Design objectives versus manageable administration.

Retirement actuaries design the plans, value the plan assets and liabilities, and determine benefit entitlements. They are mindful of the acceptable range of contributions to the plan based on the regulatory environment and the budgetary constraints of plan sponsors. They assess and monitor the risks and evaluate the current financial conditions of a plan—especially assets and liabilities—to provide benefits to employees and assure employer solvency, regardless of whether it is the employer or the employee who manages the plan's investment. To do this, the retirement actuary determines the amount of money required to pay for benefits and determines the appropriate contributions as well as the timing of those contributions. Some retirement actuaries also explain the effects of different investment choices and recommend investment policy to help clients meet their objectives.

2.5.4 Health Insurance

2.5.4.1 Risks

The health area of practice is primarily concerned with two risks; the risk that an individual has inadequate health care due to cost or inaccessibility and the risk that an individual has inadequate income caused by a health problem. Whether an individual has adequate health care depends greatly on the health care system and how it is financed.

A health care system provides a structure for a collection of public or private health care providers that determines how the provider services are delivered to individuals. Financing of health care differs by country. Services may be paid for by the government, by individuals, or by employers, and risks may be borne by the government, individuals, employers, health care providers, or private insurers.

The health actuary manages the product risks of health insurance by taking into consideration not only the expected or average health care costs, but also the interdependent effect of:

- Risk pools associated with differing customers;
- Selection by participants;
- Negotiated payment methods with providers;
- Relationship of benefit levels to the cost of the insured event to the participant;
- Relationship of benefit levels to the normal income of the participant;
- Health industry cost management practices;
- Availability of similar benefits from other sources;
- Tax and regulatory requirements;
- Legal restrictions; and
- Various forms of marketing and potential markets.

2.5.4.2 Financial security systems

Programs intended to address the risk of inadequate health care include government plans, contracts with provider organizations (hospital/physician groups, pharmaceutical benefit management firms or PBMs), including for-profit companies, and private (individual or group) health insurance and managed care policies. The risk of inadequate income due to a health problem is generally addressed through individual and group disability insurance policies.

2.5.4.3 The actuary's contributions

Health actuaries manage the financing and delivery of health care and health-related benefit packages and their associated risks. The health practice is diverse. Some examples of the range of issues, benefit types and customer groups the health actuary is involved with include:

- Employers, insurance companies, managed care organizations and health care providers;
- Individual and group purchasers of health care services;
- Fully insured and self-insured benefits;
- Small group and large group purchases;
- Active and retiree insureds;
- Long-term (disability insurance and long-term care) and short-term insurance products;
- Medical and nonmedical plans;
- Direct insurance providers and reinsurance companies;
- Special populations (e.g., Medicaid risk); and
- Government-provided benefits (social insurance).

Health actuaries design health care and health-related benefit packages to meet the competing objectives of those who fund, those who provide, and those who deliver health care services and benefit packages. Recipients of health care are certainly concerned with quality. They also typically desire low premiums, freedom of choice of providers, and comprehensive coverage. At the same time, health insurers need to remain viable. The health actuary is faced with competing objectives and the need for tradeoffs and balance.

The health practice area currently embodies a variety of product lines. Actuaries in the health practice area may work on macro-level issues, developing health care policy, and measuring its effect on the roles of public and private insurance. As a result, they are directly involved in the social insurance delivery of health care and health insurance products. They are also involved in plan design, including individual and group managed care and nonmanaged care medical plans, nonmedical product lines such as dental and disability income, long-term care, and employee benefit planning.

The actuary aligned with the health area of practice contributes to pricing, valuation, cost/benefit analyses (both short and long term) and other types of financial analyses. Accurate pricing requires measuring claim cost trends and forecasting future trends. The health actuary also conducts studies and analyses in areas such as population health and medical-technology effectiveness. Additionally, health actuaries are involved in managing the risks of health care providers.

The health practice overlaps with other areas of actuarial practice. For example, disability benefits are typically an area of focus for retirement benefits. Therefore, although an actuary may identify health as a specialty area, there is a role for health actuaries in other areas of practice as well. Conversely, retirement benefits actuaries tend to perform health care calculations.

2.5.5 Casualty

2.5.5.1 Risks

The casualty practice area addresses the risk of financial loss as a result of accident or injury or damage to property. Casualty actuarial practice deals with a very wide range of risks. On the personal side, individuals buy automobile insurance against losses arising out of damage they might do to others, either to their bodies or to their vehicles (or, for example, to utility poles), and for damage that might be done to their own vehicle such as by accident, by a hailstorm, or by theft. Individuals buy homeowners' insurance for their houses or apartments. And they may buy additional coverage to protect them from lawsuits, called personal umbrella coverage.

Companies buy insurance for risks involving vehicles. They buy insurance for their factories, stores, offices, and so on. They can buy coverage for business interruption due to a storm or power failure. They buy coverage for the medical expense and lost wages of their employees under the workers compensation statutes, which vary significantly by state and by type of employee. They buy insurance to cover their liability if someone is injured on their premises or by their products. Doctors, lawyers, and other professionals buy malpractice coverage for their professional liability. Airlines cover their aircraft and their liability for accidents. The range of risks covered by casualty actuaries is very great, and the actuaries must understand the characteristics of those risks.

2.5.5.2 Financial security systems

Financial security systems that address the risks of interest to the casualty actuary include insurance companies that provide property, automobile, and liability insurance coverage as well as workers compensation plans.

2.5.5.3 The actuary's contribution

In many respects, the functions a casualty actuary performs are similar to those of a life actuary. Casualty actuaries help set price, determine value, and conduct financial analysis of the various types of insurance and workers compensation.

The key commonalities between the casualty and life actuarial functions are pricing and reserving. It is vital to set an adequate yet fair price. Actuaries are involved in analyzing past experience and projecting the future cost of coverage, building in expense provisions, and helping to set a fair and adequate price.

Their work involves risk classification. In personal automobile insurance, for instance, key classification variables include age and experience of the driver, mileage, make/model/year of the vehicle, and location where the vehicle is garaged and driven. In homeowners insurance, key variables are location and construction (think of hurricane or earthquake risk). In medical malpractice, key variables are specialty and location. Neurosurgeons pay more than pediatricians, for instance, and New York is more expensive than Wisconsin because of differences in tort laws and the willingness of New York juries to award large verdicts—not because the doctors are better in Wisconsin. Setting a fair and adequate price also involves product design. Many casualty policies have cost-sharing provisions such as limits and deductibles, both of which affect claims and therefore price.

Reserving is a key responsibility for casualty actuaries. In some lines of business, it can take years for claims to be filed and paid. Sometimes, this is due to congestion in the courts. Actuaries have to use the most current data to project how much will ultimately be paid for accidents that have already occurred and help the insurance company set aside sufficient funds. This is a key component of the financial reporting of insurers.

The work that casualty actuaries perform differs from the work of life actuaries, specifically with respect to the range of associated risks. Loss distributions by size also differ in the casualty area of practice, although this is also true of medical expense coverage and some disability income coverage. Some casualty insurance products are characterized by many relatively small claims such as damages to personal automobiles. But others experience many small claims and a few very large claims, with major implications for both pricing and reserving. Actuaries work with distributions of losses by size to estimate the effect of policy limits and deductibles. Insurance companies buy reinsurance, that is, insurance on insurance, to protect themselves against large claims and against hurricanes, earthquakes, and other natural disasters. These distributions of losses by size are important in the pricing of reinsurance, in determining how much risk the insurance company should retain for itself, and how much it should "lay off" to the reinsurer.

Casualty insurance typically involves short-term policies. Most casualty insurance is for a term of one year, although shorter and longer terms occur. Unlike life insurance, or some forms of disability insurance, in which coverage is for many years or where renewability is guaranteed, casualty insurance can be re-priced and re-underwritten at each renewal.

Other areas in which casualty insurance differs from life insurance include claim expense and concentration:

- **Claim Expense.** Insurers spend significant amounts handling claims, which can be a significant cost, especially in the liability area, where lawyers and experts are required. Claim expense must be properly analyzed for both pricing and reserving.
- **Concentration.** While the law of large numbers can help reduce the variability of experience, there is another phenomenon called concentration of risk. If an insurance company has written all the homeowners policies in a Florida city that has been hit by a major hurricane, its loss experience will be worse. Actuaries can help manage this risk by modeling, by developing guidelines for the underwriters, and by analyzing alternative reinsurance arrangements.

2.6 Key Competencies for Actuaries

What are the key competencies that actuaries need to be successful?

The following was published on the Society of Actuaries website:[13]

> A competency is defined as a skill, knowledge, ability or behavioral characteristic associated with a specific profession.

That article also states:

> Today's actuaries use their advanced technical skills to satisfy increasingly complex business, decision-making and management demands. However, other nontechnical skills are also central to the actuary's success as a well-rounded business professional and advisor.

Actuaries apply their knowledge and technical and enabling skills on day-to-day work assignments. ***Technical competencies*** comprise the actuary's specialized knowledge, skills, and abilities. ***Enabling competencies*** include the general knowledge, skills, and abilities relevant for all professionals.

2.6.1 Technical and Enabling Skills

Varying levels of proficiency among professionals can be found within technical and enabling skills. Actuaries display progressively higher levels of technical and enabling skill proficiencies with experience and career progression. Proficiency levels reflect a continuum of expertise. Examples include moving from novice to expert, moving from having some knowledge and experience to being known as a leader in the field, or being a contributor on the way to being a shaper.

2.6.1.1 Technical skills and analytical problem solving

The following are some key technical skills for actuaries.

Applied Actuarial Analysis. Competency in actuarial science is the foundation of the actuarial profession. Actuaries often address problems relating to uncertain future events. Because insurance is based on scientific actuarial principles, financial aspects of uncertainties, such as premature death, can be exchanged for the certainty of a premium payment. Pension and social security programs require actuarial analysis based on contingencies, such as length of employment, covered earnings, and mortality. Investments and other financial transactions involving risk or uncertainty can also be modeled using actuarial techniques. In a dynamic and rapidly changing world, your knowledge must be continuously expanded to meet increasingly complex problems and to enhance the value added by actuarial analysis.

General Business Skills. The professional designation of "actuary" confirms that you have a broad knowledge of business, business disciplines, and management. Consistent with business needs and your professional organization's basic education requirements, actuaries have knowledge and an understanding of accounting, business law, economics, and corporate finance.

13 Society of Actuaries (2011).

Quantitative Skills. Actuaries are recognized for their expertise in the quantitative skills area. Actuaries demonstrate mathematical, analytical, and financial modeling skills while assessing, anticipating, and managing risk. They demonstrate the ability to apply advanced mathematics in a business or financial context. The quantitative skill set includes:

- Calculus, linear algebra, and probability;
- Mathematical and applied statistics;
- Financial mathematics;
- Contingency, frequency, severity, aggregate loss, and credibility models;
- Parametric and nonparametric models and
- Computer applications, languages, and programming.

Specialized Skills. Specialization comes with progression through education, examination, and on-the-job experience.

2.6.1.2 Enabling skills

Enabling skills include the general knowledge, skills, and abilities relevant to all professionals. Enabling skills are nontechnical, general skills that complement the actuary's technical skills. They are central to the actuary's success as a well-rounded business professional and advisor. The following is a list of some key enabling skills.

Change Enablement. Change is continuous and often rapid. Actuaries apply systematic thinking to change initiatives and act to overcome barriers to change and support change. Implementing change effectively involves developing and executing strategies and action plans.

Communication. Communication skills include both oral and written communication. Oral communication refers to both speaking and listening skills. Written communication refers to both writing and reading skills. The successful actuary communicates complex issues clearly, accurately, confidently, and persuasively in an individual setting or in a group discussion or presentation and uses language that is appropriate for the audience. Effective listening and reading helps the actuary clarify messages and relate understanding. Effective writing and speaking provides clear and effective expression of ideas.

Knowledge Management and Self-Development. A professional actively pursues opportunities to acquire and maximize knowledge, share knowledge, and learn from others. Staying current on new approaches, techniques, and tools relevant to the profession helps the actuary identify, create, and implement effective solutions.

Leadership. Leadership skills include setting direction and leading change, influencing, decision making, negotiation, and people management and development. Leadership skills apply to all positions, that is, an actuary does not need to be an executive in an organization to demonstrate leadership skills. Acting as a positive role model to others, setting clear and realistic priorities, taking initiative to identify and address issues, and acting within a context of achieving shared organizational goals are all examples of leadership skills.

Project Management. The actuary clearly defines and manages assignments and projects consistent with scope. Effective project management includes planning to prioritize and organize work and implementing processes to ensure delivery of high-quality products or services. Project management is central to planning and delivering quality work while managing risks and meeting goals.

Relationship Management. Collaborating and networking help actuaries to establish, build, and maintain value-added relationships, both internal and external to the organization of the actuary. Effective business relationships cultivate respect and trust.

Teamwork. The actuary is often a member of a team. Cooperation and collaboration with others (actuaries and nonactuaries) contribute to shared goals and effective performance.

2.6.1.3 Blending technical and enabling skills

Professionals take personal responsibility for seeking opportunities that will enhance their skills. It is important for an actuary to stay current with cultural and social trends, demographics, government and regulations, and the business and economic environment, as well as developments in particular areas of theory and practice that affect the actuary's work.

The combination of technical and enabling skills developed by an actuary are often referred to as "business savvy" or "business acumen."

The definition of business acumen used in Society of Actuaries' (SOA's) market research is: Broad-based knowledge of business disciplines, used to grasp the whole of a problem or situation and develop creative, implementable solutions. The actuary with business acumen perceives quickly the essence of business situations and acts accordingly; devises creative, systemic solutions to problems; balances attention between tactical detail and a broad strategic view; gets results by building processes that work and continuously improves them; exhibits a broad knowledge of business disciplines beyond their own areas of expertise.

Continuing Education. While a newly credentialed actuary has developed a certain level of knowledge and expertise, this should not be regarded as the end of an actuary's education. These educational accomplishments are a vital part of an actuary's progress. While achieving an actuarial designation is important, continuing training and practical experience are what qualifies an actuary to practice and to give advice on specific issues. A combination of educational achievements, practical experiences, and formal qualifications permit actuaries to practice within their areas of expertise.

2.6.2 The SOA Competency Framework

The following was published on the SOA website:[14]

> The SOA's Competency Framework for Actuaries is a tool to help actuaries make decisions related to their individual professional development and career management plans. It applies systematic, sound approaches to selecting professional development opportunities, focusing on the skills needed to go beyond technical and specific actuarial analysis.
>
> The goal is to promote professional development and lifelong learning that meets the needs of members, their employers and the public. In addition, new tools are being developed to support the framework, including a self-assessment that will identify individual strengths and opportunities for additional skill development.

14 Society of Actuaries (2011).

> A competency is defined as a skill, knowledge, ability or behavioral characteristic associated with a specific profession.

A comprehensive discussion of the competency framework is provided in an article by Eadie, Hall, and Powills (2009). The process of developing the framework began with having members brainstorm responses to the statement "Looking 3 to 5 years into the future, to be valued for their professionalism, technical expertise and business acumen, actuaries must have or develop skills that include..." More than 1,500 statements were received that were then distilled into 100 statements. The next step was to have a sample of members sort and group the statement, looking for similarities. Respondents were then asked to give names to the groupings they had created. Combining these results produced the eight competencies that make up the framework. They are, in no particular order:

1. Communication—Demonstrating the listening, writing, and speaking skills required to effectively address diverse technical and nontechnical audiences in both formal and informal settings.
2. Professional Values—Adhering to standards of professional conduct and practice where all business interactions are based on a foundation of integrity, honesty, and impartiality.
3. External Forces and Industry Knowledge—Identifying and incorporating the implications of economic, social, regulatory, geo-political, and business changes into the design and delivery of actuarial solutions.
4. Leadership—Initiating, innovating, inspiring, creating, or otherwise acting to influence others regardless of level or role toward a common good.
5. Relationship Management and Interpersonal Collaboration—Creating mutually beneficial relationships and work processes toward a common goal.
6. Technical Skills and Analytical Problem Solving—Applying the actuarial knowledge, skills, and judgment required to provide value-added services.
7. Strategic Insight and Integration—Anticipating trends and strategically aligning actuarial practice with broader organizational business goals.
8. Results-Oriented Solutions—Providing effective problem solving that addresses relevant interests and needs.

This list aligns well with the discussions previously in this chapter. For example, two of the key components of being a professional are here (competencies 2 and 6), and of all them work together to describe actuaries as creative problem solvers.

CHAPTER 3
The Actuarial Control Cycle

3.1 Introduction

The control cycle concept is not new, and it is something you almost certainly employ on a regular basis. For example, suppose you must decide on the best way to travel to work. Your first step is to understand the problem and its dimensions. It is not enough merely to get yourself to work. You will likely consider the amount of time for travel and its variability. Other factors are cost, comfort, and convenience. Your next step will be to evaluate a variety of options such as driving, carpooling, or taking various types of public transportation. You will then select the mode that appears to best meet your needs. If the process were to end here, it would be a decision process, but not a control cycle. The final step is to monitor the results of your decision. You might formally keep track of the time of your daily commute and its costs or just form a general impression of how it is meeting your needs. If the results are not to your satisfaction, you can use this information to restart the process. Maybe you discover that speed is more important (versus cost) than you anticipated. Perhaps the carpool you joined does not provide you with sufficient flexibility. Armed with new objectives and/or facts, a revised approach to commuting may be selected.

This is the essence of a control cycle approach: Understand the problem, make a decision, and then monitor the results, making changes as appropriate. A formal definition from BusinessDictionary.com is:

> Continuously repeating cycle of planning, monitoring, assessing, comparing, correcting, and improving plans, processes, and practices.[1]

A high-level overview is presented in Bellis (2004). She notes that

> The expression 'Actuarial Control Cycle' (ACC) is used in two ways: as a model to describe the fundamental nature of actuarial work, and as the name of a subject which since 1996 has formed Part 2 of the Australian actuarial education system. (p. 14)

She also notes that there has been criticism of this concept:

> The ACC has been criticized . . . as being no more than a commonsense feedback loop, which will not necessarily fit every actuarial task, and which is neither a new concept nor uniquely actuarial. . . . Such criticism has not prevented acceptance of the ACC as a useful structure for educational purposes. (p. 15)

As will shortly be evident, many entities have defined something called the Actuarial Control Cycle. There is no agreement about what modifications should be made to the basic control cycle to make it actuarial. And even once modified, the resulting process would likely apply to other professions.

In the following discussion, you will be introduced to a few of the manifestations of the Actuarial Control Cycle that have been developed. In the end, what is important is not the ability

1 www.businessdictionary.com/definition/control-cycle.html, accessed September 5, 2010.

to replicate one of them faithfully in your actuarial work, but rather to leave you with a foundation for doing quality work. A beneficial use of the Actuarial Control Cycle is to provide a framework for introducing new actuaries to the work they are preparing to do. This approach has been formally adopted by several actuarial associations as part of their education process. Examples include:

- Society of Actuaries—Fundamentals of Actuarial Practice Course
- Institute of Actuaries of Australia—Part II
- Faculty and Institute of Actuaries—CA1

3.2 Versions and Evolution of the Actuarial Control Cycle

3.2.1 Jeremy Goford's Control Cycle

The origin of the control cycle concept in actuarial work is often traced to the paper "The Control Cycle: Financial Control of a Life Assurance Company" by Jeremy Goford (1985). A good summary of the paper is provided by Andrew Summerfield (2007). This view of the control cycle was confined to the specific case of profit testing as an example of a control cycle. The cycle steps proposed were:

1. Initial assumptions
2. Profit test
3. Model
4. Analysis of surplus
5. Monitoring

After step five, there is a revision of assumptions and the process is repeated.

Goford (1985) points out that one benefit is satisfying "the need to communicate to shareholders the links between profit testing and the company's actual results."

3.2.2 Institute of Actuaries of Australia

In the mid-1990s, the Institute changed their curriculum to remove the separation of topics by product and instead focus on techniques that are relevant across all practice areas. The control cycle was adopted as the organizing principle for presenting this material. In an article explaining these changes to SOA readers, Knox and Lyon (1995) point out some advantages of this approach (p. 6):

- Furnishes an actuarial framework for later subjects;
- Concentrates on principles, approaches, and problem solving, without unnecessary attention to legislation and other details covered in later subjects;
- Builds upon the mathematically-based skills taught in the earlier subjects;
- Applies the cycle to a wide range of problems, thereby highlighting the opportunity for actuarial expertise to be applied in the wider field;
- Supplies a broad and flexible syllabus that can be easily updated with contemporary examples; and
- Provides for improved job opportunities as students will have better problem-solving and analytical skills in both the traditional and wider areas.

They go on to describe the aim of the control cycle subject (p. 7).

> The aim of the actuarial control cycle subject is to provide the student with the generalized actuarial approach necessary for tackling a range of commercial problems, including those associated with risk-based products and others offered by financial institutions. The subject is not specific to any single area of practice but draws examples and implications from many areas of work. This includes investments, finance, life insurance, general insurance, and superannuation, as well as non-traditional areas of actuarial endeavor.

To support this curricular change, in 2003 the Institute published *Understanding Actuarial Management: The Actuarial Control Cycle.*[2] The book was written to be the foundational textbook for Part II of the Institute's professional accreditation program.

The book presented the control cycle as a three-step process:

1. Understand, identify, and specify the problem.
2. Develop and implement the solution.
3. Monitor and respond to experience.

As with all cycles, the process is then repeated as often as necessary. The book added three additional features to the control cycle that make it more relevant to actuarial practice.

- Investments are critical to actuarial work. On page 2, a diagram indicates that it comes between Steps 2 and 3, although investments are likely to be a consideration at all steps.
- Professionalism informs all of actuarial work. In addition to the expectation that actuaries will do quality work, professionalism also implies that actuaries serve the public as well as their client.
- The economic and commercial environment has a significant impact on the actuary's work.

A key feature of the Institute's adoption of the control cycle is that the education is delivered through university courses and distance education.

3.2.3 Society of Actuaries

In 2001, the Society of Actuaries (SOA) began a project to redesign its education system. Among the many problems identified was that the introduction to actuarial practice was not successful from either learning or examining perspectives. Candidates learned a lot of facts about products and actuarial work, but with limited depth or understanding that could be carried forward. Two key issues were how the material should be organized and how it should be presented. For the first, the experiences of the Australian Institute and the UK Actuarial Profession showed how the control cycle provides an excellent organizing principle. As the others had done, the SOA abandoned the silo approach of treating each product and practice area separately. Unlike those organizations, the SOA did not have a well-developed means of delivering education through universities. As a result, it was decided to deliver this material through online education.

2 Bellis et. al. (2003).

The online course was titled the Fundamentals of Actuarial Practice (FAP) and became required for candidates in 2006. *Understanding Actuarial Management* was adopted as the core text for the course. As presented in FAP, the control cycle is:

- Define the problem.
- Design the solution.
- Monitor the results.

Unlike the previous presentation, there is no order to these steps. Movement between them can be in any direction. As with the Australian version, the process is surrounded by professionalism and an awareness of external forces.

In an article introducing the course to SOA members and candidates,[3] a list of benefits of this new approach is provided (p. 8).

> Within the context of the control cycle as a problem-solving framework, candidates will have an increased understanding of:
>
> - The role of the professional actuary.
> - Actuarial work/functions.
> - Competencies expected of all actuaries.
> - How core external forces integrate into actuarial work.
> - Key concepts within the context of common actuarial problems.
> - Traditional and nontraditional problems.
> - Common models for each practice area.
> - Selecting assumptions and how the process and considerations are critical to finalizing the design solution and monitoring results.
> - The application of the complete cycle and interrelationships between each cycle component.

With curriculum convergence in Australia, the United Kingdom, and the United States, it was appropriate to consider a revision of the core textbook. In 2010, the second edition of *Understanding Actuarial Management* was published.[4] Aside from making the book more relevant for all three organizations, the book has significantly expanded material on risk management.

Chapter 1 of the book explains what makes a control cycle actuarial:

> What makes the Actuarial Control Cycle distinctly actuarial is the nature of the work carried out at each stage of the cycle. The problem will usually (though not always) involve uncertain future cash flows. The process of defining the problem includes understanding the background, fully identifying all the issues and specifying them clearly to ensure that the client and the actuary agree on the work to be done. The design of a solution will almost always involve modeling. The actuary may have ongoing responsibility for monitoring the experience as it develops and advising on the response, or may seek to build flexibility into the solution. (p. 3)

---

3 Society of Actuaries (2003).

4 Bellis, et. al. (2010).

3.2.4 Another View from the Institute of Actuaries of Australia

In 2006, Julian Gribble[5] published an article summarizing an extended view of the Actuarial Control Cycle. He adds a word, to arrive at the Actuarial Practice and Control Cycle. He begins with the same three core items as the other versions, applying them to the development of models (in the most general sense) and calling this the "Analytic Cycle." Each item is linked to the others and the cycle can be progressed in any direction. He makes the following comment:

> This Analytic Cycle, provides the 'techie stuff,' which is important, but it is not the whole game. This is a necessary, but not sufficient, component of the ultimate business solution being reached. One way of characterising this is that it is one thing to get the numbers, but the real value add comes when you can make the numbers talk!

The Analytic Cycle is then embedded into a "Professional Cycle." There are four aspects to this, again with no particular order, but interlinked. These elements are:

- Professionalism—Includes compliance with professional guidance and standards, adherence to a code of conduct and responsibility to the public.
- Governance—Overseeing the management and control of the project, including risk management aspects.
- Environment—Includes legal, regulatory and other business constraints and how they may change over time.
- Implementation—In the end, it is the outcome that is judged and the best decisions will not succeed unless carefully implemented.

Pictorially, this can be presented as in Figure 3.1.

FIGURE 3.1 Julian Gribble's Control Cycle

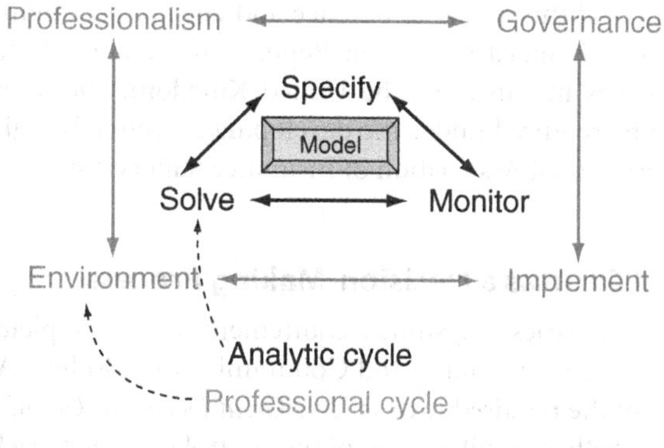

Gribble then continues:

> The Professional Cycle provides a context for analyses and options to be considered by businesses for making their decisions. . . . Again, the professional cycle is a necessary, but not sufficient, requirement for the ultimate business solution to be reached.

5 Gribble (2006).

Surrounding and supporting the Professional Cycle there is a set of more general attributes including judgment and materiality, integrity and ethics, communication and interpretation, intellectual exchange with the broader business and academic community, and business acumen. . . .

Ultimately, if the messages being sent are not received then, in effect, they were not sent and the work may as well not have been done. The application of these capabilities to an actuarial control process leads to Actuarial Practice. So, in summary we have [for Actuarial Control and Practice]:

Identify the problem
Models
+ Analytic cycle
+ Professional cycle
= Actuarial control cycle
+ Application to financial services
= Actuarial control
+ Actuarial capabilities
= Actuarial practice

Actuaries become valuable when they are engaging in Actuarial Practice. It is at that point, reflecting all the identified capabilities, not just the technical ones, that the focus changes to that of the users of the actuarial services rather than the providers.

The broad applicability of this actuarial practice and control paradigm is embedded in the concept of the annual Financial Condition Report, an established statutory requirement for insurance companies in Australia, the United Kingdom, and several other countries. The report is also to be required under the developing Solvency II regime in Europe and is endorsed by the International Association of Insurance Supervisors.

3.2.5 The Control Cycle as a Decision-Making Process

Part of the Society of Actuaries' Capstone (requirements to be completed just prior to earning fellowship) is the Decision Making and Communication Module. At the time this book is being written, one of the required texts is *How Great Decisions Get Made* by Don Maruska (2004). His steps are another manifestation of the control cycle approach:

1. Enlist everyone, discover shared hopes, and uncover the real issues. These provide a means to organize the task of defining the problem.
2. Identify options, gather the right information, get everything on the table, write down choices, and map solutions. This sets out a path to determining a solution.
3. Be prepared with alternatives and celebrate results. These do not map as well to the monitoring phase, but he does advise decision makers to look for changes that may require corrections and to prepare for that possibility.

3.2.6 Other Cycles and Cycles Within Cycles

The FAP course introduces several other cycles that relate to actuarial work. They will be briefly described here. The first is a Risk Control Cycle:

- Strategic planning;
- Short-term risk management; and
- Long-term risk management.

These are enabled through an overall enterprise risk management framework that includes monitoring and controls. The cycle also notes some commonly used strategies such as reinsurance, selection of risks, asset liability management, and hedging. Just as the Actuarial Control Cycle combines an understanding of the problem and environment with the technical skill to design a solution, the Risk Control Cycle combines a broad understanding of risks with actuarial tools to manage them.

A second cycle is the Model Control Cycle:

- Define the model;
- Build the model; and
- Maintain the model.

Here, it is assumed that the problem has already been stated and the work is confined to turning that statement into a model that can be used to provide a solution. This typically takes place between the problem definition and solution design phases.

The third cycle is the Assumption Control Cycle:

- Select assumptions;
- Quantify assumptions; and
- Monitor assumptions.

This takes place during the design solutions phase as the model is calibrated and refined.

The final cycle is the Monitoring Control Cycle:

- Data gathering;
- Analysis of results; and
- Feedback and recommendations.

This is an explication of how the results monitoring phase is carried out.

3.3 An Expanded Discussion of the Control Cycle

In this section, we expand on the steps in the control cycle. It will be followed by a section with several examples. The key steps in the control cycle, as noted previously, are to define the problem, design the solution, and monitor the results.

3.3.1 Define the Problem

How would you "Define the Problem?" Sometimes, the problem will be defined for you by a client or by your manager. Did they get it right? At other times, a problem will be identified by you. Did you get it right? In either case, you must effectively communicate and document the problem for all the stakeholders. The communication and documentation must identify the nature and potential effect of the risks involved.

Before you proceed to the second stage of the control cycle—Design the Solution—it is imperative that all parties, including you, your client, and your manager, understand the problem and agree that it has been defined appropriately. Only then should you move forward to consider the risks identified in the Design the Solution stage.

3.3.2 Design the Solution

During the Design the Solution stage, it is necessary that you constantly consider whether you are solving the right problem. Did you really define the problem properly? Have you identified and are you making provision for all the material risks? Are the risks you identified truly material? Let's have no million-dollar solutions to $10 problems. During the Design the Solution stage, you must communicate the potential solutions to all parties, document your work, and have your work peer-reviewed by other actuaries. You will note that three words are keys to each stage in the process: define, design, and monitor. The control cycle not only describes the big picture, but it is also embedded throughout.

The solution design will vary greatly, depending on the type of problem. It may be necessary to develop a model on which tests can be run. The model must incorporate the ability to test each of the critical risks. The assumptions used in building the model must be selected carefully and must be consistent with the material risks identified in the definition of the problem.

3.3.3 Monitor the Results

The third stage, Monitor the Results, distinguishes an actuarial solution from other solutions. Actuarial solutions characteristically extend over many years. As an actuary, you will undoubtedly monitor solutions designed by other actuaries. The monitoring process often leads to a new problem to be defined, solved, and monitored.

An actuarial solution must continue to be monitored—often beyond the career or lifetime of the original problem solver or solution designer—which is why the process requires excellent documentation and communication among actuaries. The monitoring often involves an ongoing review of financial results to determine whether the original solution remains valid.

The actions used to fix a flawed solution will vary dramatically, depending on the circumstances. Consider that some insurance policies that were sold during the 1940s remain in force today. These policies may have had face amounts of only $500. The current cost to process and send a letter to the policyholder may now be considerably greater than the annual premium. That possibility was probably not contemplated in the original solution. What, if anything, can be done about it now? Since the amounts are so small compared to current policies, does it even matter? Monitoring past solutions often gives you additional factors to consider as you develop solutions to new problems.

Here's another example. As a group, women generally live longer than men. As a result, men were subject to higher life insurance rates than women. In recent years, however, legislation has required insurers to use unisex mortality tables. What do you do? Use a mortality table based on blended male and female rates? Use male rates for everyone? Unisex mortality, then, is a new problem created by changing external forces that requires the review of existing solutions.

The strength of the control cycle is that it provides a problem-solving framework that can be consistently reviewed, refined, and applied. As discussed previously, the solution can involve multiple applications of the control cycle, depending on the nature of the problem.

3.4 Control Cycle Examples

3.4.1 Health Insurance and the Control Cycle

Health insurance is an area in which problems are constantly changing and evolving. Each year, the demographics of the groups being insured change. New pharmaceutical and improved health care delivery services regularly appear. The rate of increase in health care costs is highly variable. Health care regulators are under constant pressure to change the rules. These changing external forces require the actuary to regularly redefine the problems and re-establish solution designs. Solutions must be easily and quickly modified to reflect the changing environment.

3.4.2 Life Insurance and the Control Cycle

Life insurance is the product the public has traditionally associated with actuaries. The development and success of life insurance, in its many forms, established the need for and the delivery of services by actuaries.

The basic problem for the company is how an insurer, with a high degree of assurance, can collect a relatively small amount of cash on a regular basis from each of a large group of clients and then have sufficient funds to pay out a substantial amount upon the death of relatively few of its clients. Premature death has a small probability of occurrence over the short term, but such a death can be financially devastating to the client's family. The insurer and the insured both depend on the actuary to develop a solution that properly balances their diverse interests.

In North America, the proliferation of life insurance has led to external forces that are particular to the life insurance industry. Regulators have put many rules into place, such as requirements to establish reserve funds that the insurer sets aside so that money is available when a death occurs and to provide minimum cash values so that the insured is guaranteed some cash upon the surrender of certain life insurance contracts. Regulators also require many detailed reports on the financial status of an insurer and each of its product lines. Life insurance is a contract that can be applied over a short term or over a lifetime. Life insurance products can offer guaranteed or variable premiums. They can be issued to an individual or to a group. Each life insurance contract has its own unique risks.

A life insurance solution to the premature death problem has many aspects. What form of premium will be collected? What are the insurer's anticipated expenses? What is the target profit? What investment return can the insurer attain with the collected premiums? How will insured lives be selected through the underwriting process? What are sufficient reserves? What reserves are required?

What is the possibility that the insured will voluntarily or involuntarily cease premium payments? What happens if the insured stops premium payments? What is the regulatory environment?

While monitoring the results, the actuary must be satisfied that both the insurer and the insured have achieved—or will achieve—the desired results. During this process, the actuary must continually consider the answers to the many questions presented previously.

3.4.3 Credit or Loan Insurance and the Control Cycle

Credit insurance is a contract that pays the outstanding loan balance should the borrower die before the loan is repaid. It can be issued to an individual borrower, or a financial institution can insure a class of loans.

Similar to individual life insurance, the basic problem is the ability to provide an amount of money on the death of the insured. In contrast to individual life insurance, however, the amount of the death benefit is equal to the outstanding loan balance at the date of death, so the insurer's obligation is unknown until death occurs. The cost of insurance depends on whether the borrower makes regular payments of a specified amount or if the borrower makes special loan repayments. The amount insured over time is often not known with certainty when the insurance is purchased. The form of premium payment can further expand the problem. Will a single premium—such as a lump sum amount added to the loan—be used? Will a monthly premium based on the outstanding balance at the beginning of the month be used? Each has its own advantages.

An acceptable solution will be dependent on the premium payment method, the insurer's anticipated expenses and target profit, the regulatory environment, and the possibility that the insured will pay off the loan early or will default on loan payments. Generally, credit insurers will not hold the same type of reserve as for individual life insurance. For credit insurance, the insurer will hold unearned premium reserves in cases in which a single premium was paid or an incurred but not reported reserve to recognize the delay that occurs between the date of death and the filing of a claim.

In monitoring the results, the actuary must again be satisfied that both the insurer and the insured have or will achieve the desired result.

3.4.4 Disability Insurance and the Control Cycle

Disability insurance contracts pay a specified monthly amount to a person who has become disabled and is unable to work. They can be issued to an individual or to a company that wishes to insure a key employee and/or to cover business expenses (such as to replace an employee for a period of time). In contrast to life insurance, where death is final, people do recover from some disabilities; therefore, the basic problem is much different.

Disability insurance programs require actuarial knowledge and experience. In addition to mortality rates, the actuary must consider rates at which people are expected to become disabled (disability incidence rates), and the rates that the disability income will cease because the disabled person recovers (disability recovery rates). An actuary must determine the amount of money required to continue payments to people receiving disability income.

When applying the control cycle to disability insurance products, the transition between Define the Problem and Develop the Solution is critical and complex. Instead of a single lump sum, we now want to provide a monthly benefit that is payable only while the insured remains disabled. Further, we must recognize whether benefits are payable when the insured cannot perform his or her own job or any job, or a combination of the two. If the insured recovers, under what conditions do benefits become payable again? The solution will depend on the length of the benefit period, the contingency of becoming disabled, the contingency of recovery, the contingency of death, and the waiting period before benefits begin. As for other types of insurance, several factors must also be considered, including the insurer's anticipated expenses and target profit; the investment return of the insurer; and the underwriting process. Other factors to be considered include the reserves required so that funds are available when a disability occurs, the possibility that the insured will voluntarily or involuntarily cease premium payments, and the regulatory environment.

One issue with disability insurance is that there will be claims that the actuary does not know about but will need to include in his or her estimates (e.g., incurred claims where information is not available because of the waiting period). Reserving for these incurred but not reported (IBNR) claims needs to be taken into consideration.

3.4.5 Annuities and the Control Cycle

This product is the opposite of life insurance. Generally, a lump sum is paid upfront by the insured to the insurer. The insurer then pays a predetermined income to the annuitant (the insured) for as long as the annuitant lives. The basic problem is how to make certain that, at any point in time, the insurer has sufficient funds to guarantee payment of all future benefits. The insurer's risk has changed from the possibility that an individual will die at a younger than expected age to the annuitant living longer than expected. What will happen if mortality rates decline?

To design the solution, the investment of the lump sum premium will be critical. What happens if the firm does not earn enough with its investments? In contrast to other insurance, annuity pricing changes almost daily, since the long-term rates at which the lump sum can be invested can fluctuate. Annuity markets are competitive. What do you do if your firm's competitors offer substantially lower premium rates? Actuaries project annuity cash flows for a number of years (25, for instance) and select assets for investment that significantly increase the possibility that investment cash flows will match the annuity cash flows.

For annuities, monitoring the results is probably the most important part of the control cycle. The actuary must again be satisfied that both the insurer and the insured have or will achieve the desired result. Annuities can cause "reserve strain" for an insurer since regulations and actuarial standards of practice may require the company to hold an amount in reserve that is greater than the single premium the insurer received. This extra reserve strain comes out of the insurer's own surplus capital. The insurer can release the extra reserve over time. The existence of this reserve strain, however, means that in monitoring the results, the actuary must be careful to maintain premiums at a level that does not attract more business than the insurer can accept without unreasonably impinging on available capital. There is no opportunity to adjust the premium since it is paid up front. Instead of receiving monthly premiums, the insurer is paying monthly benefits. The payments can be made over a very long period of time and may be subject to inflationary pressure on expense. It is also important to periodically check to make sure that the annuitant is still living (but this is not an actuary's responsibility). Direct deposit forms of payment make this even more important. The adjustments that the actuary can trigger as a result of monitoring are likely to be in the area of reserves and pricing for new annuities.

3.4.6 Pension Plans and the Control Cycle

The problem definition for pension plans can be quite complex. How much will an employee need for retirement? Who owns the funds generated? Should annuities be purchased from insurance companies? How should the assets be invested? How does the pension fund affect the plan sponsor's finances? How much contribution should be made now? How are contributions expected to evolve over time? All of these problems are routinely addressed by actuaries.

The pension actuary must develop a solution that generates a fund where payments are made and contributions are deposited. At any point in time, the fund must have sufficient assets to either purchase annuities for retiring plan members or to make monthly payments to all retired plan members. In addition, the fund must be at a level so that, in combination with future contributions, the future liabilities can be met. Risks include not only the mortality risk found in annuities, but also the demographic risks of the group. Variations in either the number of older members retiring or the number of younger members joining the plan can have significant impact.

Designing the solution will be dependent, in part, on the goals of the employer or plan sponsor. The plan design may establish the ultimate pension based on each member's final average earnings, career average earnings, or even a flat benefit per year of service. The regulatory environment is very much an overriding factor with pension plans.

Monitoring the results is the primary—and by far the most time-consuming—aspect of the actuary's role. Constant changes to plan demographics, investment returns, and regulations require the actuary to continually review the plan's risks and any underlying assumptions. Pension plans epitomize the concept that an "acceptable solution" implies a result that is dynamic. Pension solutions are developed in a manner that permits ongoing recognition of and adjustment for evolving contingent events. The transition from problem to solution to monitoring of results is constant for pension plans. New problems may emerge at any time. The actuary must consider not only ongoing liabilities but also the plan's ability to pay benefits if the plan sponsor becomes insolvent.

3.4.7 Criminal Rate of Interest and the Control Cycle

At the opposite extreme from pension plans are certain actuarial problems in which there is a "correct answer," and it is not necessary to pursue the evolving and dynamic "acceptable or optimal solution." Generally, this type of problem is one in which the actuary takes a retrospective look at a problem and calculates a particular value. An example is a regulation found in some jurisdictions that specifies the maximum interest rate that can be charged on a loan.

In Canada, for instance, the lender has committed a crime if the effective annual rate of interest on a loan is greater than 60 percent. The Canadian criminal code specifies that an actuary must calculate the effective annual rate of interest. The problem and its definition here is quite simple. The actuary is given a stream of loan advances and loan payments and asked to calculate the effective annual rate of interest from the date of the first advance to the date of the last payment. The solution is a calculated interest rate. For situations such as Criminal Rate of Interest, where there is a "correct answer," designing the solution is much more critical than monitoring the results since the answer is static rather than dynamic.

3.4.8 Automobile Insurance and the Control Cycle

Casualty insurance, which includes automobile insurance, varies fundamentally from life insurance. A key difference is that the benefit payable under most casualty policies is an amount that "indemnifies" the insured for actual damages rather than providing payment of a specific amount, as is typical with life insurance. Casualty products typically cover a variety of risks under the same policy. For example, an auto insurance policy can provide coverage against some or all of theft, collision, personal injury, fire, and property damage. There may be deductibles, limits, or coinsurance arrangements for some or all of the categories.

The problems in auto insurance therefore require the analysis of many more factors than for life insurance. Each component of the coverage may require a distinct premium.

The solution design will be dependent on many factors. The premium for each segment may vary not only with the age and driving record of the insured but also with the age and model of the vehicle and the location of the primary driver's residence. Depending on jurisdiction, government can have a very direct effect on both the premium and the coverage provided.

When monitoring the results, the actuary can generally take advantage of the fact that rates are typically guaranteed for only one year at a time.

3.5 Some Conclusions about Actuarial Work and the Control Cycle

Previously, it was noted that the control cycle was not unique to actuaries, but there are aspects of the control cycle as discussed here that are particularly relevant to actuarial work. It was also noted that while many people do things similar to what actuaries do, there are elements that make actuarial work unique.

3.5.1 Temporal Congruence

A common misconception about actuaries, even among actuaries, is that they focus almost totally on future or prospective events. This is not true. Solutions must be based not only on the present to the future (prospectively) but also on the past to the present (retrospectively). If the solution does not reconcile the past to the future, it is time to step back and reevaluate. Sometimes, a retrospective review is possible only through an actuarial model of the solution. A retrospective review is almost always necessary as results of an actuarial solution are monitored.

3.5.2 Additivity

A second actuarial fact is that the pieces to a solution must add up. For any given contingency, the probability of it happening plus the probability of it not happening must, of course, equal one. Therefore, results without consideration of the contingency must always equal the sum of the results if the contingency occurs added to the sum of the results if the contingency does not occur. In today's high-tech world, this basic fundamental truth is sometimes overlooked as information is churned out using sophisticated methods based on high volumes of data. Application of the control cycle should avoid this potential flaw.

3.5.3 Solvability

Compared to many other scientific endeavors, there is typically no single, correct solution in most actuarial problems. There is often an optimal solution, one that is acceptable to all stakeholders. The term "correct answer" implies the ability to predict the exact result. This cannot be done with certainty when considering contingent events. On the other hand, the term "optimal solution" implies a result that is within a range of acceptability, is dynamic, and has been developed in a manner that permits an ongoing recognition of—and adjustment for—evolving contingent events (i.e., managing the risk). The control cycle is ideal to enable management of an optimal solution.

3.5.4 Revisiting Professionalism

The control cycle provides a mechanism for the actuary to manage risks with temporal congruence, additivity, and solvability in mind. Professionalism surrounds the three stages, and external forces exert their influence from outside.

The ability to describe the control cycle illustrates that the actuary brings professionalism and an awareness of external forces to all of aspects of his work. Professionalism and external forces together form an effective "context" for the three major stages of the control cycle.

The control cycle is not a static process with distinct steps but rather a dynamic process with constant overlap and transition among the primary stages.

When defining the problem, the actuary must be clear about the goals of the major stakeholders. How can potentially conflicting goals be reconciled within the external force of a particular regulatory environment? As the actuary designs the solution, various activities will be required. These activities could include, but are not limited to, building mathematical models, identifying model parameters, and setting assumptions. During Design the Solution, the actuary will continue to consider the problem definition and the interaction between the definition and the solution. Is the solution complete? Does the model effectively simulate results? Should the problem definition change?

Once the solution is implemented, the actuary monitors the results against expectations. During this stage, the actuary addresses questions like:

- Did the model produce useful results?
- Are the assumptions appropriate?

CHAPTER 4

Principles of Actuarial Science

In 2008, a joint committee of the Casualty Actuarial Society and SOA completed a task of writing a document that sets out the principles that underlie actuarial science. The document is available at the SOA website and in the online resources for this book. From the introduction:[1]

> The objective of *Principles Underlying Actuarial Science* is to articulate the current understanding of the significant principles that form the scientific framework underlying all areas of actuarial practice. The intended audience includes practicing actuaries, researchers and others, such as representatives of standard-setting organizations. (p. 5)

As may be clear from the previous chapters, it is difficult to define the scope of actuarial work. The scope of actuarial work is outlined in "Principles Underlying Actuarial Science" as follows:

> Actuarial science is primarily concerned with the study of consequences of events that involve risk and uncertainty. Actuarial practice identifies, analyzes and assists in the management of the outcomes—including costs and benefits—associated with events that involve risk and uncertainty. Understanding the principles underlying actuarial science enables actuaries to develop models of such events and other techniques to solve practical problems.
>
> To gain insights about future possibilities, the actuary depends on observation and wisdom gained through prior experience. Actuaries use these observations and experience to construct, validate and apply models. Actuaries continually incorporate additional observations and insights into their models. This feedback cycle systematically addresses discrepancies between these models and observed reality.
>
> Actuarial practice, in turn, is concerned with the assessment of the economic consequences associated with phenomena that are subject to uncertainty. This practice requires an understanding of the principles underlying several fields, including statistics, economics and risk management, as well as the principles of modeling, valuation and risk classification.
>
> Actuaries solve business problems in which the mitigation of negative consequences and the exploitation of positive consequences of risk play major roles. Thus, actuaries must be familiar with the principles of the management of fields in which they work, including insurance, health care and retirement systems, investment portfolios and the risks individuals face. Actuarial models can be developed to solve most of the typical problems that require analysis of the consequences of risk and uncertainty. (pp. 6 and 7)

The paper points out that much of actuarial science and actuarial practice uses concepts and techniques from other areas. This is particularly evident in the first two of "Principles Underlying Actuarial Science's" four sections.

1 Allaben, et. al. (2008).

Section 1 establishes a statistical framework. For the statistical techniques used in actuarial work to succeed, future experience must be somewhat predictable based on past experience. Further, the probabilistic structure of future experience must be able to be estimated using random samples. Since the work is based on probabilistic models, actuaries should not be completely judged on the accuracy of their forecasts, but rather on the quality of the methods used to make those forecasts.

Section 2 covers economics and in particular how organizations and individuals respond to incentives and disincentives. This leads to concepts such as the time value of money and risk aversion, adverse election, and moral hazard. These are all key concepts that any practicing actuary should master.

The last two sections relate more directly to actuarial work. Section 3 covers risk management and modeling. In particular, it states that it is possible to construct models that describe the behavior of financial security systems. Such models can then be used to manage the risks inherent in financial security systems. Risk management concepts such as pooling and hedging are described. All practicing actuaries must be fully aware of these concepts.

The final section covers financial security systems. Related topics such as risk classification, rate structures, and anti-selection—which relate to the control and management of financial security system risks—are introduced.

The concepts identified in "Principles Underlying Actuarial Science" provide another outline of actuarial practice, concepts, and work.

Actuaries do not work to predict the future. They work to manage the future sustainability of the financial security systems that are important to us all.

PART 2
INVESTMENTS

Toby A. White

CHAPTER 5

Introduction and External Factors

5.1 Overview of Investments Section

The next seven chapters explore basic concepts and issues relating to finance and investments. Although they are written primarily for a general audience, for which little prior knowledge is assumed, there are some places where increased emphasis is placed on the insurance or actuarial perspective.

Chapter 5 provides background on some external factors that affect investment decisions. Chapter 6 is an introduction to the basic principles of interest theory, including the accumulation and discounting of cash flows, types of interest rates, capital budgeting techniques, and various annuity structures (including loans and bonds). Chapter 7 is an overview of asset types and distinguishes between basic underlying assets such as bonds, stocks, and various low-risk securities and derivatives such as forwards, futures, and swaps.

Chapter 8 begins with some basic investment concepts and problems, proceeds to develop a mean-variance framework for investment analysis, and concludes by discussing more complex investment issues such as diversification, asset allocation, and performance evaluation. Chapter 9 introduces standard finance models such as the Capital Asset Pricing Model (CAPM), Arbitrage Pricing Theory (APT), cash flow projection models, and behavioral finance models and discusses both the data sources and parameter estimates that relate to these models.

Chapter 10 provides more detail on interest rates and yield curves through a discussion of the term structure of interest rates, while also distinguishing between interest rate and reinvestment rate risk and between spot and forward rates. Finally, Chapter 11 is an overview of core asset and liability management practices, both for corporations in general and as pertains specifically to life insurance companies; such practices include duration, convexity, immunization, and various matching strategies.

5.2 External Factors Affecting Investment Decisions

External factors are important when making investment decisions and can have as much, if not more, influence on the decisions being made than any individual characteristics or constraints. The main categories of external factors, all of which will be discussed, include cultural and social values, demographics, governmental influences, and the economic/business environment, which encompasses issues like the business cycle, taxes, and inflation.

In developing an investment strategy, each individual or company considers its risk tolerance, market outlook, and the effects on its liabilities. For example, risk tolerance affects the work of actuaries in all practice areas, especially as it pertains to clients and employers. Different companies have different risk tolerances, depending on factors such as the company's surplus position, the emphasis placed on earnings stability, the time horizon of the associated investment strategy, the economic outlook, and the ability of the organization to manage risk. Many of these external forces are interconnected, and thus not independent.

5.2.1 Cultural/Social Values

Investment decisions are influenced jointly by social trends, cultural beliefs, and economic trends. Social trends include the ever-expanding array of investment choices, the increasing use of the Internet for investing, day trading, investor confidence (or overconfidence), and socially responsible investing (SRI).

Socially responsible investing refers to an investment strategy that simultaneously attempts to maximize financial return and satisfy both social and environmental aims. SRI incorporates three sub-strategies: screening, shareholder advocacy, and community investing. With screening, social and/or environmental criteria are used to decide whether or not an investment should be undertaken. Shareholder advocacy involves efforts taken to continually improve corporate practices from an ownership perspective. In community investing, funds are allocated toward community projects or organizations that are not as favored by traditional financing activities. Financial service organizations are increasingly creating investment products and funds with social and environmental aspects to which investors can direct their premiums.

Changing cultural beliefs with regard to family versus individual responsibility can also affect the design of government programs such as Social Security. If a society has stronger dependence on family units, it will depend less on government to fill any gaps in retirement funding. Furthermore, whereas past generations have held the government relatively accountable for their financial stability post-retirement, both current and future generations are becoming increasingly self-reliant. Specifically, both individual savings and employer-sponsored savings plans are becoming more essential to maintain one's standard of living. In a recent (2010) Gallup poll, more U.S. non-retirees say that 401(k) and IRAs will be a significant source of retirement income (45 percent) than will Social Security (34 percent) (Jones, 2010). Note that this change of attitudes may not necessarily be by choice, but may instead relate to the looming cost-benefit shortfall of the U.S. Social Security program (Leonhardt, 2010).

5.2.2 Demographics

Companies need to provide products that match the investment needs of their customers, and these needs change over time and with age. Actuaries use demographic information, recent experience, and projections of current trends to arrive at the assumptions needed to develop investment policies.

An individual's age is perhaps the most essential demographic variable that affects investment projections. Individuals in their early working years (25–44) tend to invest more aggressively than those closer to retirement because they have more time to make up for any short-term investment losses. However, as workers approach retirement age, their investment objectives will shift from growth (capital appreciation) to income (capital preservation) considerations.

EXAMPLE 5.1

You are an investment advisor with two clients. Client A is age 30, married with two young children, and has given you 50,000 to invest. Client B is age 60, married with two grown children, and has given you 500,000 to invest. What are some differences in the investment strategies you would recommend to these two clients?

Solution: The strategy for Client A should be more aggressive, with emphasis on capital appreciation, especially since Client A will need to accumulate funds for upcoming large expenditures such as buying a house or funding the children's college education. In contrast, the strategy for Client B should be more conservative (i.e., lower risk tolerance relative to Client A), with emphasis on preserving the majority of the \$500,000 of capital that has been accumulated to date. Client B will be reaching retirement age soon and being able to provide a retirement income so that Client B can maintain a standard of living should be a paramount concern.

Still, as the retirement age for full Social Security benefits will gradually increase (by 2027) from 65 to 67, workers may need to defer the reallocation of funds from growth to income. Furthermore, due to advances in health care and medical technology, life expectancy is becoming longer. Thus, retirees will need more savings, achieved by obtaining a high enough return, and at controlled risk levels, to provide for a comfortable retirement that may last well beyond their retirement age.

Also, an increasing number of "retirees" are returning to work after having initially quit their jobs. This decision may be motivated by a continued desire to feel worthwhile and productive. However, some return to work for financial reasons, either to supplement their retirement income to maintain previously achieved standards of living or to support what is expected to be a long retirement. Investment options for these groups may need to be longer-term and more liquid than in the past.

5.2.3 Governmental Influences

The government influences finance and investment decisions through regulatory, fiscal, and monetary policies. Here, we discuss such influences from the perspective of corporate investors who have a fiduciary responsibility to their shareholders. Likewise, institutional investors such as insurance companies must make investment decisions that are aligned with the well-being of their policyholders. Regulations are imposed so that institutional investors will have safety of principal, stability of value, sufficient liquidity, appropriate diversification, and a reasonable relationship between assets and liabilities. The extent of regulation will differ substantially by industry, country, and region.

In the United States, the Securities and Exchange Commission (SEC) is the primary body for financial regulation. The SEC requires full disclosure of relevant information relating to the issuance of new securities and also regulates securities exchanges, over-the-counter (OTC) trading, brokers, and dealers. The Investment Company Act of 1940 required that public offerings of securities be registered with the SEC. This act was replaced in 2010 by The Dodd-Frank Wall Street Reform and Consumer Protection Act, which promotes accountability and transparency in the financial system and seeks to end "too big to fail"-type government bailouts. The Federal Reserve regulates bank lending and also sets margin requirements on stocks and options. The Commodity Futures Trading Commission (CFTC) regulates the trading of futures contracts. Some states also regulate security trading in an attempt to prevent fraud.

The Sarbanes-Oxley Act of 2002 imposed new responsibilities on public companies when communicating with investors. It was an outgrowth of several accounting frauds, including Enron and Worldcom. This act created the Public Company Accounting Oversight Board (overseen by the SEC), required that auditors cannot simultaneously perform non-audit services for the firm they are auditing, required the CEO/CFO to validate their firm's financial reports, ensured that the opinions of research analysts are independent, and required disclosure of any potential conflicts of interest. Significant penalties are now imposed for non-compliance, which makes the due diligence work actuaries do more important than ever before.

On a more global scale, the Basel Committee on Banking Supervision, which provides a forum for cooperation on matters of banking oversight, has developed an international framework for measuring capital from a banking perspective. The primary objective is to strengthen the stability of worldwide banks while also maintaining competitive equality. Ideally, the Basel framework, which includes minimum capital requirements, supervisory review and market discipline, will cause the banking industry to adapt stronger risk management practices.

There are also regulations specific to life insurance companies and/or pension plans. For example, a U.S. life insurer's asset portfolio can only have a small amount invested in foreign assets. There are limits pertaining to single investments and specific asset classes (e.g., bonds, stocks, mortgages and real estate). Under the Employee Retirement Income Security Act (ERISA) of 1974, investment managers are mandated to diversify pension plan assets, so as to minimize the risk of large losses. Furthermore, investment managers have a "fiduciary liability," as defined by law, and are thus held to a higher standard by society when managing the assets of others.

Fiscal policy relates to a government's spending and taxation actions. To stimulate a nation's economy, policymakers can either increase government spending or decrease tax levels (or both), whereas reverse actions lead to an economic contraction. Fiscal policy can be effective but is not always easy to implement. Actuaries working in finance and investments must be aware of tax structure. For example, in the United States, capital gains have often been taxed at lower rates than ordinary interest income. Also, investments in municipal bonds are tax-advantaged in that interest earned is exempt from federal taxes (and from state taxes if the holder is a resident of that state).

To help combat an economic recession, the government may cut individual tax rates, as this will encourage increased consumption. Corporate tax rates can also be reduced, so as to encourage business investment, which includes possible increases in research and development, technological updates, or an increased ability to hire additional employees. To control an economy that may be growing too fast, the government may introduce temporary surtaxes or excess profit taxes and/or reverse some of the tax cuts that were made when the economy was not doing as well.

Monetary policy relates to the supply of money. As the money supply is increased, short-term interest rates will fall, which will eventually encourage investment and consumption;

however, inflationary effects may also set in. Decreases in the money supply will cause interest rates to rise, tend to rein in an economy that is growing too fast and also act as a deterrent against expanding inflation rates. The three main tools for monetary policy include the government's open market operations (where bonds are bought and sold), the setting of the discount rate, and reserve requirements as pertains to banks. The buying of bonds, the lowering of the discount rate, and the lowering of reserve requirements are all consistent with expansionary monetary policy.

5.2.4 Economic/Business Environment

Investment behavior is also related to the prevailing conditions in the economic and business environment. An unfavorable economic climate may induce some investors to abandon certain sectors, asset types, or individual securities. For example, in times of trouble, investors may reallocate funds to Treasuries or gold or simply keep significant amounts of money outside the market altogether. Also, with all the occurrences of accounting fraud over the last 10–15 years, investor trust and confidence may have significantly eroded.

When actuaries develop solutions within economic and business contexts, they must consider issues relating to portfolio management, asset allocation, fixed-income securities, and globalization. For both retirement funds and insurance products, there is often a long time horizon between when funds/premiums are collected from individuals and when benefits/claims are paid out. The investment actuary is charged with managing asset portfolios so that payments can be made when due, both on a short- and long-term basis.

Effective portfolio management requires knowledge about the various capital markets and an understanding of an investor's objectives and constraints, so that the optimal combination of assets can be formed. Note that as an investor's circumstances change over time, portfolio strategies will have to be updated. With both pension funds and insurance companies, the portfolio manager must not only represent the interests of individuals/policyholders, but also consider the shareholders of the institution they support.

Asset allocation concerns the asset classes that will be utilized and the proportion of total assets allocated to each class. According to studies, asset allocations have greater effects on determining overall return than individual security selection. There are three steps to a typical asset allocation process. First, the portfolio manager should identify the fund's objective; for both insurance companies and pension funds, this is often the maximization of surplus (i.e., the excess of assets over liabilities). Second, the efficient frontier should be formed, whereby either expected surplus is maximized for a given level of risk (as measured by standard deviation), or risk is minimized for a given level of surplus. Third, the ultimate mix must be tailored to the individual investor and examined to see if any regulatory constraints (e.g., limits) have been violated. Note that the manager can conduct either active or passive allocation, depending on the frequency for which changes in the portfolio mix are enacted.

Fixed income securities are especially useful for pension funds and insurance companies because they mature at predetermined times and amounts (provided there is no default), so that there is less uncertainty with respect to assets being sufficient to cover liabilities. Still, returns can vary depending on interest rate levels, the shape of the yield curve, the spread above risk-free rates, and the perceived risk of the issuing company. Furthermore, as mortality, morbidity, and retiree/policyholder behavior deviate from assumptions (not to mention defaults and calls/prepayments), payment levels may vary, so that exact cash flow matching strategies will fail. Immunization is often employed as an alternative to cash flow matching whereby duration and/or convexity may be matched.

If the asset manager is allowed to invest globally, instead of just nationally or regionally, opportunities for diversification will increase. This will lead to more optimal risk-return relationships; in other words, the efficient frontier will expand outward. As worldwide financial markets become more integrated and previous obstacles to international investing dissipate, more investors will be encouraged to take advantage of the additional choices inherent in foreign investments.

5.2.4.1 Business cycle

When choosing between several alternatives, it is imperative that each alternative be compared over the same time period. If the alternatives are of the same length, but are compared over different time periods, then it is likely that business cycles will affect the comparison. For example, if one alternative takes place mostly around the peak of a business cycle and the other occurs near a low point, the first alternative will appear to be superior and meaningful differences will be obscured. Now, if two alternatives are of different length, where the length of the longer alternative is a multiple of that of the shorter alternative, and the shorter alternative's period coincides with a typical business cycle, a valid comparison can still be made. The necessary adjustment is to repeat the shorter alternative until its time period matches that of the longer alternative.

5.2.4.2 Taxes

Actuaries must be careful to distinguish between before-tax cash flows and after-tax cash flows. When comparing alternatives, if a uniform tax rate is applied to all profit levels (where profit = revenues net of expenses), then the optimal decision remains consistent, regardless of whether pre- or post-tax cash flows were utilized. However, a flat tax structure is rare in practice. Furthermore, the cash flows reported to the taxing authority are not true cash flows but are tax-adjusted to reflect the specific tax aspects applying to each. Thus, firms must keep two records of cash flows, one for tax purposes and the other to make decisions.

5.2.4.3 Inflation

Cash flows can be described using either actual dollar values or using values that reflect purchasing power relative to a previous time point. If the inflation rate is given by f, and a good is priced at 1 today, it will be priced at $1+f$ one year ahead; in fact, inflation accrues just like compound interest, so the price of that same good k years ahead would be $(1+f)^k$ assuming a constant inflation rate.

Purchasing power is defined in terms of "constant" or "real" dollars, relative to some reference year. For example, if 2005 is the reference year, and we are looking at real dollar prices five years ahead (in 2010), those prices would be relative to what actual prices were in 2005, rather than what actual or "nominal" prices are in 2010. Regardless of whether real cash flows or nominal cash flows are used, it is essential to not go back and forth between the two, but remain on a consistent basis when making comparisons.

If r is the nominal interest rate and r_0 is the real interest rate, then the relationship between these two rates and the expected inflation rate f, which is often referred to as the Fisher hypothesis, is: $1 + r = (1 + r_0)(1 + f)$. In words, while money increases nominally at the rate $1+ r$, the real increase in money, as measured by the effect of purchasing power, occurs at the rate $1 + r_0$. Note that $r = (1 + r_0)(1 + f) - 1 = r_0 + f - r_0f$. Thus, if the expected inflation rate is relatively small, then the nominal rate of interest can be approximated by $r = r_0 + f$.

EXAMPLE 5.2

If the real interest rate is 4% per year, and the expected inflation rate is 3%, what is the approximate nominal interest rate? What is the exact nominal interest rate, as implied by the Fisher hypothesis?

Solution: The approximate nominal interest rate is: $r = r_0 + f = 0.04 + 0.03 = 0.07 =$ 7%. The exact nominal interest rate, as inferred from the Fisher equation is:

$$r = [(1 + r_0)(1 + f)] - 1 = [(1.04)(1.03)] - 1 = 0.0712 = 7.12\%.$$

CHAPTER 6

Interest Theory

6.1 Types of Interest Rates

Interest is necessary to compensate a lender for use of its capital by a borrower over the time period for which the borrower uses this capital. Let's begin with a simple example, where a single amount K is lent now (at $t = 0$) from the lender to the borrower and will be returned to the lender with interest at some future time $t > 0$. Then, at time t, the cash flow exchanged will be $K(1 + i)^t$, where i is the interest rate.

Note that $(1 + i)^t$ is only one type of *accumulation function*, which is a function that, given a single investment of 1 at time zero, provides the accumulated value of that investment at time t. We denote the accumulation function as $a(t)$, whereby $a(0) = 1$, and $a(t)$ is typically a continuous increasing function of t. The accumulation function $(1 + i)^t$ is called *compound interest*, while the most common alternative accumulation function is $a(t) = 1 + it$, which is called *simple interest*.

We can also define an amount function $A(t)$, which is related to the accumulation function, based on the amount of the initial amount lent (K). From the lender's perspective, K can be thought of as an initial deposit into a fund. Then, $A(0) = K$, and in general, $A(t) = Ka(t)$, which is the amount in the fund at time t. Furthermore, the amount of interest the investor earns between any two time points, t_1 and t_2 (where $t_2 > t_1$), is the difference in the amount function at those times (i.e., $A(t_2) - A(t_1)$). Thus, using the previous example, where $a(t) = (1 + i)^t$, $t_1 = 0$, and $t_2 = 1$, then $A(1) - A(0) = Ka(1) - Ka(0) = K(1 + i) - K = Ki$, the amount of interest earned on the borrowed amount over the first year.

EXAMPLE 6.1

If 10,000 is deposited into an account now that earns an annual effective compound interest rate of 5% per year and no further deposits are made, what amount of interest is earned by this fund during the fourth year of the investment?

Solution: The amount of interest earned during the fourth year (i.e., between $t = 3$ and $t = 4$) is $A(4) - A(3) = 10{,}000[(1.05)^4 - (1.05)^3] = 578.81$.

6.1.1 Simple Interest versus Compound Interest

With compound interest (i.e., $a(t) = (1 + i)^t$), any interest earned in earlier periods can be applied to the fund balance and is automatically reinvested in future periods. Thus, the term *compound* refers to the process where interest is reinvested (or compounded) to earn additional interest.

EXAMPLE 6.2

If 100 is invested for two years, the annual interest rate is 5% and the fund accumulates according to compound interest, then what is the accumulated value of the investment after two years? Also, what amount of interest is earned by this fund during the second year of the investment?

Solution: The accumulated value of the investment after two years is $A(2) = 100a(2) = 100(1.05)^2 = 110.25$. Also, $A(1) = 100(1.05)^1 = 105$. Thus, the amount of interest earned in the second year is $A(2) - A(1) = 110.25 - 105 = 5.25$, rather than 5. The amount 5.25 can be interpreted as the 5 (=0.05*100) earned on the original principal (between times one and two), along with the 0.25 (=0.05*5) earned on the 5 interest earned in the first year.

With simple interest (i.e., $a(t) = 1 + it$), unlike with compound interest, the amount of interest earned each period remains constant.

EXAMPLE 6.3

If 100 is invested for two years, the annual interest rate is 5%, and the fund accumulates according to simple interest, then what is the accumulated value of the investment after two years? Also, what amount of interest is earned by this fund during the second year of the investment?

Solution: The accumulated value of the investment after two years is $A(2) = 100a(2) = 100[1 + 0.05(2)] = 110$. Also, $A(1) = 100a(1) = 100(1.05) = 105$. Thus, the amount of interest earned in the second year is $A(2) - A(1) = 110 - 105 = 5$, which is the same as what was earned in the first year. Thus, when simple interest is employed, there is no compounding of interest.

In practice, compound interest is almost universally employed if the investment period is one year or longer. However, for short-term investment periods, such as fractional periods within a year, simple interest may be utilized, as it is easier to calculate and understand and is a close approximation to what would be obtained if compound interest were applied over the same interval.

EXAMPLE 6.4

If 100 is invested at 5% interest and $t = 1/12$ (in years), so that the investment period is one month, then what is the accumulated value of 100 one month from now under simple interest? Under compound interest?

Solution: Under simple interest, $A(1/12) = 100(1 + 0.05/12) = 100.42$. Under compound interest, $A(1/12) = 100(1.05)^{1/12} = 100.41$, which is just a penny less. Note that if $t = 1$, simple interest and compound interest produce the same accumulated value because $(1 + i)^1 = 1 + i(1) = 1 + i$. However, if $t < 1$, simple interest will produce larger amounts, whereas if $t > 1$, compound interest will produce larger amounts.

From now on, unless otherwise stated, assume that compound interest is being utilized rather than simple interest.

6.1.2 Effective, Nominal, and Periodic Rates

So far, when employing the notation i, we have been implicitly assuming that i was an annual effective rate of interest. More formally, this represents the amount of money that one unit invested at time zero will earn at time one. Then, if we wish to accumulate a cash flow forward in time (for any value of t), the appropriate accumulation function is $a(t) = (1 + i)^t$, recalling that we now assume compound interest. Likewise, if we wish to discount a future cash flow backward in time, the appropriate discount function is $1/a(t) = 1/(1 + i)^t = (1 + i)^{-t}$. A common notation, especially for actuaries, is $v = 1/(1 + i)$ and thus $1/a(t) = v^t$. Assuming that $i > 0$, as is usually the case, then $v < 1$. Then, if we wish to find the present value of K, where K is to be paid in the future (at time t), it is $K/(1 + i)^t = Kv^t$, which is less than K.

What if the period over which interest is earned is of some frequency other than annual? For example, many corporate bonds pay semi-annual coupons, and many common stocks pay quarterly dividends. In these cases, when cash flows are accumulated or discounted, it may be easier to work with an interest rate that is of the same relative frequency as the frequency at which cash flows are paid. Both *nominal* and *periodic* interest rates accomplish this purpose, but in slightly different ways.

Nominal rates are employed when interest is paid more (or less) frequently than once per year. The terms *payable, convertible,* and *compounded* are used interchangeably to describe the application of nominal interest rates. A nominal interest rate of $i^{(m)}$ payable m times per year implies that the interest rate corresponding to each subperiod of length $1/m$ during the year is $i^{(m)}/m$. Here, m is the number of subperiods per year for which interest is paid and typically corresponds to the number of cash flows occurring during the year.

EXAMPLE 6.5

If the nominal interest rate is 10% payable semi-annually, what is the semi-annual interest rate?

Solution: Here. $i^{(2)} = 0.1$ (because there are two semi-annual periods in a year), and the semi-annual rate is $i^{(2)}/2 = 0.1/2 = 0.05 = 5\%$.

For corporate bonds with semi-annual coupons, $m = 2$, and for common stocks with quarterly dividends, $m = 4$. Note that while $i^{(m)}$ is the nominal rate, which is quoted on an annualized basis, it is $i^{(m)}/m$ that represents the true rate for each subperiod during the year. In fact $i^{(m)}/m$ is often called the *per-period rate.*

It is also possible that the per-period rate may need to be determined directly from an annual effective rate (if the annual nominal rate is not given), which is slightly more difficult than just dividing by m, as was the case when converting from an annual nominal rate to a per-period rate. The per-period rate is the solution for j in the following equation: $1 + i = (1 + j)^m$, so that $j = (1 + i)^{1/m} - 1$. Here, j represents the interest rate for one such subperiod within the year.

EXAMPLE 6.6

If the annual effective interest rate is 10%, but an equivalent six-month rate is desired, what is this equivalent semi-annual rate?

Solution: The equation of value is: $1.1 = (1 + j)^2$, where j is the six-month rate. Solving this equation, $j = 1.1^{1/2} - 1 = 0.0488 = 4.88\%$ (approximately), and not 5% as with the nominal-to-per-period conversion.

6.1.3 Continuous Compounding

What if it is assumed that interest is convertible continuously, instead of at discrete times throughout a year? This corresponds to the nominal case described previously, but with an infinitely large m. Then, δ_t, which is called the *force of interest*, measures the intensity at which interest is operating at an instantaneous moment in time.

To develop this concept, we first need to generalize the concept of a nominal rate of interest for arbitrary accumulation functions. For a period running from t to $t + h$, the equivalent nominal annual rate is

$$i_t^{1/h} = \frac{a(t+h) - a(t)}{ha(t)}.$$

For compound interest, this becomes

$$i_t^{1/h} = \frac{(1+i)^{t+h} - (1+i)^t}{h(1+i)^t} = \frac{(1+i)^h - 1}{h} = m[(1+i)^{1/m} - 1] = i^{(m)}$$

Where $m = 1/h$.

Now suppose the time period becomes infinitesimally small. Define

$$\delta_t = \lim_{h\to 0} i_t^{1/h} = \frac{1}{a(t)} \lim_{h\to 0} \frac{a(t+h) - a(t)}{h} = \frac{a'(t)}{a(t)}$$

provided the accumulation function is differentiable.

It can also be shown using a Taylor series expansion (see Kellison, 2008, p. 33) that for compound interest $\lim_{m\to\infty} i^{(m)} = \delta$, so that δ can be interpreted as a nominal rate of interest convertible continuously.

For compound interest,

$$\delta_t = (1+i)^{-t} \frac{d}{dt}(1+i)^t = (1+i)^{-t}(1+i)^t \ln(1+i) = \ln(1+i) = \delta.$$

In this case, the force of interest is constant over time.

The differential equation can be solved for $a(t) = \exp\left(\int_0^t \delta_r dr\right)$. For compound interest this becomes $a(t) = e^{t\delta}$.

EXAMPLE 6.7

If 100 is invested at a force of interest of $\delta = 0.05$, then what is the accumulated value after two years?

Solution: The accumulated value after two years will be $A(2) = 100e^{0.05(2)} = 110.52$, which is a little higher than if we had just used an effective annual interest rate of 5% (see the 110.25 value from before) because the continuous compounding of interest occurs more frequently than the annual compounding of interest.

6.2 Two Approaches to Interest

There are two primary approaches when using interest rates to value an investment. The first is a rate of return approach, whereby if given a set of cash flows, an investor calculates the interest rate being earned. The second is a discounted cash flow or net present value analysis, whereby if given a particular interest rate (e.g., perhaps one that is tied to some market interest rate or one that is reflective of a company's cost of capital), an investor calculates the net worth, in today's dollars, of all the future expected cash flows that will be earned.

In this section, the two approaches will be treated as theoretical constructs. In Section 6.3, we will show how these approaches can be used in making investment decisions.

6.2.1 Rate of Return

Consider an investment that produces a sequence of known cash flows at known times. Let those cash flows be $C_0, C_1, \ldots, C_n$ with cash flow C_k occurring at time t_k. Assume that $0 = t_0 < t_1 < \cdots < t_n$ and $C_0 < 0$. Negative cash flows are interpreted as money paid by the investor while positive cash flows represent income or withdrawals. For now, we will assume that withdrawals in excess of the fund balance at that time are not permitted. Also note that there is always an opposite perspective in that cash going out from one party is always cash going in to another party.

For such a sequence of cash flows, the investor may want to measure the investment's performance by calculating a *rate of return*. One measure of rate of return is the rate that causes the sum of the discounted (to time zero) cash flows to be zero. In this context, the rate of return may also be referred to as the *yield rate* or as the *Internal Rate of Return (IRR)*. The equation to solve is

$$0 = \sum_{k=0}^{n} C_k(1 + i)^{-t_k}.$$

One way to think of the yield rate is that if C_0 is invested in a fund earning that rate, there will be exactly enough money in principal and interest to provide the cash flows. Generally, the higher the yield rate, the more attractive the project.

EXAMPLE 6.8

You are offered an opportunity to invest 100 today and then receive 10 one year from now and 115 two years from now. What is the IRR for this investment?

Solution: The equation to solve is $0 = -100 + 10(1 + i)^{-1} + 115(1 + i)^{-2}$. This can be changed into a quadratic equation in $x = 1 + i$: $100x^2 - 10x - 115 = 0$. The solution is $x = 1.1235$ for an IRR of 12.35%.

It is easy to conceive of a situation with a negative IRR. This implies that the investor would be better off not investing the funds at all.

EXAMPLE 6.9

You are offered an opportunity to invest 100 today and then receive 10 one year from now and 80 two years from now. What is the IRR for this investment?

Solution: The equation to solve is $0 = -100 + 10(1 + i)^{-1} + 80(1 + i)^{-2}$. This can be changed into a quadratic equation in $x = 1 + i : 100x^2 - 10x - 80 = 0$. The solution is $x = 0.9458$ for an IRR of -5.42%.

In the examples presented, there was a unique solution greater than -100%. It is possible to construct situations where there are multiple feasible (greater than -100%) solutions. As will be noted in the next section, this is one drawback of the IRR approach to valuing an investment.

It is also possible for the interest rate to vary over the investment horizon, so that every period for which the interest rate is constant must be analyzed separately. In fact, interest rates do not typically remain constant for long. However, throughout this chapter, unless otherwise stated, we will assume a level interest rate throughout the investment horizon.

6.2.2 Net Present Value

Before introducing the second approach, we introduce the concepts of *accumulated value, future value, present value,* and *current value.* Consider a simple investment structure, where a single cash flow is invested at $t = 0$ and allowed to accumulate for n years. Let this investment be a deposit in an interest-bearing bank account, where the interest rate is level throughout the investment horizon and is known in advance. If this rate is positive, as is almost always the case, then we can speak of the account's *accumulated value* at $t_1 = n$, which will be higher than the amount of the initial deposit.

An alternative investment structure is one in which no capital is contributed today, but a certain, fixed amount is to be received at some time in the future. However, due to the time value of money, again assuming that interest rates are positive, that amount (whatever it is), which is often called the *future value*, will be worth less in today's dollars than it will be at the time in which it is received. The *present value* is simply the current investment necessary to produce this future value. Note that *accumulated value* and *future value*, although introduced here in different contexts, are used interchangeably. Going forward, we will use *accumulated value.*

An important distinction between present value and accumulated value, even if there is more than one cash flow involved, is that with present value calculations, all cash flows are discounted back to the present (time zero), while with accumulated value calculations, all cash flows are accumulated forward to some future point in time (often, the end of the investment period). It is also possible to choose an intermediate time point for cash flow valuation, where some cash flows must be accumulated forward to that time and others must be discounted back to that time. In that case, we call the value of the cash flow structure the *current value* as of that time.

When calculating the present value, the initial investment (C_0) may be included or excluded. When it is included, the term *net present value* (NPV) is often used. There is a connection between NPV and IRR in that when the NPV is calculated at the IRR, by definition it is zero. When the initial investment is excluded, the present value (PV) can be interpreted as the initial investment that would force the IRR (or one of the solutions to the IRR equation) to match the interest rate used for determining the present value.

Once the cash flows are determined, there are no decisions to make when determining IRR. However, for NPV or PV, the interest rate used in the calculation must be determined by the analyst. This will be discussed further in Section 6.3.

EXAMPLE 6.10

The project in Example 6.8 generates a cash flow of 10 at time one and 115 at time two. If 100 is to be invested in this project, what are the PV and NPV at 10%?

Solution: When doing PV and NPV calculations, the investment is usually treated as a negative amount and the returns as positive. The PV is $10(1.1)^{-1} + 115(1.1)^{-2} = 104.13$. The NPV is $104.13 - 100 = 4.13$.

6.3 Capital Budgeting

Both an investor and an institution may have tough choices to make when allocating a scarce amount of capital among several alternative cash flow structures. The investor must choose from a pool of investments, each of which provides certain cash flows at certain times. An institution may be choosing between various projects to fund with its capital resources, each of which is expected to generate cash flows. In either case, the choice will be made based on an analysis of the cash flows.

As discussed in Section 6.2, there are two primary methods by which both investors and institutions may make good choices: NPV and IRR.

6.3.1 Net Present Value

The NPV method is usually considered the better of the two methods because it tackles the primary goal of investment management, which is maximizing shareholder wealth. NPV measures the extent to which a corporate project contributes to shareholder wealth, or equivalently, the extent to which an investment adds value to an investor's portfolio. Going forward, we will assume the perspective of an individual investor rather than that of a corporate institution.

Let C_k represent the net cash flow at time t_k, with deposits (or investments) considered as negative cash flows and withdrawals (or returns) considered as positive cash flows. Note that if there is a deposit and a withdrawal at the same time, the two transactions are netted against each other. Also, let i be the per-period interest rate. For illustrative purposes, we will assume that i is an annual effective rate of interest. In practice, i may be set at the company's overall cost of capital. However, if a project is perceived as more risky than the average project the company typically undertakes, then a higher i may be chosen. Likewise, if the project is less risky than average, a lower rate may be more appropriate. Then, an investment's NPV is the sum of all discounted cash flows, where each cash flow is discounted at rate i from the time at which it occurs back to now (time zero). In equation form, we have:

$$NPV = \sum_{k=0}^{n} C_{t_k}(1 + i)^{-t_k}$$

Typically, an investment has a single deposit or outflow at time zero followed by multiple returns or inflows at various future points in time. That is, $C_0 < 0$ and $C_1, \ldots, C_n > 0$. For example, an investor in a coupon-paying bond pays the bond's price at time zero and receives periodic coupons in the future, along with the bond's face amount when it matures. In this case, unless the cash flows are indexed to inflation, and ignoring the possibility that the issuer of the bond may default on some or all of the payments, they are all fixed in advance so that the NPV for a given interest rate can be determined exactly. However, an investor in a dividend-paying stock pays the stock's price at time zero and receives periodic dividends on the stock in the future. Now, neither the timing nor the amount of such dividends is guaranteed, so that the NPV can only be estimated, rather than known for sure.

When using the NPV method to choose among investment alternatives, it is imperative to know whether the alternatives are independent or mutually exclusive. The alternatives are (mutually) independent if the cash flows of any particular alternative have no effect on the cash flows of any other alternative. In this case, any alternative with positive NPV should be accepted, whereas alternatives with negative (or zero) NPV should be rejected.

In contrast, if the alternatives are mutually exclusive, only one (by definition) can be accepted. For example, maybe the investor is choosing from among several small-cap growth stocks, each requiring an equal amount of initial investment, but due to portfolio diversification constraints, there is room for only one such stock in the portfolio. Then, only the stock with the highest estimated NPV should be considered for acceptance, where acceptance would occur if and only if that stock had a positive estimated NPV, with discounting done using the company's overall cost of capital possibly adjusted for risk.

EXAMPLE 6.11

Project A requires an initial investment of 100,000 and is expected to return 20,000 in one year, 40,000 in two years, and 70,000 in three years. Project B requires an initial investment of 100,000 and is expected to return 10,000 in one year, 30,000 in two years, and 90,000 in three years. Find the NPVs of both projects, using an annual effective interest rate of 10%, and then determine which of the two projects should be accepted, assuming the projects are independent. What if they are mutually exclusive?

Solution: NPV for Project A:

$$-100{,}000 + \frac{20{,}000}{1.1} + \frac{40{,}000}{(1.1)^2} + \frac{70{,}000}{(1.1)^3} =$$

$$-100{,}000 + 18{,}181.82 + 33{,}057.85 + 52{,}592.04 = 3{,}831.71.$$

NPV for Project B:

$$-100{,}000 + \frac{10{,}000}{1.1} + \frac{30{,}000}{(1.1)^2} + \frac{90{,}000}{(1.1)^3} =$$

$$-100{,}000 + 9{,}090.91 + 24{,}793.39 + 67{,}618.33 = 1{,}502.63.$$

If the two projects are independent, both projects should be accepted as NPV(Project A) > 0 and NPV(Project B) > 0. However, if the two projects are mutually exclusive, then only Project A should be accepted, since NPV (Project A) > NPV (Project B).

6.3.2 Internal Rate of Return

An asset's yield rate is defined as the discount rate that forces the present value at the time of the investment of the cash inflows to equal the asset's price. Equivalently, it is the rate that forces the NPV to be zero. When doing capital budgeting, this yield rate is the IRR. The equation to solve is

$$NPV = \sum_{k=0}^{n} C_{t_k}(1 + i)^{-t_k} = 0.$$

Now, solving for the IRR (or IRRs, as the there may be more than one solution) that satisfy NPV = 0 is not as trivial as calculating the NPV when given a specific interest rate. For example, if the inflows are all made at integer times so $t_1 = 1, t_2 = 2, \ldots, t_n = n$, then solving for the IRR(s) is equivalent to finding the roots of an nth-degree polynomial. In practice, there are two primary methods for doing this. The crudest is trial and error, which is generally not recommended. The other involves a programmatic approach, using either a financial calculator or some computing software function (e.g., Excel has one). When using a financial calculator, all the individual cash flows need to be entered before the IRR button can be applied. While the equation will almost always have multiple solutions, only interest rates greater than −100 percent are acceptable solutions (we assume it is not possible to lose more than what is invested). Often, but not always, there will be only one solution that meets this criterion.

The IRR is an estimate of an investment's periodic rate of return. The investor may have a target rate that the investment must exceed before being considered. The target rate is often the cost of capital, or perhaps the risk-adjusted return on capital (RAROC). Then, for independent investments, any investment with an IRR exceeding this target rate should be accepted, as long as the investor can afford to commit to all such investments. However, if the IRR falls below the target rate, even if the IRR is positive, then the investment should be rejected. For mutually exclusive investments, only the investment with the highest IRR should be accepted and only if that investment's IRR also exceeds the target rate. Note that for independent projects, the NPV and IRR methods always produce the same accept/reject decision, provided that the NPV is calculated using the target rate. For mutually exclusive projects, it is possible for the two methods to produce conflicts. This will only occur (and in fact, is guaranteed to occur) when the cost of capital is less than the one interest rate that causes the NPV for two competing projects to be equal. If a conflict does occur, the NPV method is usually chosen as the tiebreaker. For example, a small project may have a high IRR, but a low NPV (because few dollars are invested), while a larger project may have a lower IRR, but generate more gain in dollars (and thus have a higher NPV). If only one can be selected, the one that generates more gain is usually preferable.

EXAMPLE 6.12

Project A requires an initial investment of 100,000 and is expected to return 20,000 in one year, 40,000 in two years, and 70,000 in three years. Project B requires an initial investment of 100,000 and is expected to return 10,000 in one year, 30,000 in two years, and 90,000 in three years. Find the Internal Rate of Return on each project, and then, if the company's cost of capital is 10%, determine which of the two projects should be accepted if the projects are independent. What if they are mutually exclusive?

Solution: For Project A the IRR equation to solve is:

$$-100{,}000 + \frac{20{,}000}{1 + IRR} + \frac{40{,}000}{(1 + IRR)^2} + \frac{70{,}000}{(1 + IRR)^3} = 0.$$

Using either trial and error, or a numerical calculation procedure, IRR = 11.79%.

Solution: For Project B, the IRR equation to solve is:

$$-100{,}000 + \frac{10{,}000}{1 + IRR} + \frac{30{,}000}{(1 + IRR)^2} + \frac{90{,}000}{(1 + IRR)^3} = 0.$$

The solution is IRR = 10.64%.

If the two projects are independent, both projects should be accepted as IRR (Project A) $>$ 10% and IRR (Project B) $>$ 10%. However, if the two projects are mutually exclusive, then only Project A should be accepted, since IRR (Project A) $>$ IRR (Project B).

The IRR method can be problematic when solving the NPV = 0 equation produces multiple solutions. There are two types of cash flow structures: normal and non-normal. A normal structure occurs when one or more cash outflows are then followed by a series of cash inflows, so that there is only one change in sign in the cash flows over time. In such cases, the IRR (if a real root exists) is guaranteed to be unique. Fortunately, many investments have normal cash flow structures, so that the potential problem of multiple IRRs is avoided.

A non-normal structure occurs when some future cash outflows are made subsequent to the commencement of future cash inflows, so that there are multiple changes in sign on the cash flows over time. In this case, the maximum number of IRRs, or yield rates, will be equal to the number of sign changes. For example, if an investment requires deposits not just at time zero, but also at times three and five, whereas the cash inflows are received at times one, two, four, and six, then the signs of the cash flows are (−, +, +, −, +, −, +) so that there are 5 different changes in sign. In such an example, there may be five IRRs that solve the NPV = 0 solution (although there could also be fewer, and even if there are 5 roots, some of them may be complex rather than real roots). However, if the outstanding accumulated fund balance is positive throughout the investment horizon, the yield rate is still guaranteed to be unique. When there are multiple roots, there is no reason to believe that any one root is a more accurate portrayal of the investment's true measure of return than any other root. Note that in such cases, financial calculators may not show all such roots, but algorithmically converge to one of the roots, and there is no reason to believe that this particular root is the best choice.

EXAMPLE 6.13

In Example 6.12, are the IRRs (for both Projects A and B) guaranteed to be unique?

Solution: Yes, because both projects have a single outflow followed by multiple inflows, so that there is only one change in sign. In other words, the cash flow structure of both projects consists of normal cash flows rather than non-normal cash flows.

EXAMPLE 6.14

Determine the IRR for the following set of cash flows: $C_0 = -100$, $C_1 = 150$, $C_2 = -40$.

Solution: The equation to solve is $0 = -100 + 150v - 40v^2$. The roots of this quadratic equation are $v = 0.86722$ and $v = 2.88278$, which translate to IRRs of 15.31% and −65.31%. In this case, because the investment is profitable (returning 150 on an undiscounted, aggregate investment of 140), the positive IRR is the reasonable choice.

6.4 Annuities

When cash flows vary in systematic fashion, it is possible to come up with simplified expressions for an investment's present value, rather than just summing all the discounted cash flows individually. This is especially true when payments are made at equal intervals of time. Such sequences of payments are called *annuities*. For now, we will assume that all payment amounts are also equal, so that we are valuing a level annuity. We will also assume that future payments are certain to be made and are not contingent on some event occurring or not occurring. Thus, we will be valuing what is called an annuity-certain, as opposed to a contingent (e.g., life) annuity. Finally, we will assume that the payment period, which is the common interval between annuity payments, coincides with the frequency at which the interest rate is quoted. Note that if the interest rate is quoted on some other frequency, the simplest valuation approach is to calculate the rate that is on the same frequency as the payment period, and then work in per-period units (rather than with annual units, for instance).

6.4.1 Annuity-Due, Ordinary Annuity, and Deferred Annuity

Level-payment annuities-certain can be classified by the time at which the first payment is made. If the payments begin immediately (i.e., at the same time as the valuation date), then the structure is called an *annuity-due*. Then, such payments are made at the beginning of each of the annuity's subsequent periods. For now, we will also assume that the number of periods is finite, but we will relax this assumption later.

In formula terms, let K be the amount of each payment, and let i be the per-period interest rate, so that $v = \dfrac{1}{1+i}$ is the per-period discount factor. Then, the present value of an annuity due with n total payments is $K + Kv + Kv^2 + \cdots + Kv^{n-1}$. Note that here, the last, or nth payment occurs at the beginning of the nth period, which is at $t = n - 1$. This present value (PV) can be simplified using geometric series, that is, $PV = K(1 + v + \cdots + v^{n-1}) = K\sum_{t=0}^{n-1} v^t = K\left[\dfrac{1 - v^{(n-1)+1}}{1 - v}\right] = K\left[\dfrac{1 - v^n}{1 - v}\right]$. Using standard actuarial symbols, this can also be written as $K\ddot{a}_{\overline{n}|}$, where the two dots over the annuity symbol denote that each payment occurs at the beginning the period.

EXAMPLE 6.15

Calculate the present value of a 10-year annuity that pays 100 each month, with each payment occurring at the beginning of the month (and the first payment due now), assuming a nominal interest rate of 12% convertible monthly.

Solution: The present value of this annuity is:

$$100\ddot{a}_{\overline{120}|0.01} = 100\left[\frac{1 - (1.01)^{-120}}{1 - (1.01)^{-1}}\right] = 100(70.3975) = 7{,}039.75.$$

Note that the annuity symbol has the interest rate after the "angle." This is an optional part of the notation and is often used if the interest rate is not otherwise clear.

If the first payment is at the end of the first period, then the structure is called an *ordinary annuity*. Note that conceptually, the end of the first period is considered to be the same time as the beginning of the second period, so that the end of the first period is exactly one period later than the beginning of the first period. This annuity is called ordinary because it is the most commonly observed structure in practice, that is, the investor pays a price for an asset at time zero and then gets cash flows at the end of each period until the security's term expires. It is also known as an *immediate annuity*.

The present value of an ordinary annuity with n total payments is $Kv + Kv^2 + \cdots + Kv^n$. Note that here, the last, or nth payment occurs at the end of the nth period, which is at $t = n$. This PV can also be simplified using geometric series, that is,

$$PV = K(v + v^2 + \cdots + v^n) = Kv(1 + v + \cdots + v^{n-1})$$

$$= Kv\frac{1 - v^n}{1 - v} = K\frac{1 - v^n}{(1 + i)(1 - v)} = K\frac{1 - v^n}{i}.$$

Using standard actuarial symbols, this can also be written as $Ka_{\overline{n}|}$.

EXAMPLE 6.16

Calculate the present value of a 10-year annuity that pays 100 each month, with each payment occurring at the end of the month (and the first payment due one month from now), assuming a nominal interest rate of 12% convertible monthly.

Solution: The present value of this annuity is:

$$100a_{\overline{120}|0.01} = 100\left[\frac{1-(1.01)^{-120}}{0.01}\right] = 100(69.7005) = 6{,}970.05.$$

Note that 6,970.05 = 7,039.75/1.01, where 7,039.75 is the answer to Example 6.15. In Example 6.16, all 120 payments are being received one month later (and are thus discounted for one additional month when converting to today's dollars).

If the cash flows received by the investor do not begin until two or more periods after the initial valuation date, then those cash flows are said to form a *deferred annuity*. A deferred annuity is valued the same as an ordinary annuity (or an annuity-due), except that the entire stream of cash flows is discounted back by the length of the deferral period.

For example, consider an m-year, n-payment deferred annuity, whereby the first of n payments occurs exactly m years following the initial valuation date. Then, the last such payment occurs at time $t = m + n - 1$. Then, the PV can be written

$$PV = Kv^m + Kv^{m+1} + \cdots + Kv^{m+n-1}$$
$$= Kv^m(1 + v + \cdots + v^{n-1}) = Kv^m\ddot{a}_{\overline{n}|}.$$

This is the same as the expression for a non-deferred annuity-due, except that all cash flows are shifted backward m periods. Note that this present value could have also been written as $Kv^{m-1}(v + v^2 + \cdots + v^n) = Kv^{m-1}a_{\overline{n}|} = K\frac{v^{n-1} - v^{m+n-1}}{i}$, which is the same as the expression for a non-deferred ordinary annuity, except that all cash flows are shifted back $m - 1$ periods.

EXAMPLE 6.17

Find the present value of a 10-year annuity that pays 100 each month, with each payment occurring at the end of the month, but the first payment does not occur until three years from now, assuming a nominal interest rate of 12% convertible monthly.

Solution: The present value of this annuity is:

$$100(v^{36})\ddot{a}_{\overline{120}|0.01} = 100(1.01)^{-36}\left[\frac{1-(1.01)^{-120}}{1-(1.01)^{-1}}\right]$$
$$= 100(0.698925)(70.3975) = 4{,}920.26.$$

Note that 4,920.26 = 7,039.75/(1.01)^{36}, where 7,039.75 is the answer to Example 6.15, because now all 120 payments are being received three years, or 36 months, later (and are thus discounted for three additional years when converting to today's dollars).

Although we focus on present value calculations here, due to our asset valuation perspective, the corresponding formulae for accumulated values of assets or funds follow quite easily. Specifically, assuming that the interest rate remains level throughout the investment horizon, and letting AV denote accumulated value, we have $AV_n = PV(1+i)^n$. Note that there is a subscript on AV because accumulated value is always calculated with reference to a specific future time. Because present value is always calculated at time zero, no subscript is needed. Thus, rather than writing all the corresponding formulae for the accumulated value of each type of annuity, we can use the link below (once we've calculated the present value) to develop the corresponding accumulated value. For example, the accumulated value (at time n) of an n-period ordinary annuity, paying K per period, is

$$AV_n = K\frac{1-v^n}{i}(1+i)^n = K\frac{(1+i)^n - 1}{i} = Ks_{\overline{n|}}.$$

6.4.2 Varying Annuities

Now, we will relax the assumption that all payment amounts must be level. However, we will still insist that the time interval between payments remains constant and that the payment amounts vary in some systematic fashion. Specifically, as is commonly the case in both asset and fund valuation, assume that the payment amounts increase (or decrease) by a flat percentage amount each period. In other words, the payment amounts vary in geometric progression so that each subsequent payment is r percent greater than the previous payment (where r can be either positive or negative). Such an assumption might relate to the adjustment of cash flows for inflation, or in the case of a stock, the expected growth rate of future dividends.

Starting with an ordinary annuity construct, where there are n payment periods, and the payments are made at $t = 1, 2, \ldots, n$, assume the first payment is of amount K (as before). However, now the subsequent payments are $K(1+r)$ at time two, $K(1+r)^2$ at time three and, finally, $K(1+r)^{n-1}$ at time n. Then, the present value can be written as:

$$PV = Kv + K(1+r)v^2 + K(1+r)^2v^3 + \cdots + K(1+r)^{n-1}v^n$$

$$= Kv\sum_{t=0}^{n-1}[(1+r)v]^t = Kv\left\{\frac{1-[(1+r)v]^n}{1-[(1+r)v]}\right\} = \frac{K}{1+i}\left\{\frac{1-[(1+r)v]^n}{1-[(1+r)/(1+i)]}\right\}$$

$$= K\left\{\frac{1-[(1+r)v]^n}{(1+i)-(1+r)}\right\} = K\left\{\frac{1-[(1+r)v]^n}{i-r}\right\}.$$

EXAMPLE 6.18

Calculate the present value of a 50-year ordinary annuity (with annual payments), where the first payment is 1,000, and each subsequent payment is 5% greater than the previous payment. Assume an annual effective interest rate of 8%.

Solution: The required values are $K = 1{,}000$, $r = 0.05$ and $i = 0.08$. The present value of this annuity is

$$1{,}000\left\{\frac{1-[1.05/1.08]^{50}}{0.08-0.05}\right\} = 25{,}183.36.$$

Similar formulae are available for the present value of varying-payment annuity-due and deferred-annuity structures, along with their corresponding accumulated value counterparts. However, we will leave such derivations to the reader. Another commonly cited varying payment structure is when the payments vary in arithmetic progression (e.g., 5, 10, 15, 20, 25, . . . , 95, 100). However, since such structures are rarely observed in practice, this will not be covered here.

6.4.3 Perpetuities/Stocks

Another variation on the annuity structures already discussed is having payments that continue forever. When the time horizon is infinite, the annuities formed from the cash flows are called *perpetuities*. Although most assets have finite time horizons, some assets, such as common and preferred stocks, are valued as if they were held into perpetuity. Here, we consider two types of stock valuation, one in which the dividends are assumed to be constant and one where the dividends increase in geometric fashion.

The assumption of constant dividends is equivalent to assuming that there will be no growth rate in future dividends from their current level. The price of a stock (now) is the present value of all future dividends, and even if the stock is subsequently sold sometime in the future, its price should still reflect the present value of all future dividends at that time, so that the current price is the sum of all future dividends (both before and after the stock purchaser subsequently sells the stock).

Assuming that a dividend will be paid at the end of each period, with the first dividend D occurring one period after the investor buys the stock, we can easily develop the stock's price, or present value. We just adapt the ordinary annuity valuation approach applied previously, but now substitute D for K, and also let n tend to infinity. When dividends remain constant, the present value is

$$\begin{aligned} PV &= D(v + v^2 + v^3 + \cdots) = \lim_{n \to \infty} D(v + v^2 + v^3 + \cdots + v^n) \\ &= \lim_{n \to \infty} D\left[\frac{1 - v^n}{i}\right] = D\left[\frac{1 - 0}{i}\right] = \frac{D}{i} \end{aligned}$$

provided $v < 1$. Using actuarial notation, this can be written as $PV = Da_{\overline{\infty}|}$.

EXAMPLE 6.19

Calculate the theoretical value of a stock share that is expected to pay constant dividends of two per quarter forever, with the first dividend occurring three months from now. Assume a nominal interest rate of 8% convertible quarterly.

Solution: The theoretical value of this stock is the present value of future dividends, where $D = 2$ and $i = 0.08/4 = 0.02$. Thus, the stock's theoretical value is $2/0.02 = 100$.

We can apply the same procedure to the case where dividends increase in geometric fashion, which is equivalent to assuming that there is a constant (but non-zero) growth rate in future dividends. Let g be the dividend growth rate, that is, the dividend paid at time t is $D(1 + g)^{t-1}$. We make the additional assumption that $g < i$, otherwise, the present value of dividends would not converge to a finite number. Then, the present value of such a perpetuity is

$$
\begin{aligned}
PV &= Dv + D(1+g)v^2 + D(1+g)^2v^3 + \cdots \\
&= \lim_{n\to\infty} Dv[1 + (1+g)v + (1+g)^2v^2 + \cdots + (1+g)^n v^n] \\
&= \lim_{n\to\infty} D\left\{ v\frac{1-[(1+g)v]^{n+1}}{1-(1+g)v} \right\} = D\left[\frac{1-0}{i-g}\right] = \frac{D}{i-g}.
\end{aligned}
$$

EXAMPLE 6.20

Calculate the theoretical value of a stock share that is expected to pay quarterly dividends forever, where the first dividend of two occurs three months from now, and each subsequent dividend is 1% greater than the previous dividend. Assume a nominal interest rate of 8% convertible quarterly.

Solution: The theoretical value of this stock is the present value of future dividends, where $D = 2$, $g = 0.01$, and $i = 0.08/4 = 0.02$. Thus, the stock's theoretical value is

$$\frac{2}{0.02 - 0.01} = \frac{2}{0.01} = 200.$$

Note that this valuation is twice as high as that obtained in Example 6.19, where the growth rate in dividends was assumed to be zero.

6.4.4 Loans

One of the most common applications of annuities in finance and banking is mortgage loans. A traditional loan can be viewed as an annuity and analyzed accordingly. The investor is the lender (usually a bank) who lends, or invests, the loan amount L to a borrower at $t = 0$. In return, the borrower must repay the entire amount borrowed according to some agreed upon schedule, and at some agreed upon interest rate, so that the future cash flows returning to the lender consist partly of principal (the amount borrowed) and partly of interest.

We will assume that the borrower makes level payments at the end of each of n periods (until the loan is completely paid off) and that the interest rate remains constant throughout the life of the loan. Initially, we will also assume that the borrower makes all such payments on time and in full, no more and no less. Denoting this periodic payment as R, the loan's fixed interest rate as i (quoted on a per-period basis), and the number of periods until the loan is paid off as n, the initial amount of the loan must be equivalent to the present value of all cash flows the lender will ultimately receive from the borrower. Using actuarial notation that we have already established, $L = PV = Ra_{\overline{n}|i}$.

EXAMPLE 6.21

If you have just received a 200,000 loan to be repaid by equal payments at the end of each month for the next 30 years and have a fixed nominal interest rate of 6% convertible monthly, what is the amount of your monthly payment?

Solution: The monthly interest rate is 0.06/12 = 0.005 = 0.5%. The amount of the payment will be: $R = \dfrac{L}{a_{\overline{n}|i}} = \dfrac{200{,}000}{a_{\overline{360}|0.005}} = \dfrac{200{,}000}{166.7916} = 1{,}199.10.$

While L is the outstanding loan balance at time zero (before any time has passed and before any payments have made on the loan), we can also calculate outstanding loan balances at intermediate times (after some, but not all, payments have been made). Suppose that we are at integer time t, where $0 < t < n$, and that a loan payment has just been made; thus, in total, t payments of R have been made, and n-t payments remain. Then, the outstanding loan balance at time t (denoted B_t) must be the present value of the remaining payments to be made. Thus, $B_t = Ra_{\overline{n-t}|i}$.

EXAMPLE 6.22

Returning to Example 6.21, where you took out a 200,000, 30-year loan at a nominal interest rate of 6% convertible monthly, what will your outstanding loan balance be immediately after your 120th payment (i.e., 10 years from now)?

Solution: The outstanding loan balance 10 years from now, or just after the 120th payment, is $B_{120} = Ra_{\overline{360-120}|0.005} = 1{,}199.10a_{\overline{240}|0.005} = 1{,}199.10(139.580772) =$ 167,371.30.

Note that even though we are only one third of the way through our loan's time horizon (10 years from now,) less than one sixth of the original loan principal has been paid off by this time. This is because in the loan's early periods, a relatively greater proportion of the loan's level payment is allocated to interest rather than principal repayment.

Now, by our previous assumptions, the loan balance at time n, B_n, must be 0. The process of reducing the loan balance from its initial level of L at time zero to its terminal value of 0 at time n is called *amortizing the loan* and is often expressed in an amortization schedule or table. Besides showing the outstanding loan balance at any point in time, such schedules also show the portions of each level loan payment R that comprise principal repayment P_t and interest payment I_t. Specifically, $R = P_t + I_t$, so that while R remains level in total, its components vary by period. Typically, in the early part of the traditional loan repayment time horizon, the interest payments will dominate the principal payments; thereafter, the interest payments will decrease and the principal payments will increase so that by the later part of the loan term, the principal payments will dominate the interest payments. It can be shown that $P_t = Rv^{n-t+1}$ and $I_t = R(1 - v^{n-t+1})$.

EXAMPLE 6.23

Returning to Example 6.22, where you took out a 200,000, 30-year loan at a nominal interest rate of 6% convertible monthly, and you calculated your outstanding loan balance immediately after the 120th payment, what proportion of the 120th payment is interest (versus principal repayment)? Compare these proportions to those obtained by decomposing the 240th payment into interest and principal repayment.

Solution: The amount of principal repaid in the 120th payment is $P_{120} = Rv^{241} = 1{,}199.10(1.005)^{-241} = 360.44$, which is 30.06% of the total payment. Thus, the remaining 69.94% of the 120th payment is allocated to interest. The amount of principal repaid in the 240th payment is $P_{240} = Rv^{121} = 1{,}199.10(1.005)^{-121} = 655.79$, which is 54.69% of the total payment. Thus, the remaining 45.31% of the 240th payment is allocated to interest. We observe that the proportion of the payment allocated to repaying the loan's principal increases as the loan approaches maturity.

Other key relationships contained within the amortization schedule are mostly recursive. For example, $I_t = B_{t-1}i$, which implies that the end-of-period interest payment is a function of both the interest rate and the loan balance at the beginning of the period. Also, $B_t = B_{t-1} - P_t$, which implies that it is only principal repayments (and not interest payments) that can contribute toward reducing periodic loan balances. In fact, the sum of all principal repayments from time one to time n must be equivalent to the initial loan amount.

6.4.5 Bonds

Another standard application of annuities among investment choices arises when pricing bonds that pay periodic coupons. Most coupon-paying bonds pay coupons on a semi-annual basis, so that it helps to discount cash flows using a six-month interest rate. When an investor buys a bond for price P (at time zero), there is an expected receipt of two future cash flow streams.

The simpler cash flow stream is a single cash flow, called the redemption value or face amount, which is returned to the investor on the bond's maturity date, and is typically of the same order of magnitude as (but not necessarily identical to) the bond's price. The other cash flow stream consists of periodic coupons returned to the investor at the end of each of n coupon periods. These coupons are similar to the interest payments the lender receives from the borrower in the loan structure, except that the coupons are typically level (because no principal is being returned to the bond purchaser prior to maturity), unlike a loan's interest payments, which are decreasing as the loan balance declines.

Coupon amounts are based on the bond's par value (F), usually a round number like 1,000 or 10,000, which is often the same as the bond's face amount (C). Specifically, the coupon amount is Fr, where r is the per-period coupon rate. Then, the price of the bond (at time zero) can be easily determined as the present value of all future cash flows. In formula terms, $P = Fra_{\overline{n}|i} + \dfrac{C}{(1+i)^n}$. In words, the price consists of the coupon-related annuity along with the single redemption value cash flow, discounted back n periods to the present.

EXAMPLE 6.24

Calculate the price of a 1,000 par value 10-year bond that can be redeemed at 100 above par, and has semi-annual coupons payable at 12% convertible semi-annually, if the bond is bought to yield 8% convertible semiannually.

Solution: Here, $F = 1{,}000$, $r = 0.12/2 = 0.06$, $n = 10*2 = 20$, $C = 1{,}100$, and $i = 0.08/2 = 0.04$.

Thus, we have:

$$P = Fra_{\overline{n}|i} + \frac{C}{(1+i)^n} = (1{,}000)(0.06)a_{\overline{20}|0.04} + \frac{1{,}100}{(1.04)^{20}}$$
$$= 815.42 + 502.03 = 1{,}317.45.$$

As with loans, bonds can be sold by the original purchaser prior to the bond's maturity. The appropriate sale price is the present value of the remaining coupons along with the discounted face amount (which is now being discounted over a shorter time period). Naturally, the interest rate at the time of sale could be different than the original i. With bonds, there is an inverse relationship between prices and interest rates.

6.5 EXERCISES

6.1 Assume all cash flows are made annually and that the annual effective interest rate is 8%. Also, unless otherwise noted, assume that the investment horizon lasts 30 years. Find the present value (at $t = 0$) and the accumulated value (at $t = 30$) for each of the following investment structures:

a) A 20-year level-payment deferred-annuity, where payments of \$1,000 are made at $t = 11, 12, \ldots,$ and 30.

b) A 30-year geometrically varying ordinary annuity, where the first payment is 1,000, and each subsequent payment is 10% higher than the previous payment.

c) A stock paying annual end-of- year dividends into perpetuity, where the first dividend (at $t = 1$) is 5, the growth rate in dividends is 20% for the next 5 years (through $t = 6$), and the growth rate in dividends is 5% thereafter (after $t = 6$ and continuing forever).

d) A 30-year loan with end-of-year payments, where each of the first 15 payments is 1,000, and each of the last 15 payments is 2,000.

e) A 30-year bond paying annual end-of-year coupons, where the coupon rate is 6%, the par value is 10,000, and the bond is redeemable at par.

For the next three problem parts, assume you are the recipient of the cash flows that correspond to the structures given in a), b), and c) above and that you are able to reinvest the cash flows in a separate fund, according to the particular interest rate structure given in each problem part.

f) Calculate the amount of interest earned between $t = 11$ and $t = 13$ on the deferred annuity from part a), using simple interest of 10% per year.

g) Calculate the amount of interest earned between $t = 1$ and $t = 3$ on the geometrically varying annuity from part b), using a constant force of interest of 10%.

h) Calculate the amount of interest earned between $t = 1$ and $t = 3$ on the dividend-paying stock from part c), using a nominal rate of interest of 10% convertible quarterly.

i) For the loan from part d), calculate the outstanding loan balance at $t = 1$ and $t = 2$, and find the amounts of the first and second loan payments that are allocated to interest and principal repayment.

j) For the bond from part e), if no coupons were paid (instead of 6% coupons), what would the new discounted bond price be if the redemption value were to remain unchanged at 10,000?

6.2 You are the Chief Financial Officer for your company and must decide whether or not to undertake each of three projects. Each project requires an initial investment today and then will provide future cash flows through the next 10 years. The projects are labeled X, Y, and Z and have the following cash flow structures (where t represents time in the units defined in the project description).

-Project X requires an initial investment of 100,000, and provides 10 annual end-of-year cash flows of $C_t = 10{,}000 + 1{,}500(t - 1)$.

-Project Y requires an initial investment of 50,000 and provides 20 semi-annual end-of-period cash flows of $C_t = 5{,}000(1.03)^{t-1}$.

-Project Z requires an initial investment of 25,000 and provides 40 quarterly end-of-period cash flows of $C_t = 4{,}000$. However, this project also requires a second investment five years from now of 50,000.

For parts a), b), and c), assume the annual effective interest rate is 10%.

a) Calculate the Net Present Value of Project X.
b) Calculate the Net Present Value of Project Y.
c) Calculate the Net Present Value of Project Z.
d) Calculate the Internal Rate of Return for Project X.
e) Calculate the Internal Rate of Return for Project Y.
f) Calculate the Internal Rate of Return for Project Z.
g) If the three projects are independent, which project(s), if any, will be undertaken?
h) If the three projects are mutually exclusive, which project(s), if any, will be undertaken?
i) Did NPV and IRR produce the same ranking of the three projects?
Will this always be the case?
j) Play around with the interest assumption (currently at 10%), and see if there is a range for which the rankings obtained from a)–c) change.

CHAPTER 7
Asset Types

This chapter provides an introduction to the basic asset types employed by both insurance companies and financial services organizations and distinguishes between underlying assets and derivatives, which have value dependent on underlying assets. We begin with an overview of some low-risk assets like savings deposits, money market instruments, and U.S. government securities. Then, we introduce the concepts of bonds and stocks, and discuss types and characteristics of each. Next, we offer a basic discussion of derivatives, such as forward contracts, futures contracts, commodity and interest rate swaps, and call and put options. Finally, we mention other assets that are specific to insurance company portfolios.

7.1 Underlying Assets

An underlying asset has value in and of itself, rather than having value that is derived from some other asset. This is in contrast to derivatives (discussed later in this chapter), which have value that depends on the value of some underlying asset. Below, we discuss three major classes of underlying assets: low-risk fixed-income securities, bonds (of higher risk), and stocks.

7.1.1 Low-Risk, Fixed-Income Securities

Fixed-income securities provide a mostly certain cash flow stream to an investor over a pre-specified amount of time. However, there are still risks involved with fixed-income securities and, in some cases, the amount and timing of the promised cash flow stream can vary according to contingent circumstances. For example, the security might go into default, which could cause the income stream to be partially or fully delayed or even discontinued. There are three types of fixed-income securities that have virtually no default risk—savings deposits, money market instruments, and U.S. government securities.

7.1.1.1 Savings deposits

Interest-bearing savings deposits are primarily offered by commercial banks and in the United States are guaranteed (up to a specified amount) by the federal government. A demand deposit pays a rate of interest that depends on current economic conditions and must be maintained in a bank account for a minimum length of time (e.g., six months) to prevent early withdrawal penalties. A certificate of deposit (CD) operates similarly, except that the amount of interest paid depends on the pre-specified length of time the depositor promises to hold the money in the account. CDs are issued in standard denominations such as 1,000 or 10,000 and can be bought and sold in a securities market.

7.1.1.2 Money market instruments

Loans made from banks to corporations that are short term (i.e., one year or less) form the basis of money market instruments. Examples of money market instruments include commercial paper, bankers' acceptances, Eurodollar deposits, and Eurodollar CDs. Commercial paper consists of unsecured loans and is therefore not guaranteed by any collateral. With a banker's acceptance, if one company buys something from another company, and then agrees to make payment within a certain period of time, a third-party bank can *accept* this promise and act as back-up to ensure this payment will be made; note that this acceptance can be traded in secondary markets, once the bank accepts the ultimate responsibility for payment. Eurodollar deposits are dollar-denominated but held in non-U.S. banks; similarly, Eurodollar CDs are dollar-denominated but issued by non-U.S. banks. Investors can also temporarily hold cash reserves in money market accounts that pay a very low rate of interest until they decide where else to employ such funds.

7.1.1.3 U.S. government securities

The U.S. government issues many types of fixed-income securities in order to obtain loans of varying maturities. Since these securities are backed by the government itself, they have almost no credit risk (i.e., extremely low probability of default).

Treasury bills (T-bills) have terms to maturity of either 13, 26, or 52 weeks and are issued in denominations of $10,000 or more. They are highly liquid and can be sold easily prior to the maturity date. At issue, these are priced at a discount to reflect the time value of money. Thus, if the face amount is $100,000, a 52-week T-bill might sell for $97,500.

Treasury notes (T-notes) have maturities between 1 and 10 years and may be issued in smaller denominations relative to T-bills. Also, unlike T-bills, the holder receives periodic, fixed, pre-determined semi-annual coupons across the entire holding period. At maturity, the holder also received the note's face value.

Treasury bonds (T-bonds) have maturities exceeding 10 years; otherwise, they are similar in structure to T-notes. One unique feature of T-bonds is that they are callable after some initial period of call protection; then, the Treasury (i.e., the issuer) can call the bond back, thus forcing the investor to redeem the bond early.

There are more complex variations on basic Treasury securities, such as STRIPS and TIPS. With STRIPS (Separate Trading of Registered Interest and Principal of Securities), the coupons are *stripped* from the T-bonds and then repackaged into separate securities, each resembling a zero-coupon bond (albeit with varying maturities).[1] With TIPS (Treasury Inflation Protection Securities), both the coupons and face amount are indexed to future changes in the Consumer Price Index, which is the standard proxy for measuring inflation in the U.S. economy.

7.1.2 Bonds

Bonds represent the greatest volume of trading in fixed-income securities. They are issued not only by the federal government but also by state governments and municipalities and by corporations. Before delving into all the types of bonds, let's begin with a general definition of a bond.

Most generally, when an issuer sells a bond to an investor, that issuer has the obligation to return cash flows to the investor at times that are pre-specified in the bond's contract.

---

1 The term *coupon* comes from the fact that, at one time, bonds had physical books containing coupons that could be redeemed for the periodic interest payments.

The largest such cash flow is the face amount, or redemption value, which is paid at maturity and is often equal to the bond's par value. The purpose of the par value, which is often a large round number like 1,000 or 10,000, is to help determine the amount of periodic coupon payments the investor receives each coupon period. Specifically, the coupon amounts are equal to the par value times the coupon rate. Typically, coupons are paid on a semi-annual basis (note that the coupon rate is quoted as an annual nominal rate convertible semi-annually) at the end of each six-month period until the bond's maturity. Thus, at maturity, there are two cash flows: the last coupon payment and the redemption value.

The original price of a bond, at time of issue, reflects the present value of both cash flow streams, that is, a bond's price is the present value of all coupons to be received, which form a level annuity, and the present value of the redemption value, which is a single cash flow. Bond issuers sell bonds in order to raise capital immediately and generally use coupon rates that are close to the prevailing market interest rates.

If the redemption value equals the par value, and the coupon rate is equivalent to the market interest rate (which is used to discount the bond's cash flows), then the bond's price will be equivalent to its redemption value. However, if the redemption value equals the par value, and the coupon rate is higher than the interest rate, the bond will sell at a *premium*, that is, at a price higher than the redemption value. Likewise, if the coupon rate is lower than the interest rate, the bond will sell at a *discount*, that is, at a price lower than the redemption value. A special type of bond is a zero-coupon (or accumulation) bond, which by definition has a coupon rate of zero, and therefore sells at a heavy discount relative to its face amount.

In the United States, most bonds have a small bid-ask spread, so that dealers (financial intermediaries) will buy the bond from the issuer at the bid price and then sell the bond to the investor at the higher ask price. Bond prices are quoted in thirty-seconds of a point, relative to a standard level of 100; if the face amount is other than 100, multiply the price quote by the corresponding multiple of 100.

EXAMPLE 7.1

If a bond's face amount is 1000, and the price is quoted at 105 11/32, then what is the actual price of the bond?

Solution: The bond's actual price is $[1{,}000/100][105 + (11/32)] = 10(105.34375) = 1{,}053.44$.

When the sale date does not occur on a coupon payment date, bond quotations also include accrued interest. The accrued interest payment is made at the date of sale and is added to the price, since the new bondholder will benefit from receiving the entire upcoming coupon payment. This extra amount can be approximated by the fraction of the current coupon period that has already elapsed by the sale date times the full coupon amount.[2]

2 The approximation method employed here is called the *practical method* and is the simplest among competing approximation methods. For a more complete discussion of other approximation methods used, see Kellison (2008), Section 6.5.

EXAMPLE 7.2

If coupons on a bond are paid on June 15 and December 15, and the coupon amounts are 50 each, but the date of sale is August 1, then what is the accrued interest payment?

Solution: $(47/183)50 = 12.84$, where 47 is the number of days between June 15 and August 1, and 183 is the number of days between June 15 and December 15.

7.1.2.1 Types of bond issuer

There are several different types of bond issuers. Here, we discuss some common issuers other than the U.S. government. Corporate bonds are issued by companies that want to raise capital for both everyday operations and new ventures. Corporate bonds are less liquid than and can vary substantially with respect to credit quality, which depends in turn on the strength of the issuing company and the characteristics of the bond itself.

Municipal bonds are issued by both state and local governments and are classified as either general obligation or revenue bonds. General obligation bonds are backed directly by a government agency, whereas revenue bonds may also be supported by revenues pertaining to the project the bond issue is funding. The primary advantage of *munis*, as municipal bonds are often called, from an investor's perspective, is that the interest income from coupons is exempt from both federal income tax and from any state and local taxes from the state of issue. As a result, investors must accept lower yields on these bonds relative to otherwise equivalent corporate bonds.

7.1.2.2 Characteristics

The specific characteristics of each bond issue are laid out in an *indenture*, which is the official contract of bond terms. For example, a bond could be callable if the issuer is allowed to call back, or redeem, the bond (for a predetermined price) prior to maturity at certain specified times. The issuer will choose to do this at the time that is most to their advantage, which is likely to be at the time that is most disadvantageous. In a declining interest rate environment, the issuer will be more motivated to call the bond early, so as to refinance, or issue a new bond with lower coupon payments. Callable bonds are priced lower than otherwise equivalent non-callable bonds because the issuer has the option to control the timing of cash flows.

A bond could also be *putable* if the investor is allowed to put back the bond early, which means that the issuer must pay the face amount prior to the maturity date, should the investor request such payment. This will occur in a rising interest rate environment whereby the investor could then roll over the funds received into a new bond with higher coupon payments. Putable bonds are priced higher than otherwise equivalent non-putable bonds because the investor now has this option.

Some bonds contain a sinking fund provision to ensure an orderly retirement of the bond issue. Here, the issuer must make periodic pre-defined payments of parts of the redemption value, effectively buying back a portion of the outstanding bond amount each period. The fund is usually held by an independent party. A failure to satisfy the sinking fund provision may constitute a default on the bond. There may also be covenants in the indenture that limit the amount of additional debt the issuer can utilize after an initial bond is issued. This is meant to further protect the bondholder, so as to prevent the issuer from becoming so leveraged that, if adverse economic or company scenarios occur, the original bond may go into default. Also, in the event of bankruptcy, there may be terms that specify which bondholders get paid first and in what amount.

Rating agencies assess the riskiness inherent in various corporate bond issues and assign a letter grade that reflects their estimate of the bond's credit risk. Note that such agencies, like Moody's and Standard & Poor's (S&P), came under fire during the recent financial crisis for severely underestimating the risk involved for many bonds with complex structures, such as mortgage-backed securities (MBS) and collateralized debt obligations (CDOs). However, on a long-term historical basis, a bond's rating has been strongly correlated with its default frequency. As T-bonds are backed by the credit of the federal government, they are generally rated high since their probabilities of default are near zero.

There are two primary categories for a bond's rating: *investment-grade* and *high-yield* (or junk). Using S&P's rating classifications as an example, the highest investment grade is AAA, and the next highest (investment) grades are AA, A, and BBB, respectively. All grades at BB and below are considered high-yield; more specifically, grades of BB and B are labeled *speculative*, whereas the lowest grades are CCC, CC, C, and D, where the probability of default increases with each grade decline.

When assigning a rating, the agencies consider the financial status of the bond's issuer as measured by various financial ratios and the bond's terms as reflected in the indenture. Note that the changes or trends in these ratings may be even more important than the absolute level of the ratings themselves. Just because a bond has an unfavorable rating does not imply that all investors should avoid it; in fact, the reason these bonds are labeled as high-yield is that they can potentially yield high returns if the investor receives the bond's scheduled cash flows. If default risk is adequately diversified, the investor may be more than fairly compensated for this risk, even if a few of the bonds in the investor's portfolio default. Furthermore, if a bond goes into default, the investor may not lose all promised cash flows but may still recover a portion of these cash flows as scheduled or at a later time.

7.1.3 Stocks

Just like bondholders, stockholders have two different sources of cash flows from their investment. However, unlike bondholders, neither of these two sources consists of fixed income. First, there are periodic dividends; however, the amount of dividends, along with the decision as to whether or not dividends will be issued at all, is not fixed in advance. The process of setting dividend levels is made by the corporation's board. Second, stockholders can benefit from capital appreciation, or growth, but only if the stock price rises over their investment horizon. Note that the amount of appreciation is partially determined by when the stockholder decides to sell the stock they originally bought, so that, unlike bonds, the stock has no predetermined maturity date like bonds.

The current price of a stock share is whatever the market price happens to be. However, the intrinsic value of a stock share, which represents a stock's "true," or "theoretical" value must be estimated, and is equal to the present value of all future dividends. If the intrinsic value is greater than the current market value, this is an indication that the stock is currently undervalued (and that a "buy" recommendation may be warranted). Likewise, if the intrinsic value is less than the current market value, this indicates that the stock may be currently overvalued (and that a "sell" recommendation may be preferred).

The most common frequency for how often dividends are paid is quarterly, since this coincides with a firm's quarterly earnings reports. The dividends being discounted are only an estimate, since no one can say for sure what these dividend amounts will be. For simplicity, it is often assumed that dividends will grow at a constant rate so that the theoretical value of a stock price can be easily estimated using geometrically varying annuities, as illustrated in Section 6.4.2. Another, slightly more complicated variation that applies more to newer and smaller firms is to assume a two-stage growth model. Here, dividends are assumed to grow at a supernormal growth rate for a small number of years, but thereafter, a much lower, more normal growth rate is established. Note that stock valuations do not include the sale price of a stock because it is assumed that the stock is held into perpetuity. This assumption works from a valuation perspective because even if the stock were sold at a future point in time, its theoretical sale price would still be the present value of future dividends from the point of sale; thus, the current price is just estimated as the present value of all dividends, which includes those before the point of this hypothetical sale and those afterward as well.

When companies issue stock, the investor obtains rights that pertain to certain company operations. For example, the owners have a claim on the company's earnings, as represented either through an immediate dividend payout, or possibly in the continued reinvestment of those earnings, which should ideally lead to appreciation in the stock price. In fact, when prospects are bright, most rational stockholders would prefer to have a lower dividend payout and instead enjoy the potential benefit of capital growth. Shareholders also elect a company's board of directors, who then appoint the upper-level managers of the company. If the company becomes bankrupt, the shareholders have limited liability; the most they can lose is the original amount they invested in the stock. However, in the event of bankruptcy, stockholders are last in priority relative to all other claimants; that is, stockholders will only receive what is left over (if anything) after bondholders have already been paid.

7.1.3.1 Types of stock

Companies can issue shares of stocks in multiple ways, depending on their size and how long they have been in existence. When the company is originated, the owners supply their own capital and have shares in the company in proportion to what is contributed. At this point, the company is privately held. To become publicly held, so that public trading of shares is possible, the company must hire an investment banking firm to help arrange for an *initial public offering* (IPO) of the company's stock.

An existing publicly held company can also decide to issue new shares. Then, additional capital will be invested in the firm by either previously existing or new investors. If there are new investors, then the ownership percentage for each original investor will be diluted. The company may also split stock shares, so that the price per share is divided up into smaller pieces while the overall number of shares will multiply. However, this does not result in any additional paid-in capital or ownership dilution.

A publicly held company can also decide to become privately held once again, which results in a reverse IPO, or leveraged buyout. Here, a group of individuals buys back stock shares and runs the company for a short period of time, perhaps hoping to improve the efficiency of operations. Then they may take the company public again by selling shares to public investors at a significant mark-up from the price at which they bought them when the leveraged buyout took place.

7.1.3.2 Characteristics

Once an individual acquires shares of a company's stock, they can transfer ownership to other individuals without the permission of the original issuer. Thus, there is an active secondary market for stock-related transactions. The secondary market consists of both exchange trading and OTC trading. In the United States, there are two primary stock exchanges, both based in lower Manhattan: the New York Stock Exchange (NYSE) and the American Stock Exchange. The owners of exchanges are considered brokers who can buy or sell on the exchange. Brokers profit from commissions on each trade, regardless of whether they buy or sell.

Stocks are also traded an on OTC basis. The National Association of Securities Dealers Automated Quotation system (NASDAQ) is responsible for the majority of OTC trading in the United States. NASDAQ consists of a network of dealers who trade on behalf of their customers. Dealers profit from the bid-ask spread, since they buy at the lower bid price but sell at the higher ask price. Now, most trading is done electronically rather than right on the trading floor. It is also possible for transactions to occur directly among individuals and institutions, so that no brokers or dealers need be involved.

Stock transactions can be the result of market orders, limit orders, or stop orders. Most transactions are market orders, whereby the broker attempts to get the best readily available price for the client, but makes no guarantee as to what this price will be. By contrast, if the client places a limit order to buy a stock at a specific price, the broker will only execute this order if the stock price is at or below this level; likewise, if the client places a limit order to sell a stock at a specific price, the broker will only execute this order if the stock price is at or above this level. A stop, or stop-loss order, commands the broker to sell a stock if the price falls down to a specific level, so as to limit the client's losses. Similarly, a stop order can be placed to buy a stock if the price rises up to a specific level. Both limit and stop orders need not be ever executed if the stock moves in the opposite direction as specified by the particular order. Usually, limit and stop orders expire after a certain period of time, but they can also be *good-until-cancelled.*

A stock transaction is typically thought of as buying the stock initially and selling the stock at some future time; however, when these positions are reversed, a *short sale* is formed. Here, a trader sells the stock initially, and then buys it back at some future time, thus hoping to profit from a decline in the stock price. Since the trader does not own the stock at the initial point of sale, it is necessary to borrow the shares from a second party before selling them to a third party.

With a short sale, any dividends that accrue during the time between when the shorter sells and repurchases the stock are credited to the second party (i.e., the party who lent the short seller the shares) from the short seller's account. In addition, short sellers must establish a margin account to protect this second party from non-repayment of the borrowed shares in case the stock price actually goes up. Note that the short seller's losses are potentially unlimited since stock prices have no upper bound. This is in contrast to the maximum loss amount from a long position, which is limited to the amount of the original funds invested. The initial margin amount is usually set at 50 percent of the stock's price and is an asset of the short seller. Thus, the short seller earns interest on deposits into the margin account, which is a component of the total return. If the margin account balance becomes too low, the short seller may have to deposit additional funds, as specified by any *maintenance margin* requirements.

7.2 Derivatives

A financial derivative is a security whose value is derived from the value of some other underlying asset. The use of derivatives increased substantially in the 1970s when currencies were first allowed to float (after the gold standard was abandoned) and oil prices became highly volatile due to OPEC's reduction in the oil supply. Recently, the popularity of, and uses for, derivatives has continued to expand in various risk management contexts.

There are two primary purposes for derivatives: hedging and speculation, although after the recent financial crisis, hedging is likely to become the more respected of the two purposes. When companies and traders want to reduce or more effectively manage their risk exposure, they can utilize derivatives in a hedging context (i.e., to reduce losses if their particular market view is not ultimately realized). Derivatives can also be used in speculative fashion to make more highly leveraged bets that a particular price movement will occur; if this move does occur, gains can be magnified considerably. However, if the opposite move occurs and the position is unhedged, the investor can suffer enormous losses. Below, we introduce the main categories of derivatives, including forward contracts, futures contracts, swaps, and both call and put options.

7.2.1 Forward Contracts

7.2.1.1 Characteristics

A forward contract consists of an obligation to buy (or sell) a specific amount of some commodity at a pre-specified price and at a pre-specified time in the future. Both parties to the contract (i.e., the buyer and the seller) are obligated to fulfill the contract terms at the pre-specified future time. The buyer is said to have the long position, and the seller the short position. For example, one year from now, the buyer will pay 10,000 to the seller; in exchange, the seller will deliver 10 ounces of gold to the buyer. Note that in many cases, the seller will not actually provide the gold but rather the current market value of 10 ounces of gold.

The official forward contract is spelled out in a legal document. Note that the underlying asset need not be a physical commodity (like oil or soybeans) but can also be an interest rate instrument or a foreign currency. A unique characteristic of forward contracts is that there is no initial premium made; the only cash flow occurs when the good is delivered from the seller to the buyer. Thus, the market for forward contracts differs from spot markets where the underlying asset is paid for and delivered (almost) immediately.

7.2.1.2 Pricing

When forming the theoretical value of a forward contract, it is assumed that there are no transaction costs, no storage costs to hold the underlying asset between now and time T (the time at which the asset is to be delivered), and that it is also possible to sell the underlying asset (what the seller is to deliver at time T) short. Let S be the spot price of the underlying asset at time zero, and let F be the corresponding forward price at time T. Suppose an investor buys one unit of a commodity right now at price S and simultaneously enters into a short forward contract, whereby one unit of the underlying asset will be delivered at time T in exchange for price F. Then, the price charged at time T should be $F = Se^{rT}$, where r is the prevailing risk-free continuously compounded interest rate used to accumulate (or discount) cash flows. Equivalently, $S = Fe^{-rT}$. In practice, traders of both forward contracts and futures contracts use a slightly higher rate than the risk-free T-bill rate to reflect the extra default risk involved with forward contracts relative to government-issued securities.

EXAMPLE 7.3

Suppose a share of a non-dividend-paying stock costs 50 today, and the annual continuously compounded risk-free rate is 6%. How much should a two-year forward contract for this stock cost (assuming this cash flow is paid two years from now)?

Solution: For a stock without dividends, the forward price is the future value of the initial stock price. Thus, $F = Se^{rT} = 50e^{0.06(2)} = 50e^{0.12} = 56.37$.

Although the spot price at time zero has no variability (i.e., it is known), the spot price of the underlying asset can change from its original level. Let S_T be the spot price at time T. If $S_T > F$, the long position in the forward contract will be profitable since the commodity will be purchased for the lower price F instead of the market price S_T. However, if $S_T < F$, it is preferable to be in the short position since the long position is still obligated to buy the commodity at F, while the seller receives the higher price of F rather than the market price of S_T.

If transaction costs (e.g., fees, bid-ask spreads, and differences in rates for borrowing and lending) are non-negligible, the previous analysis becomes more complex. If the underlying asset is a physical commodity, there may be considerable storage costs. For example, anything edible will need to be preserved appropriately; also, an expensive asset such as gold will entail vault rental and insurance fees. If the underlying asset is financial but less tangible than gold, although there may be no storage costs, there could still be cash flows incurred between now and time T. For example, a stock may have dividend payments and a bond may have coupon payments. These cash flows go to the current owner of the security, just as the storage costs mentioned before do. Neither the cash flows from financial assets nor the storage costs from physical commodities affect the party that assumes ownership at time T, that is, until ownership is transferred at that time.

It is also possible to transact in prepaid forward contracts. Here, although the delivery of the underlying asset still does not occur until time T, the price paid by the buyer who will eventually receive this asset is paid now. Not surprisingly, the value of a prepaid forward, often denoted F^P, is related to F as follows: $F^P = PV(F)$, where $PV(F)$ is the present value of F, when discounting back from time T to now. Note that if there are no storage costs or expected intermediate cash flows, then $F^P = S$, the current spot price. For example, the prepaid forward price on a non-dividend paying stock is simply the current value of the stock.

EXAMPLE 7.4

Suppose a share of a non-dividend-paying stock costs 50 today, and the annual continuously compounded risk-free rate is 6%. How much should a two-year pre-paid forward contract for this stock cost (right now)?

Solution: For a stock without dividends, the prepaid forward price is the same as the initial stock price, which is 50. Also, the pre-paid forward price is the discounted forward price from Example 7.3, that is, $F^P = PV(F) = Se^{rT}e^{-rT} = S = 50$.

7.2.2 Futures Contracts

7.2.2.1 Characteristics

Futures contracts are similar to forward contracts, except that futures are traded on an organized exchange. With exchanges, contract terms are more standardized, and it is easier for individuals to find counterparties to take the other side of the transaction. In fact, the exchange may act as a counterparty to both sides of a transaction (i.e., the buyer and seller) so as to minimize the risk that one counterparty may default and not fulfill their side of the contract. Forward contracts are tailored to the individual parties involved, so that multiple identical contracts that should be priced equivalently might actually be priced differently. The prices of futures contracts are more consistent.

Forward contracts are not traded, so that no market price is ever established. However, for futures contracts, as market conditions change, the price can be adjusted. Moreover, futures contracts can be traded and easily settled prior to maturity. Let F_t be the futures price at time t (in days). Then, the initial futures price is F_0, and one day later, the price for a newly issued futures contract (with the same terms) is F_1. The price of all the futures contracts issued on the previous day then changes from F_0 to F_1. Then, the contract parties will either pay or be paid the difference between F_0 and F_1 because at the contract's maturity, F_1 will be the cash amount exchanged rather than F_0. This process is called *marking to market* and is further clarified by the following example.

EXAMPLE 7.5

The 3-month (91 days) futures price on a stock is 28. You enter into 25 long futures contracts, where each futures contract has a size 50 times that of the stock price. The exchange requires an initial margin of 10% of the initial notional amount, and the margin account earns interest at a 6% annualized continuously compounded rate. Suppose the futures price is marked to market each day, and the futures price falls to 27 one day after the original contracts are bought. Calculate the margin account balance at this time (i.e., one day ahead).

Solution: The notional amount is $25 \times 50 \times 28 = 35{,}000$, so that the initial margin account balance is $10\% \times 35{,}000 = 3{,}500$. When the price falls by 1 after one day, this reflects a loss of $25 \times 50 \times (28 - 27) = 1{,}250$. We can either pay this loss to our counterparty directly, or allow it to be incorporated into the margin account balance. If taking the latter approach, the new margin account balance will be $3{,}500e^{0.06(1/365)} - 1{,}250 = 2{,}250.58$.

As noted in the example, both the long and short parties to a futures contract must open a margin account with a broker, where the initial margin balance is set at 5–10% of the value of the futures contract. At the end of each trading day, the margin accounts are marked to market, so that if the futures price increases, the long party receives a deposit into their margin account whereas the short party must draw from their margin account to pay the difference. If the futures price goes down, cash flows in the opposite direction would occur. Thus, by the maturity date, the futures price may be quite different from what it was initially, but because marking-to-market has occurred throughout, both parties can readily fulfill their obligation. Note that the significant majority of futures contracts have their positions settled prior to maturity.

EXAMPLE 7.6

Returning to Example 7.5, assume the futures contract is not closed out early but is held until maturity, and the marking to market process continues on a daily basis throughout the 91-day time horizon. Also, suppose the margin account balance has actually increased to 5,000 by the end of the 91 days (which reflects an overall upward trend in the stock's price over this time). Calculate the 3-month profit on the long position in the futures contract.

Solution: The 3-month profit on this position will be the final margin account balance minus the future value of the initial margin account balance. In this case, the profit will be $5{,}000 - 3{,}500e^{0.06(91/365)} = 1{,}447.25$. Note that the profit for the counterparty (i.e., the short position) will be negative since this position will have had a decrease rather than an increase in the margin account over the 91-day time period.

Another purpose of margin accounts is that they help guarantee that each party will not default on their obligations. If a margin account (after several adverse price moves) drops below a minimum level, which is usually around 75% of the initial margin (called the maintenance margin), the contract holder is given a margin call to replenish the margin account to at least the original minimum level. If this contract holder cannot fulfill terms of the margin call, the futures contract will be closed out. Although margin accounts on futures contracts do not pay interest directly, many brokers allow low-risk securities like T-bills to serve as margin so that the margin account will earn a modest interest rate.

7.2.2.2 Pricing

At any point in time during the existence of a futures contract, there is only one price that matters—the delivery price. The value of futures contracts prior to delivery is conceptually zero because, due to the marking to market process, the margin accounts envelop any price changes directly. The prices of futures contracts are also closely related to the prices of otherwise equivalent forward contracts. However, there is a subtle difference. With forward contracts, there is no initial cash flow and, in fact, no cash flow at all until maturity. With futures contracts, because of marking to market, there is a cash flow each day that reflects the change in the futures price from the previous day.

Now, if interest rates are deterministic (i.e., non-random), then forward and futures prices must still be the same in order to preclude arbitrage opportunities. However, if interest rates are not deterministic, the prices may legitimately differ, albeit by not a very large amount. More specifically, if interest rates are positively correlated with futures prices, the futures price will exceed an otherwise equivalent forward contract because the marking to market process becomes advantageous to the one holding the long position in the futures contract. The reverse is true when interest rates are negatively correlated with futures prices because then, marking to market will work against the party with a long position.

7.2.3 Swaps

A swap is an agreement to exchange one cash flow stream for another. Although swaps are often tailored toward the specific investment objectives of the parties involved, the most common type of a swap is a plain vanilla swap. Here, one party agrees to swap a series of uncertain payments for a series of fixed payments. If one party currently has an uncertain liability stream, which will produce large losses if payment levels increased, that party could enter into a swap to pay a predictable schedule of fixed liabilities instead.

For example, let party A be the fixed-rate payer where the amount of each periodic payment equals a fixed rate of interest times the notional principal amount. (The term *notional* means "in name only," since there really is no principal involved, so that the only purpose of the notional amount is to set the level of the fixed payments). Then, let party B be the floating-rate (or variable-rate) payer who is obligated to pay a floating rate of interest applied to the same notional amount. LIBOR (London Interbank Offered Rate) is often used as a basis for the rate from which floating rates are set.

When the floating rate is higher than the fixed rate, A pays the difference to B and vice versa. The effect is that party A, who was the floating-rate payer prior to the swap, has now become a fixed-rate payer.

7.2.3.1 Value of interest rate swaps

In the context of a plain vanilla interest rate swap, let r be the fixed rate of interest, N be the notional amount, and M be the number of periods in the swap. Also, let $(c_1, c_2, \ldots, c_M)$ be the sequence of floating rates observed across all M swap dates. Then, since party A is the swap's fixed-rate payer and floating-rate receiver as described previously, the cash flows received by A will be $N(c_1 - r, c_2 - r, \ldots, c_M - r)$. Let V be the value of the swap from party A's perspective. It can be computed by summing the present value of the M cash flows. Thus, $V = N\sum_{t=1}^{M}(c_t - r)v^t$, where v^t is an appropriate discount factor from t back to 0, as reflected in the current term structure of interest rates. Note that the value of the swap from party B's perspective is just $-V$. Given that the floating rates are not known in advance, it is uncertain which of the two parties will have positive value from doing the swap. Parties usually enter into a swap with no money changing hands at time zero, and thus the fixed swap rate r is usually set so that $E(V) = 0$.

EXAMPLE 7.7

You enter into a 3-year interest rate swap on a notional amount of 1,000,000, where you will be the fixed-rate payer and the floating-rate receiver. The fixed rate is determined to be 5%, and the floating rates at times 1, 2, and 3, turn out to be 4%, 6%, and 7%, respectively. If the 1-year, 2-year, and 3-year spot rates (at the time the swap is conceived) are 4.5%, 5.5%, and 6.5%, calculate the value of the swap (also at the time the swap is conceived).

Solution: The value of this interest rate swap from your perspective (i.e., the fixed-rate payer and floating-rate receiver) is:

$$V = N\sum_{t=1}^{M}(c_t - r)v^t$$

$$= 1{,}000{,}000\left\{\left[\frac{.04 - .05}{(1.045)^1}\right] + \left[\frac{.06 - .05}{(1.055)^2}\right] + \left[\frac{.07 - .05}{(1.065)^3}\right]\right\}$$

$$= 1{,}000{,}000(-.00956938 + .00890452 + .01655698)$$

$$= 1{,}000{,}000(.01589212) = 15{,}892.12.$$

7.2.3.2 Value of commodity swaps

A swap can also be thought of as a series of forward contracts. This idea is perhaps best illustrated with commodity swaps, which are like interest rate swaps except that now payments are based on commodity prices instead of interest rates. For example, if a company must purchase oil each month but is concerned that oil prices may fluctuate too wildly, they can enter into a commodity swap that will effectively exchange their variable-payment structure for a more stable fixed-payment structure. All they must do is find a counterparty willing to engage in this swap.

Assume that party A prefers to pay a fixed per-unit amount X each period when buying the commodity and that in each of the M periods, party A will buy N units of the commodity. Also, let $S_1, S_2, \ldots, S_M$ be the sequence of spot prices for the commodity observed across all M swap dates. Then, since party A is the swap's fixed-level payer and variable-level receiver, the net cash flow received by party A will be $N(S_1 - X, S_2 - X, \ldots, S_M - X)$. Thus, $V = N\sum_{t=1}^{M}(S_t - X)v^t$ where v^t is once again an appropriate discount factor from t back to 0, as reflected in the current term structure of interest rates. Usually, the fixed price X is set so that $E(V) = 0$.

EXAMPLE 7.8

You enter into a three-year commodity swap to buy 500,000 barrels of oil at the end of each year, where you will be the fixed-level payer and the variable-level receiver. The per-unit forward prices for oil barrels to be delivered at times 1, 2, and 3, are 100, 110, and 120, respectively. *Note that these forward prices are the expected spot prices at times 1–3.* The total cost of the swap is akin to buying 3 pre-paid forward contracts but then spreading that cost over three years with level payments. If the one-year, two-year, and three-year spot rates (at the time the swap is conceived) are 4.5%, 5.5%, and 6.5%, calculate the fixed per-barrel amount you must pay each year.

Solution: The fixed per-barrel amount to be paid at times 1, 2, and 3 is X, where X is the solution to $N\sum_{t=1}^{M} F_t v^t = N\sum_{t=1}^{M} X v^t$, or $X = \frac{\sum_{t=1}^{M} F_t v^t}{\sum_{t=1}^{M} v^t}$. Thus, we have:

$$X = \frac{\sum_{t=1}^{M} F_t v^t}{\sum_{t=1}^{M} v^t} = \frac{\frac{100}{1.045} + \frac{110}{(1.055)^2} + \frac{120}{(1.065)^3}}{\frac{1}{1.045} + \frac{1}{(1.055)^2} + \frac{1}{(1.065)^3}} = \frac{293.8655}{2.6832} \approx 109.52.$$

7.2.4 Options

The distinguishing feature of options, as compared with forward contracts, is that the option holder has the right (option) but not the obligation, to comply with the contract terms. Thus, options are asymmetric in that one party has the power to take advantage of the other, and the other party then must comply with the option holder's decision. Another key distinguishing feature of options is that the option holder must pay an initial premium in exchange for the possibility that they might take advantage of the other party at some future time. With forwards, there are no initial premiums or cash exchange, and both parties must comply with the contract terms.

7.2.4.1 Call options

There are two types of basic options, depending on whether the option buyer can eventually have the choice of buying or selling some underlying asset. A call option gives its holder the right to buy some underlying asset (e.g., a stock) at a fixed price at some future point in time. This price is called the exercise or strike price and is denoted by K. It is set when the option is purchased. European-style options can be exercised only at the option's maturity date, whereas American-style options can be exercised at any time prior to maturity. There are also Bermuda-style options, which can be exercised during a limited pre-specified time period between the option's inception and maturity. For all three exercise styles just mentioned, the option becomes worthless if not exercised by the maturity date.

The option holder may choose to exercise a call option (at maturity or at any other contractually permissible time) when $S_t > K$. In this case, the underlying asset can be bought at the strike price K, which will be lower than the asset's current spot price S_t. If early exercise is allowed, it may be advantageous to the option holder to delay exercise in the hope of a greater return. However, if $S_t < K$, then the option holder will never choose to exercise the option because that asset could be bought on the open market for the lower price S_t. Thus, the payoff for exercising a long position in a call option at time t is non-negative, specifically being $\max(S_t - K, 0)$. Having a positive payoff does not imply that the overall strategy was profitable, since the initial option premium must be taken into account. More formally, the profit from exercising a long position in a call option at time t is the payoff on the option less the accumulated value of the initial cost: $\text{Profit}_t = \max(S_t - K, 0) - Ce^{rt}$, where r is the annualized continuously compounded interest rate and C is the price of the call option.

EXAMPLE 7.9

One year ago, you bought at a price of 10 a one-year, 40-strike European call option on a non-dividend-paying stock. The current stock price is 55, and you have just exercised the call option. If the annual continuously compounded interest rate is 6%, what is your profit from purchasing the call option?

Solution: The profit on the call option is: $\text{Profit}_t = \max(S_t - K, 0) - Ce^{rt} = \max(55 - 40, 0) - 10e^{0.06(1)} = 15 - 10.62 = 4.38$.

A short position in the call option involves receiving the option premium up front, but then having to possibly sell the underlying asset for less than market value (specifically at price K) if and when the option holder decides to exercise the option. Both the payoff and profit for the short position are the opposite of what they would be for the corresponding long position. This relationship is true for any asset or derivative, not just for options.

7.2.4.2 Put options

In contrast to a call option, a put option gives its holder the right to *sell* the underlying asset at a fixed price at some future point in time. The option holder may choose to exercise a put option when $S_t < K$. The underlying asset can then be sold at the strike price K, which will be higher than the asset's current spot price. However, if $S_t > K$, then the option holder will choose not to exercise the option because that asset could be sold on the open market for the higher price S_t.

Arguing as in the discussion of call options, $\text{Profit}_t = \max(K - S_t, 0) - Pe^{rt}$, where P is the price of the put option. A short position in the put option involves receiving the option premium up front, but then having to possibly buy S_t for more than market value (specifically at price K) if and when the option holder decides to exercise the option.

EXAMPLE 7.10

One year ago, you bought at a price of 5 a one-year, 40-strike European put option on a non-dividend-paying stock. The current stock price is 55, and you have to decide whether or not to exercise the put option. If the annual continuously compounded interest rate is 6%, what is your profit from purchasing the put option?

Solution: The profit on the put option position is:

$\text{Profit}_t = \max(K - S_t, 0) - Pe^{rt} = \max(40 - 55, 0) - 5e^{0.06(1)} = 0 - 5.31$
$= -5.31$.

Note that while the call option in Example 7.9 was *in the money*, the put option in this example is *out of the money* at expiration.

One difference between call and put options is that with call options, the short option position owns the underlying asset during the life of the option contract; with put options, the long option position owns the underlying asset until the option contract is exercised or expires.

7.3 Assets Used in Insurance Company Portfolios

Insurance companies must manage large quantities of assets, and achieving an acceptable return on these asset portfolios is an essential component in realizing consistent success. Although it would be nice to always make investment decisions that maximize expected return, there are various constraints that must be considered. For example, risk must be controlled, especially if there are policyholders who are depending on their insurer to provide economic security over the long term.

Before constructing investment portfolios, it is necessary to establish high-level objectives. At a minimum, such objectives should include minimum return requirements and maximum risk limits. These objectives can be tailored to the type of product supported. For example, insurance products require assets to be sufficient for paying liabilities that arise from future claims so that there may be considerable constraints on assuming additional risk. However, investment-oriented products are supposed to provide retirement income, often many years into the future, thus allowing for greater assumed risk levels and higher expected return. To prevent insurance companies from taking excessive risks that threaten either the firm's solvency or the general welfare of its policyholders, there are various regulatory constraints. For instance, there are maximum limits on each type of investment, based on a percentage of total assets or total surplus. This might apply to both individual assets and entire asset classes. There may also be restrictions on an asset's quality and liquidity.

Much of this discussion is specific to insurance companies in the United States, but the general concepts apply more widely.

7.3.1 Life Insurance Companies

The asset portfolio of a life insurer may be segmented into a general account and various separate accounts. The general account is used to support traditional fixed-type liability payments while the separate accounts tend to support investment-related products like variable annuities, variable universal life, and pension products. The separate accounts are subject to less regulation with respect to investment restrictions than is the general account, although the general account tends to be much larger. Investment objectives for insurers must balance the conservative goal of meeting obligations to policyholders and the more aggressive goals of contributing to earnings and surplus growth, along with maintaining the ability to be competitive in the marketplace, since higher returns will lower the cost of insurance.

Life insurance companies tend to invest over a more long-term horizon, using a mix primarily of stocks, bonds, mortgages, real estate, and policy loans. Because of the nature of life insurance in the United States, the majority of assets are in fixed income investments like corporate bonds. Specifically, bonds are appropriate for managing the relationship between assets and liabilities and for setting pricing assumption yields. Government bonds are also employed to a lesser degree to provide liquidity in case of cash flow emergencies. Common stock is a less significant asset class component, due to the high variability in the timing and amount of cash flows. Also, there are often limits on the proportion of portfolio assets that can be allocated to equities, although since these limits exist only for the general account, separate accounts often have very high equity weightings.

Mortgages, real estate, policy loans, and cash equivalents are also utilized in small part. Note that policy loans are not the responsibility of the investment department since it is the policyholder who has the option to affect cash flows. Finally, derivatives like options, futures, and swaps are often incorporated as hedging vehicles to minimize asset/liability risk.

7.3.2 Property and Casualty Insurance Companies

In contrast to life insurance companies, property and casualty (P&C) insurers tend to have a more short-term horizon, focusing on municipal bonds, government bonds, and cash. P&C firms are also likely to have relatively higher quality and higher liquidity assets available. Also, historically, investment operations relating to P&C insurance have been smaller in scope than those relating to life insurance and have received much less attention from P&C management than underwriting operations. This is because investment income for P&C insurers tends to be much less volatile than underwriting profits.

The primary asset class utilized by P&C insurers is bonds, which includes government, municipal, and corporate issues. Traditionally, municipals were popular because of their tax-exempt status, but recently taxable bonds have become increasingly popular, both because of their higher yields and their potential use to offset underwriting losses. As for the term of these debt securities, a healthy mix of intermediate and long-term debt is incorporated to capitalize on the higher yields relative to comparable short-term debt.

The next most popular asset classes are common and preferred stocks. Real estate is not weighted very heavily, as valuation and investment restrictions discourage its use, although a small real estate component may serve to foster portfolio diversification.

7.3.3 Pensions and Retirement Funds

The investment performance of a pension plan affects the employees' benefits for defined contribution plans. Many plans may have limits on the proportion of total assets that are issued by the employer (e.g., the company's own stock). In addition, states may have laws regulating limits on asset class holdings and may prescribe that investments be chosen from among an approved list. For defined contribution plans, although employer contributions remain level, it is the plan participants who assume the investment risk, which may cause benefits to vary considerably. Now, the sponsor has a greater responsibility to invest assets prudently and may be subject to legal liability if failing to do so. In particular, a very conservative investment plan may be appropriate for participants approaching retirement age, although for younger, new entrants, a more aggressive approach may be warranted.

Due to the long-term nature of pension funding, there are not many forbidden assets or asset classes. Asset allocation weightings tend to comprise about 60 percent equities, 30 percent in intermediate-to-long-term bonds, and 10 percent in short-term cash equivalents. Of course, these weights will vary based on the needs and characteristics of plan participants. There may also be limited assets in real estate and mortgage instruments, commodities, and derivatives. Common stocks tend to be more heavily weighted than bonds because over the long term, they have historically outperformed fixed-income investments. When bonds are used, longer-term bonds are again preferred to shorter-term bonds due to expected higher yields. A good mix of government and corporate bonds are utilized, where Treasury Bills may also be employed to provide short-term liquidity. If real estate is incorporated at all, it is usually through commercial rather than residential properties.

CHAPTER 8

Investing/Portfolio Management

This chapter covers many of the issues and concepts affecting investment decisions. We begin with introductory issues such as the comparison of investment alternatives, along with arbitrage and risk aversion, and discuss basic investment problems such as valuation, hedging, and the formation of portfolios. Then, we cover the calculation of means, variances (and standard deviations), covariances, and correlations in a portfolio context. The chapter concludes with an overview of some more complex investment issues like diversification, asset allocation, the incorporation of a risk-free asset, and performance evaluation.

8.1 Introductory Investment Issues

8.1.1 Investment Concepts

There are some basic terms to be familiar with before getting too deep into investment problems and concepts. These include the comparison principle, arbitrage, and risk aversion. Briefly, the comparison principle discusses how alternative investment options may be compared so that the optimal option(s) may be selected. Arbitrage is the opportunity to earn a positive return without assuming any risk. Risk aversion implies that an investor would select the alternative with the lowest amount of risk, given that all alternatives have the same expected return.

8.1.1.1 Comparison Principle

Investment decisions frequently involve choosing the best option from among a set of limited alternatives. The information used to make investment decisions comes primarily from financial markets. The comparison principle states that each investment option under consideration can be compared based on a selected evaluation criterion that uses data from financial markets. An example, presented in Chapter 6, states that the alternative with the highest net present value or perhaps the highest internal rate of return should be selected.

The simplest example is when the choice is either to undertake the project or not. We assume that money is available to invest in this project. We also assume that the alternative of doing nothing is an investment in a risk-free security such as a Treasury bill, where interest is earned while the investor waits for other opportunities.

EXAMPLE 8.1

Suppose the prevailing one-year interest rate on a Treasury bill is 6%. Also, suppose the investor is offered a project that produces a guaranteed return of X% in one year. What are the appropriate decision rules for various ranges of X?

Solution: If $X > 6\%$, a rational investor will accept the opportunity to do the project; if $X < 6\%$, the project will be rejected.

8.1.1.2 Arbitrage

Arbitrage is the process of earning a guaranteed positive return without investing anything, or equivalently, without assuming any risk. Although arbitrage opportunities are quite rare in practice, they do exist and can be exploited for a very brief period of time. As the saying goes, there may be such a thing as a "free lunch." However, such opportunities are fleeting, as typically market equilibrium is quickly restored, especially now that the trading of securities is so much more technologically advanced.

In markets with heavy trading volume the *law of one price* is said to generally preclude arbitrage opportunities, that is, if two different securities have identical characteristics, then they must be valued at the same price. Otherwise, a trader could exploit any non-zero price differential and make an immediate risk-free profit.

EXAMPLE 8.2

Ignoring transaction costs, if a stock share can be purchased from one-market maker at 39.99, and immediately be sold to another market-maker at 40.01 (without anything having changed inherently about the security itself), then a small arbitrage has been demonstrated. If 10,000 shares are exchanged, what arbitrage profit is possible?

Solution: The arbitrage profit is $10{,}000(40.01 - 39.99) = 200$.

8.1.1.3 Risk Aversion

There are three general risk-classifications for investors: risk-seeking, risk-neutral, and risk-averse. To demonstrate the difference between these three types, consider the following example.

EXAMPLE 8.3

An investor invests 10,000 today and is offered the choice between two cash flow structures, both to be received one year from now.

Choice I: 11,000 with 100% probability
Choice II: 9,000 with 50% probability, and 13,000 with 50% probability

Show that the expected return for the two choices is exactly the same.

Solution: With Choice I, the investor has a certain 10% return, since $\frac{11{,}000 - 10{,}000}{10{,}000} = \frac{1{,}000}{10{,}000} = 10\%$. In contrast, the return on Choice II is uncertain. There is a 50% chance that the investor will lose 10%, as $\frac{9{,}000 - 10{,}000}{10{,}000} = \frac{-1{,}000}{10{,}000} = -10\%$. Similarly, there is a 50% chance that the investor will gain 30%. Then, the **expected** return for Choice II is 10%, which is the same as the expected (and actual realized) return from Choice I.

The risk-neutral investor will be completely indifferent between Choices I and II. However, the risk-seeking investor will take a chance on Choice II, hoping for the 30% return, but knowing that there is an equal chance for a 10% loss. Finally, the risk-averse investor will not speculate on Choice II but instead settle for Choice I, taking the sure thing. Note that both options have the same initial cost and the same expected return, but that Choice I is guaranteed whereas Choice II has variability. More formally, the risk aversion principle states that if two investment choices have the same mean but different levels of risk (which we will later measure by variance or standard deviation), a rational risk-averse investor will prefer the choice with lower risk.

8.1.2 Investment Problems

8.1.2.1 Valuation

Any investment opportunity can be evaluated based on the present value of all cash flows that will be returned on the original investment. In other words, how much must be invested now in order to receive pre-specified amounts at pre-specified times in the future?

EXAMPLE 8.4

If the one-year interest rate is 5% and a cash flow of 1,000 is to be received one year from now, what price should be paid today?

Solution: The price that should be paid today is $\frac{1{,}000}{1.05} = 952.38$. Thus, 952.38 must be invested today in order to receive 1,000 one-year from now.

The example assumed two things that may not necessarily be true. First, the amount of the time-one cash flow (1,000) was known, but future cash flows are not always known, and instead may have to be estimated. Thus, valuation may depend on expected discounted cash flows rather than just discounted cash flows. Second, we assumed that there was only one initial outflow that formed the basis of the investment; in practice, an investor can make multiple deposits into a fund at multiple points in time. The Net Present Value method addresses this possibility by letting any deposit into a fund be denoted as a negative return.

8.1.2.2 Hedging

Hedging is used to reduce risk rather than to increase return and, in fact, it is likely to decrease return. It can be applied in both an investment setting or in the context of everyday company operations. When hedging is used to limit potential losses, it takes on the form of insurance.

EXAMPLE 8.5

From an investment perspective, if an investor has a long position in a stock, but is worried that the price of the stock may go down, a European put option on that stock can be purchased. What will happen if the stock price is below the option's strike price at expiration? What will happen if it is above the option's strike price at expiration?

Solution: If the stock price subsequently falls below the option's strike price K, the investor can still sell the stock at the floor price K. However, if the stock price subsequently rises, the investor will let the put option expire worthless and may still have a nice profit, which has only been reduced by the accumulated value of the price paid for the option.

EXAMPLE 8.6

From the perspective of everyday company operations, a firm with production costs that depend heavily on the price of one particular input might hedge using futures contracts. In the absence of hedging, the firm's profits would be too heavily dependent on movement in the prices of that key input. That is, if the price increased substantially from current levels, the firm might have a big loss, but if the price decreased from expected levels, the firm might reap additional profits. When hedging with a long position in futures contracts (on the key input), what will happen to the firm's profits if the key input price increases? Decreases?

Solution: If the key input price changes in either direction, the value of the futures contract will also change in the same direction, so that the net effect of this price change on profits is zero.

Note a conceptual difference between Example 8.5, which relies on put options, and Example 8.6, which relies on futures contracts. With a long position in put options, the investor eliminates severe losses, although to obtain this protection, the investor must pay the initial option premium. However, with a long (or short) position in futures contracts, the investor eliminates the possibility of both gains and losses, while also not needing to pay any initial premium.

8.1.2.3 Portfolio Selection and Consumption/Framing

Other common investment problems include portfolio selection and consumption/framing. The portfolio selection problem seeks to balance risk and return considerations, while allocating a fixed amount of capital appropriately. The individual (or corporate) investor has many choices for how to allocate funds, both at the asset class level and at the individual security level. More detailed information on the construction of portfolios is provided later in this chapter.

The consumption/framing problem has to do with tailoring (i.e., framing) an investment strategy to the individual circumstances of the investor. From an individual's perspective, both age and family status play key roles in investment decisions because of the different consumption behaviors that have been observed across these demographic variables.

EXAMPLE 8.7

Contrast the basic investment objectives (e.g., income versus growth) for a young, single, upwardly-mobile individual and an elderly retired married couple with several dependent children. Also, comment on what these objectives might be for a public university's endowment fund.

Solution: A young, single, upwardly-mobile individual will not have a high need for current income from investments, but instead will likely prefer growth, or capital appreciation. Meanwhile, an elderly retired married couple with several dependent children will prefer a steady, predictable stream of income and will have a much lower risk tolerance. From a corporate perspective, consider a public university endowment fund. This will have both income and growth needs. It will need income to fund current operations, which might include scholarships, faculty positions, and periodic technology fees. However, it must also consider growth objectives that can potentially support more long-term, school-related projects (e.g., a new research center, a music theater, or a sports facility).

8.2 Mean-Variance Analysis

8.2.1 Individual Asset Perspective

Initially, we will assume that there is only a single asset and a single investment period. More specifically, assume the asset is bought only at the beginning of the investment period and then held throughout the period. At the end of the investment period, we can measure the return on the asset. If we sell this asset at the end of the investment period, the gain (or loss) is said to be *realized*; otherwise, it is *unrealized*.

Let X_0 be the original amount invested and X_1 be the value of the same investment one year later. Then the total return (R) on the investment is $R = \frac{X_1}{X_0}$. More commonly, an investment's level of success is defined as a rate of return (r), where $r = \frac{X_1 - X_0}{X_0}$. Note that this expression can be solved for $X_1 = X_0(1 + r)$, which shows how a rate of return can resemble an interest rate. Also, $r = R - 1$ or $R = 1 + r$.

EXAMPLE 8.8

You invest 10,000 on July 1, 2009, and make no further deposits or withdrawals over the next year. On July 1, 2010, your account balance is 11,693.27. What is the total return on your investment? Also, what is the rate of return on your investment?

Solution: The total return on your investment is 11,693.27/10,000 = 1.1693 = 116.93%. The rate of return on your investment is (11,693.27 − 10,000)/10,000 = 0.1693 = 16.93%.

Typically, an initial position in an investment is long, with the investor planning to short the investment at some future time. When the timing of these two positions is reversed, this is called a *short sale*. Suppose party A is the investor who would like to take a short position and party B is an interested buyer. However, party A does not yet own the asset and so must borrow the asset from a third party, party C, who does already own it. From party A's perspective, X_0 is received right away, which is the cash received from party B. At the same time, party A delivers the borrowed asset to party B. Then, at some pre-specified time in the future, say one year later, party A must buy back the asset from party B, at its current value, X_1. Party A then returns the borrowed asset to party C. Party A enters the short sale due to a belief that the asset value will decline from time zero to time one, producing a profit of $X_0 - X_1$, However, if the asset price goes up, party A will have a loss because the time-one buyback price will be higher than the initial sale price.

EXAMPLE 8.9

You short-sell 50 shares of a non-dividend-paying stock for 100 per share and buy all 50 shares back one year later at the lower price of 92.35 per share. Assuming no transaction costs, no interest, and no existence of a margin account, what is the profit on your one-year transaction? What would your profit be if instead, the price one year later had increased to 146.79?

Solution: Under the first scenario, your one-year profit is $50 \times (100 - 92.35) = 50 \times 7.65 = 382.50$. Under the second scenario, your one-year profit is $50 \times (100 - 146.79) = 50 \times (-46.79) = -2{,}339.50$. Note that with short sales, there is no upper bound on how much can be lost (since the stock price can increase without limit), which very much motivates the need for a margin account.

Since there is no theoretical upper limit on what the time-one buyback price will be, the process of short selling is more risky than going long. This is especially true, given that the majority of assets are more likely to increase than decrease in value over time. Thus, short selling may be prohibited by certain financial institutions. If allowed, the short seller may have to establish an initial margin account as collateral and subsequently maintain this account at or above minimum levels if adverse price movements in the asset precipitate margin calls. Going forward, we will assume that short selling of assets is allowed. Also, if the asset shorted pays cash flows (e.g., dividends on stock) during the time period during which the short seller is short, those cash flows must be paid by the short seller to the person from whom the stock was borrowed (in the example, party A pays these intermediate cash flows to party C).

8.2.2 Portfolio-based Perspective

Now, instead of allowing the investment to comprise a single asset, assume that n different assets are available. Then, a portfolio can be formed that comprises various combinations, or weights, of these n assets. Note that some of these weights might be zero, so that the portfolio need not contain all n assets. Like before, assume that X_0 is the initial amount to be invested, but now, it must be allocated among n assets.

Specifically, let $X_0 = \sum_{i=1}^{n} X_{0i}$, where each X_{0i} represents the amount invested in asset i, for $i = 1, 2, \ldots, n$. Note that long positions in asset i will produce a positive value for X_{0i} and short positions will produce a negative value for X_{0i}. The amounts of individual assets invested can be expressed as weights with respect to the total amount invested, that is, $X_{0i} = w_i X_0$, where w_i is the fraction of the portfolio invested in asset i. It must be true that $\sum_{i=1}^{n} w_i = 1$, although there are no bounds on the individual weights (the w_i) if short selling is allowed, so that some weights may be negative and others more than one.

Both a portfolio's total return and rate of return are equal to the weighted sum of the corresponding individual asset returns, with the weights defined as before. For example, if R_i is the total return on asset i and r_i is the rate of return on asset i, then the portfolio's total return is

$$R = \frac{\sum_{i=1}^{n} X_{1i}}{X_0} = \frac{\sum_{i=1}^{n} R_i X_{0i}}{X_0} = \frac{\sum_{i=1}^{n} R_i w_i X_0}{X_0} = \frac{X_0 \sum_{i=1}^{n} w_i R_i}{X_0} = \sum_{i=1}^{n} w_i R_i.$$

The portfolio's rate of return is

$$r = R - 1 = \left[\sum_{i=1}^{n} w_i R_i\right] - 1 = \left[\sum_{i=1}^{n} w_i (1 + r_i)\right] - 1 = \left[\sum_{i=1}^{n} w_i + \sum_{i=1}^{n} w_i r_i\right] - 1$$
$$= \left[1 + \sum_{i=1}^{n} w_i r_i\right] - 1 = \sum_{i=1}^{n} w_i r_i.$$

EXAMPLE 8.10

You own a portfolio of three stocks, all of which were purchased one year ago. At that time, you allocated 50,000 to Stock A, 30,000 to Stock B, and 20,000 to Stock C. The one-year rates-of-return for the three stocks (from the time of purchase until now) were 10%, 20%, and −15%, respectively. What was the one-year rate of return on your portfolio?

Solution: The weight for Stock A is 50,000/(50,000 + 30,000 + 20,000) = 0.5. Similarly, the weight for Stock B is 0.3, and the weight for Stock C is 0.2. Thus, the one-year portfolio return is $\sum_{i=1}^{n} w_i r_i = (0.5)(.10) + (0.3)(.20) + (0.2)(-.15) = 0.05 + 0.06 - 0.03 = 0.08 = 8\%$.

8.2.3 Expected Value and Variance

The previous analyses of returns assumed a retrospective time frame, that is, an initial amount X_0 is invested and allowed to grow to X_1, and then at time one we are able to calculate returns based on what occurred in the past year. What if instead, we want a current (time zero) prospective forecast of what returns will be in one year? Since the value of our current investment one year ahead is not certain, variability must be captured.

Let Y be a random variable representing an asset's annual rate of return. Conceptually, Y should be continuous, since any real number (greater than or equal to −1) could be a possible rate of return. However, we will assume initially that Y is discrete and can take on only one of a small, finite number of values, $y_1, y_2, \ldots, y_m$. Then, there is a non-zero probability (p_j), for $j = 1, 2, \ldots, m$, that Y could assume the value y_j. That is, $\Pr(Y = y_j) = p_j$, where each p_j satisfies $0 \le p_j \le 1$ and $\sum_{j=1}^{m} p_j = 1$.

The probabilities may follow a named distribution with a probability mass function, such as binomial, or may be a listing of all the probabilities (the p_js) for each j (e.g., $p_1 = 0.3$, $p_2 = 0.5$ and $p_3 = 0.2$). In either case, the expected value of Y is $E(Y) = \sum_{j=1}^{m} y_j p_j$.

Note that if Y_1 and Y_2 are two distinct random variables (they may or may not have the same distribution), then $E(Y_1 + Y_2) = E(Y_1) + E(Y_2)$. Also, if a and b are constants, then,

$$E(Y + a) = E(Y) + a,$$
$$E(aY) = aE(Y),$$
$$E(a) = a, \text{ and}$$
$$E(aY_1 + bY_2) = aE(Y_1) + bE(Y_2).$$

The expected value forms a point forecast for what a rate of return might be one year ahead. It would be desirable to also have some idea of how likely the actual return will be close to the expected return. For example, if the investor knows that there is a 90 percent chance that the one-year rate of return will be between 5 percent and 15 percent (where 10 percent is the expected value), then the investor will have much more information than if just knowing the expected return is 10 percent.

Here, we are talking about variability, or deviations, from the expected value. One measure of deviation is the *variance* of the random variable, which is the expected squared deviation from the mean. Then, letting $E(Y) = \mu$, we have:

$$Var(Y) = E[(Y - \mu)^2] = E(Y^2 - 2\mu Y + \mu^2) = E(Y^2) - 2\mu E(Y) + \mu^2$$
$$= E(Y^2) - 2\mu^2 + \mu^2 = E(Y^2) - \mu^2 = E(Y^2) - [E(Y)]^2.$$

A more popular concept, as a measure of spread, is the standard deviation (s.d.), which is the square root of the variance. Then, denoting $s.d.(Y)$ as σ (so that $Var(Y) = \sigma^2$), we have: $s.d.(Y) = \sqrt{Var(Y)} = \sqrt{E(Y^2) - [E(Y)]^2}$.

Note that if Y_1 and Y_2 are two distinct and **independent** random variables (again, they may or may not have the same distribution), then $Var(Y_1 + Y_2) = Var(Y_1) + Var(Y_2)$. By independent, we mean that knowing the value of one random variable will have no effect on the probability distribution of the other random variable. This independence assumption will be relaxed in the section on covariance and correlation. Also, if a and b are constants, then

$$Var(Y + a) = Var(Y),$$
$$Var(aY) = a^2 Var(Y),$$
$$Var(a) = 0, \text{ and}$$
$$Var(aY_1 + bY_2) = a^2 Var(Y_1) + b^2 Var(Y_2), \text{if } Y_1 \text{ and } Y_2 \text{ are independent.}$$

Now that we have developed expected values, variances, and standard deviations for the returns of individual securities, we can apply these same concepts in a portfolio setting. Let Y_p be the random variable representing a portfolio's rate of return and let Y_i be the random variable representing asset i's individual rate of return. Then,

$$Y_p = w_1 Y_1 + w_2 Y_2 + \cdots + w_n Y_n$$
$$E(Y_p) = w_1 E(Y_1) + w_2 E(Y_2) + \cdots + w_n E(Y_n).$$

EXAMPLE 8.11

You invest 50,000 in Stock A, 30,000 in Stock B, and 20,000 in Stock C. You expect the three stocks to earn 10%, 15%, and 5%, respectively, over the next year. What is the expected return on your three-stock portfolio over this year?

Solution: The weight for Stock A is 50,000/(50,000 + 30,000 + 20,000) = 0.5. Similarly, the weight for Stock B is 0.3 and the weight for Stock C is 0.2. Thus, the one-year expected portfolio return is 0.5(0.10) + 0.3(0.15) + 0.2(0.05) = 0.05 + 0.045 + 0.10 = 0.105 = 10.5%.

If all n individual assets are mutually independent (not an especially realistic assumption), then,

$$\begin{aligned} Var(Y_p) &= Var(w_1 Y_1 + w_2 Y_2 + \cdots + w_n Y_n) \\ &= w_1^2 Var(Y_1) + w_2^2 Var(Y_2) + \cdots + w_n^2 Var(Y_n). \end{aligned}$$

EXAMPLE 8.12

Using the same data you used in Example 8.11, you are also given that the standard deviation of returns for Stocks A, B, and C are 40%, 60%, and 20%, respectively. If the returns on the three stocks are mutually independent, what is the variance of your three-stock portfolio's return over the year? What is the corresponding standard deviation?

Solution: The one-year variance of portfolio returns is $0.5^2(0.40)^2 + 0.3^2(0.60)^2 + 0.2^2(0.20)^2 = (0.25)(0.16) + (0.09)(0.36) + (0.04)(0.04) = 0.0400 + 0.0324 + 0.0016 = 0.074$. Thus, the standard deviation of portfolio returns is $(0.074)^{0.5} = 0.272 = 27.2\%$.

8.2.4 Covariance and Correlation

What if Y_1 and Y_2 are no longer independent, but instead are associated in some way? In other words, what if knowing the value of Y_1 changes the probability distribution of Y_2? One measure of dependence is the covariance between Y_1 and Y_2. Letting $E(Y_1) = \mu_1$ and $E(Y_2) = \mu_2$, the covariance is

$$\begin{aligned} \sigma_{12} = Cov(Y_1, Y_2) &= E[(Y_1 - \mu_1)(Y_2 - \mu_2)] = E(Y_1 Y_2 - \mu_1 Y_2 - Y_1 \mu_2 + \mu_1 \mu_2) \\ &= E(Y_1 Y_2) - \mu_1\mu_2 - \mu_1\mu_2 + \mu_1\mu_2 = E(Y_1 Y_2) - E(Y_1)E(Y_2). \end{aligned}$$

Now, there are three cases with respect to the relationship between Y_1 and Y_2. First, if Y_1 and Y_2 are independent, then they are said to be uncorrelated. In this case, $E(Y_1 Y_2) = E(Y_1)E(Y_2)$ and thus $\sigma_{12} = 0$. Recall that the converse is not true in that a zero covariance does not imply independence. Second, if $\sigma_{12} > 0$ the two variables are said to be positively associated. It indicates that if the first variable has a large value, the second variable is likely to also have a large value. Similarly, if $\sigma_{12} < 0$, the two variables are said to be negatively associated. When the first variable has a large value, the second variable is likely to have a small value. Most pairs of stocks tend to move up together and down together (largely because of market effects) and thus tend to have positive correlation.[1]

One problem with covariance as a measure of association is that it has no readily interpretable scale. An alternative measure is the correlation, $\rho_{12} = Corr(Y_1,Y_2) = \dfrac{Cov(Y_1,Y_2)}{\sqrt{Var(Y_1)Var(Y_2)}} = \dfrac{\sigma_{12}}{\sigma_1\sigma_2}$. Correlation is a dimensionless quantity with $-1 \le \rho_{12} \le 1$. When Y_1 and Y_2 are independent, $\rho_{12} = 0$. Note that a correlation of one implies perfect **linear** association, that is, $Y_1 = aY_2 + b$. Other functional relationships yield perfect predictability but need not have a perfect correlation. Note that $Corr(Y_1,Y_1) = \dfrac{Cov(Y_1,Y_1)}{\sqrt{Var(Y_1)Var(Y_1)}} = \dfrac{Var(Y_1)}{Var(Y_1)} = 1$.

If Y_1 and Y_2 are two distinct random variables that are **not** necessarily independent, then

$$\begin{aligned} Var(Y_1 + Y_2) &= E\{[(Y_1 + Y_2) - (\mu_1 + \mu_2)]^2\} = E\{[(Y_1 - \mu_1) + (Y_2 - \mu_2)]^2\} \\ &= E[(Y_1 - \mu_1)^2 + (Y_1 - \mu_1)^2 + 2(Y_1 - \mu_1)(Y_2 - \mu_2)] \\ &= E[(Y_1 - \mu_1)^2] + E[(Y_1 - \mu_1)^2] + 2E[(Y_1 - \mu_1)(Y_2 - \mu_2)] \\ &= Var(Y_1) + Var(Y_2) + 2Cov(Y_1,Y_2). \end{aligned}$$

Finally, returning to the portfolio-based perspective, but now allowing for dependence among any pair of random variables,

$$Var(Y_p) = Var(w_1Y_1 + w_2Y_2 + \cdots + w_nY_n) = \sum_{i=1}^{n}\sum_{j=1}^{n} w_iw_j\sigma_{ij} = \sum_{i=1}^{n}\sum_{j=1}^{n} w_iw_j\rho_{ij}\sigma_i\sigma_j.$$

Note that when $j = i$ then $w_iw_i\sigma_{ii} = w_i^2Var(Y_i)$.

EXAMPLE 8.13

Use the same data you used in Example 8.12, but now assume that the returns on the three stocks are correlated. Specifically, the correlation coefficient between the returns of Stocks A and B is 0.7; also, the correlation coefficient between the returns of Stocks A and C is 0.55; finally, the correlation coefficient between the returns of Stocks B and C is 0.45. Now, what is the variance of your three-stock portfolio's return over the year? What is the corresponding standard deviation?

Solution: The one-year variance of portfolio returns is (0.3)(0.5)(0.7)(0.4)(0.6) + (0.3)(0.2)(0.55)(0.4)(0.2) + (0.5)(0.2)(0.45)(0.6)(0.2) = 0.0332. The standard deviation of portfolio returns is $(0.0332)^{.5} = 0.182 = 18.2\%$. Note that this is lower than the corresponding answer to Example 8.12 (when the three stocks were mutually uncorrelated), which was 27.2%.

1 It is not hard to conceive of stocks that may be negatively correlated. For example, as gold prices rise, mining stocks may increase in value while jewelry store stocks may decrease in value.

8.3 Other Issues

8.3.1 Diversification

Generally, a portfolio with a small number of assets will have greater risk than one with a larger number of assets. In the extreme, consider a portfolio of a single asset. Even if that asset has a decent expected rate of return, the risk assumed may be large because if that asset loses significant value, the portfolio will lose value as well. The other extreme is a portfolio that somehow contains every single asset publicly available in the market (the *market portfolio*). This portfolio will be relatively immune to incurring significant losses if only a small number of assets do poorly. This is the principle of diversification.

Note that there are barriers to owning every asset in the market, specifically transaction costs and constraints an investor might have with respect to return requirements. Furthermore, even a completely diversified portfolio still has some risk, since there are two types of risk, and only one can be diversified away. Firm-specific risk can be substantially reduced (and virtually eliminated) as more and more assets are added to the portfolio. However, systematic risk, which permeates the entire market and does not depend on the welfare of specific firms, will remain.

Here, when we discuss risk in a portfolio context, we will use portfolio variance, or equivalently, portfolio standard deviation, as our risk measure. Recall the formula for a portfolio's variance, given the weights each individual asset contributes to overall portfolio capital and the entire correlation structure between each pair of portfolio assets; that is,

$$Var(Y_p) = \sum_{i=1}^{n}\sum_{j=1}^{n} w_i w_j \sigma_{ij} = \sum_{i=1}^{n}\sum_{j=1}^{n} w_i w_j \rho_{ij}\sigma_i\sigma_j .$$

To demonstrate the powerful effect diversification has on reducing firm-specific risk, consider an example where a portfolio comprises equal amounts of a large number (n) of mutually uncorrelated assets, all with the same variance. Then, $w_1 = \cdots = w_n = 1/n$, $\sigma_{ij} = 0, i \neq j$, and $\sigma_{ii} = \sigma^2$. The portfolio variance is

$$Var(Y_p) = \sum_{i=1}^{n}\sum_{j=1}^{n} w_i w_j \sigma_{ij} = \frac{1}{n}\frac{1}{n}\sum_{i=1}^{n}\sum_{j=1}^{n}\sigma_{ij} = n^{-2}\sum_{i=1}^{n}\sigma^2 = n^{-1}\sigma^2.$$

Thus, it is easy to see that, in this example, portfolio variance (and thus risk) is inversely related to the number of assets in the portfolio. The reduction in portfolio variance, on a percentage basis, is especially pronounced at relatively small values of n (see Example 8.14).

EXAMPLE 8.14

When comparing a portfolio with two stocks to one with 10 stocks, using the same assumptions as stated in the previous paragraph, by how much will the 10-stock portfolio variance be reduced, when compared to the two-stock portfolio?

Solution: The portfolio with two stocks will have a variance of $\sigma^2/2$, whereas the portfolio with 10 stocks will have a variance of $\sigma^2/10$, which is only 1/5 as large as the variance of the two-stock portfolio; thus, variance was reduced by 80%.

However, assets do not tend to be mutually uncorrelated and can, in fact, have significant positive correlation. However, there are still benefits to diversification.

EXAMPLE 8.15

Consider a variation on our previous example (when all assets were mutually uncorrelated) where now, each pair of different assets has correlation 0.5, that is, $\rho_{ij} = 0.5, i \neq j$. Retaining the other assumptions, derive the revised formula for the variance of portfolio returns.

Solution: Now, the variance of portfolio returns is given by:

$$Var(Y_p) = \sum_{i=1}^{n}\sum_{j=1}^{n} w_i w_j \rho_{ij}\sigma_i\sigma_j = \frac{1}{n}\frac{1}{n}\sigma^2\sum_{i=1}^{n}\sum_{j=1}^{n}\rho_{ij}$$

$$= n^{-2}\sigma^2[n + n(n-1)0.5] = \frac{\sigma^2}{2n} + \frac{\sigma^2}{2}.$$

Note that there are $n(n-1)$ terms in the double summation for which $i \neq j$. In this example, $\sigma^2/2n$ represents the firm-specific risk, which can be continually reduced as more and more assets are added to the portfolio. The second term, $\sigma^2/2$ represents the risk that remains (i.e., the non-diversifiable or systematic risk). Thus, even if we have every asset possible in our portfolio, the portfolio variance cannot go below $\sigma^2/2$.

8.3.2 Asset Allocation

The investment process is often described in two stages. The first stage is asset allocation, where decisions are made about which asset classes should be used and about how much of the total amount invested is allocated to each of these classes. The second stage is security selection, where decisions are made about which securities to invest in, along with the dollar amount allocated to each security. Investors who perform the asset allocation stage first, who then subsequently select individual securities, are utilizing a top-down approach. This is more common than the alternative, bottom-up approach whereby the individual securities are selected before any asset class constraints are considered. Here, we focus on the first stage, the asset allocation process. Note that this is arguably the more important stage because the majority of variability in per period returns is explained more by asset allocation decisions than by individual security selection.

To decide on an appropriate asset mix, the investment manager must balance the available investment opportunities with the investor's individual preferences. Before assessing the investment opportunities, an investment goal must be established, such as a specific growth in asset value as measured by rate of return over a pre-specified time horizon, or a required surplus of assets over liabilities at a specific point in time. Then calculate the expected value and variance (or standard deviation) of returns for different types of asset mixes. This analysis will incorporate a probability distribution for all the different returns that could be earned, along with an assumed covariance structure among multiple asset class returns. Naturally, if two portfolios have equal expected returns, the one with lower variability (risk) will be preferred. Also, if two portfolios have equal volatility, the one with higher expected returns will be preferred.

After analyzing the available opportunities in the capital markets, the investor's unique preferences can be incorporated. One such preference is the level of risk tolerance the investor is able to assume. This can be defined as the extra variance that will offset a unit of extra expected return, so that the investor's expected utility remains level. In the end, the investor selects an asset mix with the greatest expected utility, while simultaneously satisfying any constraints that may exist. Examples of constraints might include cash flows that are required at certain times in the future (perhaps to match liabilities), or minimum rates of return that must be earned (perhaps to guarantee minimum returns to another party while still keeping some investment income for profit). Other constraints involve provisions for liquidity, the need to keep up with inflation, and checking that no legal limits are exceeded on any one asset class (or asset).

When deciding on the number of asset classes, the principle of parsimony applies. Specifically, the number of asset classes should be relatively small, and each chosen class should be materially different from each other chosen class. The manager should determine a set of well-defined factors that will largely drive the potential returns of each asset class while also ensuring that most of these factors do not apply to multiple classes. In other words, if the factors associated with various asset classes employed are reasonably uncorrelated, the resulting asset mix will have greater diversification power. The expected returns of each chosen asset class should not be highly positively correlated with either each other or with the overall market. The idea is that total portfolio risk will be less than the sum of its parts if both the asset classes and the individual assets within each asset class are not perfectly positively correlated. This is especially important in times of extreme market moves or volatility, where portfolios that are underdiversified can suffer extreme losses quite quickly.

Once the appropriate number and type of asset classes is chosen, the investment process is often completed by choosing representative individual assets from a small set of lists, where each list corresponds with a particular asset class. Thus, a manager who prefers a top-down approach will expend greater efforts on doing the asset allocation phase correctly, while not focusing as much on individual security selection. Still, the same principles discussed above (i.e., those pertaining to expected return, standard deviation of returns, and correlation structure among various individual asset returns, along with the principles of parsimony and diversification) apply at the security selection phase as well.

8.3.3 Incorporating a Risk-free Asset

To this point, we have assumed that all n assets in our portfolio are risky. In other words, each asset has some variability as to what return it will produce, that is, $\sigma > 0$. In contrast, a risk-free asset has a known, certain future stream of cash flows and thus has no risk or variability, so that $\sigma = 0$. This can be conceptualized as borrowing or lending cash at some predetermined risk-free rate.

As to how the incorporation of a risk-free asset affects portfolio returns and standard deviations, consider a two-asset portfolio, where one asset is risk-free (denote this asset *rf*), and the other asset is risky (denote this asset *rsk*). Let w_{rsk} be the portfolio weight corresponding to the risk asset and let w_{rf} be the portfolio weight corresponding to the risk-free asset. Because the weights of the two assets must sum to 1, we have $w_{rsk} + w_{rf} = 1$, or $w_{rsk} = 1 - w_{rf}$.

The weights need not be between zero and one because when an individual borrows (as opposed to lends) at the risk-free rate w_{rf} will be negative. Then, the expected portfolio return is,

$$E(Y_p) = E(w_{rf}Y_{rf} + w_{rsk}Y_{rsk}) = w_{rf}E(Y_{rf}) + (1 - w_{rf})E(Y_{rsk})$$
$$= w_{rf}r + (1 - w_{rf})\mu_{rsk}$$

where r is the risk-free rate and μ_{rsk} is the expected return on the risky asset. Note that the random variable Y_{rf} is a constant and has no variability.

EXAMPLE 8.16

Consider a portfolio with two assets, a risky asset and a risk-free asset. The expected return on the risky asset is 10%, while the return on the risk-free asset is guaranteed to be 4%. If two-thirds of an investor's dollars are allocated to the risky asset, what will be the expected return on the portfolio?

Solution: If $w_{rsk} = 2/3$, then $w_{rf} = 1-(2/3) = 1/3$. Then, the expected portfolio return will be $(1/3)(0.04) + (2/3)(0.10) = 0.08 = 8\%$.

Before calculating this two-asset portfolio's standard deviation, note that the correlation (and covariance) between the risky asset's return (a random variable) and the risk-free return (a constant) is 0. This is because the correlation between a random variable and a constant must be 0, since knowing the value of the random variable will have no effect on the value of the constant, which is already known. Then,

$$Var(Y_p) = w_{rf}^2Var(Y_{rf}) + w_{rf}w_{rsk}Cov(Y_{rf}, Y_{rsk}) + (1 - w_{rf})^2Var(Y_{rsk})$$
$$= (1 - w_{rf})^2\sigma_{rsk}^2.$$

This implies that the portfolio standard deviation is $(1 - w_{rf})\sigma_{rsk} = w_{rsk}\sigma_{rsk}$.

EXAMPLE 8.17

Using the same data you used in Example 8.16, you are also given that the standard deviation of returns for the risky asset is 30%. What is the variance of your two-asset portfolio's return over the year? What is the corresponding standard deviation?

Solution: The portfolio variance is given by $(1 - w_{rf})^2\sigma_{rsk}^2 = (1 - (1/3))^2(0.3)^2 = 0.04$. The corresponding standard deviation is $(0.04)^{0.5} = 0.20 = 20\%$, which is exactly two-thirds of the 30% standard deviation for the risky asset.

Thus, portfolio risk is linearly proportional to the proportion of the portfolio invested in the risky asset. Furthermore, since the risky asset is likely to have a higher expected return than the risk-free asset (to compensate the investor for the additional risk assumed), then it is clear that the portfolio's expected return will also increase as the portfolio's risk level increases.

8.3.4 Performance Evaluation

When evaluating the performance of a portfolio, or any individual asset in the portfolio, a retrospective calculation that summarizes both mean returns and the volatility of those returns over time is needed. This involves taking the time frame under study and dividing it into several smaller, equally sized time periods. For example, if we have 10 years of year-end stock price data, we can use the annual year-end prices to form the average annual realized return and the standard deviation of those returns. Alternatively, if we have a single year of month-end stock price data, we can use the month-end prices to form the average monthly return and the standard deviation of the monthly returns.

In general, let n be the number of observation periods, T be the length of time of the investment, and h be T/n, the length of each observation period. Let r_i^p be an estimate of the effective return from time $(i - 1)h$ to time ih for $i = 1, 2, \ldots, n$. Similarly, let r_i^c be an estimate of the continuously compounded return over that period. Depending on how the returns are estimated, it may be that $r_i^c = ln(1 + r_i^p)$.[2] The average return over the time period is best estimated as

$$\bar{r}^p = \left[\prod_{i=1}^{n}(1 + r_i^p)\right]^{1/n} - 1 \text{ and } \bar{r}^c = \frac{1}{n}\sum_{i=1}^{n} r_i^c$$

The first formula is for a geometric mean, which reflects compounding of effective returns. An approximation to the first formula (using the first term of the Taylor series expansion) is $\bar{r}^p = \frac{1}{n}\sum_{i=1}^{n} r_i^p$, which is the arithmetic mean. If using this approximation, it is important to be aware of any error that may be introduced. The error increases with the variability of the set of returns. These rates can be annualized by computing $(1 + \bar{r}^p)^{1/h} - 1$ and $\bar{r}^c/h$ respectively.

As for calculating the standard deviation, which measures the volatility inherent in the per-period returns (where h is the size of each period), we can start by calculating the sample variance of all n observed returns. This is $s^2 = \frac{\sum_{i=1}^{n}(r_i - \bar{r})^2}{n - 1}$. Then, the sample standard deviation is the square root of the sample variance $s = \sqrt{\frac{\sum_{i=1}^{n}(r_i - \bar{r})^2}{n - 1}}$. It is common for volatility to be calculated only for continuously compounded returns. In this case, the annualized standard deviation is $s/\sqrt{h}$, provided the per-period returns are independent. It is important to note that all of the formulas for means and volatilities assume that both measures are constant throughout the time period.

EXAMPLE 8.18

You are given the monthly effective returns for a stock throughout an entire calendar year. From January through December, they are 0.03, −0.02, −0.04, 0.06, 0, 0.01, −0.03, 0.05, 0.09, −0.05, 0, and 0.02. Calculate the sample mean of monthly effective returns using both the geometric and arithmetic means. Then convert these

---

2 These rates may need to be estimated if there are cash flows during the observation period. See Kellison (2009, Sections 7.5 and 7.6).

returns to continuously compounded returns and calculate the sample mean of the converted returns. Compare this value to the one obtained using the geometric mean of effective returns. Now calculate the sample standard deviation of monthly returns for this calendar year, using only the continuously compounded returns. Finally, convert all these values from a monthly to a yearly basis.

Solution: The three formulas for the average produce

$$\bar{r}^p = [1.03(0.98)\cdots(1.02)]^{1/12} - 1 = 0.00919$$

$$\bar{r}^p \approx (0.03 - 0.02 + \cdots + 0.02)/12 = 0.01$$

$$\bar{r}^c = [\ln(1.03) + \ln(0.98) + \cdots + \ln(1.02)]/12 = 0.00915.$$

Note that converting the effective rate based on a geometric average to a continuously compounded rate produces $\ln(1 + 0.00919) = 0.00915$. Thus, these two approaches are internally consistent.

The variance is

$$s^2 = \frac{(0.02956 - 0.00915)^2 + \cdots + (0.01980 - 0.00915)^2}{11} = 0.001745.$$

The standard deviation is 0.04177.

The annualized means (using $h = 1/12$ and ignoring the approximate mean) are $(1 + 0.00919)^{12} - 1 = 0.11602$ and $12(0.00915) = 0.10977$. As before, the two are equivalent in that $\ln(1.11602) = 0.10977$. Converting the approximate mean produces $(1 + 0.01)^{12} - 1 = 0.12683$, exaggerating the difference. The annualized volatility is $0.04177\sqrt{12} = 0.14471$.

8.4 EXERCISES

8.1 You are given data in Table 8.1 concerning three stocks, where $P(0)$ is the current price and the three $P(1)$ columns represent forecasts of each stock's price one year from now in bad, normal, and good economic environments. You are also given the probability that each of these economic states will occur. Ultimately, you will choose only one of these three stocks for your portfolio.

TABLE 8.1 Values for Exercise 8.1

	$P(0)$	$P(1)_{bad}$	$P(1)_{normal}$	$P(1)_{good}$
Stock A	20.00	12.00	22.00	32.00
Stock B	50.00	35.00	59.00	X
Stock C	80.00	64.00	84.00	Y
Probability (Econ. State)		0.20	0.50	0.30

a) If all three stocks (A, B, and C) have the same expected return, calculate the $P(1)_{good}$ values for X (Stock B) and Y (Stock C).

b) Calculate the expected price, $P(1)$, one year from now, for all three stocks, and verify that both the expected returns and total returns are the same for all three stocks.

c) Calculate the stand-alone risk for each stock, as measured by the probability-weighted standard deviation of returns for one year.

d) If you are a *risk-neutral* investor, which of the three stocks will you prefer (if any) and why? If you are a *risk-averse* investor, which of the three stocks will you most prefer and why? Finally, if you are a *risk-seeking* investor, which of the three stocks will you most prefer and why?

For parts e), f), and g), let $X = 75$ and $Y = 112$ (instead of the values you solved for in part a) that forced the mean returns to be equal). When comparing stocks with relatively high expected return and risk to those with relatively low expected return and risk, another way to rank such stocks is by using the coefficient of variation, which is the ratio of the standard deviation of returns to the mean return.

e) Calculate the revised expected returns for Stocks B and C.

f) Calculate the revised standard deviation of returns for Stocks B and C.

g) If you are a *risk-averse* investor, which of the three stocks will you now most prefer and why (based on the coefficient of variation)?

For parts h), i), and j), use monthly stock price data given in Table 8.2 for the year starting at time 0 (in the scale above) and ending at time 12 (in months). Assume all prices are end-of-month prices.

TABLE 8.2 Stock prices for Exercise 8.1

Time (in months)	Prices for Stock A	Prices for Stock B	Prices for Stock C
0	\$20.00	\$50.00	\$80.00
1	\$18.86	\$47.81	\$81.93
2	\$19.53	\$46.99	\$78.53
3	\$18.56	\$46.05	\$82.09
4	\$20.43	\$48.40	\$86.57
5	\$20.90	\$46.73	\$81.85
6	\$22.76	\$52.54	\$88.28
7	\$21.08	\$50.09	\$84.42
8	\$24.61	\$56.84	\$93.21
9	\$25.04	\$58.35	\$89.30
10	\$22.91	\$56.02	\$86.56
11	\$23.73	\$55.75	\$87.62
12	\$22.74	\$58.47	\$86.73

h) Estimate the mean continuously compounded monthly return for all three stocks. Hint: the *continuously compounded* return for the month starting at time $t - 1$ and ending at time t is exactly $\ln(S_t/S_{t-1})$.

i) Once you have all the monthly returns, estimate the monthly volatility for all three stocks, that is, find the standard deviation of all 12 monthly returns (separately, for each stock).

j) Convert your answers from parts h) and i), which are both on a (continuously compounded) monthly scale, to the corresponding (continuously compounded) annualized measures.

8.2 Use the same three stocks (with supporting assumptions and data) that were used in Exercise 8.1. Use $X = 75$ and $Y = 112$, as was used for parts d)–f). Now, you are doing a portfolio-based analysis with the following additional assumptions:

- You invest 10,000 at the beginning of the year (time zero), and are interested in predicting the value of your portfolio at the end of the year.
- 20% of your investment is made in Stock A.
- 48% of your investment is made in Stock B.
- 32% of your investment is made in Stock C.
- You expect the correlation between the returns on Stocks A and B to be 0.8.
- You expect the correlation between the returns on Stocks A and C to be 0.6.
- You expect the correlation between the returns on Stocks B and C to be 0.7.

a) What is the expected return of your portfolio one year from now, given the three-state model used in Exercise 8.1 (for parts d–f)?

b) If the stock prices progress as given in Table 8.2, what will be the realized return on your portfolio one year from now?

c) What is the standard deviation of your portfolio return one year from now, given the three-state model used in Exercise 8.1 (for parts d–f)?

d) How would your answer to part c) change if you had instead assumed that the returns on the three stocks were mutually uncorrelated?

e) How would your answer to part c) change if you had instead assumed that the returns on Stocks A and B were perfectly positively correlated, but that the returns on Stock C were perfectly negatively correlated with both Stock A and (separately) Stock B.

f) How would your answers to both parts a) and c) change if you included only two of the three stocks in your portfolio (assuming the same correlation structure as given originally, and assuming that your *relative* portfolio weights would remain unchanged from before)?

g) How would your answers to both parts a) and c) change if you added two new stocks to the portfolio that had returns that were completely uncorrelated with those of the original three stocks (and each other)? Assume here that you invest 5,000 *extra* in each of these two new stocks, while maintaining the same capital investment (in dollars and *relative* weights) as before in the original three stocks. Also, assume that the mean return and standard deviation of returns for the two new stocks match that of Stocks B and C.

For parts h), i), and j), assume you invest half of your 10,000 in your original three-stock portfolio (in the same *relative* weightings as before). Now, though, you will invest the remaining half in a risk-free asset that will pay a 5% return in one year. Thus, your portfolio has four assets.

h) Recalculate the portfolio's expected return one year from now.

i) Recalculate the portfolio's realized return one year from now (if prices progress according to the same table used in part b).

j) Recalculate the standard deviation of your portfolio return one year from now. Compare your answers for a)–c) to those for h)–j), and justify the differences you observe.

CHAPTER 9

Finance Models and Data

9.1 Capital Asset Pricing Model

9.1.1 Market Equilibrium

One of the most essential investment problems is to estimate the appropriate price of a risky asset. Here, we develop such an approach within the mean-variance framework established in Chapter 8. Specifically, assume that all investors are mean-variance optimizers. That is, given a risk tolerance (as measured by variance or standard deviation), they seek to maximize expected return, or equivalently, given a return target, they seek to minimize risk. Furthermore, assume that there is a commonly known risk-free rate for borrowing or lending a risk-free asset and there are no transaction costs.

We continue with a few assumptions about investors. First, assume there is a well-defined set of risky investments from which they may choose. Second, assume they all are all mean-variance optimizers, but with differing risk tolerances. Then they will all choose the same fund from within the set of risky investments along with a proportion of the risk-free asset. This is often referred to (in finance textbooks) as the "one-fund theorem," and is a result of standard mean-variance portfolio theory. The only quantity that varies is the proportion of each investor's portfolio that is assigned to the risk-free asset; those with low risk tolerance will prefer a greater proportion of the risk-free asset, and those with higher risk appetite will prefer a smaller proportion of the risk-free asset.

In particular, if the available set of risky investments is all the equities available in the market, then the fund will be the *market portfolio*. It is the weighted sum of all stock shares, where the weights are proportional to a particular stock's representation in the entire equity market. These weights can also be conceived of as the ratio of an asset's total capital value to the market's total capital value and are called capitalization weights. Note that these weights are proportional to total market capitalization rather than the number of shares held.

Why must the optimal portfolio be equal to the market portfolio? The answer to this question is known as "the equilibrium argument," which is as follows. Initially, a large group of investors (all of whom are solving a common mean-variance portfolio optimization) acquire portfolios based on common estimates for the means, variances, and covariances among asset returns, where returns depend on both initial and final asset prices. Then, if the market demand for certain assets does not correspond with the supply currently available, prices will change until demand and supply are matched exactly, and hence equilibrium is established. Thus, prices will continually adjust until the market becomes efficient and, after such adjustments have taken place, this efficient portfolio is the same as the market portfolio.

9.1.2 Beta

The Beta of an asset (denoted β) reflects the extent to which the asset covaries with the market portfolio. Beta measures a stock's volatility relative to the market, where a stock that is representative of a typical market stock, and thus has average risk, will have $\beta = 1$. Such a stock tends to move up when the market increases, moves down when the market declines, and expresses similar percentage changes in price over time when compared to the market portfolio. Mathematically, a stock's β can be expressed as: $\beta_S = \rho_{S,M}\left(\frac{\sigma_S}{\sigma_M}\right)$, where $\rho_{S,M}$ is the correlation coefficient between the stock's returns and the returns on the market, σ_S is the volatility of the stock's returns, and σ_M is the volatility of the market returns. In a simple linear regression context, where the return on the stock is the dependent variable and the return on the market is the independent variable, β_S represents the slope coefficient, or qualitatively, the tendency of the stock's returns to relate to changes in the market. More formally, β_S is the rate of change in the stock's return for a unit change in the market return.

Stocks with relatively high beta (i.e., $\beta > 1$) will also tend to move up and down in sync with the market but will do so in greater percentage amounts. Since $\rho_{S,M} \leq 1$, then if $\beta > 1$, it must be true that $\sigma_S > \sigma_M$. Such stocks are considered more risky due to this extra volatility. Meanwhile, stocks with relatively low (but positive) beta (i.e., $0 < \beta < 1$) will still tend to move together with the market but will do so in lesser percentage amounts. Note: If $\beta < 1$, it is not necessarily true that $\sigma_S \leq \sigma_M$ (because again, $\rho_{S,M} \leq 1$); however, σ_S will be more likely to be lower, relative to σ_M, than when $\beta > 1$. Such stocks are considered less risky due to the lower volatility.

EXAMPLE 9.1

Consider two stocks, A and B. The standard deviation of returns on Stock A is 50%, and the standard deviation of returns on Stock B is 25%. The correlation coefficient between the returns on Stock A and the returns on the market is 0.8, and the correlation coefficient between the returns on Stock B and the returns on the market is 0.6. The standard deviation of returns on the market is 30%. Compare the beta coefficients of Stocks A and B.

Solution: Using $\beta_A = \rho_{A,M}\left(\frac{\sigma_A}{\sigma_M}\right)$, the beta for Stock A is 0.8(0.5/0.3) = 1.33. Similarly, the beta for Stock B is 0.6(0.25/0.3) = 0.50. Thus, based on the beta coefficients of the two stocks, Stock A is considerably more risky than Stock B.

Beta can also be stated in terms of variances and covariances with respect to the market portfolio. Specifically, letting $\sigma_{S,M}$ be the covariance between the asset's returns and the returns on the market portfolio, and letting σ_M^2 be the variance of the market portfolio returns, then: $\beta = \frac{\sigma_{S,M}}{\sigma_M^2} = \frac{Cov(r_S, r_M)}{Var(r_M)}$. This implies that the excess return on an individual asset is directly proportional (via β) to its covariance with the market portfolio.

It is theoretically possible for beta to be close to 0, or even less than 0. If an asset's beta is zero, this implies that the asset is uncorrelated with the market, so that market trends at large have no relationship to the asset's price movements. Although extremely rare in practice, an asset with negative beta will be inversely correlated with market trends. Such assets provide excellent diversification potential, as they perform relatively well when most other assets perform poorly, and can thus reduce portfolio risk substantially when combined with assets that mimic the market's general trends.

Most stocks have beta coefficients between 0.5 and 1.5. The actual beta coefficients used for each stock are typically estimated based on about one year's worth of weekly price data, which includes the tracking of an individual company's stock, along with the corresponding market data. Unless a company experiences material changes in its inherent composition, its beta is not likely to change much through time. In general, aggressive, highly leveraged companies will have relatively high betas, whereas more conservative companies will have lower betas. It is typical for betas to vary significantly by industry. However, many of the major players in a particular industry may have beta coefficients that are close together.

Beta for a portfolio of assets, β_p, is the weighted average of the betas for all individual assets in the portfolio. Here, assuming a total of n stocks in the portfolio, the weights (given by $w_1, w_2, \ldots, w_n$) are the same as the weights used to define the portfolio. For example, if 20% of the portfolio's total value is composed of the stock labeled "3," then $w_3 = 0.2$. In formula terms, $\beta_p = \sum_{i=1}^{n} w_i \beta_i$. This is the same type of formula (with the same interpretation for the weights) that was used to define a portfolio's return: $r_p = \sum_{i=1}^{n} w_i r_i$.

EXAMPLE 9.2

You have a portfolio of three stocks, each with a different beta coefficient. One-half of your portfolio is invested in Stock A, one-third is invested in Stock B, and the remaining portion is invested in Stock C. The beta of Stock A is 30% higher than that of the market portfolio, the beta of Stock B is 20% lower than that of the market portfolio, and the Beta of Stock C is equal to that of the market portfolio. What is the beta for your three-stock portfolio?

Solution: First, note that $\beta_A = 1.3, \beta_B = 0.8, \beta_C = 1.0$. Second, note that $w_A = 1/2, w_B = 1/3, w_C = 1/6$. Then, the beta for your three-stock portfolio is: $\beta_p = \sum_{i=1}^{n} w_i \beta_i = (1/2)(1.3) + (1/3)(0.8) + (1/6)(1.0) = 1.05$. This is slightly more risky than holding the market portfolio itself.

9.1.3 The Capital Market Line

The capital market line (CML) shows the relationship between a portfolio's expected rate of return $E(r_p)$ (y axis) and risk, as measured by the standard deviation of the portfolio returns σ_p (x axis). The line is upward sloping and begins at the coordinate $(0, r_f)$ because the only portfolio that has a standard deviation of zero is one that contains only the risk-free asset. Then, the line proceeds upward to the right, so that as risk levels increase, so will expected return levels. One key point of interest on the CML is the market portfolio, which is located at the coordinate $(\sigma_M, E(r_M))$, where $E(r_M)$ is the expected value of the market rate of return, and σ_M is the standard deviation of the market rate of return.

The equation for the CML is: $E(r_p) = r_f + \left(\frac{E(r_M) - r_f}{\sigma_M}\right)\sigma_p$. Thus, since the slope-intercept form for a line is $y = mx + b$, we can see that r_f is the y-intercept (as discussed previously), and $\frac{E(r_M) - r_f}{\sigma_M}$ is the slope. The slope is often labeled the "price of risk" and reflects the amount by which the market portfolio's expected rate of return must increase for each unit increase in the market portfolio's standard deviation.

9.1.4 Capital Asset Pricing Model

The Capital Asset Pricing Model (CAPM) predicts an asset's expected return given its level of risk. This enables investors to have benchmark rates of return when comparing competing investment choices. Assuming the market portfolio is efficient, the expected return for any individual asset i must be: $E(r_i) = r_f + \beta_i[E(r_M) - r_f]$, where $\beta_i = \rho_{i,M}\left(\frac{\sigma_i}{\sigma_M}\right)$. For a detailed proof of this statement, see Section 7.3 of Luenberger (1998). Again, returning to the slope-intercept form for a line, r_f is the y-intercept, and β_i is the slope. This line, which is commonly known as the Security Market Line (SML) (and is discussed in greater detail in Section 9.1.5), is often written as $E(r_i) - r_f = \beta_i[E(r_M) - r_f]$ to emphasize that $E(r_i) - r_f$ is the excess of the expected rate of return over the risk-free asset. Then, noting that $E(r_M) - r_f$ is the excess of the expected rate of return on the market portfolio over the risk-free asset, we see that the two excess return measures are clearly linked by the beta coefficient; that is, the excess return on an individual asset is directly proportional (via β) to the excess return on the market portfolio. Note that $E(r_i) - r_f$ is also called the risk premium for asset i, and $E(r_M) - r_f$ is commonly referred to as the market risk premium. Thus, β_i can also be determined as the ratio of two risk premiums, that is, $\beta_i = \frac{E(r_i) - r_f}{E(r_M) - r_f}$.

EXAMPLE 9.3

The risk-free asset has a guaranteed return of 4%, and the expected market return is 10%. Calculate the expected return on a security with a beta coefficient of 1.20. Then, calculate the expected return on a security with a beta coefficient of 0.75. By how much did the expected return decrease, when beta dropped from 1.20 to 0.75?

Solution: The SML from CAPM states that $E(r_i) = r_f + \beta_i[E(r_m) - r_f]$. Thus, if Beta = 1.20, the expected return = 0.04 + 1.2(0.10 – 0.04) = 0.04 + 0.072 = 0.112 = 11.2%. However, if Beta = 0.75, the expected return = 0.04 + 0.75(0.10 – 0.04) = 0.04 + 0.045 = 0.085 = 8.5%. Thus, when Beta drops from 1.20 to 0.75, the expected return falls 2.7% from 11.2% to 8.5%.

9.1.5 The SML

While the CML relates expected return to risk (via standard deviation) from the context of an efficient portfolio, the SML relates expected return to risk (via beta) from the context of an efficient individual asset. We will now relate the SML to the CAPM.

The security market line (SML) for equity i shows the relationship between expected rate of return $E(r_i)$ (y axis) and the relationship between the asset and the market, as measured by β (x axis). Thus, the SML is just a graphical relationship of CAPM. Like with the CML, the SML is upward sloping and begins at the coordinate $(0,r_f)$. As β increases, the expected rate of return will increase. One key point of interest on the SML is the market portfolio, which is located at the coordinate $(1,E(r_M))$, where $E(r_M)$ is the expected value of the market rate of return, and 1 is the beta coefficient corresponding with the market portfolio. By definition, the market portfolio must have $\beta = 1$ because the market always moves identically to changes in itself.

9.1.6 Risk Types

CAPM can also be expressed in terms of a random return rather than an expected return. Then, a stochastic error term must be introduced to make both sides of the CAPM equation balance. Specifically, if we let r_i replace $E(r_i)$, where r_i is the random rate of return on asset i, then CAPM says: $r_i = r_f + \beta_i(r_M - r_f) + \varepsilon_i$. Here, ε_i is a random variable with expectation 0 that is uncorrelated with the market portfolio.

Conceptually, ε_i can be defined as the unexpected component of an asset's return due to events that are specific to the individual firm only (and not to the entire market). Thus, $E(\varepsilon_i) = 0$, and $Cov(\varepsilon_i, r_M) = 0$. Then, if we let $\sigma^2_{\varepsilon_i} = Var(\varepsilon_i)$, we can decompose the total variance $\sigma_i^2 = Var(r_i)$ into the sum of two component variances. Specifically, we have:

$$\begin{aligned}\sigma_i^2 &= Var[r_f + \beta_i(r_M - r_f) + \varepsilon_i]\\ &= Var(\beta_i r_M + \varepsilon_i) = Var(\beta_i r_M) + Var(\varepsilon_i) + Cov(\beta_i r_M, \varepsilon_i)\\ &= \beta_i^2\sigma_M^2 + \sigma^2_{\varepsilon_i}.\end{aligned}$$

9.1.6.1 Systematic risk

The first component of the total variance is $\beta_i^2\sigma_M^2$, which is known as systematic, or market risk. This type of risk cannot be diversified away by investing in a higher number of individual firms because every asset incorporates this risk. Specifically, this is the variance attributable to the uncertainty of macroeconomic factors (e.g., inflation, interest rates, the economy, unemployment, and general price levels).

9.1.6.2 Firm-specific risk

The second component of the total variance is $\sigma^2_{\varepsilon_i}$, which is known as non-systematic, or firm-specific risk. This type of risk can be reduced and nearly eliminated by increasing the number of securities in the portfolio. Specifically, this is the variance attributable to firm-specific uncertainty. A portfolio with a small number of assets will have significant firm-specific risk because there is a non-negligible chance that many of the firms may experience adverse outcomes at once. However, if the portfolio has a larger number of assets, the chances are much greater that some firms will have positive outcomes that offset the firms with adverse outcomes. These adverse outcomes may be caused by random, unsystematic events such as lawsuits, strikes, unsuccessful marketing and/or research and development programs, or losing a major contract with either an existing or potential business partner. Note that all of these events are specific to the individual firms and are not necessarily correlated to general market trends.

9.1.7 Implications of CAPM

While CAPM is a theoretical construct (because it depends on assumptions that are not strictly true), it is frequently implemented in practice through the use of index funds. CAPM is based on the assumption that the optimally efficient investor should hold the market portfolio consisting of risky assets and supplement that with the risk-free asset. If the market is restricted to the world of available equity assets, then the investor should buy shares in all of these stocks, in proportion to the amount that is available in the market as a whole. The investor would also buy a specific amount of risk-free securities like U.S. T-bills, where the proportion of the total amount invested that is allocated to the T-bills would be inversely related to the investor's risk tolerance.

Thus, CAPM precludes any analysis of individual securities and instead favors *index funds*, which are mutual funds specifically designed to match the market portfolio. The term *index* relates to funds that mimic the assets contained within various financial indices. For example, an S&P 500 index fund includes small components of all 500 stocks in the S&P 500, which in aggregate, are meant to represent overall market trends. Other index funds could be designed to be more or less broad than the S&P 500. A broader index fund might include all publicly available securities but might be prohibitive to obtain due to transaction costs. A less broad fund might seek to replicate some subset of the market (e.g., a specific sector, industry, or country), which would likely not be representative of the market as a whole.

Thus, CAPM followers are inherently implementing a passive investment strategy and assume that no investor has any informational advantage beyond what is already publicly available and reflected in current market prices. In contrast, those who prefer active strategies believe they can do better than the average, market-replicating investor. Active investors believe they have unique information or insight that will potentially allow them to outperform the market. In reality, the majority of investors employ an asset management style that lies between passive and active extremes. Many of these investors will begin with the market portfolio (or an index fund) as a starting point and then look to tailor or tweak those holdings to their specific investment objectives or market views.

9.2 Other Financial Modeling Frameworks

There are other modeling frameworks besides CAPM. They are introduced in this section.

9.2.1 Factor Models

The mean-variance framework previously discussed requires the specification of a large number of parameters, due to all the asset returns, variances, and covariances that must be estimated. As the number of assets in a portfolio becomes even moderately large, the estimation of all these parameters becomes cumbersome. Factor models address this issue by requiring a much smaller number of parameters to be estimated.

With factor models, the randomness inherent in the returns of the portfolio assets can be attributed to a small number of underlying sources, which are called *factors*. Determining the factors to use is no trivial task, but once appropriate factors have been identified, analysis proceeds somewhat smoothly.

There are three types of factors that may be included in investment models. First, there are external factors, which account for macroeconomic measures like gross domestic product (GDP), consumer price index (CPI), and unemployment. Second, there are firm-specific factors, which include various financial ratios from the balance sheet and income statement like the price-earnings ratio, dividend-payout ratio, and debt-to-equity ratio. Third, there are extracted factors that can be considered a compromise between the systematic and firm-specific factors just mentioned. Examples include the rate of return on the market portfolio, the rate of return on a similar security to the one being modeled, and the average return of all securities within the industry of the asset being modeled.

The simplest factor model is a single-factor model: $r_i = a_i + b_i f + \varepsilon_i$. Here, r_i is the rate of return on the ith asset in a portfolio of n assets, which is partially predicted by the factor f. Both a_i and b_i are fixed constants and represent intercept and slope coefficients, respectively. The constant b_i is especially noteworthy because it is the factor loading that reveals the sensitivity of the asset return to the factor f. The final term, ε_i is an error term, where $E(\varepsilon_i) = 0$, and the error terms for the collection of assets, $\varepsilon_1, \varepsilon_2, \ldots, \varepsilon_n$, are uncorrelated with each other and with the factor f. Furthermore, the variances of the ε_i are known for $i = 1, 2, \ldots, n$.

EXAMPLE 9.4

You use a factor model with one factor to predict the expected return on a stock in the period ahead. Based on past data, you have estimated the intercept and slope coefficients for your factor model to be 0.05 and −2, respectively. If the factor represents the expected annual change in the unemployment rate, calculate the expected return if unemployment is expected to fall by 3%. Also, calculate the expected return if unemployment is expected to increase by 2%.

Solution: The single-factor model, as it pertains to security i is: $r_i = a_i + b_i f + \varepsilon_i$. Taking the expected value of both sides, we have $E(r_i) = a_i + b_i E(f)$, since $E(\varepsilon_i) = 0$. Thus, if $E(f) = -0.03$, then the expected return on the stock will be $0.05 - 2(-0.03) = 0.11 = 11\%$. However, if $E(f) = 0.02$, then the expected return on the stock will be $0.05 - 2(0.02) = 0.01 = 1\%$.

There is no reason why factor models cannot contain multiple factors. In fact, most factor models relating to U.S. stocks contain anywhere between 3 and 15 factors. For example, a two-factor model might look like $r_i = a_i + b_{1i} f_1 + b_{2i} f_2 + \varepsilon_i$. These models do not assume that f_1 and f_2 are uncorrelated. In fact, the multiple factors contained within these models are often strongly correlated. Although this correlation adds additional complexity to the modeling process, the number of parameters that need be estimated is still significantly below what is required for a mean-variance analysis that relies on a fully unstructured covariance matrix.

EXAMPLE 9.5

Returning to Example 9.4, now assume that there is a second factor that affects the expected return on the stock. Specifically, let the first factor still be the change in unemployment, and let the second (new) factor be the change in inflation. Based on past data, you have estimated the intercept coefficient to be 0.05 and the slope coefficients for the two factors to be −2 and 1.2, respectively. Now, calculate the expected return if unemployment is expected to fall by 3%, but inflation is expected to increase by 1.5%.

Solution: The two-factor model, as pertains to security *i* is: $r_i = a_i + b_{1i}f_1 + b_{2i}f_2 + \varepsilon_i$. Taking the expected value of both sides, with $E(f_1) = -0.03$ and $E(f_2) = 0.015$, then the expected return on the stock is $0.05 - 2(-0.03) + 1.2(0.015) = 0.128 = 12.8\%$.

9.2.1.1 Arbitrage Pricing Theory

One primary factor-based alternative to the CAPM is arbitrage pricing theory (APT). Unlike CAPM, which requires the valuation of portfolio-based returns and risk, APT more simply assumes that investors prefer greater returns to lesser returns. APT also assumes that the universe of available assets must be infinitely large and that all assets must be materially different from each other.

As a starting point, consider a single-factor model, but with no error term, that is, $r_i = a_i + b_i f$, and assume that all assets satisfy this model. Because the error term is absent, then any uncertainty in the asset return must be fully explained by the uncertainty in the factor *f*. For example, we can predict what the return will be in the upcoming period, based on the current value of *f*. However, the actual return will depend on the future value of *f*, which will not necessarily correspond with the current value of *f* used to form the predicted return. Thus, the difference between the predicted return and the actual return will be explained by the difference between the current and future values of *f*. The key revelation from APT is that the values of a_i and b_i must be related in order to preclude an arbitrage opportunity.

Now, suppose there are *m* factors in the model and *n* assets in the portfolio. Then, the return for asset *i* can be written as: $r_i = a_i + \sum_{j=1}^{m} b_{ji}f_j$, for $i = 1, 2, \ldots, n$. Furthermore, it can be shown that there are constants $\theta_0, \theta_1, \ldots, \theta_m$ such that: $E(r_i) = \theta_0 + \sum_{j=1}^{m} b_{ji}\theta_j$, for $i = 1, 2, \ldots, n$. The connection between these two equations is as follows. If all the b_{ji} values are zero, then there is no risk and $a_i = \theta_0$ for all *i*. This implies that all the assets are risk-free, which is consistent with the assumption that there is a single risk-free rate that applies to such assets. However, if any $b_{ji} \neq 0$, then $E(r_i)$ will change in proportion to b_{ji}, where θ_j is the "price of risk" associated with the factor f_j. Then, as $E(f_j)$ increases, so will $E(r_i)$. Note that, as stated previously, we do not know what f_j will be in the future (hence the incorporated randomness), and it is the future rather than the current value of f_j that will help determine the realized return r_i.

9.2.1.2 Comparing CAPM and APT

Although CAPM is usually not considered to be a factor model, it can be looked at as one. Recall that CAPM states: $E(r_i) - r_f = \beta_i[E(r_M) - r_f]$. The corresponding factor model is: $r_i - r_f = \alpha_i + \beta_i(r_M - r_f) + \varepsilon_i$. Thus, CAPM is like a single-factor model, where the factor is r_M, the market rate of return. Note that the constant risk-free rate has been subtracted from both sides of the equation, so that the model is in terms of excess returns ($[r_i - r_f]$ versus $[r_M - r_f]$) rather than pure returns (r_i versus r_M). Other differences between CAPM and traditional factor models are that CAPM assumes the one-factor model intercept (a_i) is 0 and that there is no error term.

CAPM can also be related to the APT formulation introduced previously. Specifically, for a single-factor APT, if $f = r_M$, $\theta_0 = r_f$ and $\theta_1 = E(r_M) - r_f$, then the two models match exactly. Starting with the APT notation (with $m = 1$), we can convert to the CAPM model. Note that b_i (the APT notation for the single-factor loading) is used interchangeably here with β_i (the CAPM notation for beta). It can be shown that the reason different assets have different beta coefficients is that they have different factor loadings. This is a further theoretical connection between the two modeling frameworks.

9.2.2 Cash Flow Projection Models

Cash flow projection models are necessary because changes in interest rates can affect a company's surplus position, as defined by the gap between assets and liabilities. For an insurance company, asset cash flows consist mostly of dividends on stocks, coupons on bonds, and both the funds needed to buy these stocks/bonds (which are negative cash flows) and the funds received upon selling or redeeming them. Liability cash flows consist mostly of the net of claims and expenses over premiums.

Surplus, $S(i)$, can be defined as a function of the interest rate and the corresponding asset and liability cash flow levels; specifically, $S(i) = \sum_t A(t)(1+i)^{-t} - \sum_t L(t)(1+i)^{-t}$. Here, $A(t)$ and $L(t)$ reflect the various asset and liability cash flows, respectively, at time t, and i is the valuation interest rate.

Suppose our goal is to minimize the effects of interest rate changes. One way to do this is to force $S'(i) = 0$. Thus, we have:

$$S'(i) = \sum_t -tA(t)(1+i)^{-t-1} - \sum_t -tL(t)(1+i)^{-t-1} = 0,$$

so that

$$\sum_t -tA(t)(1+i)^{-t-1} = \sum_t -tL(t)(1+i)^{-t-1},$$

or

$$\sum_t tA(t)(1+i)^{-t} = \sum_t tL(t)(1+i)^{-t}.$$

Note that we have made the simplifying assumptions that both the asset and liability cash flows are independent of interest rates themselves and that only parallel shifts in the yield curve are allowed.

EXAMPLE 9.6

You are an asset-liability manager who wants to minimize the effects of interest rate changes on your company's surplus position. Suppose you have a known liability of 100,000, due two years from now, and a known asset cash flow of 50,000 due one year from now. You want to buy another asset that provides exactly the right amount of cash flow (X) two years from now so that $S'(i) = 0$. If the annual effective rate of interest is 8%, what should this cash flow amount (X) be?

Solution: For $S'(i) = 0$, we must have $\sum_t tA(t)(1 + i)^{-t} = \sum_t tL(t)(1 + i)^{-t}$. Thus, $\frac{1(50{,}000)}{1.08} + \frac{2(X)}{(1.08)^2} = \frac{2(100{,}000)}{(1.08)^2}$. This can be solved for $X = 73{,}000$. Note that the surplus amount is then: $S(0.08) = \frac{50{,}000}{1.08} + \frac{73{,}000 - 100{,}000}{(1.08)^2} = 23{,}148.15$. If the interest rate were to move in either direction, $S(i)$ would produce a slightly smaller amount than 23,148.15, but the overall effect on surplus would be minimal. For example, if the interest rate drops to zero, $S(0) = 23{,}000$ and if it doubles to 16%, $S(0.16) = 23{,}038.05$, both close to $S(0.08)$.

Thus, the goal is to manage both asset and liability cash flows to immunize the surplus from interest rate changes. To help manage adverse changes in asset cash flows, the investment manager can hedge by buying derivatives contracts, or adapt other risk-reducing techniques, noting that stochastic analysis may be required. To help manage adverse changes in liability cash flows, a carefully considered policy design is prudent (so that policyholders will be less likely to exploit the insurance company when the company is particularly vulnerable). In the optimal scenario, asset cash flows will match liability cash flows at all times for which such cash flows occur, causing the surplus to continually remain at 0.

However, exact matching is difficult, if not impossible, to achieve in practice; even if executed successfully, the company's investment strategy may become overly conservative leading to significant reduction in expected return. Furthermore, in insurance contexts, although liability cash flows can be projected to some degree of accuracy, the actual cash flows that ensue will deviate from what was expected and create at least some mismatching. Asset cash flows can be somewhat unpredictable. For example, consider an equity investment in a start-up firm, where both the timing and amount of future dividends are uncertain. More broadly, unexpected changes in macroeconomic factors may have significant impact on the term structure of interest rates, as reflected in the yield curve, which could cause some asset cash flows to deviate from that originally forecasted.

Cash flow projection models are most useful for life insurance products with long-term savings elements, as well as for pension plans, and both long-term care and disability insurance. The common factor in all these product types is that interest rate changes may materially affect the balance between assets and liabilities to the point where a company's surplus position can become dangerously low. For example, consider a deferred life annuity, where policyholder funds may be withdrawn, subject to minimum withdrawal benefits. Then, if interest rates are high, these withdrawals may cause the company to sell off assets at deflated prices, which can create a loss in surplus.

Simulation is often used in conjunction with cash flow projection models, especially when interest-sensitive assets are a major component of a company's asset portfolio. The more randomness inherent in either asset or liability cash flows, the greater the benefit of a simulation study. The output from all the iterations of a simulation will produce a distribution of net cash flows at various future points in time. Then, management can effect policy changes to achieve a specific risk management goal. For example, management might take action to minimize the probability of some adverse result occurring, where this probability is estimated from the simulation results.

9.2.3 Behavioral Finance Models

Behavioral finance models allow for explanations of real-world phenomena that appear to be inconsistent with the more traditional, rational, utility-maximization models that have already been discussed. For example, there are traditional stochastic models for stock returns that work fairly well across the majority of the stock price distribution. However, at the tails, such models often break down, at times severely, under-predicting the occurrences of extreme outcomes. The stock market bubble of the late 1990s and early 2000s saw extreme rates of return at both high and low ends of the spectrum. This is evidence that there may be irrational forces that affect market behavior. The same is true with respect to product design, that is, not all policyholders will behave according to rational, theoretically induced expectations. For example, there is a perception that certain causes of death are more common than they actually are (accidents and cancer, for instance), which artificially inflates the demand for insurance products that cover deaths relating to these causes.

Consider the efficient market hypothesis (EMH), which if completely true, would render behavioral finance models useless. The EMH states that market prices reflect all available information, that prices move randomly, and that investors behave rationally. Thus, if the EMH was actually true, attempts at outperforming the market would be a waste of time, or equivalently, if an investor did beat the market, it would be due to random chance, rather than any unique insight or skill. However, there is much data that both refutes the validity of the EMH and identifies various market anomalies that cannot be accounted for by the EMH. These data motivate the need for a different modeling framework—one that is encompassed by behavioral finance models.

Focusing on the word *behavior*, these models attempt to incorporate systematic deviations from decisions made using optimization models, deviations that link cognitive psychology with the world of financial economics. Both human emotion and cognitive error are utilized to explain how investors make decisions. This contrasts with more traditional analytical models that may be better able to predict future results in a rigorous fashion. Here, 10 investor behaviors that lead to violations of the EMH (i.e., market anomalies) are discussed. The experienced investment manager may be able to steer clear of some of these behaviors, so that they might make more informed and objective investment decisions.

- Overconfidence—On average, investors are more confident in their own abilities than they should be, based on their true ability level. Overconfidence causes some investors to trade too often (e.g., day traders), since these individuals continually believe they have superior abilities, relative to the market.
- Self-Attribution Bias—When investors succeed, they too often attribute their success to skill, but when they fail, they too often blame their failure on bad luck. This causes investors to sell winning stocks too soon (so as to accumulate pride) and to hold on to losing stocks too long (so as to avoid regret).
- Optimism—More than half of all investors believe that they will be more successful than the investor at the 50th percentile (however success is defined), but of course, only half can be above this median level. This is similar to the "overconfidence" behavior described previously, but here the reference group consists of an aggregate population of investors, whereas before, the reference party was the individual investor himself or herself.
- Sample Size Neglect—Too often, conclusions are inferred from too small a sample size. The smaller the sample size, the greater the chance that a spurious conclusion might be drawn (i.e., one that was obtained from random chance rather than resulting from a true underlying process).
- Belief Perseverance—After investors form their initial opinions, they will be resistant to deviate from such opinions; more specifically, they will give greater weight to evidence that supports their prior opinions than they will to evidence that contradicts these opinions.
- Anchoring—When an analyst must form an initial estimate, there is often little or no basis for what this value should be. However, the level of the initial estimate has great bearing on what future, revised estimates will be. Thus, these future estimates may be biased, based on the "anchor" or level of the initial estimate.
- Risk Aversion—Especially on a short-term basis, most investors feel greater pain from a loss than they do glee from a gain. Such investors would rather have nothing happen than to have a bunch of gains and losses that effectively cancel out in aggregate.
- Prediction Addiction—Many analysts desperately try to mine a dataset in order to find patterns that will lead to superior predictive ability. While some of these patterns may be legitimate, other patterns may be of only short-term use (or perhaps no use at all) and have no relation to what will happen in the long term.
- Hindsight Bias—Sometimes, after an event has already occurred, an analyst claims to have predicted this event (successfully) at a previous time. However, the same analyst may have also predicted other events previously that did not come to fruition.
- Framing/Persuasion Effect—Conclusions may be influenced more by how a question or concept is framed rather than from a more thorough analysis. Likewise, corporate decisions may be influenced more by who is supporting the decision rather than how well constructed the supporting arguments are.

Note that behavioral finance has only been around for about 30 years, and although much progress has been made in understanding many of these market anomalies academically, there is still much work to be done. For example, there needs to be a better connection developed between the ten behaviors mentioned and a predictive modeling framework that incorporates such behaviors. Thus, one should not be too quick to dismiss the EMH altogether.

9.3 Data and Estimation

9.3.1 Sources of Data

Actuaries need access to data for several reasons, including pricing of existing products, development of new products, calculation of reserves, and analysis of trends. The best and most important source of data is whatever is already available internally. Much of a company's actuarial analysis revolves around previous claim experience, so that if rates for a block of previously existing business need to be updated, past experience will be the primary source of information. However, if a company wants to price new benefits, develop new product lines, or expand into new geographic areas, external data sources may also be required. Note that external data may also be necessary if a company's volume of business to date is not yet sufficient to produce credible experience. External data sources can also be used to verify that internally produced data is reasonable and consistent with macro-level trends.

There are several sources for external data, some of which are free, and some which may be quite expensive. Federal government publications are primarily cost-free and easily obtainable in electronic format. Examples include data from the U.S. Census, the CPI, and the National Health Interview Survey (NHIS). The SOA also offers numerous actuarial-oriented publications containing data that pertains to insured populations. Note that insured populations will behave differently than the general populations analyzed in federal government publications. Examples of actuarial publications include serials (*Transactions* and *Records* from the SOA), reports, and tables. Much of this can be found directly on the SOA website (www.soa.org). Other external sources of data (which may not be free) include state and regional organizations and pricing manuals from major actuarial consulting firms.

9.3.2 Estimating Model Parameters

When employing a mean-variance framework like CAPM or APT to help construct an investment portfolio, it is necessary to assign numerical values to all the parameters of the model. These parameters represent the expected asset returns, the standard deviations of those returns, and the covariances among the returns of different assets. It is also necessary to choose the length of time for the investment period for which the returns are calculated. Common choices are one week, one month, or one year.

The most obvious approach is to use the past to estimate the future, that is, historical data of various asset returns should be incorporated to predict what will happen with these assets in the future. Although this approach is convenient, since such data is plentiful and readily available, it is not necessarily reliable for predictive purposes. This is especially true with respect to predicting expected future returns, which may have little or no relation to what has happened in the past. However, past volatility is more closely related to expected future volatility; also, the covariances between separate asset returns are likely to be more homogeneous through time than are the returns of individual assets.

Suppose we are interested in estimating an asset's mean return over a period of time T and during that period, observations are available at intervals of time h. Let n be the number of such intervals, and thus $T = nh$, where the values are set to ensure that n is an integer. Note that this is the same framework used in Section 8.3.4. One difference is that here we are concerned with a single asset and not a portfolio. Then, it is reasonable to work with the asset's value at the end of each period. Let S_t be the asset's value at the end of the tth period (which is at time th). The usual estimate of the continuously compounded return for that period is $r_t = \ln(S_t/S_{t-1}),\ t = 1, \ldots, n$. Then, an unbiased estimate of the mean return is

$$\bar{r} = \frac{1}{n}\sum_{t=1}^{n} r_t = \frac{1}{n}\sum_{t=1}^{n}[\ln(S_t) - \ln(S_{t-1})] = \frac{1}{n}[\ln(S_n) - \ln(S_0)] = \frac{1}{n}\ln(S_n/S_0).$$

It may seem odd that the intermediate values are not needed, but because the mean return is assumed constant over the period, all we need know is the total growth of the asset over the period. As in Section 8.3.4, this can be converted to an annual rate by dividing by h. Then, converting this annual continuously compounded rate to an annual effective rate produces

$$\bar{r}_{eff} = \exp(\bar{r}/h) - 1 = \exp\left[\frac{\ln(S_n/S_0)}{nh}\right] - 1 = (S_n/S_0)^{1/T} - 1.$$

This is simply the effective rate that after T years allows the investment to grow from its initial to its final value.

We might be interested in the accuracy of this estimator. We know that the variance of a sample mean is the variance of a single observation divided by the sample size. Let σ_h^2 be the variance of the asset's return over a period of length h. Then,

$$Var(\bar{r}^h) = \frac{\sigma_h^2}{n}$$

where the superscript is a reminder that the average is calculated over observations taken every h years. Keeping the time period T fixed, it appears that increasing n (i.e., taking observations more frequently) will lead to a smaller variance and thus a more accurate estimator. However, as the interval shrinks, the volatility of a return measured over that interval also shrinks. In fact, $\sigma_h^2 = \sigma^2 h$, where σ^2 is the variance of annual returns. Then $Var(\bar{r}^h) = \frac{\sigma_h^2}{n} = \frac{\sigma^2 h}{Th} = \frac{\sigma^2}{T}$, and thus the accuracy of the estimator depends only on the length of the time period and not the number of observations taken within that period. This should have been obvious upon noting that if the estimator does not depend on the intermediate observations, then its accuracy should not depend on the number of such observations. The only way to reduce the variance of the estimator is to use a longer time period. However, doing so introduces the problem that the returns might not have a stable mean or variance over a longer period.

Thus, there is a limit to the degree of accuracy with which we can estimate the mean return of an asset. This phenomenon is sometimes called *mean blur*.

The variance can be estimated with the usual variance formula as given in Section 8.3.4. If the returns have a normal distribution (which is equivalent to assuming asset prices have a lognormal distribution, not an unreasonable assumption), then the variance of the estimated variance is

$$Var(s^2) = \frac{2\sigma_h^4}{n-1} = \frac{2\sigma^4 h^2}{T/n - 1} \approx \frac{2\sigma^4 h^2}{h} = 2\sigma^4 h.$$

Thus, accuracy can be increased by reducing the value of h.

EXAMPLE 9.7

You are given the monthly effective returns for a stock throughout an entire calendar year. From January through December, they are 0.03, −0.02, −0.04, 0.06, 0, 0.01, −0.03, 0.05, 0.09, −0.05, 0, and 0.02. From Example 8.18, the monthly sample mean and variance of the continuously compounded return are 0.00915 and 0.001745. Determine a 95% confidence interval for the mean monthly return. Then, determine the standard deviation of the estimator for the variance.

Solution: The variance of the monthly sample mean is 0.001745/12 = 0.000145 and the standard deviation is 0.012059. A 95% confidence interval is calculated as (0.00915 − 1.96 × 0.012059, 0.00915 + 1.96 × 0.012059), where 1.96 is the appropriate z-score from the Normal distribution. This produces a confidence interval of −0.0145 to 0.0328. In this case, one year was not sufficient to provide a reasonably accurate estimate. The variance of the variance estimator is $2(0.001745)^2/11 =$ 0.000000554 for a standard deviation of 0.000744.

As for factor models, the blur effect does hamper the estimation of the intercept, or a term, and this is called a blur. Specifically, the standard deviation of the estimate of a will often be larger than the size of the estimate itself. However, this blur effect does not apply as much to the factor loadings, that is, the b terms can be estimated to a greater degree of accuracy relative to their specific magnitudes.

9.3.3 Updating Estimates based on New Experience

Focusing on improving estimation procedures for the expected returns of individual assets, what other information or structure can be incorporated beyond past or historical returns? Perhaps the analyst or modeler can utilize information that is more prospective in nature, data that might indicate what an asset's future prospects might be. Such data could be inferred from a painstaking analysis of a company's financial statements, including the balance sheet, income statement, statement of cash flows, and statement of shareholder's equity. Furthermore, knowledge of a company's upcoming business plan might be useful as it relates to future projects, management style, level of competition, and the projected market for the goods and services the company offers. Even the opinions of other analysts and the news media may be incorporated, as can an analyst's own opinions, as formed over years of experience in researching a company.

An alternative modeling framework might incorporate credibility, in either a Bühlmann or a Bayesian context. With Bühlmann credibility, the analyst uses a weighted average of the sample mean ($\bar{r}$, as estimated previously) and a more broadly defined mean. This latter measure may reflect a more theoretical mean that might be associated with an asset, or it could represent a data-based mean, as calculated over a longer period of time; in either case, this broader mean might be determined more from qualitative than quantitative considerations. Then, as recent data comes in that may deviate from the assumed level of the broader mean, the estimate for μ can be updated (i.e., shifted away from the broader mean and toward the sample mean).

With Bayesian estimation, a (prior) probability distribution is assigned to what the per-period mean could be. Note that this is not a single value, as with the broader mean described previously for Bühlmann credibility, but an entire range of values. Then, as new data comes in, the distributional assumption for the per-period mean gets updated. In statistical terms, a posterior distribution is formed for the per-period mean, given the data that has been observed, where the posterior distribution will differ from the prior distribution that did not condition on any observed data. The posterior distribution is related to the prior distribution and the model distribution, where the model distribution relates to the data, given a particular value of the per-period mean, μ. Note that the model distribution assumes that data observations are conditionally independent given μ. For more details on both types of credibility, see Klugman, Panjer, and Willmot (2008, Chapter 20).

9.4 EXERCISES

9.1 **a)** Extract all the daily closing prices for the calendar year 2010 (from 12/31/2009–12/31/2010) for the low-beta stock Coca-Cola (Symbol: KO), the high-beta stock Best Buy (Symbol: BBY), and a proxy for the market, the S&P 500 Index (Symbol: ^GSPC). See the following website for a simple way to extract this data: http://www.optiontradingtips.com/options101/volatility.html. Then, once you are on this website, click on the Historical Volatility.xls link. Note that these prices are also available in the provided model solutions spreadsheet. Then, based on the formula $r_t = \ln(S_t/S_{t-1})$, calculate the continuously compounded daily returns for all 252 trading days in 2010.

b) Using the data provided, estimate the annualized volatility for both Coca-Cola and Best Buy, along with the annualized volatility for the S&P 500 Index. Note: To convert from daily volatility to annualized volatility, use 365 days (not 252 days).

c) Using the data provided, calculate the correlation coefficient between the returns on Coca-Cola and the S&P 500. Do the same between the returns on Best Buy and the S&P 500. Also, calculate the correlation coefficient between the returns on Coca-Cola and Best Buy, and explain why this is so much lower than the two correlations you calculated between each stock and the market.

d) Based on your answers to parts b) and c), estimate the beta coefficient for each of the two given stocks. How do these estimates compare to the latest published Beta values for these two stocks? Why might there be differences between your estimates and the published values?

e) If the risk-free rate of return (as estimated from the returns on either T-bills or T-bonds) is 4%, and the market risk premium is 5%, use the *published* Beta values you found in part d) to calculate the required rate of return for both Coca-Cola and Best Buy.

f) Calculate the continuously compounded realized returns for calendar year 2010 for both Coca-Cola and Best Buy. In each case, were the required returns from part e) satisfied or not?

g) Assuming that the S&P 500 is representative of the market at large, what should the beta coefficient be for an index fund that mimics the S&P 500? Then, repeat parts e) and f), as pertains to the S&P 500 index.

For parts h) through j), assume a portfolio context. At the beginning of 2011, you decided to invest 15% of your after-tax salary for 2010. Your pre-tax salary for that year was 75,000, of which 28% was removed for taxes. You decided to put 2,500 into an S&P 500 index fund, 1,000 into a mystery stock that has no correlation with market returns and the rest into Coca-Cola and Best Buy, with twice as much invested in Best Buy (versus Coca-Cola).

h) Calculate the portfolio weights for each of the four components.

i) Calculate the portfolio beta, based on your weights from part h). Note: Now, use the estimated betas from part d) (rather than the currently published betas) for both Coca-Cola and Best Buy.

j) Calculate the required return for 2011, based on the portfolio beta you calculated in part i). Also, assume you had taken the same strategy one year earlier (with the same salary and tax structure). What would your realized portfolio return (on a continuously compounded basis) have been in 2010, if the mystery stock had doubled in value from the beginning of 2010 to the end of 2010?

CHAPTER 10

The Term Structure of Interest Rates

10.1 Interest Rates

10.1.1 Risks

10.1.1.1 Interest rate risk

Both insurance companies and other financial service organizations can encounter problems when interest rates change. Interest rate risk is defined as the risk of losses due to changes in interest rates. These losses may be due to changes in interest rate levels or could be from changes in the shape of the yield curve.

From an insurance company perspective, consider an asset cash flow and a liability cash flow. The asset cash flow includes investment income (e.g., dividends from stocks and coupons from bonds, along with the net cash flows from stock and bond sales and purchases) and principal repayments (e.g., the repayment of policy loans and the redemption value from bonds). The liability cash flow includes the net of policy claims, surrenders, and associated expenses over premium income received. Note that in a young and growing company, the liability cash flow may be quite small, or even negative, because the policyholders (in aggregate) will not yet have surrendered much or have incurred many claims. Then, net cash flow, on a per period basis, is the difference between that period's asset cash flow and liability cash flow. If, in aggregate, the liabilities exceed the assets, net cash flow will be negative. Then, the company must either liquidate assets or borrow to cover the cash shortfall.

Now, if interest rates have risen during a time period when net cash flow is negative, capital losses may occur when bonds and other fixed-income securities are liquidated. This is a classic example of interest rate risk. There is an inverse relationship between interest rates and the value of most fixed-income securities, so that increases in interest rates will result in lower prices at the point of sale than when the securities were bought (presumably when rates were lower). Longer-term securities will have greater exposure to the same interest rate increase than shorter-term securities do because of time-value-of-money effects.

EXAMPLE 10.1

If a 1,000 par value 10-year bond that can be redeemed at 100 above par is bought to yield 8% convertible semi-annually, and the bond has semi-annual coupons payable at 12% convertible semi-annually, its price will be 1,317.45. (See Example 6.24 for this calculation). Immediately after the bond's purchase, the yield rate increases to 10% convertible semi-annually. If you then decide to sell the bond (perhaps because you fear interest rates will go up even further), what will be the sale price, and how much capital will you have lost on your investment?

Solution: Here, $F = 1{,}000$, $r = 0.12/2 = 0.06$, $n = 10 \times 2 = 20$, $C = 1{,}100$, and $i = 0.10/2 = 0.05$.

Thus, we have

$$P = Fra_{\overline{n}|i} + \frac{C}{(1+i)^n} = (1{,}000)(0.06)a_{\overline{20}|0.05} + \frac{1{,}100}{(1.05)^{20}}$$

$$= 747.73 + 414.58 = 1{,}162.31.$$

Hence, the amount of capital lost is 1,317.45 − 1,162.31 = 155.14.

10.1.1.2 Reinvestment rate risk

If total assets exceed total liabilities, then net cash flow will be positive. If net cash flow is positive, then there will be excess cash available to be reinvested. Now, if interest rates have fallen during the time period when net cash flow is positive, reductions in income may occur when expiring bonds and other fixed-income securities are reinvested in securities with income payments tied to the lower interest rates. This is an example of reinvestment rate risk.

Both interest rate risk and reinvestment risk, referred to as "C-3" risk by the actuary C.L. Trowbridge, can be amplified when interest rate options are embedded in an insurance company's assets and liabilities. Interest rate options are derivatives whose value is derived from interest rate levels. With respect to interest rate risk, where rates have gone up, rational policyholders will have extra incentive to surrender their policies so that they can reinvest their cash values elsewhere and earn higher rates of return. Such policyholders may also take out policy loans and be able to invest the proceeds at a higher rate of return than the interest rate the insurance company charges. Thus, by granting surrender and policy loan options, companies may have to liquidate assets when interest rates increase, leading to losses.

As for reinvestment rate risk, when interest rates decrease, the insurance company may lose control of a portion of its asset portfolio. For example, issuers of callable bonds will be more likely to call those bonds early so that they can replace those bonds with ones requiring lower periodic coupons.

EXAMPLE 10.2

Five years ago, you invested in a 10-year bond that paid annual 5% coupons, was redeemable at its par value of 1,000, and was bought to yield 5%. After five years, the issuer has the option to call the bond at par. The annual interest rate has declined to 3% and so the issuer decides to call the bond. The best you can do is use the 1,000 to buy a five-year bond redeemable at its par value of 1,000 and with 3% annual coupons. What is the present value of all the income you will lose as a result of this action?

Solution: Here, the term "income" refers to the coupons received. Originally, your last five coupons were all $0.05 \times 1{,}000 = 50$, but under the new bond, your five coupons will all be $0.03 \times 1{,}000 = 30$. Thus, you lose 20 each coupon period so that PV (income lost) $= 20a_{\overline{5}|0.03} = 20(4.5797) = 91.59$.

Also, for similar reasons, borrowers may decide to prepay or refinance their mortgages. Note that in both of these examples, the insurance company is the counterparty (i.e., the investor in the callable bonds and the lender of the mortgage) and will be disadvantaged by interest rate decreases. For investors with long-term investment horizons, reinvestment risk is especially prevalent when holding short-term bonds, because when such bonds expire and have to be rolled over (so as to retain the income benefits that accrue to the investor), the income received will decline as interest rates fall.

EXAMPLE 10.3

You are a loan officer for a bank. Ten years ago, you lent 300,000 to an individual seeking a residential mortgage; it was a 30-year, level, monthly-payment loan at a fixed interest rate of 9% convertible monthly. Just after receiving the borrower's 120th payment, you learn that the borrower wishes to refinance the outstanding loan balance at the new lower rate of 4.8% convertible monthly. Assuming that the borrower wishes to repay the loan in 20 years (instead of 30 years from now) and that there are no refinancing fees (i.e., closing costs), by how much does the monthly payment decline?

Solution: The monthly payment under the original loan structure, based on an interest rate of $0.09/12 = 0.0075$, is $R = \frac{L}{a_{\overline{n}|i}} = \frac{300{,}000}{a_{\overline{360}|0.0075}} = \frac{300{,}000}{124.2819} = 2{,}413.87$. One hundred twenty payments later, the outstanding loan balance is $B_{120} = Ra_{\overline{360-120}|0.0075} = 2{,}413.87a_{\overline{240}|0.0075} = 2{,}413.87(111.144954) = 268{,}289.47$.

However, when the interest rate falls to $0.0048/12 = 0.004$, the new monthly payment, R^*, based on $i^* = 0.004$, will be: $R^* = \frac{B_{120}}{a_{\overline{240}|i^*}} = \frac{268{,}289.47}{a_{\overline{240}|0.004}} = \frac{268{,}289.47}{154.0933} = 1{,}741.08$. This is a decline in income (for the bank) of $2{,}413.87 - 1{,}741.08 = 672.79$ per month.

10.1.2 Assumptions

10.1.2.1 Interest rate determinants and their effect on investment income

A pricing actuary must incorporate any investment income earned on the asset portfolio that supports the product. To do this appropriately, the actuary must understand how and why the interest rates used to calculate investment income vary over time.

There is a strong relationship between market conditions and interest rate levels. When interest rates and inflation rates are low, market conditions are more favorable. Note that most previous economic downturns tend to have been associated with high interest and inflation rates, although the most recent recession (beginning in late 2007) featured primarily low interest and inflation rates The government can artificially manipulate the level of interest rates to achieve a particular monetary policy. For example, in an economic downturn, the U.S. Federal Reserve might lower rates so as to stimulate the economy; in contrast, when times are good and growth may be occurring too quickly, rates might be raised so as to preserve the value of currency.

There are many factors that affect interest rate levels, including duration (or investment horizon), the amount of default risk and asset class. First, interest rates tend to be higher for longer-term securities because there is a greater risk of price declines due to future rate increases for longer-term bonds versus shorter-term bonds. Second, two bonds of similar maturity (or duration) might have different yield rates if the estimated default risk differs between the two. Naturally, the riskier bond will pay greater interest income to compensate the investor for assuming this additional risk. Third, interest rates also vary by asset class; mortgages, for instance, pay higher rates than bonds of similar risk levels because of the additional expenses associated with the servicing of loans.

Many long-term insurance products pay investment income based on cumulative cash flows. Here, in a product's early years, asset levels may be insufficient to support a product, as measured by solvency reserves. Then, the negative cash flows create negative interest income, whereby the company borrows internally from its owners. However, in later years, when assets typically exceed reserves, the interest earned on the excess will contribute further to building up this excess. Note that a company does not earn investment income on reserves, but only on the assets backing those reserves. The investment income on cumulative cash flows is then used to calculate asset shares, which helps determine how assets and investment income are allocated between various group and individual policyholders.

Policy loans are another application of how investment income affects insurance products. Here, the policyholder is allowed to borrow money from the insurer, while using the policy's cash value (or death benefit if the insured dies before repayment) as collateral. The company then collects interest from the policyholder. Due to the collateralized nature of policy loans, the insurance company has little need to worry about the policyholder defaulting on these loans, especially relative to other invested assets. However, there is the worry that the loan balance may rise to equal the cash value, which will trigger a surrender, whereby future profits are lost. The company may either track interest separately for policy loans versus invested assets, or if the two rates are not materially different, they can use a single rate that is a weighted-average of the two rates when pricing the associated product.

As for invested assets, the company must credit interest so as to allocate interest income to its various policies. This is particularly relevant for participating policies (i.e., those that pay dividends), along with policies where benefits are tied directly to investment earnings. When crediting interest, the company may utilize either the portfolio rate method or the investment year (new money rate) method. The portfolio rate method uses average rates earned over a past number of years, and is less volatile due to this averaging effect. However, this method is problematic when rates are increasing because investors may avoid making new deposits (and may even make withdrawals) into a fund crediting interest at a lower rate than what is currently available in the market. The investment year method addresses this problem by acknowledging both the date of investment and the current date. For more background on these two methods, see Kellison (2008, pp. 274–276). Total investment income consists of interest earned on assets already in place at the end of the previous year, interest earned on cash flows occurring during the current year, and interest earned on policy loans.

10.1.2.2 Trends in interest rate movements

For insurance products with significant investment components, it can be dangerous to guarantee (or even project) current levels of rates too far into the future, as many past insurance company failures have demonstrated. A simple alternative, if guarantees are to be included, is to guarantee a low interest rate but to credit additional interest income to the policyholder if current economic conditions are favorable. This strategy shifts the interest rate risk from the company to the policyholder. In Chapter 11, more complex strategies for managing interest rate risk will be presented.

EXAMPLE 10.4

Consider a life insurance product where the cash value is guaranteed to accumulate at a minimum interest rate of 3% per year. In return for this guarantee, whenever annual market interest rates are greater than 3%, the insurance company will credit interest income at a rate that is 3% plus 75% of the excess of the prevailing market interest rate over 3%. If the prevailing annual market interest rates over a five-year period are 5%, 4%, 2%, 2.5%, and 3.5%, what rates are applied to these policies over the five-year period?

Solution: In year one, the credited rate is $0.03 + 0.75(0.05 - 0.03) = 4.5\%$. In year two, the credited rate is $0.03 + 0.75(0.04 - 0.03) = 3.75\%$. In years three and four (each), the credited rate is 3%, since both 2% and 2.5% are less than the guaranteed rate. In year five, the credited rate is $0.035 + 0.75(0.035 - 0.03) = 3.875\%$.

Both the level and volatility of interest rates are highly unpredictable and can vary substantially by country. For nations with relatively slow moving rates, like the United States, insurance companies will often assume that these rates will persist into the short-term future while subtracting a small amount in order to establish a margin for adverse movement. In general, short-term interest rates (e.g., time horizon = 90 days) have tended to be more volatile than long-term rates (e.g., time horizon = 10 years), while longer-term rates have been much more positively correlated across nations than short-term rates. In normal interest rate environments, long-term rates will exceed short-term rates due to the maturity risk premium discussed previously. However, this need not always be the case; if short rates exceed long rates, the yield curve is said to be inverted or downward sloping.

10.2 Yield Curves

The yield curve is a graphical representation of how interest rates vary with time to maturity. Common points on the yield curve, where the x axis represents years to maturity and the y axis represents the yield rate, include 90 days (3 months), 180 days (6 months), and 1, 2, 3, 5, 7, 10, 20, and 30 years. Figure 10.1 presents a yield curve for March 1, 2011 based on U.S. Treasuries.[1]

Interestingly, the points on the yield curve usually lie on a smooth curve. It should be noted that for the curve in Figure 10.1 the values have been smoothed by use of a cubic spline, and so the smoothness is a result of the methodology. The typical shape is one that rises gradually over time and at a decreasing rate (i.e., the curve is concave). However, there are other possible graphical representations. When short-term rates increase quickly, but this increase

1 U.S. Department of the Treasury (2011).

FIGURE 10.1 Daily Treasury Yield Curve Rates

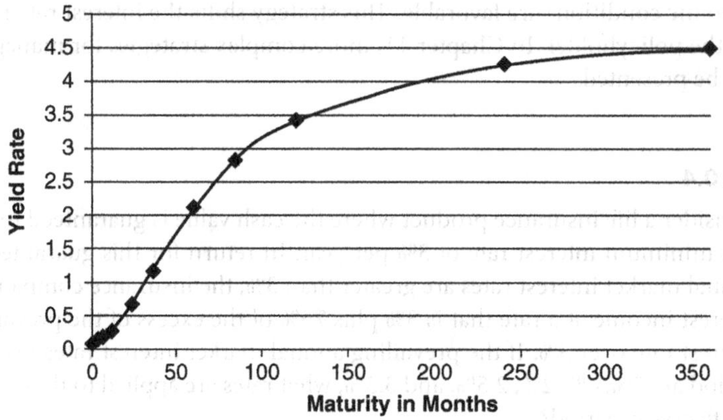

is expected to be temporary, long-term rates will remain near their previous levels. Then, the yield curve may be downward sloping, which is often termed *inverted.* Humped, undulating, and relatively flat shapes are also possible. A flat yield curve implies that there is no additional risk premium for a bond's increasing term to maturity.

Note that each rating class for bonds, as determined by rating agencies such as Moody's or Standard & Poor's, will have a unique yield curve associated with it. For example, a 10-year AAA investment grade bond will have a lower yield rate than an otherwise equivalent 10-year high-yield bond. If a particular bond has a yield rate that differs materially from what the standard yield curve for its rating and maturity would indicate, this is probably due to that bond's specific individual features. Some of these features were discussed in the section on bonds in Chapter 7.

10.2.1 Spot Rates

Spot rates are the most basic building blocks when defining the term structure of interest rates. On an annualized basis, let s_t be the interest rate used to discount a cash flow made at time t back to time 0. Thus, s_1 is the one-year spot-rate and s_2 is the two-year spot rate. Note that when using s_2 to discount a time-two cash flow, we use s_2 not only to go back from time two to time one, but also to go back from time one to time zero. This is different from the situation where a particular interest rate (i_2) is used to discount cash flows back from time two to time one, and a separate interest rate (i_1) is used to discount cash flows back from time one to time zero.

EXAMPLE 10.5

What is the present value of a 1,000 cash flow made two years from now, where $s_1 = 0.04$ and $s_2 = 0.05$?

Solution: The present value is $\dfrac{1{,}000}{(1 + 0.05)^2} = 907.03$. Thus, the one-year spot rate, s_1, is never used in this calculation. Also note that we assumed the spot rates are annual effective rates, but if they are instead continuously compounded rates, then this present value is $1{,}000e^{-0.05(2)} = 904.84$. Going forward, annual effective rates will be presumed.

Note that spot rates can be thought of as the yield to maturities on zero-coupon bonds since such bonds have only single cash flows that occur at maturity. In the preceding example, think of 5% as the yield rate, 1,000 as the redemption value (or face amount), and $907.03 as the bond's initial (time zero) price.

However, spot rates can also be used to evaluate coupon-paying bonds or any fixed-income security with a predictable series of future cash flows.

EXAMPLE 10.6

Consider a five-year bond with level annual 6% coupons and 1,000 par value that matures at par and is subject to the following sequence of spot rates:

$$s_1 = 0.04,\ s_2 = 0.05,\ s_3 = 0.058,\ s_4 = 0.065,\ s_5 = 0.07.$$

Note that this series of spot rates follows the most typically observed pattern on the yield curve, that is, the curve is increasing but at a decreasing rate. What is the bond's price, or present value? Also, what is the bond's level annualized yield to maturity?

Solution: First, note that the annual coupon is 1,000(0.06) = 60. Then, the bond's price is given by

$$\frac{60}{(1.04)} + \frac{60}{(1.05)^2} + \frac{60}{(1.058)^3} + \frac{60}{(1.065)^4} + \frac{(60 + 1{,}000)}{(1.07)^5} = 965.18.$$

The bond's level annualized yield to maturity is the common rate that, if used to discount all the cash flows, would produce an equivalent price (965.18). This rate, which can be solved for using a financial calculator, numerical methods or by trial and error, is 6.8457% because

$$\frac{60}{(1.068457)} + \frac{60}{(1.068457)^2} + \frac{60}{(1.068457)^3} + \frac{60}{(1.068457)^4} + \frac{(60 + 1{,}000)}{(1.068457)^5} = 965.18.$$

Note: the reason why 6.8457% is so close to the upper range of the spot rates ($s_5 = 0.07$ in particular) is that the redemption value (which occurs at time five) is so much larger than any individual coupon amount. Also note that because the bond's annualized yield is higher than the coupon rate (i.e., 6.8457% > 6%), the bond's price must be less than its redemption value (i.e., 965.18 < 1,000). Finally, note that a spot rate curve is distinct from a yield curve; for instance, the 6.8457% rate would be the time-five rate on the yield curve (for bonds of this type), whereas the 7% rate would be the time-five rate on the spot rate curve. Note that the spot rate curve relates strictly to yields on zero-coupon bonds, whereas yield curves in general relate to whatever investment instrument is being examined.

One problem with spot rates is that they are not always readily available. Typical lengths of zero-coupon bonds include those maturing at 1, 2, 3, 5, 7, 10, 20, and 30 years. Thus, we do not immediately have spot rates at the other maturities such as 4, 8, or 25 years. However, we can still infer what these rates are by starting with the shorter given spot rates and subsequently working forward to generate the rates for longer maturities. This procedure is called the bootstrap method.

For example, assume that we know s_1 and know both the price and all cash flows for a two-year coupon-paying bond. We can then solve for s_2.

EXAMPLE 10.7

Let $s_1 = 0.04$, and consider a bond that provides 60 at time one and 1,060 at time two. If the current price of the bond is 1,019.14, what is s_2?

Solution: The equation for the bond's price is a function of s_2 and is given by: $1{,}019.14 = \dfrac{60}{1.04} + \dfrac{60 + 1{,}000}{(1 + s_2)^2}$. This can be solved for $s_2 = 0.05$.

Then, if we have both s_1 and s_2, we can repeat the same procedure to next get s_3, given the price and all cash flows for a three-year bond. We can then continue to generate each subsequent spot rate until we have defined the entire spot rate curve.

10.2.2 Forward Rates

What if you want to set a rate today for which money is borrowed between two dates in the future? In Chapter 7, we discussed a forward contract, where two parties agree at some future date to exchange a good for a price determined today. A forward rate is a similar concept with respect to the timing of cash flows. It can be defined as the expected spot rate for a time period that begins in the future.

For example, assume both the one-year and two-year spot rates are known, and that a company needs to borrow K now, which will be repaid in full (with interest) two years from now. This firm has two choices. The first choice is to borrow K for two years at the two-year spot rate. The second choice is to borrow K for one year at the one-year spot rate, and then apply the one-year spot rate in effect for the second year, which is the forward rate (established now, at time zero) from time one to time two. If we label this forward rate f, then we can solve for f as the rate for which the company is indifferent between the two choices, that is, the amount the company owes at time two is:

$$K(1 + s_2)^2 = K(1 + s_1)(1 + f), \text{ or } f = \frac{(1 + s_2)^2}{(1 + s_1)} - 1.$$

EXAMPLE 10.8

If the one- and two-year spot rates are 4% and 5%, respectively, what is the annualized forward rate f between times one and two? Also, what would one unit of currency invested at time zero be worth after two years?

Solution: The annualized forward rate f, between times one and two, is $(1.05)^2/1.04 - 1 = 0.060096$ so that $1(1.05)^2 = 1(1.04)(1.060096) = 1.1025$. Note that if the two choices (Choice 1: s_2 for each of two years; Choice 2: s_1 for year one and f for year two, where f in this context is the observed market forward rate instead of the forward rate implied by the given spot rates) do not produce the same accumulated value at time two, then there will be an arbitrage opportunity for either the borrower or lender, depending on which choice produces the higher time-two value.

This discussion assumes that the borrower establishes the agreement for the second year's loan today. If the borrower waits until time one, the loan will be made at whatever rate is available at that time.

The notion of forward rates can be extended to any future time period of any length. Just as for spot rates, forward rates are typically expressed on an annualized basis. Then, sticking with annual periods (to keep things simple), let s_a be the a-year spot rate, and let s_b be the b-year spot rate, where $b > a$. Then, if we break up the b years into the first a years and the subsequent $b - a$ years, we must have: $(1 + s_b)^b = (1 + s_a)^a(1 + f_{a,b})^{b-a}$, where $f_{a,b}$ is the (annualized) forward rate for the time period from a to b. As before, we can solve for

$$f_{a,b} = \left[\frac{(1 + s_b)^b}{(1 + s_a)^a}\right]^{\frac{1}{b-a}} - 1.$$

EXAMPLE 10.9

If the two-year spot rate is 5% and the five-year spot rate is 7%, then what is the annualized forward rate $f_{2,5}$ between times two and five? Also, what would one unit of currency invested at time zero be worth after five years?

Solution: The annualized forward rate $f_{2,5}$ between times two and five is $[(1.07)^5/(1.02)^2]^{1/3} = 0.083545$, so that $1(1.07)^5 = 1(1.05)^2(1.083545)^3 = 1.4026$.

Note that any spot rate s_t can be written as, and is equal to, $f_{0,t}$. Also, if there are n given spot rates (including the forward rates that start at time zero), then there will be $n(n + 1)/2$ forward rates that are implied by the spot rate curve. For example, if $n = 5$, so that s_1, s_2, s_3, s_4, s_5 are given, then the following 15 forward rates can be derived: $f_{0,1}, f_{0.2}, f_{0,3}, f_{0,4}, f_{0,5}, f_{1,2}, f_{1,3}, f_{1,4}, f_{1,5}, f_{2,3}, f_{2,4}, f_{2,5}, f_{3,4}, f_{3,5}, f_{4,5}$.

10.2.3 Explanations for Term Structure

Most yield curves (and spot rate curves for that matter) are not typically flat. In fact, the pattern of sharply increasing rates at short-term maturities, followed by gradually increasing rates as maturity lengthens, is observed empirically more often than might be anticipated. There are three possible theories that help explain yield curve patterns: expectations theory, liquidity preference, and market segmentation. The first two are consistent with the standard yield curve shape explained previously, whereas the third (market segmentation) does not necessarily support any discernible pattern.

The expectations theory states that spot rates are a function of the expectation of what interest rate levels will be in the future. In other words, the forward rate is exactly what the market expects the corresponding spot rate to be in the future. When comparing rates across time that have identical ranges for the time horizons, if the majority of individuals believe that an n-year spot rate will be higher in the future than it is now (i.e., an n-year forward rate will be higher starting at time t than the n-year spot rate is right now), this will cause the $(n+t)$-year spot rate to be higher than the n-year spot rate. This in turn will cause the yield curve to rise. Why might the majority of investors believe that spot rates will be higher in the future? It may be because most people believe inflation will rise, which will require an accompanying increase in nominal rates of interest (to maintain similar levels of the real rate of interest). Note that yield rates are nominal rates and not real rates, whereas real rates are net of inflation. Also, note that this particular theory is counterintuitive and is not widely held as the primary explanation for normal yield curve patterns.

The liquidity preference theory states that most investors prefer short-term, fixed-income securities to otherwise equivalent long-term securities. Thus, to induce investors to invest in longer-term securities, an extra yield premium must be incorporated. Why might the majority of investors have a preference for shorter-term securities? It may be because investors do not like to have significant capital tied up for long periods of time. In other words, investors have a preference for more liquid, cash-accessible investments. Also, as mentioned previously, shorter-term bonds are less price-sensitive to interest rate changes than longer-term bonds, and therefore have less interest rate risk. Thus, long-term bonds should have higher yields to reflect this extra risk.

Market segmentation theory states that the market demand for fixed-income securities is segmented by term to maturity. More specifically, investors who prefer longer-term bonds are different from those who prefer shorter-term bonds. Thus, there is no reason to believe that short-term rates and long-term rates should be correlated. In fact, a literal interpretation of this theory is that all spot rates are mutually independent. A more relaxed view of market segmentation would suggest that investors shift between market segments only when one segment becomes more relatively attractive versus another. Then, although adjacent points on the yield curve would have to be close together, there would not have to be any discernible pattern.

10.2.4 Short Rates and Floating-rate Bonds

Up to now, we have been assuming that bonds are strictly fixed-income securities, and thus have level coupons, where the coupon amount is set when the bond is initially established and not altered thereafter. However, an investor can also buy floating-rate bonds. Here, although both the par value and maturity date remain fixed, the periodic coupon payments are a function of current (short) rates of interest. Short rates are simply forward rates that exist for only a single period. Denote the short rate from time k to time k+1 as $r_k = f_{k,k+1}$, where k is the number of years from now. Then, $(1 + s_k)^k = (1 + r_0)(1 + r_1) \cdots (1 + r_{k-1})$ and $(1 + f_{a,b})^{b-a} = (1 + r_a)(1 + r_{a+1}) \cdots (1 + r_{b-1})$.

EXAMPLE 10.10

If the two-year spot rate is 6%, the five-year spot rate is 8%, and the annualized forward rate between times three and five is 10%, what is the short rate between times two and three?

Solution: We are given $s_2 = 0.06$, $s_5 = 0.08$ and $f_{3,5} = 0.10$, and need to find $r_2 = f_{2,3}$. The appropriate equation of value is: $(1.06)^2(1 + r_2)(1.10)^2 = (1.08)^5$, so that:

$$r_2 = \{(1.08)^5[(1.06)^2(1.10)^2]\} - 1 = 0.080741 = 8.0741\%.$$

When a floating-rate bond is issued, the first coupon amount (to be paid at the end of the first coupon period) is based on the short rate that existed at issue. The coupon amount is the par value times the beginning-of-period short rate. Then, the coupon rate is reset to whatever the short rate has become at the time when the second coupon period starts; then, the second coupon amount, paid at the end of the second coupon period would be the par value times the second short rate (which was determined at the beginning of the second coupon period). This process continues all the way through the end of the last coupon period, which is when the bond matures.

Assuming the bond can be redeemed at par, note that at any reset point, the floating-rate bond's value will be exactly par. This can be proved by a backward argument starting with valuing the bond on the last reset point (i.e., the start of the last coupon period). At this point in time, the bond's value is the sum of two discounted cash flows received at maturity (the redemption value and last coupon) discounted back one period at the current short rate. Since this same short rate is also used to determine the coupon amount, the value of these two cash flows one period earlier must be par. Continuing backward, the same relationship will hold. For example, two periods back from maturity, the bond's value is the discounted sum of its value one period back (which we just calculated to be par) plus the present value of the second-to-last coupon paid (which depends on the second-to-last short rate). Both of these cash flows are then discounted back one more period at the second-to-last short rate, which in total is par.

10.3 EXERCISES

10.1 These exercises are applications of interest rate and reinvestment risk.

a) Ten years ago, you purchased a 30-year 10,000 bond, redeemable at par, with a coupon rate of 8% convertible semi-annually. At the date of purchase, the bond was bought to yield 10% convertible semi-annually. However, just a minute ago, the nominal yield rate increased to 12% convertible semi-annually. If you were to sell the bond now, how much less would you receive compared to if you had sold the bond before the yield rate increased? What kind of risk is shown here?

b) One year ago, you purchased a one-year 1,000 bond, redeemable at par, with a coupon rate of 6% convertible semi-annually. At the date of purchase, the bond was bought to yield 6% convertible semi-annually. This bond has just expired, and you plan to use the proceeds from the redemption value to purchase a new one-year bond (now). However, interest rates have fallen so that the new bond will have a coupon rate of 4% convertible semi-annually. Assume the new bond also has a yield rate that matches its coupon rate and can be redeemed at par (1,000). By how much is the income received from the second bond reduced from the income received from the first bond? What kind of risk is shown here?

c) Five years ago, you (a mortgage loan officer at the local bank) lent 100,000 to a borrower who was buying a home. In return, the borrower would make level monthly payments for

15 years at a nominal interest rate of 6% convertible monthly. However, now (at time 5) the borrower has received a large inheritance and wishes to prepay the entire outstanding loan balance. You use the exact amount of the proceeds (i.e., the loan balance prepaid) to make a new fixed-monthly-payment 10-year loan. However, the nominal interest rate has dropped to 4.8% convertible monthly. By how much is the income received from the new loan's payment reduced from the income received from the original loan's payment? What kind of risk is shown here?

10.2 These exercises correspond to yield curves and spot rates.

a) You estimate the following spot rates on a 10-year yield curve:

$s_1 = 0.050$ $s_2 = 0.060$ $s_3 = 0.069$ $s_4 = 0.077$ $s_5 = 0.084$
$s_6 = 0.090$ $s_7 = 0.094$ $s_8 = 0.097$ $s_9 = 0.099$ $s_{10} = 0.100$

Calculate the price of a 10-year annual coupon bond that is redeemable at par = 10,000 and pays 7.5% coupons.

b) If the yield curve given in part a) were to experience a parallel shift of 1% (additive) upward, recalculate the bond's price. Do the same for a 1% (additive) parallel shift downward.

c) Calculate a level annualized yield to maturity that would produce the same prices as given in part a) and for both parts of b).

10.3 These exercises correspond to the bootstrap method and forward rates.

a) You are given the following prices of bonds with 10% annual coupons, all of which are redeemable at par = 1,000. Here, the notation P_t means that the bond's term to maturity is t years ahead.

$P_1 = 1{,}018.52$ $P_2 = 1{,}010.00$ $P_3 = 1{,}002.44$
$P_4 = 1{,}030.39$ $P_5 = 1{,}078.91$

Derive the spot rates (for $t = 1, 2, 3, 4$, and 5) implied by the given bond prices, using the bootstrap method.

b) Now that you have a sequence of spot rates $\{s_t\}$ for $t = 1, 2, 3, 4, 5$ from part a), calculate the short rates for all five years during the bond's term.

c) Also, using the spot rates $\{s_t\}$ from part a), calculate the annualized forward rate from $t = 1$ to $t = 3$. Do the same from $t = 3$ to $t = 5$.

d) Calculate the price of a five-year floating-rate bond, where the annual coupons are based on the short rate (from part b) for each year. For example, the first coupon will be the par value (still 1,000) times the short rate (from part a)) for the first year (i.e., from $t = 0$ to $t = 1$). Discount all cash flows using an annual effective interest rate of 9%.

CHAPTER 11
Asset and Liability Management

11.1 Interest Rate Sensitivity

11.1.1 Duration

As mentioned in Chapter 10, long-term bonds are generally more sensitive to changes in interest rates than short-term bonds. However, there are additional factors beyond a bond's term-to-maturity that affect interest rate sensitivity, especially when analyzing coupon-paying bonds. An alternative, more descriptive measure of the "length" of a fixed-income security is *duration*. Duration is the weighted average of the times at which all cash flows are made, where the weights reflect the present values of each cash flow.

11.1.1.1 Macaulay duration

If i is the per-period effective rate of interest, and C_t represents the amount of cash flow returned on a security at time t, then the security's duration, D, is given by: $D = \dfrac{\sum_t tC_t/(1+i)^t}{\sum_t C_t/(1+i)^t}$.

This is often called *Macaulay duration* (in honor of R. F. Macaulay who first introduced the concept in 1938), so as to be distinguishable from other types of duration that we will discuss later.

EXAMPLE 11.1

What is the duration of a security that will pay 5,000 in one year, 10,000 in two years, and 20,000 in three years, if the annual effective interest rate is 12%?

Solution: With $C_1 = 5{,}000$, $C_2 = 10{,}000$, $C_3 = 20{,}000$,

$$D = \frac{\sum_t tC_t/(1.12)^t}{\sum_t C_t/(1.12)^t} = \frac{\frac{(1)(5{,}000)}{(1.12)^1} + \frac{(2)(10{,}000)}{(1.12)^2} + \frac{(3)(20{,}000)}{(1.12)^3}}{\frac{5{,}000}{(1.12)^1} + \frac{10{,}000}{(1.12)^2} + \frac{20{,}000}{(1.12)^3}}$$

$$= \frac{4{,}464.29 + 15{,}943.88 + 42{,}706.81}{4{,}464.29 + 7{,}971.94 + 14{,}235.60} = \frac{63{,}114.98}{26{,}671.83} = 2.37.$$

Note that the denominator for D is also the present value, or fair price, of the security right now, which is 26,671.83.

The sum is taken over all times at which the security's cash flows occur, which need not be restricted to the integers (or even vary in any systematic fashion). Note that the cash flow corresponding to the price paid to purchase the security at time zero is excluded; thus, there is an implicit assumption that the security is already owned before computing duration.

Assuming all the cash flows in the duration formula are positive, then it can easily be inferred that D must be between 0 and n, where n is the time at which the last cash flow is received. For coupon-paying bonds, which typically also return the face amount at the end of the last coupon period, n is the number of coupon periods. When coupons are paid annually, n is on an annual scale. However, if coupons are paid semi-annually, as is often the case, n is the number of semi-annual periods, and i is the semi-annual rate. Note that a 10-year bond with semi-annual coupons will have $n=20$ coupon periods and might have a duration between 10 and 20. For zero-coupon bonds, the duration and term to maturity are both equal to n, since there is only one cash flow to be analyzed, and that occurs at time n.

For coupon bonds, the duration will be less than n, but still might be close to n (especially for shorter-term bonds), since the weight on the terminal cash flow is typically much higher than the weights on all the coupons, even when accounting for the time value of money. However, as the term to maturity lengthens, the time value of money becomes more powerful, that is, as $n \rightarrow \infty$, it is not true that $D \rightarrow \infty$ as well. Instead, D will converge to a finite limit that is independent of the coupon rate. In fact, the size of the coupon rate does not affect the value of D greatly, although the lower the coupon rate, the higher D will be, given a specific value of n.

EXAMPLE 11.2

Evaluate $\lim\limits_{n\rightarrow\infty} D$ to show that D converges to a finite limit as the time horizon of a security becomes infinitely large and that this limit is independent of the coupon rate r. Assume $i > 0$.

Solution: It can be shown, using the formula for D and the actuarial notation introduced in Chapter 6, that the duration for an n-year coupon-paying bond that can be redeemed at par is $D = \dfrac{r\left[\dfrac{\ddot{a}_{\overline{n|}} - nv^n}{i}\right] + nv^n}{ra_{\overline{n|}} + v^n}$. Then,

$$\lim_{n\rightarrow\infty} D = \lim_{n\rightarrow\infty} \frac{r\left[\dfrac{\ddot{a}_{\overline{n|}} - nv^n}{i}\right] + nv^n}{ra_{\overline{n|}} + v^n} = \lim_{n\rightarrow\infty} \frac{\dfrac{r}{i}\left[\left(\dfrac{1-v^n}{[i/(1+i)]}\right) - nv^n\right] + nv^n}{r\left(\dfrac{1-v^n}{i}\right) + v^n}$$

$$= \frac{\dfrac{r}{i}\left[\left(\dfrac{1-\lim\limits_{n\rightarrow\infty} v^n}{[i/(1+i)]}\right) - n\lim\limits_{n\rightarrow\infty} v^n\right] + n\lim\limits_{n\rightarrow\infty} v^n}{r\left(\dfrac{1-\lim\limits_{n\rightarrow\infty} v^n}{i}\right) + \lim\limits_{n\rightarrow\infty} v^n} = \frac{\dfrac{r}{i}\left[\left(\dfrac{1-0}{[i/(1+i)]}\right) - 0\right] + 0}{r\left(\dfrac{1-0}{i}\right) + 0}$$

$$= \frac{\left(\dfrac{1+i}{i^2}\right)}{\left(\dfrac{1}{i}\right)} = \frac{1+i}{i}.$$

The ratio $\dfrac{1+i}{i}$ is both finite and independent of the coupon rate r.

EXAMPLE 11.3

The formula for D, as introduced in Example 11.2, is a function of the coupon rate r. Take the derivative of this function, with respect to r, to show that D and r are inversely related, that is, show that this derivative must be negative. Assume that $i > 0$.

Solution: We can write D as a function of r; that is

$$D(r) = \frac{r\left[\frac{\ddot{a}_{\overline{n}|} - nv^n}{i}\right] + nv^n}{ra_{\overline{n}|} + v^n}.$$

Then, the derivative, using the ratio or quotient rule, is

$$D'(r) = \frac{(ra_{\overline{n}|} + v^n)\left[\frac{\ddot{a}_{\overline{n}|} - nv^n}{i}\right] - \left(r\left[\frac{\ddot{a}_{\overline{n}|} - nv^n}{i}\right] + nv^n\right)a_{\overline{n}|}}{(ra_{\overline{n}|} + v^n)^2}$$

$$= \frac{v^n\left[\frac{\ddot{a}_{\overline{n}|} - nv^n}{i}\right] - nv^n a_{\overline{n}|}}{(ra_{\overline{n}|} + v^n)^2}$$

$$= \frac{v^n\left(\left[\frac{\ddot{a}_{\overline{n}|} - nv^n}{i}\right] - na_{\overline{n}|}\right)}{(ra_{\overline{n}|} + v^n)^2} = \frac{v^n\left(\left[\frac{\ddot{a}_{\overline{n}|} - nv^n}{i}\right] - n\left(\frac{1 - v^n}{i}\right)\right)}{(ra_{\overline{n}|} + v^n)^2}$$

$$= \frac{v^n\left[\frac{\ddot{a}_{\overline{n}|} - n}{i}\right]}{(ra_{\overline{n}|} + v^n)^2}.$$

The denominator of the derivative is positive, since it is the square of a non-zero number. As for the numerator, both v^n and i are positive. However, $\ddot{a}_{\overline{n}|} - n < 0$ because $\ddot{a}_{\overline{n}|} < n$, due to the assumption of a positive interest rate. Thus, $D'(r) < 0$.

11.1.1.2 Modified duration

It is also true that D is inversely related to i. We can use this fact to develop the related concept of *modified duration*. First, we write the denominator of D as $P(i)$, which is the price of the security when evaluated at the per-period interest rate i. Thus, $P(i) = \sum_t C_t/(1+i)^t = \sum_t C_t(1+i)^{-t}$. Now, if we are interested in the *relative* rate of change in $P(i)$ as i changes, we can calculate the ratio $\frac{P'(i)}{P(i)}$, where $P'(i)$ is the instantaneous rate of change in $P(i)$ as i changes. Note that the effect of dividing $P'(i)$ by $P(i)$ is to control for the initial size of $P(i)$ itself. Then,

$$P'(i) = \frac{d[P(i)]}{di} = \frac{d[\sum_t C_t(1+i)^{-t}]}{di} = \sum_t -tC_t(1+i)^{-t-1}.$$

Combining this with the definition for $P(i)$,

$$\frac{P'(i)}{P(i)} = \frac{\sum_t -tC_t(1+i)^{-t-1}}{\sum_t C_t(1+i)^{-t}} = \frac{-1}{1+i}\frac{\sum_t tC_t(1+i)^{-t}}{\sum_t C_t(1+i)^{-t}} = \frac{-D}{1+i}.$$

To make this ratio positive, multiply both sides by -1 to obtain $\frac{-P'(i)}{P(i)} = \frac{D}{1+i}$, which is positive since $P'(i)$ is always negative. This revised ratio, $\frac{D}{1+i}$ is called both the *volatility* (V) and equivalently, the *modified duration* of a security, where the Macaulay duration is D. Here, V is a measure of the interest rate sensitivity of the security's future cash flows.

EXAMPLE 11.4

Return to the security in Example 11.1, where 5,000 is received in one year, 10,000 which is positive is received in two years, and 20,000 is received in three years. The annual effective rate of interest is 12%. Evaluate the derivative of the price function at $i = 12\%$, and verify that the volatility of this security is equivalent to your duration answer from Example 11.1 divided by 1.12.

Solution: Here,

$$P'(i=0.12) = \sum_t -tCF_t(1.12)^{-t-1} = -\left[\frac{(1)5{,}000}{(1.12)^2} + \frac{(2)10{,}000}{(1.12)^3} + \frac{(3)20{,}000}{(1.12)^4}\right]$$
$$= -[3{,}985.97 + 14{,}235.60 + 38{,}131.08] = -56{,}352.65.$$

Thus, the volatility is $\frac{-P'(i)}{P(i)} = \frac{-(-56{,}352.65)}{26{,}671.83} = 2.11 = \frac{2.37}{1.12} = \frac{D}{1+i}$.

Note that we can also approximate $P'(i)$ by the ratio $\frac{\Delta P}{\Delta i} = \frac{P(i+h) - P(i)}{(i+h) - i}$, where h is the amount that the interest rate is shocked ($h > 0$ if this shock is upward). Then, from before, since $-P'(i) = VP(i)$, we can write $\frac{P(i+h) - P(i)}{(i+h) - i} \cong -VP(i)$. Thus, $P(i+h) - P(i) \cong hVP(i)$ or $P(i+h) \cong P(i)(1 - hV)$.

Thus, given the security's modified duration, we can approximate the change in the security's price when the yield rate changes from i to $i + h$.

EXAMPLE 11.5

For the security used in Example 11.1 and Example 11.4 (with duration 2.37 and volatility 2.11), the current price (using $i = 12\%$) was previously shown to be 26,671.83. Based on the approximation to the derivative mentioned previously, calculate the estimated price of this security if the interest rate were 10% instead of 12%. Then, to examine how precise your estimate was, calculate the exact price at $i = 10\%$.

Solution: The approximate price is given by: $P(i+h) \cong P(i)(1-hV)$, where $i = 0.12$, $h = -0.02$, $V = 2.1128$.

Thus,

$$P(0.12 - 0.02) = P(0.10) \cong P(0.12)[1 - (-0.02)(2.1128)]$$
$$= 26{,}671.83(1 + .042256) = 27{,}798.88.$$

The exact price at $i = 10\%$ is

$$\frac{5{,}000}{(1.10)^1} + \frac{10{,}000}{(1.10)^2} + \frac{20{,}000}{(1.10)^3} = 4{,}545.45 + 8{,}264.46 + 15{,}026.30 = 27{,}836.21.$$

Thus, the approximation is low, but only by $(27{,}836.21 - 27{,}798.88) = 37.33$.

11.1.1.3 Effective duration

An alternative approximation to $P'(i)$ allows for the possibility that the interest rate might change in either direction; it could either increase to $i + h$, or it could decrease to $i - h$, where now we insist that $h > 0$. Specifically, let $P'(i) \cong \dfrac{P(i+h) - P(i-h)}{(i+h) - (i-h)}$. Note that $P'(i)$ is still negative since $P(i+h) < P(i-h)$ for fixed-income securities where prices are inversely related to interest rates. Define *effective duration* using the negative of this approximation to the derivative (so that it becomes positive). That is,

$$D_e = \frac{P(i-h) - P(i+h)}{2hP(i)}$$

Effective duration is useful when it is easy to compute the present value at the three interest rates used in the formula, but more difficult to obtain the exact derivative.

EXAMPLE 11.6

For the security used in the previous examples (with Macaulay duration 2.37 and modified duration 2.11), calculate the effective duration, assuming a 2% increase and 2% decrease in interest rates from the original 12% interest rate level.

Solution: In Example 11.1, it was shown that $P(0.12) = 26{,}671.83$ and in Example 11.5, it was shown that $P(0.10) = 27{,}798.88$. We must also find the price at $i = 14\%$, which is:

$$P(0.14) = \frac{5{,}000}{(1.14)^1} + \frac{10{,}000}{(1.14)^2} + \frac{20{,}000}{(1.14)^3} = 4{,}385.96 + 7{,}694.68 + 13{,}499.43 =$$
25,580.07.

Then, the effective duration, based on $h = 0.02$ is:

$$D_e = \frac{P(i+h) - P(i-h)}{2hP(i)} = \frac{P(0.14) - P(0.10)}{2(0.02)P(0.12)}$$
$$= \frac{27{,}798.88 - \$25{,}580.07}{2(.02)(26{,}671.83)} = \frac{2{,}218.81}{1{,}066.87} = 2.08.$$

11.1.1.4 Portfolio duration

Consider a portfolio of bonds that all have the same yield to maturity. Then, the duration of the entire portfolio can be calculated as the weighted sum of the durations of the individual bonds. Here, the individual bond durations are weighted by the individual bond prices, relative to the value of the whole portfolio.

If the portfolio has m such bonds, and the price and (Macaulay) duration of each bond (for $j = 1, 2, \ldots, m$) are given by P_j and D_j, respectively, so that the value of the entire portfolio is $P = \sum_{j=1}^{m} P_j$, then the formula for the portfolio duration (D_P) is:

$$D_P = \sum_{j=1}^{m} \frac{P_j}{P} D_j = \frac{\sum_{j=1}^{m} P_j D_j}{\sum_{j=1}^{m} P_j}.$$

EXAMPLE 11.7

You have just bought three two-year bonds, and have thus formed a bond portfolio. Bond one is a zero-coupon bond, bond two is a coupon bond that pays annual 6% coupons, and bond three is a coupon bond that pays coupons at 6% convertible semi-annually. If all three bonds can be redeemed at par = 1,000, and the annual effective interest rate is 5%, what is the duration of the entire portfolio?

Solution: First, we must find the price and duration of all three bonds. Note that the price of each bond is given in the denominator of the respective duration formula. For bond one,

$$D_1 = \frac{(2)\frac{1{,}000}{(1.05)^2}}{\frac{1{,}000}{(1.05)^2}} = \frac{2(907.03)}{907.03} = 2.00, \text{ where } P_1 = 907.03.$$

For bond two,

$$D_2 = \frac{(1)\frac{60}{(1.05)^1} + (2)\frac{1{,}060}{(1.05)^2}}{\frac{60}{(1.05)^1} + \frac{1{,}060}{(1.05)^2}} = \frac{57.14 + 1{,}922.90}{57.14 + 961.45} = \frac{1{,}980.04}{1{,}018.59} = 1.94,$$

where $P_2 = 1{,}018.59$.

For bond three,

$$D_3 = \frac{(0.5)\frac{30}{(1.05)^{0.5}} + (1)\frac{30}{(1.05)^1} + (1.5)\frac{30}{(1.05)^{1.5}} + (2)\frac{1{,}030}{(1.05)^2}}{\frac{30}{(1.05)^{0.5}} + \frac{30}{(1.05)^1} + \frac{30}{(1.05)^{1.5}} + \frac{1{,}030}{(1.05)^2}}$$

$$= \frac{14.64 + 28.57 + 41.82 + 1{,}868.48}{29.28 + 28.57 + 27.88 + 934.24} = \frac{1{,}953.51}{1{,}019.97} = 1.92,$$

where $P_3 = 1{,}019.97$. Thus, the duration of the entire portfolio is:

$$D_P = \frac{\sum_{j=1}^{m} P_j D_j}{\sum_{j=1}^{m} P_j} = \frac{(907.03)(2) + (1{,}018.59)(1.9439) + (1{,}019.97)(1.9153)}{907.03 + 1{,}018.59 + 1{,}019.97}$$

$$= \frac{5{,}747.65}{2{,}945.59} = 1.9513.$$

Of course, it is also possible that the individual bonds do not all have the same yield to maturity. However, portfolio duration can still be approximated by the weighted-sum approach given previously if a single yield to maturity is substituted for all of the varying yields. The actuary will have to justify the methodology used to estimate the portfolio's aggregate yield as a function of the yields on all the individual bonds.

11.1.2 Convexity

The duration-related price-yield approximations given previously can be improved further by incorporating a second-order term. From a graphical perspective, modified duration (V) measures the *relative* slope of the price-yield curve at a given interest rate, which leads to a first-order approximation for $P(i + h) - P(i)$ for a given interest rate shock h. In contrast, convexity is the *relative* curvature of the price-yield curve at a given interest rate, which leads to a second-order approximation for $P(i + h) - P(i)$.

The approximation is based on a Taylor series expansion. The second-order approximation for any function is

$$P(i + h) \cong P(i) + hP'(i) + h^2 P''(i)/2.$$

Define *convexity* as

$$C = \frac{P''(i)}{P(i)}.$$

Note that the term *convexity* relates to the fact that the price-yield curve is convex in shape because the second derivative is always positive. This indicates that the curve is decreasing (as interest rates increase) and does so at a decreasing rate. This shape can be visualized by thinking of a cereal bowl, but only focusing on the left half of the bowl (i.e., the downward-sloping part). Note also that, just as we calculate $P'(i) = \sum_t -tC_t(1 + i)^{-t-1}$, we can also calculate the second derivative as $P''(i) = \sum_t (-t)(-t - 1)C_t(1 + i)^{-t-2} = \sum_t (t)(t + 1)C_t(1 + i)^{-t-2}$.

Thus, the exact convexity for a security is given by $C = \dfrac{P''(i)}{P(i)} = \dfrac{\sum_t (t)(t + 1)C_t(1 + i)^{-t-2}}{\sum_t C_t(1 + i)^{-t}}$.

EXAMPLE 11.8

What is the convexity of the security for the example used throughout this chapter?

Solution: Using the formula for C, we have:

$$C = \frac{\sum_t (t)(t+1)C_t(1+i)^{-t-2}}{\sum_t C_t(1+i)^{-t}}$$

$$= \frac{\frac{(1)(2)(5{,}000)}{(1.12)^3} + \frac{(2)(3)(10{,}000)}{(1.12)^4} + \frac{(3)(4)(20{,}000)}{(1.12)^5}}{\frac{5{,}000}{(1.12)^1} + \frac{10{,}000}{(1.12)^2} + \frac{20{,}000}{(1.12)^3}}$$

$$= \frac{7{,}117.80 + 38{,}131.08 + 136{,}182.45}{4{,}464.29 + 7{,}971.94 + 14{,}235.60} = \frac{181{,}431.33}{26{,}671.83} = 6.80.$$

Putting together the second-order Taylor series approximation and the definitions for both C and V, we can construct a new and improved formula for the approximate value of $P(i+h)$ for a given interest rate shock h. Now, we have

$$\begin{aligned} P(i+h) &\cong P(i) + hP'(i) + h^2P''(i)/2 \\ &= P(i) + h[-VP(i)] + h^2CP(i)/2 \\ &= P(i)(1 - hV + h^2C/2). \end{aligned}$$

We could also develop formulas for effective convexity and portfolio convexity that correspond to those shown previously for effective duration and portfolio duration. Effective convexity is given by $C_e = \frac{P(i+h) - 2P(i) + P(i-h)}{h^2P(i)}$, which relies on a finite difference approximation to the second derivative. Portfolio convexity is given by $C_P = \sum_{j=1}^{m} \frac{P_j}{P} C_j = \frac{\sum_{j=1}^{m} P_j C_j}{\sum_{j=1}^{m} P_j}$, which is again the weighted sum of the convexities of the individual bonds.

EXAMPLE 11.9

For the security used in the examples in this chapter (with duration 2.37, volatility 2.11, and convexity 6.80), the current price (using $i = 12\%$) was previously shown to be 26,671.83, and the current price (using $i = 10\%$) was previously shown to be 27,836.21. Based on the improved, second-order approximation to the derivative mentioned previously, calculate the estimated price of this security if the interest rate was 10% instead of 12%. Then, compare the accuracy in your new approximation (relative to the exact price when the interest rate is 10%) to the accuracy you calculated in Example 11.5.

Solution: The approximate price is given by: $P(i + h) \cong P(i)(1 - hV + h^2C/2)$, where $i = 0.12$, $h = -0.02$, $V = 2.1128$, $C = 6.8024$. Thus,

$$P(0.10) = P(0.12 - 0.02) \cong P(0.12)[1 - (-0.02)(2.1128) + (-0.02)^2(6.8024/2)]$$
$$= 26{,}671.83(1 + .042256 + .001360) = 27{,}835.16.$$

Now, the approximation is only low by $(27{,}836.21 - 27{,}835.16) = 1.05$, which is significantly less than the error of 37.33 from the first-order approximation in Example 11.5.

11.2 Immunization

11.2.1 Redington Immunization

A primary goal of insurance companies is to manage the risks associated with the products they sell. For example, they need to seek protection from the risk that interest rates will change to their detriment. When forming an asset portfolio consisting of bonds, a primary objective should be to protect against both interest rate risk and reinvestment risk. For more background on these two related types of risk, see Section 10.1 on interest rates.

Life insurance companies will have recurring obligations, or liabilities, in the future that must be met by the cash flows from their asset portfolios. As a starting point, a company's investment manager might purchase zero-coupon bonds with maturities and face amounts that match the expected timing and size of future liabilities. However, these types of bonds are available only in maturities of various round numbers of months or years. Thus, not every liability due date can be matched. Furthermore, if T-bonds are utilized, the company will have lower expected yield than many other alternative investments. Of course, if riskier investments, (e.g., corporate bonds) are utilized, future cash flows are uncertain (e.g., due to defaults).

Immunization is an alternative to the exact cash flow matching technique described previously, and can protect a portfolio's value against changes in interest rates. This is also referred to as *Redington immunization* as it was introduced by F. M. Redington in 1952. Here, the goal is to construct an asset portfolio that has a reasonable chance of providing cash flows at the time they are needed to pay the liabilities, regardless of how future interest rates may move. There are three requirements needed to achieve immunization. First, the present value of the asset portfolio should be equal to the present value of the liability portfolio. Second, the modified duration of the asset portfolio should be equal to the modified duration of the liability portfolio. Third, the convexity of the asset portfolio should be *greater* than the convexity of the liability portfolio. These requirements will be discussed in more detail.

The simplest (and therefore least effective) requirement for immunization is to ensure that the asset portfolio is equivalent to the liability stream in present value. Define each cash-flow, C_t, to be $C_t = A_t - L_t$, where some cash flows are asset flows, others are liability flows, and others are the net of asset cash flows over liability cash flows (if they occur simultaneously). Then, this condition for immunization implies that the value of the net portfolio equal zero, that is, $P(i) = \sum_t C_t(1 + i)^{-t} = \sum_t (A_t - L_t)(1 + i)^{-t} = 0$, so that $\sum_t A_t(1 + i)^{-t} = \sum_t L_t(1 + i)^{-t}$.

For example, if cash is needed to pay off some liability, the investment manager can sell the appropriate amount of the asset portfolio; then, the liability will be paid off, and the asset portfolio will still have the same present value as that of the remaining obligations. Likewise, if the cash flows from the existing asset portfolio are more than sufficient to cover liabilities that are due, the surplus can be reinvested in additional bonds, which will in turn maintain the required present value equilibrium. This approach is limited because any change in interest rates or cash flows will lead to gains or losses. Because of this limitation, when assets and liabilities are equal only in present value (i.e., only the first of the three requirements is satisfied), they are not said to be immunized.

In reality, interest rates are dynamic, and changes in those rates will generally not affect the asset and liability portfolios in identical ways. The asset and liability portfolios can then easily become misaligned. Thus, as a second requirement, the process of immunization also forces the modified duration of the asset portfolio to match the modified duration of the liability portfolio.

To see this, set a goal of $P'(i) = 0$ so that small changes in the interest rate will have no effect on the net value of the assets and liabilities. Then,

$$\begin{aligned} 0 = P'(i) &= \sum_t [(-t)(A_t - L_t)(1+i)^{-t-1}] \\ &= \sum_t [(-t)A_t(1+i)^{-t-1}] - \sum_t [(-t)L_t(1+i)^{-t-1}] \\ &= -D_A P_A(i) + D_L P_L(i). \end{aligned}$$

Here D_A and D_L are the durations of the assets and liabilities, respectively. Because we have already forced the present values of assets and liabilities to be equal, forcing the derivative to be zero is equivalent to requiring that the asset and liability durations match.

The final condition for immunization is that the convexity of the asset portfolio exceed the convexity of the liability portfolio. To see why this is needed, first recall the Taylor Series expansion: $P(i+h) \cong P(i) + hP'(i) + h^2P''(i)/2$. Because the first two terms have been forced to be zero, we have $P(i+h) \cong h^2P''(i)/2$. As long as the second derivative is positive, a small change in the interest rate will cause the net position to be positive with asset values exceeding liabilities. Then, $0 < P''(i) = \sum_t [(-t)(-t-1)(A_t - L_t)(1+i)^{-t-2}] = C_A P_A(i) - C_L P_L(i)$.

Thus, the convexity of the asset portfolio must exceed the convexity of the liability portfolio.

Another way to view this is note that if these conditions ($P'(i) = 0$ and $P''(i) > 0$) are true, the function $P(i)$ will have a local minimum at the current interest rate. This implies that small changes in interest rates *in either direction* lead to increases in $P(i)$, the present value of surplus cash flows. More specifically, if the interest rate decreases, both asset and liability present values will increase, but asset values will increase by a greater amount. Also, if the interest rate increases, both asset and liability present values will decrease, but asset values will decrease by a lesser amount.

Once immunization is achieved at a given interest rate level, and then interest rates change, the asset and liability portfolios, theoretically, should still be approximately matched. However, as time passes and interest rates change further, the adjusted portfolio values may no longer be immunized at the new rate levels. As a result, the portfolio may need to be rebalanced. Rebalancing may either be done at regular intervals or when the difference in asset and liability durations exceeds a specified amount.

There are limitations with respect to basic immunization strategies. First, we have assumed that all assets earn the same yield to maturity, whereas it is more generally true that longer-term assets have higher expected yields than shorter-term assets. For more discussion on why this is the case, see the various explanations for term structure in Section 10.2. Second, we have also assumed that only parallel shifts in the yield curve are allowed, so that when yields change, they do so by the same amount across all maturity levels. In reality, this is not necessarily the case. Third, immunization requires the estimation of liability cash flows. In practice, both the timing and amount of these cash flows is subject to great variability. Finally, this technique only works for small changes in interest rates, although the next section introduces an extension that applies to larger incremental changes.

11.2.2 Full Immunization

We now explore an immunization-type method that works with changes in interest rates of any magnitude. Consider the case where a single liability of amount L_t is due at some known time in the future (time t). The concept of *full immunization* requires two assets to be held, where the first asset provides a cash inflow of A at time $t - a$ (where $a < t$), and the second asset provides a cash inflow of B at time $t + b$, where times a and b are both positive. Thus, the timing of the cash flow from the first asset precedes the liability cash flow, and the timing of the cash flow from the second asset occurs after the liability cash flow.

If any two of the four constants (A, B, a, b) are given, two equations can be solved for the remaining unknown constants. Using time t as the valuation date for both equations, and insisting that both $P(i) = 0$ and $P'(i) = 0$, as with Redington immunization, we have:

$$P(i) = A(1+i)^a - L_t + B(1+i)^{-b} = 0, \text{ or } A(1+i)^a + B(1+i)^{-b} = L_t.$$
$$P'(i) = Aa(1+i)^{a-1} - Bb(1+i)^{-b-1} = 0, \text{ or } Aa(1+i)^a - Bb(1+i)^{-b} = 0.$$

Now, if the first equation is multiplied by a and then subtracted from the second equation (or if the first equation is multiplied by b and then added to the second equation), we can eliminate one of the unknown variables, solve for the other one, and then plug back in and solve for the one we originally eliminated.

To see why this approach provides immunization over large changes in the interest rate, consider the second derivative $P''(i) = Aa(a-1)(1+i)^{a-2} + Bb(b+1)(1+i)^{-b-2}$. Substituting $Aa(1+i)^a = Bb(1+i)^{-b}$ from the second equation gives

$$\begin{aligned} P''(i) &= Bb(a-1)(1+i)^{-b-2} + Bb(b+1)(1+i)^{-b-2} \\ &= Bb(1+i)^{-b-2}(a+b) > 0. \end{aligned}$$

Because every term in the second derivative is positive, the derivative is positive not only at the current interest rate (which is all that Redington immunization ensured) but at all value of i. With the present value function being convex, and having a minimum at the current interest rate, the present value must be positive at all interest rates, not just those nearby.

EXAMPLE 11.10

A liability of 1,000,000 is due five years from now. This obligation will be met by two asset cash flows, one of amount A that occurs three years from now, and the other of amount B that occurs six years from now. If the annual effective interest rate is 10%, and a full immunization strategy is adapted, calculate A and B.

Solution: The first equation becomes $A(1.1)^2 + B(1.1)^{-1} = 1{,}000{,}000$. The second equation is $(2A)(1.1)^2 - (1B)(1.1)^{-1} = 0$. Now, If we add these two equations together, we can eliminate the unknown B. This yields $3A(1.1)^2 = 1{,}000{,}000$. Thus, $A = \dfrac{1{,}000{,}000}{3(1.1)^2} = 275{,}482.09$. Finally, we can use this value for A in one of our original equations so that we can solve for B. Using $A(1.1)^2 + B(1.1)^{-1} = 1{,}000{,}000$, we see that $B(1.1)^{-1} = 1{,}000{,}000 - A(1.1)^2$. Thus,

$$B = (1.1)[1{,}000{,}000 - 275{,}482.09(1.1)^2] = 733{,}333.33.$$

With these values, $P(i) = 275{,}482(1 + i) + 733{,}333(1 + i)^{-2} - 1{,}000{,}000$. Figure 11.1 shows that the value is positive at all interest rates.

FIGURE 11.1 Full Immunization

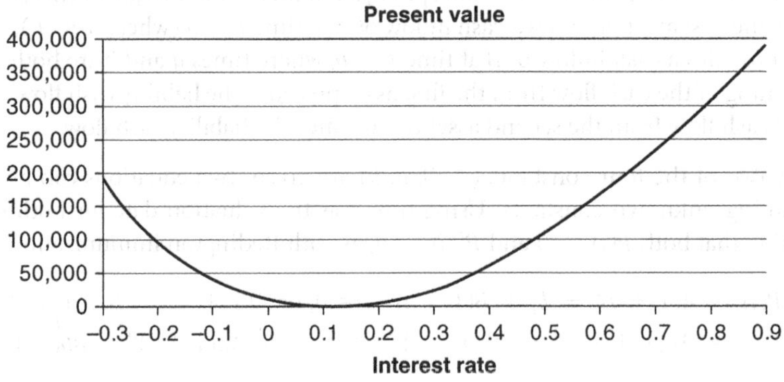

Note that there may not necessarily be a unique solution (or any solution at all) when the pair of unknowns are either a and B, or A and B (Kellison, 2009, p. 487). However, for the other four possible combinations for the two unknowns, there will always be a unique solution. Note also that full immunization can be applied to more than just one liability and two assets; however, for each liability cash flow, the manager must structure assets so that two asset cash flows will be available, one occurring before, and the other occurring after the appropriate liability cash flow. Also, as interest rates change, rebalancing may be required, just as it was for Redington immunization.

11.3 More on Asset and Liability Matching

11.3.1 Exact Matching

To match asset and liability cash flows exactly, which is sometimes called dedication or absolute matching, the investment manager begins by matching the final liability cash flow and then working backward to the present time. Once assets are constructed to match the cash flows of the longest-term liabilities, the manager proceeds to match the next-longest liability cash flows. Note that the assets used to match the longest liabilities may also produce cash flows before that time, and these intermediate-timed cash flows must be accounted for when matching shorter-term liabilities.

EXAMPLE 11.11

A company has two known liabilities, both occurring in the future. The first liability is 30,000 and is due one year from now. The second liability is 50,000 and is due two years from now. To match these liabilities exactly, there are two types of bonds available to purchase. Bond A is a one-year 7% annual coupon bond with a 6% annualized yield rate. Bond B is a two-year 9% annual coupon bond with an 8% annualized yield rate. Both bonds have par value = 1,000 and can be redeemed at par. How many units of each bond should be purchased to exactly match the two liabilities? Assume you are allowed to buy a fractional (i.e., non-integer) number of units. Also, what is the total cost of these bonds?

Solution: The first step is to match the latest liability cash flow, which is 50,000 two-years ahead. The only asset available for this purpose is Bond B (because Bond A expires one year from now). At time two, one unit of Bond B supplies a cash flow of 1,000 (redemption value) + 90 (coupon amount) = 1,090. However, we need 50,000. Thus, the correct number of units for Bond B is (50,000/1,090) = 45.872. Note that this will also partially match our liability cash flow at time 1, since 45.872 units of Bond B will supply a total coupon amount of $90 \times 45.872 = 4{,}128.44$ at time one. Our total liability cash flow is 30,000 at time one. Thus, there remains 30,000 − 4,128.44 = 25,871.56 to be matched from Bond A. At time one, one unit of Bond A supplies a cash flow of 1,000 (redemption value) + 70 (coupon amount) = 1,070. Thus, the correct number of units for Bond B is (25,871.56/1,070) = 24.179.

Finally, the total cost of our bond portfolio that is needed to match these two liabilities exactly will be based on the cost of each bond. The cost of Bond A is $\frac{70 + 1{,}000}{1.06} = \frac{1{,}070}{1.06} = 1{,}009.43$ and for Bond B it is $\frac{90}{1.08} + \frac{90 + 1{,}000}{(1.08)^2} = 1{,}017.83$.
Thus, the total cost is: 24.179(1,009.43) + 45.872(1,107.83) = 71,096.50.

Note that this amount is less than the sum of the two liabilities due (80,000) because the amount invested now will grow in time to pay off the two future liabilities exactly.

Of course, the primary problem with an exact matching strategy is that neither the asset nor the liability cash flows can be known accurately very far out into the future. Liability cash flows can be estimated, but their exact timing and amount depend on the occurrence (and severity) of uncertain events. Asset cash flows are more easily predicted but can still be variable if there are defaults (or prepayments) or changes in either interest rates or expected return levels. Furthermore, as mentioned before, even if the correct matching asset strategy was known with certainty, there is no guarantee that such a strategy can be implemented; for example, the universe of available assets is not infinite and in fact may be restrictive with respect to maturity term, cash flow income dates, and return requirements.

11.3.2 Horizon Matching

We have already discussed duration matching and immunization strategies that attempt to protect a company from changes in interest rates. Another strategy that may be employed is *horizon matching*, a hybrid between exact matching and duration matching. Here, in the first 5–10 years, assets are bought to match the liability cash flows as exactly as possible. Note that during this period, cash flows are easier to predict than when farther out on the investment horizon and thus easier to match. There are also likely to be assets available at these shorter maturities. The remaining liability cash flows (i.e., those more than 10 years out) are matched using duration matching. As time goes on, so that the later cash flows become nearer to the present, adjustments are made so that there is a shift from duration matching to more exact matching.

11.4 Asset and Liability Management Risk Measures for Life Insurance Companies

A life insurance company faces many different types of risk. Pricing/underwriting risk relates to mortality, morbidity, and lapse assumptions; investment risk relates to interest rates, equity returns, and default rates; and operational risk relates to regulatory reform and systems and administrative capabilities. In order to manage all of these risks, the actuary must be able to measure and quantify risk. Asset and liability management (ALM) is the process of managing risks that result from mismatches between assets and liabilities. For both banks and insurance companies, ALM can help achieve corporate objectives in a risk-controlled manner.

11.4.1 Types of Risk Measure Methodologies

11.4.1.1 Point estimates

There are four primary types of risk measures employed by life insurance actuaries in an ALM context: point estimates, scenario testing, stochastic modeling, and dynamic modeling. The simplest approach is a point estimate, which is a static measure calculated at a specific point in time. An example of a point estimate is the present value of a series of cash flows, the determination of which is based on a single scenario or set of assumptions. Point estimates, such as reserve levels or mortality ratios, are easy to calculate and understand but are limited in value as risk measures due to their static, one-dimensional nature.

11.4.1.2 Scenario testing

Scenario testing extends point estimation by generating a set of point estimates, one estimate for each scenario, taken across a broad range of scenarios. There may be a base case that reflects all pertinent assumptions at their best estimate levels. Then, the assumptions can be varied one at a time, keeping all the other assumptions at their base level. This special case of scenario testing is often referred to as sensitivity analysis. The goal is to examine the direction and magnitude of changes in some metric for a given assumption change. Scenario testing may also involve altering several assumptions from their base level simultaneously; for example, there may be a best-case scenario where all the assumptions are set at levels that produce favorable results and, more importantly, there will likely also be a worst-case scenario, where the assumptions are set at levels that produce unfavorable results. Because no probability weights are assigned to each scenario, this form of testing is often referred to as deterministic modeling.

The primary benefit of scenario testing is to identify risk exposures under various "what-if," or stressed, situations. This methodology can account for more possible future events than point estimation and is more tractable and efficient than stochastic modeling. Disadvantages of scenario testing are that numerous assumptions are required, the choosing of scenarios is more of an art than a science, and no indication of the likelihood of any scenario occurring is given. Furthermore, scenario testing is not adequate for the quantification of downside tail risk.

11.4.1.3 Stochastic modeling

Stochastic modeling extends scenario testing by randomly generating scenarios based on a particular probability distribution. There could be a separate distribution for every assumption, but a good model will account for the correlation structure between assumption levels, that is, a multivariate model that incorporates dependencies among assumptions should be used. The end result is the formation of an entire distribution of point estimates, one for each generated scenario, rather than just the small number of point estimates that were generated under the deterministic environment.

As with scenario testing, stochastic modeling can take into account a multitude of future events and environments. However, it outdoes scenario testing both with respect to its incorporation of probability weights for each scenario and its quantification of downside tail risk. The disadvantage of stochastic modeling is its general complexity. It requires even more assumptions than deterministic modeling and involves greater computing power and time. Also, the results obtained remain sensitive to the model's original assumptions.

11.4.1.4 Dynamic modeling

Whereas stochastic modeling stops once the scenarios are generated, dynamic modeling goes one step further by incorporating potential reactions to the outcomes of each scenario. In other words, if a specific scenario is generated, instead of just calculating a point estimate of some given metric (e.g., present value of cash flows), dynamic modeling will predict policyholder behavior within the context of that particular environment. For example, in a rising interest rate environment, policy lapses will be higher for certain interest sensitive products, and this in turn may cause the company to alter their crediting rate strategy going forward. While dynamic modeling is the most realistic simulation of what might actually happen, it is also the most complex and least tractable modeling process.

11.4.2 Brief History of ALM Risk Measures

11.4.2.1 1970s and before

In the 1950s and early 1960s, the North American economic environment was fairly stable, insurance products were simple relative to what they are today, and statutory valuation interest rates were prescribed by regulators. Thus, the only risk measures needed were point estimates used to determine reserve levels and mortality ratios. However, around the mid-1960s, inflation rates increased sharply, and a higher and more volatile interest rate environment emerged.

This increased volatility produced levels of variability previously unseen in predictive processes, which consequently precipitated the need for improved risk management analytics.

By the 1970s, increases in policy loans and surrenders led to life insurance companies developing new interest sensitive products such as adjustable-rate annuities and universal life. Subsequently, assets with both higher risk and expected return levels were bought to support the new liabilities. Technological advances also allowed for more complex methodology as relates to cash flow projection. Meanwhile, many simple ALM risk measures, such as net present value, duration, convexity, and spread (i.e., the excess of the asset portfolio yield over the liability portfolio yield), were being implemented.

11.4.2.2 1980s

Inflation and interest rate levels hit double-digits in the early 1980s, while new insurance product development was oriented almost entirely toward investment and savings vehicles. Increased competition within the life insurance industry necessitated companies to focus on achieving higher yields in their asset portfolios, which led to increased risk exposure levels. By the late 1980s, high-profile failures of various established life insurance companies highlighted the need for further improvements in ALM in particular and risk management in general.

Several variations on duration, convexity, and spread emerged during this period. For example, both key rate duration and spread duration were introduced. Key rate duration measures the sensitivity of a security's price to a yield curve shift at a specific point (key rate), while the rest of the yield curve remains constant. Spread duration measures the sensitivity of a security's price to changes in the security's spread over a risk-free rate; option adjusted spread is a similar measure, which is the spread that when added to a risk-free yield curve, will cause the present value of asset cash flows to equal its market price. Finally, and most importantly, cash flow testing, scenario testing, and stress (sensitivity) testing were all ratcheted up, with increased emphasis on demonstrating that a company's surplus position would have a high probability of being adequate over a long period of time, even in the most pessimistic economic and business environments.

11.4.2.3 1990s

More financial institutions suffered considerable losses in the early- to mid-1990s due to investment mismanagement or poor ALM practices. Meanwhile, the use of financial derivatives, which started in the 1970s, proliferated considerably. Fixed income returns were low relative to stock returns during this period, which caused life insurance companies to become more involved in equity-linked products where many of the investment risks were passed on to the policyholder. To remain competitive, many companies offered guaranteed minimum death benefits, income benefits, and maturity benefits—all of which created additional risk exposure.

To measure this risk, the use of both stochastic modeling and dynamic modeling increased. There was particular emphasis on measuring the left-hand, or downside tail, of a particular metric's distribution. Value at Risk (VaR) became popular, which estimates the maximum loss over a specified time horizon at a given confidence level. Furthermore, additional risk measures were incorporated, such as the option Greeks (delta, gamma, theta, vega, rho, and psi), which measure the price sensitivity of derivatives when one of the pricing inputs (underlying asset value, time to maturity, volatility of underlying asset returns, interest rate, and underlying asset dividend, etc.) changes.

11.4.2.4 2000s and beyond

The early years of the 21st century saw sky-high volatility levels in both equity returns and interest rates. There were also some catastrophic corporate defaults (e.g., Enron and Worldcom). The market crises of both 2000–2001 and 2008–2009, although not necessarily caused by inadequate ALM practices, were in some cases exacerbated by poor risk planning and control. Conditional tail expectation (CTE) was introduced as an improvement to VaR. CTE is the average amount of a loss, given that the loss exceeds a specific quantile. Thus, in contrast to VaR, CTE incorporates the magnitude of losses even below a specifically requested level, instead of just identifying the amount of losses at this level. Also, throughout the last 10 years, enterprise risk management (ERM) has become more common among insurance companies. Here, companies can manage their risk, both financial and non-financial, across all levels of the company, but in a highly strategic and coordinated manner.

ALM risk measures are still evolving, as companies continue to globalize, technology continues to improve, and ERM continues to advance. It is expected that in the future, increased emphasis will be placed on the following risk measures: extreme value (downside tail) risk, embedded option valuation, credit and counterparty risk, liquidity risk, and foreign currency risk.

11.5 EXERCISES

11.1 You wish to compare the cash flow structures of the following two assets, where the annual effective rate of interest used to value both assets is 6%.

Asset A is a 30-year 10,000 par value bond with 7.5% annual coupons.

Asset B is a 30-year 250,000 mortgage loan with annual end-of-year payments. The first 10 payments are 10,000, the second 10 payments are X, and the final 10 payments are 2X.

a) Calculate the price for Asset A and solve for the payment X for Asset B.

b) Calculate and compare the Macaulay durations for Assets A and B.

c) Calculate and compare the modified durations for Assets A and B.

d) If the interest rate were to change from 6% to 5% (or 7%), estimate the new price of Assets A and B as a function of volatility. Compare your estimates to the actual prices of Assets A and B at 5% (or 7%).

e) Based on your answers to part d) (the exact versions), calculate the effective durations for Assets A and B, and compare your estimates to the actual modified durations you calculated in part c).

f) Calculate the Macaulay duration for a portfolio containing both Assets A and B.

g) Calculate and compare the convexities for Assets A and B.

h) If the interest rate were to change from 6% to 5% (or 7%), estimate the new price of Assets A and B as a function of volatility and convexity. Compare your estimates to those obtained from part d).

i) Based on your answers to part d) (the exact versions), calculate the effective convexities for Assets A and B, and compare your estimates to the actual convexities you calculated in part g).

j) Calculate the convexity for a portfolio containing both Assets A and B.

11.2 Consider the following assets:

Asset A_1 is a one-year annual coupon par value bond with C = 1,000 and r = 8%.
Asset A_2 is a two-year zero-coupon bond with C = X.
Asset A_3 is a three-year annual coupon par value bond with C = 1000 and r = 10%.
Asset A_4 is a four-year zero-coupon bond with C = Y.
Asset A_5 is a five-year annual coupon par value bond with C = 1000 and r = 12%.
You are expecting to pay the following liabilities within the next few years:
$L_1 = 800$ $L_2 = 1{,}000$, $L_3 = 1{,}800$, $L_4 = 1{,}000$, and $L_5 = 800$ (where L_t is notation for a liability being paid *t* years ahead). Assume an annual effective interest rate of 10% is used throughout this problem.

a) Set up an equation (using all five assets and all five liabilities) containing X and Y that satisfies the first condition for Redington immunization (i.e., $PV_{Assets} = PV_{Liabilities}$).

b) Set up an equation containing X and Y that satisfies the 2nd condition for Redington immunization (i.e., $Duration_{Assets} = Duration_{Liabilities}$).

c) Use the two equations you have established to solve for X and Y.

d) Using your answers from part c), determine whether or not the third condition for Redington immunization will hold (i.e., $Convexity_{Assets} > Convexity_{Liabilities}$).

For parts, e), f), and g), assume there is a single liability outflow of 1,800 at time three.

e) Asset A provides a single time-two inflow of X, and asset B provides a single time-four inflow of Y. Use full immunization to solve for X and Y.

f) Asset A provides a time-two inflow of 1,000, and asset B provides a time-*t* ($t > 3$) inflow of Y. Use full immunization to solve for *t* and Y.

g) Asset A provides a time-*t* ($t < 3$) inflow of 1,000, and asset B provides a time-four inflow of Y. Use full immunization to solve for *t* and Y.

For parts h), i), and j), return to the original five assets and liabilities. Let X (for A_2) and Y (for A_4) have the same values that were obtained in part c).

h) Calculate the number of units of Assets A_2 and A_4 needed to exactly match Liabilities L_2 and L_4.

i) Calculate the number of units of Assets A_1, A_2, and A_3 needed to exactly match Liabilities L_1, L_2, and L_3.

j) Calculate the number of units of Assets A_1, A_2, A_3, A_4, and A_5 needed to exactly match Liabilities L_1, L_2, L_3, L_4, and L_5.

PART 3

Life Insurance and Annuities

Jeffrey A. Beckley

CHAPTER 12

Introduction

In this section, we will discuss individual life and annuity products. Chapter 13 provides a description of the types of life insurance and annuity products offered in the United States and Canada. This section also introduces commonly used terms in individual life insurance and annuity products.

Chapter 14 discusses some of the external forces that influence individual life insurance and annuity products.

Chapters 15 through 17 cover pricing and profit testing for individual life and annuity products. Chapter 15 introduces pricing of life and annuity products by defining profits and discusses how the definition of profits is influenced by accounting systems. Further, we define the various profit measures that may be used in development of new products. Chapter 16 discusses approaches to profit testing and pricing tools. It also provides detailed formulas and analysis of book profits and sources of profit. Chapter 17 covers the inputs into the profit testing process.

Chapter 18 discusses regulatory influences including reserves, nonforfeiture requirements, and taxes. Chapter 19 covers monitoring results, and Chapter 20 closes out the discussion of individual life and annuity products.

CHAPTER 13

Types of Coverage

Life insurance companies offer a variety of individual life insurance and annuity coverages. In this chapter, we consider common life insurance and annuity products. The agreement between the *life insurance company* and the *policy owner* is a legal contract called a *policy.* The policy specifies the rights and obligations of both the life insurance company and the policy owner.

13.1 Life Insurance

In its most basic form, life insurance pays a *death benefit* upon the death of the *insured* during the period of the life insurance coverage. Life insurance can be classified in several ways. For our purposes, life insurance will be classified as whole life insurance or term insurance. After discussing whole life and term insurance, we will discuss additional benefits that may be attached to life insurance policies using riders.

13.1.1 Whole Life

As implied by the name, whole life provides coverage that lasts until death or all of life. When the insured dies, a death benefit is paid to the *beneficiary* of the policy. Some whole life policies contain a *maturity date.* The policy will end on the maturity date even if the insured is still alive. If the policy reaches its maturity date it is said to have *matured* or endowed and a payment is made by the life insurance company on the maturity date to the policy owner. The amount paid is called an *endowment* and is typically equal to the death benefit of the policy on the maturity date. The maturity date for whole life insurance is typically at an advanced attained age such as attained age 95 or 100. Newer products may mature at age 121 as that is the end of the 2001 Commissioner's Standard Ordinary table. In the United States, the Internal Revenue Code (IRC) defines how life insurance policies are taxed. Under the IRC, a life insurance policy that endows for the full death benefit prior to attained age 95 is not considered life insurance. For this reason, policies which endow earlier than age 95 are not sold in the United States.

Prior to 1986, when the IRC was changed to reflect the definition of life insurance, endowment policies were commonly sold in the United States. For example, a 10-year endowment policy provides a death benefit for 10 years. If the insured is still alive at the end of 10 years, then an endowment equal to the death benefit is paid to the policy owner. While such endowment policies are no longer sold in the United States, they are popular in other countries. Endowment policies provide a combination of protection from death during the coverage period and a savings element with a payoff in the form of an endowment.

In return for the payment of the death benefit, the policy owner makes payments, called *premiums,* to the life insurance company while the insured is alive. The premiums for some policies are payable until the death of the insured. For other policies, the premiums are for a limited period of time such as to age 65 or for 20 years. Some products only require a single premium at issue.

13.1.1.1 Parties to a life policy

It should be noted that we have introduced four parties to the life insurance policy—the life insurance company, the policy owner, the insured, and the beneficiary. As mentioned previously, the life insurance policy is a contract between the life insurance company and the policy owner. However, the insured and the beneficiary are certainly interested parties to the agreement. The payment of benefits (death benefits or an endowment) is based on the status (dead or alive at the maturity age) of the insured. If the insured dies, the beneficiary[1] will receive the death benefit. It is important to note who pays and who receives the cash flows under a life insurance policy.

- The life insurance company pays the benefits (death or endowment) and receives the premiums based on the status of the insured.
- The policy owner pays the premiums and receives the endowment benefit if a policy matures.
- The beneficiary receives the death benefit if the insured dies. The beneficiary does not make any payments. It should be noted that the policy owner has the right to change the beneficiary[2] if desired.
- The insured does not receive or pay any cash flows.

As we discuss other cash flows related to life insurance and annuity policies, you should pay attention to which party is paying or receiving the cash flows.

It is possible for the same person to have more than one role. For example, the policy owner and the beneficiary may be the same person. Also, the policy owner and the insured may be the same person. However, it is not very common for the insured and the beneficiary to be the same person because when the insured dies, the beneficiary would also die. If the insured and the beneficiary is the same person, then the death benefits paid go into the estate of the insured and are distributed to the heirs of the estate. If the beneficiary is not the same as the insured, but predeceases the insured, then the death benefits go into the estate of the beneficiary.[3] When the beneficiary predeceases the insured, the policy owner will often exercise the previously discussed right to name a new beneficiary.

In our discussion so far, it has been inferred that there is only one insured for each life insurance policy. While this is generally true, it is not always true. Life insurance policies can cover two insureds.[4] Such policies are called *joint life policies* and the payment of the death benefit depends on both lives. A policy that pays the death benefit upon the first death of the two insureds is called *first-to-die* policy. An example of the use of a first-to-die policy is to

1 A policy can have multiple beneficiaries. For example, the beneficiaries may be the children of the insured. Alternatively, the policy owner can name multiple beneficiaries and what portion of the death benefit is to be paid to each beneficiary.

2 The policy owner can name an irrevocable beneficiary. Once an irrevocable beneficiary is named, the beneficiary cannot be changed.

3 The policy owner can name contingent beneficiaries. A contingent beneficiary will receive the death benefits if the primary beneficiary predeceases the insured. For example, the wife of the insured may be the primary beneficiary with the children of the insured being named as the contingent beneficiaries. In this case, the wife of the insured will receive the death benefits if she is alive. In that case, the children of the insured will not receive any of the death proceeds. However, if the wife predeceases the insured, then the death benefits would be paid to the children.

4 Theoretically, a life insurance policy could cover any number of insureds. While a few life insurance policies have been sold to cover more than two insureds, such policies have never sold well in the marketplace because the need for such policies is very limited.

provide coverage on a husband and wife so that when one of them dies, the other could use the death benefit to pay off a mortgage loan. A policy that pays upon the second death of the two insureds is called a *second-to-die* policy or *survivorship* policy. Second-to-die policies are typically sold so the death benefit can be used to pay estate taxes upon the death of the second insured. With second-to-die policies, there is no benefit paid upon the first death. The premiums for a second-to-die policy are typically paid until the second death. However, there are second-to-die policies where the premium stops upon the first death.

13.1.1.2 Nonforfeiture benefits

Under a life insurance policy, the life insurance company is obligated to provide the benefits guaranteed by the contract as long as the policy owner pays the premiums. If the policy owner does not pay the premium, then the contract between the policy owner and the life insurance company as originally established is terminated. At termination, under a whole life policy, the life insurance company may be required by regulation to:

- Pay the policy owner an amount in cash—this is known as the *cash value;*
- Provide a reduced death benefit without the policy owner being required to pay more premiums; or
- Provide a death benefit for the current amount of the death benefit, but the coverage will terminate earlier than it would have if the policy owner had continued to pay the premiums.

These options are known as *nonforfeiture* options. In the United States, these options are required by regulation. It should be noted that the regulations provide a minimum amount that must be provided to the policy owner. The life insurance company is permitted to provide a greater nonforfeiture benefit. Nonforfeiture benefits will be discussed in greater detail in Section 18.3.

13.1.2 Types of Whole Life

Whole life products can take several forms. Here we classify whole life products into four categories.

- Traditional life;
- Universal life;
- Variable life; and
- Equity-indexed life.

There are considerable similarities between these different categories, but also substantial differences.

13.1.2.1 Traditional life

A traditional whole life normally provides a level death benefit and requires a level premium during the premium paying period. A level death benefit means that the death benefit does not change over time. Similarly, a level premium means that the policy owner pays the same premium each time a premium is due. It does not change over time. When the death benefit is level and a level premium is payable for as long as the insured is alive, the policy is called an *ordinary life* policy.

13.1.2.1.1 Premium payment period

As mentioned earlier, the premium paying period may only be for a specified time frame. These are called *limited-pay* whole life policies. When the premiums are not payable for life, the most prevalent premium options are:

- A single premium at issue of the policy;
- Premiums payable for a period of time, typically 10 or 20 years; and
- Premiums payable to a specified age such as 65, 95, or 100.

In all cases, premiums are only paid while the insured is alive. If the policy is issued with a premium paying period to age 65 and the insured dies when she is 55, the policy owner does not have to pay additional premiums.

13.1.2.1.2 Timing of premium payments

When the premium is a single premium, that single premium is paid at the time the policy is issued (when the contract becomes effective). When a policy is issued with periodic payments, annual premiums may be paid once per year at the beginning of the policy year. A policy year begins on the day the policy was issued and goes for one year. For example, a policy issued on November 29 has policy years that start on November 29 and end on the following November 28.

Alternatively, premiums may be paid more frequently than annually. The frequency with which premiums are paid is called the *premium mode*. The most common premium modes are:

- Annually—Paid once per year at the beginning of the policy year. For our sample policy issued on November 29, each annual premium during the premium paying period is due on November 29;
- Semi-annually—Paid twice per policy year or every six months. For our sample policy, the premium is due on November 29 and May 29 of each year during the premium paying period;
- Quarterly—Paid four times per policy year or every three months. For our sample policy, the premium is due on November 29, February 28, May 29, and August 29. Note that the premium for February is due on the 28th since February 29 does not occur every year; and
- Monthly—Paid 12 times per year or each month. For our sample policy, the premiums are due on the 29th of the each month except for February when the premium is due on the 28th.

When premiums are paid more frequently than annually, the premiums charged reflect a loss of interest and the additional expense of collecting premiums more frequently. Table 13.1 provides an example of the amount of premium to be paid based on the premium mode.

TABLE 13.1 Premium Modes

Premium Mode	Modal Premium	Total Premium for a Policy Year
Annual	1,000	1,000
Semi-annual	520	1,040
Quarterly	265	1,060
Monthly	90	1,080

The policy owner has the option of electing the premium mode used to pay the premium. The policy owner can change the premium mode during the premium paying period. For example, the policy owner could start paying annual premiums and then switch to monthly premiums later. Generally, the life insurance company should be indifferent to the premium mode selected because the modal premiums should reflect the additional costs associated with each premium mode. These additional costs include interest lost because premiums are paid later and the cost of billing and processing more frequent premium payments. It usually does not include the loss of premium in the year of death because most life insurance policies provide for a refund of premium beyond the month of death. For example, if a policy owner pays an annual premium of 1,200 on January 1 and then dies in May, premium of 700 for the months of June through December would be refunded as part of the death claim.

13.1.2.1.3 Nonlevel premiums

While most policies have level premiums, this is not always the case. For some policies, the premiums increase over time. For some policies, the premiums may even decrease over time.

Graded premium whole life is probably the most common version with increasing premiums. It provides a level death benefit but the premiums start out very low and increase every year for a specified period of time. After the specified period of time, the premiums remain level for the remainder of the premium paying period. The period of time during which premiums increase may be stated as a number of years (such as 30 years) from the date of issue or it may be stated as an attained age (such as premiums increase until attained age 75). The premium pattern for graded premium whole life allows an applicant to purchase a whole life policy for a lower initial premium, but still guarantees the coverage will last for the insured's lifetime. It is also thought that the policy owner's salary will increase with time and these increased earnings will allow the policy owner to pay the increased premiums in future years. Finally, many times, graded premium whole life competes with term insurance, which is discussed later.

Another common life insurance product where the premiums are not level is a policy aimed at juveniles. This policy provides whole life insurance and is only sold with a juvenile insured, typically issue ages 0 to 17. The initial premium paid at the time the policy is issued provides coverage to attained age 25. Beginning at attained age 25, level premiums are paid each year to maintain the coverage for life. This policy is often bought by the juvenile insured's parents or grandparents with the idea that if the juvenile wants to maintain the coverage when she is 25, she can begin paying the premiums at that time. By the time the juvenile is 25, she may be able to afford the premiums. Another advantage of this product is that the insurability of the juvenile insured is guaranteed when the policy issued. Therefore, at age 25, the insured does not need to prove that she is healthy. If the insured has become uninsurable since the issue of the product, she still can maintain coverage at standard rates.

An example of a policy with a decreasing premium is a whole life policy where the premiums decrease at attained age 65. For example, the premiums may reduce by 50 percent at age 65. The reason for such a pattern is the belief that when people retire, their income will decrease and therefore, their expenses (life insurance premiums) should also decrease.

We have discussed three examples of policies with nonlevel premiums. In each case, there is a particular marketing reason for development of the product. This is generally true of all products with nonlevel premiums. Each such product is targeted at a market niche or to assist a sales approach.

13.1.2.1.4 Nonlevel death benefits

Just as there are whole life products with level death benefits and nonlevel premiums, there are whole life products with level premiums, but nonlevel death benefits. These products also often have particular marketing reasons for development.

The most common whole life product with nonlevel death benefits is a graded death benefit whole life. One version has a reduced benefit in the first two or three policy years with the ultimate death benefit being level after the two or three year grading period. For example, the death benefit in the first year is 10 percent of the ultimate death benefit while the death benefit in the second year is 40 percent of the ultimate death benefit. Beginning in the third year, the full death benefit is provided.

FIGURE 13.1 Application for a policy with full underwriting

2. Name – Last, First, Middle Initial	Relationship	Date of Birth	State of Birth	Sex	Marital Status	Social Security No.	Driver's License No.
Proposed Insured:							
Spouse/Joint/Other Insured:							
Owner if OWP:							
Dependent #1:							
Dependent #2:							
Dependent #3:							

	YES	NO
17. Has anyone in Section 2:		
a. used nicotine in any form in the past 12 months? If yes, indicate type ☐ cigarettes ☐ cigars ☐ pipe ☐ chewing ☐ snuff ☐ other_________ (nicotine replacement products)	☐	☐
b. used nicotine in any form in the past and quit? If yes, date last used? ___________	☐	☐
18. Does anyone in Section 2 now have or in the past ten years had:		
a. tuberculosis, asthma, disease or disorder of lungs or respiratory system?	☐	☐
b. high or low blood pressure or disease or disorder of heart or circulatory system?	☐	☐
c. disease or disorder of digestive system (stomach, intestines, liver, gallbladder)?	☐	☐
d. mental or nervous disorder, paralysis, convulsions, epilepsy, disease or disorder of the brain or nervous system?	☐	☐
e. gravel, stone, colic, stricture, prostate trouble, or any other disorder of the urinary or reproductive system?	☐	☐
f. rheumatism, rheumatic fever, arthritis, disease or disorder of muscles, bones, or joints?	☐	☐
g. rectal disorders, rupture, venereal diseases, cancer, diabetes, goiter, disease or disorder of the endocrine system?	☐	☐
h. impaired sight or hearing or any disease or disorder of the eyes or ears?	☐	☐
i. Acquired Immune Deficiency Syndrome (AIDS), AIDS Related Complex (ARC), or AIDS related conditions?	☐	☐
20. Has anyone in Section 2:		
a. had a chronic cough, significant weight change (other than normal growth of children), chronic fatigue, diarrhea, or enlarged glands within the past two years?	☐	☐
b. had an electrocardiogram, x-ray, blood test, or any other diagnostic tests within the past five years?	☐	☐
c. tested positive for antibodies to the AIDS (Human T-cell Lymphotropic, Type III, HTLV-III) virus within the past ten years?	☐	☐
d. consulted a medical practitioner or received hospital or sanitorium care in the past five years other than listed in Section 16?	☐	☐
e. been declined, postponed, limited, or had a policy issued other than as applied for on any life, health, or disability insurance or reinstatement thereof in the past five years?	☐	☐
f. had, been advised to have, or contemplated any surgical procedure or operation within the past ten years?	☐	☐
21. Is any female listed in Section 2 now pregnant? If yes, date due?	☐	☐

19. Give full details to questions requiring additional information. Include name of applicable person, conditions, dates, physicians, hospitals, addresses.

One of the risks for a life insurance company is that of premature death or higher than expected mortality. When a person applies to buy a life insurance policy, the life insurance company evaluates the health of the applicant using a process called underwriting. Underwriting verifies that an applicant is healthy. If an applicant is not healthy, the life insurance company will decline the application or charge a higher premium for the policy.

A graded death benefit whole life policy is normally sold with limited underwriting. For example, Figure 13.1 is a typical application for a fully underwritten life insurance policy. Figure 13.2 is a typical application for a graded death benefit whole life policy with limited underwriting. If you look at the health questions in each application, you can see that the questions in Figure 13.2 are

FIGURE 13.1 (*Continued*)

22. Is anyone in Section 2:		
a. now under the observation of a medical practitioner or receiving any kind of medical treatment?	☐	☐
b. aware of any symptoms for which you have not yet consulted a medical practitioner?	☐	☐
23. a. In the past 5 years has anyone in Section 2 been advised by a medical professional to have any tests, surgery, treatment, or further medical evaluation that have not been performed?	☐	☐
b. Does anyone in Section 2 have any medical test results pending?	☐	☐
24. Has anyone in Section 2 **ever**:		
a. been rejected, deferred, or discharged by the armed forces for a physical or mental condition?	☐	☐
b. used (other than prescribed by a physician) narcotics, LSD, cocaine, amphetamines, barbiturates, or marijuana; or been dependent upon alcohol, drugs or narcotics (whether prescribed by a physician or not); or been treated, or been advised to seek treatment or counseling for alcohol or drug usage; or been arrested for DUI or substance violation?	☐	☐
c. had a driver's license revoked or suspended or ever been arrested or convicted for other than a misdemeanor; or had in the past two years two or more moving violations or two or more vehicle accidents?	☐	☐
d. engaged in or contemplated engaging in skin diving, racing, any other hazardous sport or any type of flying as a pilot or crew member in the past five years? If yes, complete Hazardous Sports Questionnaire (form number 13-398), or Racing Questionnaire (13-399), or Aviation Supplement (12-163).	☐	☐
e. applied for or received any kind of benefits, pension, or disability for any injury, sickness or impaired condition in the past five years?	☐	☐
25. Is any application for any other life or disability income insurance now pending or contemplated with this company or any other company?	☐	☐
26. A. Does anyone in your family now have or in the past 10 years had cancer, heart, or kidney disease? If yes, give details in Section 19:	**YES** ☐	**NO** ☐

B.	Age if living	Cause of Death	Age at Death
Father			
Mother			
Siblings			

FIGURE 13.2 Application for a policy with limited underwriting

1. Last Name	First Name	Middle Initial	Date of Birth (M-D-Y)	State of Birth	☐ Male ☐ Female
Marital Status	Height	Weight	Social Security Number	U.S. Citizen: ☐ Yes ☐ No *If no:* 1. Give immigration status/type of visa: ________ 2. Please submit IRS Form W-8 Ben if proposed insured is to be the owner.	
Street Address	City	State	Zip Code	Phone Number ( )	

9. Has the proposed insured used nicotine in any form in the past 12 months?	☐ Yes	☐ No

	YES	NO
11.a. Do you currently receive kidney dialysis or require oxygen use or have you received or been told that you need an organ transplant or have you been diagnosed as having a terminal illness? (Terminal illness is defined as any illness diagnosed that would reasonably be expected to cause death within twenty-four (24) months.)	☐	☐
11.b. Do you require assistance to feed, bathe, dress or take your own medication or are you currently confined to a hospital, nursing home, mental facility, hospice, or require home health care?	☐	☐
11.c. Have you ever tested positive for the AIDS virus or been diagnosed or treated, or recommended for treatment for AIDS (Acquired Immune Deficiency Syndrome), ARC (AIDS Related Complex) or any other immune disorder?	☐	☐
11.d. In the past twelve (12) months:	YES	NO
1. Other than for temporary or minor conditions, have you been hospitalized two or more times?	☐	☐
2. Other than preventive, maintenance or risk lowering medications prescribed, have you been treated for or diagnosed with any cancer (other than Basal Cell skin cancer), heart attack, stroke, or had heart surgery (including angioplasty)?	☐	☐
3. Have you used any illegal drugs, been treated for or advised to have treatment for drug abuse?	☐	☐

much less thorough. The cost of the higher mortality associated with the less thorough underwriting is partially offset by the lower death benefits in the early years.

There are some whole life insurance policies that are issued with no underwriting. These are typically called *guaranteed issue* policies because an applicant will be issued a policy simply by applying. These policies usually provide a return of premium death benefit for the first two or three years of the policy. Sometimes, the early death benefit will be slightly larger, such as 110 percent of the premium paid. The purpose of this reduced death benefit is to discourage an applicant who is terminally ill and expecting to die in the next two or three years from applying for this policy. There is no real benefit to such an applicant since they would just get their premiums (perhaps 10 percent more) back.[5]

Table 13.2 compares the death benefits for level benefit whole life, graded death benefit whole life and guaranteed issue whole life policies.

TABLE 13.2 Policies with Nonlevel Benefits

Policy Year	Level Death Benefit	Graded Premium Whole Life	Guaranteed Issue Whole Life[6]
1	10,000	1,000	440
2	10,000	4,000	880
3	10,000	10,000	10,000

5 For these policies to be profitable, the life insurance company must rely on the agent to provide field underwriting. In other words, the agent must not sell these policies to an insured that is clearly very ill. The life insurance company will usually have mechanisms in place to discourage the issue of these products to terminally ill applicants. For example, the life insurance company will usually require the agent to repay to the company any commissions paid to the agent if the insured dies during the first two years of the policy. Also, life insurance companies will generally terminate any agent who develops a history of selling policies to terminally ill applicants.

6 Based on a death benefit of 110 percent of premium paid in the first two years and an annual premium of $400.

Another whole life insurance product with a nonlevel death benefit is a policy sold to provide insurance on juvenile insureds. The policy typically has a level death benefit until a certain attained age such as 25 at which time the death benefit will increase substantially such as five times the original amount. These policies are called *jumping juvenile* policies. The premium may remain level after the change in death benefit, but most of the time the premium also increases. So, we see a whole life policy can have both a nonlevel death benefit and a nonlevel premium.

The marketing concept for jumping juvenile policies is that once a young insured has completed college and joined the workforce, he needs more life insurance and can also afford to pay a higher premium.

13.1.2.1.5 Participating policies

Life insurance policies can be sold on a *participating* or a *nonparticipating* basis. A participating (or par) policy pays dividends while a nonparticipating (or nonpar) policy does not pay dividends. A *dividend* is intended to return the *divisible surplus* of a life insurance company to the policy owner. The concept of a par policy is that the life insurance company will return some of the profits on the policy to the policyholder. The total amount of the profits to be returned is called the divisible surplus and this amount is determined annually by the life insurance company. It is important to understand that not all profits generated are returned to the policy owner. Some profits are retained to support future growth and to provide assurance that the company can pay future benefits, even under adverse future experience. Profits may also be distributed to the company's stockholders as stock dividends, which are different from policy dividends.

Once the divisible surplus for the company is determined, then the dividends for each participating policy within the life insurance company are determined. The dividends for individual policies are determined based on the *contribution principle.* The contribution principle is that aggregate divisible surplus should be allocated to individual policies in proportion to the amount of surplus that each individual policy contributed to divisible surplus.

Dividends are typically paid annually on the policy anniversary. The policy owner may have several options as to the use of the dividends. For example, the dividend may be:

- Paid in cash to the policy owner;
- Left with the life insurance company to accumulate with interest;
- Used to reduce the premium that is due;
- Used to purchase paid-up additions. Paid-up additions are additional amounts of death benefit for the remaining period of the policy purchased by using the dividend as a single premium. In subsequent years, paid-up additions normally earn dividends on top of the dividends earned by the policy; or
- Used to purchase one-year term insurance. One-year term insurance is an additional amount of death benefit that only lasts for one year, purchased by using the dividend as a single premium.

There are other dividend options offered by some policies, but the five listed are the most common.

Some life insurance policies also pay termination (or terminal) dividends which are paid upon termination of the policy. They may be paid upon death, maturity, or surrender. Termination dividends reflect the release of surplus that is necessary to support that individual policy. Termination dividends are always paid in cash.

13.1.2.1.6 Indeterminate premium policies

Life insurance policies may also be sold with *indeterminate* premiums. When a life insurance policy has indeterminate premiums, the policy has a premium that is currently charged to the policy owner. However, the life insurance company has the right to change the premium being charged, either up or down. The life insurance policy will contain a guaranteed maximum premium, and the company cannot increase the premium above the guaranteed maximum premium.

For example, a life insurance policy may have a current premium of 500 and a guaranteed maximum premium of 700. The life insurance company has the right to change the premium up or down, but not to exceed 700. If mortality on these policies is better than anticipated, then the company could decrease the premium to 475 (or some other amount) to reflect the favorable mortality. In this case, the policy owner would start paying the lower premium. If on the other hand, if mortality was worse than expected, the life insurance company could increase the premium to 550 (or some other amount) to reflect the adverse experience. If the mortality was so bad that the premium should be increased to 800, the life insurance company could only increase it to 700 as the policy guarantees that the premium will never exceed this amount.

It should be noted that any change of premium occurs for all policyholders who own the same policy form. The premiums cannot be changed by individual insured. In other words, if the health of an insured deteriorated, her premiums could not be increased unless all the premiums for the same policy form were increased. Furthermore, the premiums for all insureds could only be changed if the aggregate mortality was worse than expected.

13.1.2.1.7 Nonguaranteed elements

Dividends and indeterminate premiums are two types of *nonguaranteed elements*. Nonguaranteed elements are cost components of a life insurance policy that can be changed in the future. There is typically a guarantee contained in the policy such that the nonguaranteed element cannot go above or below that guarantee. For example, with indeterminate premiums, as discussed, the life insurance policy will contain a maximum premium. For dividends, the minimum dividend is zero, so a life insurance company cannot decrease the dividends below zero. Other types of contract with nonguaranteed elements (e.g., universal life) will be discussed later.

The purpose of nonguaranteed elements is to allow life insurance companies to reflect current experience that they are unwilling to guarantee for the length of the policy, which can be over 100 years. For example, in the late 1970s and early 1980s, short-term interest rates exceeded 15 percent, and long-term interest rates exceeded 10 percent (an inverted yield curve). While life insurance companies wanted to reflect this high level of interest rates in their premiums,[7]

7 To some extent, life insurance companies were forced to reflect the high level of interest rates (whether they wanted to or not) in the pricing of their products to compete with other financial products such as bank certificates of deposits. Also, some life insurance companies were reflecting the high level of interest rates, which forced other life insurance companies to also reflect those high rates in order to compete.

they were unwilling to guarantee premiums (or other nonguaranteed elements) for long periods based on these interest rates. Therefore, they developed a current premium based on the current interest rate environment but set a guaranteed premium based on a lower interest rate they felt could be sustained over the life of the policy.

As another example, with the low interest rates of 2010, life insurance companies were reluctant to determine premiums based on the assumption that interest rates are going to be higher in the future. However, if interest rates do increase in the future, a company may want to decrease the premium (or adjust other nonguaranteed elements) to reflect the higher interest rates. A reduction in the premium may be necessary to prevent a policy owner from replacing the current policy with a new policy reflecting the higher interest rate in a lower premium.

The examples use interest rate as the variable affecting the premium. However, the nonguaranteed elements could also be changed to reflect actual mortality experience, persistency experience, or expense experience.

The actuary typically recommends the level of the nonguaranteed elements. There are Actuarial Standards of Practice (ASOPs) the actuary must comply with in making such recommendations. In the United States, ASOP No. 15, *Dividends for Individual Participating Life Insurance, Annuities, and Disability Insurance* covers determination of dividends for participating policies while ASOP No. 1, *Nonguaranteed Charges or Benefits for Life Insurance Policies and Annuity Contracts* covers the determination of other nonguaranteed elements. In Canada, the Actuarial Standards Board has adopted a standard: *Recommendations—Dividend Determination and Illustration.* Additionally, there are regulatory requirements in certain states in the United States.

13.1.2.1.8 Economatic life policies

An economatic life (EOL) policy is set up to use the dividends to maintain coverage, which permits the initial premium to be very low. These plans are set up with a guaranteed death benefit that is not level. For example, the death benefit is 100,000 for the first two years and then is 80,000 thereafter. Additionally, the policy is set up to pay annual dividends beginning at the end of the second year. Each year, the dividend will be used to purchase a combination of one-year term insurance and paid-up additions such that the death benefit is brought back to 100,000. Remember that paid-up additions provide a permanent death benefit while one-year term only provides a death benefit for one year. Over time, the dividend will purchase enough paid-up additions to replace the 20,000 of death benefit reduction.

EXAMPLE 13.1

Table 13.3 is an illustration of how such a policy works.[8] For the policy owner, the risk of the EOL policy is that dividends will decrease in the future and not be large enough to purchase sufficient term and paid-up additions to keep the total death

8 The calculations supporting Table 13.3 and many of the tables in this section are included in a spreadsheet available in the online material supporting this book.

benefit level. EOL policies typically provide the policy owner the right to pay additional premiums to bring the death benefit up to the original death benefit if the dividends are not sufficient to maintain the level death benefit.

TABLE 13.3 Economatic Policy Example

Policy Year	Guaranteed Death Benefit	Dividend	Paid-Up Additions	One-Year Term Insurance	Total Death Benefit
1	100,000.00	0.00	0.00	0.00	100,000.00
2	100,000.00	100.00	0.00	0.00	100,000.00
3	80,000.00	150.00	345.63	19,654.37	100,000.00
4	80,000.00	200.00	895.44	19,104.56	100,000.00
5	80,000.00	250.00	1,637.42	18,362.58	100,000.00
6	80,000.00	300.00	2,557.22	17,442.78	100,000.00
7	80,000.00	350.00	3,642.51	16,357.49	100,000.00
8	80,000.00	400.00	4,881.53	15,118.47	100,000.00
9	80,000.00	450.00	6,263.87	13,736.13	100,000.00
10	80,000.00	500.00	7,780.93	12,219.07	100,000.00
11	80,000.00	550.00	9,425.12	10,574.88	100,000.00
12	80,000.00	600.00	11,190.46	8,809.54	100,000.00
13	80,000.00	650.00	13,072.26	6,927.74	100,000.00
14	80,000.00	700.00	15,065.20	4,934.80	100,000.00
15	80,000.00	750.00	17,162.54	2,837.46	100,000.00
16	80,000.00	800.00	19,358.72	641.28	100,000.00
17	80,000.00	850.00	21,632.24	0.00	101,632.24
18	80,000.00	900.00	23,970.27	0.00	103,970.27
19	80,000.00	950.00	26,367.09	0.00	106,367.09
20	80,000.00	1,000.00	28,817.47	0.00	108,817.47

13.1.2.2 Universal life

As with a traditional life insurance policy, a *universal life* (UL) insurance policy (also known as interest-sensitive whole life) provides a death benefit in return for the payment of premiums. However, UL offers considerably more flexibility than is offered in a traditional policy. This is the advantage of UL over traditional life. The disadvantage of UL is that it does not offer the same guarantees that are offered by traditional life. We will explore these differences later in this section.

UL policies were first offered in the 1970s in response to the high interest rate environment discussed in Section 13.1.2.1.7. UL now has a market share of approximately 40 percent,[9] which is roughly twice the market share for traditional whole life. (The remaining market share is split between variable life—segregated funds in Canada—and term insurance. Both will be discussed later.)

9 Graham (2011).

When a premium is paid on a UL policy, the premium (less any related expense charges) is deposited in a fund for that policy. The fund then earns interest on the fund balance. There is an interest rate (typically 3 or 4 percent) that is guaranteed, but the company may credit a higher interest rate if they are earning a higher interest rate. The interest rate is a nonguaranteed element. Each month, an amount is deducted from the fund value. This amount is called the *monthly deduction* and reflects any expense charges and a charge for providing the death benefit. The expense charges (including those deducted when a premium is paid) may also be a nonguaranteed element. In other words, the policy may have a guaranteed maximum expense charge, but the life insurance company may choose to charge less. The charge for providing the death benefit is called the *cost of insurance* and is calculated as the *net amount at risk* multiplied by the cost of insurance rate, which depends on the insured's current age, gender and other factors. The net amount at risk is the death benefit less the fund value after the expense charges. In terms of a formula, the monthly deduction is:

$$\textit{Monthly Deduction} = \frac{\textit{Death Benefit} - (\textit{Fund Value} - \textit{Expense Charges})}{1+i} \times \textit{Cost Of Insurance Rates} + \textit{Expense Charges}$$

The following should be noted:

- The monthly deduction is deducted at the start of each month. Therefore, the present value of the cost of insurance is deducted from the fund value. The $1 + i$ is included in the formula to reflect the present value where i is the monthly interest rate. Note that i is the guaranteed interest rate even if the company is crediting a higher interest rate.
- The cost of insurance rates generally increase each policy year to reflect the increased probability of death.
- The expense charges are deducted from the fund value because the fund value is determined before there is any deduction for expenses. Additionally, while not explicitly shown, the fund value will reflect any premium paid on the date that the monthly deduction is calculated.
- The expense charge gets included in the monthly deduction. Subtracting the expense charge from the fund value to calculate the net amount at risk does not actually deduct the expense charge from the fund value. It merely makes for an accurate calculation of the net amount at risk.

EXAMPLE 13.2

Table 13.4 shows the progression of the account value for a UL policy for one policy year.

The online reference material for this book has a spreadsheet supporting these calculations as well as calculations for months 13 through 60.

TABLE 13.4 Universal Life Account Values

Policy Month	Premium	Premium Expense Charge	Net Premium	Per Policy Expense Charge	Per 1,000 Expense Charge	Death Benefit	Net Amount at Risk	Cost of Insurance Rate Per 1,000	Monthly Deduction	Fund Value after Monthly Deduction	Interest on Fund Value	Fund Value End of Month
1	1,000.00	30.00	970.00	6.00	5.00	100,000	98,717.82	0.093333	20.21	949.79	3.87	953.66
2	-	-	-	6.00	5.00	100,000	98,734.11	0.093333	20.22	933.44	3.80	937.24
3	-	-	-	6.00	5.00	100,000	98,750.47	0.093333	20.22	917.03	3.74	920.76
4	-	-	-	6.00	5.00	100,000	98,766.90	0.093333	20.22	900.54	3.67	904.21
5	-	-	-	6.00	5.00	100,000	98,783.40	0.093333	20.22	883.99	3.60	887.60
6	-	-	-	6.00	5.00	100,000	98,799.96	0.093333	20.22	867.37	3.53	870.91
7	-	-	-	6.00	5.00	100,000	98,816.59	0.093333	20.22	850.69	3.47	854.15
8	-	-	-	6.00	5.00	100,000	98,833.29	0.093333	20.22	833.93	3.40	837.32
9	-	-	-	6.00	5.00	100,000	98,850.07	0.093333	20.23	817.10	3.33	820.43
10	-	-	-	6.00	5.00	100,000	98,866.91	0.093333	20.23	800.20	3.26	803.46
11	-	-	-	6.00	5.00	100,000	98,883.82	0.093333	20.23	783.23	3.19	786.42
12	-	-	-	6.00	5.00	100,000	98,900.80	0.093333	20.23	766.19	3.12	769.31

13.1.2.2.1 Premiums

UL may have fixed premiums (fixed premium UL) or flexible premiums (flexible premium UL). When the policy has fixed premiums, the premiums are the same as for a traditional life. That is, they must be paid, can be level or nonlevel, may be for life or for a limited pay period, may be guaranteed or indeterminate, and can be paid annually or more frequently. There may be some flexibility once certain conditions have been met. For example, if the fund value exceeds a certain level, then the premium may be skipped.

A flexible premium UL has considerable flexibility as to the timing and amount of premiums. The primary requirement is that sufficient premium be paid to maintain a positive fund value. Therefore, at any point in time, the premiums paid plus the interest earned in the fund must be greater than the premium related expense charges and the monthly deductions. While there is considerable flexibility, many flexible premium UL policies are sold on the basis of an assumed level premium payment made consistently through the lifetime of the policy.

Some flexible premium UL policies do have some premium payment requirements. For example, some policies may require a premium to be paid for the first few years such as the first five years. Additionally, some flexible premium UL policies have a *secondary guarantee* that is based on paying premiums on a consistent basis. Secondary guarantees are discussed in Section 13.1.2.2.3.

13.1.2.2.2 Death benefits

For UL insurance policies, the death benefit is a function of the *specified amount* and the *death benefit option*. The policy owner selects both the specified amount and the death benefit option when the policy is purchased. The death benefit options are:

- Level death benefit (also known as Option 1). With this death benefit option, the death benefit is equal to the specified amount. Therefore, the death benefit is level[10]; and
- Increasing death benefit (also known as Option 2). With this death benefit option, the death benefit is the specified amount plus the fund value. Therefore, as the fund value goes up, so does the death benefit, which is why the name is *increasing death benefit*. It should be noted that if the fund value decreases then the death benefit will also decrease. The fund value will decrease when the expense and cost of insurance charges exceed the sum of the premiums being paid and the interest being earned on the fund.

These two death benefit options are available on almost any UL policy. Additional death benefit options are offered by some UL policies. For example, some policies offer a death benefit equal to the specified amount plus the sum of the premiums paid. This is often referred to as a return of premium death benefit option.

UL policies will generally allow the policy owner to switch death benefit options after the policy has been issued. There may be an adjustment to the specified amount or other

10 In reality, the death benefit may increase even if this option is selected as the Internal Revenue Code in the United States requires that a life insurance policy maintain a certain net amount at risk, if the policy owner wishes to avoid some adverse tax consequences. Therefore, if the fund value for a policy gets sufficiently close to the death benefit, the death benefit will be increased to maintain the required net amount at risk.

requirements to make sure that the policy owner does not use this option to the disadvantage of the insurance company. For example, a policy is issued with a level death benefit option, a specified amount of 100,000 and has a current fund value of 40,000. Now the policy owner wants to change to an increasing death benefit. At that point, the specified amount would be decreased to 60,000. This means that the death benefit immediately after the change will be the same as the death benefit immediately before the change. It also means that there has been no increase in the net amount at risk. Therefore, if the insured is in bad health, the insurance company is indifferent to the change because they would have to pay the same death benefit immediately before or after the change. While it is true that the death benefit after the change has occurred will be different than it would have been if the change had never occurred, the net amount at risk will not be increasing so the insurance company is indifferent to the change.

Additional death benefit flexibility is available under most UL policies as these policies generally allow the policy owner to increase or decrease the specified amount while the policy is in force. Any increase in the specified amount will result in an increased net amount at risk so such an increase is subject to additional underwriting at the time of increase. Generally, a decrease is not subject to any other conditions except maintaining a minimum specified amount. Death benefit flexibility is generally limited on traditional whole life policies although some flexibility is available through riders, which will be discussed later.

13.1.2.2.3 Secondary guarantees

As discussed in the UL introductory paragraph, the disadvantage of UL when compared to traditional life policies is the lack of guarantees. In order to address this disadvantage, life insurance companies have introduced *secondary guarantees*. A secondary guarantee provides a guarantee to the policy owner that the policy will not terminate prior to the death of the insured (even if the fund value goes to zero) if the policy owner meets certain requirements. The requirements can be premium-based or based on a *shadow account*.

Premium-based requirements are easy to understand. Provided the policy owner pays a certain premium, the policy is guaranteed not to terminate. The premium that the policy owner must pay under the secondary guarantee is lower than the premium that would be necessary if the premium were calculated using the guaranteed interest rates, expense charges, and mortality charges of the universal life policy.

For example, if we calculated the level premium that must be paid for a UL policy based on the guaranteed interest rate of 4 percent and the guaranteed expense and mortality charges, we might get a premium of 2,700. However, the secondary guarantee may state that the policy will stay in force if the cumulative premium paid exceeds a benchmark stated in the policy. For our example, the cumulative premium paid must always be greater than 2,000 times the number of completed policy years. Therefore, by the end of the first policy year, the policy owner would have had to pay at least 2,000. By the end of the second policy year, the policy owner would have had to pay at least 4,000, etc. This benchmark premium will usually be based on assumptions that are reasonable at the time that the policy was issued. For our example, the 2,000 was based on an interest rate of 5 percent. If the policy owner pays a premium of 2,000 and the interest rate being credited reduces to 4 percent (or any rate below

5 percent), then the fund value of the policy could go to zero. If there was not a secondary guarantee, the policy would lapse if the fund value goes to zero. However, with the secondary guarantee, as long as the policy owner continues to pay 2,000 each year, the universal life policy will still be in force even though there is no fund value.

Shadow-account based requirements are not as simple as premium-based requirements, but they have the same function, which is to permit the policy owner to pay a level premium over the life of the UL contract and guarantee that the policy will continue. Just as with the premium-based example in the previous paragraph, the level premium using the shadow account is lower than would be available based on the guaranteed interest rate and expense and mortality charges that apply to the primary fund value in the UL policy. When the secondary guarantee is shadow-account based, the UL policy effectively has a second fund value that is calculated with a different interest rate, expense charges, and mortality charges than the primary fund value. This shadow account is only used to determine whether the policy stays in force. The shadow account is not available to the policy owner for other purposes such as policy loans, partial withdrawals, and to determine the cash value.

It should be noted that under either type of secondary guarantee, if the policy owner does not pay sufficient premium to maintain the secondary guarantee, it does not necessarily mean that the policy will terminate at that time. It just means that the secondary guarantee terminates, and the UL policy will function just as any UL without a secondary guarantee. For our premium based example, the policy owner was required to pay a premium of 2,000 per year to maintain the secondary guarantee—the guarantee that the policy would not lapse even if the account value reduced to zero. Let's assume that the policy owner has been paying a premium of 2,000 each year for 10 years. During that time, interest rates have been at 6 percent, which is above the guaranteed interest rate of 4 percent. The 6 percent interest rate has also been above the 5 percent interest rate that was used to calculate the benchmark premium of 2,000. Because of the higher interest rate, the fund value has been growing substantially, and the policy owner decides to reduce the premium being paid from 2,000 to 1,600. When the policyholder reduces the premium in the 11th policy year to 1,600, the secondary guarantee will terminate because the total premiums paid ($2{,}000 \times 10 + 1{,}600 = 21{,}600$) will be less than the benchmark premium times the number of years that the policy has been in force ($2{,}000 \times 11 = 22{,}000$). However, even though the secondary guarantee terminates at this time, the policy does not terminate because the fund value is still positive. Further, the policy will remain in force in the future as long as the fund value remains positive.

13.1.2.2.4 Participating UL policies

The vast majority of UL policies are nonparticipating. Most of the participating UL policies have never paid a dividend as the other nonguaranteed elements within the policy are adjusted, so there is no divisible surplus generated by these policies. When a dividend is paid, it is added to the fund value or paid in cash.

13.1.2.2.5 Nonguaranteed elements

For traditional life, we discussed dividends and indeterminate premiums as the two types of nonguaranteed elements. UL policies may contain additional nonguaranteed elements. For a flexible premium UL, possible nonguaranteed elements include the following.

The interest rate paid on the fund value

The UL policy contains a guaranteed interest rate, which is typically in the range of 3 to 4 percent. Policies issued in the late 1970s and during the 1980s, when interest rates were higher, may have had guaranteed interest rates as high as 6 percent. At the company's option, a higher interest rate than the one guaranteed may be paid. The actual or current credited interest rate will generally be based on the interest rate earned on the investments that the insurance company has backing the UL fund values. The current credited rate is usually calculated as the earned rate less an interest rate *spread*. The spread is determined when the actuary prices the product.

For example, for a UL policy, suppose the spread is 150 basis points[11] (1.50 percent), and the guaranteed rate is 4 percent. If the company is earning 6 percent on its investments, it will credit a rate of 4.5 percent. If the company is earning a rate of 5 percent, it will have to credit a rate of 4 percent since this is the guaranteed interest rate. Therefore, the company will not be able to earn the spread determined in pricing.[12] This means that the insurance company will earn less profit than desired or may even suffer a loss.

The purpose of the interest rate spread, which is determined by the company and is not contractually specified, is to generate profit for the company or to help offset expenses if the expense charges are not sufficient to cover the actual expenses.

The assets supporting the fund values for universal life are invested in the *general account* of the life insurance company. The general account of the life insurance company is the invested and other assets of a life insurance company that are available to pay claims and benefits. The assets in the general account are usually fixed income securities such as bonds and mortgages. The assets in the general account are determined by the life insurance company. The policy owners do not have a direct interest in the assets of the general account.

Assets supporting traditional life policies are also invested in the general account and in similar assets to those supporting the UL policies.

Cost of insurance charges

The policy will contain guaranteed cost of insurance charges. The actual cost of insurance charges are generally less than the guaranteed charges. The guaranteed cost of insurance charges are usually equal to the prevailing Commissioner's Standard Ordinary (CSO) mortality table at the time the policy was issued. For example, for policies issued in 1985, the guaranteed cost of insurance rates were based on the 1980 CSO Table. The guaranteed and current cost of insurance rates will usually vary by gender (male versus female) and by premium class (usually smoker versus nonsmoker). The life insurance company has the right to set lower current cost of insurance rates prior to the policy being issued. However, once the policy has been issued with lower rates, there are regulatory (and possibly contractual) impediments to changing the current cost of insurance rates on policies that are in force. Generally, to change the

11 A basis point is 0.01 percent so 150 basis points is 1.5 percent. Basis points is usually abbreviated as bp so the spread would be expressed as 150 bp.

12 When the company is not able to pay a credited interest rate equal to the earned interest rate less the spread due to the guaranteed interest rate, this is known as interest rate compression. Interest rate compression occurs during long periods of low interest rates such as the period from 2005 to 2011. This is also known as *spread compression*.

current cost of insurance rates on in force policies, the company must demonstrate that actual mortality is different from the mortality expected at the time that the product was priced.

Expense charges

Expense charges for a UL policy may take several forms. The expense charge may be a percent of premium, a dollar amount per month, an amount per 1,000 of specified amount or per net amount at risk, or may even be expressed as a percent of the cost of insurance rate or of the fund value. The policy will always have a guaranteed maximum expense charge for each form of expense charge. The company may charge the guaranteed expense charges, in which case the expense charge is not a nonguaranteed element. However, for many UL policies, the company will charge an expense charge that is lower than the guaranteed expense charge.

The expense charges may, but do not have to, cover the expenses incurred by the company. Most of the time, the expense charges will not cover all the expenses incurred, particularly commission expenses. The expense incurred over and above the expense charges will be covered by interest rate spread or margins in the actual mortality charges.

Policyholder dividends

As mentioned, UL policies may be participating.

The nonguaranteed elements for flexible premium UL are also present in fixed premium UL. In addition, fixed premium UL may have two other nonguaranteed elements.

Indeterminate premiums

Fixed premium UL may have indeterminate premiums just as traditional life insurance policies.

Death benefits

With some fixed premium UL policies, the death benefit may be a nonguaranteed element. In such cases, there is a current death benefit, which is projected to be level, but the life insurance company has the right to reduce the death benefit in the future. The policy will have a minimum guaranteed death benefit below which the current death benefit may not be reduced.

For example, a policy may be issued with a death benefit of 50,000 with the expectation that if nothing changes, the death benefit will remain at 50,000 until the policy ends. However, the policy may only guarantee that the death benefit will be at least 50,000 for the first 10 years and at least 40,000 thereafter. The policy will usually provide the policy owner the option of paying additional premium to maintain the death benefit at 50,000 if the company decided to decrease the amount in the future.

A fixed premium UL with a nonguaranteed death benefit functions very similar to the economatic whole life policy previously discussed. Instead of dividends being used to "buy" the nonguaranteed death benefit each year, the interest earnings in excess of the guaranteed interest rate and the gains on mortality charges are used to "buy" the additional death benefit to keep the death benefit level. Also, just as with the economatic plan, if experience is worse than anticipated and the death benefit would need to be reduced, the policy owner has the right to pay additional premiums to keep the death benefit level. These types of changes cannot be made at the whim of the company or to increase profits. The contract will generally specify under what circumstances the changes can be made. Further, regulations in certain jurisdictions also require justification for such changes.

13.1.2.2.6 Surrender values

UL policies provide nonforfeiture benefits. For most UL policies, the only nonforfeiture benefit provided is a cash surrender value. The cash surrender value is generally determined as the fund value less a surrender charge, if any. Typically, there is a surrender charge during the first ten to twenty years that the policy is in force. Thereafter, the surrender charge is zero, meaning that the cash surrender value is equal to the fund value.

As was noted in Section 13.1.1.2, insurance regulations provide a minimum amount that must be provided to the policy owner. For UL policies, the regulations establish a maximum surrender charge. Surrender charges can be less than the maximum. Nonforfeiture benefits will be discussed in greater detail in Section 18.3.

13.1.2.3 Variable life

A *variable life* insurance policy can take a form similar to traditional life or a form similar to universal life in which case it is generally referred to as *variable universal life* (VUL). The primary difference between traditional life and UL and their variable life versions is that the policy owner determines how funds supporting the contract are invested and assumes the investment risk as a result. In Canada, these products may be referred to as *segregated fund products.*

For variable life in a traditional policy form, funds supporting the cash value of the policy are invested in one or more *separate accounts.* This is contrasted with the assets supporting the traditional life and universal life liabilities where the funds are invested in the general account of the insurer as described in Section 13.1.2.2.5. These separate accounts may be mutual funds or similar vehicles that have specific investment objectives. The policy owner determines how the cash value is invested by selecting the funds to invest in and what percentage of the cash value goes into each fund. Once again, this is different from the general account where the insurer determines how the funds are invested. Another major difference between the funds in the general account and the funds in the separate account is that the funds in the separate account can only be used to support the liabilities of the associated variable life policies. If the life insurance company becomes insolvent, the assets in the separate account are not available to other policies supported by the general account.

The death benefit and cash value are determined daily based on the returns in the separate accounts. The policy generally includes an *assumed interest rate* (AIR). If the returns exceed the AIR, then the cash value and the death benefit will increase. If the returns are less than the AIR, the cash value and the death benefit will decrease.

For VUL, the fund value is invested in separate accounts at the direction of the policy owner. With VUL, the specified amount does not change based on the investment returns. Therefore, the death benefit does not change unless the death benefit option is option 2. However, the fund value does reflect actual returns from the separate accounts.

In many cases, the life insurance company will offer the owner of a variable life policy the option of investing in the general account of the insurance company. By investing in the general account, the policy will act very similar to a nonvariable policy. The fixed account guarantees a minimum interest rate and credits an interest rate based on the return of the assets in the insurance company, if higher.

EXAMPLE 13.3

Table 13.5 shows the progression of the account value for a UL policy for one policy year.

TABLE 13.5 Variable Life Fund Progression

Policy Month	Premium	Premium Expense Charge	Net Premium	Per Policy Expense Charge	Per 1,000 Expense Charge	Death Benefit	Net Amount at Risk	Cost of Insurance Rate Per 1000	Monthly Deduction	Fund Value After Monthly Deduction	Investment Return on Fund Value	Fund Value End of Month
1	1,000.00	30.00	970.00	6.00	5.00	100,000	98,717.82	0.093333	20.21	949.79	23.59	973.37
2	-	-	-	6.00	5.00	100,000	98,714.46	0.093333	20.21	953.16	(0.36)	952.80
3	-	-	-	6.00	5.00	100,000	98,734.97	0.093333	20.22	932.58	9.62	942.20
4	-	-	-	6.00	5.00	100,000	98,745.53	0.093333	20.22	921.99	10.56	932.55
5	-	-	-	6.00	5.00	100,000	98,755.15	0.093333	20.22	912.34	(29.29)	883.05
6	-	-	-	6.00	5.00	100,000	98,804.49	0.093333	20.22	862.82	(0.64)	862.18
7	-	-	-	6.00	5.00	100,000	98,825.29	0.093333	20.22	841.96	3.61	845.57
8	-	-	-	6.00	5.00	100,000	98,841.85	0.093333	20.23	825.34	17.01	842.35
9	-	-	-	6.00	5.00	100,000	98,845.05	0.093333	20.23	822.13	19.67	841.80
10	-	-	-	6.00	5.00	100,000	98,845.61	0.093333	20.23	821.57	25.40	846.97
11	-	-	-	6.00	5.00	100,000	98,840.45	0.093333	20.23	826.75	13.04	839.79
12	-	-	-	6.00	5.00	100,000	98,847.61	0.093333	20.23	819.56	9.74	829.30

The online reference material for this book has a spreadsheet supporting these calculations as well as calculations for months 13 through 60.

When the funds are invested in a separate account, the policy owner has assumed the investment risk. The life insurance company does not guarantee a return[13] on the separate account and returns can be negative. The assumption of the investment risk by the policy owner has certain implications.

- In the United States, the product is considered both life insurance and a security. Therefore, it must satisfy the requirements of both the state insurance departments who regulate life insurance and of the Securities Exchange Commission (SEC) who regulate securities. In Canada, the Canadian Security Administrators (CSA) has ceded authority to the insurance regulators in Canada. The regulation of the insurance products is generally governed by the provincial insurance regulators while the regulation of solvency is generally regulated by Office of the Superintendent of Financial Institutions (OSFI).
- Since it is considered a security in the United States, it must be sold by registered representatives who have a security license. Additionally, the policy owner must receive a prospectus, which provides detailed disclosure regarding the policy. In Canada, segregated fund products are not considered to be a security so the agent does not need a security license.
- Since the policy owner is assuming considerably more risk, the policy owner should also have a higher expected return. With nonvariable life products, the insurance company (which has the investment risk) generally invests in fixed income vehicles (bonds and mortgages) to support the contracts. The separate accounts that support variable products are typically invested in equities (stocks). Historically, over the long term, equities have outperformed fixed income investments.

With nonvariable life insurance, one of the sources of profit for the insurance company is the difference between what they earn on the invested assets and the interest rate that they pay on the policy. With the UL contract, this difference is specifically identified as the spread. For traditional life, the "spread" is not as clearly identified to the policy owner but is still an expected source of profit. For variable life insurance products, the policy owner gets the investment returns from the separate account, but the policy owner does not get the entire return as there is a fee deducted and paid to the life insurance company. This fee is specifically identified as a Mortality and Expense (M&E) charge. For example, if the M&E charge is 0.60 percent (60 basis points or 60 bp), Table 13.6 indicates the gross return in the separate account and net return to the policy:

TABLE 13.6 Variable Life Investment Credit

Separate Account Gross Return	M&E Charge	Net Return to Policy
8.00%	0.60%	7.40%
0.00%	0.60%	−0.60%
−8.00%	0.60%	−8.60%

For variable life insurance, the insurance company will make its "spread" regardless of performance, unlike the nonvariable life insurance product.

In all other aspects, the variable life product functions the same as its nonvariable counterpart.

13 The life insurance company may provide a minimum guarantee through a rider (which requires additional premium). These guarantees will be discussed later.

13.1.2.4 Indexed life

Indexed life (also known as *equity-indexed life*) is a cross between variable and nonvariable life. Indexed life is generally sold as a UL policy form but can take the form of traditional life. If indexed life is a UL, the interest rate credited to the fund value is based on an external index such as the Standard and Poor's 500 (S&P 500). If the external index increases during a policy year, the interest credited will increase. Generally, the amount of interest credited to the fund value only reflects a portion of the return on the index. Mechanisms used to limit the upside return include:

- A participation rate. The policy owner only receives a portion of the return on the index. For example, the participation rate might be 70 percent. Therefore, if the S&P 500 Index increased by 10 percent, the life insurance company would credit the policy with 7 percent;
- A cap. The return to the policy owner will not exceed a certain amount (the cap) no matter what the return. For example, if the cap was 10 percent and the S&P 500 Index increased by 15 percent, the life insurance company would credit 10 percent to the policy; and
- A spread. The policy owner receives the return of the index less a spread. For example, if the spread was 5 percent and the S&P 500 Index returned 12 percent, the life insurance company would credit 7 percent to the policy.

It is common for indexed life policies to include a combination of the above mechanisms in determining the interest rate credited to the fund value. One method is not necessarily more favorable to the policy owner than another as results will vary depending on what happens to the index.

If the index stays flat or decreases during the policy year, the life insurance company provides a minimal guarantee. The minimal guarantee may be that the return credited to the fund value will never be negative or it may guarantee a small positive return each year such as 2 percent. Because of this guarantee, indexed life has not been considered a security.[14] Therefore, it does not need to be sold by registered representatives nor is a prospectus required.

When indexed life takes the form of traditional life, typically the product is participating and the dividends paid are a function of an external index.

For indexed life, the life insurance company may provide more than one external index that can be used as a basis for the interest rate. The policy owner may be able to choose which index(es) will be used and what percent of the fund value is allocated to each index. This is similar to the multiple separate accounts with variable life. As with variable life, the life insurance company may also offer the policy owner the option of investing in the general account of the insurance company.

Indexed life tends to appeal to the policy owner who is willing to accept more investment risk relative to UL, but wants downside protection that is not present in a variable product. The life insurance company protects itself by using a combination of fixed income investments and options on the indexes to assure a profit over and above the index based return.

In all other aspects, the indexed life product functions the same as its nonvariable counterpart.

---

14 There have been recent actions by the SEC to treat equity-indexed products as securities. However, those SEC proposals have been overturned by the U.S. judicial system.

13.1.3 Term Insurance

Term insurance provides coverage that lasts for a specified term. If the insured dies during the specified term, a death benefit is paid to the beneficiary of the policy. If the insured lives to the end of the specified term, then life insurance coverage ends with no benefit being paid. The term of coverage may be for a specified period such as 10 years or may be to a specified age such as age 95. Term insurance is intended to cover life insurance needs that are temporary, permitting the purchaser to match his needs with the coverage.

Term insurance may be sold as a stand-alone policy or it may be attached to another life insurance policy as a rider. We will discuss riders in greater detail later.

As with whole life, the policy owner pays premiums to the life insurance company while the insured is alive. The premiums for some policies are payable until the death of the insured. For term insurance, the premiums are often level for the term period. However, this is not always the case. Some policies only require premiums for a period that is shorter than the term of life insurance. For example, some term coverage is purchased by paying a single premium at issue of the term policy. Another common premium pattern is for premiums to increase annually to reflect the annual increase in the probability of death. Finally, a common variation on the premium pattern is level premiums for some period (e.g., 20 years) followed by annually increasing premiums for the remainder of the term.

Term life can take many forms. It may provide a level death benefit for a period of time such as 20-year level term or term to age 95. Alternatively, it may provide a decreasing death benefit for a period of time such as 30-year decreasing term. The death benefit for decreasing term may decrease uniformly over the life of the policy or the death benefit may follow the unpaid balance on a loan such as a mortgage loan.

13.1.3.1 Parties to a term life policy

The parties to a term life insurance policy are the same as the parties to a whole life policy—the life insurance company, the policy owner, the insured, and the beneficiary. As discussed under whole life, term policies can be sold with two insureds as either a first-to-die or second-to-die policy.

13.1.3.2 Nonforfeiture benefits

Generally, term insurance does not offer nonforfeiture benefits. However, some term insurance policies do have nonforfeiture benefits. For example, nonforfeiture benefits may be required if the term insurance covers a long period of time or goes to an older age. Nonforfeiture benefits are discussed in more detail in Section 18.3.

13.1.3.3 Conversion privilege

Most term insurance contains a conversion privilege. The conversion privilege gives the policy owner a right (option) to convert to a whole life policy without evidence of insurance. The option can be valuable to the policy owner if the health of the insured deteriorates during the term policy and the policy owner would not be able to purchase life insurance on the insured after the term insurance ends. The conversion option allows the policy owner to trade in the term insurance policy for a whole life policy. Obviously, the premium for the whole life will be higher, but the coverage would not terminate.

The conversion privilege is typically limited such as being available for the first 10 years of the term insurance or prior to attained age 60. This is to prevent too much anti-selection against the life insurance company. There is a cost associated with the conversion privilege since the mortality experience on a conversion policy will be substantially worse than the mortality experience for a fully underwritten policy. This cost is included in the premiums of the term insurance.

Finally, it should be noted that a conversion privilege is not required and some term policies do not include a conversion option.

13.1.4 Types of Term Insurance

Term insurance products can take several forms. We classify term insurance products into seven categories.

- Level term for a period with an annual renewable term tail;
- Level renewable term;
- Annual renewable term;
- Term to 100;
- Decreasing term;
- Deposit term; and
- Family coverage.

There are considerable similarities between these different categories, but also substantial differences.

13.1.4.1 Level term for a period with an annual renewable term tail

The most popular term product in the United States today is one that provides a level death benefit to an extended attained age, most commonly attained age 95. The premiums for the coverage are level for a period of time and then increase annually thereafter until the end of the term period. The period during which the premiums are level is may be 10, 15, 20, 25, or 30 years. The most common periods are 10 or 20 years.

Premiums may be paid annually or modally as was the case with whole life. The premiums are required to keep the policy in force. There is no flexibility with regard to the premiums as there is with UL policies.

Generally, these term policies are sold with the expectation that at the end of the level premium period, the policy owner will stop paying premiums and the policy will terminate without value.[15] The premium increase at the end of the level term period is substantial. It may increase by a factor of ten or more. When the premium increases that much, most policy owners will stop paying premiums. For some policy owners, they may no longer need insurance on the insured. For many policy owners, they will be able to purchase new insurance on the insured at a cheaper price, provided the insured is healthy enough to qualify for new

15 The termination of a policy without value due to the policyholder ceasing premium payments is referred to as a *lapse*. The termination of a policy with a surrender value due to the policyholder ceasing premium payments is referred to as a *surrender*.

insurance. For some policy owners who would like to retain the coverage on the insured, the increased premiums will be so much higher that they will decide not to pay the premium even if the insured is not healthy enough to qualify for a new policy. Thus, the only policies that will remain in force are policies on unhealthy insureds who could not qualify for new insurance, but can afford the premium and believe that it is to their financial advantage to keep the policy.

EXAMPLE 13.4

For example, a $1-million-term insurance policy with level premiums for 30 years was issued to a person age 30. The annual premium for the first 30 years is 1,400. The annual premium for the 31st year is 15,000 and for the 32nd year is 17,500. At the end of 30 years, the insured is 60 and has been told that he has terminal cancer with a life expectancy of less than 2 years. What will the policy owner do at this point? Clearly, the insured is not healthy enough to qualify for a new policy. However, if the medical prognosis is correct, the life insurance company will have to pay a $1-million death benefit in the next 2 years if the policy owner pays the premiums due prior to the insured's death. Assuming the insured dies in the next 2 years, the only rational decision for the policy owner is to pay the premiums (up to 32,500) until the insured dies.

The next logical question is why would an insurance company put themselves into a position where a policy owner has the option of keeping the coverage if they are unhealthy and terminating coverage if they are healthy? Reasons include:

- The product structure (level premiums followed by escalating annual premiums) allows these term policies to avoid nonforfeiture options under the Standard Nonforfeiture Law, which is the law prescribing minimum nonforfeiture values in the United States.
- Prior to 2000, this product structure resulted in reserves being minimized. With minimal reserves and no nonforfeiture values, the premiums for such term insurance were very low. This product design became popular with both the agents selling insurance and the public buying insurance. As such, there was a strong market demand of term insurance with this structure. In 2000, the law in the United States changed to require larger reserves. However, because of the market design, life insurance companies have continued to sell term with this structure despite the higher reserve requirements.
- Finally, not all policy owner behavior is rational. Some policies will remain on healthy insureds as the policy owners will continue to pay the much higher premiums. Life insurance companies believe that in total, the premiums collected will exceed the life insurance benefits paid.

In 2010, the Society of Actuaries published the first experience study that looks at the lapse rate at the end of the level term period and the resultant mortality for those do not lapse.[16]

16 Society of Actuaries, 2010a, Lapse and Mortality Experience of Post-Level Premium Period Term Plans, http://www.soa.org/research/research-projects/life-insurance/research-shock-lapse-report.aspx, accessed August 17, 2011. The two research reports and accompanying spreadsheet are available in the book's online resources.

13.1.4.1.1 Nonguaranteed elements

Dividends for traditional life policies were discussed in Section 13.1.2.1.5. While some term insurance has been sold with dividends, it is not very common.

Indeterminate premiums for traditional life policies were discussed in Section 13.1.2.1.6. Term insurance in general, and term with a level premium for a period with an annual renewable term tail in particular, is often sold with indeterminate premiums, which may be changed in the future. The most common indeterminate premium design is for the premiums during the level term period to be guaranteed and the annually increasing premiums to be indeterminate. This design provides the life insurance company with some protection if the mortality experience after the level term period is substantially worse than anticipated.

For some products, the premiums are not guaranteed during the level premium period. For example, the premiums may be guaranteed for 10 years at 1,000. For the next twenty years, the guaranteed premiums may be 2,500, but the current (expected) premium during those 20 years is 1,000. This design clearly provides risk protection to the life insurance company, but has a difficult time competing with a product that guarantees a level premium for 30 years.

13.1.4.2 Level renewable term

Level renewable term provides a period of level death benefit coverage that is purchased by level premiums. At the end of the specified period of coverage, the policy can be renewed for another period of time, generally equal to the same period of time as the original period. The premium during the renewal period will once again be level, but be higher than the original premium. For example, a 10-year level renewable term policy will provide a death benefit of 100,000 for the first 10 years for an annual premium of 400. At the end of the 10 years, the policy owner has the right to renew the policy for another 10 years for a death benefit of 100,000 and an annual premium of 700.

Several points should be noted:

- The option to renew is a policy owner option. The life insurance company does not have an option. If the policy owner wants to renew, the life insurance company must renew the policy.
- The renewal takes place without any underwriting or evidence of insurability being required. In other words, the insured does not need to be in good health to renew the policy. Some policies give the policy owner the option of lowering the premium by providing evidence that the insured is in good health. This option is called *re-entry.*
- The periods of level coverage are typically for 5, 10, 15, or 20 years.
- The policy generally is renewable to attained age 70. In other words, if the policy was bought at age 25 and is a 20-year policy, it can be renewed at age 45 and again at age 65. However, if it is renewed at age 65, it is renewed for a short period—5 years to take it to age 70. The termination at age 70 is standard because term insurance that goes beyond attained age 70 must provide nonforfeiture options under the U.S. Standard Nonforfeiture Law.

Premiums may be paid annually or modally and may be fixed or indeterminate. Premiums may also be attained age or select and ultimate. When premiums are attained age, they are merely a function of attained age. Therefore, a person who bought the policy 10 years ago at age 40 and is now renewing at age 50 would pay the same premium as a person who is buying a brand new policy at age 50. Select and ultimate premiums mean that the premium to be paid is a function of both the issue age and duration of the policy. For example, see Table 13.7.

TABLE 13.7 Renewable Term Premiums

	Renewal Premium for Person Current Age 50 Who Bought the Policy at Age 40	Premium for a Person Current Age 50 Who Just Bought the Policy
Attained Age Premium	22.00	22.00
Select and Ultimate Premium	25.00	20.00

There is an increase in lapse rates at the end of the level period when the policy renews and the premium increases. However, the spike in lapse rates is not nearly as large as the spike under level term for a period with an annual renewable term tail because the jump in premium is not as substantial.

13.1.4.3 Annually renewable term

Annually renewable term (ART), also called *yearly renewable term* (YRT), provides level coverage each year in return for the payment of a premium. At the end of each year, the policy owner has the option to renew the coverage for an increased premium. One way to think about ART is that it is just level renewable term, but where the renewal period is one year. The discussion about level renewable term is applicable to ART except that ART is generally renewable beyond attained age 70 since the ART design eliminates the need for nonforfeiture values under the U.S. Standard Nonforfeiture Law.

ART was very popular in the 1970s. During the 1980s, its popularity decreased substantially due to low premiums on level term for a period with an annual renewable term tail. While the initial premium for ART is lower, the present value of the premiums for level term for a period with an annual renewable term tail is substantially less than the present value of the premiums for ART.

13.1.4.4 Term to age 100

Term to age 100 provides a level death benefit to attained age 100 in return for a level premium to attained age 100. This is a popular product in Canada. It is generally not available in the United States. In the United States, term to age 100 requires cash values and nonforfeiture benefits close to those of whole life. In Canada, no nonforfeiture values are required. This permits a much lower premium and a more marketable product.

Term to age 100 is a *lapse-supported* product. A lapse-supported product is a product that is more profitable if there are more lapses. For term to 100, the premiums are level while the mortality curve is increasing. This is illustrated in Figure 13.3. In the early years of the policy, the premiums exceed the death claims. However, in the later years of the policy, the death claims exceed the premiums. Therefore, if fewer policyholders lapse then there are more

FIGURE 13.3 Comparison of premiums and mortality

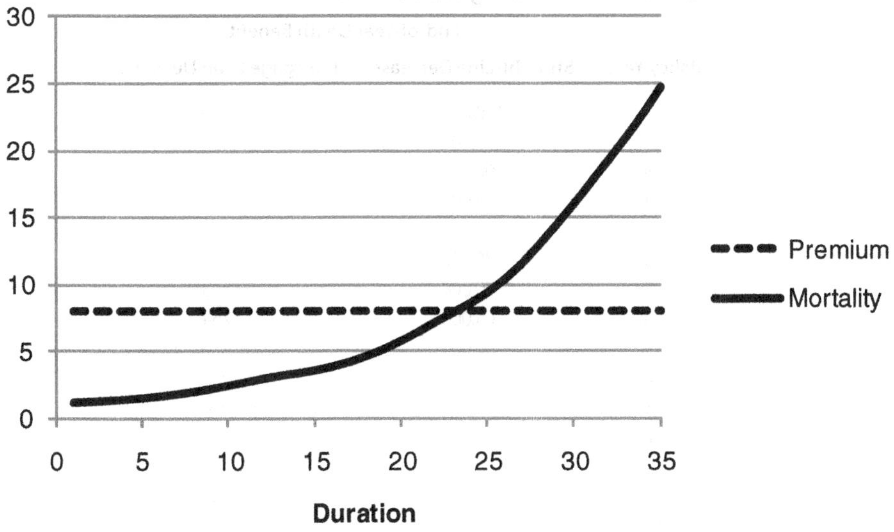

policyholders in the later years when the mortality costs exceed the premiums, resulting in larger costs and potential losses for the insurance company. For lapse-supported products, the lapse rates are a critical component in the pricing and reserving of these products. We will discuss this more in later chapters.

13.1.4.5 Decreasing term

The term products all have a level death benefit. Some term insurance products have a decreasing death benefit. These decreasing term products typically have a target market where the insurance needs are decreasing, so the death benefit follows the insurance needs.

Decreasing term is often sold to cover a specific debt such as a mortgage loan with the intent that the insurance will pay off the debt if the insured were to die. Mortgage term insurance typically provides coverage for 10, 15, 20, 25, or 30 years. The premiums are generally level during the premium paying period. The premium paying period may be the length of coverage or a shorter period. The shorter period usually is 80 percent of the coverage period. For example, the premiums for a 20-year decreasing term would be payable for 16 years.

The death benefit for mortgage term insurance may be decreasing in a straight line or may follow the outstanding balance for a mortgage given a set interest rate.

EXAMPLE 13.5

Table 13.8 lists the death benefits for 20-year decreasing term for both a straight line decrease and a death benefit that follows a 20-year mortgage with an interest rate of 6% compounded monthly. The initial death benefit is 100,000.

TABLE 13.8 Decreasing Term Benefits

	End-of-Year Death Benefit	
Policy Year	Straight-Line Decrease	Mortgage Loan Decrease
1	100,000	97,559
2	95,000	94,738
3	90,000	91,744
4	85,000	88,565
5	80,000	85,190
6	75,000	81,607
7	70,000	77,803
8	65,000	73,764
9	60,000	69,476
10	55,000	64,923
11	50,000	60,090
12	45,000	54,959
13	40,000	49,511
14	35,000	43,727
15	30,000	37,586
16	25,000	31,067
17	20,000	24,146
18	15,000	16,797
19	10,000	8,996
20	5,000	713

For some decreasing term insurance products, the death benefit actually decreases monthly to more closely follow the outstanding balance of a mortgage with monthly payments. That is the case for the coverage in Table 13.8. To see the formulas used to create this table, see the Excel file included with the online resources.

Another form of decreasing term insurance is commonly referred to as *credit life* insurance. Once again, the purpose of credit life insurance is to provide life insurance coverage on debt. Credit life is typically sold in conjunction with a consumer loan such as a loan to purchase an automobile. Credit life insurance has a single premium that is financed (becomes part of the loan balance). The term of coverage is the same as the consumer loan (e.g., 5 years). Credit life is sold with two death benefit options, which are referred to as gross coverage or net coverage. Gross coverage provides a death benefit that is equal to the sum of the remaining loan payments. Net coverage provides a death benefit equal to the outstanding balance of the consumer loan at any point in time. Under either coverage, the death benefit changes monthly as the loan is being repaid with monthly payments.

EXAMPLE 13.6

Table 13.9 lists the death benefits for a three-year consumer loan for 10,000 with an interest rate of 9% compounded monthly.

TABLE 13.9 Credit Life Death Benefits

	Monthly Death Benefit	
Month	**Gross Coverage**	**Net Coverage**
1	11,448	10,000
2	11,130	9,757
3	10,812	9,512
4	10,494	9,266
5	10,176	9,017
6	9,858	8,767
7	9,540	8,514
8	9,222	8,260
9	8,904	8,004
10	8,586	7,746
11	8,268	7,486
12	7,950	7,225
13	7,632	6,961
14	7,314	6,695
15	6,996	6,427
16	6,678	6,157
17	6,360	5,886
18	6,042	5,612
19	5,724	5,336
20	5,406	5,058
21	5,088	4,778
22	4,770	4,496
23	4,452	4,211
24	4,134	3,925
25	3,816	3,636
26	3,498	3,346
27	3,180	3,053
28	2,862	2,758
29	2,544	2,460
30	2,226	2,161
31	1,908	1,859
32	1,590	1,555
33	1,272	1,248
34	954	940
35	636	629
36	318	316

To see the formulas used to create this table, see the Excel file included with the online resources. Under our loan, the monthly payment is $\frac{10{,}000}{a_{\overline{36}|0.75\%}} = 318.00$. The death benefit under gross coverage is the number of remaining payments multiplied by the amount of the payment. For example, during the 13th month, there are 24 payments remaining so the death benefit is $318.00(24) = 7{,}632$.

Under net coverage, the death benefit is the outstanding balance of the loan. For our example, the death benefit in the 13th month is $318.00a_{\overline{24}|0.75\%} = 6{,}960.75$.

It should also be noted that credit life insurance is often sold in conjunction with credit disability insurance. The credit life will pay if the insured dies and the credit disability insurance will pay if the insured becomes disabled.

13.1.4.6 Deposit term

Deposit term was popular in the late 1970s and early 1980s. It provides a level death benefit, typically for 10 years. The premiums are level except for the first premium, which is much higher. The name deposit term is used because the excess of the first year premium over the renewal premiums as often referred to as a "deposit" during the sales process. At the end of the term period, the policy owner typically has two options:

- The policy terminates and the deposit is returned to the policy owner, typically with interest; or
- The term policy is automatically converted to a whole life policy with the deposit being used to pay the first annual premium for the whole life policy.

Deposit term was popular because the agent who sold the policy received commission on the entire first year premium including the deposit. This resulted in very high commissions to the agent relative to other term coverages. The deposit also provided an incentive for the policy owner to keep the policy in force in order to receive the deposit plus interest at the end of the policy term.

13.1.4.7 Family coverage

Term insurance coverage is often sold to cover family members. *Family coverage* is usually sold as a rider attached to another life insurance policy.

Spouse insurance is sold as a rider attached to another life insurance policy. It provides life insurance on the spouse of the insured of the life insurance policy. For example, Brad and Jacquelyn Smith are married. Jacquelyn purchases a life insurance policy on her own life. She also purchases a spouse insurance rider. Jacquelyn is the insured (and policy owner) for the life insurance policy. Brad is the insured for the spouse insurance rider. If Brad dies, the death benefit of the spouse insurance will be paid. The death benefit for spouse insurance is typically level and terminates at either attained age 65 or 70. Premiums are level and for the same period as the death benefit.

Children's term insurance is sold as a rider attached to a life insurance policy and provides a death benefit on all children of the insured of the life insurance policy. The death benefit is level and a flat amount which usually does not exceed 5,000. For example, the Smiths have two children. Jacquelyn also attaches a children's term rider to the policy that she purchased. The children's term insurance will pay a death benefit 5,000 for each Smith child that was to die. Additionally, if the Smiths have more children,[17] the new children will be covered by the rider even though they did not exist at the time the rider was purchased.

17 "Have more children" includes children added through adoption as well as added to the family through birth.

The rider normally terminates at attained age 65 of the insured parent (Jacquelyn in our example). The coverage for each child usually terminates at age 21 or 24 of each child if that is earlier. Level premiums are payable until the rider terminates (age 65 of the insured parent). It is possible that as the family ages that all children will be older than 21 (or 24) and no child will be covered under the rider. At this point, the policy owner may want to terminate the rider unless additional children are anticipated. The rider can be terminated without terminating the life insurance policy to which it is attached.

Family term insurance is a combination of spouse term insurance and children's term insurance combined into one life insurance rider.

Family income insurance is the final family coverage that we will discuss. Family income insurance is often provided as a rider, but can also be sold as a standalone policy. Family income insurance typically has a coverage period of 20 years or to age 65. The death benefit is a monthly benefit that will be paid from the time of death until the end of the coverage period. For a 20-year coverage period, if the insured dies at the end of the first year of coverage, a monthly benefit (such as 500) is paid at the end of each month for 19 years. On the other hand, if the insured died at the end of the 15th year of coverage, a monthly benefit (for the same 500 amount) is payable for 5 years. Therefore, family income insurance provides a decreasing death benefit as the number of payments decreases each month that the insured lives. It is not uncommon to guarantee a minimum number of monthly benefit payments so that the death benefit does not become so small that it has relatively little value compared to the premium. For example, there may be a minimum of 24 monthly payments guaranteed so if the insured dies during the last two years of coverage, the beneficiary will receive 24 monthly payments. The premiums for family income insurance are typically level and payable for the period of coverage.

13.1.5 Endowment Insurance

Like term insurance, *endowment insurance* also provides life insurance coverage for a specified period of time. However, unlike term, if the insured lives to the end of the term period, an endowment is paid to the policy owner. The amount of the endowment is usually equal to the death benefit that would have been paid if the insured had died. However, the endowment could be for a different amount. The death benefit is usually level for the term of the coverage.

The premiums for endowment insurance are almost always level over the term of coverage. There are adverse tax consequences for endowment insurance that terminates before attained age 95 in the United States and before 85 in Canada. Therefore, coverages that terminate prior to these ages are no longer offered. There are endowment insurance coverages that endow at these older ages, but they are very similar to whole life insurance since most insureds die or surrender prior to the endowment age.

13.1.6 Riders

Riders add additional benefits to a life insurance policy whether it is a whole life policy or a term policy. The life insurance policy is often referred to as the base policy. The rider may provide additional life insurance death benefit on the base policy insured or may add life insurance coverage on another person who becomes the insured for that rider. Riders may add supplemental benefits to life insurance policies. These supplemental benefits are triggered by an event other than death.

As mentioned, riders are attached to the base policy, they cannot be purchased separately. If the base policy terminates, the rider must also terminate unless there is a specific provision in the rider to allow it to continue.

Among the many riders available, we will cover the following:

- Term insurance
- Disability waiver
- Payor waiver
- Accidental death benefit
- Return of premium
- Accelerated death benefit
- Critical illness
- Long-term care
- Miscellaneous

13.1.6.1 Term insurance

Term insurance can be written as a base policy or as a rider attached to a base policy. All the forms of term insurance described previously with the exception of credit life insurance are available as term riders to whole life policies. The primary difference between term insurance policies and term insurance riders is that the term rider will generally terminate if the base policy terminates. There are exceptions in that certain family coverages contain a provision that allows the rider to continue to provide coverage on the remaining family members, usually without additional premium payment.

When term insurance riders are attached to a universal life or a VUL insurance policy, the cost of the coverage is deducted from the fund value in the form of cost of insurance charges based on the amount of death benefit provided by the term insurance and based on the life being insured (whether that is the base insured, the spouse or even a third life). The cost of insurance charges are added to the Monthly Deduction. The monthly deduction for the rider is calculated as:

$$\text{Monthly Deduction} = \frac{\text{Death Benefit Of Rider}}{1+i} \times \text{Cost Of Insurance Rates} + \text{Expense Charges}$$

These cost of insurance charges generally increase each policy year to reflect the increased probability of death of the insured just as the cost of insurance charges on the base policy increases. The expense charges are almost always zero.

13.1.6.2 Disability waiver

Disability waiver (usually just waiver) is a supplemental benefit that waives the premium for the life insurance policy if the insured becomes disabled. The definition of disability will be in the rider. Waiving the premium means that the policy owner does not have to pay the premium. The premium will continue to be waived as long as the insured remains disabled.

For UL or VUL, waiver takes a slightly different format. Some life insurance companies offer waiver of the monthly deduction for UL coverages. With the monthly deductions being waived, the fund value of the policy will grow with interest during the period of disability since there are no deductions being taken. Therefore, the policy is guaranteed to stay in force during the insured's disability.

The other approach for disability waiver for universal life contracts is waiver of a specified premium. The amount of the specified premium is selected by the policy owner at the time that the policy is purchased. Under this approach, the life insurance company will credit the UL policy with a premium payment on a periodic basis as if the policy owner had paid the premium. The specified premium will be reduced by any premium related expense charges and the net premium will be added to the fund value of the policy. This crediting of specified premiums will continue as long as the insured is disabled. Even if the policy owner pays premiums, the specified premiums will continue to be credited if the insured is disabled. Unlike waiver of monthly deduction, with waiver of specified amount, there is no guarantee that the fund value will continue to grow. If the premium being credited less the premium expense charges is smaller than the monthly deduction, the fund value can actually decrease over time. If the fund value decreases to zero, the policy will terminate unless the policy owner pays additional premiums.

Disability waiver coverage usually ends at age 60 or 65 even if the life insurance coverage continues beyond age 65. For example, on a whole life, the life insurance coverage continues until death, but the disability waiver will end at age 60 or 65. However, if the insured is disabled at the date that the disability waiver coverage would end, the premiums (or monthly deductions) will continue to be waived until the insured is no longer disabled. Often, because of the older attained age and normal retirement age, a person who is disabled at age 60 or 65 is presumed to be disabled for her remaining lifetime.

Since disability waiver waives the premiums of the base policy, once the premiums have ended, then disability waiver also ends. For example, if a 20-pay whole life policy is issued to a person age 25, waiver will terminate at attained age 45 when the premiums on the based policy terminate.

The premium payment period (or period for monthly deductions for UL coverages) for disability waiver will be the same as the coverage period (to attained age 60 or 65, or the premium payment period for the base policy, if shorter). The premiums for disability waiver will usually follow the pattern of the premiums of the base policy (level if the premiums for the base policy are level and will increase annually if the premiums on the base policy increase annually). For universal life coverages, the costs for the disability waiver are added to the monthly deduction and subtracted from the fund value. The cost of insurance is usually expressed as a percent of the other monthly deduction for waiver of monthly deduction or a percent of the specified premium for waiver of specified premium. These percentages typically increase with attained age as the probability of disability increases with age.

13.1.6.3 Payor waiver

Payor waiver is a rider that is very similar to disability waiver except the benefit is paid if the premium payor is disabled as opposed to the disability of the insured. While not a particularly popular benefit, this rider tends to be used if the insured is a minor. The payor is generally the policy owner, but could be someone else.

13.1.6.4 Accidental death benefit

This rider provides an additional death benefit if the cause of death was an accident. An accident is defined in the rider. For example, a whole life policy with a death benefit of 100,000 and an accidental death benefit rider with a death benefit of 100,000 will pay 100,000 upon death from natural causes and 200,000 upon death from accidental causes. For this reason, accidental death benefit is often known as *double indemnity*.

Accidental death benefit riders typically terminate at attained age 70. However, in some cases, the rider may provide coverage to the end of the base policy, which may be whole life. The premiums are payable for the length of the coverage, but not beyond the premium paying period of the base policy. The premiums are generally level. For UL coverages, the cost of the rider is included in the monthly deduction that is subtracted from fund value. The cost of insurance rider charges for this rider are often level as the cost of accidental death benefit coverage tends to be fairly level.

13.1.6.5 Return of premium

A *return of premium rider* has recently become a popular attachment to term insurance. This rider provides for the return of the premiums paid (without interest) if the policy owner keeps the policy in force for a certain period of time.

This rider is normally attached to level term for a period with an annual renewable term tail. At the end of the level term period, the rider returns the sum of the premiums paid. For example, if the level term period was 20 years and the premium each year was 1,000, then at the end of 20 years the return of premium rider would return the premium paid of 20,000. The return of premiums would be paid to the policy owner and the return of premium rider would terminate at that time.

If the policy owner stops paying premiums prior to the end of the period, a partial refund of premiums will be paid. This partial refund of premiums is required by law in the United States.

There is a premium that is charged for the return of premium rider. Therefore, the total premium paid by the policyholder is higher than the premium that would be paid without the return of premium rider. In our example, the total premium is 1,000. Without the return of premium rider, the premium might have been 350. The sum of the premiums paid for the return of premium rider is also returned at the time the premiums for the term coverage are returned. Similarly, premiums charged for other riders such as disability waiver are also returned.

A reasonable question is how the life insurance company can afford to return the premiums. The death benefits paid during the term period as well as the expenses and profits of the life insurance company must be covered. These costs (and profit) are generated primarily from two sources. First, the life insurance company collects the premiums over the term period and only returns the premiums at the end of the term period. During this time, the life insurance company invests the premiums and generates investment earnings. These investment earnings are not returned to the policy owner and can be used to cover benefits, expenses and profits.

Let's go back to our example of a level term period of 20 years with a premium of 1,000. Let's assume that a policy owner pays the premiums for 20 years. If the premium is paid annually at the beginning of the year and the life insurance company earns 6 percent on the premiums over those 20 years, then the premiums will have accumulated to $1{,}000\ddot{s}_{\overline{20}|6\%} = 38{,}993$. Therefore, even though the life insurance company must pay the policy owner 20,000 in a premium refund, 18,993 is available to offset the benefits and expenses paid on other policies and to generate a profit for the company.

The second source is from gains when the policy owner lapses or stops paying premium before the end of the term period. As mentioned, if the policy owner stops paying premiums, then return of premium rider only pays a partial refund of premium. The premiums that are not refunded are used to pay the benefits and expenses and generate profits.

Let's look at our example for a policy where the policy owner stops paying premiums after 10 years. As we noted, the policy owner will only receive a partial refund of premiums which in this case is 30 percent of the premiums paid. Therefore, the life insurance company would have collected 10 premiums of 1,000 which with interest would have accumulated to $1{,}000\ddot{s}_{\overline{10}|6\%} = 13{,}972$. The refund to the policy owner is 3,000 (30 percent of 10 premiums of 1,000). The difference of 10,972 consisting of investment gains of 3,972 and gain on lapse of 7,000 are used to pay the benefits and expenses and generate profits. Because the life insurance company benefits from additional lapses under a return of premium rider, the product with the return of premium rider is a lapse-supported product.

13.1.6.6 Accelerated death benefit rider

An *accelerated death benefit rider* is aptly named as the rider provides for the payment of all or part of the death benefit of a life insurance in advance of the death of the insured. The death benefit will be accelerated if certain conditions or triggers are satisfied.

The benefit amount is paid to the policy owner, not to the insured or to the beneficiary. The amount of the benefit is based on the death benefit of the life insurance policy. Some riders pay a benefit of 50 percent of the death benefit. Other riders pay 100 percent of the death benefit. While riders paying either 50 percent or 100 percent of the death benefit are the most common, there are riders that pay other amounts.

When the rider accelerates 100 percent of the death benefit, then the life insurance policy terminates and there is no benefit payable upon the death of the insured. If less than 100 percent of the death benefit is accelerated, then the life insurance policy continues. The amount payable upon death is reduced by the amount that was accelerated.

The most common condition for triggering an accelerated death benefit payment is terminal illness, that is, an expectation that death will occur shortly, usually within 6 or 12 months. Other conditions used by some riders include entry into a nursing home or occurrence of a specific disease or condition such as stroke, heart attack or certain cancers. These conditions must be certified by a medical doctor for the benefits to be payable.

The riders that are triggered by terminal illness are usually attached to life insurance policies at no additional cost to the policyholder. The cost to the insurance company is the loss of interest for the period (estimated to be 6 or 12 months) between the payment of the accelerated death benefit and the actual death of the insured. This accelerated death benefit or the death benefit paid on death are usually adjusted for this loss of interest. Under one approach, the accelerated death benefit is reduced by the interest before it is paid to the policy owner.

For example, a 100,000 life insurance policy has a rider that accelerates 50 percent of the death benefit if the insured is expected to die within 12 months. The insured is diagnosed as terminally ill and the policy owner elects to accelerate the death benefit. The amount accelerated will be 50,000 (50 percent of the death benefit), but the actual cash paid to the policy owner will be 47,000. The difference of 3,000 is kept by the insurance company and reflects loss of interest. The 3,000 can be calculated as 6 percent interest for 12 months on 50,000. Under this approach, the amount payable upon death is 50,000 (the original 100,000 death benefit less the 50,000 that was accelerated).

The other approach to compensating for the lost interest is to establish an interest bearing lien equal to the accelerated death benefit against the ultimate death benefit. Under this approach, for the example where 50 percent of the 100,000 death benefit is accelerated, the amount of cash that would be paid to the policy owner as an accelerated death benefit would be 50,000. Then a 50,000 lien would be established against the death benefit. The lien would earn interest at 6 percent per annum. If the insured died six months later, then the amount paid as a death benefit would be the death benefit less the lien accumulated with interest. Therefore, the payment is $100{,}000 - 50{,}000(1.06)^{0.5} = 48{,}522$.

For accelerated death benefit riders where the trigger is entry to a nursing home or occurrence of a specified disease or condition, a premium is usually charged as it can be several years between occurrence of the trigger and the payment of the death benefit.

13.1.6.7 Critical illness rider

Critical illness riders can take two forms. One is where an accelerated death benefit is paid, which was discussed in the previous section. The other form pays a benefit when a critical illness occurs. However, this benefit does not reduce the death benefit. The benefit that is paid to the policy owner is usually a single lump sum benefit. If the insured dies later, the full death benefit of the life policy is payable.

Critical illness riders are popular in some countries (e.g., South Africa), but few have been sold in North America.

13.1.6.8 Long-term care

The combination of a life insurance policy and long-term care rider has been sold by some companies over the last 10 years. This combination has been gaining market share and is now being offered by more life insurance companies.

The combination of a life insurance policy and a long-term care rider typically provides monthly benefits to the policy owner if the insured meets certain conditions. Those conditions could be entry into a nursing home, receiving home health care or could be defined in terms of activities of daily living.[18] If the conditions are met, then a monthly benefit expressed in terms of the death benefit of the life insurance policy is paid as long as the

18 Activities of daily living are commonly used to determine if an insured is eligible for long-term care insurance benefits. These are routine activities that people tend do each day without needing assistance. There are normally six activities of daily living: eating, bathing, dressing, toileting, transferring (walking), and continence.

insured continues to qualify under the terms of the rider. For example, the monthly benefit could be 4 percent of the death benefit. The death benefit of the life insurance policy will be reduced by each monthly benefit payment until the death benefit is exhausted. For our example of 4 percent per month, the death benefit of the life insurance policy would be exhausted after 25 months (4% × 25 months = 100%). Once the death benefit of the life insurance policy is exhausted, then the long-term care rider will continue the same monthly benefit for an additional period of time specified in the rider. This additional period of time is usually 12, 24, or 36 months.

There is a premium charged for the long-term care rider.

13.1.6.9 Insurability riders

Insurability riders guarantee that additional life insurance death benefit can be purchased on the insured in the future without evidence of insurability. Therefore, the policy owner can purchase life insurance on an unhealthy insured based on premium rates for a healthy insured. The riders take two forms.

One form is called guaranteed purchase option (GPO) or guaranteed insurability option (GIO). This form of an insurability rider provides the option to purchase a new whole life policy if the rider is attached to a whole life policy, or the option to increase the specified amount of the existing policy if attached to UL policy. The policy owner typically has this option at certain attained ages such as 25, 28, 31, 34, 37, and 40. Additionally, certain special events such as marriage or the birth of a child may trigger an option to purchase additional insurance. The amount of the additional life insurance death benefit will be specified by the rider. If the policy owner does not exercise the option to purchase additional coverage, they still have the right to exercise future options. In other words, if at attained age 25, the policy owner decides that she does not want to buy additional life insurance, she will still have the option of buying additional insurance at future option dates. For this reason, there is considerable anti-selection that takes place at each option date. Those that are unhealthy will almost certainly exercise the option while those that are healthy are less likely to exercise the option.

There is a premium charged for GPO or GIO to cover the cost of anti-selection.

Another form of insurability rider is a cost of living adjustment (COLA) rider. This rider, when attached to a UL policy, provides that the specified amount of the UL contract will increase each year by the amount of the increase in the CPI. For example, if the specified amount for a policy is 120,000 and the CPI increases by 3 percent, then the specified amount will increase to 123,600. These increases occur automatically each year without any required action from the policy owner. The policy owner has the right to reject the increase if she wants. However, once an increase is rejected, no further increases will occur. Because the increase occurs automatically and because the increases cease upon rejection of an increase, there is little anti-selection on a cost of living adjustment rider. Therefore, there is generally no premium associated with a cost of living adjustment rider. While there is no premium for such a rider, as the specified amount of the universal life contract increases, the cost of insurance deductions from the account value do increase to reflect the new death benefit.

13.1.7 EXERCISES

13.1 Create a spreadsheet to calculate the monthly Fund Value for the first 10 years for a UL policy with a specified amount of 50,000 issued to a female age 45. The UL policy has the following parameters.

- Expense charges of 5% of premium and 10 per policy per month. There is also a charge of 0.06 per 1,000 of specified amount for the first five years. After five years, the per 1,000 expense charge is zero;
- Guaranteed interest rate of 4.5%;
- Current interest rate of 6%; and
- The annual cost of insurance charge is 85% of the 2001 CSO Female Age Last Birthday Smoker rates. The monthly charge is 1/12th the annual mortality rate.

A monthly premium of 100 is paid on this policy.

You can get the 2001 CSO Female Age Last Birthday Smoker mortality rates from the spreadsheet of mortality rates available as part of the online resources for this book.

13.2 Six years ago, Jordan purchased a UL policy with a premium-based secondary guarantee. The benchmark premium for the secondary guarantee is 1,500 per year. Jordan has paid a premium of 1,800 per year for each of the last six years. Jordan is having financial difficulties and wants to pay the minimum amount into his universal life contract over the next three years. However, he wants to be sure that the secondary guarantee on his contract remains in effect. Calculate the amount that Jordan will pay in each of the next three years if he pays the minimum amount each year.

13.3 Create a spreadsheet to calculate the monthly Fund Value for the first 20 years for a variable UL policy issued on December 31, 1990, with a specified amount of 75,000 issued to a male age 50. The UL policy has the following parameters.

- Expense charges of 4% of premium and 7 per policy per month. There is also a charge of 0.06 per 1,000 of specified amount for the first 10 years. After 10 years, the per 1,000 expense charge is zero;
- The fund value is invested in the S&P 500 Index;
- M&E Charge of 125 bp; and
- The annual cost of insurance charge is 85% of the 2001 CSO Male Age Last Birthday Nonsmoker rates. The monthly charge is 1/12th the annual mortality rate.
- The net amount at risk is calculated using an annual effective interest rate of 4%.

A quarterly premium of 700 is paid on this policy.

You can get the 2001 CSO Male Age Last Birthday Nonsmoker mortality rates from the spreadsheet of mortality rates available as part of the online resources for this book. You can get the S&P 500 returns from the spreadsheet FAP S&P 500 Returns.xlsx included in the online resources.

13.4 Compare and contrast the graded premium whole life product described in Section 13.1.2.1.3 with the annually renewable term product described in Section 13.1.4.3.

13.5 Consider the life insurance products listed below. Which are lapse supported products? State reasons to support your conclusions.

a) Whole Life Insurance
b) Universal Life Insurance policy with secondary guarantees
c) Universal Life Insurance policy with level cost of insurance rates
d) Level Term for a Period with an Annual Renewable Term Tail
e) Level Renewable Term
f) Annually Renewable Term

13.6 Jenna buys a used car for 15,000. She pays 7,000 from her savings account and takes out a loan of 8,000. The loan will be repaid over 24 months at an interest rate of 12% compounded monthly. If Jenna purchases credit life insurance covering the gross outstanding balance, what will her death benefit be in during the 5th month of the loan?

What would her death benefit be during the 5th month of the loan if she had purchased net coverage?

Will the death benefit under net coverage ever exceed the death benefit under gross coverage?

13.2 Annuities

In its most basic form, an annuity is a savings account where the amount saved is paid out to the annuitant in future years. The amount in the annuity may be paid as a lump sum or may be paid as periodic payments over time. As with life insurance, annuities can be classified in several ways. For our purposes, we will consider *deferred annuities* and *payout annuities.*

13.2.1 Deferred Annuity

A deferred annuity is a fund into which the policy owner deposits premium(s). The policy owner may deposit a single premium or may pay more than one premium. The amount in the fund accrues interest. The interest on deferred annuities is determined:

- Based on the investment returns earned by the company (a fixed annuity);
- Based on a mutual fund or separate account (a variable annuity); or
- Based on the returns of a stock index such as the S&P 500 (an indexed annuity).

At some point in the future, the policy owner of the deferred annuity may surrender the deferred annuity for a lump sum or for a series of payments under a payout annuity. Payout annuities will be discussed later. These benefits (a lump sum or a series of payments) are referred to as annuity benefits. A deferred annuity will have a maturity date. If the deferred annuity has not been surrendered prior to the maturity date, the annuity benefits will begin on the maturity date.

If the policy owner dies prior to payout, then a death benefit, generally equal to the fund value, will be paid to the beneficiary.

13.2.1.1 Parties to a deferred annuity contract

As with a life insurance policy, there are various parties to the contract. These parties are the life insurance company, the policy owner, and the beneficiary. The annuity contract is between the policy owner and the life insurance company. As with a life insurance contract, the beneficiary is a peripheral party to the agreement.

With an annuity contract, the cash flows occur as follows:

- The life insurance company pays the benefits (death benefits or annuity benefits) and receives the premiums.
- The policy owner pays the premiums and receives the annuity benefits.
- The beneficiary receives the death benefits if the policy owner dies. The beneficiary does not make any payments.

Generally, the policy owner and the beneficiary will not be the same person since benefits are triggered by the death of the policy owner.

13.2.1.2 Nonforfeiture benefits

Deferred annuities must provide a nonforfeiture benefit. For a deferred annuity, the non-forforfeiture options are generally a cash payment upon surrender of the deferred annuity. However, the Standard Nonforfeiture Law for annuities does not require a cash surrender option. A paid up annuity option is required if a cash surrender benefit is not provided. Just as with life insurance, the regulation requires a minimum nonforfeiture value, but life insurance companies are free to offer higher benefits.

Nonforfeiture requirements are discussed in detail in Section 18.3.

13.2.2 Types of Deferred Annuities

Deferred annuity products can take several forms. For the purpose of our discussions, we will classify deferred annuities into three categories as follows:

- Fixed deferred annuities;
- Variable deferred annuities; and
- Indexed deferred annuities.

As with life insurance, there are significant differences and similarities between these different categories.

13.2.2.1 Fixed deferred annuities

The premiums for a fixed deferred annuity are invested in the general account of the life insurance company. The value of the annuity does not vary with the value of the underlying assets. This is the reason that these annuities are referred to as "fixed." In Section 13.2.2.2 we will discuss variable annuities, where the value of the annuity does vary with the underlying assets.

13.2.2.1.1 Premium payments

The timing of premium payments for a deferred annuity may be fixed or may be flexible. Many deferred annuity contracts are sold as single premium contracts. The policy owner only pays one premium, which must be paid at the time the annuity contract is sold so the timing of the premium payment is fixed. The amount of the premium that must be paid is flexible, subject to a minimum (such as 10,000) and a maximum (such as 1 million). A life insurance company will generally waive the maximum except under extra-ordinary situations such as disruptions in the investment market.

The alternative to a single premium deferred annuity is a flexible premium contract. Within certain limits, a flexible premium contract allows the policy owner to pay premiums of any amount and at any time. One common requirement is that a minimum premium (such as 2,000) must be paid prior to the issue of the deferred annuity. Generally, thereafter, the policyholder may pay additional premiums at any time subject to a minimum (such as 100) and a maximum (such as 1 million).

Prior to the mid-1970s, most annuities that were sold had fixed premium payments. These annuities required periodic premium payments for a specified amount. When flexible premium deferred annuities were introduced in the mid-1970s, fixed premium annuities were no longer sold.

13.2.2.1.2 Fund value

When a premium is received by the insurance company, the premium less any expense charges is deposited into a fund. Typically, no expense charges are deducted although a few companies do deduct any premium taxes that must be paid on the premium. The fund is increased with interest. For a fixed deferred annuity, the interest rate credited on the fund will be based on the interest rates that the life insurance company earns on its investments. A deferred annuity contract will guarantee a minimum interest rate. This minimum interest rate is typically around 3 percent, but can be as low as 1 percent.

As with a UL contract, the interest rate is a nonguaranteed element and functions in the same manner. The actual or current credited interest rate will generally be based on the earned interest rate on the investments that the insurance company has backing the annuity funds. The current credited rate is usually calculated as the earned rate less a spread where the spread is determined in pricing. The example provided in Section 13.1.2.2 for UL is applicable to a fixed deferred annuity.

Unlike UL, there are no charges that are deducted from this fund on a regular basis except for a few annuity contracts that deduct an expense charge (e.g., 40) once a year.

Table 13.10 shows the fund value at the end of each policy year that develops for a single premium deferred annuity where the single premium was 50,000 and the credited interest rate was 6 percent each year for 20 years.[19]

TABLE 13.10 Deferred Annuity Fund Values

End of Year	Account Value	End of Year	Account Value
1	53,000.00	11	94,914.93
2	56,180.00	12	100,609.82
3	59,550.80	13	106,646.41
4	63,123.85	14	113,045.20
5	66,911.28	15	119,827.91
6	70,925.96	16	127,017.58
7	75,181.51	17	134,638.64
8	79,692.40	18	142,716.96
9	84,473.95	19	151,279.98
10	89,542.38	20	160,356.77

To see the formulas used to create this table, see the Excel file included with the online resources.

The fund value (also known as account value) of the deferred annuity is the basis of the annuity and death benefits for the contract. As mentioned previously, the annuity benefits are paid out as a lump sum or as periodic payments under a payout annuity. This may occur at any time if the policy owner elects to surrender the annuity and must occur at the maturity date if the annuity is still in force at that time. If the benefits are paid as periodic payments, the full fund value (without any adjustments) is typically used as a single premium to purchase a payout annuity. Payout annuities are discussed later.

19 It is not realistic for the credited interest rate to stay level for all 20 years. The credited interest rate is determined periodically by the insurance company using the earned interest rate. The redetermination usually occurs quarterly or annually but can occur more frequently in a volatile interest rate environment.

When the annuity benefit is taken as a lump sum, there are two adjustments that may be made to the fund value prior to the payment of a lump sum. These adjustments are:

- Surrender charges; and
- Market value adjustment.

13.2.2.1.3 Surrender charges

If the deferred annuity contract is surrendered for a lump sum soon after it is issued, the fund value will be reduced by a surrender charge prior to the payment of the lump sum. The surrender charge may take many forms. However, a typical surrender charge is expressed as a percentage of the fund value. The surrender charge will decrease over time to zero. Table 13.11 provides a sample surrender charge.

TABLE 13.11 Surrender Charges

Surrender during Policy Year	Surrender Charge as a Percent of Fund Value
1	9%
2	8%
3	7%
4	6%
5	5%
6	4%
7	3%
8	2%
9	1%
10+	0%

EXAMPLE 13.7

We will work through an example to illustrate how the surrender charge works. If a policy has a fund value of 59,550.80 at the end of the third policy year and is surrendered at that time, the surrender charge is 7%. Therefore, the surrender charge amount is

$$\begin{aligned}\text{Surrender Charge} &= (\text{Fund Value})(\text{Surrender Charge Percent})\\ &= (59{,}550.80)(0.07) = 4{,}168.56.\end{aligned}$$

The amount paid as a lump sum is

$$\text{Fund Value} - \text{Surrender Charge} = 59{,}550.80 - 4{,}168.56 = 55{,}382.24.$$

Many deferred annuity contracts allow the policy owner to withdraw a portion of the fund value without a surrender charge. This is known as a partial free withdrawal. A common partial free withdrawal allows the policy owner to withdraw up to 10% of the fund value each policy year without a surrender charge.

EXAMPLE 13.8

If our sample deferred annuity contained such an option, then at the end of the third year, the policy owner could withdraw up to 10% of the account value without a surrender charge. The maximum partial free withdrawal is

$$\text{Partial Free Withdrawal} = (\text{Fund Value})(\text{Free Withdrawal Percentage})$$
$$= (59{,}550.80)(0.10) = 5{,}955.08.$$

This would give the policy owner the ability to withdraw 5,955.08 from the annuity contract without a surrender charge. If the policy owner wanted to surrender the entire contract and the contract had a 10% free withdrawal provision, then the policy owner could withdraw the 10% of the fund value without a surrender charge and the surrender charge only applies to the remaining 90% of the fund value. The following formula illustrates this calculation.

$$\text{Surrender Charge} = (\text{Fund Value less Partial Free Withdrawal})(\text{Surrender Charge Percent})$$
$$= (59{,}550.80 - 5{,}955.08)(0.07) = 3{,}751.70.$$

The surrender charge and partial free withdrawal illustrated in Example 13.8 is fairly representative of those in the United States market. However, the surrender charges and partial free withdrawals are not standardized. The surrender charges on some products are considerably higher and may last much longer than those illustrated while other annuities have lower surrender charges or shorter surrender charge periods. Partial free withdrawal provisions also vary substantially with some products not even offering a partial free withdrawal privilege.

The purpose of the surrender charge is to discourage the surrender of the deferred annuity contract shortly after it is issued. The life insurance company incurs considerable expense (mostly related to commissions payable to the agent who sold the annuity) in issuing the policy. Those expenses are recovered over time from the interest rate spread. However, if the policy is surrendered too soon after it was issued, the life insurance company will not have a chance to recover the issue expenses. Therefore, the surrender charge can be used to recover the expenses.

13.2.2.1.4 Market value adjustment

Some deferred annuities include a *market value adjustment* (MVA). The MVA is only applied upon surrender of the contract and may increase or decrease the fund value. The MVA is intended to reflect the change in the value of the assets supporting the annuity fund values when there are changes in the yield curves in the financial markets. When the annuity is surrendered, it is assumed that the life insurance company must liquidate the assets supporting that annuity. The assets will be liquidated at market value and any gain or loss on the sale of the asset will be reflected in the MVA.

As you may recall, the value of a bond will increase when interest rates decrease and vice versa. The MVA is intended to roughly reflect the change in value of the bond. Therefore, the MVA results in an increase in the value of the annuity if the interest rate on the date of surrender is lower than the interest rate on the date of issue. Similarly, if the interest rate has increased since issue, then the MVA will reduce the value available from the annuity.

Most MVAs are only effective during the surrender charge period (nine years in Table 13.11) as an insurance company is assumed to be able to immunize against surrender after the surrender charge period.

EXAMPLE 13.9

An example of an MVA formula is:

$(Fund\ Value)(A - B)(\,^{MR}/_{12}\,)$ where

Fund Value is the fund value of the annuity.

A is the yield rate on 10-year Treasury Notes on the date of issue as a decimal.

B is the yield rate on 10-year Treasury Notes on the date of surrender as a decimal.

MR is the number of months remaining until the surrender charge ceases.

Consider an annuity purchased on January 1, 2005 when 10-year Treasury Notes are yielding 4.23%. The annuity has a 9-year surrender charge period. The annuity is surrendered on February 1, 2010. The fund value at that time is 67,236.97. On February 1, 2010, the yield on 10-year Treasury Notes is 3.68%. The MVA that is added to the fund value upon surrender is:

$$(67{,}236.97)(0.0423 - 0.0368)\left(\frac{47}{12}\right) = 1{,}448.40.$$

It should be noted that most deferred annuity contracts do not contain an MVA.

13.2.2.1.5 Minimum nonforfeiture requirements

In the United States, the Standard Nonforfeiture Law for annuities does not require a value be available for surrender prior to the maturity date. However, if a value is made available by the life insurance company, the Standard Nonforfeiture Law specifies a minimum value that must be provided.[20] The minimum nonforfeiture requirement generally limits the size of the surrender charge and/or market value adjustment.

13.2.2.1.6 Death benefits

If the policy owner dies, a death benefit is paid. The death benefit is usually equal to the fund value of the annuity. For some annuities the death benefit may be the surrender value, which means the fund value would be adjusted by the surrender charge or MVA, if any.

13.2.2.2 Variable deferred annuities

Variable deferred annuities have many similarities to fixed deferred annuities. Therefore, we will just highlight the major differences. To the extent that we do not discuss a feature that

20 Most annuities sold in the United States offer a nonforfeiture value as the marketplace generally requires it for competitive reasons.

was mentioned for fixed deferred annuities, then that feature should be assumed to be the same for variable deferred annuities.

The primary difference between fixed deferred annuities and variable deferred annuities is the method of determining the return on the fund value of the annuity. As with variable life, funds supporting the fund value of the annuity are invested in one or more separate accounts. These separate accounts may be mutual funds or similar vehicles that have specific investment objectives. The policy owner determines how the fund value is invested by selecting the funds and what percentage of the fund value goes into each fund. The death benefit and cash value are determined daily based on the returns in the separate accounts.

In many cases, the life insurance company will offer the policy owner the option of investing in the general account of the insurance company. By investing in the general account, the policy will act very similar to a general deferred annuity. The general account guarantees a minimum interest rate and credits an interest rate based on the return of the assets in the insurance company, if higher.

When the funds are invested in a separate account, the policy owner has assumed the investment risk. The life insurance company does not guarantee a return[21] on the separate account and returns can be negative. The assumption of the investment risk by the policy owner has the same implications as for variable life. See Section 13.1.2.3 for a discussion of these implications.

With a fixed deferred annuity, the primary (if not only) source of profit for the insurance company is the difference between what they earn on the invested assets and the interest rate that they pay on the policy. As with variable life insurance products, the policy owner of a variable annuity gets the investment returns from the separate account, but the policy owner does not get the entire return as there is a fee deducted and paid to the life insurance company. This fee is again specifically identified as a M&E charge and works the same as for variable life. See Section 13.1.2.3.

An additional difference is that a variable deferred annuity without an option to invest in the general account of the life insurance company will not contain an MVA. If a variable deferred annuity does allow the policy owner to invest in the general account of the life insurance company, then the annuity may have an MVA. In that case, the MVA will only apply to the portion of the fund value in the general account.

13.2.2.3 Indexed deferred annuity

An *indexed deferred annuity* (also known as an *equity-indexed annuity*) is a cross between variable and nonvariable. As with indexed universal life, the interest rate credited to the fund value on the indexed deferred annuity is based on an external index such as the S&P 500. If the external index increases during the participation period, the interest credited will be positive. If the index decreases during the participation period, the interest rate will be floored at zero. In other words, the product guarantees that the fund value will not decrease. Generally, the amount of interest credited to the fund value only reflects a portion of the return on the index. Mechanisms used to limit the upside return are the same as for indexed life. See Section 13.1.2.4.

21 The life insurance company may provide a minimum guarantee through a rider. These guarantees will be discussed later.

The life insurance company may provide more than one external index that can be used as a basis for the interest rate. The policy owner may be able to choose which index(es) will be used and what percent of the fund value is allocated to each index. This is similar to the multiple separate accounts with variable life. As with variable deferred annuities, the life insurance company may also offer the policy owner the option of investing in the general account of the insurance company.

An MVA may be included in an indexed deferred annuity. For an indexed deferred annuity, the MVA will apply to the entire fund value just as it does for a fixed deferred annuity.

In all other aspects, the indexed deferred annuities functions the same as its nonvariable counterpart.

13.2.3 Types of Riders

For variable deferred annuities, benefits can be added by riders. We will cover the following:

- Guaranteed minimum death benefit; and
- Guaranteed living benefits.

13.2.3.1 Guaranteed minimum death benefit

As mentioned, the fund value (and therefore the death benefit) for a variable deferred annuity can increase or decrease as the separate account increases or decreases. While the long-term trend for stock investments is up, it is normal for the stock market to fluctuate up and down. Since investment in a variable deferred annuity is considered a long-term investment, the stock market fluctuations are not a problem, as the policy owner can wait until the market recovers. However, if the policy owner dies during a down market, then the variable deferred annuity may be liquidated at that time. Therefore, life insurance companies offer a rider to protect the policy owner from this possibility. The *guaranteed minimum death benefit* (GMDB) rider provides a guaranteed death benefit for a variable deferred annuity. This guarantee can take various forms. Three examples will be presented.

A *return of premium* provision guarantees that the death benefit will never be less than the premium paid (less any withdrawals that have been taken). Therefore, if the fund value of the variable annuity is less than the premium paid in and the policy owner dies, the beneficiary will receive the premium paid in.

A *high water mark* provision guarantees that the death benefit will be the highest fund value on any policy anniversary.

A *roll-up* provision guarantees that the death benefit is the premium accumulated at a set interest rate such as 5 percent. Such a death benefit will be adjusted for any partial withdrawals.

EXAMPLE 13.10

A variable deferred annuity was issued on November 29, 2005. The fund value on that date was 50,000. The fund value on each subsequent November 29 is listed in Table 13.12. On June 1, 2010, the policy owner died with a fund value of 44,000.

TABLE 13.12 Fund Values

November 29,	Fund Value
2006	55,000
2007	57,000
2008	39,000
2009	43,000

Under a return of premium provision, the death benefit is the 50,000 that was invested.

Under a high water mark provision, the death benefit is 57,000 as this was the highest fund value on any past anniversary and it is higher than the fund value at death. It should be noted that the fund value could have been higher than 57,000 at some point during the contract, but we only look at the high water mark on the anniversaries

Under a roll-up benefit at 5% the death benefit is[22] $50{,}000(1.05)^{4.419178} = 62{,}031.07$. The death benefit in this case is higher under the roll-up GMDB, but this is not always the case.

There is a charge for these GMDB riders, which is expressed as a annual percentage of the fund value. For example, the charge might be 50 basis points.[23] Finally, it should be noted that this benefit is only available upon death. Therefore, it provides limited downside protection to the policy owner.

13.2.3.2 Guaranteed living benefits

Guaranteed living benefits (GLB) riders provided a guaranteed benefit while the policy owner is still alive. The benefit is only available after some period of time such as 10 years and usually requires that the policy owner maintain the funds in diversified separate accounts.

There is a charge for GLB riders just as there are for GMDB riders. The charge for GLB riders are usually larger as there is more opportunity for the policy owner to select against the life insurance company since the policy owner does not have to die to activate the benefit.

The GLB riders can take several forms. The most common are now discussed.

A *guaranteed minimum income benefit* (GMIB) rider provides a guarantee that after a certain period of time (e.g., 10 years) the policy owner can convert the variable deferred annuity into an annuity that pays an income benefit. The amount available to determine the income benefit will be the greater of the fund value or the premiums accumulated at a specified interest rate such as 5 percent. It should be noted that this value is not available as a lump sum, but only available as an income benefit.

A *guaranteed withdrawal value* (GWV) rider allows the policy owner to recoup the premium paid over a specified period (usually between 8 and 15 years) through withdrawals.

22 This is based on 4 years and 153 days.

23 This is equivalent to 0.50%.

For example, the policy owner may withdraw 8 percent of the premium paid for 12.5 years. This results in 100 percent return of premium. The rider usually allows for step-ups every 5 years. In other words, at each step up point, if the fund value is higher than the premiums paid in, then the new basis for the withdrawal benefit will be the fund value instead of the premiums. Once again, this benefit is not available as a lump sum, but only as withdrawals over a period of time.

A *guaranteed fund value* rider provides a guaranteed minimum fund value that can be withdrawn as a lump sum under certain conditions. This rider guarantees the fund value will not be less than the premiums paid as long as the premiums are left with the life insurance company for a certain number of years such as 10. Furthermore, this rider usually has specific investment requirements, which must be followed over the 10-year period. If the requirements are followed, then the policy owner will have a guarantee of return of premium at anytime following the minimum holding period.

A *lifetime benefits* rider guarantees a lifetime income to the policy owner. The benefit guarantees an annual lifetime benefit typically equal to 4 to 6 percent of the premium for as long as the policy owner is alive. The benefit will increase if the variable annuity experiences strong investment performance. The cost of this rider is a function of the age of the policy owner. Therefore the cost of the benefit will vary by age or the amount payable will vary with age. Once again, this is an income benefit and not available as a lump sum.

EXAMPLE 13.11

A variable deferred annuity was issued on January 1, 2000. The premium paid on that date was 100,000. The fund value on each subsequent January 1 is listed in Table 13.13.

TABLE 13.13 Fund Values

January 1,	Fund Value
2001	110,000
2002	105,000
2003	115,000
2004	120,000
2005	125,000
2006	100,000
2007	110,000
2008	70,000
2009	90,000
2010	110,000

Under each of the following scenarios, determine the benefits that would be provided by the GLB riders.

Scenario 1: A guaranteed minimum income benefit rider attached to the policy provides a guarantee that after 10 years, the policy owner can convert the variable deferred annuity into an annuity that pays an income benefit. The amount available to determine the income benefit will be the greater of the fund value or the premiums accumulated at 4%. Therefore, the amount used to determine the income benefit is the greater of

$$110{,}000 \text{ and } 100{,}000(1.04)^{10} = 148{,}024.$$

This could be used to buy a monthly income of 1,184.19 payable for the life of the annuitant. Without the guaranteed minimum income rider, the monthly income would have only been 800.[24]

Scenario 2: A guaranteed withdrawal value rider is attached. This rider allows the policy owner to recoup the premium paid over a ten year period provided the annuity has been in force for at least 10 years. The rider returns 100% of the premium. The rider also provides a step up every 5 years following issue. Therefore, the amount that the policy owner could withdraw each year for the next 10 years is

$$\textit{Max}(\text{Premium Paid; Account Value at end of 5th year; Account Value at end of 10th year}) \div 10 = \textit{Max}(100{,}000;125{,}000;110{,}000) \div 10 = 12{,}500.$$

Scenario 3: A guaranteed fund value rider is attached to the policy that guarantees that the surrender value of the annuity will not be less than the premium paid less any withdrawals provided the policy has been in force for 8 years. If the policy owner surrendered the policy at the end of 10 years, the surrender value would be 110,000 since the fund value at that time exceeds the premiums paid of 100,000. Under this scenario, the guaranteed fund value rider would not have affected the surrender value. However, if the annuity had been surrendered at the end of the eighth year, the surrender value that would have been paid would have been 100,000 as the premiums paid exceeded the fund value of 70,000.

Scenario 4: A *lifetime benefits* rider is attached to the annuity policy. It guarantees a lifetime income to the policy owner equal to six percent of the base amount. The base amount is the greater of the premium paid and the account value at the end of each 5-year period following issue. Therefore, the annual lifetime benefit guaranteed at the end of 10 years is:

$$\textit{Max}(\text{Premium Paid; Account Value at end of 5th year; Account Value at end of 10th year}) \times 0.06 = \textit{Max}(100{,}000;125{,}000;110{,}000) \times 0.06 = 7{,}500.$$

While this amount is lower than the amount paid under the guaranteed withdrawal value rider, the 7,500 is paid for the life of the annuitant, not just for 10 years.

13.2.4 Payout Annuity

A payout annuity is a series of periodic payments made by the life insurance company to the policy owner. The series of payments may be guaranteed for a period of time (such as 10 years) or may only be payable if the annuitant is alive. If the policy owner dies and additional payments are to be made, those additional payments are made to the beneficiary.

---

24 These monthly incomes are based on an illustrative rate of 8 per 1,000.

A payout annuity originates from a deferred annuity when the policy owner elects to begin receiving payments under the annuity contract. In this case, the payout annuity is a continuation of the deferred annuity contract. In other words, a new contract is not issued.

A payout annuity contract may also originate as a new contract in which the policy owner pays a single premium to the life insurance company in return for the series of future period payments. In this case the product is generally known as a *single premium immediate annuity.*

13.2.4.1 Parties to a payout annuity contract

The parties to a payout annuity include the same parties as deferred annuity plus the annuitant. Since the other parties have already been discussed, we will only discuss the annuitant here. If the payments of a payout annuity are based on a person being alive, then the annuitant's life is the basis of those payments. Most of the time, the annuitant and the policy owner will be the same person.

13.2.4.2 Payments

Payments under a payout annuity can be guaranteed or contingent.

13.2.4.2.1 Guaranteed payments

Guaranteed payments are precisely as named. These payments are guaranteed to occur. For example, the payout annuity may guarantee a payment of 1,000 on the first of each month for 20 years (a total of 240 payments).

13.2.4.2.2 Life contingent payments

Contingent payments are usually contingent upon the life of the annuitant. If the annuitant is alive on the date the payment is to be made, then the payment is made. If the annuitant is not alive, then the life insurance company no longer makes payments. If the annuitant dies shortly after the payments under the payout annuity begin, then the life insurance company makes very few payments to the policy owner. On the other hand, if the annuitant lives a long time, the life insurance company can make payments for many years.

Life contingent payments expose the life insurance company to longevity risk. In other words, the longer the annuitant lives, the more the life insurance company must pay. Therefore, if the annuitant lives longer than expected, the life insurance company will lose money. We can contrast that with a life insurance policy where the life insurance company will lose money if the insured dies too early. For this reason, life insurance and payout annuities can be considered as having opposite risks and are, therefore, natural hedges.

Payments can also be based on other contingencies. For example, an annuity may provide for payments to an employee's spouse if the employee dies. Those payments will continue to the spouse until the spouse remarries. Upon remarriage, the payments cease.

There are common options available under a payout annuity. We have already discussed the first two.

- Guaranteed or certain payments;
- Life annuity;

- Certain and life payments. This is a combination of the two previous options. The payments continue as long as the annuitant is alive, but are guaranteed for some period of time, even if the annuitant is not alive. For example, a payout annuity could provide a monthly payout for 240 months or the life of the annuitant, whichever is longer. Therefore, if the annuitant dies in the first 240 months, payments will continue and stop after the 240th payment. If the annuitant lives longer than 240 months, the monthly payments will continue until the annuitant dies; and
- Joint annuity. Under a joint annuity, the payments are contingent on more than one life. Most of the time, such annuities are based on two lives, frequently the lives of a husband and wife. The payments under the annuity will continue as long as at least one of the annuitants is alive.

One of the options for a certain and life annuity is called a *refund annuity*. Under a refund annuity, the payments continue for the life of the annuitant, but guarantee that the payments will at least sum to the premium paid to purchase the payout annuity. For example, James purchases a refund payout annuity for 100,000. The monthly payments are 1,000 per month. Therefore, if James dies before 100 monthly payments are made, the payments will continue until 100 payments are made so that the total amount paid back to the policy owner and beneficiary would total the premium paid of 100,000.

13.2.4.2.3 Nonlevel payments

The payments under a payout annuity are generally level but do not have to be level. We will cover four instances where the payments are not level:

- Inflation adjusted benefits;
- Variable payout annuity;
- Joint annuities; and
- Structured Settlements.

13.2.4.2.3.1 Inflation adjusted benefits

Some payout annuities adjust the payment amount for inflation. In the United States, the payments each year might increase based on the change in the CPI. For example, during 2009, Jordan received monthly annuity payments of 400. Jordan's annuity provides that his payments will increase each calendar year based on changes in the CPI. The CPI in December of 2008 was 210.228 while the CPI in December 2009 was 215.949. Therefore, Jordan's payments during 2010 are $400(215.949/210.228) = 410.89$.

13.2.4.2.3.2 Variable payout annuity

As with variable life insurance and a variable deferred annuity, the assets backing a variable payout annuity are invested in separate accounts at the direction of the policy owner. The payments under the variable payout annuity will then reflect the returns on the separate accounts. The initial payments will reflect an AIR. If the returns on the separate accounts exceed the AIR, then the amount of the payments will increase. If the returns are less than the AIR, then the amount of the payments will decrease. Payment changes are generally done on an annual basis for administrative purposes and reflect the return on the separate accounts for the last year.

The first variable annuity was issued by the Teachers Insurance and Annuity Association in 1952. It is based on the premise that for the most part investment earnings at any time reflect a modest fixed amount plus inflation. If this premise is true, then increasing annuity payments by the difference between actual earnings and a modest fixed amount (the AIR) will create a pattern that mimics inflation. However, unlike policies that directly incorporate inflation, these increases create no risk to the insurance company. The following is a proof of that fact.

Consider a variable payout annuity with annual payments at the beginning of each year. The following notation will be used:

- i is the AIR set for the policy.
- j_t is the actual investment rate earned in year t.
- F_t is the amount in the insurance company's separate account that supports this annuity. The annuity begins with the annuitant using F_0 to purchase the annuity.
- B_t is the annuity payment received at time t.
- l_t is the number of annuitants alive at time t. Because this demonstration is about investment rates and benefit adjustments, it is assumed that the annuitants die according to the mortality table used to establish the initial benefit. The company will bear the longevity risk.

Using the AIR, the amount of annuity that can be purchased is

$$B_0 = F_0 l_0 / \sum_{t=0}^{n-1} (1+i)^{-t} l_t$$

where n is the time at which all annuitants have died. By the terms of the annuity, benefits are adjusted by (noting that it is the ratio, not the difference, that is used)

$$B_t = B_{t-1}(1+j_t)/(1+i) = B_0(1+j_t)\cdots(1+j_1)/(1+i)^{t.}$$

The fund value once all the annuitants have died is the accumulated value of the initial fund less the accumulated value of all benefits paid. All accumulations are done using the actual investment rate. Assume that l_0 people each purchase this annuity. Then the final fund value is

$$F_n = l_0 F_0 (1+j_n)\cdots(1+j_1) - \sum_{t=0}^{n-1} l_t B_t (1+j_n)\cdots(1+j_{t+1})$$

$$= l_0 F_0 (1+j_n)\cdots(1+j_1) - \sum_{t=0}^{n-1} l_t B_0 \frac{(1+j_t)\cdots(1+j_1)}{(1+i)^t}(1+j_n)\cdots(1+j_{t+1})$$

$$= (1+j_n)\cdots(1+j_1)\left[l_0 F_0 - \sum_{t=0}^{n-1} l_t B_0 (1+i)^{-t} \right] = 0.$$

Thus, no matter what the actual investment returns turn out to be, the fund will provide exactly the promised benefits.

EXAMPLE 13.12

A 97-year-old individual has 100,000 to invest in a variable annuity. The mortality table has $l_{97} = 10$, $l_{98} = 7$, $l_{99} = 3$, and $l_{100} = 0$. The AIR is 3%. Show that if investment earnings are 6%, 7%, and 5% over the next three years, the insurance company will neither gain nor lose money.

With this investment, the initial annuity payment is

$$\frac{100{,}000(10)}{10 + 7(1.03)^{-1} + 3(1.03)^{-2}} = 50{,}958.26.$$

At the end of the first year, the fund (assuming 10 policies were sold) has $10(100{,}000 - 50{,}958.26)(1.06) = 519{,}842.44$. The remaining 7 annuitants begin the second year with a payment of $50{,}958.26(1.06)/(1.03) = 52{,}442.48$ and at the end of the year the fund has $[519{,}842.44 - 7(52{,}442.48)](1.07) = 163{,}437.24$. The final annuity payment is $52{,}442.48(1.07)/(1.03) = 54{,}479.08$. After making this payment, the fund has $163{,}437.24 - 3(54{,}479.08) = 0$. The investment earnings in year three are irrelevant because there is no money to invest and no further annuity payments to be made.

There is a spreadsheet available in the online resources that uses a 10-year period and allows you to vary the various factors and see that the ending fund balance is always zero.

13.2.4.2.3.3 Joint annuities

Joint annuities often provide for a change in the amount of the payment upon the first death. The reduction may be independent of the order of death or may be dependent on the order of death.

EXAMPLE 13.13

With a joint and 2/3 survivor annuity, the payment reduces to 2/3 the original payment upon the first death. If Doug and Mary have a joint and 2/3 survivor annuity that pays 600 per month, upon the death of either Doug or Mary, the payment will reduce to 400 per month. The justification for such a reduction is that upon the first death, the survivor will need less income since there is only one person alive. In return, a larger payment can be provided while both are alive.

Now suppose Doug retires and his employer provides a payout annuity that is based on both his life and that of his wife, Mary. The annuity is for 600 per month as long as Doug is alive. However, if Mary is the only one alive, the annuity will only pay 400. In other words, it provides the following payments:

Status	Payment
Doug and Mary Alive	600
Doug Alive, Mary Dead	600
Mary Alive, Doug Dead	400

The logic behind such an annuity is that Doug earned the retirement benefit and should not receive a reduction in the payment as long as he is alive. However, as above, if Doug dies, Mary will not need as much income because her expenses will be less than the combined expenses of Doug and Mary.

13.2.4.2.3.4 Structured settlements

A structured settlement is a special payout annuity usually in conjunction with the settlement of a lawsuit. The payments are negotiated between the parties of the lawsuit or are determined by the court as part of the settlement. The defendant is required to purchase a structured settlement from a life insurance company to assure that required future payments will be made. Future payments may be certain (guaranteed), may be life contingent, or both. The payments frequently vary over time and may contain large lump sum payments at certain milestone dates. For example, if the plaintiff is a child, there might be large payments at ages 18, 19, 20, and 21 with the intent that these payments will cover the of cost college for the child.

The mortality table used to calculate the cost of structured settlements is often a special mortality table intended to reflect mortality of the injured party, who often has a shortened life expectancy due to the events that caused the lawsuit. Substandard mortality tables may also be used for reserves as mentioned in Section 18.2.3.3.

13.2.5 EXERCISES

13.7 Complete Table 13.14 for each annuity scenario listed below.

TABLE 13.14 Table to Be Completed for Exercise 13.7

End of Year	Premium at Beginning of Year	Fund Value	Surrender Value
1			
2			
...			
20			

Annuity Scenario 1: A single premium fixed annuity with a premium of 100,000. The interest rate credited is 5% for the first 10 years and 6% during years 11–20. The annuity has the surrender charges listed in Table 13.11. There is no partial free withdrawal or MVA.

Annuity Scenario 2: A single premium fixed annuity with a premium of 75,000. The interest rate credited is 8% for all years. The annuity has the surrender charges listed in Table 13.11. The policy owner can withdraw up to 10% of the account value without a surrender charge. There is no MVA.

Annuity Scenario 3: A single premium fixed annuity with a premium of 100,000. The interest rate credited is 5% for all years. The annuity has the surrender charges listed in Table 13.11. The annuity also has the MVA formula in Example 13.9.

There is no MVA after the end of the surrender charge. The yield rate on 10-year Treasury Notes on the date of issue was 5.5%. The yield rate on 10-year Treasury Notes on the date of surrender was

5.0%. The policy owner can withdraw up to 10% of the account value without a surrender charge or MVA. The surrender value for the fund value that is subject to the surrender charge and MVA is determined by first adjusting the fund value by the MVA and then applying the surrender charge to that balance.

Annuity Scenario 4: A flexible premium fixed annuity has an annual premium of 5,000 paid at the beginning of each year. The interest rate for all years is 6%. The annuity has the surrender charges listed in Table 13.11. The policy owner can withdraw up to 10% of the account value without a surrender charge. There is no MVA.

13.8 Jean bought a variable annuity on December 31, 2000 by paying a premium of 100,000. The fund value was invested in a mutual fund that exactly replicated the S&P 500 Index. There were no expense charges except for an M&E charge of 75 bp.
Show that the end of the year fund value for this annuity is given in Table 13.15.

TABLE 13.15 Development of Fund Values

End of Year	S&P 500 Index	Premium at Beginning of Year	Fund Value	Total Fund Value Charge
	1320.280			0.750%
2001	1148.083	100,000.00	86,207.54	
2002	879.819	-	65,417.52	
2003	1111.916	-	82,184.05	
2004	1211.916	-	88,958.93	
2005	1248.293	-	90,961.91	
2006	1400.634	-	101,380.67	
2007	1468.355	-	105,522.08	
2008	903.255	-	64,120.22	
2009	1115.100	-	78,677.77	
2010	1257.636	-	88,144.55	

1. If the variable annuity had a guaranteed minimum death benefit that guaranteed a return of premium, determine the death benefit that would be paid on:
   a) December 31, 2006
   b) December 31, 2008
   c) December 31, 2010

   Assume that this benefit is included in the variable annuity that Jean purchased and that there is no additional cost for this benefit.
2. Jean adds a guaranteed minimum death benefit rider with a high water mark provision. The rider provides a death benefit equal to the highest fund value on any past anniversary. The cost to add this rider is an annual fund charge of 10 bp. Determine the death benefit that would be paid on:
   a) December 31, 2006
   b) December 31, 2008
   c) December 31, 2010

   Note that you will have to recalculate the fund values based on the M&E charge of 75 bp plus the rider charge of 10 bp for a total charge of 85 bp.

3. Jean adds a guaranteed minimum death benefit rider with a roll-up provision using 4%. (This is instead of the rider in 3, not in addition to the rider in 3.) The cost to add the rider with a roll-up provision is an annual fund charge of 25 bp. Determine the death benefit that would be paid on:
   a) December 31, 2006
   b) December 31, 2008
   c) December 31, 2010

Note that you will have to recalculate the fund values.

13.9 James bought a variable annuity on December 31, 2000 by paying a premium of 100,000. The fund value was invested in a mutual fund that exactly replicated the S&P 500 Index. There were no expense charges except for an M&E charge of 50 bp.
James has the choice of the following four GLB riders:

Rider 1 provides a guaranteed minimum income benefit after 10 years. The income benefit will be determined using the greater of the fund value or the premium accumulated at an annual effective interest rate of 3%. The cost for this rider is 30 bp.

Rider 2 provides a guaranteed withdrawal value of 20% of the premium per year over 5 years once 10 years has passed. This rider does not include a step up provision. The cost for this rider is 20 bp.

Rider 3 is a guaranteed fund value rider that provides the policy owner may withdraw as a lump sum the greater of the current fund value, the premium paid, or the highest fund value at the end of each five-year period after issue. The funds must be invested in the stock market at all times. The cost of this rider is 35 bp.

Rider 4 is a lifetime benefits rider. It guarantees a lifetime benefit of 6.5% of the base amount. The base amount is the greater of the premium paid or the fund value at the end of each five-year period following issue. The cost for this rider is 30 bp.

Determine:

1. Under Rider 1, the monthly income James could receive at the end of 10 years if the payout rate was 6 per 1,000 of value.
2. Under Rider 2, the amount that James could withdraw each year for 5 years.
3. Under Rider 3, the amount that James would receive if he surrendered his contract at the end of 10 years.
4. Under Rider 4, the lifetime annual income that James could receive after 10 years.

13.10 Using the spreadsheet provided with Example 13.12, calculate the annual payout each year for 10 years under a variable payout annuity issued to an annuitant age 90 that is invested in the S&P 500 Index as of December 31, 1995. The AIR on the annuity is 4%. The single premium paid is one million.
Assume the following mortality table:

Age	l_x	Age	l_x
90	20	96	10
91	19	97	7
92	18	98	4
93	16	99	2
94	14	100	0
95	12		

CHAPTER 14
External Forces and Life and Annuity Products

There are several external factors that influence the life and annuity products offered in countries around the world. We will discuss four factors related to the North American market:

- Cultural and social factors;
- Demographics;
- Economic and business environment; and
- Government and regulatory.

14.1 Cultural and Social Factors

14.1.1 Demand for Life Insurance

In North America, cultural/social and demographic forces have resulted in a slow continuous decline in demand for life insurance; hence insurance companies have needed to do two things:

- Remake themselves as major participants in the annuity/savings market; and
- Vastly increase the complexity of life insurance products to compete in a shrinking market.

The first was facilitated by the fact that annuity products enjoy a tax-preferred status. The second was facilitated by advancing computer technology.

14.1.1.1 The need for life insurance.

North Americans are characterized by a relatively high degree of individualism and self-sufficiency. Each adult member of these societies is expected to manage the financial risk of untimely death. Family and friends are generally not expected to help manage this risk. Products are designed to meet different risk profiles and play a significant role in wealth accumulation and preservation.

14.1.2 Attitudes Toward Discrimination

Societal attitudes toward discrimination will determine the underwriting bases that can be employed in determining prices for insurance products. As late as 1960, some U.S. life insurance companies priced life insurance products on the basis of race. African Americans were charged higher premiums than Caucasians. This was due to the fact African Americans had lower life expectancies than Caucasians. As society changed in its attitude toward racial discrimination, race-based pricing began to be regarded as unfair and became illegal.

Although it might be viewed as discriminatory, gender-based pricing of life insurance and annuity products in the United States is generally not viewed as unfair or illegal. With the exception of Montana, where gender based life product pricing is not permitted, it is accepted that differences in longevity between males and females are real and can be reflected in life insurance pricing.

It is interesting to note that in 2011, the highest court of the European Union ruled that insurers could no longer charge different premium or offer different benefits to men and women because it is gender discrimination. This ruling applied to all types of insurance (not just life insurance) as well as the benefits provided by pension plans.

14.2 Demographic Trends

Demographic trends affect the demand for life insurance and annuity products throughout the world. In North America, the most influential trends have been the aging population and the increasing number of female wage earners.

The percentage of population in North America over the age of 65 will be increasing significantly over the next 15 years as the Baby Boomers age.[1] The Baby Boomer generation is influential because of its size, but also because of its financial affluence. The aging of this population over the last 15 years has influenced the demand for life and annuity products during that period and is bound to influence the demand for products in the future.

Another major demographic influence has been the increase in the number of female wage earners. For families with two adults, this results in two wage earners in the family. This increases the wealth and disposable income of these families.

Life insurance companies have experienced a strong growth in the demand for savings products, particularly deferred annuity products. The growth has been driven by the aging population. As the Baby Boomers approach retirement age, they have increased their savings rate. The life insurance industry has benefited from this increase by aggressively pursuing the savings dollars with innovative deferred annuity products. The indexed deferred annuity and the various riders attached to variable deferred annuities discussed in the previous chapter have all been introduced over the last 10 years to attract additional money into life insurance company products.

To a lesser extent, the increase in two wage earner families has also positively influenced deferred annuity sales as these families have more income and can afford to save more than a similarly situated family with only one wage earner.

There has been a strong increase in the demand for long-term care products as the population ages. Long-term care is considered a health product and is not discussed in detail in this section. However, the need for long-term care has led to some innovative combinations of life insurance and long-term care insurance riders. This combination was described in Section 13.1.6.8.

During the period from 2000 to 2010, a few life insurance companies have also sold a combination of deferred annuity with long-term care benefits. The long-term care benefits were linked to the fund value of the deferred annuity. Payments for long-term care reduce the fund value of the annuity. The reduction was generally not on a one-for-one basis. In other words, the fund value was only reduced by a portion (e.g., 80 percent) of the amount paid as long term care benefits. Beginning in 2010, the U.S. government has changed the way that

1 While there is no definitive definition, the Baby Boomer generation is generally considered to be those born between 1946 and 1964.

such benefits are taxed making an annuity-long term care combination more attractive. As a result, many additional life insurance companies have entered this market.

Over the last 10 years, there has been a gradual reduction in the demand for life insurance products.[2] While there has been a growth in certain markets, the overall trend has been downward. Part of this decrease is attributable to demographic trends. Families with two wage earners feel less need for life insurance protection. If one wage earner dies, the family may feel that they could get along on the other wage earner's income. Both wage earners may have group life insurance provided by their employer so there is less need to buy life insurance. Families with two wage earners and no children may not see the need for any life insurance. If one wage earner dies, the other wage earner will be self-sufficient and there are no children with whom to be concerned.

While the overall demand for life insurance has decreased, there has been a growth in life insurance sales in certain segments, which has been driven by demographic trends. For example, life insurance can be purchased for estate tax planning purposes. In many countries, there is a tax that is imposed by the government upon the transfer of an estate from the deceased to the heirs of the deceased. Life insurance may be purchased to help pay this estate tax upon the death of the insured. In the United States, life insurance that pays upon the death of the last survivor is usually purchased as there is no tax upon the transfer of the estate between spouses.

Another growth area for life insurance has been policies purchased to cover final expenses. These are generally smaller policies issued at an older age with limited underwriting. A specialized market is the pre-need market in which the insured purchases a life insurance policy in combination with a pre-planned funeral. In the pre-need market, the funeral home sells the life insurance policy at the time the funeral is planned. The death benefit of the insurance policy will pay for the funeral upon the death of the insured. Most of the pre-need policies are sold with a single premium. Other final expense policies are generally whole life insurance with premiums payable for life.

Other expanding markets are women and the elderly. Since more women are employed, there is a greater need for life insurance. Since a larger proportion of the population is older, there is greater demand for life insurance at older ages.

Life insurance companies and their actuaries have been exploring methods of providing protection against a person living too long. This is often referred to as *longevity insurance.* The main risk being insured is that a person will live too long and as a result will exhaust their retirement savings prior to death. For example, single premium immediate annuities as described in Section 13.2.4 could be considered to be longevity insurance. They provide a lifetime income as long as the annuitant is alive. While the demand for immediate annuities is expected to grow, they have not been popular in the United States. The primary reason probably is that purchasers consider them relatively expensive for the benefit paid.

A few life insurance companies in the United States have recently developed a deferred immediate annuity that is more deserving of the title of longevity insurance. This product is

2 This is based on the number of individual life insurance policies issued from 1999 to 2009. The number of policies issued has decreased at an annualized rate of 1.4 percent per year over the last 10 years. American Council of Life Insurers 2010 Life Insurers Fact Book, Washington, DC, Page 66, Table 7.1.

designed to pay the annuitant a benefit beginning at a designated older age such as age 85. The potential downside of this policy is that if the annuitant dies before the designated age, then no benefit is paid to the annuitant or the annuitant's beneficiaries. This permits the payout amount to be increased substantially due to survivorship.

EXAMPLE 14.1

James wants to purchase a deferred payout annuity. James has his 55th birthday today. Using the 2000 Annuity Table with interest at 6%, calculate the single premium James would have to pay today for each of the following deferred annuities. Assume there are no expenses in the premium.

- The annuity will pay an annual income of 50,000 on his birthday beginning at age 85. If James dies prior to age 85, no benefit will be paid.
- The annuity will pay an annual income of 50,000 on his birthday beginning at age 85. If James dies prior to age 85, his premium will be returned without interest.
- The annuity will pay an annual income of 50,000 on his birthday beginning at age 85. If James dies prior to age 85, his premium will be returned with interest at 6%.

For the first annuity with no death benefit, the single premium is

$$\sum_{t=30}^{\infty} v^t \, {}_tp_{55} = 26{,}984.21.$$

For the second annuity with a death benefit of a return of premium without interest, the single premium is

$$\frac{\left(\sum_{t=30}^{\infty} v^t \, {}_tp_{55}\right)}{\left(1 - \sum_{t=0}^{29} v^{t+0.5} \, {}_tp_{55} q_{55+t}\right)} = 32{,}625.40.$$

For the third annuity with a death benefit of a return of premium with interest, the single premium is

$$\frac{\left(\sum_{t=30}^{\infty} v^t \, {}_tp_{55}\right)}{\left(1 - \sum_{t=0}^{29} v^{t+0.5}(1+i)^{t+0.5} \, {}_tp_{55} q_{55+t}\right)} = \frac{\left(\sum_{t=30}^{\infty} v^t \, {}_tp_{55}\right)}{\left(1 - \sum_{t=0}^{29} {}_tp_{55} q_{55+t}\right)}$$

$$= \frac{\left(\sum_{t=30}^{\infty} v^t \, {}_tp_{55}\right)}{{}_{30}p_{55}} = v^{30} \sum_{t=0}^{\infty} v^t \, {}_tp_{85} = 54{,}307.69.$$

A spreadsheet detailing these calculations is included in the online material supporting this text.

It is obvious that a significantly lower premium is required when no death benefit is paid.

14.2.1 EXERCISE

14.1 Julie wants to purchase a deferred payout annuity by paying a single premium of 10,000 today. Today is Julie's 25th birthday. Using the 2000 Annuity Table with interest at 8%, calculate the annual payment that Julie would receive beginning at age 75 under each of the following deferred annuities. Assume there are no expenses in the premium.

- The annuity will pay an annual income on Julie's birthday beginning at age 75. If Julie dies prior to age 75, no benefit will be paid.
- The annuity will pay an annual income on Julie's birthday beginning at age 75. If Julie dies prior to age 75, her premium will be returned without interest.
- The annuity will pay an annual income on Julie's birthday beginning at age 75. If Julie dies prior to age 75, her premium will be returned with interest at 8%.

14.3 Economic and Business Environment

14.3.1 Investment Markets and Investment Returns

Economic factors such as economic cycles, inflation and deflation, as well as investment markets and investment returns, influence a life insurance company. For example, premium payment patterns can be influenced by investment markets and returns. If investment returns are higher than expected, fewer premiums might be paid into the contract because less premium would be needed to keep the policy in force.

14.3.2 Interest Rates

Interest rates merit special mention here because they influence a variety of financial considerations. Typical life insurance asset earnings are influenced by the level of interest rates. Crediting rates for products such as deferred annuities and universal life are generally related to the current level of interest rates. Extreme situations can develop when the actual earned rates of the assets backing the liability approach a product's guaranteed crediting rate. Reserve valuation rates are a function of specific treasury rates in the year prior to issue. Even a variable product's performance can be influenced by the level of interest rates since the return of equity and other asset classes in the separate account vary by the movement of interest rates.

14.3.3 Economic Cycles

An economic cycle can also influence the insurance industry. For instance, in a recessionary phase there may be fewer mergers and acquisitions due to the strained current financial situations of both the acquirer and the acquired. A prolonged period of strong or poor performance of the stock market can influence the sales of variable products.

14.3.4 Temporary Market Conditions

Even temporary market conditions can wreak havoc on life insurance companies' financial performance. Whereas the discussion so far has emphasized more common financial characteristics such as risk and return characteristics of assets, liquidity and lack of diversification can also result in grave financial consequences. For example, in 1991 Executive Life failed due primarily to an excessive exposure to junk bonds at a time when the junk bond market plummeted. Mutual Benefit also failed that year primarily as a result of excessive investment in commercial mortgages and real estate during a weak economy that led to corporate downsizing and empty office space.

A more recent example was the financial crisis of 2008 and 2009. It resulted in the collapse of and, in some cases, the bailout by the national government of large financial institutions. Stock markets suffered large losses on a global basis.

The financial crisis was triggered by a liquidity shortfall in the United States banking system. The collapse of the U.S. housing market caused values of securities based on the real estate prices to plummet. Many life insurance companies in the United States participated heavily in these securities. A few life insurance companies failed as a result of the severe reduction in the value of these and related assets. Further, as a result, many of life insurance companies suffered significant reductions in their capital and surplus.

14.3.5 Mergers and Acquisitions

The highly competitive life insurance industry comprises firms of various sizes. There is a general view that the U.S. insurance market is oversaturated and that some consolidation over the next few years is expected, especially since merger activity was fairly slow over the recent relatively weak economic period from 2008 to 2010. Possible benefits of merging include operational expense savings, enhanced distribution channels, better risk distribution, stronger financial positions, and tax benefits.

14.3.6 Corporate Structure

The life insurance industry includes firms with various profiles. The players range from large companies that offer a broad variety of products through very large and diverse distribution channels to small companies that specialize in niche markets.

While most life insurance companies are stock companies, there are also life insurance companies that use a mutual company structure. The major difference between the stock and mutual structures is that the latter is owned by the policy owners with profits effectively being distributed via policy dividends. Management objectives, product design and financial reporting have significant differences in these two corporate models.

14.4 Government Influences

Regulation and globalization is another important environmental trend. Globalization is international business activity and is influenced by large multinational companies and international acquisitions and alliances. According to Jennifer Rankin (2003) several factors now exist that are sparking an increased interest in globalization. For instance, many countries are moving away from government control and their protectionist pasts to take a more market-driven approach to their economy. They are changing insurance regulations to encourage a stable, properly managed and thriving industry. Countries such as India are privatizing state-owned companies and opening up their markets to investment by foreign companies.

To sell products in international markets, a company must become familiar with the different characteristics of the target business environment such as the target market itself, insurance and general business regulations, taxation policies, business practices, and standards of practice. Product designs must meet the needs of the local consumers such that previously successful domestic products may not now be appropriate. Product assumptions such as mortality and lapse rates may be very different than they were when priced for a U.S. market. In addition, financial reporting and taxation may be significantly different in these international domains. Operating expenses can be significantly different abroad as factors such as workers' rights and real estate costs must be considered. Investment opportunities may also vary from domestic markets.

14.4.1 Regulation

The life insurance industry in most countries is highly regulated. These regulations have a major influence on the products offered. Regulations may be imposed by the federal government or by state or provincial governments. In some cases, even local governments may impose regulations.

As stated by Callahan, et. al. (2000):

> [M]ost governments regulate insurance through solvency laws and market conduct laws. ***Solvency laws*** are designed to ensure that insurance companies are able to meet their debts and pay policy benefits when they come due. Generally, these laws regulate an insurer's capitalization, liquidity, investments, reserves, and policy design. ***Market conduct laws*** are designed to ensure that insurance companies conduct their businesses fairly and ethically. These laws regulate a range of company operations, including company management, marketing, underwriting, policyholder service, and claims.

In the United States, solvency and market conduct issues are generally regulated at the state level. In Canada, market conduct issues are regulated at the provincial level while solvency issues are regulated at the federal level. For most other countries, both market conduct and solvency issues are regulated at the federal level.

In the United States, life and annuity products must comply with the Standard Nonforfeiture Law, which is considered a market conduct law as it requires that the life insurance company provide certain minimum benefits upon the termination of a life insurance or annuity contract.[3] When the Standard Nonforfeiture Law requires nonforfeiture values, the law requires a cash surrender value that will be paid in cash to the policy owner when the contract is terminated.

The Standard Nonforfeiture Law specifies the minimum cash surrender value that must be provided. The life insurance company can provide a larger cash surrender value if they want to do so. For traditional life insurance policies, the cash value is usually determined by a formula specified in the Standard Nonforfeiture Law. For UL, VUL, and deferred annuities, the cash value is usually calculated as the fund value less a surrender charge. In this case, the Standard Nonforfeiture Law will specify the maximum surrender charge that may be deducted from the fund value.

3 There are certain exceptions where nonforfeiture values do not have to be provided. For example, as previously mentioned, for term insurance that ends prior to attained age 70.

In addition to the cash surrender value, for life insurance contracts, the Standard Nonforfeiture Law requires that an actuarially equivalent paid up insurance option also be provided to the policy owner.

In Canada, nonforfeiture values are not required.

Nonforfeiture requirements are discussed in detail in Section 18.3.

Life insurance contracts and annuity contracts are long-term contracts that can last in excess of 80 years. The life insurance company is making a promise to pay amount(s) in the future in return for the payment of premiums now. Therefore, the life insurance company is incurring a liability as it collects the premium. Regulation requires that life insurance companies record these liabilities on their balance sheets. These liabilities are called reserves. To assure the solvency of the life insurance company, assets equal to or in excess of the reserves must be maintained by the company. These assets are then available to pay the promised benefits in the future when they come due.

The regulations of all countries as part of their solvency laws require life insurance companies to hold reserves. However, there is no general uniformity as to the reserving methods across different countries. Even within a country, there may be multiple methods of calculating reserves. For example, in the United States, it is common for a life insurance company to calculate at least three sets of reserves. Statutory reserves are required to be used for financial statements submitted to state insurance regulators. Tax reserves are required to calculate income for the purpose of calculating federal income taxes. Finally, when reporting income according to Generally Accepted Accounting Principles (GAAP), then GAAP reserves are required. GAAP statements are generally required for stock companies registered with the Securities and Exchange Commission.

While reserves do not affect the total profits earned by a life insurance product, they do determine how the profits are recognized. Therefore, a change in the reserve requirements will change the pattern of profits that emerge from a life insurance product. The adoption of more strenuous reserve requirements results in profits emerging later than under a less strenuous reserve requirement. Since reserve requirements are determined by regulation (or accounting bodies for GAAP), reserve requirements are an external force.

We will discuss reserves in greater detail in Section 18.1.

14.4.2 Taxes

Besides direct regulation as discussed, the methods by which a government taxes both corporations and individuals have a big effect on life insurance companies and their products. For individuals, income taxes and inheritance taxes tend to have the largest influence. For corporations, premium taxes and income taxes will be considered.

Most countries impose an income tax on individuals. Also, life insurance and annuity products often receive a favorable tax treatment. Therefore, the purchase of life insurance products or annuities may be driven by the desire to eliminate or reduce the taxes to be paid. In the United States, individuals are taxed on income. Life insurance and annuities receive favorable tax treatment and may be used to defer payment of taxes, possibly indefinitely in the case of life insurance.

14.4.2.1 Individual income taxes in the United States

Life insurance products are defined in the IRC. If a product meets this definition, then it receives favorable tax treatment as the *inside buildup* is not taxable and the proceeds paid on death are not taxable to the beneficiary. Furthermore, under certain circumstances, the premiums may be deductible if paid by a corporation.

The inside buildup on a life insurance policy is the growth of the cash surrender value of the policy. For UL and VUL products, the fund value earns interest each month which increases the fund value. Under U.S. tax law, the interest that is earned is not taxed as long as the policy remains in force. If the policy remains in force until the death of the insured, then the inside buildup is never taxed. For traditional policies, while the mechanics are not as transparent, the cash surrender values function similarly to the fund values and part of the growth in the cash surrender values are due to the interest earned.

If a life insurance policy is surrendered, then at that time, any gain in the contract is taxable. Generally, the gain in the policy is the value received in excess of the premiums paid. It should be noted that this gain will be less than the interest earned by the policy because the cost of the life insurance protection and expenses associated with the policy is also reflected in the surrender value.

EXAMPLE 14.2

James buys a 100,000 whole life policy with a single premium of 34,000. Twenty years later, when he is 65, he surrenders the policy for its cash surrender value of 53,000. The gain on the contract is 53,000 − 34,000 = 19,000. This amount would be included as taxable income in the year that he surrenders the contract.

If the insurance company took the 34,000 single premium and invested it at 4.5% interest, at the end of 20 years, the single premium would have grown to approximately 82,000.[4] The difference between the 82,000 and 53,000 includes the cost of insurance protection, expenses, and profit for the life insurance company.

When the insured dies, the death benefit is paid to the beneficiary. The beneficiary does not have to pay taxes on the death benefit. Therefore, life insurance can be used to transfer wealth tax-free.

Deferred annuities in the United States also enjoy tax-free inside buildup as long as the deferred annuity remains in force. If the annuity is surrendered for its cash surrender value, then any gain in the contract is taxable. Generally, the gain in the policy is the value received in excess of the premiums paid. Unlike life insurance, upon the death of the annuity owner, the gain in the contract will be taxable to the beneficiary.

These tax advantages are important to life insurance companies. Individuals and corporations purchase life insurance and annuity contracts to take advantage of tax status. Corporations may purchase life insurance policies as an investment vehicle because they expect the life insurance policy to provide a better after-tax return than would be provided by other investments that do not receive the same tax preferences. There are life insurance companies that have large blocks

---

4 $34{,}000(1.045)^{20} = 81{,}998$.

of Corporate Owned Life Insurance (COLI) and/or large blocks of Bank Owned Life Insurance (BOLI). COLI and BOLI are generally purchased because of the tax preferences.

As with corporations, wealthy individuals may also purchase life insurance to take advantage of the tax preferences. Similarly, many of the purchasers of deferred annuities buy the deferred annuity because the interest earned is not taxed until it is received upon termination of the annuity.

These tax preferences are available because the U.S. government has made a conscious decision that life insurance and annuities are important vehicles in protecting the financial security of the policy owners. Of course, this could change in the future as the government recognizes that these tax preferences may not be used for the intended purposes. For example, in 1982, the tax laws were changed such that a deferred annuity surrendered prior to attained age 59½ is not only subject to taxes on any gain in the contract, but is also subject to a 10 percent penalty tax on the gain over and above the normal income tax.

14.4.2.2 Inheritance tax

In the United States, a deceased's estate may be subject to inheritance taxes when it is passed to the heirs of the estate. Life insurance policies have been developed that target this market. The death benefits from these policies are paid to the heirs as beneficiaries and can be used to pay the inheritance tax. This is especially attractive because the death benefit is not taxable to the beneficiary.

This market has been in a state of flux in the United States as the inheritance tax has been uncertain. For example, during 2010, there is no inheritance tax. However, the inheritance tax will again be in place in 2011.

14.4.2.3 Corporate taxes

Just as the actions of an individual or corporation purchasing life insurance are influenced by tax laws, the actions of a life insurance company are influenced by tax laws. One of the primary influences of tax laws is on the products offered by the life insurance company. First, in the United States, the Internal Revenue Code includes a definition of life insurance. Therefore, almost invariably, life insurance products are designed to remain within this definition so the policy receives the favorable tax treatment. Secondly, life insurance and annuity products are often developed and marketed to take advantage of the tax preferences given to them. As mentioned, COLI and BOLI are only viable because of the tax deferral that occurs in life insurance. Deferred annuities are often compared on an after tax basis with other investments, which emphasizes the advantage of deferring of taxes on the interest income earned.

Life insurance companies also are tax payers and these taxes are a second way in which tax laws influence life insurance companies. The taxes paid are typically premium taxes and income taxes. Premium taxes are usually a percent of the premium collected. Premium taxes in the United States vary by product and state. They are typically low for annuities with there being no premium tax in many states. For life insurance, premium taxes are typically about two percent, but may exceed five percent in certain jurisdictions. The costs are typically built into the premiums that the policy owner pays.

Life insurance companies are also subject to federal income taxes and generally life insurers attempt to minimize the income taxes paid.

CHAPTER 15
Pricing

When an actuary at a life insurance company determines the premiums and other elements of a life insurance policy or deferred annuity, this is generically referred to as pricing. There are many elements used in the pricing of a life insurance policy or a deferred annuity and we will explore those elements in this chapter. Those elements include:

- Profitability of the product;
- Pricing methodology;
- Pricing tools;
- Pricing inputs including investment returns, expenses, mortality and persistency;
- Compliance with regulatory requirements, including nonforfeiture benefits and reserves; and
- Taxes.

In this chapter, when we refer to a *product*, we are referring to either a life insurance policy or an annuity. To the extent that our discussion is specific to a life insurance policy or an annuity, we will reference those specifically. Otherwise, when we discuss a product, we are referring to either.

15.1 Measuring Profitability

15.1.1 Definition of Profits

Profits can be thought of as the amount of money that a life insurance company has left over once the product is no longer in force. However, in determining the profitability of a product, the pattern of the profits is also important. For example, Table 15.1 lists the year-by-year profits for two products being priced.

TABLE 15.1 Book Profits for Two Products

Policy Year	Book Profits for Product 1	Book Profits for Product 2
1	(1,000)	(2,000)
2	–	(600)
3	100	–
4	150	50
5	200	125
6	250	200
7	300	275
8	350	350
9	400	425
10	450	500
11	500	575
12	550	650

(Continued)

TABLE 15.1 Book Profits for Two Products *(Continued)*

Policy Year	Book Profits for Product 1	Book Profits for Product 2
13	600	725
14	650	800
15	700	875
16	750	950
17	800	1,025
18	850	1,100
19	900	1,175
20	950	1,250
Total	**8,450**	**8,450**

As you review these two profit streams, you will note:

- The total profits over the 20-year period are the same;
- The emergence of the profits over those 20 years is considerably different. Product 1 generates profits much earlier that Product 2; and
- For both products, there is a loss (negative profit) during the first year or two of the product. This is a common profit pattern especially for life insurance policies. We will discuss this more later.

If you were the actuary for a life insurance company, which of these profit patterns would you prefer? Most companies would prefer the profit pattern for Product 1 because it generated profits earlier than Product 2. This permits the life insurance company to use those profits to support more new products or to provide dividends for the stockholders of the company.

You might think that measuring the profitability for a product during pricing such as in Table 15.1 would be a relatively straightforward process. Unfortunately, that is not the case. First, there are multiple accounting frameworks that can be used to measure profits. The difference in profits could be entirely due to different patterns of establishing reserves. Reserves do not affect the overall profits from a given product. The reserves only affect the pattern of profits. The total amount of earnings only depends on the cash flows, which are not affected by the accounting basis or reserve basis.

Additionally, there are many different methods of measuring profits. While we will consider these complexities shortly, for now we will ignore these differences.

15.1.2 Book Profits

You will note that the profits in Table 15.1 are labeled as *Book Profits.* Book Profits is the standard method of measuring profits during pricing. Book Profits only reflect the profits for each year generated by the product being priced. Book Profits do not include investment income earned on previous duration's gains or losses. In general, Book Profits are calculated as:

$$BP_t = Prem_t + I_t - E_t - B_t - \Delta Res - \Delta ReqSur$$

Where:

- BP_t is the Book Profit at the end of Period t;
- $Prem_t$ is the premium in period t;
- I_t is the investment income earned on the cash flows, reserves and required surplus during period t;
- E_t is the expenses (including taxes and commissions) during period t;
- B_t is the benefits paid during period t;
- ΔRes is the increase in the reserves during period t; and
- $\Delta ReqSur$ is the increase in required surplus during period t.

Books profits and their use in the pricing of life insurance products were first introduced in a ground breaking paper by James C. H. Anderson (1959).[1] More than 50 years later, Anderson's paper still provides the basic underpinnings for the pricing work and models used by actuaries. We will explore book profits in detail in Section 16.4.

It should be noted that while the Anderson Method was originally directed at life insurance, the concept is applicable across most long term insurance products sold by life insurance companies including deferred and payout annuities and individual health insurance products.

15.1.3 Accounting System

The measurement of some of the items in the definition of book profits is a function of the accounting system being used to price the product. In the United States, life insurance companies commonly report financial results to state regulators on an accounting basis that is referred to as Statutory Accounting while they report profits to their shareholders and the financial markets using a GAAP Accounting basis. In Canada, the same accounting method is used to report profits to regulators as to the financial markets and the company's shareholders. However, this method is not the same as either method used in the United States although it is closer to GAAP than to Statutory.

The accounting basis used in pricing can affect most of the components of book profits listed. The reserves required by a life insurance company are completely a function of the accounting system. Additionally, the recognition of premiums and expenses can be a function of the accounting basis. For example, Statutory Accounting requires that all expenses incurred be recognized immediately. Therefore, expenses associated with the issue of the policy are immediately recognized as a reduction in profits. On the other hand, under GAAP Accounting, certain expenses are considered to be deferrable which means that they are recognized over the life of the policy instead of immediately when the policy issued.

Additionally, since required surplus is often a function of reserves, it can also be function of the accounting basis. Finally, investment income is a function of both reserves and required surplus so it also is determined by the accounting system. Therefore, the only item that is not a function of the accounting system is the benefits component.

1 A copy is available at: http://www.soa.org/library/research/transactions-of-society-of-actuaries/1959/january/tsa59v11n30ab42.pdf and is available with the book's online resources.

In Section 18.1, we will discuss reserves in detail. In the meantime, our discussions will assume that reserves are based on the accounting system in use without specifying the accounting system. It should be noted that in the United States, most companies price products using the Statutory Accounting basis.

15.2 Profit Measures

While a pricing model will produce a series of periodic book profits similar to Table 15.1, these periodic profits are summarized into a single metric that can be used to compare the profits from several different scenarios. These single metrics are called pricing measures and we will discuss the most common of those pricing measures.

15.2.1 Return on Investment

The most widely used profit measure is the *return on investment* (ROI), which is the internal rate of return calculated treating negative book profits as investments and positive book profits as returns. The internal rate of return is the interest rate at which the present value of the book profits is zero.

When working with book profits, it is important to distinguish between the profits on a block of policies sold and profits on a single policy. When working with a single policy (which is what is done in all the examples here) the profits are per policy sold, not per surviving policy (as is often the case in reserve calculations). This reflects the fact that for each policy sold there is a probability that in a later year it will generate no book profits (because the insured has died or the policy has lapsed or surrendered).

EXAMPLE 15.1

The following book profits resulted over a three-year period:

End of Year	Book Profit
1	−100
2	50
3	66

The ROI over 3 years for this pattern of book profits is 10% since

$$-100(v^1) + 50(v^2) + 66(v^3) = 0 \text{ where } v = (1.1)^{-1}.$$

The ROI cannot usually be calculated directly using algebra. It can be determined using an iterative approach, a financial calculator or the IRR functionality of a spreadsheet. The ROI for our two profit patterns in Table 15.1 are 23.3% for Product 1 and 12.2% for Product 2. These are calculated in the spreadsheet for Table 15.1 that is included with the online reference material for this book.

Generally, a larger ROI is preferable to a lower ROI. For Table 15.1, Product 1 generates a substantially higher ROI. This is consistent with our earlier intuitive observation that the profit pattern for Product 1 was better than the profit pattern for Product 2. Our conclusion at that time was that since both products had the same total profits and the profits emerged earlier on Product 1, then the profit pattern for Product 1 was preferable. The ROI for Product 1 is higher precisely because the profits emerge earlier.

Each life insurance company that uses ROI as a profit measure will determine what ROI is acceptable for the product being priced. Generally, the profit objective in terms of ROI is in the range of 8 to 15 percent. The ROI will be at the high end of this range for products with a higher risk (the profits are less certain). Additionally, the target ROI will often fluctuate with interest rates available on investments. In other words, if interest rates are low, a lower ROI will be acceptable. This is reasonable since you can view the initial losses incurred when a product is issued to be an investment by the life insurance company's owners and the ROI is the return on that investment. If they are going to "invest" by selling new policies of a given product, the life insurance company should compare expected return on that product with the available returns on other investments.

There are potential pitfalls or problems with ROI. One problem is that the ROI may not exist. For example, if all book profits are positive (or negative), then an ROI cannot be calculated. Additionally, depending on the pattern of book profits, it is possible to have multiple ROIs or the ROI may be an imaginary number.

Another potential pitfall is that certain profit patterns can generate a misleading ROI.

EXAMPLE 15.2

Consider Product 3 from Table 15.2.

TABLE 15.2 Product 3 Book Profits per Policy

Year	Book Profit	Year	Book Profit
1	−0.10	11	0
2	0	12	0
3	0.20	13	0
4	0	14	0
5	0	15	0
6	0	16	0
7	0	17	0
8	0	18	0
9	0	19	0
10	0	20	0

The ROI for this product is 41.4%. However, the book profits for this product are very small, and in most cases, a life insurance company probably would not want to issue a product that produced such meager book profits. The ROI is very large despite the relatively small profits because the original investment (negative profit in the first year) is very small.

EXAMPLE 15.3

Now look at the pattern of profits in Table 15.3 for Product 4.

TABLE 15.3 Product 4 book Profits

Year	Book Profit	Year	Book Profit
1	3	11	−1
2	2	12	−1
3	1	13	−1
4	0	14	−1
5	−1	15	−1
6	−1	16	−1
7	−1	17	−1
8	−1	18	−1
9	−1	19	−1
10	−1	20	−1

This pattern of book profits and losses generates an ROI of 10.5%. However, clearly this set of book profits is not acceptable. Note that if all the signs are changed the product becomes acceptable while the ROI stays at 10.5%. That is because the ROI makes the present value zero and thus the sign on the cash flows is not relevant. Furthermore, larger losses in the later years would actually increase the ROI.

The main point is that while the ROI is the most commonly used profit measure, it cannot be used without actuarial judgment. The actuary should always visually inspect the book profits to assure that unreasonable or unacceptable book profits are not generating an acceptable ROI because of these potential flaws.

15.2.2 Profit Margin

Another common profit measure is the *profit margin.* The profit margin is the present value of book profits divided by the present value of the premiums. The present values are calculated using a specified interest rate. Some companies use an interest rate that is equal to the expected investment earnings rate being used in pricing the product. Other companies use a higher interest rate to reflect the higher risk (variability of returns) in selling an insurance product as opposed to traditional investments. The higher interest rate will generally result in a lower profit margin. Profit margins expected in pricing are generally in the 4 to 7-percent range. In other words, the present value of profits is generally targeted to be 4 to 7 percent of the present value of premiums.

EXAMPLE 15.4

We will demonstrate the calculation of the profit margin with Product 5 in Table 15.4.

TABLE 15.4 Product 5

End of Year	Book Profit	Premiums
1	−100	50
2	50	45
3	66	40

If we calculate the profit margin at an annual interest rate of 5%, we make the following calculation:

$$\text{Profit Margin} = \frac{-100v + 50v^2 + 66v^3}{50 + 45v + 40v^2} = 0.05519 \text{ where } v = (1.05)^{-1}.$$

Our profit margin is 5.5%.

You will note that we have assumed that the premiums are at the beginning of the year. If this is not true (e.g., premiums are paid monthly), then the present value of premiums should be adjusted appropriately. We have also assumed that the book profits are at the end of the year. Based on our definition of book profits, that will always be the case.

You will also note that the premium decreases each year. As noted, calculations are based on policies sold and thus some insureds will die and some policy owners will stop paying premiums. Therefore, even if the product has a level premium, the actual premiums received per policy sold will not be level.

Profit margin as a profit measure is used more frequently on term insurance as the initial investment on term insurance may be small. As we noted, the ROI may not return reasonable results if the initial investment is small. It should also be noted the Profit margin can be calculated and produces reasonable results even if there are profits in all years.

Many life insurance companies look at both the profit margin and the ROI when they price products.

15.2.3 Spread Margin

A profit measure that is used primarily for deferred annuities is *spread margin*. Spread margin is not as standardized as ROI and profit margin. Spread margin expresses the profit as a percent of the fund value. This method is also referred to as *return on assets.*

The spread margin may be calculated as the present value of profits divided by the present value of the annual fund values. The present values are generally calculated at the earned rates and the beginning of the year fund values are used.

EXAMPLE 15.5

Consider the three-year period with the profits and fund values in Table 15.5.

TABLE 15.5 Spread Margin Example

Year	Book Profit	Beginning-of-Year Fund Values
1	10	5000
2	50	5250
3	60	5512

If we calculate the spread margin at an annual interest rate of 6%, we make the following calculation:

$$\text{Spread Margin} = \frac{10v + 50v^2 + 60v^3}{5000 + 5250v + 5512v^2} = 0.00702 \text{ where } v = (1.06)^{-1}.$$

This would generally be expressed as 70 bp.

As an alternative, the spread margin may be calculated on an annual basis as the profit divided by the account value. Then if a spread margin over a time period is desired, an arithmetic average is used.

EXAMPLE 15.6

Table 15.6 provides the calculation using the same values as in Example 15.6.

TABLE 15.6 Alternative Spread Margin Calculation

Year	Book Profit	Beginning-of-Year Fund Values	Annual Spread Margin
1	10	5,000	0.20%[2]
2	50	5,250	0.95%
3	60	5,512	1.09%

If a spread margin was desired over the three-year period, it is calculated as

$$\frac{0.0020 + 0.0095 + 0.0109}{3} = 0.0075 \text{ or } 0.75\% \text{ or } 75\,\text{bp}.$$

It should be noted that the two methods of calculating the spread margin produce slightly different results. Furthermore, it should be noted that, in practice, other variations may also be used.

15.2.4 Return on Equity

Return on equity (ROE) measures profits generated as a percent of equity. The ROE is usually calculated on an annual basis and then an arithmetic average is taken over the period of interest. ROE is used when a GAAP accounting basis is used. Under GAAP accounting, the profits are generally positive in all years. When this is the case, an ROI cannot be calculated. Therefore, an alternative profit measure must be used. ROE is an alternative measure that is often used in these circumstances. The equity used in the denominator will usually include both equity generated by the product and required surplus.

2 Calculated as 10/5,000. The other values in this column are similarly calculated.

As mentioned in Section 15.2.2, profit margin could also be used as the alternative measure. ROE is generally used when the company wants a measure that is more consistent with ROI.

EXAMPLE 15.7

Assume the profits and equity as in Table 15.7.

TABLE 15.7 ROE Example

Year	Profit	Equity	Annual ROE
1	0.5	8	6.25%[3]
2	1.0	9	11.11%
3	0.9	10	9.00%
4	0.8	11	7.27%
5	0.7	10	7.00%

The ROE for the five-year period is calculated as:

$$\frac{0.0625 + 0.1111 + 0.0900 + 0.0727 + 0.0700}{5} = 0.0813 = 8.13\%.$$

15.2.5 Other Measures

There are other measures or profit objectives used by life insurance companies. Generally, these other measures are secondary measures. For example, the life insurance company will look first at ROI or profit margin and then will look at other measures to be sure they are in an acceptable range.

We will discuss three of these secondary measures here:

- Surplus strain;
- Break-even year; and
- Assets as a percent of reserves.

15.2.5.1 Surplus strain

Under statutory accounting, there is usually a substantial loss in the first year that a life insurance policy is issued. This loss is known as *surplus strain*. When used as a profit measure, surplus strain is usually expressed as a percent of the first year premium. For example, if the first year premium was 100 and the first year loss was 70, the surplus strain is 70 percent. Unlike most profit measures where a larger value is preferred, the company wants to minimize the surplus strain since it measures the amount of surplus that must be invested in the first year that the product is issued.

3 Calculated as 0.50/8. The other values in this column are similarly calculated.

15.2.5.2 Break-even year

This measure is also related to the surplus strain in the first year of a life insurance product. The break-even year is the policy year during which the total profits with interest since issue becomes positive. For example, a life insurance company issues a life policy with a loss in the first year. After that initial loss, the life policy starts to generate gains, but it is the fourth year before the total profits become positive, then the break-even year will be four. It is not unusual for a life insurance product to break even as late as the 10th year.

15.2.5.3 Assets as a percent of reserves

To some extent, this measure is also related to surplus strain. This measure states that the assets accumulated at some future duration must be a certain percent of the reserves. For example, the assets after 15 years must be at least 105% of the reserves at the end of 15 years.

15.2.6 EXERCISES

15.1 If the profits for Product 4 in Table 15.3 were changed to -2 for years 11 through 20, calculate the ROI.

15.2 Calculate the profit margin for Product 5 (Table 15.4) using an annual interest rate of 6%.

15.3 Use the profits in Table 15.5 to calculate the spread margin using an annual interest rate of 8%.

15.4 You are given the information in Table 15.8 for a whole life policy based on statutory accounting and reserves.

TABLE 15.8 Values for Exercise 15.4

Policy Year	Premium Income	Book Profit with Required Surplus	Assets	Reserves	Surplus without Required Surplus
1	1,000.00	(179.59)	(158.62)	–	(158.62)
2	799.73	5.59	458.44	607.70	(149.27)
3	703.45	3.96	995.27	1,136.56	(141.29)
4	646.80	14.08	1,486.91	1,610.71	(123.80)
5	601.12	14.37	1,944.92	2,051.23	(106.32)
6	564.60	18.46	2,375.99	2,461.01	(85.02)
7	533.06	22.31	2,788.43	2,848.28	(59.84)
8	505.88	27.03	3,190.36	3,220.00	(29.64)
9	482.55	33.45	3,570.92	3,563.71	7.21
10	460.22	39.77	3,931.14	3,880.34	50.81
11	438.86	58.65	4,284.71	4,170.71	114.00
12	418.39	59.73	4,616.11	4,436.34	179.77
13	398.79	58.16	4,925.16	4,679.52	245.64
14	379.97	56.00	5,213.59	4,902.53	311.06
15	361.92	56.71	5,484.69	5,105.86	378.82
16	344.63	57.24	5,737.84	5,288.88	448.96
17	328.07	58.46	5,973.35	5,451.12	522.23
18	312.20	60.48	6,192.01	5,592.49	599.53
19	296.99	61.20	6,392.38	5,712.60	679.78
20	282.38	63.17	6,575.03	5,810.76	764.28

The information in Table 15.8 is included in a spreadsheet available as part of the online resources available with this book.

a. Calculate the ROI over 20 years for this product.
b. Calculate the Profit Margin over 20 years for this product using an annual interest rate of 5.5%.
c. Calculate the Profit Margin over 20 years for this product using the ROI from Part a as the interest rate.
d. Explain why your answer to Part c is zero.
e. Calculate the surplus strain for this product.
f. Calculate the break-even year for this product.
g. Calculate the assets as a percent of reserves at the end of 10 years, 15 years, and 20 years.

15.5 You are given the values in Table 15.9 for a whole life policy based on GAAP accounting and reserves.

TABLE 15.9 Values for Exercise 15.5

Policy Year	GAAP Net Income	Surplus with Required Surplus
1	31.34	52.97
2	28.66	92.06
3	29.77	132.56
4	31.91	174.73
5	34.27	218.69
6	36.93	264.74
7	39.78	313.23
8	42.81	364.44
9	46.09	418.37
10	49.40	474.99
11	52.69	534.30
12	55.86	596.23
13	59.10	660.92
14	62.34	728.37
15	65.49	798.44
16	68.69	871.26
17	71.90	946.81
18	75.09	1,025.06
19	78.34	1,106.10
20	81.56	1,189.85

The information in Table 15.9 is included in a spreadsheet available as part of the online resources available with this book.

a. Calculate the ROE for this product.
b. Explain why you cannot calculate a ROI for this product based on the GAAP results in Table 15.9.

15.6 You are given the values in Table 15.10 for a deferred annuity product.

TABLE 15.10 Values for Exercise 15.6

Policy Year	Book Profit	Beginning-of-the-Year Fund Value
1	100.00	100,000.00
2	1,003.95	102,820.00
3	1,023.02	104,629.63
4	1,063.41	105,362.04
5	1,105.07	104,982.74
6	1,148.02	103,491.98
7	1,192.29	100,925.38
8	1,237.91	97,352.62
9	2,302.44	82,555.02
10	2,280.69	74,382.08

The information in Table 15.10 is included in a spreadsheet available as part of the online resources available with this book.

a. Calculate the spread margin using the approach in Example 15.5 and an annual effective interest rate of 5.0%.

b. Calculate the spread margin using the approach in Example 15.6.

CHAPTER 16
Profit Testing

Profit testing is a critical component of product pricing. Profit testing is the process through which the actuary determines the profits that will result from a given set of assumptions and premiums. Profit testing will usually involve several iterations as the initial premiums and assumptions virtually never produce the desired profits.

16.1 Approaches to Profit Testing

16.1.1 Cell-Based Approach

One approach is a cell-based approach to profit testing. A cell is a given issue age, gender, and premium class. For example, a male age 35 nonsmoker would be a cell. A cell-based approach determines profit for each pricing cell using the assumptions and premiums for that cell. Each cell is expected to produce appropriate profits, which are generally about the same for each cell. The advantage of such an approach is that the distribution of business issued does not affect the aggregate profits. In other words, if most of the business is expected to be issued at ages 35 and younger, but the actual issues are predominately at age 55 and older, the aggregate profits will still be maintained because each cell produces acceptable profits.

It should be noted that a cell-based approach does not develop premiums and test the profits for every possible age, but generally for representative ages such as quinquennial or decennial ages. The premiums for the remaining ages are developed using interpolation.

There are many tools that are used to implement a cell-based approach to profit testing. One approach is an asset share.[1] An asset share is a model of a single policy cell that projects cash flows and other financial information (such as reserves) for a policy in that cell. The projection may be for the possible life of the policy or for a shorter period of time such as 20 or 30 years. An asset share can be used to project future balance sheets and income statements on multiple accounting bases as well as calculate the book profits and the profit measures that we discussed in Chapter 15. We will discuss asset shares in more detail later.

16.1.2 Model Office Approach

A model office approach is an approach where a life insurance product is priced in the aggregate. In this approach, the life insurance company will identify representative cells. For example, the life insurance company could use the following cells:

Male, Nonsmoker, Ages 5, 15, 25, 35, 45, 55, 65
Male, Smoker, Ages 25, 35, 45, 55, 65
Female, Nonsmoker, Ages 5, 15, 25, 35, 45, 55, 65
Female, Smoker, Ages 25, 35, 45, 55, 65

---

1 The term *asset share* was originally so named because it can be used to determine the assets attributable to an individual policy—that policy's share of assets—asset share.

The life insurance company determines what proportion of the policy being priced will be issued to each of the 24 cells. Profit tests are run on each of the cells and then the total aggregate profits are determined by combining the results from each of the cells using the proportion in each cell as the weight. These aggregate results are used to determine the profit measures and acceptability of the profits. In a model office approach, the profits of the individual cells are generally not considered. If the aggregate profit meets the profit objectives of the life insurance company, then the product pricing is considered sufficient.

EXAMPLE 16.1

For simplicity, assume that a life insurance company is profit testing a five-year term insurance policy. The company is using a four-cell model office with cells for ages 25, 35, 45, and 55. The book profits for each cell are listed in Table 16.1. The ROI for each cell is listed at the bottom of Table 16.1. The ROI for each cell varies. The company's goal is to achieve an ROI of 12%. The ROI for each cell except for age 35 meets our overall objective.

TABLE 16.1 Model Office Book Profits and ROI

Distribution of Issues	25%	25%	25%	25%	
	Issue Age				
Year	Age 25	Age 35	Age 45	Age 55	Total
1	−100.00	−150.00	−250.00	−500.00	−250.00
2	25.00	0.00	60.00	90.00	43.75
3	40.00	40.00	100.00	200.00	95.00
4	40.00	60.00	100.00	200.00	100.00
5	40.00	60.00	100.00	200.00	100.00
ROI	15.5%	2.1%	15.1%	12.8%	11.9%

The company assumes that sales of this term product will be evenly distributed between each cell, resulting in the aggregate book profits and aggregate ROI of 11.9% which is very close to the company's goal of 12%. It should be noted that the aggregate ROI is calculated using the aggregate profits. Calculating a weighted average ROI using the ROI of each cell is not correct.

The problem with a model office approach is that if the distribution of issues is not as expected, the profits can be substantially impacted. What will the ROI be if the actual distribution of sales is 20% for each of ages 25, 45, and 55 with 40% of the sales being at age 35? Using the spreadsheet included in the on line resources, Table 16.2 shows the results.

As expected, the ROI decreases to 10.6%, which is well below the company's objective of 12%. This is distribution risk.

TABLE 16.2 Model Office Book Profits and ROI

Distribution of Issues	20%	40%	20%	20%	
	Issue Age				
Year	Age 25	Age 35	Age 45	Age 55	Total
1	−100.00	−150.00	−250.00	−500.00	−230.00
2	25.00	0.00	60.00	90.00	35.00
3	40.00	40.00	100.00	200.00	84.00
4	40.00	60.00	100.00	200.00	92.00
5	40.00	60.00	100.00	200.00	92.00
ROI	15.5%	2.1%	15.1%	12.8%	10.6%

16.1.3 Deterministic Approach

In a deterministic approach, a company uses one set of assumptions during profit testing. This one set of assumptions is the basis used to determine the premiums and the resultant profits. A deterministic approach is reasonable when a company is confident that the assumptions used will be realized. It is commonly used to price whole life and term insurance.

In addition to the one set of scenarios used for pricing the product, the company may also calculate profits under several other scenarios in order to understand the effect of variance from the expected assumptions. The company may run tests with variations in lapses, expenses, mortality and investment returns. These additional scenarios are usually referred to as sensitivity tests. For example, the following scenarios might be used:

- 80% of expected lapses and surrenders
- 120% of expected lapses and surrenders
- 120% of expected expenses
- 120% of expected mortality for life insurance
- 80% of expected mortality for annuities
- 80% of expected investment returns

These sensitivity tests will inform the company of the change in profits that will occur under each of these scenarios. Note that these scenarios are intended to test adverse experience—higher expenses, worse mortality, and lower investment returns. For lapse, both higher and lower lapse rates are being tested. Sometimes the effect of lapse rate variances is counter-intuitive. For some products such as level premium term insurance, lower lapse rates may adversely affect the profits of the company.

In Bellis, et. al. (2010, p. 379), it is stated:

> For sensitivity testing, it is tempting to pick arbitrary changes to assumptions, such as increases or decreases of 10 percent. These are easy to understand but they don't tell you how likely the changes are.

The example clearly uses arbitrary changes to assumptions. While arbitrary adjustment do not give us the likelihood of the changes, they do tell us how sensitive to the products profits are to the changes in assumptions. This identifies the primary risks for the company and they can monitor those risks as experience develops.

Bellis, et. al. (2010, p. 379) also states:

> There are alternatives. For example:
>
> - Changes can reflect past experience. For example, the sensitivity range for an assumption could reflect a 95 percent confidence interval around the mean. However, this approach may not allow for extreme but plausible events or may be skewed by the nature of experience over the time being considered.
> - Another approach is to have a story behind each sensitivity that explains why the assumptions might turn out to be at a different value—perhaps one that seems quite extreme but is still plausible. This is not easy to do, but it is a very useful exercise to attempt. A story can make it useful to communicate the sensitivity results to others.

For life insurance products, most companies do not have sufficient data to calculate a confidence interval for determining the range of sensitivity tests. However, using past experience to determine historically worst case tests is often a good approach and does provide a basis for development of a story to support the sensitivity test.

16.1.4 Multiple Scenario Approach

Under a multiple scenario approach, several scenarios are used for profit testing. A multiple scenario approach is often used for flexible premium universal life products. Since the premium is flexible, the policy owner controls when the premium is paid and its amount. A company might complete profit testing using the following four premium payment patterns:

- A single premium paid at issue;
- A level premium paid over the life of the policy;
- A decreasing amount of premium paid each policy year; and
- Premium equal to the minimum amount of premium will be paid each year.

EXAMPLE 16.2

An illustration of premium patterns for a male age 35 is shown in Table 16.3.

These premium patterns were calculated using the universal life policy from Exercise 13.1 with a specified amount of 100,000.

Premium Pattern 1 assumes that the policy owner pays a single premium in the first year. This premium was calculated as the maximum premium allowed under the IRC.

Premium Pattern 2 is the level premium that must be paid to mature the policy for the specified amount at age 96. Maturing the policy for the specified amount means that the fund value of the policy at age 96 is equal to the specified amount.

TABLE 16.3 Premium Pattern for Profit Testing

Policy Year	Premium Pattern 1	Premium Pattern 2	Premium Pattern 3	Premium Pattern 4
1	24,704	795	795	294
2	-	795	755	299
3	-	795	717	304
4	-	795	682	312
5	-	795	648	319
6	-	795	615	319
7	-	795	584	319
8	-	795	555	319
9	-	795	527	319
10	-	795	501	319
11	-	795	476	319
12	-	795	452	319
13	-	795	430	319
14	-	795	408	319
15	-	795	388	319
16	-	795	368	385
17	-	795	350	450
18	-	795	332	480
19	-	795	316	525
20	-	795	300	570

Premium Pattern 3 starts with the premium calculated for Premium Pattern 2. However, each premium thereafter is 95% of the premium paid in the previous year. Premiums for universal life policies are flexible. If a policyholder does not pay a premium, the policy does not terminate unless the fund value goes to zero. Therefore, this pattern reflects the assumption that each year some policyholders will not pay the premium. Further, the number of policyholders skipping the premium will increase with time since issue.

Premium Pattern 4 assumes that the policy owner will pay the minimum premium permitted each year to keep the policy in force. Under this pattern of premiums, the fund value will be approximately zero at all times. You may wonder why the premium remains level during policy years 5–15. If you review the design of the product from Exercise 13.1, the per 1,000 expense charge goes to zero in the sixth policy year. Therefore, a premium of 319 is sufficient to keep the policy in force for those years. In year 16, the premiums must start increasing again as the cost of insurance rates have increased enough require a higher premium.

Premium Pattern 1 and Premium Pattern 4 are the two extremes in the premium payment pattern. By testing these premium payment patterns, the actuary can determine if an extreme premium payment pattern can cause profitability issues with a universal life product. With Premium Pattern 1, the fund value will be maximized. This means that the net amount at risk (the specified amount less the fund value) will be minimized. Therefore, the profits from the cost of insurance rates will be minimized. However, since the fund value is maximized, the profit from the interest rate spread will be maximized. With Premium Pattern 4, the fund value is minimized, resulting in a large net amount at risk. Under this premium pattern, the profits from interest spread will be minimal while profits from cost of insurance will be maximized. If the profits from these two sources (interest spread and cost of insurance charges) are balanced, then both premium patterns hopefully generate reasonable profits.

Under a multiple scenario approach, the elements of the policy are adjusted so that acceptable profits are generated under each of the scenarios. For a universal life product, the elements of the policy that can be adjusted include the cost of insurance charges, the expense charges and the interest rate credited to the fund value. These must be balanced so that the product will generate acceptable profits across all the premium scenarios. Using the above scenarios, if a single premium is paid, then the policy will have a large fund value and a smaller net amount at risk (specified amount less the fund value). However, if the minimum amount of premium is paid each year, then the product will have a very small fund value and a large net amount at risk. Profits from the investment spread are driven by the fund value while profits from mortality charges are a function of the net amount at risk. Under the single premium scenario, most of the profits will be driven by the investment spread while under the minimum premium scenario, the profits will be driven by the cost of insurance charges. By profit testing under both scenarios, a company can balance the profits being generated from each source so that the profits under any premium payment scenario will be acceptable.

Under a multiple scenario approach, it is still common to run sensitivity tests to ascertain the effect of variations in other assumptions.

16.1.5 Stochastic Approach

A stochastic approach is a multiple scenario approach where hundreds or thousands of scenarios are tested. Each scenario is stochastically generated from a distribution of possible scenarios.

A stochastic approach is generally used with guaranteed minimum death benefits or guaranteed living benefits attached to a variable annuity. Under these riders, the benefits to be paid as well the charges that will be collected are a function of the future returns of the equity markets. While these could be priced using a multiple scenario approach, such an approach does not provide a distribution of results weighted by probabilities and will often miss some of the most adverse scenarios.

EXAMPLE 16.3

The annual return on a variable annuity is determined using a stochastic model. The stochastic model assumes that each year, the annual return is distributed as follows:

Possible Return	−15%	−5%	0	+6%	+12%	+20%
Probability	10%	20%	20%	20%	20%	10%

In practice, a more complex model will be used that takes into account the various investments made and correlations between investments and through time.

Assume a single premium of 50,000 is paid. Determine the distribution of the 10th year fund value using Monte Carlo simulation with 10,000 trials.

This can be set up in a spreadsheet. We will use a uniform distribution to simulate our returns. The spreadsheet in the online reference material has a model that stochastically projects the 10th year fund value for one trial.

There is a second tab in the spreadsheet that was used to calculate 10,000 trials. The 10th year account value is listed for each of the 10,000 trials. We can use this distribution to determine various attributes such as mean (67,487) and standard deviation (20,470).

With a stochastic approach, sensitivity testing is not necessary unless there are variables that are not being tested in the stochastic scenarios.

16.1.6 Micro Pricing

Micro Pricing is the most common approach used to price life insurance products. Micro pricing is a cost-plus approach to determining premiums or profits during profit testing. A cost-plus approach quantifies the various costs associated with a product. For example, for a term life insurance product, the costs include:

- Mortality costs—Death Benefits to be paid;
- Distribution costs—Commissions paid to agents;
- Other expense costs—Issue and maintenance expenses as well of premium taxes;
- Capital costs—Use of capital that must be allocated to support this business has a cost; and
- Federal income taxes.

Once the costs have been quantified, then a desired profit can be added to these costs and the premium is the sum of the costs plus the desired profit. Of course, this approach may lead to a premium that is unacceptable in the market as the premium may be too high to be competitive with similar products being offered by other companies.

A similar cost-plus approach is to determine the desired premium based on the premiums being used by competitors. Once this is done, the costs determined above can be deducted from the premium to determine the resultant profit. If the resultant profit is acceptable, then the pricing process is complete. In reality, the initial premium seldom results in an acceptable profit and an iterative process is used to adjust costs, proposed premiums, and profits until an acceptable combination is obtained.

It should be noted that very few of the costs are fixed. Obviously, the distribution costs can be changed by changing the commissions that are paid to agents. While less obvious, the mortality costs can be changed by changing the thoroughness of the underwriting. Finally, it may even be possible to change the other expense cost. If the product is being priced with fully allocated expenses, a shift to marginal expenses or a reallocation of expenses among products would result in a change in the other expense costs. Fully allocated expenses and marginal expenses are discussed in Section 17.5.1.

Finally, under a micro pricing process, the premiums, associated costs, and profits are calculated on a per unit basis. Therefore, an average cost is used for each unit. There is an implicit assumption that costs will not change as the number of units of a product are sold. This is generally not a true statement as the expenses per unit are clearly a function of the number of units sold.

As an example,[2] the product development process generally is a flat cost without regard to the number of units of a product that are sold. Suppose the cost to develop a new whole life product is 100,000. The company expects to sell 500 million of death benefit each year for four years with this new product. Therefore, the product development cost included in the premium for this product is:

$$\frac{100,000}{500,000(4)} = 0.05 \text{ per } 1,000.$$

However, if the product sells better than anticipated, the cost per unit will be less. If the product sells one billion of death benefit per year for four years, the cost will actually be 0.025 per 1,000. On the other hand, if the product sells fewer units than anticipated, the cost could be significantly higher. If the company only sells 100 million of death benefit for the next two years (and stops selling the product due to low sales at that time), then the cost would actually be 0.50 per 1,000.

As we have just demonstrated, the cost per unit will generally vary with the number of units sold. However, a simplifying assumption of a constant cost is necessary for this approach. It is generally an acceptable assumption as long as the range of the variance of units sold is within a reasonably narrow range.

16.1.7 Macro Pricing

Macro Pricing is a concept that was introduced by Chalke (1991).[3] In this paper, Chalke states that the use of a cost-plus based pricing approach has flaws. He postulates that a pricing model based on economic concepts is a better approach to pricing life insurance products.

Under an economic-based approach, a life insurance company would always attempt to maximize total profits as opposed to attempting to meet a per unit based profit margin. A reduction in the price of a product with the associated reduction in per unit profit could result in maximizing total profits if the number of units of the product sold increases sufficiently to offset the reduction in per unit profit.

---

2 This example ignores the time value of money for simplicity purposes. These types of calculations will normally incorporate the effect of interest in the calculations. They may also reflect a probability distribution in the calculation of expected values.

3 Available online at http://www.soa.org/library/monographs/50th-anniversary/product-development-section/1999/january/m-as99-3-02.pdf. This paper is available with the book's online resources.

As an example, for a term insurance product, the premium is 1 per 1,000 of death benefit. At a premium of 1, the profit margin is 0.10 and the company expects to sell 200 million of death benefit. This results in a total profit of $200{,}000{,}000\,\frac{0.10}{1000} = 20{,}000$.

However, if the premium was reduced to 0.95 per 1,000 of death benefit, the company expects to sell 500 million of death benefit. Unless other changes were made to the term product, the reduction in premium also reduces the profit margin. If the resultant profit margin decreases by the amount of the decrease in the premium,[4] then resultant profit margin is 0.05 per 1,000. In that case, with a price of 0.95 per 1,000, the total profit generated is $500{,}000{,}000\,\frac{0.05}{1000} = 25{,}000$ which produces more total profit.

Chalke also points out that the demand curve for a product is a function of more than just the price of the product. For example, for life insurance products, it is also a function of the compensation paid to the distribution system. Agents are more apt to sell a product that generates more compensation for them than a product that produces lower compensation. Therefore, in macro pricing approach, a three dimensional demand curve must be developed and used to evaluate the various scenarios.

Macro pricing is not used extensively in the product development process for life insurance products for a variety of reasons. One of the main reasons is that development of demand curves for life insurance products is challenging and incorrect assumptions can be costly.

16.2 Pricing Tools

All pricing tools are models. As Bellis, et. al. (2010, p. 364) states:

> A model is a representation of reality. Actuaries build models that approximate the financial implications related to products. Models are never precisely correct but they are useful in managing risk. Some models are very simple and some are complex.

The pricing model that we will use in this book is the asset share.

16.3 Asset Shares

As stated in Section 16.1.1, an asset share is a model of a single policy cell that projects cash flows and other financial information (such as reserves) for a policy in that cell. An asset share can be used to project future balance sheets and income statements on multiple accounting bases as well as calculate the book profits and the profit measures. When a model office approach to pricing is used, a series of cells (asset shares) are combined to produce the results for the model office.

---

4 There are reasons that this may not be true, but for the purposes of this example, we will make that assumption. One reason that this might not be true is that additional economies of scale may be achieved by increasing the sales by 250 percent, which would reduce the expenses for this product. Another reason is the effect of federal income taxes could change the pattern of profit.

As we know from Section 15.1.2, in order to calculate book profits, we need a model that will project premiums, investment income, expenses, benefits, reserves and required capital. Once we have the book profits we can calculate the profit measures. These same items are needed to project balance sheets and income statement. In order to project these items, our model needs to incorporate the product features and our assumptions. When multiple scenarios or stochastic scenarios are used, then an asset share is created for each scenario.

EXAMPLE 16.4

Table 16.4 is an example of an asset share calculation. This model is included in a spreadsheet in the online resources for this book. This spreadsheet includes the formulas for each cell.

The first several columns of Tables 16.4a and 16.4b are the assumptions that are the basis for the asset share. This asset share is for a 35-year-old male nonsmoker for a

TABLE 16.4a Asset Share Calculation

	Assumptions
Issue Age	35
Pricing Horizon - Years	30
Premium Rate Per Unit	
Premium Rate Per Unit	12.50
Policy Fee	50
Average Size in 1000's	100
Acquisition Expense - Per Policy	100
Required Capital	
Percent of Reserves	4.80%
Percent of Claims	4.20%
Percent of Premiums	4.20%
Percent of NAAR	0.00%
Per Policy	0
Federal Income Taxes:	
DAC Proxy Percent	7.70%
DAC Amortization Period	10
Federal Income Tax Rate	34.00%
Present Value Discount Rate	5.50%
Valuation Interest Rate	4.00%
Valuation Mortality Table	2001 CSO Male ALB Nonsmoker
Tax Reserve Interest Rate	4.50%
Tax Reserve Mortality Table	2001 CSO Male ALB Nonsmoker
Cash Value Interest Rate	5.00%
Cash Value Mortality Table	2001 CSO Male ALB Nonsmoker

TABLE 16.4b

							Expenses									Dividends	
Duration	Death Benefit per Unit	Premium Pattern	Mortality Rates	Mortality Factors	Lapse Rates	Commission Rates	Percent of Premium	Premium Tax Rates	Per Unit	Per Policy	Per Claim	Per Surrender	Per Lapse	Gross Investment Rate	Investment Expense	Policyholder	Termination
1	1000	1	0.00031	0.70	0.200	0.800	0.2	0.025	0.75	40	0	0	0	0.055	0	0	0
2	1000	1	0.00042	0.70	0.120	0.100	0	0.025	0	40	0	0	0	0.055	0	0	0
3	1000	1	0.00053	0.70	0.080	0.100	0	0.025	0	40	0	0	0	0.055	0	0	0
4	1000	1	0.00064	0.70	0.060	0.080	0	0.025	0	40	0	0	0	0.055	0	0	0
5	1000	1	0.00075	0.70	0.050	0.080	0	0.025	0	40	0	0	0	0.055	0	0	0
6	1000	1	0.00085	0.70	0.050	0.080	0	0.025	0	40	0	0	0	0.055	0	0	0
7	1000	1	0.00096	0.70	0.050	0.080	0	0.025	0	40	0	0	0	0.055	0	0	0
8	1000	1	0.00109	0.70	0.050	0.080	0	0.025	0	40	0	0	0	0.055	0	0	0
9	1000	1	0.00122	0.70	0.050	0.080	0	0.025	0	40	0	0	0	0.055	0	0	0
10	1000	1	0.00138	0.70	0.050	0.080	0	0.025	0	40	0	0	0	0.055	0	0	0
11	1000	1	0.00157	0.70	0.050	0.030	0	0.025	0	40	0	0	0	0.055	0	0	0
12	1000	1	0.00180	0.70	0.050	0.030	0	0.025	0	40	0	0	0	0.055	0	0	0
13	1000	1	0.00206	0.70	0.050	0.030	0	0.025	0	40	0	0	0	0.055	0	0	0
14	1000	1	0.00233	0.70	0.050	0.030	0	0.025	0	40	0	0	0	0.055	0	0	0
15	1000	1	0.00258	0.70	0.050	0.030	0	0.025	0	40	0	0	0	0.055	0	0	0
16	1000	1	0.00282	0.70	0.050	0.030	0	0.025	0	40	0	0	0	0.055	0	0	0
17	1000	1	0.00309	0.70	0.050	0.030	0	0.025	0	40	0	0	0	0.055	0	0	0
18	1000	1	0.00339	0.70	0.050	0.030	0	0.025	0	40	0	0	0	0.055	0	0	0
19	1000	1	0.00376	0.70	0.050	0.030	0	0.025	0	40	0	0	0	0.055	0	0	0
20	1000	1	0.00415	0.70	0.050	0.030	0	0.025	0	40	0	0	0	0.055	0	0	0
21	1000	1	0.00464	0.70	0.050	0.030	0	0.025	0	40	0	0	0	0.055	0	0	0
22	1000	1	0.00518	0.70	0.050	0.030	0	0.025	0	40	0	0	0	0.055	0	0	0
23	1000	1	0.00575	0.70	0.050	0.030	0	0.025	0	40	0	0	0	0.055	0	0	0
24	1000	1	0.00636	0.70	0.050	0.030	0	0.025	0	40	0	0	0	0.055	0	0	0
25	1000	1	0.00699	0.70	0.050	0.030	0	0.025	0	40	0	0	0	0.055	0	0	0
26	1000	1	0.00821	0.70	0.050	0.030	0	0.025	0	40	0	0	0	0.055	0	0	0
27	1000	1	0.009230	0.70	0.050	0.030	0	0.025	0	40	0	0	0	0.055	0	0	0
28	1000	1	0.010430	0.70	0.050	0.030	0	0.025	0	40	0	0	0	0.055	0	0	0
29	1000	1	0.011730	0.70	0.050	0.030	0	0.025	0	40	0	0	0	0.055	0	0	0
30	1000	1	0.013100	0.70	0.050	0.030	0	0.025	0	40	0	0	0	0.055	0	0	0

TABLE 16.4c

Year	Attained Age	Attained Age	In Force BOM	Deaths	Lapses	In Force EOM	Premium Income	Net Investment Income	Total Income	Death Claims	Surrender Benefits	Commissions	Expen[…] Beg of Year
1	35		1.00000	0.0002170	0.19996	0.79983	13.00	(0.13)	12.87	0.22	-	10.40	4.68
2	36		0.79983	0.0002351	0.09595	0.70364	10.40	0.37	10.76	0.24	-	1.04	0.26
3	37		0.70364	0.0002611	0.05627	0.64711	9.15	0.73	9.88	0.26	0.19	0.91	0.23
4	38		0.64711	0.0002899	0.03881	0.60801	8.41	1.07	9.49	0.29	0.46	0.67	0.21
5	39		0.60801	0.0003192	0.03038	0.57731	7.90	1.39	9.29	0.32	0.63	0.63	0.20
6	40		0.57731	0.0003435	0.02885	0.54811	7.50	1.68	9.19	0.34	0.86	0.60	0.19
7	41		0.54811	0.0003683	0.02739	0.52036	7.13	1.95	9.08	0.37	1.08	0.57	0.18
8	42		0.52036	0.0003970	0.02600	0.49396	6.76	2.20	8.97	0.40	1.28	0.54	0.17
9	43		0.49396	0.0004218	0.02468	0.46886	6.42	2.43	8.85	0.42	1.47	0.51	0.16
10	44		0.46886	0.0004529	0.02342	0.44499	6.10	2.64	8.73	0.45	1.64	0.49	0.15
11	45		0.44499	0.0004890	0.02223	0.42228	5.78	2.84	8.63	0.49	1.80	0.17	0.14
12	46		0.42228	0.0005321	0.02109	0.40066	5.49	3.03	8.52	0.53	1.95	0.16	0.14
13	47		0.40066	0.0005777	0.02000	0.38008	5.21	3.19	8.40	0.58	2.08	0.16	0.1
14	48		0.38008	0.0006199	0.01897	0.36048	4.94	3.34	8.28	0.62	2.20	0.15	0.1
15	49		0.36048	0.0006510	0.01799	0.34184	4.69	3.47	8.16	0.65	2.32	0.14	0.1
16	50		0.34184	0.0006748	0.01706	0.32411	4.44	3.59	8.04	0.67	2.42	0.13	0.1
17	51		0.32411	0.0007010	0.01617	0.30724	4.21	3.70	7.91	0.70	2.51	0.13	0.1
18	52		0.30724	0.0007291	0.01533	0.29118	3.99	3.80	7.79	0.73	2.60	0.12	0.1
19	53		0.29118	0.0007664	0.01452	0.27589	3.79	3.88	7.66	0.77	2.67	0.11	0.0
20	54		0.27589	0.0008015	0.01375	0.26134	3.59	3.95	7.54	0.80	2.73	0.11	0.0
21	55		0.26134	0.0008488	0.01302	0.24747	3.40	4.02	7.41	0.85	2.78	0.10	0.0
22	56		0.24747	0.0008973	0.01233	0.23424	3.22	4.07	7.28	0.90	2.82	0.10	0.0
23	57		0.23424	0.0009428	0.01166	0.22163	3.05	4.11	7.16	0.94	2.85	0.09	0.0
24	58		0.22163	0.0009867	0.01103	0.20961	2.88	4.15	7.03	0.99	2.87	0.09	0.0
25	59		0.20961	0.0010256	0.01043	0.19816	2.72	4.18	6.90	1.03	2.89	0.08	0.0
26	60		0.19816	0.0011388	0.00985	0.18717	2.58	4.20	6.77	1.14	2.89	0.08	0.0
27	61		0.18717	0.0012093	0.00930	0.17666	2.43	4.21	6.64	1.21	2.89	0.07	0.0
28	62		0.17666	0.0012898	0.00877	0.16660	2.30	4.21	6.51	1.29	2.88	0.07	0.0
29	63		0.16660	0.0013680	0.00826	0.15697	2.17	4.21	6.37	1.37	2.85	0.06	0.0
30	64		0.15697	0.0014394	0.00778	0.14776	2.04	4.20	6.24	1.44	2.82	0.06	0.0

Expenses Mid of Year	Expenses End of Year	Increase in Reserves	Benefits and Expenses	Net Income before Taxes and Dividends	Dividends	Net Income before Taxes	Taxes	Net Income	Book Profit before Required Surplus	Required Surplus	Net Investment Income on Required Surplus	Book Profit with Required Surplus
0.36	-	(0.00)	15.65	(2.78)	-	(2.78)	(0.62)	(2.16)	(2.16)	0.56	-	(2.71)
0.30	-	6.7240	8.56	2.21	-	2.21	1.21	1.00	1.08	0.77	0.02	0.88
0.27	-	5.8540	7.72	2.16	-	2.16	1.32	0.83	0.88	1.00	0.03	0.68
0.25	-	5.4428	7.33	2.16	-	2.16	1.45	0.70	0.72	1.23	0.04	0.52
0.24	-	5.1789	7.20	2.09	-	2.09	1.55	0.54	0.53	1.46	0.04	0.34
0.23	-	4.7904	7.01	2.17	-	2.17	1.69	0.49	0.45	1.67	0.05	0.29
0.21	-	4.4160	6.83	2.25	-	2.25	1.80	0.45	0.39	1.87	0.06	0.26
0.20	-	4.0514	6.65	2.32	-	2.32	1.90	0.42	0.35	2.05	0.07	0.24
0.19	-	3.6982	6.46	2.39	-	2.39	1.99	0.40	0.32	2.21	0.07	0.23
0.18	-	3.3606	6.28	2.45	-	2.45	2.06	0.39	0.30	2.36	0.08	0.23
0.17	-	3.0384	5.82	2.81	-	2.81	2.24	0.57	0.46	2.50	0.09	0.41
0.16	-	2.7383	5.68	2.83	-	2.83	2.30	0.53	0.40	2.62	0.09	0.37
0.16	-	2.4718	5.57	2.83	-	2.83	2.34	0.49	0.34	2.73	0.10	0.32
0.15	-	2.2354	5.48	2.80	-	2.80	2.36	0.44	0.27	2.83	0.10	0.27
0.14	-	2.0038	5.37	2.79	-	2.79	2.37	0.41	0.23	2.91	0.10	0.25
0.13	-	1.7727	5.25	2.79	-	2.79	2.38	0.41	0.21	2.99	0.11	0.24
0.13	-	1.5406	5.11	2.80	-	2.80	2.39	0.41	0.20	3.05	0.11	0.24
0.12	-	1.3100	4.97	2.81	-	2.81	2.39	0.43	0.20	3.11	0.11	0.25
0.11	-	1.0836	4.84	2.83	-	2.83	2.38	0.45	0.20	3.15	0.11	0.27
0.11	-	0.8529	4.69	2.85	-	2.85	2.37	0.48	0.22	3.19	0.11	0.30
0.10	-	0.6276	4.54	2.87	-	2.87	2.35	0.52	0.24	3.21	0.12	0.33
0.10	-	0.4195	4.41	2.88	-	2.88	2.32	0.56	0.26	3.23	0.12	0.36
0.09	-	0.2350	4.29	2.87	-	2.87	2.28	0.59	0.27	3.23	0.12	0.38
0.09	-	0.0684	4.17	2.85	-	2.85	2.24	0.61	0.28	3.23	0.12	0.39
0.08	-	(0.0959)	4.05	2.85	-	2.85	2.20	0.65	0.29	3.22	0.12	0.42
0.08	-	(0.2874)	3.96	2.81	-	2.81	2.14	0.67	0.28	3.21	0.12	0.42
0.07	-	(0.4712)	3.84	2.81	-	2.81	2.09	0.72	0.31	3.18	0.12	0.45
0.07	-	(0.6581)	3.70	2.80	-	2.80	2.04	0.76	0.33	3.15	0.12	0.48
0.06	-	(0.8353)	3.57	2.80	-	2.80	1.99	0.82	0.35	3.10	0.11	0.51
0.06	-	(0.9950)	3.44	2.80	-	2.80	1.94	0.86	0.37	3.05	0.11	0.53

TABLE 16.4d Balance Sheet

Year	Attained Age	Invested Assets	Deferred Premiums	Total Assets	Reserves	Dividends Apportioned	Total Liabilities	Surplus
0		-	-	-	-	-	-	-
1	35	(2.16)	-	(2.16)	(0.00)	-	(0.00)	(2.16)
2	36	5.56	-	5.56	6.72	-	6.72	(1.16)
3	37	12.25	-	12.25	12.58	-	12.58	(0.32)
4	38	18.40	-	18.40	18.02	-	18.02	0.38
5	39	24.12	-	24.12	23.20	-	23.20	0.92
6	40	29.40	-	29.40	27.99	-	27.99	1.41
7	41	34.26	-	34.26	32.41	-	32.41	1.85
8	42	38.73	-	38.73	36.46	-	36.46	2.27
9	43	42.83	-	42.83	40.16	-	40.16	2.67
10	44	46.58	-	46.58	43.52	-	43.52	3.07
11	45	50.19	-	50.19	46.55	-	46.55	3.64
12	46	53.47	-	53.47	49.29	-	49.29	4.17
13	47	56.43	-	56.43	51.76	-	51.76	4.66
14	48	59.10	-	59.10	54.00	-	54.00	5.10
15	49	61.52	-	61.52	56.00	-	56.00	5.52
16	50	63.70	-	63.70	57.78	-	57.78	5.92
17	51	65.65	-	65.65	59.32	-	59.32	6.34
18	52	67.39	-	67.39	60.63	-	60.63	6.76
19	53	68.92	-	68.92	61.71	-	61.71	7.21
20	54	70.26	-	70.26	62.56	-	62.56	7.70
21	55	71.41	-	71.41	63.19	-	63.19	8.22
22	56	72.39	-	72.39	63.61	-	63.61	8.77
23	57	73.21	-	73.21	63.85	-	63.85	9.36
24	58	73.89	-	73.89	63.91	-	63.91	9.98
25	59	74.45	-	74.45	63.82	-	63.82	10.63
26	60	74.83	-	74.83	63.53	-	63.53	11.30
27	61	75.08	-	75.08	63.06	-	63.06	12.02
28	62	75.18	-	75.18	62.40	-	62.40	12.78
29	63	75.16	-	75.16	61.57	-	61.57	13.60
30	64	75.03	-	75.03	60.57	-	60.57	14.46

TABLE 16.4e

Profit Measures	
Return on Investment	
20 Years =>	15.3%
Break-even Year	
Year =>	4
Profit Margin =>	3.45%

whole life insurance policy. The projection period is for 30 years. These assumptions appear in the first worksheet of the spreadsheet. The spreadsheet is set up so that the issue age, gender, smoking status, and projection period as well as the assumptions can be changed in the assumption section of the spreadsheet.

The next two tables in the asset share project an income statement (Table 16.4c) and balance sheet (Table 16.4d) using U.S. statutory accounting as the basis. These are the next two worksheets in the spreadsheet. The profit and accumulated surplus is calculated assuming that the profits are retained within the company. Additionally, the book profits are calculated. The book profits are equivalent the profits that would be distributed each year if profits were distributed each year.

The book profits can be used to calculate the various profit measures (Table 16.4e) that are discussed in Section 15.2.

The statutory reserves, tax reserves, and cash surrender values are not listed in the asset share table but are calculated in the last three worksheets of the spreadsheet. These calculated values are used to determine the increase in reserves, surrender benefits, and taxes in the income statement.

16.4 Analysis of Book Profits

We will now look at Book Profits in substantially more detail. In Section 15.1.2, we introduced book profits and defined them at a high level as:

$$BP_t = Prem_t + I_t - E_t - B_t - \Delta Res - \Delta ReqSur$$

Where:

- BP_t is the Book Profit at the end of Period t;
- $Prem_t$ is the premium in period t;
- I_t is the investment income earned on the cash flows, reserves and required surplus during period t;
- E_t is the expenses (including taxes and commissions) during period t;
- B_t is the benefits paid during period t;
- ΔRes is the increase in the reserves during period t; and
- $\Delta ReqSur$ is the increase in required surplus during period t.

We will now define Book Profits in a more complete formula as:

$$\begin{aligned} BP_t = {} & ({}_{t-1}V + RS_{t-1} + P_{t-1})(1 + i) - DB_t \cdot q_t(1 + i)^{0.5} - CV_t \cdot w_t - Div_t(1 - q_t) \\ & - E_t^{BOP}(1 + i) - E_t^{MOP}(1 + i)^{0.5} - E_t^{EOP} - ({}_tV + RS_t)(1 - q_t - w_t). \end{aligned}$$

To reconcile this formula to our previous formula,

$Prem_t$, the premium at the beginning of period t (time t-1), is P_{t-1}.

I_t, the investment income earned on the cash flows, reserves, and required surplus during period t, is

$$({}_{t-1}V + RS_{t-1} + P_{t-1})i - DB_t \cdot q_t[(1 + i)^{0.5} - 1] - E_t^{BOP}i - E_t^{MOP}[(1 + i)^{0.5} - 1].$$

E_t, the expenses (including taxes and commissions) during period t, is $E_t^{BOP} + E_t^{MOP} + E_t^{EOP}$.

B_t, the benefits paid during period t, is $DB_t \cdot q_t + CV_t \cdot w_t + Div_t(1 - q_t)$.

ΔRes, the increase in the reserves during period t, is ${}_tV - {}_{t-1}V(1 - q_t - w_t)$.

$\Delta ReqSur$, the increase in required surplus during period t, is $RS_t - RS_{t-1}(1 - q_t - w_t)$.

When Anderson developed his original book value formula, the only significant difference was that required surplus (to be discussed in Section 16.4.1.8) was not included. The concept of required surplus was developed in the 1990s.

Another difference was that Anderson developed a formula where all calculations were completed on an annual basis. Today, with the much more powerful computer resources that are available, calculations are generally done on a monthly basis with monthly book profits accumulated to the end of the year to determine the end of the year book profit. Our remaining discussion will assume that each period is one month.

16.4.1 Components of Book Profits

We will now look further at each of the components of Book Profits.

16.4.1.1 Reserves

The ΔRes Component of Book Profits reflects the increase in reserves. The increase in reserve reflects both the change in the reserve on an in force per policy basis which is ${}_tV - {}_{t-1}V$, but also the fact that for those policy owners that die or withdraw, the life insurance company no longer needs to hold a reserve. The release of reserve for death or withdrawal is ${}_tV(q_t + w_t)$ which is negative in our book profit formula because this reserve no longer needs to be held.

In Section 15.1.3, we discussed accounting systems and pointed out that reserves are a function of the accounting system. Furthermore, we pointed out that other items in the book profit formula may also be a function of reserves such as required surplus. All components of the book profit calculation need to be completed on a consistent basis. Reserves are discussed in detail in Section 18.1.

The most common basis used for pricing products in the United States is based on the statutory accounting framework. When this accounting framework is used, then the reserves to be used in the book value calculations are statutory reserves. Statutory reserves vary by product and are discussed in Section 18.1.2.1.

16.4.1.2 Premiums

Premiums are paid by the policy owner to the life insurance company. Premiums may seem like a simple concept. However, this is not necessarily that case. First, we will consider traditional life policies and fixed premium universal life policies. Then we will consider flexible premium policies.

16.4.1.2.1 Traditional life and fixed premium universal life

For traditional life and other fixed premium policies, premiums are typically expressed as a rate per thousand of death benefit. However, that rate will be a function of the characteristics of the insured. For example, the premiums will usually vary by the gender and issue age of the insured. Additionally, the premiums may reflect the health of the insured. A person who is not in the best health will often be charged a higher premium, which is called a substandard premium. Even for those eligible for standard premiums because of good health, the premiums may vary by other characteristics such as smoker versus nonsmoker.

The premiums may also be a function of policy size. Larger policies are often charged a lower overall premium per 1,000 of death benefit due to economies of scale. In particular, many of the expenses (discussed in Section 16.4.1.6) associated with a life insurance policy are a fixed amount so the cost per 1,000 reduces as the policy size increases. For example, if it costs 50 per year to administer the policy, then the cost per 1,000 for a policy of 10,000 will be 5 where the cost per 1,000 for a policy of 100,000 is only 0.50. These differences in cost per 1,000 are typically reflected through premium banding or through a policy fee.

EXAMPLE 16.5

When premiums are banded, then the premium rate per 1,000 will vary by policy size. For example, Table 16.5 lists banded premium rates.

TABLE 16.5 Banded Premium Rates

Issue Age	Premium Rate per 1,000 Size 25,000 to 99,999	Premium Rate per 1,000 Size 100,000 to 499,999	Premium Rate per 1,000 Size 500,000 and over
35	10.00	9.00	8.25
36	10.25	9.25	8.50
37	10.55	9.55	8.80
38	10.90	9.90	9.15
39	11.30	10.30	9.55
40	11.80	10.80	10.05

For a policy of 50,000 on an insured age 35, the total premium is 500 (50 units of 1,000 multiplied by the premium rate of 10.00 per 1,000). For a policy of 500,000 on an insured of age 35, the total premium is 4,125.

One of the implications from banded premium rates is that certain amounts at the top of each band will never be sold because it is to the policy owner's benefit to move up to the next band since more insurance can be purchased for less premium. Using Table 16.5, we can see this for an insured at age 35 who wants to purchase 90,000 of life insurance. The premium for 90,000 is 900. However, if we look at the premium for 100,000, it is also 900. Therefore, it is to the advantage of the policy owner to purchase a policy for 100,000 since the premium will be the same and there will be an additional death benefit of 10,000. As a matter of fact, for an insured age 35, amounts greater than or equal to 90,000 will never be sold because it will always be to the policyholder's advantage to purchase a 100,000 policy.

If the premiums are calculated using a policy fee, then the total premiums paid for a policy is calculated as:

$$\text{Total Premium} = (\text{Premium Per 1000})(\text{Number of Units of 1000}) + \text{Policy Fee}.$$

EXAMPLE 16.6

If the policy fee is 125 and the premium rates are given in Table 16.6, the premium for 100,000 is $(8.00)(100) + 125 = 925$ and the premium for 90,000 is $(8.00)(90) + 125 = 845$. With a policy fee structure, we no longer have a problem with discontinuities in the gross premiums.

TABLE 16.6 Premiums with a Policy Fee

Issue Age	Premium Rate Per 1,000
35	8.00
36	8.25
37	8.55
38	8.90
39	9.30
40	9.80

The advantages of premiums based on a policy fee are:

- Equity. The policy fee approach results in greater equity, assuming that the policy fee reflects the per policy expense costs. With banded premiums, the difference in costs can be reflected across the bands, but within the band, the larger policies are still subsidizing the smaller policies. For example, Table 16.7 lists the total premium per 1,000 for three different size policies. These are based on the two previous examples.

TABLE 16.7 Difference between Using Bands and a Policy Fee

Face Amount	Premium per 1,000 Banded Premiums	Premium per 1,000 Policy Fee
25,000	10.00	13.00
62,500	10.00	10.00
80,000	10.00	9.56

- Continuity of Face amounts. With a policy fee, we do not have the discontinuity of face amounts as discussed previously for banded premiums.

The advantages of banded premiums are:

- Simplicity. It is easier to look up a premium in a table and multiply it by the number of 1,000s than it is to look up a number in a table, multiply it by the number of 1,000s and then add a policy fee.
- Perception. Many agents look at the policy fee as an additional charge to the policy owner on top of the premium as opposed to part of the premium.

It should also be noted that for some life insurance products, premiums may be banded and also contain a policy fee. While this is not common, such products do exist.

The fact that premiums can be paid in different modes also must be considered. As discussed in Section 13.1.2.1.2, the premiums for different modes usually reflect an additional charge for the loss of interest and additional costs associated with the modal premiums. This additional premium charge (as well as the associated lost investment income and expenses) should be reflected in the book profit.

Finally, if premiums are not level, then we must reflect any changes to premiums in our book profits.

From the standpoint of our Book Profits formula, $Prem_t$ will be the premium allocated to period t. This allocation must be consistent with the reserves being used in our calculation. Where the reserves reflect the modal premium, $Prem_t$ will be the cash premium received in each period. This is generally true of GAAP and Canadian CALM reserves and may be true for U.S. Statutory reserves.

If the reserves do not reflect modal premiums, then the premiums allocated to each period must be adjusted to the same basis as the reserves. For example, in U.S. statutory accounting, reserves for traditional life policies are frequently calculated assuming that annual premiums are paid. If this is done in pricing, then the premiums must also be adjusted even if the premiums are paid on another mode such as monthly or quarterly. This adjustment is completed by accruing premium income under the accounting method. The accrued premium is not cash premium, but an accounting adjustment to reflect premium expected to be received in the future. This adjustment is known as the deferred premium adjustment.

EXAMPLE 16.7

The annual premium is 1,000 and the monthly premium is 90. If reserves are calculated based on annual premiums, but the premiums are actually paid monthly, then premiums during the policy year (assuming no terminations) would be reflected as in Table 16.8.

TABLE 16.8 Monthly Premiums

Policy Month	Cash Premiums	Deferred Premiums	$Prem_t$
1	90	990	1,080
2	90	900	0
3	90	810	0
4	90	720	0
5	90	630	0
6	90	540	0
7	90	450	0
8	90	360	0
9	90	270	0
10	90	180	0
11	90	90	0
12	90	0	0

Under this scenario, $Prem_t$ = Cash Premiums + Increase in Deferred Premiums. In the first month, $Prem_t$ is cash premium of 90 plus increase in deferred premiums of 990. In the second month, $Prem_t$ is cash premium of 90 plus increase in deferred premium of −90 which is zero.

This deferred premium adjustment complicates the calculation of book profits. Besides the adjustment, the investment income (discussed in Section 17.1) on premiums is only earned on the cash portion.

16.4.1.2.2 Flexible premium policies

As the name clearly implies, a flexible premium policy (universal life or deferred annuity) does not have set premiums that must be paid. Often times, there will be an initial premium that is required. Further, there may be expected premiums based on secondary guarantees in the contract. However, the policy owner has final control of whether a premium will be paid or not. When the premium is not paid, the policy will not necessarily terminate unless the fund value of the contract goes to zero. Therefore, the actuary generally relies on company experience and/or actuarial judgment to estimate the premiums that will be paid under flexible premium policies.

In estimating the premiums to be paid, the actuary will usually make assumptions regarding premium suspension rates. Premium suspension rates are the percentage of policies that will stop paying premiums in any policy year.

EXAMPLE 16.8

If the premium in the first year is assumed to be 1,000 and the premium suspension rate is 10% in all future years, then the premiums for the first five years are estimated to be as in Table 16.9.

TABLE 16.9 Premium Suspension

Policy Year	Premium
1	1,000
2	900
3	810
4	729
5	656

A common approach, as discussed in Section 16.1.4, is to run a variety of premium assumptions and to try to balance the various mortality and expense charges against the fund value so that the book profits that result will be acceptable under any premium pattern. This is generally not an easy task.

16.4.1.3 Premium component

Book Profits are normally calculated on a per 1,000 of death benefit basis. Therefore, $Prem_t$ needs to:

- Be on a per 1,000 basis;
- Reflect the policy mode and any mode adjustments; and
- Adjust the policy fee (if any) to a per 1,000 basis.

Since the policy fee is on a per policy basis, we must adjust it to a per 1,000 basis. We do this using the average policy size in 1,000s. The average policy size in 1,000s can be calculated from similar policies sold by the life insurance company or can be estimated by the actuary. The policy fee per 1,000 will then be calculated as:

$$\frac{PolicyFee}{AveSize}$$

Therefore, the premium for Book Profit can be summarized as:

$$Prem_t = \left[PremPer1000_t + \frac{PolicyFee}{AveSize} \right] (ModeFactor).$$

EXAMPLE 16.9

Using the premiums in Table 16.6 with a policy fee of 125 and an average size of 125,000, the monthly premium if the mode factor is 0.09 is

$$Prem_t = \left(8.00 + \frac{125.00}{125} \right) (0.09) = 0.81.$$

It should be noted that for flexible premium policies, there is generally no policy fee and the premium per 1,000 reflects the premium suspension rate. Further, the mode factor generally is just one divided by the number of payments per year. For example, for monthly mode, the mode factor would be 1/12.

Finally, in many cases, the object of our pricing will be to determine premiums. If this is the case, then we will need to determine premiums using an iterative approach until we have acceptable premiums.[5] This is generally done by using an estimated premium and adjusting it up or down until we get to an accepted premium.

5 An acceptable premium can be defined in a number of ways. A premium should generate sufficient profits for the life insurance company, but must also be competitive with other products being offered by the life insurance company as well as the competitors of the life insurance company. A life insurer may also have other restraints on the premium which must be considered.

16.4.1.4 Benefits

In our formula for book profits, B_t is the benefits paid during period t, which is

$$DB_t q_t + CV_t w_t + Div_t(1 - q_t)$$

We will now discuss each component of the benefits.

DB_t represents the death benefit payable in period t. If the death benefit is level, then DB_t will be level and will not be a function of t. If the profit testing is based on a unit of 1,000 of death benefit, then $DB_t = 1{,}000$.

In Section 13.1.2.1.5, we discussed terminal dividends (dividends paid upon termination of the policy). If the policy pays terminal dividends upon death, then DB_t must reflect the terminal dividends. The symbol q_t is the probability of death in period t. It is one of the assumptions that we will discuss further in Section 17.3.

CV_t represents the cash value payable upon surrender in period t. The cash value is generally not level during a period (month or year). Therefore, it is generally assumed that if premiums are paid to the end of the period that any surrenders or withdrawals will occur at the end of the month. Since most calculations take place on a per unit basis, then CV_t will be the cash value per unit, which for a level death benefit product will be per 1,000.

If the policyholder stops paying premiums, they may elect other nonforfeiture options such as paid-up insurance. These other options are generally ignored on the basis that they are actuarially equivalent to the cash value and therefore, it is simpler to just assume everyone takes the cash value.

If the policy pays terminal dividends on surrender, then CV_t must reflect the terminal dividends. The symbol w_t is the probability of withdrawal at the end of period t. It is one of the assumptions that we will discuss further in Section 17.4.

For annuity contracts, the unit used in the calculation is usually an amount of premium (such as per 10,000 of single premium or per 1,000 of annual premium) instead of an amount of death benefit (such as per 1,000).

Div_t represents the dividend payable at the end of period t. The dividend is normally only payable at the end of the policy year to policyholders surviving to that point. The dividends will be on a per unit basis. The determination of dividends is discussed in the next section.

The dividend factor is multiplied by $1 - q_t$, which reflects the assumption that the dividend is only payable if the policy is in force at the end of the period. The dividend is assumed to be paid to those that withdraw because withdrawals are assumed to occur at the end of period t. If the assumptions that dividends are only paid to those in force at the end of the year is wrong, then the benefits portion of the formula must be modified appropriately. For example, some companies pay a policyholder dividend to policyholders who die during the year. If this is the case, then DB_t would need to be adjusted to reflect the payment of that dividend on death or the Div_t component would need to be adjusted to reflect payment of a dividend each period for those that die during the period.

16.4.1.5 Dividends

Dividends are intended to return the *divisible surplus* of a life insurance company to the policy owner. The concept of a participating (par) policy is that the life insurance company will return some of the profits on the policy to the policyholder. The amount of the profits to be returned is called the divisible surplus and this amount is determined annually by the life insurance company. Divisible surplus is determined at the life insurance company level. The allocation of divisible surplus to individual policies should be determined using the *contribution principal*. The contribution principal states that the allocation of the divisible surplus should be proportional to the contribution that a policy makes to divisible surplus.

Dividends are usually determined using a three-factor formula. The three factors reflect contributions to divisible surplus from:

- Investment return in excess of that guaranteed in the policy;
- Mortality gains from mortality better than that assumed in the policy; and
- Gains from other sources such as expenses less than assumed in pricing. This third factor is often referred to as loading.

A typical dividend formula is

$$Div_t = (i_t^D - i_t^G)({}_{t-1}V + {}^VP_{t-1}) + (q_t^G - q_t^D)(DB_t - {}_tV)$$
$$+ (1 + i_t^D)[G_t(1 - c_{t-1}) - {}^VP_{t-1} - e_{t-1}].$$

The first term is the investment return in excess of that guaranteed in the policy. The second term reflects the mortality gains and the last term is the loading factor.

As for the investment factor:

i_t^D = the investment rate assumed to be earned for calculating the dividend. This is usually less than the actual rate earned because as we stated previously, the life insurance company keeps part of the gains from in force policies to fund future growth and provide additional assurance that the company will be able to meet its obligations.

i_t^G = the interest rate guaranteed by the life insurance policy. Typically, this is the interest rate used to calculate the reserves for the policy.

$(i_t^D - i_t^G)$ reflects the difference in the two investment rates. This difference is multiplied by $({}_{t-1}V + {}^VP_{t-1})$ which is the initial reserve consisting the reserve at the end of the previous period plus the net valuation premium paid at the start of period t. $({}_{t-1}V + {}^VP_{t-1})$ are the assets at the beginning of period t that are supporting the policy and on which the company would be earning investment income. The valuation premium is the premium that is used to calculate the reserves. For statutory reserves in the United States, the valuation premium and the reserve are calculated using only an interest rate and mortality table. When the valuation premium is calculated on this basis, it is referred to as a net valuation premium. Valuation premiums will be discussed further in Section 18.2.2.7.

As for the mortality factor:

q_t^G = the mortality rate guaranteed by the life insurance policy. Typically, this is the mortality rate used to calculate the reserves for the policy.

q_t^D = mortality rate assumed to be incurred for calculating the dividend. This is usually higher than the actual rate incurred because, once again, the life insurance company keeps part of the gains.

$(q_t^G - q_t^D)$ reflects the difference in the two mortality rates. This difference is multiplied by $(DB_t - {}_tV)$, which is death benefit payable in period t less the reserve at the end of period t. $(DB_t - {}_tV)$ is usually referred to as the *net amount at risk.* This is the amount that the life insurance company would have to pay over and above the reserve if the insured died. Therefore, it is the amount that the life insurance company has at risk. Multiplying the net amount at risk by the difference between the guaranteed mortality and the dividend mortality reflects (a portion of) the gain from favorable mortality.

As for the loading term, it can be rearranged to be $(1 + i_t^D)(G_{t-1} - {}^VP_{t-1} - G_{t-1} \cdot c_{t-1} - e_{t-1})$ which reflects:

$G_{t-1} - {}^VP_{t-1}$ represents the difference between the gross premium collected from the policy owner and the net valuation premium used to calculate the reserves. This difference is the amount that is available to cover expenses. The percent of premium expenses are expressed as $G_{t-1} \cdot c_{t-1}$ where G_{t-1} is the Gross Premium and c_{t-1} is the percent of that premium used to cover expenses, which includes commissions. Finally, e_{t-1} is all other expenses. The amount available to contribute to a dividend is increased with interest for the period as the premiums and expenses are assumed to occur at the start of the period.

16.4.1.6 Expenses

The expenses in the book profit formula are split between those that occur at the beginning of the period, at the middle of the period, and at the end of the period. The expenses include commissions paid and taxes.

We will discuss commissions, taxes and other expenses separately.

16.4.1.6.1 Commissions

Commissions for life insurance products and annuities are normally a percentage of the premium collected. For life insurance, the commissions in the first year will typically be substantially higher than the commissions in later years. For example, commissions might be 100 percent of the premium in the first year and 8 percent of premiums in years two and later. If the premium includes a policy fee, then the policy fee may or may not be commissionable. If the policy fee is not commissionable, then the commission is just a percentage of the premium without the policy fee. Since premiums are paid at the start of a period, these commissions are included in the expenses at the start of the period.

Commissions on fund-based products such as a deferred annuity or UL can be based on a percent of the fund value. These are called *trailer commissions* and are used to incent the agent to encourage the policy owner to keep funds with the life insurance company. Trailer commissions are normally paid at the end of a policy year or perhaps are paid at the end of each quarter or month. On an annualized basis, the trailer commission might be 0.5 percent and would be included in the expenses at the end of the period.

16.4.1.6.2 Taxes

In the United States, life insurance companies pay premium taxes and federal income taxes (FIT).

Premium taxes are paid to local and state governments and are a percent of premium. Premium taxes can run as high as 5 or 6 percent in certain locations, but are typically in the range of 1.5 to 2.5 percent. Premium taxes also may vary by product with annuities having lower or no premium taxes. Since the premium taxes are associated with premiums, they are assumed to be incurred at the start of each period at the same time that the premium is paid.

FIT are paid to the federal government and are a function of income. Income is defined by law and regulations and will not be the same as the income reported on either a statutory or a GAAP basis. For example, income for FIT purposes uses tax reserves, which are calculated as specified by tax law. FIT will be ignored in our discussions as inclusion of FIT is beyond the scope of this book.

In Canada, for currently issued policies, the reserves used to determine income tax are the same as the reserves used for financial reporting.

16.4.1.6.3 Other expenses

Other expenses include issue and maintenance expenses and are typically classified in one of four categories:

- Percent of premium;
- Per policy;
- Per unit or per 1,000; and
- Per decrement.

16.4.1.6.3.1 Percent of premium expenses

Expenses related to premiums should be expressed as a percent of premium expense. Besides commissions and premium taxes, there are often other expenses that are highly or completely correlated with premiums. For example, many life insurance companies provide a bonus to their marketing executives based on the amount of new life and annuity sales. These bonuses will usually be related to premiums collected on new policies.

16.4.1.6.3.2 Per policy expense

Expenses that do not vary by policy size or amount of premium should be expressed as per policy expenses. Most maintenance expenses fit this description. The cost of administering a policy on the computer does not vary with policy size or amount of premium. Neither does the cost of changing the address or beneficiary. Even billing the policy owner for the premium or processing the premium when it is received does not vary by policy size or premium amount. These maintenance expenses are generally assumed to occur uniformly throughout the policy year so they are included in the expenses in the middle of the period.

In addition to maintenance expenses, some issue expenses are best expressed as per policy expenses. For example, the cost of printing and assembling the policy and mailing it to the policy owner as well as entering the necessary data into the administration system does not vary by policy size or premium amount. Also, certain underwriting expenses are best expressed as a per policy expense. For example, in the United States, most life insurance companies routinely query the Medical Information Bureau (MIB).[6] The cost to query the MIB is the same regardless of policy size. Issue expenses are assumed to occur at the beginning of the period.

16.4.1.6.3.3 Per unit or per 1,000 expense

Expenses that are primarily a function of policy size should be expressed as per unit or per 1,000. For example, the underwriting requirements for life insurance policies increase as the amount of insurance being purchased increases. For a small policy, the life insurance company may issue the policy without additional information other than that provided by the application and MIB. For a large policy, the life insurance company will require the applicant to complete a physical examination, which may include specific tests such as an electrocardiogram (ECG or EKG). Therefore, the cost of underwriting is highly correlated with the policy size.

Some life insurance companies treat a portion of the maintenance expense as a per unit expense. These life insurance companies believe that a large life insurance policy will incur additional expenses. One example of such additional expenses is reinsurance costs. Life insurance companies have a maximum amount of insurance that they are willing to retain (known as their retention limit). If they sell a life insurance policy that has a larger death benefit, then the life insurance company will reinsure a portion of that policy with another life insurance company. The life insurance company will pay a premium to the reinsurer and the reinsurance company will pay a portion of the death benefit if the insured dies. Since the reinsurer intends to make a profit, clearly there is a cost to the life insurance company that is buying reinsurance.

Another reason that a portion of the maintenance expense may be treated as per unit is because life insurance companies will often provide extra services to policy owners with larger face amounts. For example, if a policy with a large death benefit is considering surrendering their policy, a company will often spend additional resources to try to conserve the policy.

16.4.1.6.3.4 Per decrement expense

A life insurance policy can cease to be in force for several reasons. However, whatever the reason, there are generally additional expenses associated with the termination of the policy. For example, if the insured dies, then the life insurance company must pay the claim, which results in additional expenses (such as writing the check, verifying that the insured is dead and locating the correct beneficiary). If the policy owner decides that the life insurance policy is no longer needed, then the policy will either be surrendered for its cash value or lapse

---

6 The Medical Information Bureau, generally known as MIB, facilitates sharing of underwriting information among member companies. Per the MIB, "This data acts as the vehicle to steer the underwriter's investigation, providing the insurance industry with a more complete and accurate picture of an insurance applicant's health situation." http://www.mib.com/html/about_mib_inc.html, accessed October 12, 2011.

without value if there is no cash value. A surrender will generally be more expensive than a lapse because the life insurance company will have to write a check to the policy owner for the cash value of the policy.

Death claims are assumed to occur uniformly throughout the period so this expense is assigned to the middle of the period. Surrenders and lapses are assumed to occur at the end of the period so these expenses are assigned to the end of the year.

16.4.1.7 Investment income

The investment income component (I_t) of book profit reflects investment income on assets at the beginning of the period (${}_{t-1}V + RS_{t-1}$) plus investment income on the cash flows during the period. Premium (P_t) and expenses at the beginning of the period (E_t^{BOP}) earn investment income for the entire period since they are assumed to occur at the start of the period. Death Claims ($DB_t q_t$) and expenses at the middle of the month (E_t^{MOP}) are assumed to occur uniformly throughout the period so on the average, they earn investment income for one half of the period.

16.4.1.8 Required surplus

A life insurance company is required to maintain a certain level of surplus depending on the risks that the company has assumed. The minimum surplus requirement is referred to as *risk-based capital* (RBC). RBC is defined by law or regulation in the United States and Canada. In the United States, it is defined by the laws and regulations developed by the National Association of Insurance Commissioners (NAIC). Most U.S. companies have a goal of maintaining a surplus equal to 250 to 350 percent of RBC. In Canada, RBC is determined by the Office of the Superintendent of Financial Institutions (OSFI). OSFI publishes "Minimum Continuing Capital and Surplus Requirements" (MCCSR) for life insurance companies. MCCSR contains a risk-based capital formula and detailed directions on the calculation of RBC.

Whenever a policy is sold, surplus must be allocated to support that policy. This is known as required surplus and is an additional cost for the life insurance company when it issues a new policy. The required surplus right before the policy is issued is zero, and it is also zero once the policy is no longer in force. However, while the policy is in force, the company must hold the required surplus. Any increase in required surplus reduces the book profits and any decrease increases the book profits. Because the required surplus generally increases in the early policy years and decreases in the later policy years, it tends to reduce the early book profits and increase the later book profits. The effect is to delay the time at which the company can lay claim to the profits generated by the policy, thus the effect of RBC is to provide a cushion in case things go bad and the expected profits are not realized.

Required surplus is usually expressed as a combination of various policy components reflecting the statutory requirements of RBC in the United States and Canada. For example, it might be the sum of the following:

- five percent of reserves;
- four percent of the difference between claims paid and the reserves associated with those claims; and
- four percent of premiums.

Each company develops its own formula for required surplus. However, most of the required surplus formulas used are based on the statutory RBC formula. For example, the RBC requirements are a function of the assets held by the company. Riskier assets require larger RBC. Therefore, the factor applied to the reserves (as a proxy for assets) will vary by company and generally be a reflection of the type and quality of the assets expected to be used to support the product.

These formulas also vary by product as the statutory RBC requirements in the United States and Canada reflect the risks associated with the given product. Therefore, life insurance products will have different formulas than deferred annuities, which will be different from payout annuities. Even within life insurance products, the formula may be different. For example, a variable life product where the policy owner is assuming the investment risk will require less capital than a nonvariable product where the life insurance company has the risk.

16.5 Sources of Profit

It is common for the actuary to want to fully understand the profits that are being generated by a product. One method of understanding the profits being generated by a product is to split the profits into the sources of profit. The typical sources of profit are:

- Gains from interest;
- Gains from mortality;
- Gains from expenses
- Gains from persistency
- Gains from required surplus; and
- Gains from dividends.[7]

16.5.1 Derivation of Sources of Profit

We start with our book profit formula from Section 5.4, which was:

$$\begin{aligned} BP_t = {} & ({}_{t-1}V + RS_{t-1} + P_{t-1})(1+i) - DB_t \cdot q_t(1+i)^{0.5} - CV_t \cdot w_t - Div_t(1-q_t) \\ & - E_t^{BOP}(1+i) - E_t^{MOP}(1+i)^{0.5} - E_t^{EOP} - ({}_tV + RS_t)(1 - q_t - w_t). \end{aligned}$$

We will make a simplifying assumption that death benefits are paid at the end of the year of death and get this formula:[8]

$$\begin{aligned} BP_t = {} & ({}_{t-1}V + RS_{t-1} + P_{t-1})(1+i) - DB_t \cdot q_t - CV_t \cdot w_t - Div_t(1-q_t) \\ & - E_t^{BOP}(1+i) - E_t^{MOP}(1+i)^{0.5} - E_t^{EOP} - ({}_tV + RS_t)(1 - q_t - w_t). \end{aligned}$$

7 "Gains from dividends" is actually a misnomer as dividends can only result in a reduction in profits as the dividend returns profit to the policy owner. Therefore, the gain from dividends will always be a negative.

8 Using this simplifying assumption allows us to arrive a formula that intuitively makes sense. Without this assumption, our gains from mortality does not reduce to a simple intuitive formula. Algebraically, we can develop such a formula. See Exercise 16.8.

Further, we should also note that from the recursive reserve formula:

${}_tV = ({}_{t-1}V + {}^VP_{t-1})(1 + i^G) - q_t^G(DB_t - {}_tV) - w_t^G(CV_t - {}_tV)$ where ${}^VP_t$ is the premium used to determine reserves, i^G is the interest rate, q_t^G is the mortality rate, and w_t^G is the withdrawal rate used to determine reserves.

Now, we rewrite the book profit formula by adding and subtracting ${}_tV$ in the last line.

$$\begin{aligned} BP_t = {} & ({}_{t-1}V + RS_{t-1} + P_{t-1})(1 + i) - DB_t \cdot q_t - CV_t \cdot w_t - Div_t(1 - q_t) \\ & - E_t^{BOP}(1 + i) - E_t^{MOP}(1 + i)^{0.5} - E_t^{EOP} - ({}_tV + RS_t)(1 - q_t - w_t) \\ & + {}_tV - [({}_{t-1}V + {}^VP_{t-1})(1 + i^G) - q_t^G(DB_t - {}_tV) - w_t^G(CV_t - {}_tV)]. \end{aligned}$$

Finally, we rearrange the book profit formula to get:

$$\begin{aligned} BP_t = {} & ({}^VP_{t-1} + {}_{t-1}V)(i - i^G) \\ & + (q_t^G - q_t)(DB_t - {}_tV) \\ & + (P_{t-1} - {}^VP_{t-1})(1 + i) - E_t^{BOP}(1 + i) - E_t^{MOP}(1 + i)^{0.5} - E_t^{EOP} \\ & + (w_t - w_t^G)({}_tV - CV_t) \\ & + RS_{t-1}(1 + i) - RS_t(1 - q_t - w_t) \\ & - Div_t(1 - q_t). \end{aligned}$$

We can look at this formula as follows:

BP_t = Gain from interest
+ Gain from mortality
+ Gain from expenses
+ Gains from persistency
+ Gain from required surplus
+ Gain from dividends.

16.5.2 Analysis of Sources of Profit

The source of profits formula can be used at time of pricing to determine expected profits. It can also be used to analyze the actual profits after the product has been issued. In either case, while the results may be useful, it is not necessarily indicative of satisfactory or unsatisfactory results. While it would be nice to have products that were expected to and actually did generate profits from each of the above sources (except dividends), in reality, many products are priced to generate profits from certain sources while generating losses from other sources. If the aggregate profit is acceptable, there generally is not a problem with such a product.

After a product is issued, it is instructive to compare the expected profits by source with the actual profits by source. If the actual profits by source are materially different from the expected profits by source, then the life insurance company should investigate why these differences are occurring. Further, upon understanding the reason for the deviation in experience, the life insurance company can decide what, if any, management actions are appropriate. For example, if the gain from interest is lower than expected, then the company may review its investment policy to determine if it is consistent with that used in pricing. It could also decide to adjust nonguaranteed elements (interest rates being credited or dividends being paid) if there are nonguaranteed elements in the product. In some cases, there may not be any management action that can be taken. It is still important for the life insurance company to understand why experience is deviating from expected as such an understanding may be useful in avoiding a similar occurrence in the future.

16.5.3 Comparison to Dividend Formula

It is instructive to compare the three factor dividend formula from Section 16.4.1.5 with the six factor source of profits formula. The dividend formula is

$$\begin{aligned} Div_t = (i_t^D - i_t^G)({}_{t-1}V + {}^VP_t) + (q_t^G - q_t^D)(DB_t - {}_tV) \\ + (1 + i_t^D)[G_{t-1}(1 - c_{t-1}) - {}^VP_{t-1} - e_{t-1}]. \end{aligned}$$

A close comparison shows that the first three factors of the source of profits formula have the same form as the divided formula. While the form is the same, the factors are not all the same. In particular, in the source of profit formula, i and q_t reflect actual investment return and actual mortality experience. However, the equivalent items in the dividend formula, i_t^D and q_t^D, are the investment rate and mortality used to calculate the dividends. Generally, $i_t^D < i$ and $q_t^D > q_t$ because the life insurance company does not return all profits to the policyholder. The life insurance company will keep a portion of the profits to provide a buffer against unexpected losses and to build sufficient capital to support continued growth.

The last three factors in the source of profits formula generally do not appear in the dividend formula. The gains from dividends do not appear because we are determining the dividend. Required surplus is an allocation of the company's surplus used to support the product while it is in force. It is not surplus generated by the product and as such, the gains from required surplus should not be paid out as dividends. Finally, gains from persistency are generally not paid as dividends. In many cases, there is not a material difference between the CV_t and ${}_tV$ so this factor would contribute little to the dividends. Secondly, termination of policies may generate profits if ${}_tV > CV_t$, but in the long term it generally decreases the profits as the policy is not going to generate profits in the future.

16.6 Company Models

Our discussion in this chapter has included cell-based models (looking at results of a single cell) as well as a model office where the results of several cells are combined to produce the results for a group of policies. While these approaches are commonly used to price life insurance products, for many other tasks, an actuary needs a more robust financial model. For example, the actuary may want to develop a model that will project the future financial results of a block of business or the company as a whole. These models may include the liability side of the business only or the model may project both assets and liabilities. Such models, which we will call *company models*, can be used for cash flow testing, gross premium valuations and to determine the value of a company. While company models are significantly more complicated than single cell models or model offices, the building blocks for company models are single cell models or model offices.

16.6.1 Seriatim Company Model

In the most granular company model, but in many senses the simplest model, we build a single cell model for each policy, and then add together the results of each cell to get the total results for the company. Even in this case, a cell may be used for multiple policies. For example, if two policies have essentially the same demographics, then the same cell can be used for both policies. This is true even if the policies were not issued at the same time. For example, assume two traditional whole life policies were issued to two female nonsmokers who were both age 35 at the time of issue. However, one policy was issued on January 1, 2009, and the other policy was issued on January 1, 2010. If these are identical policies with the same expected cash flows, we can use the same cell for both policies. If we wanted to model results for 2011, we would take the results of the third year of the single cell projection, which represents the 2011 projection for a policy issued on January 1, 2009, and add the results from the second year of the single cell projection which represents the 2011 projection for the policy issued on January 1, 2010. To further illustrate, suppose the traditional whole life cell for this policy projects premiums as follows:

Policy Year	Premium per Policy
1	900
2	800
3	720
4	660

Our company model for these two policies would project a 2011 premium of 720.00 + 800.00 = 1,520.00.

This same approach would be used for each cash flow and for reserves and book profits.

16.6.2 Grouped Company Model

In most cases, a seriatim company model is not reasonable or feasible. The cost of a seriatim model is substantial and generally not justified. Therefore, most company models use a grouped approach. The steps in developing a grouped approach are:

- Step 1: Develop single-cell projections that represent a large percentage of the business in force in the company or block of business that is being modeled;
- Step 2: Assign each policy being modeled to the cell that best represents that policy;

- Step 3: Multiply the results of the each single cell projection developed in Step 1 by the number of units or policies assigned to that cell in Step 2; and
- Step 4: Accumulate the results of Step 3 to develop the company projection.

The first two steps tend to be very labor intensive and time consuming. Additionally, each step is interrelated. Single-cell projections need to be developed for all critical products. The actuary must review each and every product and determine if the product is important enough to model or if it can be modeled with another product. Further, once it is determined that a product will be modeled, then the number of cells necessary to model that product must be determined. Finally, for each cell that will be modeled all the relevant information must be entered into the software that will be used to complete the company model.

Once the first two steps are completed, the last two steps are generally completed by the software. Therefore, while these steps may take time, they are not very labor intensive.

16.6.2.1 Single-cell projections

Single-cell projections need to be developed that will cover the majority of the business being modeled. These cells are generally defined by product, issue age, gender, and premium class. Other parameters may also be incorporated. For example, if assumptions or product features vary by year of issue, then year of issue might be another parameter.

16.6.2.2 Assigning policies to cells

Even within the parameters list in Section 16.6.2.1, cells are not developed for every possible value of the parameter. For example, if a product is sold at issue ages 0 to 80, then cells could be developed for issue ages 5, 15, 25, 35, 45, 55, 65, and 75. Then, the policies issued at ages 0 through 9 would be assigned to the cell for issue age 5, the policies issued at ages 10 through 19 would be assigned to the cell for issue age 15, etc.

However, for the product parameter, a general rule of thumb is that single-cell projections should be developed to cover about 80 percent of the business being modeled where the 80 percent is measured by the number of policies, the amount of reserves, and face amount being modeled. One way to accomplish this is to take each product and sort by the number of policies, amount of reserves and face amount. Take the smallest number of products such that 80 percent of each category is covered and model those products. The remaining products are grouped or modeled into the modeled products based on the model product that is closest to the unmodeled product.

16.6.2.3 Accumulating the results

Once we have the single-cell projections and have assigned each policy to a cell, the final two steps in the process can be completed. We multiply each cell by the number of units that have been assigned to that cell when the policies are assigned to the cells. The basis for each single-cell projection must match the assignment of the units to the cells. Normally the single-cell projections are completed on a per unit basis. For example, for life insurance policies, a unit could be 1,000 of death benefit. Then we would multiply by the number of 1,000s of death benefit that were assigned to that cell.

16.6.3 Complications of a Company Model

16.6.3.1 Policy year versus calendar year

Company models are done on a policy year basis or a calendar year basis. A policy year is based on the date that the policy was issued. If a policy is issued on July 1, 2011, then the first policy year is from July 1, 2011, to June 30, 2012. Each subsequent policy year runs from July 1 to June 30. A calendar year basis looks at results from January 1 to December 31.

For company models involving new business or pricing (or repricing), a policy year basis is usually used. For most other purposes, a calendar year basis is used. Our single-cell projections need to be on the same basis or converted to the same basis. Most single-cell projections are done on a policy year basis so for a calendar year projection, they must be converted to a calendar year basis. Today, most projections are actually completed on a monthly basis, so converting to a calendar year basis is very simple. For example, if all the policies are assumed to be issued on July 1 of a year, then the results for the first 6 months of our project would be in one calendar year, the results for months 7 through 18 would be in another calendar year, and so on.

16.6.3.2 Flexibility of the model

As mentioned previously, building a model is time consuming and labor intensive. Furthermore, a model is seldom used just once or for only one purpose. Therefore, building a model that is flexible, easily updated, and adaptable is important. The actuary needs to keep this in mind when the model is initially developed.

Assumptions that are not product specific should be entered into the model in the aggregate and not at the product level. For example, the same interest rate scenarios are generally used for all products and should be entered in the aggregate. This permits flexibility and allows assumptions that change frequently to be changed one place in the model.

Product features, on the other hand, are generally built into each cell of the model. For example, the premium rate charged is generally cell specific and will not change in the future so building it into each cell is appropriate.

16.6.3.3 Output of a model

The output of a company model should reflect the use of that model. However, for most uses, it is desirable to have output that follows a standard income statement and balance sheet. This facilitates the validation of the model (discussed in Section 16.6.3.4). Furthermore, output that follows a standard income statement and balance sheet will facilitate non-actuaries understanding the model and its results.

16.6.3.4 Validation of a company model

A critical step in any model is the validation of the model. Once the model has been run, the output must be reviewed to verify that it reasonably reflects reality and does not contain errors. There are generally two levels of validation—static validation and dynamic validation.

In static validation, the beginning balances in the company model are compared to the actual balances on the date that the projection begins. Balances that are compared might include the number of policies, amount of death benefit, and the account value and surrender value for deferred annuities or universal or variable life. The beginning balances in the model should be approximately equal to the actual balances on the date that the projection begins.

In a dynamic validation, the income statement items for the first year of the projection are compared to the appropriate income statement items for the last two or three years. The progression from the actual historic values to the projection values should be reasonable and smooth. For example, the premium collected over the last three years could be compared to the premium projected during the first year of the company model.

An alternative method of completing a dynamic validation is programmed into some modeling software. These software packages use the input in the model to "backcast" an income statement and balance sheet for the year prior to the model start date. The results of this backcast year can be compared to the actual results over the last year as a method of verifying that the model is doing a good job of modeling the company.

A good model will also allow the actuary to "drill down" into results. Drill down means that the results from only a portion of the model can be reviewed. This could be at the product level or all the way down at a single cell level. The ability to drill down provides a way to understand unusual results once they are identified. It is also a good idea to select a number of cells for review at a detailed level to verify that the model is working correctly. This is especially important for a new model.

16.6.3.5 Simplified approaches

In some cases, a simplified model may produce as good a projection as a detailed model. These cases are usually for relatively simple liabilities. An example is a block of deferred annuities where a portfolio interest rate is being paid. The whole block of annuities may be easily projected just based on an interest rate, an expense cost and a termination rate. There may be no economic justification to project these annuity policies using a detailed, single-cell model.

16.7 EXERCISES

16.1 Using the premiums in Table 16.5, calculate:

1. The premium for 50,000 of insurance for a person age 40;
2. The premium for 150,000 of insurance for a person age 38;
3. The premium for 750,000 of insurance for a person age 36.

16.2 Ryan, age 35, wants to buy 925,000 of life insurance. Using the premiums in Table 16.5, can Ryan actually buy 925,000 of insurance? If not, determine the amount of life insurance that Ryan will buy. Determine the premium that Ryan will pay.

16.3 Using the premiums in Table 16.6 and a policy fee of 125, calculate:

1. The premium for 50,000 of insurance for a person age 40;
2. The premium for 150,000 of insurance for a person age 38;
3. The premium for 750,000 of insurance for a person age 36.

16.4 Ryan, age 35, wants to buy 925,000 of life insurance. Using the premiums in Table 16.6 with a policy fee of 125, what premium would Ryan pay?

16.5 Develop the premiums to be assumed during the first 20 years for a flexible premium UL policy where the first year premium is expected to be 2,000. Assume that the premium suspension rate will be 10% for the second premium, 7.5% for the third premium and 5% for each subsequent premium.

16.6 Using the premiums in Table 16.6, calculate the modal premiums per 1,000, $Prem_t$, to be used to calculate book profits for an insured age 40. Assume an average size of 200,000 and use the following mode factors in your calculations:

Premium Mode	Mode Factor
Semi-Annual	0.525
Quarterly	0.265
Monthly	0.090

16.7 Using the banded premiums in Table 16.5, calculate the modal premiums per 1,000, $Prem_t$, to be used to calculate book profits for an insured age 40. Assume an average size of 600,000 and use the following mode factors in your calculations:

Premium Mode	Mode Factor
Semi-Annual	0.525
Quarterly	0.265
Monthly	0.090

16.8 Derive a source of profits formula if we assume that the death benefits are paid in the middle of the year. In that case, our recursive reserve formula is

$${}_tV = ({}_{t-1}V + {}^VP_{t-1})(1 + i^G) - q_t^G[DB_t(1 + i^G)^{0.5} - {}_tV] - w_t^G(CV_t - {}_tV).$$

CHAPTER 17

Inputs for Profit Testing

17.1 Investment Income

Investment income is earned on the assets accumulated by a life insurance policy. In pricing a life insurance product, we will incorporate investment income based on the interest rates that we expect to earn during the life of the policy. Our expected interest rates will be a function of:

- Anticipated investment strategy;
- Current interest rate environment;
- Investment earnings rates on currently owned assets; and
- Policy provisions to allow post-issue adjustments.

Since investment returns vary by the duration of the investment (e.g., 5 year versus 20 year), quality of investment and type of investment (e.g., bonds versus mortgages), the intended investment strategy is critical to determining the expected investment income. Of course, the investment strategy also needs to reflect asset-liability matching requirements. Finally, the investment income must reflect the potential default costs associated with the investment strategy.

Life insurance policies that are participating or contain nonguaranteed elements permit adjustments to be made to the cost of the policy if the actual investment earnings are different from the expected investment earnings. The expected investment earnings for such policies will typically be more aggressive than for policies which do not contain such provisions. For example, a company might use the investment returns in Table 17.1.

TABLE 17.1 Investment Returns Assumed for Pricing

Duration	Participating Whole Life	Nonparticipating Whole Life
1–5	7.0 %	7.0%
6	7.0%	6.6%
7	7.0%	6.2%
8	7.0%	5.8%
9	7.0%	5.4%
10+	7.0%	5.0%

17.2 Equity Returns

Equity returns are important in pricing a variable annuity or variable life insurance product. Since equity returns can fluctuate substantially, a standard approach is to generate a variety of equity return scenarios. These scenarios are then used during the pricing process to examine the potential results of each scenario.

The variety of scenarios may be generated using a deterministic approach with the scenarios reflecting past historical equity returns or the actuary's judgment. However, the most common approach is to generate scenarios using a stochastic generator. A large number of scenarios may be generated with scenario reduction techniques being used to summarize these stochastic scenarios into a more manageable number of scenarios that are used for pricing.

17.3 Mortality

One of the key inputs for pricing a life insurance product is the mortality expected to occur in the future on the product being priced. The expected mortality may be a function of:

- Age;
- Gender;
- Duration since issue;
- Premium class (e.g., smoker or nonsmoker);
- Underwriting (full underwriting versus limited underwriting); and
- Distribution system.

The expected mortality may be developed based on the individual company's past experience. However, many companies do not have sufficient or statistically credible data to develop their own mortality tables. These companies will generally use industry experience compiled by organizations such as the Society of Actuaries. The expected mortality may be expressed as a percent of the industry experience based on company specific mortality studies or industry studies.

Mortality assumptions for deferred annuities have less importance because the death benefit on a deferred annuity is generally approximately equal to the reserve. Therefore, the payment of death benefit under a deferred annuity is completely or substantially offset by the release of the reserve that is held.

Mortality assumptions for payout annuities are important if the payments are life contingent. Very few life insurance companies have sufficient mortality experience on payout annuities to develop their own mortality assumptions. Therefore, almost all companies use industry experience as the basis for their mortality assumptions.

It should be noted that for payout annuities, if actual mortality is higher than expected, the company will experience a gain as the company will pay out less than was expected at the time of pricing.

17.4 Persistency

A policy persists if it stays in force and does not lapse or surrender. A lapse is usually considered to be the termination of a policy with no cash value. Surrender is usually used to refer to a policy that terminates with a cash surrender value. Persistency assumptions are often expressed as the probability of lapse or surrender.

For a life insurance product, the expected persistency may be a function of:

- Age;
- Duration since issue; and
- Distribution system.

Because lapses and surrenders occur much more frequently than deaths, most life insurance companies have sufficient experience to develop their own persistency tables. However, many companies still use industry experience, which is generally compiled by the Life Insurance Marketing Research Association in the United States in collaboration with the Society of Actuaries. The most recent study was published in 2009 using data from 2004–2005 (an update is expected in late 2011 or early 2012).[1] As with mortality, the probability of lapse or surrender is often expressed as a percent of the industry experience.

The persistency assumption for deferred annuities is very important. If a deferred annuity surrenders, then it cannot generate future profits. A high surrender rate means that sufficient profits will not be generated in the future to amortize the initial expenses and commissions paid.

Surrender assumptions for deferred annuities are generally a function of the surrender charge. The surrender charge is an impediment to lapses as the policy owner often does not wish to pay the surrender charge. An example of a surrender assumption for deferred annuities is

$$15\% - \textit{Surrender Charge Percent.}$$

For example, if the surrender charge is 6 percent in the fifth policy year, then the assumed surrender rate in the fifth policy year will bc 9 percent.

Payout annuities are priced assuming no lapse or surrender rates. Generally, payout annuities do not provide an option to surrender or lapse. See Section 18.3.2 for further discussion.

17.5 Expenses

Types of expenses are described in detail in Section 16.4.1.6. A company can use various approaches to determining the expense assumptions to use in the pricing of products.

17.5.1 Fully Allocated Expenses versus Marginal Expenses

The company may use *fully allocated* expenses or *marginal* expenses. With fully allocated expenses, all expenses of the company are included in the development of expense assumptions used to price a life insurance product. With marginal expenses, the expense assumptions used to price a product will only reflect the additional costs expected to be generated by the new product.

The most common difference between fully allocated expenses and marginal expenses is overhead. An example of overhead is the salaries of senior officers of the company such as the chief executive officer, chief financial officer, and chief actuary. With fully allocated expenses, the cost of the senior officers is included in the expense assumptions used to price new business. The concept is that all policies benefit from the expertise of the senior officers. Therefore, all policies should bear the costs of overhead. With marginal expenses, overhead expenses are generally not included since selling a new product will not result in additional

1 Society of Actuaries and LIMRA (2009). The paper and accompanying spreadsheet are available with the book's online resources.

overhead. For example, the company will not hire additional senior officers just because a new product is being sold.

17.5.2 Expense Analysis

A company may use a very detailed process to develop these expenses. One such approach is a functional cost study. In a functional cost study, each employee of the company keeps detailed track of the time spent on each task. This tracking of time by task is generally done for a short period of time such as two weeks to one month. Based on this analysis the employee's salary and related expenses (cost of benefits, implied "rent" for the portion of the office allocated to that employee, etc.) are assigned to various functions such as issue of new policies, servicing of existing policies and marketing.

Alternatively, a company may use a less rigorous approach. The company may allocate expenses to various functions using various approximations or rules of thumb. For example, the company may allocate 60 percent of expenses to the generation of new business and 40 percent of expenses to servicing in force business. The expenses associated with new business will be split between the various categories of expenses—per policy, per 1,000, percent of premium and per decrement. Once the aggregate expenses are allocated to each category, then aggregate expenses allocated to each category is divided by the number of units in each category.

EXAMPLE 17.1

A life insurance company has the following information available to determine expense assumptions.

- Total expenses related to life insurance incurred in a year is 1,000,000.
- Total life insurance policies issued during year was 1,500.
- Total annualized premium on policies issued during the year was 1,200,000.
- Total death benefit for policies issued during the year was 150,000,000.
- Total life insurance policies in force at the start of the year was 12,000.
- Total life insurance policies in force at the end of the year was 13,000.
- The company allocates 55% of total expenses to maintaining the in force policies and 45% to the generation of new business.
- Maintenance expenses are allocated on a per policy basis.
- For the expenses associated with new business, 60% are allocated per policy, 25% are allocated per 1,000 of death benefit and 15% are allocated as a percent of premium.

Determine the expense assumptions based on this information.

Our maintenance expense assumption is

$$\textit{Maintenance Per Policy} = \frac{(1{,}000{,}000)(0.55)}{(12{,}000 + 13{,}000)/2} = 44.00.$$

The denominator is the average number of policies in force during the year.

Our issue expenses are

$$Issue\ Expense\ Per\ Policy = \frac{1{,}000{,}000(0.45)(0.60)}{1{,}500} = 180.00$$

$$Issue\ Expense\ Per\ 1000 = \frac{1{,}000{,}000(0.45)(0.25)}{150{,}000} = 0.75$$

$$Issue\ Expense\ as\ Percent\ of\ Premium = \frac{1{,}000{,}000(0.45)(0.15)}{1{,}200{,}000} = 5.625\%.$$

Some companies use industry or benchmark assumptions. For small companies or larger companies entering into a new market, using industry average expenses as a benchmark for pricing may be necessary to compete with other companies marketing the same or similar products. The justification for using such assumptions is that the company will grow and achieve economies of scale over time that will reduce actual expenses below the benchmark expenses. Without the use of such expenses, the company could never expect to grow sufficiently since the products would not be competitive in the marketplace.

One source of benchmark expenses are studies conducted by the Society of Actuaries. One such study is completed annually to produce the Generally Recognized Expense Table. These are commonly known as GRET expenses. These expenses are available for use in testing by the Illustration Actuary.[2] However, they can also be used for pricing. One problem with the GRET expenses is that they have fluctuated substantially from year to year. These tables are prepared by the SOA and approved by the NAIC.[3]

17.6 EXERCISES

17.1 A life insurance company has the following information available to determine expense assumptions.

- Total expenses related to life insurance incurred in a year is 3,000,000.
- Total life insurance policies issued during year was 8,000.
- Total annualized premium on policies issued during the year was 6,000,000.
- Total death benefit for policies issued during the year was 7 billion.
- Total life insurance policies in force at the start of the year was 50,000.
- Total life insurance policies in force at the end of the year was 52,000.
- The company allocates 40% of total expenses to maintaining the in force policies and 60% to the generation of new business.
- Maintenance expenses are allocated on a per policy basis.
- For the expenses associated with new business, 60% are allocated per policy, 20% are allocated per 1,000 of death benefit and 20% are allocated as a percent of premium.

Determine the expense assumptions that would be developed based on this nformation.

2 Testing by the Illustration Actuary must be completed annually but is beyond the scope of this book.

3 A copy of the 2012 proposed draft is available at http://www.naic.org/documents/committees_a_latf_110720_soa_2012_gret_analysis.pdf.

CHAPTER 18
Regulatory Influences on Profit Testing

18.1 Reserves

18.1.1 General

A life insurance or annuity contract generally obligates a life insurance company to make payments (death benefits or annuity payments) in the future in return for the policy owner making premium payments. Therefore, the life insurance company has a future liability. This liability needs to be recorded on the balance sheet of the life insurance company. The reserve is this liability. It is important to understand that the reserve is merely an estimate of this liability.

18.1.2 Types of Reserves

Reserves have many purposes. In the following sections, reserve types are identified by their purpose. The purpose tends to drive the methods, models and assumptions used.

18.1.2.1 Statutory reserves

Reserves may be prescribed by law. These reserves are generally called statutory reserves and must be used in the financial statements filed with regulatory authorities. Statutory reserves contain a level of conservatism as the reserves are intended to assure that the life insurance company will be able to meet its future obligations. Thus, the main purpose of these reserves is to protect the company's policy owners and beneficiaries.

Statutory reserves may be fully prescribed by law. For example, in the United States, both the model and the assumptions used to calculate minimum statutory reserves are defined by law. A life insurance company in the United States can hold a higher reserve, but may not hold a reserve lower than the prescribed reserve.

Statutory reserves may also be principles based. For principles-based statutory reserves, the law will require that an insurance company hold a reserve, but the model and/or the assumptions will not be specified. In this case, the actuary, using any prescribed guidance from the law or from professional standards, will be responsible for determining the appropriate model and assumptions to use in calculating the reserve. Many jurisdictions, including Canada, use a principles-based approach to calculating statutory reserves. At the current time, the United States is considering adoption of principles-based reserves for policies issued in the future.

A principles-based approach relies on actuarial judgment and professionalism as well as a variety of models. A principles-based approach to reserves generally is based on the following concepts.

- It captures all of the significant financial risks, benefits, and guarantees associated with the contracts including the "tail risk" and the funding of the risks;
- It uses risk analysis and risk management techniques to quantify the risks and is guided by the evolving practice and expanding knowledge in the measurement and

management of risk. This may include, to the extent required for an appropriate assessment of the underlying risks, stochastic models and other means of analysis that properly reflect the risks of the underlying contracts;
- It incorporates assumptions and methods that are consistent with, but not necessarily identical to, those used by the company in pricing or overall risk management;
- It permits the use of company experience, based on the availability of relevant insurance company experience and its degree of credibility, to establish assumptions for risks over which the company has some degree of control; and
- It provides for the use of assumptions that contain an appropriate level of conservatism when viewed in the aggregate and that, together with the methods used, recognize the solvency objective of statutory reserves.

18.1.2.2 GAAP reserves

In the United States, financial results for life insurance companies are generally reported to shareholders and financial markets (as opposed to regulatory authorities) using GAAP. The reserves used in these financial statements are different from those calculated for statutory purposes. GAAP reserves are determined in accordance with accounting standards and guidance promulgated by the American Institute of Certified Public Accountants and the Financial Accounting Standards Board.

GAAP reserves for traditional, nonparticipating life insurance products are determined in accordance with Statement of Financial Accounting Standard (SFAS) 60. This is a premium-based model in that profits emerge in relation to premiums. SFAS 60 reserves generally contain a margin of conservatism known as a *provision for adverse deviation* (PAD). However, the amount of conservatism is usually less than the conservatism built into statutory reserves.

GAAP reserves for annuity and universal life type products are determined in accordance with SFAS 97. This is not a premium-based model as the profits emerge in relation to gross margins as opposed to premiums. These reserves are generally calculated on best estimate assumptions with little or no conservatism incorporated in the calculation of reserves.

For GAAP reserves established under either SFAS 60 or SFAS 97, we have stated that the reserves are less conservative than the statutory reserve. Statutory reserves and GAAP reserves serve different purposes. The purpose of statutory reserves is to help provide assurance that the life insurance company will have sufficient assets to be able to satisfy future obligations. The emphasis is on the balance sheet and not on providing a realistic income statement. GAAP reserves are realistic (with small margins) as their purpose is to appropriately allocate income between accounting periods. Here the emphasis is on the income statement.

GAAP reserves differ from statutory reserves in several ways. These include:

- GAAP reserves account for nonforfeiture benefits while statutory reserves do not;
- The assumptions used to calculate GAAP reserves are not specified but are determined by the actuary. For statutory reserves in the United States, the law specifies the assumptions that must be used to calculate the reserves; and

- GAAP reserves also explicitly reflect expenses while statutory reserves do not explicitly reflect expenses. Under GAAP accounting, most expenses that are directly related to issuing the policy are considered to be *deferred acquisition costs* (DAC). These expenses are established as a contra-liability. In GAAP financials, the DAC is then amortized over the life of the policy against either premiums or gross margins depending on the model being used.

18.1.2.3 Canadian reserves

In Canada, reserves are calculated using the Canadian asset liability method (CALM). CALM reserves are used for all purposes (reporting to regulators, shareholders, financial markets and determination of income taxes). CALM is a principles-based approach where reserves are calculated at the business segment level. Reserves are not calculated on a policy by policy level although the reserves calculated at the business segment are allocated to the policy level.

Under CALM, the cash flows from the business segment's assets and liabilities are projected until all liabilities have matured. These projections are completed under several scenarios. The base scenario and nine prescribed scenarios must be used in the CALM approach. Additional scenarios are also utilized, which can be deterministic or stochastic scenarios. For each scenario, the reserve is the amount of beginning assets necessary so the assets are forecast to be zero at the end of the projection.

The reserve is then determined by selecting one of the scenarios and using the reserve for that scenario. The reserve must be greater than the reserve required for the baseline and each of the required scenarios. If stochastic scenarios are used, then the scenario chosen should be in the range defined by the average of the highest 40 percent of scenarios and the average of the highest 20 percent of scenarios. If deterministic scenarios are used, the scenario chosen should be in the upper part of the range of scenarios.

The actuary establishes the assumptions to be used in applying CALM. The final reserve reflects a level of conservatism that is appropriate for solvency reserves and is determined by the actuary with guidance from the Canadian Institute of Actuaries and regulatory authorities.

18.1.2.4 Gross premium reserves

Gross premium reserves reflect all future cash flows under a life insurance policy or an annuity. The reserve is the present value of future cash outflows (benefits, expenses, etc.) less the present value of future cash inflows (premiums, earnings on required surplus, etc.). The future cash flows are generally completed using best estimate assumptions. Assets may be included in the projection or a fixed discount rate may be used to determine the present values.

Gross premium reserves are generally not used for financial reporting, but often are the best estimate of the true economic reserve. In other words, the gross premium reserve will be the best estimate of the true liability that the life insurance company has accepted.

18.1.2.5 Federal income tax reserves

In the United States, the IRC prescribes the reserves that must be used to determine income for the purpose of calculating FIT. The reserves prescribed by the IRC are similar to the reserves prescribed for current statutory reserves except the assumptions are generally less conservative. These reserves should be calculated and used in pricing of products if the pricing includes federal income taxes as an expense. If this is not done, then the federal income tax expense will not be accurate.

18.2 Reserve Model

We will start by developing a general reserve model. We will then take this general model and express it in terms of our cash flows as we did to calculate book profits. Finally, we will explore how this model would be modified to calculate each of the types of reserve discussed in Section 18.1.

18.2.1 General Reserve Formula

We will use the following general reserve model:

Reserve = Present Value of Future Benefits + Present Value of Future Expenses − Present Value of Future Premiums.

This model, or a modified version of it, can be used for all types of reserves discussed in Section 18.1. The assumptions that are used to calculate the present values will vary by type of reserve.

18.2.2 Detailed Reserve Formula

We will now define the reserve at time s, ${}_sV$, in a more complete formula as:

$$
\begin{aligned}
{}_sV = & \sum_{t=0} DB_{s+t+1}\,{}_tp^{(\tau)}_{x+s}q_{x+s+t}\cdot v^{t+0.5} \\
& + \sum_{t=0} CV_{s+t+1}\,{}_tp^{(\tau)}_{x+s}w_{x+s+t}\cdot v^{t+1} \\
& + \sum_{t=0} Div_{s+t+1}\,{}_tp^{(\tau)}_{x+s}(1 - q_{x+s+t})v^{t+1} \\
& + \sum_{t=0} AnnBen_{s+t+1}\,{}_tp^{(\tau)}_{x+s}(1 - q_{x+s+t})v^{t+1} \\
& + \sum_{t=0} Dis_{s+t+1}\,{}_tp^{(-dis)}_{x+s}v^{t} \\
& + \sum_{t=0} [E^{BOP}_{s+t+1}\,{}_tp^{(\tau)}_{x+s}v^{t} + E^{MOP}_{s+t+1}\,{}_tp^{(\tau)}_{x+s}(1 - q_{x+s+t})^{0.5}v^{t+0.5} + E^{EOP}_{s+t+1}\,{}_tp^{(\tau)}_{x+s}(1 - q_{x+s+t})v^{t+1}] \\
& - \sum_{t=0} {}^{V}P_{s+t}\,{}_tp^{(\tau)}_{x+s}v^{t}.
\end{aligned}
$$

The subscript x is the age at which the policy was issued. The subscript s is the time in periods (typically one year for statutory reserves or one month for gross premium reserves) from when the policy is issued and the subscript t is the time from the current time (s) at which the quantity is being evaluated. For payments such as death benefits and dividends, the subscript indicates the time period in which it was paid and not the exact time within that period it is assumed to be paid.

18.2.2.1 Mortality Component

The expression $\sum_{t=0} DB_{s+t+1}\,{}_tp^{(\tau)}_{x+s}q_{x+s+t}\cdot v^{t+0.5}$ represents the present value of future death benefits.

DB_{s+t+1} is the death benefit from time t to time t+1 from the current time s.

The expression ${}_tp^{(\tau)}_{x+s}q_{x+s+t}$ is the probability that the insured does not die or surrender for t periods in the future and then dies in the $t + 1$st period. Finally, $v^{t+0.5}$ is the interest discount assuming that the death benefit is paid in the middle of time period $t + 1$. If the death benefit is paid at a time other than the middle of time period $t + 1$, then this discount factor would need to be adjusted accordingly. Similarly, the formula makes a specific assumption about when each type of payment is made and an appropriate adjustment is needed if a different assumption is made.

We will illustrate these terms for a policy issued at age 35 that is now at time five (age 40) using one year as the time period. The contribution for the third time period ($t = 2$) will be illustrated. The mortality component is

$$DB_{5+3}({}_2p^{(\tau)}_{35+5})q_{35+5+2}\cdot v^{2+0.5} = DB_8({}_2p^{(\tau)}_{40})q_{42}\cdot v^{2.5}.$$

18.2.2.2 Surrender benefits component

The expression $\sum_{t=0} CV_{s+t+1}\,{}_tp^{(\tau)}_{x+s}w_{x+s+t}v^{t+1}$ represents the present value of future surrender benefits. CV_{s+t+1} is the cash surrender benefit from time t to time $t + 1$. CV_{s+t+1} may vary over this time period. If this is the case, then the appropriate value of CV_{s+t+1} should be used depending on the point during the period that CV_{s+t+1} is assumed to be paid. In our expression, the surrender value is assumed to be paid at the end of time period $t + 1$.

The expression ${}_tp^{(\tau)}_{x+s}w_{x+s+t}$ is the probability that the insured does not die or surrender for t periods in the future and then surrenders in the $t + 1$st period. Finally, v^{t+1} is the interest discount assuming that the surrender benefit is paid at the end of time period $t + 1$.

For our example, the contribution is

$$CV_{5+2+1}({}_2p^{(\tau)}_{35+5})w_{35+5+2}\cdot v^{2+1} = CV_8({}_2p^{(\tau)}_{40})w_{42}\cdot v^3.$$

18.2.2.3 Dividend component

The expression $\sum_{t=0} Div_{s+t+1}\,{}_tp^{(\tau)}_{x+s}(1 - q_{x+s+t})v^{t+1}$ represents the present value of future dividends. If a policy is nonparticipating, then this term does not need to be included. Div_{s+t+1} is the dividend during the time period from t to $t+1$. The expression ${}_tp^{(\tau)}_{x+s}(1 - q_{x+s+t})$ is the probability that the insured does not die or surrender for t periods in the future and then does not die in the $t + 1$st period. There is an assumption that any surrender during the $t + 1^{tst}$ period will be at the end of the period and the dividend will be paid prior to the surrender. Finally, v^{t+1} is the interest discount assuming that the dividend is paid at the end of time period t.

For our example, the contribution is

$$Div_{5+2+1}({}_2p^{(T)}_{35+5})(1 - q_{35+5+2})v^{2+1} = Div_8({}_2p^{(T)}_{40})(1 - q_{42})v^3.$$

18.2.2.4 Annuity component

The expression $\sum_{t=0} AnnBen_{s+t+1}\, {}_tp^{(T)}_{x+s}(1 - q_{x+s+t})v^{t+1}$ represents the present value of future annuity benefits. If a policy does not provide annuity benefits, then this term does not need to be included. $AnnBen_{s+t+1}$ is the annuity benefit during time period from t to $t + 1$. The expression ${}_tp^{(T)}_{x+s}(1 - q_{x+s+t})$ is the probability that the insured does not die or surrender for t periods in the future and then does not die in the t + 1st period. There is an assumption that any surrender during the t + 1st period will be at the end of the period and the annuity benefit will be paid prior to the surrender. Finally, v^{t+1} is the interest discount assuming that the annuity benefit is paid at the end of time period $t + 1$.

If the benefit is paid at the start of the period, then the formula becomes $\sum_{t=0} AnnBen_{s+t+1}\, {}_tp^{(T)}_{x+s} \cdot v^t$.

If the payments are guaranteed or certain such as an interest-only payout annuity, then the formula for the reserve is $\sum_{t=0} AnnBen_{s+t+1} \cdot v^{t+1}$. This formula assumes payments at the end of the period.

For our example, using the first version of the formula, the contribution is

$$AnnBen_{5+2+1}({}_2p^{(T)}_{35+5})(1 - q_{35+5+2})v^{2+1} = AnnBen_8({}_2p^{(T)}_{40})(1 - q_{42})v^3.$$

18.2.2.5 Disability component

The expression $\sum_{t=0} Dis_{s+t+1}\, {}_tp^{(-dis)}_{x+s} v^t$ represents the present value of future disability benefits. In most cases, for life insurance and annuity policies, this term does not need to be included as no disability benefits will be provided. The component will be necessary when the waiver of premium or waiver of monthly deduction rider is attached. Dis_{s+t+1} is the disability benefit that would be paid during time period t to $t + 1$. The expression ${}_tp^{(-dis)}_{x+s}$ is the probability that the insured will be disabled at the beginning of the t + 1st period. There is an assumption that any disability benefit is paid at the beginning of the t + 1st period since this benefit will usually be a waiver of a premium or monthly deduction, which occur at the start of a time period. Finally, v^t is the interest discount assuming that the disability benefit is paid at the beginning of the t + 1st time period.

For our example, the contribution is

$$Dis_{5+3}({}_2p^{(-dis)}_{35+5})v^2 = Dis_8({}_2p^{(-dis)}_{40})v^2.$$

18.2.2.6 Expense component

The expression

$$\sum_{t=0}[E^{BOP}_{s+t+1}\,{}_tp^{(\tau)}_{x+s}v^t + E^{MOP}_{s+t+1}\,{}_tp^{(\tau)}_{x+s}(1 - q_{x+s+t})^{0.5}v^{t+0.5} + E^{EOP}_{s+t+1}\,{}_tp^{(\tau)}_{x+s}(1 - q_{x+s+t})v^{t+1}]$$

represents the present value of future expenses. E^{BOP}_{s+t+1}, E^{MOP}_{s+t+1}, and E^{EOP}_{s+t+1} are the expenses incurred at the beginning, middle and end of the $t+1$st time period respectively.

The probability terms represent the probability that the insured has survived to the beginning of the period and then not died between then and the assigned payment date. It is assumed that surrenders are at the end of the year, so there is no need to survive this decrement. Finally, the interest discount factors are determined based on when the expense is incurred.

For the example, the contribution is

$$E^{BOP}_{5+2+1}({}_2p^{(\tau)}_{35+5})v^2 + E^{MOP}_{5+2+1}({}_2p^{(\tau)}_{35+5})(1 - q_{35+5+2})^{0.5}v^{2+0.5} + E^{EOP}_{5+2+1}({}_2p^{(\tau)}_{35+5})(1 - q_{35+5+2})v^{2+1}$$
$$= E^{BOP}_8({}_2p^{(\tau)}_{40})v^2 + E^{MOP}_8({}_2p^{(\tau)}_{40})(1 - q_{42})^{0.5}v^{2.5} + E^{EOP}_8({}_2p^{(\tau)}_{40})(1 - q_{42})v^3.$$

18.2.2.7 Premium component

Finally, the expression $\sum_{t=0} {}^VP_{s+t}\,{}_tp^{(\tau)}_{x+s} \cdot v^t$ represents the present value of future premium payments. ${}^VP_{s+t}$ represents[1] the valuation premium payable at the beginning of the $t+1$st time period which is time t. Note the use of the subscript $s+t$ rather than $s+t+1$ as in the other cases. This is because premiums are almost always paid in advance, so the subscript represents the time of the premium payment and not the period. This premium will vary depending on the type of reserve that is being calculated. For example, the gross premium will be used for a gross premium reserve. A net benefit premium will be used for U.S. statutory reserves.

There is an assumption that any premium is paid at the beginning of the $t+1$st period. Finally, v^t is the interest discount assuming that the premium is paid at the beginning of the $t+1$st time period t.

For the example, the contribution is ${}^VP_{5+2}\,{}_2p^{(\tau)}_{35+5} \cdot v^2 = {}^VP_7\,{}_2p^{(\tau)}_{40} \cdot v^2$.

18.2.3 U.S. Statutory Reserves

The most common basis used for pricing products in the United States is based on the statutory accounting framework. When this accounting framework is used, then the reserves to be used in the Book Profits calculations are statutory reserves. Statutory reserves vary by product and will be discussed for life insurance, deferred and payout annuities. Statutory reserves are specified by the Standard Valuation Law.

---

1 It should be clear by now that what is important is not getting all the symbols correct but rather ensuring that for each cash flow the appropriate probability and discount factor is applied, based on the assumptions made.

18.2.3.1 Life insurance

Statutory reserves for life insurance are calculated as the present value of future benefits less the present value of future net premiums as described in the general formula. The present values are calculated using interest and mortality only. Therefore, the only components of our reserve formula that are included are the mortality component and the premium component. The minimum reserve is specified by law and/or regulation. A greater reserve can be held by the life insurance company.

In specifying the minimum reserves, the law specifies the maximum interest rate that may be used to calculate the reserve, the mortality table that is to be used and the methodology for calculating the net premium. The maximum interest rate that can be used is dynamic, meaning that it is linked to interest rates of bonds in the U.S. market and changes automatically if interest rates change. Even so, the interest rate does not change every calendar year as the law specifies that the interest rate will only change if the change is at least 0.5 percent.

Furthermore, the interest rate that can be used is a function of the length of the life insurance contract. The interest rate for contracts that are for 10 years or less is higher than the rate for contracts which exceed 10 years, but do not exceed 20 years. For contracts that exceed 20 years, an even lower interest rate must be used. For policies issued in calendar year 2011, the maximum valuation interest rates are given in Table 18.1.

TABLE 18.1 Valuation Interest Rates

Duration of the Life Contract	Maximum Valuation Interest Rate
0 to 10 years	4.75%
More than 10 Years but not to exceed 20	4.50%
More than 20 Years	4.00%

The mortality table used changes periodically, but requires adoption by the NAIC.

The minimum reserve basis is the Commissioners Reserve Valuation Method (CRVM), which specifies how the net valuation premiums are to be determined. Under CRVM, the present value of the renewal net valuation premium at issue is equal to the sum of the present value of the benefits at issue plus an expense allowance. The renewal net valuation premium is the premium to be used after the first year. In the first year, the valuation net premium is the renewal net valuation premium less the expense allowance.[2] The expense allowance is to recognize that at the time that a life insurance policy is issued, the life insurance company incurs significant expense. The expense allowance permits the life insurance company to amortize a portion of that expense over the life of the policy. It should be noted that the expense allowance is defined by law and is not the actual or expected expenses of the company. The present value of premiums and benefits at issue are calculated on the same basis (interest rate and mortality table) as the reserves.

The Standard Valuation Law (SVL) specifies the maximum interest rate, the mortality table, and the method.

2 The renewal net valuation premium is commonly represented by the symbol β while the first year net valuation premium is commonly represented by the symbol α.

EXAMPLE 18.1

We will calculate the U.S. statutory reserves for a five-year term insurance with a level death benefit of 100,000 issued to a male nonsmoker age 70. Under 2011 rules, the maximum interest rate that we can use is 4.75%. Further, the SVL specifies the mortality table, in this case, the 2001 Commissioners Standard Ordinary mortality table for male nonsmokers. This table, along with the table for male smokers, female nonsmokers, and female smokers are included with the online resources. The relevant mortality rates for our 70-year old male nonsmoker are shown in Table 18.2.

TABLE 18.2 2001 CSO Mortality Rates

Attained Age	Mortality Rate
70	0.02527
71	0.02799
72	0.03117
73	0.03452
74	0.03812

The net benefit premium is calculated on the same basis, remembering that the net benefit premium is calculated such that present value of the net premiums at issue is equal to the sum of the present value of the benefits at issue plus the expense allowance. Therefore, assuming annual premiums:

$$^{V}P\sum_{t=0}^{4} {}_tp_{70} \cdot v^t = 100{,}000\sum_{t=0}^{4} {}_tp_{70}q_{70+t} \cdot v^{t+1} + EA.$$

Note that the death benefit is assumed to be paid at the end of the policy year. Under CRVM reserves, this is permitted. The *EA* is defined in the SVL but is beyond the scope of this book, so it is given to you as 7.0183 per 1,000 of insurance.

We can calculate ^{V}P using the information in Table 18.3.

TABLE 18.3 Net Valuation Premium Calculation

t	${}_tp_{70}v^t$	${}_tp_{70}q_{70+t}v^{t+1}$
0	1	0.024124
1	0.930530	0.023864
2	0.863470	0.025694
3	0.798621	0.026318
4	0.736088	0.026787
Total Sum	4.328708	0.127788

Therefore, $^{V}P = \dfrac{(100{,}000)(0.127788) + 100(7.0183)}{4.328708} = 3{,}114.23.$

This premium is the renewal net valuation premium. The first year net valuation premium is

$$^{V}P - EA = 3{,}114.23 - (100)(7.0183) = 2{,}412.40.$$

Our reserves are then as follows:

$$_0V = \sum_{t=0}^{4} DB_{1+t}\,{}_tp_{70}q_{70+t} \cdot v^{t+1} - ({}^VP - EA) - \sum_{t=1}^{4} {}^VP\,{}_tp_{70} \cdot v^t = 0.00$$

$$_1V = \sum_{t=0}^{3} DB_{2+t}\,{}_tp_{71}q_{71+t} \cdot v^{t+1} - \sum_{t=0}^{3} {}^VP\,{}_tp_{71} \cdot v^t = 0.00$$

$$_2V = \sum_{t=0}^{2} DB_{3+t}\,{}_tp_{72}q_{72+t} \cdot v^{t+1} - \sum_{t=0}^{2} {}^VP\,{}_tp_{72} \cdot v^t = 476.50$$

$$_3V = \sum_{t=0}^{1} DB_{4+t}\,{}_tp_{73}q_{73+t} \cdot v^{t+1} - \sum_{t=0}^{1} {}^VP\,{}_tp_{73} \cdot v^t = 665.03$$

$$_4V = DB_5\, q_{74} \cdot v^1 - {}^VP = 524.90$$

$$_5V = 0 - 0 = 0$$

The details supporting these calculations are in the online resources. If you analyze the spreadsheet closely, you will note that the reserves are actually calculated using a recursive formula, which is

$$_tV = \frac{({}_{t-1}V + NetPrem)(1 + i) - q_{70+t-1}DB_t}{1 - q_{70+t-1}}$$

Note that $_0V$ is zero and that $NetPrem$ is ${}^VP - EA$ for the first year and ${}^VP$ for renewal years. If you used the formulas above, you would get the same answers, but it would not be as efficient.

A general recursive formula is

$$_tV = \frac{\begin{array}{l}({}_{t-1}V + {}^VP_t - E_t^{BOP})(1 + i) - E_t^{MOP}(1 - q_{x+t-1})^{0.5}(1 + i)^{0.5} \\ - (E_t^{EOP} + Div_t + AnnBen_t)(1 - q_{x+t-1}) - CV_t w_{x+t-1} - DB_t q_{x+t-1}(1 + i)^{0.5}\end{array}}{p_{x+t-1}^T}$$

This formula makes the same assumptions as in the earlier development regarding the timing of payments.

The general recursive formula does not include the disability component included in the general formula in Section 18.2.2. Incorporating the costs of the disability benefit in the recursive formula is not straightforward due to multiple status possibilities.

18.2.3.2 Deferred annuities

Reserves for deferred annuities are calculated using the Commissioners Annuity Reserve Valuation Method (CARVM). CARVM at its most basic level requires that the reserves held for deferred annuities are the largest present value of future guaranteed benefits. This can be a complicated process, and the intricacies of these calculations are beyond the scope of this book. However, we will go through an example to illustrate the concept.

Actuarial Guidelines[3] have been adopted to help clarify the calculations of annuity reserves. Table 18.4 indicates the actuarial guidelines that are applicable to reserves for deferred annuities.

TABLE 18.4 Annuity Reserve Actuarial Guidelines

Type of Annuity	Applicable Actuarial Guideline
Fixed Annuities	Actuarial Guidelines 13 and 33
Variable Annuities	Actuarial Guidelines 34, 39, and 43
Indexed Annuities	Actuarial Guidelines 33 and 35

EXAMPLE 18.2

Our example will have the following features:

- Single premium deferred annuity with a premium of 50,000;
- Guaranteed interest rate of 5% for two years and 3% thereafter;
- Surrender charges of 7% in year one, 6% in year two, 5% in year three, 4% in year four, and zero thereafter;
- No partial free withdrawals;
- Death benefit is equal to the surrender value; and
- Valuation interest rate of 4.5%.

As stated, CARVM requires that the reserve be the largest present value of future guaranteed benefits. When there are multiple benefit streams (e.g., partial withdrawals, surrenders, death benefits and annuitization benefits), this can become a very complicated calculation. For our example, we have set it up so that the only benefit stream that needs to be considered is surrenders. In this case, the CARVM reserve becomes the largest present value of guaranteed future surrender values where the present value is calculated using the valuation interest rate. The valuation interest rate is dynamic and specified by the SVL just as it is for life insurance policies.

We will begin by determining the reserve on the issue date. The calculations are in Table 18.5.

TABLE 18.5 CARVM Reserve Calculation at Issue

End of Policy Year	Guaranteed Account Value	Guaranteed Surrender Value	Present Value of Surrender Value
0	50,000.00	46,500.00	46,500.00
1	52,500.00	48,825.00	46,722.49
2	55,125.00	51,817.50	47,450.83
3	56,778.75	53,939.81	47,267.27
4	58,482.11	56,142.83	47,079.20
5	60,236.58	60,236.58	48,336.91
6	62,043.67	62,043.67	47,643.07
		Greatest PV =>	48,336.91

3 Actuarial Guidelines are developed by the National Association of Insurance Commissioners to interpret and clarify laws and regulations.

The guaranteed account value is determined by increasing the single premium with guaranteed interest (5% the first two years and 3% thereafter). The guaranteed surrender value is the guaranteed account value multiplied by (1 − the surrender charge). The present value is determined by taking the present value at 4.5% interest. For example, $\frac{60{,}236.58}{(1.045)^5} = 48{,}336.91$.

Note that we can stop our projections at the end of six years because the present value will always be less. The guaranteed account value is increasing by 3%, but the present value is being calculated at 4.5%.

Now suppose the policy is 2.5 years old and has an account value of 60,000. The calculations are in Table 18.6.

TABLE 18.6 CARVM Reserve at Time 2.5

End of Policy Year	Guaranteed Account Value	Guaranteed Surrender Value	Present Value of Surrender Value
Now	60,000.00	57,000.00	57,000.00
3	60,893.35	57,848.68	56,589.43
4	62,720.15	60,211.34	56,364.27
5	64,601.75	64,601.75	57,870.01
6	66,539.81	66,539.81	57,039.34
		Greatest PV=>	57,870.01

We project the surrender values at the end of each policy year as well as on the valuation date to determine the reserve. This approach is known as *curtate* CARVM. Curtate CARVM only considers the policy year ends and it is possible that a larger present value exists at some other point in the policy year. Continuous CARVM looks at all points in time to determine the largest present value. Most states accept curtate CARVM, but some states insist on the use of continuous CARVM. The calculation of continuous CARVM is given in Table 18.7.

TABLE 18.7 Continuous CARVM Reserve at Time 2.5

End of Policy Year	Guaranteed Account Value	Guaranteed Surrender Value	Present Value of Surrender Value
Now	60,000.00	57,000.00	57,000.00
3	60,893.35	58,457.62	57,185.11
4	62,720.15	62,720.15	58,712.78
5	64,601.75	64,601.75	57,870.01
6	66,539.81	66,539.81	57,039.34
		Greatest PV=>	58,712.78

The continuous reserve is higher because the surrender charge drops from 4% to zero on the first day of the fifth policy year. We treat it as though it happened on the last day of the fourth policy year to simplify the process. With continuous CARVM, we reflect it at that point in time instead of at the end of the fifth policy year.

18.2.3.2.1 Applicability of the general reserve formula

The general reserve formula that we developed in Section 18.2.2 is still generally applicable except that we take the largest present value.

18.2.3.3 Payout annuities

The reserve for a payout annuity is the present value of future payments. Future payments that are guaranteed are discounted at interest only. Life contingent payments are discounted at both interest and survivorship. The minimum statutory reserves are determined using the maximum interest rate and the mortality table specified by statute. Reserves can be calculated using a different interest rate or mortality table, but the reserves must be equal to or greater than the minimum reserves.

The maximum interest rate is dynamic just as it is for life insurance and deferred annuities and is a function of the calendar year that the payout annuity was issued.

Structured settlements (discussed in Section 13.2.4.2.3.4) have special reserve requirements that are detailed by Actuarial Guidelines IX, IX-A, and IX-B. Guideline IX and IX-B defines acceptable interest rates while Guideline IX-A permits use of substandard annuity mortality to calculate reserves under certain circumstances.

EXAMPLE 18.3

We will calculate the reserve for a payout annuity issued to a female age 65. The payout annuity has annual payments of 1,000 at the beginning of each year. The payments are guaranteed for the first 10 years and continue thereafter as long as the annuitant is still alive. We will use an interest rate of 5% and the 2000 Annuity Mortality Table. A copy of this mortality table is included in the online resources.

Using our general reserve formula, the reserve is equal to just the annuity component. There is no premium component as the payout annuity is purchased with a single premium. Our reserve is

$$ {}_sV = \sum_{t=0}^{9-s} AnnBen_{s+t} \cdot v^t + \sum_{t=10-s}^{\infty} AnnBen_{s+t}\, {}_tp_{65+s} \cdot v^t \quad s = 0, 1, \ldots, 9, $$

$$ {}_sV = \sum_{t=0}^{\infty} AnnBen_{s+t}\, {}_tp_{65+s} \cdot v^t \quad s = 10, 11, \ldots. $$

The first formula is applicable during the first 10 years (the certain period) since the first 10 payments are guaranteed. Therefore, they are discounted with interest only, which is equivalent to setting ${}_tp_{65+s} = 1$ since the payments are certain to be made. You should also note that upon the death of the annuitant during the first 10 years, there will still be a positive reserve, although the second part of the equation, $\sum_{t=10-s}^{\infty} AnnBen_{s+t}\, {}_tp_{65+s} \cdot v^t$ becomes zero since the survival probability is zero if the annuitant is dead.

For this example, we will calculate ${}_5V$ and ${}_{15}V$. We will also calculate ${}_5V$ when the annuitant is alive and when the annuitant is deceased.

When the annuitant is deceased, then

$${}_5V = \sum_{t=0}^{4} 1{,}000v^t + \sum_{t=5}^{\infty} 1{,}000\ {}_tp_{70} \cdot v^t = 1{,}000\ddot{a}_{\overline{5}|} + 0 = 4{,}545.95.$$

When the annuitant is alive, then

$${}_5V = \sum_{t=0}^{4} 1{,}000v^t + \sum_{t=5}^{\infty} 1{,}000\ {}_tp_{70} \cdot v^t$$

$$= 1{,}000\ddot{a}_{\overline{5}|} + 1{,}000{}_{5|}\ddot{a}_{70} = 4{,}545.95 + 7{,}656.24 = 12{,}202.19.$$

For the reserve at the end of the 15th year,

$${}_{15}V = \sum_{t=0}^{\infty} 1{,}000\ {}_tp_{80} \cdot v^t = 1{,}000\ddot{a}_{80} = 8{,}635.25.$$

The details supporting these calculations are available in the online resources.

18.2.3.4 Asset adequacy analysis

Statutory reserves in the United States are subject to Asset Adequacy Analysis (AAA), which is the measurement of the capability of a block of assets to support a corresponding block of liabilities. This analysis has been performed by actuaries in the United States since 1986 for companies with business written in the state of New York (NY Regulation 126). With the adoption of the 1990 Standard Valuation Law (SVL), AAA was required for certain companies that did not pass one of several ratio tests. With the 2001 SVL, AAA became required by all companies, with an exemption test for small companies.

The AAA process requires the modeling of the assets and liabilities of a block of business to determine if the future cash in-flows will cover the future cost out-flows. AAA is measured on a going concern basis and thus takes only policies in force and does not consider future sales. The most typical method is cash flow testing; however this is not required, as other methods may be appropriate depending on the line of business (i.e., Gross Premium Valuation for a health insurance block of business).

In cash flow testing, the actuary projects the cash flows from the assets and the liabilities for several years into the future using several different interest rate scenarios. At the beginning of the projection, the book value of the assets and the liabilities are set equal to each other. If the cash inflows from the assets and liabilities are not sufficient to cover the cash outflows from the liabilities, then the actuary may need to establish additional reserves.

Cash flow testing is performed on a minimum of seven deterministic interest rate scenarios (The "New York 7" prescribed in NY Regulation 126), but most go beyond this number. Today, many companies have now incorporated not just the deterministic interest rate scenarios, but also stochastic modeling of interest rates to measure the results on hundreds or thousands of scenarios.

As part of the SVL, an actuary must issue a statement of opinion attesting to the adequacy of the reserves with regards to the assets that back those reserves. This actuary is the appointed actuary and must be appointed by the board of directors. The appointed actuary must be qualified to sign the health and life financial statement as prescribed by the American Academy of Actuaries. The Actuarial Opinion and Memorandum Model Regulation has several other requirements that also must be met, such as continuing education and not violating certain insurance laws. The appointed actuary must also prepare a memorandum with the asset adequacy analysis that details all assumptions and their justification.

18.2.4 U.S. GAAP Reserves

GAAP reserves vary by product and will be discussed below for traditional life insurance, fund-based products (universal life and deferred annuities) and payout annuities.

18.2.4.1 Traditional life insurance

GAAP reserves for traditional, nonparticipating life insurance products are determined in accordance with SFAS 60.[4] GAAP reserves typically comprise three parts—a benefit reserve, an expense reserve, and deferred acquisition costs (DAC). The aggregate GAAP reserve is determined by adding the three parts together.

The benefit reserve reflects both death benefits and surrender benefits. The expense reserve reflects maintenance expenses while the DAC reflects the capitalization and amortization of deferrable acquisition expenses. The valuation premium for each part of the GAAP reserves is calculated by setting the present value of the valuation premium equal to the present value of the benefits, maintenance expenses, or deferrable acquisition costs respectively.

The assumptions used to calculate GAAP reserves are not specified, but determined by the actuary. SFAS 60 reserves generally contain a provision for adverse deviation. However, the amount of conservatism is usually less than the conservatism built into statutory reserves. Once the assumptions are established at the time of the policy, then the assumptions are locked in and must be used for the life of the policy. The exception to this is if there is loss recognition meaning that the gross premiums and investment income in the future will not provide for the expected benefits and expenses in the future. In this case, a deficiency reserve should be established to cover this difference.

4 Financial Accounting Standards Board (2008). This document is also available with the book's online resources.

EXAMPLE 18.4

We will calculate the GAAP reserves for a whole life with a level death benefit of 100,000 issued to a male nonsmoker age 80. The policy matures at age 100 and premiums are payable to age 100. Our GAAP Reserves will be based on the following assumptions:

- Mortality follows the 2001 Valuation Basic Mortality Table Age Last Birthday.[5]
- Lapses or surrenders are 12% in the first year, 8% in the second year, and 5% thereafter.
- Commissions are 75% in the first year, 10% in the next two years, and 5% thereafter.
- Issue expenses are 250 per policy and 1.00 per 1,000 of death benefit.
- Maintenance expense is 50 per year occurring at the beginning of the year.
- Premium tax is 2% of premium.
- The net investment rate that we expect to earn is 6%.
- The Gross Annual Premium for this policy is 9,900.
- We will include a PAD in the development of reserves of 50 bp on investment earnings and 5% on mortality and maintenance expenses.

First, we note that under SFAS 60, we can defer the issue expenses and the commissions that are greater than the ultimate level of commissions of 5%. Then, we solve for our benefit premium, our expense premium, and our DAC premium.

Our premiums are found as the present value of future benefits or expenses divided by the present value of an annuity due. This results in the following premiums:

$$^{V}P = 7{,}617.28 \text{ for the GAAP benefit premium}$$

$$^{V}P = 1{,}388.83 \text{ for the DAC premium}$$

$$^{V}P = 744.11 \text{ for the GAAP expense premium}$$

Using the benefit premium, then we can find our benefit reserve as the present value of future benefits less the present value of future benefit premiums. In our general reserve formula, this is

$$\begin{aligned} {}_sV &= \sum_{t=0} DB_{s+t+1}\, {}_tp^{(\tau)}_{80+s}\, q_{80+s+t} \cdot v^{t+0.5} \\ &+ \sum_{t=0} CV_{s+t+1}\, {}_tp^{(\tau)}_{80+s} w_{80+s+t} \cdot v^{t+1} \\ &- \sum_{t=0} {}^{V}P_{s+t}\, {}_tp^{(\tau)}_{80+s} \cdot v^{t}. \end{aligned}$$

5 This table, along with any other mortality table referenced in this book, can be obtained using the SOA's Table Manager (note that a few, but not all, of the needed tables are also available with the book's online resources. The Table Manager can be accessed at http://www.soa.org/professional-interests/technology/tech-table-manager.aspx.

Our plan is nonparticipating and does not have annuity or disability benefits so those three terms have been eliminated. The valuation premium, ${}^{V}P$, used here is the premium for benefits.

Using the expense premium, then we can find our expense reserve as the present value of future expenses less the present value of future expense premiums. In our general reserve formula, this is

$$
\begin{aligned}
{}_sV = \sum_{t=0} [& E^{BOP}_{s+t+1}\, {}_tp^{(\tau)}_{80+s} \cdot v^t + E^{MOP}_{s+t+1}\, {}_tp^{(\tau)}_{80+s}(1 - q_{80+s+t})^{0.5} v^{t+0.5} \\
& + E^{EOP}_{s+t+1}\, {}_tp^{(\tau)}_{80+s}(1 - q_{80+s+t}) v^{t+1}] - \sum_{t=0} {}^{V}P_{s+t}\, {}_tp^{(\tau)}_{80+s} \cdot v^t.
\end{aligned}
$$

The expenses included in this formula are the maintenance expenses. Any acquisition expenses are not to be included. The valuation premium, ${}^{V}P$, used here is the premium for expenses.

It should be noted that if the expenses are level over time and unrelated to decrements and the premiums are level over time, the expense reserves will be zero at the end of each policy year. This is true for our product. Therefore, this element of GAAP reserves may be ignored by some life insurance companies. In that case, the maintenance expenses are just recognized in the financial statements as they are incurred.

Finally, using the DAC premium, we can find the DAC reserve as the present value of future deferrable expenses less the present value of future DAC premiums. The formula is the same as for expense reserves. The expenses included in this formula are the deferrable acquisition expenses. The valuation premium, ${}^{V}P$, used is the premium for DAC.

The DAC reserve will almost always be negative as the present value of future acquisition expenses after the first year of the policy will be small or zero. Therefore, the present value of DAC premiums will be larger resulting in a negative reserve.

For our whole life product, the GAAP reserves are given in Table 18.8.

TABLE 18.8 GAAP Reserves

End of Policy Year	Benefit Reserve	Expense Reserve	DAC	Net GAAP Reserve
1	7,341.61	0	−7,173.82	167.79
2	14,173.92	0	−7,378.86	6,795.06
3	20,485.91	0	−7,455.19	13,030.72
4	26,413.94	0	−7,057.04	19,356.90
5	31,905.04	0	−6,684.00	25,221.04
10	54,350.03	0	−4,923.21	49,426.82
15	68,368.44	0	−3,537.82	64,830.62
20	100,000.00	0	0.00	100,000.00

A spreadsheet in the online resources has all the calculations supporting these reserves.

18.2.4.2 Fund-based products

GAAP reserves for annuity and universal life type products are determined in accordance with SFAS 97.[6] This is not a premium-based model as the profits emerge in relation to gross margins as opposed to premiums. These reserves are calculated using best estimate assumptions with no provision for adverse deviation.

Under SFAS 97, premiums are not treated as revenue. Any charges assessed against the policies are revenue. This would include cost of insurance charges, expense charges, and surrender charges.

GAAP reserves for fund-based products comprise two parts—a benefit reserve and DAC. The aggregate GAAP reserve is determined by adding the two parts together.

The benefit reserve is equal to the fund value of the product without any reduction for surrender charges. Therefore, the benefit reserve is easy to determine unless the fund-based product has unique features, which are beyond the scope of this book.

Just as for traditional products, DAC reflects the capitalization and amortization of deferrable acquisition expenses. However, DAC under FAS 97 products is generally calculated on a retrospective basis as opposed to a prospective basis for traditional products. The DAC at any point is the accumulated deferred acquisition costs that have been incurred less the accumulated DAC amortization.

The present value of DAC at issue of the policy is divided by the present value of gross margins at issue to determine what percent of future gross margins will be used to amortize the DAC. This percent is essentially the valuation premium for DAC and we will call it the DAC amortization percent. Then, the amount of DAC amortized each accounting period is the actual gross margins multiplied by the DAC amortization percent.[7]

The assumptions used to calculate gross margins are not specified, but determined by the actuary. These assumptions do not contain a provision for adverse deviation. Furthermore, SFAS 97 requires an unlocking of assumptions. In other words, if the past experience has not been approximately equal to the expected, or if future experience is expected to be significantly different from previously expected experience, then the DAC amortization percent is to be redetermined based on actual experience to date and currently expected future experience. Furthermore, the amount of DAC that has already been amortized is to be adjusted to reflect the new DAC amortization percent.

To this point, we have used the term gross margins without defining them. The gross margins include:

- Investment earnings on the assets supporting the fund value less the interest credited to the fund value. Prospectively, this is generally expressed as an interest rate margin such as 1 percent;
- Cost of insurance charges less death claims paid;

6 Financial Accounting Standards Board (2008a). This document is also available with the book's online resources.

7 It should be noted that under SFAS 97, "front end loads" would also be amortized in relation to gross margins. Front end loads are not currently used very often with universal life products and virtually never with deferred annuities.

- Expenses charges less actual expenses incurred. Expense charges do not include front end charges and expenses incurred do not include acquisition expenses; and
- Surrender charges.

Gross margins should also reflect any other charges as appropriate to the product.

EXAMPLE 18.5

Our example has the following features:

- Single premium deferred annuity with a premium of 50,000 issued to a male age 70;
- Guaranteed interest rate of 5% for two years and 3% thereafter;
- Surrender charges of 7% in year one, 6% in year two, 5% in year three, 4% in year four, and zero thereafter;
- No partial free withdrawals;
- Death benefit is equal to the fund value;
- Commissions of 8% of premium paid at issue;
- Issue expenses of 100 per policy incurred at issue; and
- Maintenance expense of 50 per year in the middle of the year.

This is similar to the product that we used as an example for statutory reserves except that we have added expense information and changed the death benefit. We will also need mortality and lapse assumptions. We will assume that mortality follows the 2000 Annuity Mortality Table. This mortality table is included in the spreadsheet of mortality tables in the online resources.

For lapse, we will assume a lapse rate of 10% less the surrender charge in each year. The rates are shown in Table 18.9.

TABLE 18.9 Lapse Rates for Example 18.5

Policy Year	Lapse Rate
1	10% − 7% = 3%
2	10% − 6% = 4%
3	10% − 5% = 5%
4	10% − 4% = 6%
5 and after	10% − 0% = 10%

For this product, the benefit reserve is the fund value.

For DAC, we need the present value of deferrable acquisition costs and the present value of gross margins. For this example, the present value of deferrable acquisition costs is relatively easy. The deferrable acquisition costs are the commissions and the issue expenses. Both occur at the time of issue, so the present value is just 8% of the premium plus 100 which is equal to 4,100.

The present value of projected gross margins is not as easy to calculate. The full calculation is in the spreadsheet in the online resources. The first five years of the calculation are shown in Table 18.10.

TABLE 18.10 Calculation of Gross Margins

Year	Investment Rate	Investment Expense	Net Investment Rate	Credited Interest Rate	Surrender Charge	Mortality Rate	Lapse Rate
1	6.50%	0.25%	6.25%	5.00%	0.070	0.016979	0.030
2	6.50%	0.25%	6.25%	5.00%	0.060	0.018891	0.040
3	6.50%	0.25%	6.25%	5.00%	0.050	0.020967	0.050
4	6.50%	0.25%	6.25%	5.00%	0.040	0.023209	0.060
5	6.50%	0.25%	6.25%	5.00%	—	0.025644	0.100

For this deferred annuity, the gross margin consists of the interest spread (6.25% earned less 5.0% credited) and the surrender charges collected during the time that there is a surrender charge. Note that for this policy, deaths do not result in any profit or loss as the death benefit paid is the fund value, which is the benefit reserve. Therefore, when a death occurs, the fund value is paid out and the benefit reserve is released and there is no effect on the income statement.

You are encouraged to review the calculations in the spreadsheet.

Assuming that the actual gross margin matches the expected gross margin, the DAC at the time that the policy is issued is 4,100. The DAC one year later is:

DAC beginning of the period plus interest less gross margins multiplied by the DAC amortization percent $= 4{,}100(1.05) - 717.61(0.74422) = 3{,}770.94$.

Note that the present values and the interest rate used in the amortization process is the interest rate credited on the fund value.

18.2.4.2.1 Applicability of the general reserve formula

In Section 18.2.4.2, the formulas used to calculate GAAP reserves for the fund-based products is a retrospective formula while our generalized reserve formula is a prospective formula. Retrospective reserve formulas and prospective reserve formulas are equivalent and result in the same reserve value.[8] In most cases, a prospective reserve is easier to calculate so we have presented our general reserve formula as a prospective formula. In some cases, such as the GAAP reserves for fund-based products, a retrospective reserve is easier to calculate.

18.2.4.3 Payout annuities

The GAAP reserve for a payout annuity is the present value of future payments just as it is for statutory reserves. The only difference is that the actuary establishes the assumptions (interest and mortality) used to calculate the reserves.

8 The following demonstrates the equivalence of the two methods: Since Present Value of Future Benefits (and Expenses) at time 0 = Present Value of Future Premiums at time 0
Therefore, at any point in time in the future,
Accumulated Value of Past Benefits (and Expenses) + Present Value of Future Benefits (and Expenses) = Accumulated Value of Past Premiums + Present Value of Future Premiums
But Reserve at time t = Present Value of Future Benefits (and Expenses) − Present Value of Future Premiums
So Accumulated Value of Past Benefits (and Expenses) + Reserve at time t = Accumulated Value of Past Premiums
And Reserve at time t = Accumulated Value of Past Premiums − Accumulated Value of Past Benefits (and Expenses)

TABLE 18.10 Calculation of Gross Margins (*continued*)

Year	Fund Value BOY	Interest Gross Margin	Surrender Charges	Gross Margins	Present Value BOY	DAC Amortization Percent	DAC BOY	DAC EOY
1	50,000.00	610.31	107.31	717.61	5,509.12	74.422%	4,100.00	3,770.94
2	50,060.34	607.29	122.67	729.96	5,066.96		3,770.94	3,416.23
3	49,507.57	596.82	126.23	723.05	4,590.35		3,416.23	3,048.93
4	48,348.37	579.10	118.21	697.32	4,096.81		3,048.93	2,682.42
5	46,612.31	545.62	-	545.62	3,604.34		2,682.42	2,410.48

EXAMPLE 18.6

We will calculate the GAAP reserve for the payout annuity used in Example 18.3. We will use the same mortality table, but we will use an interest rate of 6%. The interest rate used should reflect current investment rates less a PAD.

Our reserve formula remains

$$_sV = \sum_{t=0}^{9-s} AnnBen_{s+t} \cdot v^t + \sum_{t=10-s}^{\infty} AnnBen_{s+t}\, {}_tp_{65+s} \cdot v^t \quad s = 0, 1, \ldots, 9,$$

$$_sV = \sum_{t=0}^{\infty} AnnBen_{s+t}\, {}_tp_{65+s} \cdot v^t \quad s = 10, 11, \ldots.$$

As in Example 18.3, we will calculate $_5V$ and $_{15}V$. We will calculate $_5V$ when the annuitant is alive and when the annuitant is deceased.

When the annuitant is deceased, then

$$_5V = \sum_{t=0}^{4} 1{,}000v^t + \sum_{t=5}^{\infty} 1{,}000\ {}_tp_{70} \cdot v^t = 1{,}000\ddot{a}_{\overline{5|}} + 0 = 4{,}465.11.$$

When the annuitant is alive, then

$$_5V = \sum_{t=0}^{4} 1{,}000v^t + \sum_{t=5}^{\infty} 1{,}000\ {}_tp_{70} \cdot v^t$$

$$= 1{,}000\ddot{a}_{\overline{5|}} + 1{,}000_{5|}\ddot{a}_{70} = 4{,}465.11 + 6{,}840.97 = 11{,}306.08.$$

For the reserve at the end of the 15th year,

$$_{15}V = \sum_{t=0}^{\infty} 1{,}000\ {}_tp_{80} \cdot v^t = 1{,}000\ddot{a}_{80} = 8{,}182.51.$$

The details supporting these calculations are in the online materials.

18.2.5 Canadian CALM Reserves

18.2.5.1 Overview

CALM is the statutory method required in Canada to determine policy liabilities. Full details are available in the Canadian Institute of Actuaries Standards of Practice.[9] In this section a

9 Canadian Institute of Actuaries (2011).

high-level overview of the method will be presented. This discussion is not intended to be a thorough and complete description.

CALM can be described in four steps as described in the following sections.

18.2.5.1.1 Liability without provision for adverse deviations for scenario-tested assumptions

The starting point is to select a scenario that represents expected future experience. Based on these assumptions, cash flows are projected and then accumulated with interest to the end of the projection period (the date of the last liability cash flow). The amount of starting assets required to produce zero surplus at the end of the projection period is the starting point for the reserve calculations. It represents the reserve needed under an assumption that the future turns out to be exactly as expected. This value contains no provision for adverse deviations (PFAD).

When determining the projection period, renewals must be considered if they are at the policyholder's discretion or increase the value of the policy liabilities. Reasonable policyholder expectations, such as the payment of policy dividends and adjustments to non-guaranteed elements should be included.

18.2.5.1.2 PFAD for all but the interest rate risk

The second step is to add margins to all of the non-interest cash flow assumptions. Each margin must be in the direction that increases the reserve value. This is done in a deterministic fashion. As in the base case, the reserve is the amount of starting assets that will produce zero assets at the end of the of the projection period.

18.2.5.1.3 PFAD for interest rate risk

The interest rate risk is accounted for in the third step. The base scenario is the prescribed interest rate scenario along with the margins to the other assumptions used in step two. Then additional prescribed interest rate scenarios are tested. The resulting reserve should be no less than the largest one produced from the prescribed scenarios. Additional scenarios appropriate for the insurer should also be used.

18.2.5.1.4 Adjustments

The PFAD from steps two and three can be adjusted for the impact of any policyholder pass-through features. This refers to policy provisions that place some or all of the risk on the policyholder. For example, if the policy has the policyholder assume all interest rate risk, then no step three adjustment is needed. If it is a partial transfer of risk, then the step three adjustment is reduced at this step.

18.2.5.2 Considerations

The various considerations put forth in the Standard of Practice make it clear that the approach is principles-based. A good example of this is the statement "Substance would supersede form in the selection,"[10] which indicates that it is more important to address the

10 Canadian Institute of Actuaries (2011, p. 2031, Section 2320.20).

actual impact of each policy rather than follow rules that attach to the policy's name. The example given is a universal life policy that may be technically described as a life insurance policy with annual premiums, but is actually being used by the policyholder as a single premium deferred annuity.

CALM is normally applied to each group of policies or business segment based on the company's asset-liability management practice for allocating assets to liabilities. However, it is also acceptable to calculate liabilities in the aggregate, reflecting all risks at once.

The assets used to support the liabilities are to be at the value used in the company's financial statements, typically book value, taking account of accrued investment income, adjustments for impairment, and amortized capital gains whether realized or unrealized.

If a policy contains multiple elements that operate independently, then each element is treated as a separate policy with its own projection period. In general, the projection period ends at the latest date the policyholder may keep the policy without further approval from the insurer. The actuary is to write down acquisition and similar expenses using an appropriate method that is consistent with the expected term of the policy, reasonably matches the net cash flows available to offset them and be locked in, unless there is an expectation that expenses will not be fully recoverable.

A policyholder's reasonable expectations refer to how the policyholder perceives the insurer will exercise the options given to the company by the policy. Such expectations may come from marketing materials or past practices of the company as well as general market conduct standards. Any changes in company policy that may affect expectations in the future should be incorporated. When projecting policyholder dividends, in addition to conforming to reasonable expectations, care is needed to avoid omission or double counting. Dividend projections should be consistent with the given scenario but should also recognize that insurance company policy may lag in responding to changes and market forces may also impact dividend payments.

If the insurer can offset adverse experience through actions such as changing dividends, premium rates or benefits, then it is not necessary to make a provision for such adverse deviations. However, as with dividends, care should be taken to account for forces that may cause the company to choose not to fully offset such adverse experience.

If deterministic scenarios are used, the liability should be in the upper part of the range of the selected scenarios. However, the liability must always be at least as large as the largest one from the set of prescribed scenarios. If stochastic scenarios are used, the policy liability should be based on a scenario that produces a value consistent with a 60 to 80 percent conditional tail expectation.

18.2.5.3 Interest rates

An interest rate scenario comprises an investment strategy as well as interest rates for both risk-free assets and those subject to default. An inflation assumption is to be included that is consistent with the selected interest rate scenario. The investment strategy should be consistent with the company's current investment policy. At a minimum the yield curve should reflect short, medium, and long-term rates.

The base scenario is determined in three parts:

- For the first 20 years, it is equal to the forward rates implied by the equilibrium risk free market curve.
- For year 40 and beyond, it is equal to the average of the 60 and 120 month moving averages of historic long-term Canadian risk-free bonds, annualized and rounded to the nearest 10 basis points.
- For years 20 to 40, the rates are set to provide a uniform transition.

The premium for default risk is to be consistent with risk premiums available in the market at the time of the valuation.

There are nine prescribed alternative scenarios. The following is a crude description of them.

1. Ninety percent of the risk free rate at year one and for years 20 and beyond at the lower bound of rates defined in the standard, with smooth transition from year 1 to year 20.
2. As in scenario one, but using 110 percent and the upper bound.
3. The long-term risk-free rate moves cyclically in 1 percent steps between the lower and upper bounds. The first cycle reaches the upper bound. The short-term risk-free rate changes uniformly over a period of not more than three years to 60 percent percent of the long-term rate and then remains at that level.
4. As in scenario three, but with the first cycle reaching the lower bound.
5. As in scenario three, except the short-term rate moves cyclically in 20 percent steps of the long-term rate, moving from 40 percent to 120 percent and back. It starts at the next step above the current actual percent, or at 120 percent if higher.
6. As in scenario four, with cycles for the short-term rate is in scenario five, but starting at the step below the current rate, or at 40% if lower.
7. The base scenario is used for the first year, and then 90% of the base scenario for all subsequent years.
8. As in scenario seven, but using 110 instead of 90 percent.
9. Assumes continuance of the current risk-free rates and default premiums.

As noted, other scenarios may be considered as appropriate. If stochastic modeling is used, it is necessary that it generates scenarios the produce liabilities that are outside the range produced by the prescribed deterministic scenarios.

18.2.5.4 Other assumptions

The Standard notes that there are difficulties when setting best estimates. Among them are:

- The data has limited credibility;
- Future experience is difficult to estimate;
- The risks lack homogeneity;
- Operational risks may impact future results;
- Well-established methods are not available;
- There is concentration of risk or lack of diversification; and
- Past experience may not be representative of the future.

The Standard provides specific guidance for many assumptions regarding margins for adverse deviations. In each case a low and a high margin is provided. The choice of low or high margin depends on the uncertainty in the best estimate. For many assumptions, the range of margins is 5 to 20 percent of the best estimate. There are some exceptions to this, such as life insurance mortality and asset defaults. The margins are applied in a manner to increase liabilities. It is noted that circumstances can exist where a percentage adjustment is not defined. In such cases a conservative assumption is to be set.

Specific margins are set for the following assumptions:

- Mortality (separately for insurance and annuity);
- Morbidity;
- Withdrawal and partial withdrawal;
- Anti-selective lapse;
- Expense; and
- Policyholder options.

For example, the margin for life insurance mortality is to add 0.00375 to the mortality rates for the low margin and 0.015 for the high margin.

18.2.6 Gross Premium Reserves

Gross premium reserves reflect all future cash flows under a life insurance policy or an annuity. The reserve is the present value of future cash outflows (benefits, expenses, etc.) less the present value of future cash inflows (premiums, earnings on required surplus, etc.). The future cash flows are generally determined using best estimate assumptions. Assets may be included in the projection or a fixed discount rate may be used to determine the present values.

Gross premium reserves are generally not used for financial reporting. However, gross premium reserves are often used as a method of verifying that the reserves that are actually used for financial reporting are sufficient. Since these reserves reflect best estimate assumptions and reflect all expected cash flows, these reserves present the most realistic estimate of the current liability based on current expectations.

EXAMPLE 18.7

We will use the five-year term insurance that we used in Example 18.1. The insurance has a level death benefit of 100,000 and is issued to a male nonsmoker age 70. In calculating a statutory reserve we only used an interest rate and mortality table. Both the maximum interest rate and the mortality assumptions are prescribed by law. When we calculate a gross premium reserve, we will use a realistic interest rate and mortality table. Additionally, we will incorporate expenses. Finally, the valuation premium that will be used to calculate the reserve will be the gross premium, which is why it is called a gross premium reserve.

We will use the following assumptions to calculate our gross premium reserve:

- Mortality follows the 2001 Valuation Basic Mortality Table Age Last Birthday. This mortality table can be found on the SOA's website.
- Lapses or surrenders are 12% in the first year and 8% thereafter.

- Commissions are 75% in the first year and 5% thereafter.
- Issue expenses are 100 per policy and 1.00 per 1,000 of death benefit.
- Maintenance expense is 50 per year occurring in the middle of the year.
- Premium tax is 2% of premium.
- The net investment rate that we expect to earn is 6%.
- The gross annual premium for this policy is 2,000.
- There are no nonforfeiture benefits.

Because the gross premium is used as the valuation premium, ${}^{V}P = 2{,}000$. Our reserves are then as follows:

$$
{}_sV = \sum_{t=0} DB_{s+t+1}\, {}_tp^{(\tau)}_{x+s} q_{x+s+t} \cdot v^{t+0.5}
$$

$$
+ \sum_{t=0} [E^{BOP}_{s+t+1}\, {}_tp^{(\tau)}_{x+s} \cdot v^t + E^{MOP}_{s+t+1}\, {}_tp^{(\tau)}_{x+s}(1 - q_{x+s+t})^{0.5} v^{t+0.5} + E^{EOP}_{s+t+1}\, {}_tp^{(\tau)}_{x+s}(1 - q_{x+s+t}) v^{t+1}]
$$

$$
- \sum_{t=0} {}^{V}P_{s+t}\, {}_tp^{(\tau)}_{x+s} \cdot v^t.
$$

This is our standard formula without cash values, dividends, annuity benefits and disability benefits since the five-year term insurance does not include any of these benefits.

The gross premium reserves as well as the statutory reserves calculated in Example 18.1 are listed in Table 18.11.

TABLE 18.11 Reserves for Example 18.7

Time Since Issue	Gross Premium Reserve	Statutory Reserve
0	−697.82	0.00
1	−2053.86	0.00
2	−1252.81	476.50
3	−657.24	665.03
4	−237.89	524.90
5	0	0.00

The details supporting the gross premium reserve are in the online resources.

The initial gross premium reserve is negative. This is not unusual. In particular, if the gross premium reserve is not negative at issue (time 0), then the product is expected to produce a loss. Remember that the reserve at time zero is the present value of future benefits and expenses less the present value of future gross premiums. Further, the gross premium should be sufficient to pay for all the issue costs. At any time other than time 0, these costs have already been incurred so they are not included in the present value of future benefits and expenses. However, future gross premiums still reflect these costs.

The second thing to note is that the gross premium reserves are less than the statutory reserves except at time five when the policy has expired and the reserve is zero. The fact that the gross premium reserve is less than the statutory reserve indicates that the statutory reserve is sufficient. If the gross premium reserve was greater than the statutory reserve at some durations then that would indicate that the statutory reserve was too low or not sufficient.

18.3 Nonforfeiture Requirements

Nonforfeiture requirements and options have been discussed several times. In the United States, the Standard Nonforfeiture Law (SNFL) specifies the minimum values that must be provided. A life insurance company may provide greater nonforfeiture values than the minimum.

We will discuss nonforfeiture requirements for life insurance policies, deferred annuities, and payout annuities.

18.3.1 Life Insurance Policies

18.3.1.1 Traditional life and term insurance

The nonforfeiture requirements for traditional life and term insurance are specified by the SNFL.[11]

The SNFL requires that cash surrender value be provided. The minimum cash value is specified in the law. In general, the minimum cash value is the present value of future guaranteed death benefits less the present value of future adjusted premiums. The present values are calculated using only mortality and interest, which are both specified in the law. The adjusted premium is also defined in the law.

The maximum interest rate that can be used in the nonforfeiture calculations is defined to be 125 percent of the maximum interest rate that can be used to calculate reserves. The nonforfeiture rate is rounded to the nearest 0.25 percent.

Section 18.2.3.1 describes how the maximum interest rate that can be used for reserves is determined. Furthermore, for policies issued in calendar year 2011, the maximum valuation interest rates were listed. In Table 18.12, the maximum nonforfeiture interest rates for 2011 have been added.

TABLE 18.12 Maximum Interest Rates for Reserves and Cash Values

Duration of the Life Contract	Maximum Valuation Interest Rate	Maximum Nonforfeiture Interest Rate
0 to 10 years	4.50%	5.75%
More than 10 Years but not to exceed 20	4.25%	5.25%
More than 20 Years	4.00%	5.00%

The mortality table used changes periodically, but requires adoption by the NAIC.

11 The Standard Nonforfeiture law has changed over time. Our discussion will focus on the nonforfeiture requirements for policies currently being issued at the time this book is published.

The adjusted premium is determined so that the present value of the adjusted premiums at issue is equal to the sum of the present value of the benefits at issue plus an expense allowance. The present value of premiums and benefits at issue are calculated on the same basis (interest rate and mortality table) as the reserves.

The expense allowance is:

$$0.01(AAI) + 1.25\begin{bmatrix} \textit{Net Level Premium} \\ 0.04(AAI) \end{bmatrix}$$

where

- *AAI* is the average amount of insurance, which is calculated as the arithmetic average of the death benefit at the beginning of the year for the first 10 years of the contract;
- [ ] means the minimum of the two values in the brackets; and
- *Net Level Premium* is the present value of death benefits at issue divided by the present value of an annuity of 1 at each premium due date.

EXAMPLE 18.8

Consider a whole life issued to a male nonsmoker age 70 with a 100,000 level death benefit. The maximum interest rate that we can use is 5.00%. Further, the SNFL specifies the mortality table so we will use the 2001 Commissioners Standard Ordinary mortality table for male nonsmokers.

The $AAI = 100{,}000$ since the death benefit at the beginning of each year for the first 10 years is 100,000.

$$\textit{The Net Level Premium is } \frac{100{,}000\sum_{t=0}^{\infty} {}_tp_{70}q_{70+t}\cdot v^{t+1}}{\sum_{t=0}^{\infty} {}_tp_{70}\cdot v^t} = 5{,}647.61.$$

The expense allowance is

$0.01(AAI) + 1.25\begin{bmatrix} \textit{Net Level Premium} \\ 0.04(AAI) \end{bmatrix} = 1{,}000 + 1.25(4{,}000) = 6{,}000$ since the *Net Level Premium* exceeds $0.04(AAI)$.

The adjusted premium (P^A) is:

$$P^A = \frac{100{,}000\sum_{t=0}^{\infty} {}_tp_{70}q_{70+t}\cdot v^{t+1} + \textit{ExpenseAllowance}}{\sum_{t=0}^{\infty} {}_tp_{70}\cdot v^t}$$

$$= \frac{54{,}254.32 + 6{,}000}{9.6066} = 6{,}272.18.$$

Sample cash values are then as follows:

$$ {}_0CV = \sum_{t=0}^{\infty} 100{,}000\ {}_tp_{70}q_{70+t} \cdot v^{t+1} - \sum_{t=0}^{\infty} 6{,}272.18\ {}_tp_{70} \cdot v^t = -6{,}000 $$

$$ {}_5CV = \sum_{t=0}^{\infty} 100{,}000\ {}_tp_{75}q_{75+t} \cdot v^{t+1} - \sum_{t=0}^{\infty} 6{,}272.18\ {}_tp_{75} \cdot v^t = 12{,}494.25 $$

$$ {}_{10}CV = \sum_{t=0}^{\infty} 100{,}000\ {}_tp_{80}q_{80+t} \cdot v^t - \sum_{t=0}^{\infty} 6{,}272.18\ {}_tp_{80} \cdot v^t = 30{,}514.75 $$

$$ {}_{20}CV = \sum_{t=0}^{\infty} 100{,}000\ {}_tp_{90}q_{90+t} \cdot v^t - \sum_{t=0}^{\infty} 6{,}272.18\ {}_tp_{90} \cdot v^t = 58{,}678.22 $$

The details supporting these calculations are in a spreadsheet in the online materials.

Two points to note:

- The cash value at the time that the policy is issued is the negative of the expense allowance. When the cash value is negative, the cash value is set to zero and no nonforfeiture benefits are provided. It is also worth noting that at the end of the first year the cash value is still negative resulting in a cash value of zero.
- The present values used to calculate the cash values assume that all death benefits are paid at the end of the policy year. This is permitted by the SNFL even though all companies pay the death benefit at the time of death, not at the end of the year. The assumption that death benefits are paid at the end of the year minimizes the cash values. Many companies assume that the death benefits are paid at the time of death when they actually calculate cash values, which results in larger cash values. Remember that the SNFL only establishes a minimum and companies are permitted to pay higher cash values.

In addition to the cash surrender value, for life insurance contracts, the SNFL requires that an actuarially equivalent paid-up insurance option also be provided to the policy owner. The two paid-up insurance options that are common are *reduced paid up* (RPU) and *extended term insurance* (ETI). With RPU, the same period of coverage is provided as the original policy provided. However, the death benefit is reduced and no more premiums may be paid. For ETI, the death benefit remains the same as the previous death benefit, but the period of coverage is shortened. As with RPU, no additional premiums may be paid once a policy goes on ETI.

A policy on RPU or ETI may be surrendered for its cash surrender value at any time. The cash surrender value for a policy on RPU or ETI is the present value of future benefits.

The SNFL contains a number of specified circumstances where nonforfeiture benefits are not required. These circumstances include:

- The cash values required in any policy year under the SNFL does not exceed 2.5 percent of the death benefit at the start of that policy year; and
- Term insurance with a level death benefit and level premiums where the period of term insurance does not exceed 20 year and does not go beyond age 70.

In Canada, nonforfeiture values are not required. It is not common to provide cash values on Term to 100 products. Some companies have provided cash values on their Term to 100 to try to encourage lapses, but it is not very common. Most whole life products in Canada do contain cash values. However, the cash values may be structured to be zero the first 15 years or longer.

18.3.1.2 Universal life insurance

The nonforfeiture requirements for UL insurance policies are specified by the Universal Life Insurance Model Regulation. While the SNFL discussed in the previous section defines minimum cash values on a prospective basis (present value of **future** benefits less present value of **future** adjusted premiums), minimum surrender values for UL products are defined on a retrospective basis as the accumulation with interest of:

- Premiums paid; less
- Cost of insurance and expense charges; less
- Any surrender charges.

The UL Model law limits the amount of the expense charges and surrender charges.

The UL Model law defines the following:

$$\textit{Average Renewal Expense} = \frac{\sum \textit{All Expense Charges for Policy Years } 2 - 20}{19}$$

$\textit{Excess First Year Expense Charge} = \textit{Total First Year Expense Charges} - \textit{Average Renewal Expense}$

The *Excess First Year Expense Charge* cannot be less than zero.

$\textit{Unused Initial Expense Allowance} = \textit{Initial Expense Allowance} - \textit{Excess First Year Expense Charge}$

The *Initial Expense Allowance* is the same as the Expense Allowance calculated under the SNFL in Section 18.3.1.1. If the *Unused Initial Expense Allowance* is negative, then the *Excess First Year Expense Charge* exceeds that permitted by the UL Model law.

The maximum surrender charge in policy year t is then[12]

$$\textit{Unused Initial Expense Allowance}\left(\frac{\ddot{a}_{x+t-1:\overline{n-t+1}|}}{\ddot{a}_{x:\overline{n}|}}\right)$$

where x is the issue age of the insured and n is the number of years that premiums can be paid under the UL policy.

12 It should be noted that some states have a stricter requirement, that is, the surrender charge in policy year t may not exceed $\textit{Unused Initial Expense Allowance}\left(\frac{\ddot{a}_{x+t:\overline{n-t}|}}{\ddot{a}_{x:\overline{n}|}}\right)$.

The interest rate and mortality table used to calculate the *Unused Initial Expense Allowance* and the life annuities must comply with the SNFL so they are consistent with those used for traditional life and term plans.

EXAMPLE 18.9

Calculate the maximum permitted surrender charges for a UL insurance policy issued to a male nonsmoker age 70 with a 100,000 level death benefit. Premiums are payable for the life of the insured. The expense charges are provided in Table 18.13.

TABLE 18.13 **Expense Charges for Example 18.9**

Policy Year	Expense Charge per Policy per Month	Expense Charge per Policy per 1,000 of Specified Amount
1	100	0.20
2–10	10	0.05
11 and after	5	0.00

We will use the maximum interest rate of 5.00% and the 2001 Commissioners Standard Ordinary mortality table for male nonsmokers.

$$\textit{Average Renewal Expense} = \frac{\sum \textit{All Expense Charges for Policy Years } 2-20}{19}$$

$$= \frac{(10)(9)(12) + (0.05)(100)(9)(12) + (5)(10)(12) + (0.00)(100)(10)(12)}{19}$$

$$= 116.84$$

Excess First Year Expense Charge = *Total First Year Expense Charges* − *Average Renewal Expense* = $100(12) + (0.20)(100)(12) - 116.84 = 1323.16$

Unused Initial Expense Allowance = *Initial Expense Allowance* − *Excess First Year Expense Charge* = $6000.00 - 1323.16 = 4676.84$

Note that we know the *Initial Expense Allowance* as it is the same as the Expense Allowance calculated under the SNFL in Example 18.8.

The maximum surrender charge in policy year t is then

$$\textit{Unused Initial Expense Allowance}\left(\frac{\ddot{a}_{x+t-1:\overline{n-t+1}|}}{\ddot{a}_{x:\overline{n}|}}\right)\text{, shown in Table 18.14.}$$

TABLE 18.14 Maximum Surrender Charge for Example 18.9

Policy Year	Unused Initial Expense Allowance	$\ddot{a}_{x+t-1:\overline{n-t+1}\vert}$	$\ddot{a}_{x:\overline{n}\vert}$	Maximum Surrender Charge
1	4,676.84	9.6066	9.6066	4,676.84
2	4,676.84	9.2712	9.6066	4,513.56
3	4,676.84	8.9349	9.6066	4,349.81
5	4,676.84	8.2649	9.6066	4,023.67
10	4,676.84	6.6121	9.6066	3,218.99
20	4,676.84	3.9374	9.6066	1,916.86

The details supporting these calculations are in spreadsheet in the online resources.

The UL Model law does not require a paid up insurance option be provided on UL contracts.

18.3.1.3 Variable life insurance

18.3.1.3.1 Traditional form

For variable life that follows the traditional form, the method of computing the minimum cash values shall be "such that, if the net investment return credited to the policy at all times from the date of issue should be equal to the assumed investment rate with premiums and benefits determined accordingly under the terms of the policy, then the resulting cash values and other nonforfeiture benefits must be at least equal to the minimum values required by the standard nonforfeiture law for a general account policy with such premiums and benefits. The assumed investment rate shall not exceed the maximum interest rate permitted under the standard nonforfeiture law of this state."[13]

The cash value must be determined at least monthly. In most cases, it is determined each day the market is open. The method used to determine the cash value must be filed with each state insurance department and may incorporate reasonable and necessary approximations as acceptable to the state.

The minimum cash values are further clarified by the requirements of Actuarial Guideline XXIV. This guideline defines three options for determining the minimum cash values for variable life insurance. The prospective method is the method that is typically used for the traditional form of variable life. The cash value is the present value of future benefits less the present value of future adjusted premiums. The adjusted premium is calculated on a basis consistent with the adjusted premium for traditional life and term products as described in Section 18.3.1.1.

18.3.1.3.2 Variable universal life

For VUL, the minimum cash values are also defined by Actuarial Guideline XXIV. The retrospective method or the maximum charge method is used for variable universal life.

13 Model Variable Life Insurance Law.

The retrospective method states that the minimum cash surrender value is the accumulated premiums paid less the accumulated value of the following:

- Mortality charges and rider charges where the premium for the rider is not paid separately;
- The average renewal expense for the first year;
- The actual expense charge for years after the first;
- Initial expense charges not exceeding the maximum allowable expense allowance;
- Service charges actually made; and
- Partial surrenders.

From this amount, the company may deduct any unamortized unused initial expense allowance.

The average renewal expense, initial expense charge, and unamortized unused initial expense allowance are calculated consistent with those for UL as defined in Section 18.3.1.2.

The maximum charge method defines the minimum cash value as:

- Gross premiums paid; plus
- Net investment income; less
- Administrative charges; less
- Acquisition charges; less
- Deferred acquisition charges; less
- Mortality charges and rider charges where the premium for the rider is not paid separately; less
- Service charges; less
- Partial withdrawals and partial surrender charges.

The administrative charges were limited to 5.00 per month per policy for 1986 and may be increased for inflation, but may not exceed 10.00 per month.

The acquisition charges may not exceed the sum of the following:

- 90 percent of premium received up to the net level whole life premium;
- 10 percent of all other premium;
- 10 per 1,000 of initial face amount;
- 1 per 1,000 of face amount after the first year; and
- 200 per policy.

If there is a surrender charge, it may not exceed the unamortized unused acquisition charge which is again determined is a manner consistent with that for UL as defined in Section 18.3.1.2.

18.3.2 Deferred Annuities

18.3.2.1 Fixed deferred annuities

The nonforfeiture requirements for fixed deferred annuities are specified by the Annuity Standard Nonforfeiture law.[14]

14 The Annuity Standard Nonforfeiture law has changed over time. Our discussion will be of the nonforfeiture requirements for annuities currently issued.

The Annuity Standard Nonforfeiture law requires the life insurance company to provide a paid-up annuity benefit upon the request of the policy owner or the cessation of premiums. Furthermore, if the annuity provides for the payment of a lump sum cash settlement at maturity or any other time, then a cash surrender value must be provided.[15]

The Annuity Standard Nonforfeiture law specifies a minimum nonforfeiture amount that must be provided under a fixed deferred annuity.[16] The minimum nonforfeiture amount is:

- 87.5 percent of premiums paid accumulated at the specified minimum interest rate; less
- An annual contract charge of 50 accumulated at the specified minimum interest rate; less
- Any partial surrenders or withdrawals accumulated at the specified minimum interest rate; less
- Any outstanding indebtedness including interest due and accrued.

The specified minimum interest rate is equal to the five-year constant-maturity treasury rate (or an average thereof) rounded to the nearest 0.05 percent and reduced by 1.25 percent. This rate cannot be less than 1 percent and is capped at 3 percent.

The specified minimum interest rate may be established at the time the annuity is issued and apply for the life of the annuity. Alternatively, the specified minimum interest rate as determined when the policy is issued may apply for an initial period of time and then be redetermined on a periodic basis based on the five-year constant-maturity treasury rate at that time. If the specified minimum rate is to be redetermined, the redetermination process must be described in the annuity contract.

The Annuity Standard Nonforfeiture law requires that the nonforfeiture options (paid-up annuity or cash surrender value) provide a value that is equal to or larger than the minimum nonforfeiture amount.[17] This requirement is often called the retrospective test since it is determined by looking backward and accumulating past payments less withdraws and charges.

The Annuity Standard Nonforfeiture law also has another requirement that is often referred to as the prospective test since it is calculated by looking forward. This requirement states that the cash surrender value cannot be less than the amount guaranteed to be available upon maturity discounted to the current date at an interest rate 1 percent greater than the rate guaranteed in the contract for accumulating the current value to the maturity date.[18] Therefore, if the annuity contract guarantees that an interest rate of i_g will be credited each year, the cash surrender value cannot be less than

$$CurrentAnnutyValue\left(\frac{(1+i_g)^t}{(1+i_g+0.01)^t}\right) \text{ where } t \text{ is the time to the maturity date.}$$

This is really a smoothness test, which prevents large surrender charge reductions immediately before the maturity date.

15 See Section 2 of the Annuity Standard Nonforfeiture law.
16 See Section 3 of the Annuity Standard Nonforfeiture law.
17 See Sections 4, 5, and 6 of the Annuity Standard Nonforfeiture law.
18 See Section 5 of the Annuity Standard Nonforfeiture law.

EXAMPLE 18.10

We will use the same policy as in Example 18.2.

- Single premium deferred annuity with a premium of 50,000;
- Guaranteed interest rate of 5% for two years and 3% thereafter;
- Surrender charges of 7% in year one, 6% in year two, 5% in year three, 4% in year four, and zero thereafter;
- No partial free withdrawals; and
- No annual expense charge.

Let's test this annuity to see if it complies with the Annuity Standard Nonforfeiture law. In order to complete this test, we need to know the maturity date. The Annuity Standard Nonforfeiture law states that unless the maturity date is fixed in the contract, a maturity date of the later of age 70 or 10 years from issue should be used.[19] Therefore, we will use a maturity date of 10 years from issue as this is the most stringent requirement. Our calculations generate the values in Table 18.15.

TABLE 18.15 Annuity Values for Example 18.10

Time since Issue	Fund Value[20]	Cash Surrender Value[21]	Minimum Nonforfeiture Amount[22]	Present Value of Maturity Value at $i_g + 1\%$[23]
0	50,000.00	46,500.00	45,011.00	45,411.72
1	52,500.00	48,825.00	46,309.83	48,136.42
2	55,125.00	51,817.50	47,647.62	51,024.61
3	56,778.75	53,939.81	49,025.55	53,065.59
4	58,482.11	56,142.83	50,444.82	55,188.22
5	60,236.58	60,236.58	51,906.66	57,395.75
6	62,043.67	62,043.67	53,412.36	59,691.58
7	63,904.98	63,904.98	54,963.24	62,079.24
8	65,822.13	65,822.13	56,560.63	64,562.41
9	67,796.80	67,796.80	58,205.95	67,144.90
10	69,830.70	69,830.70	59,900.63	69,830.70

A spreadsheet that details these calculations is available in the online resources.

To better understand the prospective test, let's test an alternative set of surrender charges. If the life insurance company wanted to charge a level surrender charge of

19 See Section 7 of the Annuity Standard Nonforfeiture law.

20 Premium accumulated at the guaranteed interest rate. We assume no withdrawals and there are no annual expense charges.

21 The cash surrender value is the (Fund Value)(1 – Surrender Charge).

22 The minimum nonforfeiture amount is 87.5 percent of the premium less an annual expense charge of $50 accumulated at the minimum specified rate. We have assumed the minimum specified rate is 3 percent. Further, the $50 annual expense charge is assumed to be charged at the start of the year. Note that the Annuity Standard Nonforfeiture law does not specify the timing of this charge.

23 Since the guaranteed interest rate is not level in all years, we adjust the formula given right before this example to reflect the nonlevel interest rate.

5% for the first six years of the annuity, would this comply with the Annuity Standard Nonforfeiture law? This time our calculations generate the values in Table 18.16.

TABLE 18.16 Alternative Surrender Charges for Example 18.10

Time since Issue	Fund Value	Cash Surrender Value	Minimum Nonforfeiture Amount	Present Value of Maturity Value at $i_g + 1\%$
0	50,000.00	47,500.00	45,011.00	45,411.72
1	52,500.00	49,875.00	46,309.83	48,136.42
2	55,125.00	52,368.75	47,647.62	51,024.61
3	56,778.75	53,939.81	49,025.55	53,065.59
4	58,482.11	55,558.01	50,444.82	55,188.22
5	60,236.58	57,224.75	51,906.66	57,395.75
6	62,043.67	58,941.49	53,412.36	59,691.58
7	63,904.98	63,904.98	54,963.24	62,079.24
8	65,822.13	65,822.13	56,560.63	64,562.41
9	67,796.80	67,796.80	58,205.95	67,144.90
10	69,830.70	69,830.70	59,900.63	69,830.70

As we can see, the annuity with 5% level surrender charges for six years complies with the minimum nonforfeiture amount, but it would fail the prospective test. Once again, the details of this calculation are in a spreadsheet in the online resources.

As described in Section 13.2.2.1.4, some deferred annuity contracts contain a MVA, which may increase or decrease the cash surrender available under the contract. The Annuity Standard Nonforfeiture law does not discuss MVAs. Therefore, different state insurance departments have adopted different positions when applying the Annuity Standard Nonforfeiture law to deferred annuities with MVAs. Some states require that the nonforfeiture options be greater than the minimum nonforfeiture amount after the MVA has been applied while other states only require that nonforfeiture options be greater than the minimum nonforfeiture amount prior to the MVA.

18.3.2.2 Indexed deferred annuities

Indexed deferred annuities are also subject to the Annuity Nonforfeiture law. The only difference with respect to indexed deferred annuities is that the minimum specified interest rate may be different.

Recall that the specified minimum interest rate for fixed annuities is equal to the five-year constant maturity treasury rate (or an average thereof) rounded to the nearest 0.05 percent and reduced by 1.25 percent. This rate cannot be less than 1 percent and is capped at 3 percent.

For indexed annuities, the Annuity Nonforfeiture law permits the 1.25 percent reduction to be increased by up to an additional 1 percent if there is "substantive participation in an equity index benefit."[24] Furthermore, the present value of the additional reduction in the minimum

24 See Section 3 of the Annuity Standard Nonforfeiture law.

specified interest rate cannot exceed the market value of the equity index benefit. It should be noted that the minimum specified interest rate is still floored at 1 percent.

18.3.2.3 Variable deferred annuities

The Annuity Standard Nonforfeiture law does not apply to variable deferred annuities.[25]

Variable deferred annuities generally provide a cash surrender value. However, this value is linked to the investments in the separate account whose value may increase or decrease.

18.3.3 Payout Annuities

Payout annuities are not required by regulation to provide a nonforfeiture option. As previously discussed, a payout annuity provides future payments to the annuitant. These payments may be guaranteed to occur or they may be only paid if the annuitant is alive at the time that the payment is due.

If future payments are guaranteed to occur, while not required by regulation, a payout annuity may provide for the payment of the present value of future guaranteed payments if the policy owner requests such a payment. This value, known as the *commuted value*, is determined using interest only to calculate the present value.

If payments are life contingent (only paid if the annuitant is alive), then no commuted value is available. This prevents anti-selection against the life insurance company. If an annuitant knew that she was terminally ill, then the annuitant would want to maximize the payments to be received from the life insurance company and would request a commuted value. Since the price of the payout annuity is based on the assumption that payments will stop upon death, the life insurance company cannot afford to pay out the present value of payments that would not be made if the annuitant is deceased.

18.4 Income Taxes

We discussed taxes in Section 16.4.1.6.2. We will not delve any deeper into taxes in this section. The reason for mentioning them here is so that it is clear that taxes are another area where regulation affects product pricing, reserves, and profits.

18.5 Required Surplus

Required surplus is described in Section 16.4.1.8. As noted, most of the time the required surplus is directly a function of risk-based capital, which is determined by law in the United States and Canada. As such, this is a fourth area where regulation affects product pricing, reserves and profits.

25 See Section 1 of the Annuity Standard Nonforfeiture law.

18.6 Premiums

In general, premium rates in North America are not regulated. Life insurance companies are able to set their own premium rates without regulatory approval. However, there are some regulatory requirements for premium rates.

18.6.1 Unisex

In certain circumstances, premium rates may not vary by gender despite the fact that females clearly live longer than males, which actuarially justifies lower life insurance premium rates for females.

Montana has a law that prohibits gender base premium rates. Therefore, all life insurance policies sold in Montana have unisex premium rates.

In 1983, the U.S. Supreme Court in *Arizona Governing Committee v. Norris, 103 S.Ct. 3492*, ruled that a municipal retirement plan could not provide gender-based annuity rates. This ruling in combination with earlier rulings was considered to prohibit gender-based rates for both life insurance and payout annuities offered as "qualified"[26] employee benefits. Therefore, life insurance companies selling qualified plans must use unisex rates.

18.6.2 Race Based

As discussed in Section 14.1.2, prior to 1960, some U.S. life insurance companies priced life insurance products on the basis of race. African Americans were charged higher premiums than Caucasians. This was due to the fact African Americans had lower life expectancies than Caucasians. Additionally, other life insurance companies refused to sell life insurance policies to African Americans.

Race-based pricing is now illegal. The life insurance companies that sold policies prior to the 1960s with a premium that was based on race have adjusted the premiums for those policies so that they are the same as the premiums charged for Caucasians.[27]

18.7 EXERCISES

18.1 Calculate the U.S. statutory reserves for a 20-year term insurance with a level death benefit of 250,000 issued to a female smoker age 60. Use a valuation interest rate of 4.00% and the 2001 Commissioners Standard Ordinary mortality table for female smokers. This table is included with the online resources. You are given that the expense allowance is 14.1757 per 1,000 of death benefit.

18.2 Calculate the reserves for the following single premium deferred annuity using the Commissioners Annuity Valuation Reserve Method.

- Single premium deferred annuity with a premium of 100,000;
- Guaranteed interest rate of 6% for four years and 3% thereafter;

26 A qualified plan is a plan that meets requirements of the IRC and, as a result, is eligible to receive certain tax benefits. These plans must be for the exclusive benefit of employees or their beneficiaries.

27 In some cases, the adjustment to the race-based premiums have been the result of a class action lawsuit or other regulatory action by state insurance departments. In other cases, the life insurance companies have voluntarily adjusted the premiums.

- Surrender charges of 8% in year one, 7% in year two, 6% in year three, 5% in year four and zero thereafter;
- No partial free withdrawals;
- Death benefit is equal to the surrender value; and
- Valuation interest rate of 5%.
  a) Calculate the curtate CARVM reserve at issue.
  b) Calculate the continuous CARVM reserve at issue.
  c) If the account value after 3 ½ years is 122,622.60, calculate the curtate and continuous CARVM reserve for this annuity.

18.3 A life insurance company has the payout annuities in force on December 31, 2010 as shown in Table 18.17.

TABLE 18.17 Annuities for Exercise 18.3

Policy	Payment Amount	Payment Frequency	Payment Timing	Issue Age	Issue Date	Gender of Annuitant	Description of Benefit
1	5,000	Annually	Dec 31	70	12/31/2010	Female	Payments Guaranteed for 4 more years. Life Contingent Payments thereafter.
2	100	Monthly	1st of each Month	58	12/31/2010	Female	Payments guaranteed for 10 more years—120 future payments. No Life Contingent Payments.
3	2,500	Annually	June 30	65	12/31/2010	Female	Payments guaranteed for 8 more years. No Life Contingent Payments.
4	9,000	Annually	Dec 31	80	12/31/2010	Female	All payments are life contingent—no certain payments.
5	1,000	Annually	Dec 31	64	12/31/2004	Female	The policy was issued on 12/31/2004 with the first payment on 12/31/2005. The payments at issue were guaranteed for the first 10 years and continue thereafter as long as the annuitant is still alive. The annuitant is still alive.

Determine the reserves that the company establishes for these payout annuities as of December 31, 2010. Assume an annual effective interest rate of 5% and the 2000 Annuity Mortality Table. While you can calculate the reserves using the full mortality table from the online resources, you should be able to calculate the reserve using only information given in Example 18.3.

18.4 Calculate the GAAP reserves for a whole life with a level death benefit of 500,000 issued to a male nonsmoker age 65. The policy matures at age 100 and premiums are payable to age 100. Our GAAP Reserves will be based on the following assumptions:

- Mortality follows the 2001 Valuation Basic Mortality Table Age Last Birthday. This mortality table can be found on the Society of Actuaries website;
- Lapses or surrenders are 20% in the first year, 12% in the second year, 8% in the third year, and 6% thereafter;
- Commissions are 80% in the first year, 10% in the next nine years, and 5% thereafter;

- Issue expenses are 200 per policy and 0.75 per 1,000 of death benefit;
- Maintenance expense is 60 per year occurring at the beginning of the year;
- Premium tax is 2.5% of premium;
- The net investment rate that we expect to earn is 6.25%;
- The Gross Annual Premium for this policy is 18,500;
- We will include a PAD in the development of reserves of 25 bp on investment earnings and 7.5% on mortality and maintenance expenses; and
- The cash values for this policy are listed in the online resources.

18.5 Calculate the Gross Premium reserves for a whole life with a level death benefit of 500,000 issued to a male nonsmoker age 65. The policy matures at age 100 and premiums are payable to age 100. Our Gross Premium reserves will be based on the following assumptions:

- Mortality follows the 2001 Valuation Basic Mortality Table Age Last Birthday. This mortality table can be found on the SOA's website;
- Lapses or surrenders are 20% in the first year, 12% in the second year, 8% in the third year, and 6% thereafter;
- Commissions are 80% in the first year, 10% in the next nine years, and 5% thereafter;
- Issue expenses are 200 per policy and 0.75 per 1,000 of death benefit;
- Maintenance expense is 60 per year occurring at the beginning of the year;
- Premium tax is 2.5% of premium;
- The net investment rate that we expect to earn is 6.25%;
- The Gross Annual Premium for this policy is 18,500; and
- The cash values for this policy are listed in the online resources.

Compare the gross premium reserves from this exercise with the net GAAP reserves from Exercise 18.4. Explain why the gross premium reserves are less.

18.6 Jennifer purchases a graded death benefit whole life insurance policy. The death benefits are as follows:

Policy Year	Death Benefit
1	200
2	450
3	750
4 and after	1,000

Calculate the *AAI* used to calculate the minimum cash surrender benefits under the SNFL in the United States.

18.7 Calculate the minimum cash values for a whole life with a level death benefit of 500,000 issued to a male nonsmoker age 65. The policy matures at age 100 and premiums are payable to age 100. Our Gross Premium reserves will be based on the following assumptions:

- Mortality follows the 2001 Commissioners Standard Ordinary Mortality Table Age Last Birthday. This mortality table can be found in the online resources; and
- An interest rate of 5%.

Verify that these cash values match the cash values given for Exercises 18.4 and 18.5.

18.8 Calculate the maximum surrender charge for the first 20 years of a universal life policy for a female nonsmoker age 50. The universal life policy has the following characteristics:

- The specified amount is 100,000;
- There is a monthly first year charge of 100 per policy and a monthly renewal charge of 5 per policy;
- The nonforfeiture basis is the 2001 CSO Female Age Last Birthdate nonsmoker table with interest at 4%; and
- The policy matures at age 100.

18.9 Section 18.3.2.1 describes the minimum nonforfeiture interest rate that may be credited on a fixed deferred annuity. If a company uses this approach and determines the interest rate for the next calendar year using the average five-year constant-maturity treasury rate for the month of October, determine the rate that the company would have used for each year from 2001 to 2011. You can find the five-year constant-maturity treasury rate on the Internet.

18.10 A single premium deferred annuity has a premium of 100,000. The guaranteed interest rate is 3% for all years. The surrender charges are 8% in the first year and 7% in the second year. The surrender charges continue to decrease 1% each year until they are zero for policy years 9 and later. The deferred annuity contract does not have a partial free withdrawal and there is no annual expense charge.

Create a table like Table 18.15 that compares the Fund Value, Cash Surrender Value, Minimum Nonforfeiture Amount, and Present Value of Maturity Value for integral time from 0 to 10. Assume the maturity date is 10 years from the issue date and the nonforfeiture minimum interest rate is 3%.

18.11 You are given the following deferred annuity policy:

- Single premium deferred annuity with a premium of 75,000;
- Guaranteed interest rate of 1.5% for 10 years and 3% thereafter;
- Surrender charges of 7% in year one, 6% in year two, 5% in year three, 4% in year four, and zero thereafter;
- No partial free withdrawals; and
- No annual expense charge.

Test this annuity to see if it complies with the Annuity Standard Nonforfeiture Law. We will use a maturity date of 10 years from issue. Further, the minimum specified rate under the SNFL is 2.5%.

18.12 You are given the following deferred annuity policy:

- Single premium deferred annuity with a premium of 200,000;
- Guaranteed interest rate of 3% for all years;
- The surrender charges are 9% in the first year and 8% in the second year. The surrender charges continue to decrease 1% each year until they are zero for policy years 10 and later;
- No partial free withdrawals; and
- No annual expense charge.

Test this annuity to see if it complies with the Annuity Standard Nonforfeiture Law. We will use a maturity date of 10 years from issue. Further, the minimum specified rate under the SNFL is 3.0%.

18.13 Sally bought a single premium immediate annuity exactly three years ago. The annuity that Sally bought paid 1,000 at the start of each month. Payments are made as long as Sally is alive, but not less than 120 payments. Immediately before the 37th payment, Sally requests the commuted value of the remaining certain payments. The insurance company calculates the commuted value using an annual effective interest rate of 6.25%. Determine the commuted value.

CHAPTER 19
Monitoring Results

Monitoring results is an important step for life insurance products. Chapter 17 of Bellis, et. al. (2010) titled Monitoring Experience states that the essential learning points of the chapter are:

- "Why we analyze experience;
- What we analyze; and
- How we do the analysis."

We will discuss the "Why" and "What" below.

19.1 Why Monitor Experience

At the highest level, monitoring experience occurs through the measurement of profits. However, merely monitoring profits does not allow us to truly understand what is happening with our products. For example, if profits match our expected profits, it does not mean that our experience matches our expected experience. We could have expenses in excess of expected expenses while our mortality has actually been lower than expected. Therefore, we need to monitor our experience at a more granular level to fully understand our sources of profit. This analysis also allows us to better manage our products in the future. In our example, if our expenses have exceed expected expenses, there may be management actions that we can take to bring expenses back in line with expected which would further increase our profits.

Another reason to monitor experience is that it should allow us to develop more accurate assumptions for use in pricing future products. Actual experience is a function of a life insurance company's distribution system, product, customer demographics, and service as well as other factors. It is almost always preferable to use a life insurance company's own experience to develop assumptions to be used to price new products as opposed to using industry experience.

Experience analysis is also important in the establishing of reserves and evaluating the adequacy of reserves. Experience studies allow us to evaluate the appropriateness of reserve assumptions and to make adjustments, if necessary. This is clearly true for GAAP reserves or gross premium reserves. However, it is also true for statutory reserves where the actuary has to opine on the adequacy of reserves.

19.2 What to Monitor

With life and annuity products, the primary assumptions to monitor are:

- Mortality;
- Persistency;
- Expenses;
- Investment returns; and
- Distribution of sales.

Sensitivity testing during pricing can identify the assumptions that are critical drivers of profitability. If deviation of certain assumptions does not significantly affect profits, then monitoring of these assumptions can be done less frequently.

19.2.1 Mortality

Mortality is generally a critical assumption for life insurance and for payout annuities. As such, periodic monitoring of mortality experience is very important. However, monitoring mortality is not as easy as it sounds because death is an infrequent occurrence. Therefore, it may take several years before an individual company's mortality experience will be credible.

On the other hand, mortality is generally not a major driver of profits for deferred annuities and the monitoring of mortality may not be necessary for this product.

While monitoring mortality is important, there may be limited management actions that can be taken if mortality is higher than expected. There is really nothing that the company can do to control future mortality for the policies that have already been issued. If a contract has nonguaranteed elements or dividends, then the higher mortality can be reflected in these items. Also, if the company can identify the cause of the high mortality, then additional management actions can be taken to prevent problems with any policies that will be written in the future.

19.2.2 Persistency

Monitoring lapses and surrenders is important for life insurance and deferred annuities. Generally, there are no lapses or surrenders on payout annuities. Unlike mortality, lapses and surrenders occur frequently and it does not take several years of experience before the results of experience analysis are credible.

In general, higher lapse and surrender rates are undesirable because there will then be fewer policies in force in the future to generate profits. However, for some products, higher lapse and surrender rates generate higher profits. For most level premium term insurance, higher lapses and surrenders generate higher profits. This is because the premiums for the policy are level while the mortality rates for the insured is increasing over time. If lapses and surrenders are higher in the later durations of the policy, then fewer death claims are incurred and the product is more profitable. Therefore, in completing sensitivity testing as described in Section16.1.3, it is important to test both higher and lower lapses and surrenders than expected to understand the effect of persistency variations.

19.2.3 Expenses

Managing expenses to closely match the expected expenses is crucial for all products. Unlike many other experience items, expenses can actually be managed. This is different from other items such as mortality where very little can be done to change mortality once the life insurance policy or annuity has been issued.

The first step in managing expenses is to monitor the expenses actually being incurred. Once we know the actual expenses being incurred, we can take steps to reduce expenses if they are higher than anticipated.

Many companies conduct annual expense studies as discussed in Section 17.5.2. While these expense studies can be used to set future pricing assumptions, they can also be used to compare with past expense assumptions to determine if actual expenses are consistent with expected expenses.

19.2.4 Investment Returns

Monitoring investment returns is a relatively easy task and is usually done quarterly, but can be done as frequently as monthly. For products with nonguaranteed elements, monitoring investment returns allows the insurance company to adjust the nonguaranteed elements to maintain expected profitability. For other products, analyzing investment returns allows the company to understand the emergence of profits and the adequacy of reserves.

19.2.5 Distribution of Sales

The distribution and mix of sales can be important if a product is not priced consistently for all pricing cells. In Section 16.1.2 and Example 16.1, we looked at the potential impact of variations in distribution of sales from expected. If distribution of sales can affect the profits of a product, then this should be monitored.

CHAPTER 20
Closing

In these last eight chapters, we have explored individual life and annuity products. At this point, you should:

- Understand the basic types of individual life and annuity insurance and the structure of those products;
- Understand the external forces that influence these products;
- Understand the basics of pricing individual life and annuity products including the various methods of measuring profits;
- Understand that the accounting system and the reserves determine when the profits are recognized;
- Understand the calculation of the reserves under the various accounting systems;
- Understand the inputs that are necessary to complete profit testing;
- Understand the regulatory influences on profit testing; and
- Understand the importance of monitoring results.

PART 4
RETIREMENT BENEFITS

Patricia L. Scahill

CHAPTER 21

Introduction to Retirement Plans

Actuaries are involved with many types of protection against financial loss. Retirement plans provide protection against loss of income when an individual is no longer gainfully employed on a full-time basis. The individual may have fully retired or be working a reduced schedule with the need for additional income to supplement part-time earnings.

In many insurance arrangements, the risk is outside the control of the person insured. In the case of retirement plans, the risk is generally within the control of the person insured. As a result, retirement plans operate differently from other types of insurance arrangements. In fact, the general public may not view them as insurance at all.

In addition to providing income after a person stops working full time, many retirement arrangements provide financial assistance upon death or disability. These risks are primarily outside the control of the person insured, but, from a cost perspective, they are generally minor benefits in the overall retirement arrangement. As a result, we will focus almost exclusively on the replacement of income lost after a person stops working full-time or works a reduced schedule.

In this text, we distinguish between four types of retirement programs.

- Social security pension program or system: sponsored by the government and covering a large portion of the residents of the country;
- Public pensions: retirement benefits provided by the government for its employees rather than to the broader group that is covered by a social security pension program;
- Private employer-sponsored pensions: provided by private, non-governmental employers for their employees; and
- Personal pensions: established and funded by an individual, such as an individual retirement account in the United States.

Further information on the types of pension plans is discussed in later sections.

21.1 External Forces Underlying the Need for a Retirement Income System

Although each of us can understand the need for financial security in retirement, we don't all face the same obstacles to attaining that financial security. On a global basis, many factors create the need for a retirement income financial security system. Countries have different obstacles to manage with respect to providing a system to facilitate financial security for its retired and elderly population. These obstacles and factors can be described as external forces.

21.1.1 Demographic Forces

Various studies show that the world's population is aging and that the relative size of the population at various ages is also changing over time. Several demographic factors contribute to this general aging of the population.

21.1.1.1 Mortality

As mortality decreases, individuals live longer. For example, mortality has declined resulting in significantly increased life expectancy since 1900 in the United States. Table 21.1 shows life expectancy at birth for males and females in the United States for selected years from 1900 to 2006.

TABLE 21.1 Average Number of Years of Life Remaining at Birth[1]

Year	Male	Female	Combined
1900–1902	47.88	50.70	49.24
1919–1921	55.50	57.40	56.40
1939–1941	61.60	65.89	63.62
1959–1961	66.80	73.24	68.89
1979–1981	70.11	77.62	73.88
1999–2001	74.10	79.45	76.83
2006	75.10	80.20	77.70

Other developed countries have experienced similar trends. Table 21.2 compares the life expectancy at birth for males and females in 1960 and 2006 for selected countries.

TABLE 21.2 Average Number of Years of Life Remaining at Birth[2]

	Male		Female	
Country	1960	2006	1960	2006
Australia	67.9	78.7	73.9	83.5
Canada	68.4	78.0	74.2	82.7
France	67.0	77.3	73.6	84.4
Germany	66.5	77.2	71.7	82.4
Japan	65.3	79.0	70.2	85.8
Mexico	55.8	73.2	59.2	78.1
United Kingdom	67.9	77.1	73.7	81.1
United States	66.6	75.2	73.1	80.4

Many factors contribute to the increase in life expectancy, including medical advances, better public health, and higher living standards (McGill, et. al., 2010, p. 13). Further improvements can be expected as medical science makes advances against diseases that primarily affect the elderly. However, future improvements will likely not be as rapid as those of the last century.

21.1.1.2 Fertility

The fertility rate is the expected number of children each woman would have if the current birth rate is representative over the entire fertility period for the woman. It is the most common measure of the birthrate over time (McGill, et. al., 2010, p. 11).

1 U.S. Department of Health and Human Services (2010), Table 11.

2 OECD (2010).

Table 21.3, published by the Organization for Economic Cooperation and Development (OECD), shows fertility rates for selected countries from 1962 to 2002.

TABLE 21.3 Evolution of Fertility Rates for Selected Countries[3]

Country	1962	1972	1982	1992	2002
Australia	3.43	2.74	1.93	1.89	1.76
Canada	3.76	2.02	1.64	1.69	1.50
China		4.87	2.31	1.95	1.88
France	2.80	2.42	1.91	1.73	1.86
Germany	2.44	1.74	1.51	1.29	1.34
Japan	1.98	2.14	1.77	1.50	1.32
Mexico	7.26	6.53	4.59	3.25	2.48
United Kingdom	2.88	2.20	1.78	1.79	1.64
United States	3.46	2.01	1.83	2.05	2.01

21.1.1.3 Aging

Mortality and fertility combine to have a major impact on the rate at which a society ages. The portion of the population over age 65 will increase as mortality improves and as fertility declines (Medicine Encyclopedia, 2010). We saw in the previous section that both of these trends are present in the United States, resulting in an aging population.

The U.S. population grew significantly during the last century, and the proportion of the population over age 65 grew even faster. Table 21.4 shows the total population compared to the population over age 65 from 1900 to 2000.

TABLE 21.4 Total U.S. Population and Population over Age 65 for Selected Years, 1900–2000 (in Thousands Except for Percentages)[4]

Year	Total Population	Population over 65	Percentage over 65
1900	75,995	3,080	4.05%
1910	91,972	3,950	4.29%
1920	105,711	4,933	4.67%
1930	122,775	6,634	5.40%
1940	131,669	9,019	6.85%
1950	150,697	12,270	8.14%
1960	179,323	16,560	9.23%
1970	203,302	20,266	9.97%
1980	226,542	25,550	11.28%
1990	248,718	31,084	12.50%
2000	281,422	34,992	12.43%

3 OECD (2010), Data Chart G3.1, Evolution of the total fertility rate for selected countries.

4 McGill, et. al. (2010), p. 10, citing U.S. Census Statistical Abstract of the United States, 2001, pp. 8, 14, and 23.

The following facts about global aging[5] illustrate recent trends outside the United States.

- The portion of the world's population over age 60 is expected to increase from 9 percent (almost 0.5 billion[6] people) in 1990 to nearly 16 percent of the world's population (1.4 billion people) by 2030;
- Because of medical advances and declining fertility, developing countries are aging much faster than industrialized countries; and
- It is expected that by 2030, the majority of the world's elderly will live in areas not currently considered industrialized, with more than 25 percent in China alone.

A more prosperous economy has better public health and medical care, increasing both life expectancy and the proportion of the population that reaches old age. As shown in Table 21.5, the proportion of a population over age 60 increases as the per capita gross national product (GNP) increases:

TABLE 21.5 Percentage of Population Over Age 60[7]

Per capita GNP less than \$600[8]	< 7%
Per capita GNP between \$600 and \$8,000	12% – 16%
Per capita GNP more than \$8,000	≥ 17%

A rise in the median age of a population is an indicator that the population is aging. Table 21.6 shows that between 1950 and 2005, the median age of the world's population increased from 24 to 28 years (United Nations Secretariat, 2005, p. 12).

TABLE 21.6 Median Age for the World[9]

	Median Age in Years		
Regions and Major Areas	**1950**	**2005**	**2050**
World	23.9	28.1	37.8
More developed regions	29.0	38.6	45.5
Less developed regions	21.4	25.6	36.6
Least developed countries	19.6	18.9	27.3
Africa	19.0	18.9	27.4
Asia	22.0	27.7	39.9
Latin America and the Caribbean	20.2	25.9	39.9
North America	29.8	36.3	41.5
Europe	29.7	39.0	47.1
Oceania	28.0	32.3	40.5

5 World Bank (1994, p. 1).
6 This text uses the "short scale" version of billion, meaning 1,000,000,000.
7 World Bank (1994, p. 28).
8 Per capita GNP, shown in U.S. dollars.
9 United Nations Secretariat (2005, p. 12). The median age for 2005 has been estimated from the data set used and the data was projected to 2050 using mortality and fertility assumptions.

Table 21.7 shows the age distribution of these regions, including a projection to 2050 based on medium fertility rate assumptions.

TABLE 21.7 Percentage Distribution of the 2005 Estimated and 2050 Projected Population[10]

Age Group	2005	2050
	World	
14 and under	28%	20%
15–59	61%	58%
60 and older	10%	22%
	More Developed Regions	
14 and under	17%	16%
15–59	63%	52%
60 and older	20%	32%
	Less Developed Regions	
14 and under	31%	21%
15–59	61%	59%
60 and older	8%	20%

The projected rate of aging is somewhat higher in less developed countries than the world as a whole. The portion of the population age 60 and older is expected to more than double in less developed countries, with the portion age 14 and under declining by one-third. In more developed regions, the population between ages 15 and 59 accounts for the largest projected decline.

21.1.1.4 Impact of demographics on retirement systems

In this section, we will consider the impact of demographics on a national retirement system referred to as a "pay-as-you-go" social security system. We will discuss social security systems in detail in later sections.

The relationship between workers and retirees changes as the proportion of the population over the typical retirement age increases. Workers must produce enough for both workers and retirees to consume, and workers also pay employment taxes if social security pensions are funded by payroll taxes. As a result, this worker/retiree relationship is critical to the viability of a "pay as you go" social security system.

The life expectancy during retirement years is an important factor in the cost of providing lifetime retirement benefits. The cost of a life annuity increases as the person's life expectancy increases because a larger expected number of monthly benefits will be paid. Table 21.8 shows life expectancy at age 65 for males and females in the United States for selected years from 1900 to 2006.

---

10 United Nations Secretariat (2005, p. 15).

TABLE 21.8 Average Number of Years of Life Remaining at Age 65[11]

Year	Male	Female	Combined
1900–1902	11.50	12.22	11.86
1919–1921	12.20	12.73	12.47
1939–1941	12.07	13.57	12.80
1959–1961	12.95	15.80	14.39
1979–1981	14.21	18.44	16.51
1999–2001	16.11	19.12	17.77
2006	17.00	19.70	18.50

As the global population ages, societies must be able to support the elderly. A lack of formal retirement systems places the financial responsibility for the elderly on the individual, families, the government or a combination of the three. Public welfare is the "insurer of last resort" for impoverished elderly. It is easy to see why a country with the financial wherewithal to establish a retirement income security system would do so by creating a government-sponsored social security program and by encouraging private employers to create retirement plans for their employees.

21.1.2 Social Forces

Until the late 19th century, families generally provided financial support for retired elderly (McGill, et. al., 2010, p. 3). Families tended to be geographically clustered, making it easy for younger family members to care for, or house, older relatives. Society was accustomed to the elderly being dependent on other family members, so no stigma was attached to this financial dependence.

As the economy in developed countries evolved from agrarian to industrialized and from primarily rural to primarily urban, families began to disperse. Housing itself also changed as families began to live in more compact, urban single-family housing instead of multi-family farmhouses.[12] As a result, it is not as common in industrialized countries to have an extended family living together. If not supported by family members, older citizens must be financially independent.

A study of individuals age 55 and older by the U.S. Department of Health and Human Services showed that, in 2002, 79 percent of individuals age 55 and older, including more than half of those age 85 and older, owned their own home. Further, only 11 percent of survey participants lived with a child, although more than half lived within 10 miles of a child (U.S. Department of Health and Human Services, 2007, p. 75).

21.1.3 Macroeconomic Forces

The economy has an impact on demographics and work patterns. A more economically prosperous economy enables workers to stop earning income at some point and enjoy leisure activities.

11 U.S. Department of Health and Human Services (2010), Table 11. Life expectancy by age, race, and sex: Death registration states, 1900–1902 to 1919–1921, and United States 1929 to 2006.

12 Single family is used to refer to parents and their children. Multi-family is used to refer to multiple biologically related generations or unrelated families.

As discussed previously, a society depends on current production to meet current consumption needs. The entire society is better off when the economy is growing, because it will more easily meet consumption demands. The dynamic of an aging population can result in an increasingly smaller percentage of the total population in the workforce, putting pressure on those who are working to produce enough for overall consumption demands. Younger retirement ages can put an additional strain on the overall economy.

In the early 1800s, the U.S. economy was primarily agricultural. Extended families tended to live on the farm, with the younger generation taking more responsibility for the farm and allowing the aging workers to work less or stop working entirely while still being supported by income from the family farm. By the end of the 1800s, large industrialized farms brought specialization and the need for new farm management skills (McGill, et. al, 2010, p. 5).

Urban business in the 1800s was often craft-oriented (McGill, et. al., 2010, p. 4), which did not require great physical strength and allowed workers to remain productive into old age. The industrial age also changed urban business by introducing large-scale production and its related efficiencies. However, the ability to operate machinery requires physical strength or manual dexterity, which tends to decrease with age.

By the time of the Great Depression, which began in late 1929 and didn't end until the early 1940s, only about 20 percent of workers were employed in agriculture. Much of the shift in the type of work resulted from younger workers taking urban jobs.[13] As a result, the workforce changed from agricultural to industrial as the population moved from rural to urban locations.

The increased demands on strength as well as the need for manual dexterity brought about by industrialization made it harder for older workers to perform up to expectations. Remaining in the workforce after the worker is no longer able to perform job duties adequately is sometimes referred to as retiring in place. Although the worker continues to earn a needed salary, self-esteem suffers. The employer is paying the worker more than his worth because the worker can't meet job expectations. Employers needed to find a humane way to ease older, less productive workers from the workforce.

21.1.4 Microeconomic Forces

When the world's economies were primarily agrarian, the older generation tended to own the land and therefore controlled the family's financial assets, providing sufficient financial resources for the retirement years (McGill, et. al., 2010, pp. 4–5). This changed as economies shifted to more industrialization and then into the information age. The typical worker today does not own the income source. Income is now most often generated from physical or intellectual labor expended on property owned by someone else. So the aging family member does not have a built-in transition from earning income into the retirement years.

In the early 1900s, as the economy continued its shift toward industrialization and specialization, unemployment among older workers rose as older workers were unable to find alternative

13 McGill, et. al. (2010, p. 4), citing U.S. Bureau of Census, *Historical Statistics of the United States*, Washington, D.C., U.S. Government Printing Office, 1975, pp. 139, 465.

employment. The unemployment rate for men over age 65 rose from 26.8 percent in 1890 to more than 50 percent by 1930 just after the U.S. stock market crash and the beginning of the Great Depression.[14]

Unemployment led to poverty among the elderly because adequate retirement systems were not yet in place to fill the income gap once an older worker was no longer able to be gainfully employed.

The Great Depression increased awareness of the economic plight of the elderly, leading to the development of the U.S. social security system, which began when the Social Security Act became law in 1935 (McGill, et. al., 2010, p. 3).

When measuring poverty levels among those over age 65, the OECD looks at the percentage of that population with income below one-half of the OECD median household income. Table 21.9 shows OECD old-age poverty rates in the mid-2000s.

TABLE 21.9 Old-Age Poverty Rates (mid-2000s)[15]

Country	Poverty Rate
Australia	26.9%
Canada	4.4%
France	8.8%
Germany	9.9%
Japan	22.0%
United Kingdom	10.3%
United States	23.6%

The U.S. Social Security Administration uses a different measure of old age poverty. The U.S. poverty line is defined as the amount of income needed to keep a household above a level determined by considering basic household needs including food and housing. Based on the U.S. measure of poverty, the old-age poverty rate is projected to decrease from 10.5 percent in 1997 to approximately 7.2 percent in 2020 and decrease further to 4.1 percent in 2047 (Wentworth and Pattison (2002).

Another factor contributing to the risk of poverty in old age is the decline in personal savings. The preretirement years represent the accumulation years when a person sets aside money or earns employer-provided retirement benefits so money will be available during the post-retirement distribution years. In order to consume in retirement, a person needs savings or some other source of income to replace income lost as a result of not working or working less. In 1974, individual retirement accounts were introduced that allowed U.S. citizens who did not participate in a tax-qualified retirement plan to be able to save for retirement on a tax-deferred basis.[16]

---

14 McGill, et. al. (2010, p. 5), citing *The Promise of Private Pensions: The First Hundred Years* by Steven A. Sass, Cambridge, Mass., Harvard University Press, 1970, p. 5.

15 OECD (2009).

16 Congressional Budget Office (2010). The tax aspects of retirement plans will be discussed later.

Household saving rates have declined for most OECD countries. Table 21.10 shows the decline from 1990 to 2009 for several OECD countries.

TABLE 21.10 Household Savings Rates as a Percentage of Disposable Income[17]

Country	1990	1995	2000	2005	2009
Australia	8.2%	6.4%	1.8%	−1.1%	2.5%
Canada	13.0%	9.2%	4.7%	1.6%	1.1%
France	9.4%	12.8%	12.0%	11.8%	12.3%
Germany	13.7%	11.0%	9.2%	10.5%	10.6%
Japan	13.9%	11.9%	8.6%	3.9%	2.6%
United States	7.0%	4.6%	2.3%	0.5%	1.2%

An article by Luke M. Shimek and Yi Wen (2008) published by the U.S. Federal Reserve Bank of St. Louis showed the current personal savings rate in China, still considered a poor country, to be about 25 percent. Shimek and Wen speculated on the reason for the high savings rate. Government reforms in China in the late 1970s created a shift in employment, resulting in fewer government-paid jobs and creating income uncertainty. Individuals tend to save more during economic uncertainty. In addition, the Chinese government, which previously fully subsidized the retirement period for its citizens, has been shifting the financial responsibility for retirement to individuals, increasing the need for savings. Another factor in the high Chinese savings rate is the lack of development in China's financial market and banking system, making loans difficult for an individual to obtain and requiring a substantial down payment for a home mortgage. Shimek and Wen predict that the development of the financial markets and the expansion of the social insurance retirement system may dramatically reduce China's savings rate in the future.

Inflation, resulting in an increased cost of living, can be devastating to a retiree whose income does not increase with an inflation index or who does not have surplus retirement assets to compensate for increasing expenses. The public pension in a typical industrial country is indexed for inflation, but that is not the case in developing countries. As an example of the impact, the purchasing power of non-indexed pension benefits in Venezuela fell 60 percent during the 1980s (World Bank, 1984, p. 2).

Health problems increase with age, and costly medical technology is concentrated at the end of life, which typically occurs in old age. As a result, the cost of health care increases as an individual, and as a society, ages. In the United States in 2002, more than 90 percent of individuals age 65 and older have some sort of health insurance, including government-sponsored Medicare (U.S. Department of Health and Human Services, 2007, p. 28). Even with health insurance, out-of-pocket expenditures can be significant and rise with age. During the two-year period from 2000 to 2002 in the United States, individuals over age 85 participating in a health and retirement survey reported $4,400 in out-of-pocket medical expenditures compared to $2,900 for individuals age 55 to age 64 (U.S. Department of Health and Human Services, 2007, p. 31).

17 Annex Table 23. Household Savings Rates. http://econ365.files.wordpress.com/2008/10/gross-savings-rate.pdf, Accessed November 12, 2010.

As personal income rises, a person needs more income in retirement to maintain the same standard of living. There is no agreed-to percentage of preretirement income that must be replaced in retirement to maintain the same standard of living although 70 percent is often recommended as a goal. The needed income replacement percentage is typically less than 100 percent because some expenses, such as work-related expenses, stop when a person stops working. In addition, saving for retirement is no longer necessary once a person retires.

Table 21.11 compares expected and actual changes in spending after an individual retires. The data is from a U.S. health and retirement survey.

TABLE 21.11 Expected and Actual Changes in Retirement Spending: 2000–2001[18]

		Expected Changes Before Retirement	Actual Changes After Retirement
Trips, Travel, or Vacation	Decrease	38.5%	44.7%
	Same	32.5%	30.4%
	Increase	29.0%	24.9%
Clothing	Decrease	65.2%	60.5%
	Same	32.8%	32.9%
	Increase	1.9%	6.6%
Eating Out/Food & Beverages	Decrease	52.5%	40.4%
	Same	38.6%	36.3%
	Increase	8.8%	23.3%
New Home, Home Repairs, or Household Items	Decrease	53.2%	37.1%
	Same	39.4%	45.5%
	Increase	7.4%	17.4%
Entertainment, Sports, and Hobbies	Decrease	46.4%	44.4%
	Same	40.4%	45.0%
	Increase	13.2%	10.6%
Automobile Expenses	Decrease	45.1%	29.4%
	Same	47.3%	51.0%
	Increase	7.6%	19.6%

Regardless of the income replacement percentage goal chosen, the resources needed in retirement for a person to maintain a preretirement standard of living after retirement increases as longevity increases. When this happens, greater resources are needed from the various sources of retirement income.

21.1.5 Forces Related to Personal Choices

As a result of higher income brought about by industrialization, there was less economic need to work as many hours to earn a certain amount of income as when wages were lower.

18 U.S. Department of Health and Human Services (2007, p. 53)

One result of greater wealth was an increased interest in leisure activities, which are defined as activities not related to a person's work.

In economic terms, the cost of an hour of leisure is the cost of foregoing an hour of paid work (McGill, et. al., 2010, p. 7). Everyone has a point at which an extra hour of paid work does not purchase sufficient additional goods and services to be worthwhile to the individual. As wages rise, this point represents a lower number of hours worked and leisure increases. People with sufficient savings or non-work-related income sources can enjoy a period of full-time leisure during retirement.

In the United States, Social Security reduces the benefit amount whenever the person has more than minimal earnings from employment if the benefit is received prior to the full social security retirement age (currently between age 66 and age 67, depending on year of birth). This penalty for working during early retirement can be thought of as either a leisure reward or an incentive to postpone retirement. This working-during-retirement penalty stops at full social security retirement age.

21.1.6 EXERCISES

21.1 Why is a retirement income system needed?
21.2 What is the impact of mortality and fertility on the aging of a population?
21.3 What societal trends impact the current need for a retirement income system?

21.2 History of Retirement Plans

21.2.1 Earliest Retirement Plans[19]

The earliest pension plans in the United States provided coverage for veterans. The first pensions were offered to disabled soldiers in the U.S. colonies prior to the signing of the U.S. Constitution. The Continental Congress provided pension coverage for the army and navy engaged in the Revolutionary War and Congress extended the coverage for disabled and aged veterans of specific subsequent wars. However, there was no formal pension system separate from these specific Congressional grants of pensions in certain circumstances.

These ad hoc pensions were formalized in the 1860s when Congress enacted legislation to facilitate the retirement of members of all branches of the military. President Abraham Lincoln used military pensions as a way to retire older senior officers and replace them with younger, more vibrant ones as the Civil War began. By the end of the 19th century, there were approximately 3 million people age 65 or older and 992,000 people receiving military pensions.[20]

---

19 This section is based on material from McGill, et. al., 2010, pp. 15–16.

20 McGill, et. al. (2010, p. 16) citing Craig and Wilson Clark, *A History of Public Sector Pensions in the United States*, p. 148.

21.2.2 Expansion of Pensions Beyond the Military[21]

In the mid-1850s, New York City established a pension system for its disabled police officers. Coverage for public workers soon expanded to firefighters and teachers employed in large cities. As with the military, the public workers covered by early pensions held demanding jobs critical to society.

The earliest private sector pensions were in the railroad industry where, like the Civil War era military, there was a need to encourage older workers to retire to make room for stronger, younger workers who were expected to be better able to avoid accidents. Retirement was a more socially acceptable way of dealing with an aging workforce than reassigning workers to lower-paying positions or terminating them without a pension. Because railroads were large, government-regulated entities, they were especially concerned about public perception. Retirement benefits provided railroads with a means of rewarding older workers for their years of service to the railroad, but encouraging them to retire from the workforce. This also opened promotional opportunities for younger workers.

The first North American private sector pension was established in Canada in 1874 by the Grand Trunk Railroad. The American Express Company, which began as a rail shipping company and then expanded into financial services, established the first private sector U.S. pension in 1880. The B&O (Baltimore & Ohio) Railroad soon followed suit.

By the early 1900s, pensions were offered in the banking and insurance industries as well as public utilities, higher education, and major urban public transportation systems. The financial services industries used pensions to encourage honesty and loyalty of workers.

The early pensions for higher education workers were funded by a grant from Andrew Carnegie that was expected to fund benefits for many years into the future. The Teachers Insurance Annuity Association, now commonly referred to as TIAA, was formed in 1918 by the Carnegie Foundation to manage the annuity portion of the teachers' retirement system.[22] This began the era of funded pension plans. However, in less than 20 years after the initial Carnegie grant, the following changes were made to reduce the cost of the program.

- New hires were no longer able to receive pensions.
- The retirement age for current participants had to be raised to age 70.
- The concept of vesting, where benefits are forfeited if the employee terminates before earning the required years of service, was introduced.

The higher education pension system led to an understanding of the need for a system that was adequately funded. The replacement of the Carnegie "free" pension program with one in which participants made contributions to the plan and benefits were based largely on the accumulation of those contributions changed the pension landscape, introducing a defined contribution concept where the ultimate benefit depended on the account balance rather than being a promised benefit.

---

21 This section is based on material from McGill, et. al. (2010), pp. 16–20.

22 TIAA-CREF Company History. http://www.tiaa-cref.org/public/about/press/about_us/history.html. Accessed September 22, 2010.

21.2.3 Early Pensions for U.S. Federal Government Employees

The Pendleton Civil Service Reform Act, which became law in 1883, changed the nature of most federal government employment. Rather than being based on political affiliation, employment was converted to a merit system. This was, at least partly, in response to the assassination of President James Garfield by a disgruntled supporter who felt he should receive an ambassadorship.[23]

The merit system was a great idea, and employees liked it so much they seemed not to ever want to retire. In order to create the needed turnover that rejuvenates a workforce and provides promotional opportunities to younger workers, Congress passed the Civil Service Retirement Act, which became effective on August 1, 1920.[24]

During World War II, the United States experienced significant inflation. In an attempt to control increases in the cost of goods and services, the federal government created several agencies charged with increasing total production and controlling wages and prices. As a result of wage restrictions, employers used fringe benefits to attract workers. These fringe benefit enticements included pensions, medical benefits, paid holidays and vacations. These benefits were considered non-inflationary so they were not subject to the wage control restrictions.

21.2.4 Growth of U.S. Pensions after World War II

In 1947, the Labor-Management Act (also known as the Taft-Hartley Act) was enacted, creating a duty for employers to bargain with unions over pensions. Collective bargaining is a give-and-take process. To reach an agreement on a new collective bargaining agreement, each side must typically give up something that was in their original offer or accept something the other side wants. The alternative to not reaching an agreement may be a strike by the union in which the union members refuse to work. Each side will have an idea of what is the worst case for which they are willing to settle. Union and management priorities change from year to year, but wages and benefits are typically among the most important.

The World War II wage controls in the United States created an interest in other forms of compensation such as pensions because they were not considered in applying the limit on wage increases. As pensions were granted to union employees, the company was apt to also provide similar or perhaps more generous benefits for nonunion workers. As a result, collective bargaining has helped expand private pensions.

Early pensions arose because of the need to encourage older, less effective workers to retire. This led to the concept that pensions were payment for human depreciation that occurred as a person aged. When pension benefits became part of the bargaining agreement, pensions began to be viewed as a form of deferred wages.

There has been a shift in the United States from defined benefit plans to defined contribution plans as shown in Table 21.12.

---

23 Pendleton Act. http://www.ourdocuments.gov/doc.php?doc=48. Accessed December 4, 2010

24 CSRS Retirement. http://www.opm.gov/retire/pre/csrs/index.asp. Accessed September 22, 2010.

TABLE 21.12 Number of U.S. Employer-Sponsored Retirement Plans by Type[25]

Year	Defined Benefit	Defined Contribution
1975	103,000	208,000
1983	175,000	n/a
1993	83,600	618,500

21.2.5 EXERCISES

21.4 What was the objective of the earliest retirement plans?
21.5 What types of workers were covered by early private pensions?
21.6 What led to the advance funding of early pensions for educational workers?
21.7 What led to the expansion of U.S. private pensions after World War II?
21.8 Are private pensions compensation for human depreciation, deferred wages, or both?

25 U.S. Department of Labor (1997, p. 1).

CHAPTER 22
Overview of Retirement Financial Security Systems

Financial security in retirement requires personal savings, work during retirement, financial support from family, some type of formal plan, or a combination of some or all of these. The role of the actuary comes into play with formal plans due to the need to structure the long-term funding of the plans to manage the associated retirement risks.

When an individual plans his sources of retirement income, he will factor in his personal situation. Sometimes a person will look at all other sources and determine total income needed in retirement. The shortfall can be filled by personal savings, earnings while retired, or lowering the standard of living in retirement, all of which are within the individual's control. Those who decide to save for retirement will shift consumption from their working years in order to put aside money to provide for consumption during retirement.

Our focus will be formal retirement systems that require the technical expertise of an actuary. These systems will have a specific type of plan with detailed provisions spelled out. We refer to this type of plan as a formal plan because the provisions have been formalized.

22.1 Most Common Types of Formal Retirement Plans

Formal retirement plans can be categorized in several ways. For example, plans can have different sponsors, including government, private employers, and individuals. Another way to categorize these programs is to consider how they are funded and who pays for the funding. Plans differ when considering how a person becomes eligible for benefits from the plan. Different types of plans make different promises to those who will ultimately receive benefits from the plan.

We will discuss various types of plans and their common features, dividing them by plan sponsor.

22.1.1 Government-Sponsored Plans

Government-sponsored plans are also referred to as social security systems.[1] These plans are often unfunded (pay-as-you-go) plans. Money to provide the benefits paid by these plans may come from general tax revenues, contributions (payroll taxes) paid by employers, employees, or a combination of the two.

Although it seems odd at first, a government-sponsored plan requiring employers and/ or employees to contribute to the plan is still generally considered an unfunded plan. The reason is that current contributions are used to pay current benefits. In other words, today's workers are contributing to pay benefits for those who worked in the past and who

1 In this section, we are discussing a retirement system providing coverage to a broad group of residents or citizens of the country whose government sponsors the plan. We are not talking about plans provided by a government to its employees.

are now receiving benefits from the plan. Even though a record may be kept of the contributions a person makes to the plan, typically no one is entitled to a refund of these contributions or, in a defined benefit social security program, a benefit based on their own contributions.

In order to receive benefits from the plan, the individual must be, or have been in the past, a resident of the sponsoring country. The individual is typically also required to have been employed in the sponsoring country, and perhaps also to have made contributions into the plan in order to collect benefits from the plan.

These plans usually guarantee a particular level of benefit. As we will see later, this type of plan is called a defined benefit plan because the characteristics of the benefit, rather than the characteristics of the contributions, are defined under the arrangement. The value of the benefit guarantee depends on the strength and the financial soundness of the sponsoring entity. If the sponsoring government is strong and the financial markets sound, the benefits can be expected to be paid as promised. However, even in the best situations, demographic changes can produce significant challenges to unfunded pay-as-you-go systems. We will dig deeper into these challenges in a later section.

Social security is subject to political risk. In a social security system, the decline in contributions is generally not accompanied by a decrease in the level of benefits the system provides to an individual, at least in part because of political considerations. Politicians, like the rest of us, want to keep their jobs. In order to keep their jobs, they need satisfied voters. Decreasing benefits does not satisfy retirees or those near retirement. As a result, benefit levels generally do not change when the available funds to provide those benefits decline. At some point, an adjustment will have to be made either in tax rates—in order to increase contributions to the needed level—or in benefits paid out.

A government-sponsored retirement plan covers a broad section of the population, so it can have a big impact on the financial security of older residents. In fact, government-sponsored plans are credited with lowering old-age poverty.

22.1.2 Employer-Sponsored Plans

Employer-sponsored plans can also be referred to as occupational plans. The common thread among occupational plans is that membership, or participation, in the plan is linked to employment. The majority of these plans are provided by employers for their employees. In order to receive a benefit from the plan, the person must work, or have worked, for the employer sponsoring the plan. Other types of occupational plans are provided by unions or associations for their members, so the common thread among members is their profession, trade or industry. Even though these plans are not always sponsored by a participant's employer, we will, for simplicity, refer to them all as employer-sponsored plans in our discussion.

Employer-sponsored plans are typically funded in advance by contributions from the employer. Sometimes participants also make contributions, either as a condition of receiving benefits from the plan (mandatory contributions) or on a voluntary basis in order to receive additional benefits from the plan.

Advance funding creates a pool of assets set aside to pay benefits when participants retire. These assets increase the security of the plan by making it more likely the promised benefits will be paid. They also receive investment earnings over time that help pay for the benefits and reduce the funding needed from the plan sponsor.

The plan's guarantee depends on the type of plan the sponsor provides. Plans may either provide a promised benefit when the participant retires (defined benefit plan) or promise a certain level of contributions during the participant's tenure with the sponsor (defined contribution).

Public employees may be covered by an employer-sponsored retirement program. Although these programs are government-sponsored, they are really pensions provided as a result of the relationship between the employer and employee. As discussed previously, when we discuss public or government-sponsored pensions, we refer to plans provided to the general population and not to employer-sponsored programs for governmental employees.

22.1.3 Individual Retirement Savings Arrangements

These arrangements are always fully funded with respect to the current benefits that can be provided since there is no pooling of risks. Individual retirement arrangements are often merely personal savings. Sometimes the person is able to save on a tax-advantaged basis like individual retirement accounts (IRAs) in the United States. Although these individual arrangements can be important in assuring adequate retirement income, they often do not use an actuary's expertise.[2]

The benefits guaranteed in an individual retirement arrangement depend on how the money to fund the benefits has been invested. The promise will either be the account balance if the assets have been invested in an account that earns investment income or a benefit payment if the individual has purchased an annuity.

22.1.4 EXERCISES

22.1 How is a defined benefit plan different from a defined contribution plan?

22.2 Do social security systems usually provide benefits in the form of a defined benefit plan or a defined contribution plan?

22.3 Who is typically covered by an employer-sponsored retirement plan?

22.4 Do employer-sponsored retirement plans provide benefits in the form of a defined benefit plan or a defined contribution plan?

22.5 What are the characteristics of an individual retirement plan?

22.6 What is the most common funding for each of the following?

- **a.** Social security systems
- **b.** Employer-sponsored plans
- **c.** Individual retirement plans

2 A personal actuary can help an individual establish a personal retirement program, but most people do not have available financial resources to use these services.

22.2 Government-Sponsored Social Security Systems

22.2.1 Introduction to Social Security

Social security plans (also referred to as systems) are government-sponsored and publicly funded. Although they may pay death and disability benefits, their primary purpose is financial security in retirement. Our focus will be on the retirement income aspects of social security systems.

These plans offer broad coverage. In developed countries where participation in the social security system is nearly universal, the coverage crosses all industry groups. As long as the sponsoring government has strong enforcement of its tax system, participation in the social security system will cross all economic groups. Because of the broad coverage, the social security system has a great impact on the financial security of the elderly population.

22.2.2 Objectives of Social Security Systems

Social security systems typically seek to provide some degree of individual equity as well as social adequacy. The individual equity prong can be satisfied by basing at least a portion of the benefit on pre-retirement earnings. As a result, higher-earning workers receive larger benefits than those earning lower wages, which reflect the fact that higher-earning workers pay a higher dollar amount of taxes into the social security system.

The social adequacy prong can be satisfied by providing a larger benefit as a percentage of preretirement earnings to those earning lower wages. Although the dollar amount paid to a lower-earning worker is smaller, when the benefit is considered as a percentage of pre-retirement income, the income replaced by the social security benefit is larger than the income replaced for a higher-earning worker. (We will see an example later that demonstrates these principles.)

Social security systems have one or more primary objective: savings, income redistribution and insurance. Many systems seek to satisfy all three objectives.

The savings objective, or individual equity objective as just discussed, of a social security system is the same as the savings objective for an individual. By accumulating benefits while working, a person will have money available at retirement. This objective encourages high-income workers to participate in the social security system (Scahill and McKay, 2002, p. 14).

The income redistribution objective, or social adequacy objective as just discussed, addresses the fact that high-income individuals have more personal resources to provide their own retirement savings. Low-income individuals may live paycheck to paycheck and can't save for the future. High-income workers are more apt to participate in an employer-sponsored plan and to have discretionary income they can save for retirement. Social security benefits can be designed to replace a larger portion of the first dollars of pre-retirement income and a lesser portion of higher pre-retirement income. In this way, a lower-paid individual will have a higher portion of income replaced by social security than those earning higher wages.

Consider an example from the U.S. social security system. The benefit formula starts with the average monthly wage (AMW)[3] and applies different multipliers for three levels of AMW. In 2010, the formula multiplied the first $791 of AMW by 90 percent. AMW over $791 and less than or equal to $4,586 (the next $3,795) is multiplied by 32 percent. Any AMW over $4,586 is multiplied by 15 percent.[4] Income used to calculate AMW is capped, so the wealthiest earners do not have all of their income used in the benefit formula.

Now let's look at three different levels of average monthly wages—$600, $3,700, and $8,500—and see the different income replacement rates based on pre-retirement average monthly wages. The calculations are in Table 22.1.

TABLE 22.1 Benefits and Income Replacement for Three AMW Values

AMW	Formula	Income Replacement
$600	$600 × 90% = $540.00	$540.00 ÷ $600 = 90.00%
$3,700	$791 × 90% + $2,909 × 32% = $1,642.78	$1,642.78 ÷ $3,700 = 44.40%
$8,500	$791 × 90% + $3,795 × 32% + $3,914 × 15% = $2,513.40	$2,513.40 ÷ $8,500 = 29.57%

The person with AMW equal to $8,500 has a lower percentage of income replaced by social security (29.57 percent) even though wages and contributions, as will be discussed, paid into the system were higher. As a result, the system can pay a relatively high benefit to a low-income worker by redistributing the contributions received from high-income workers to subsidize the benefit received by the low income worker.

In the United States, the contribution by the individual worker into the social security system in 2011 was 4.2 percent of taxable wages up to $106,800, with taxable earnings over $106,800 not subject to social security taxes. As a result, a person earning $50,000 will pay $2,100 ($50,000 × 4.2 percent) in social security taxes compared to $4,485.60 ($106,800 × 4.2 percent) paid by a person earning $200,000.[5]

As you can see, the two components of redistribution in the U.S. social security system are the higher income replacement for low-wage workers and a level percentage used to determine contributions into the system.

The third objective of a social security system is insurance, which protects against the probability of outliving personal savings by paying benefits in a monthly amount for the person's lifetime (World Bank, 1994, p. 10). Some social security systems provide benefit increases based on cost of living increases or increases in the average wage rate, which helps insure against a decline in purchasing power as the cost of living rises after retirement. As discussed previously, social security systems have been credited with lowering old age poverty.

---

3 Earnings on which a person pays social security taxes over the person's career are indexed so the result approximates final average earnings. The details of how average monthly wages are calculated are beyond the scope of this material.

4 Your Retirement Benefit: How it is Figured. http://www.ssa.gov/pubs/10070.html. Accessed September 26, 2010.

5 The scheduled contribution rate of 6.2% was temporarily lowered to 4.2% for 2011. At the time of this writing it is scheduled to return to 6.2% for 2012. The employer's contribution remained at 6.2%.

Most social security systems strive to meet all three objectives, but combining them can be problematic, both for efficiency and distributional reasons (World Bank, 1994, p. 12). Politicians are tempted to increase benefits to woo voters.

Protecting the benefit against erosion of purchasing power is another aspect of insurance in a social security system. The cost of living adjustments in the U.S. social security system are an example of this temptation for legislators to increase benefits. The U.S. social security program was essentially unchanged until 1950 when benefits were increased an average of 77 percent to account for cost of living increases since 1940 (Kollmann, 2000, p. 7). Cost of living increases were provided only when the social security law was amended. That changed in 1975 when automatic cost of living increases were adopted in an attempt to remove politics from the equation. Table 22.2 shows benefit increases to compensate for cost of living increases from 1950 to 1975.

TABLE 22.2 Social Security Benefit Increases from 1950 to 1975[6]

Effective Date	Percentage Increase
September 1950	77.0%
September 1952	12.5%
September 1954	13.0%
January 1959	7.0%
January 1965	7.0%
February 1968	13.0%
January 1970	15.0%
January 1971	10.0%
September 1972	20.0%
March 1974[7]	7.0%
June 1974	11.0%
June 1975	8.0%

With the automatic adjustments, an increase has been provided each year until 2009. During that period, the largest annual increases were from 1980 to 1982 when inflation was very high. From 1983 to 2008, the largest increase was 5.7 percent in 2008 and the smallest increase was 1.3 percent in 1986.

22.2.3 Funding of Social Security Programs

One way to look at the funding of a social security system is to consider when the funding takes place. In a pay-as-you-go system, current contributions are used to fund current benefit payments. There won't be an exact match, so some money will be set aside to pay future benefits when contributions exceed benefit payments and that money will be available in later years when payments exceed contributions. Still, in a pay-as-you-go system, the excess in any

6 Historical Background and Development of Social Security, pp. 27–28. http://www.ssa.gov/history/briefhistory3.html. Accessed November 5, 2010.

7 This increase was a special one only lasting until the June 1974 increase became effective.

one year is not substantial and the system is considered to be unfunded. Pay-as-you-go is the most common funding used for social security systems.

As an example of money accumulated in a trust fund for a social security system funded on a pay-as-you-go basis, consider the U.S. social security system. At the end of 2009, the U.S. social security trust fund for future retirement benefits was $2,336.8 billion.[8] The trust fund increased $133.9 billion during 2009, with 83 percent of the increase attributable to contributions from workers and employers. During 2009, benefit payments, administrative expenses, and other expenditures totaled $564.3 billion. The U.S. social security trust fund could pay approximately four years of distributions with no further contributions and ignoring future cost of living adjustments.

When the ratio of young workers to retirees is high, there are ample contributions coming into the program to pay benefits in a pay-as-you-go funding arrangement. However, in an aging population where retirees represent a higher portion of the population, it is more difficult to provide the promised benefits because contributions coming into the system will eventually be less than benefit payouts. Using the intermediate projection[9] from the report published by the U.S. Social Security Trustees, the trust fund for retirement benefits is expected to be exhausted in 2040.[10]

Further, high contributions in a mature system encourage high earners, who have income-producing options, to seek alternative sources of income and avoid paying social security taxes, adding further stress to the viability of the system.

Instead of pay-as-you-go funding, a social security system can be partially funded in advance. Contribution rates are intentionally set higher than needed to meet current benefit distribution requirements. The extra money is invested and the investment earnings are used to offset future benefit distribution requirements. Social security systems typically invest in government securities or quasi-government entities like state-owned enterprises or public housing (World Bank, 1994, p. 94). These investments typically earn below-market rates and the real rates of return can even be negative when inflation is high. However, investing public social security assets in the private sector can be problematic when those investments are influenced by political considerations.

In the early years of a social security system when there are a lot more workers than retirees, a pay-as-you-go system is cheaper than a funded system. However, as the system matures and there are proportionately more retirees than in the early years, the system's costs grow. The rate of growth depends on the number of younger workers entering the labor force relative to the increase in the retirees drawing benefits from the system.

Another way to look at the funding of a social security system is to look at the source of the funds used to pay benefits. A social security program can be funded by general revenues, payroll taxes, or both. Programs funded at least in part by payroll taxes have some relationship between wages and benefits. The level of taxes needed to support the program depends

---

8 2010 Trustees Report: Section II.B., Trust Fund Financial Operations in 2009. http://www.ssa.gov/OACT/TR/2010/II_cyoper.html#94983. Accessed November 5, 2010.

9 Social security actuaries use three sets of assumptions when preparing long-range projections. The intermediate set of assumptions is used here because it is the mid-range of the assumptions.

10 2010 Trustees Report: Section IV.B., Long-range estimates, p. 11. http://www.ssa.gov/OACT/TR/2010/IV_LRest.html#366403. Accessed November 5, 2010.

on the relative number of workers (taxpayers) to retirees (benefit recipients) and the level of benefits provided by the program.

A system with a relatively high number of workers to the number of retirees is considered an immature system. As the population ages, the relationship changes and the system is considered to be maturing. A mature pay-as-you-go system may barely have enough workers to support the benefits of retirees, or it may not have enough workers to support those benefits without raising contribution rates to an unsustainable level.

If benefits are not reduced as the system matures, higher payroll taxes are needed to be able to pay promised benefits. Workers paying those higher taxes no longer see them as contributions for future benefits, but taxes to support benefits they will never enjoy themselves. This intergenerational transfer causes societal stress and puts pressure on politicians to find a solution. Several social security systems are currently in this situation.

If workers do not believe they will receive a meaningful benefit from a social security system, they will not want to pay required taxes to support the system. When workers seek to avoid paying the payroll taxes, they create informal labor sectors (World Bank, 1994, p. 9). When they are successful at manipulating the system to receive benefits without paying the appropriate taxes, the financial integrity of the system is threatened.

Although these undesirable financial outcomes from attempted tax avoidance vary from country to country, they are most prevalent in less-developed economies that lack the legal and social infrastructure to maintain the integrity of the social security system. Developing countries are less able to enforce tax payments and have large informal sectors, each leading to financial instability of the social security system.

Workers tend to retire when they are eligible for social security benefits. This age can be the social security normal retirement age or an earlier age if the system pays benefits prior to normal retirement, as in the U.S. social security system. Generous early retirement benefits can also create a financial incentive to retire prior to the normal retirement age. Once workers fully retire, they do not have earnings from employment and they do not pay taxes to support the social security system when the system is funded through payroll taxes.

If the contribution rates have not properly anticipated the retirement patterns, especially in a system with generous (subsidized) early retirement benefits, these retirements will create financial stress to the system. In addition, high early retirement rates also put pressure on the broader economy to produce an adequate output with fewer workers.

22.2.4 Problems with Pay-as-You-Go Funding of Social Security[11]

In a pay-as-you-go system, contributions and benefits are separated because current contributions are used to pay benefits accrued in the past. Workers are not paying taxes to fund their own benefits, creating large positive transfers in the early years of the system when those receiving benefits paid very little into the system and large negative transfers in later years when benefits received are less than contributions paid. As discussed earlier, these intergenerational transfers in later years create an incentive for workers to evade the system because taxes rise to

11 This section is adapted from Scahill and McKay (1994, p. 17), in part citing World Bank (1994, p. 13).

meet the high level of benefit payouts and workers do not believe they receive adequate value for their contributions.

In a funded social security system, individuals are forced to save for retirement because taxes collected are set aside to pay benefits for that person. A pay-as-you-go system has no personal savings component so social security taxes will reduce personal savings unless individuals are motivated to save on their own.

In a program funded on a pay-as-you-go basis, the tax rates needed to provide promised benefits depend on the relationship between the people paying taxes, or contributions, into the system to the people receiving benefits from the system. In the United States, tax rates are a percentage of a person's pay up to the maximum taxable wage base limit. In the early years of the system, benefits paid out were low compared to taxes coming in and the tax rates were low. As the system has matured, tax rates have increased. In addition, the maximum taxable wage base has also increased, which is another source of increased funding.

Table 22.3 compares the tax rate and the maximum taxable wage base in five-year increments from 1937 to 2007. The tax rate shown excludes the portion allocated to the disability insurance portion of the system.

TABLE 22.3 U.S. Social Security Tax Rates and Wage Bases (1937–2007)

Calendar Year	Tax Rate[12]	Maximum Taxable Wage Base[13]
1937	1.000%	$3,000
1942	1.000%	$3,000
1947	1.000%	$3,000
1952	1.500%	$3,600
1957	2.000%	$4,200
1962	2.875%	$4,800
1967	3.550%	$6,600
1972	4.050%	$9,000
1977	4.375%	$16,500
1982	4.575%	$32,400
1987	5.200%	$43,800
1992	5.600%	$55,500
1997	5.350%	$65,400
2002	5.300%	$84,900
2007	5.300%	$97,500

Large pay-as-you-go systems often experience larger than expected payouts because of poor planning and political manipulation. The resulting high cost causes either higher social security taxes or general revenue transfers into the social security system. As a result, other governmental programs suffer from lack of adequate funding.

12 Trust Fund Data: Social Security Tax Rates. http://www.ssa.gov/OACT/ProgData/oasdiRates.html. Accessed November 6, 2010.

13 Automatic Increases: Contribution and Benefit Basis. http://www.ssa.gov/OACT/COLA/cbb.html#Series. Accessed November 6, 2010.

22.2.5 Social Security Systems around the World

Each country selects its own benefit design and financing arrangement, and these choices have far-reaching effects on the economy. The system will affect how much of the overall economy will be allocated to the elderly. It also affects the welfare of the young by influencing the size of the overall economy.

Table 22.4 shows the percentage of old-age income received from public sources such as social security for selected OECD[14] countries. Public sources include social security pensions and other government assistance.

TABLE 22.4 Percentage of Old-Age Income Received from Public Sources[15]

Country	Percentage
France	85.4%
Germany	73.1%
Japan	48.3%
United Kingdom	49.4%
United States	36.1%

In contrast to the amount received from public sources, Table 22.5 shows the public expenditures on social security pensions in 2005.

TABLE 22.5 Percentage of National Income Spent on Social Security[16]

Country	Percentage
France	12.4%
Germany	11.4%
Japan	8.7%
United Kingdom	5.7%
United States	6.0%

Eastern European countries have payroll taxes for social security pensions of 30 percent or more (World Bank, 1994, p. 26). In some cases, benefits are so high that general revenue must supplement payroll taxes to pay for the promised benefits. High taxes make it difficult to invest in other public programs and discourage employment. Over 98 percent of those over age 60 in Hungary are either retired or working in the informal sector and are not paying payroll taxes to provide promised social security benefits (World Bank, 1994, p. 26). Hungary is an example of problems faced in developing economies.

14 The OECD countries are Australia, Austria, Belgium, Canada, Chile, Czech Republic, Denmark, Finland, France, Germany, Greece, Hungary, Iceland, Ireland, Israel, Japan, Korea, Luxembourg, Mexico, Netherlands, New Zealand, Norway, Poland, Portugal, Slovak Republic, Slovenia, Spain, Sweden, Switzerland, Turkey, United Kingdom, and United States. http://www.oecd.org/countrieslist/0,3351,en_33873108_33844430_1_1_1_1_1,00.html. Accessed on November 13, 2010.

15 OECD (2009a, p. 1).

16 OECD (2009a, p. 2).

Until Argentina reformed its social security system in 1994, only three workers were available to support the benefits paid to every two retirees (World Bank, 1994, p. 26). Generous early retirement benefits contributed to this imbalance, reducing the number of workers paying taxes and increasing those receiving benefits. Argentina's pre-reform social security system was an example of generous benefits upsetting the needed balance between workers and retirees in a sustainable social security system.

During the 1980s, several publicly managed pension systems lost between 12 percent and 37 percent of their value, demonstrating a risk of advance funding of social security benefits (World Bank, 1994, p. 27). Aging populations increase the portion of gross domestic product (GDP) needed to provide social security benefits, so these losses for funded programs in aging populations can create a national financial crisis.

Data from 1995 published by the OECD and based on information from the U.S. Social Security Administration given in Table 22.6 shows the increase in the global penetration of mandatory social security systems from 1940 to 1995.

TABLE 22.6 Number of Countries with Mandatory Old Age Security Programs[17]

Year	Number of Countries
1940	33
1949	44
1958	58
1967	92
1977	114
1989	135
1993	155
1995	166

Using the same 1995 U.S. Social Security Administration data, OECD published the information in Table 22.7 on the types of mandatory social security systems in 1995. (Note that countries may have components falling into more than one type of system.)

TABLE 22.7 Types of Mandatory Old Age Security Programs in 1995[18]

Type of System	Number of Countries
No program	6
Mandatory public savings	19
Mandatory private savings	5
Non-contributory universal system	5
Contributory means-tested system	25
Contributory flat-benefit system	18
Contributory earnings-relates system	133
Total countries	166

17 OECD (1998, p. 6).
18 OECD (1998, p.6).

22.2.6 U.S. Social Security System

The U.S. social security system is a defined benefit arrangement funded on a pay-as-you-go basis. Benefits are based on earnings throughout the worker's career and taxes (contributions into the system) are based on those same wages. (See the examples in the previous section for more details.)

Any excess of contributions over benefit payments are invested in U.S. government securities or government-backed securities (i.e., the U.S. government guarantees the interest and principal). All of the investments currently are special obligation investments issued only to federal trust funds. Trust fund assets earned 5.3 percent in 2007.[19]

As demonstrated previously, the benefit formula combines principles of individual equity and social adequacy by basing benefits on average wages, but providing relatively larger benefits to lower wage earners. Because it is a defined benefit program, retirees receive a monthly benefit for their entire lifetime and cannot outlive the benefit.

Monthly benefits are further adjusted annually for cost of living increases using the percentage increase in the urban consumer price index based on the current year's third quarter index compared to the third quarter index the year before. If there is no increase in the index, benefits are not increased. If the index were to go down as it did in 2009, benefits remain the same. The index increased from 2009 to 2010, but the 2010 index was still below the 2008 index so benefits were not increased in 2011.

Table 22.8 shows how the cost of living adjustment was calculated during the recent period of low inflation.

TABLE 22.8 Calculation of U.S. Social Security Cost of Living Adjustment

Quarter End	Consumer Price Index for Quarter (CPI)[20]	$\frac{CPI_t}{CPI_{t-1}} - 1$	Social Security Cost of Living Adjustment in the Following Year[21]
September 2005	192.700		
September 2006	199.067	.03304	3.3%
September 2007	203.596	.02275	2.3%
September 2008	215.495	.05844	5.8%
September 2009	211.001	−.02085	0.0%
September 2010	214.136	.01486	0.0%

Full retirement benefits are provided at the social security normal retirement age, which is between 65 and 67, depending on year of birth. In all cases, reduced benefits are available

19 Find an Answer to Your Question: How the Social Security Trust Fund Earns Interest. http://ssa-custhelp.ssa.gov/app/answers/detail/a_id/404. Accessed September 27, 2010.

20 Automatic Increases: Average CPI by Quarter and Year. http://www.ssa.gov/OACT/STATS/avgcpi.html. Accessed November 6, 2010.

21 Automatic Increases: Cost-of-Living Adjustments. http://www.ssa.gov/OACT/COLA/colaseries.html. Accessed November 6, 2010.

beginning at age 62. The reduction to the full retirement benefits available at normal retirement age is 5/9 percent per month for the first 36 months the benefit will begin prior to social security normal retirement age and 5/12 percent per month for each additional month. This reduction is intended to approximate an actuarial reduction.

Table 22.9 shows the early retirement reductions from social security normal retirement age to age 62.[22]

TABLE 22.9 U.S. Social Security Reduction for Benefits Beginning at Age 62

Social Security Normal Retirement Age	Reduction to Age 62
65	20%
66	25%
67	30%

If a person delays commencement of social security benefits beyond the social security normal retirement age, benefits will increase each year until age 70. The increase for anyone born on or after 1943 is 8 percent per year, which creates an incentive to delay retirement.[23]

The U.S. social security system is funded exclusively by payroll taxes paid by the worker and employer. The current employee tax rate is 4.2 percent of wages up to the maximum taxable wage base. This tax rate is the total of the tax rate for old age and survivor benefits (OASI) and the tax rate for disability income benefits (DI). In 2011 the employer pays 6.2 percent so that the total tax paid is 10.4 percent.[24] An additional tax is also assessed on the employee and employer to support Medicare benefits, but these benefits are not discussed in this material. A person who is self-employed pays both the employee and employer portion of the taxes.

In 2010 and 2011, the wage base was $106,800. Social security provides retirement, death, and disability benefits. Social security taxes are paid by the employee and employer as long as the person earns income from employment. A small segment of employers are exempt from social security.

22.2.7 Canadian Social Security System

The Canadian social security system has two components. The Old Age Security benefit is a flat amount paid to all residents and it can be thought of as the social adequacy portion. The Canada (or Quebec) Pension Plan provides a benefit based on contributions into the system and can be thought of as the individual equity portion.

---

22 Social Security Benefits: Benefit Reductions for Early Retirement , 2010.

23 Retirement Planner: Delayed Retirement Credits. http://www.socialsecurity.gov/retire2/delayret.htm, Accessed September 27, 2010.

24 This difference is a temporary adjustment made in 2011. At the time of this writing the rates are scheduled to return to 6.2% for both employee and employer in 2012.

22.2.7.1 Old age security

The first component of the Canadian social security system (Old Age Security or OAS) was created by the Old Age Security Act in 1952. Benefits are funded through general tax revenues.

A fully indexed monthly benefit is paid to all residents age 65 or older as long as the person has been a resident for at least 10 years. To be eligible to receive the maximum pension benefits of $526.85 as of April 2011, a person must have been a resident for at least 40 years between age 18 and the year before benefits commence.[25] The benefit is reduced 1/40th for each year of residency less than 40. OAS benefits are reduced when a person's net income exceeds a set amount ($67,668 in 2011). The reduction is in the form of a tax paid when the person files his income tax return. The reduction is 15 percent of his net income, to a maximum of 100 percent of the OAS benefit. A person who has net income of $109,607 in 2011 and receives the maximum OAS benefit would have a reduction that would wipe out his OAS benefit.

OAS also has a guaranteed income supplement that is income-tested. This benefit typically is paid to those with no other pension available.

22.2.7.2 Canada/Quebec Pension Plan

The second component of Canadian social security is an income-based benefit. The Canada Pension Plan (CPP) became effective in 1966 and covers residents of all provinces except Quebec. The Quebec Pension Plan (QPP) covers residents of Quebec and is nearly identical to the Canada Pension Plan. For simplicity, the plans will be referred to as C/QPP.

The C/QPP provides retirement, death, and disability benefits. We will focus on the retirement benefits.

Coverage is mandatory for all employed individuals, including those who are self-employed. Full benefits, which are designed to replace approximately 25 percent of a person's earnings from employment, up to a maximum amount (Service Canada, 2011), are payable at age 65 even if the person continues working, provided the employee ceased working for a short period of time. Benefits are adjusted annually on January 1 to reflect increases in the CPI, which is effectively the price inflation index used in Canada. Reduced benefits can begin as early as age 60. A person can delay receiving C/QPP benefits beyond age 65. Benefits are increased if they begin after age 65 but prior to age 70.

C/QPP is funded through payroll taxes on the worker and employer. Contributions stop at age 70 even if the person continues to work. The contribution schedule is reviewed every three years to see if any changes are needed. The rate is currently 4.95 percent, paid by both the employee and employer,[26] on earnings over a base amount up to the maximum pensionable earnings. The contribution rate was last changed in 2003 (Service Canada, 2010). In 2011, maximum pensionable earnings were $48,300 and the base amount was $3,500. The financial goal is to have a reserve of five years of benefit payouts at all times.

25 Service Canada (2011). Note that the web link provided in the bibliography will provide the current rates at the time of access rather than the values provided here.

26 A self-employed individual pays both the employer and employee tax. Service Canada (2010).

Excess contributions in QPP are invested in market securities. CPP is moving toward a diversified portfolio with independent investment management for its excess contributions.

22.2.8 Chinese Social Security System[27]

China's social security pension system began in 1951. The original system was a pay-as-you-go funding arrangement with employers making modest contributions to local and national pools.

During the Cultural Revolution (1966–1976), state-owned enterprises (SOEs) became responsible for the social security system. Each SOE managed its own program, paying benefits from current revenues, and there was no pooling of risks. Funds previously accumulated in the national pool were used for other purposes, rather than being transferred to the SOEs who were now providing pension benefits.

Pooling was reintroduced in the late 1980s as part of a redevelopment of the social security system. The system had very generous, and costly, early retirement benefits intended to provide employment opportunities for young workers by encouraging older workers to retire. China's one-child policy caused a rapidly aging population which, along with the generous early retirement benefits, crippled the social security system.

In 1991, individual contributions were required to help shore up the system. Throughout the 1990s, various experiments took place to find the best system. It was recognized that a system in which benefits are provided entirely by the national government wasn't sustainable. China needed a three-pillar system with benefits provided by the national government, employers and employees, which is in place today. The remaining discussion will focus on the social security pillar.

It was recognized that China needed to consolidate responsibility for the social security system. In 1998, responsibility that had been spread among various departments was consolidated with the Ministry of Human Resources and Social Security.

China's current social security system was established July 1, 1997, and it was updated in 2005. It consists of two parts. One part of the social security pillar, the social pool, is funded through a contribution by employers equal to 20 percent of the entity's total wage bill. Wages used to calculate the required contributions are no less than 60 percent and no more than 300 percent of the average of the city average salary (CAS). Benefits from the social pool are also based on the CAS and the employee's indexed contribution salary.

The second part of the social security pillar, the individual account, is funded by individual contributions equal to 8 percent of wages up to 300 percent of the CAS. The accounts are credited with annual interest (about 4 percent per year in mid-2000s). Although this part is intended to be fully funded, many individual accounts are notional accounts because the actual money contributed is used by the provinces for other purposes. The individual account is converted to a life annuity when an individual begins receiving benefits. If the individual outlives the funds in the individual account, the social pool would be tapped to continue the benefit payments.

The biggest challenge faced by provinces following the restructuring of the social security system was financing pension debt that existed for benefits already in payment status.

27 Parts of this section are taken from Moo (2009).

The Chinese economy was shifting from one dominated by SOEs to one where the private sector was a growing factor. It is estimated that a majority of provinces had not properly funded the individual account portion of the program. The need to reform the system was obvious.

The Pilot Program for Improving Social Security System was promulgated by the State Council in 2000 (Wang, 2005,.p. 3). Liaoning Province, with 42 million people, was selected as a site for the pilot project because it was especially hard hit by the transition from an economy dominated by SOEs to more of a market economy.

Under the pilot, pensions are no longer provided by SOEs. The province will pay pensions even if the SOE that employed the individual can no longer afford to pay them. A large part of the funding was met by the central government during the three-year pilot period. The Liaoning experiment was successful at separating the social pool contributions from the individual account contributions. This allowed the individual account contributions to function as a funded part of the overall social security system, as was originally intended.

22.2.9 United Kingdom Social Security System

The U.K. social security system began in 1908 with means-tested,[28] non-contributory benefits (Bozio, et. al., 2010, p. 7). The Widows, Orphans and Old Age Contributory Pensions Act 1925 introduced contributory benefits. The system changed to universal coverage with the passage of the National Insurance Act 1946 (Bozio, et al., 2010, p. 8).

The U.K. social security system currently consists of four parts (Bozio, et. al., 2010, p. 4):

1. A basic state pension (BSP) funded on a pay-as-you-go basis;
2. An earnings-related benefit;
3. A flat-rate non-contributory benefit; and
4. A means-tested benefit.

The Pensions Act 2007 made further reforms, which included the following four items (Bozio, et. al., 2010, pp. 10-11):

- The normal retirement age (called the "state pension age") will increase to improve the long-term financial viability of the system.
- The BSP will be paid to a broader segment of the population in order to reduce the dependence on the means-tested benefit. This portion of the reform is accomplished by reducing the number of years of contributions required to become entitled to a full BSP benefit.
- The BSP will be indexed with the increase in wages rather than the increase in prices, which will help avoid a decrease in value of the BSP benefit when wages rise more rapidly than prices. It will also tie benefit increases more closely to increases in contributions.
- The earnings-related benefit will gradually become a flat-rate benefit.

28 Means-tested benefits are provided to lower-income or less wealthy individuals rather than to everyone. These benefits can be thought of as needs-based benefits.

22.2.10 EXERCISES

22.7 Who is covered by a social security system?

22.8 What are the three primary objectives of a social security system? Give an example of how each is achieved.

22.9 Using the formula for U.S. social security given in Section 22.2.2, calculate the social security benefit and the income replacement percentage for each of the following average monthly wages used in the benefit formula.

- **a.** $1,000
- **b.** $2,500
- **c.** $8,000

22.10 Which of the following are characteristics of a pay-as-you-go funding arrangement?

- **a.** Intergenerational transfers
- **b.** Declining tax rates as the population ages
- **c.** Trust fund assets
- **d.** Correlation between taxes paid and benefits received by an individual

22.11 Describe the two components of the Canadian social security system.

22.12 How has China's one-child policy affected its public pension system?

22.13 Compare the benefits provided by the U.K. social security system to the United States and Canadian systems.

22.3 Employer-Sponsored Retirement Programs

22.3.1 Introduction to Employer-Sponsored Retirement Programs

Employer-sponsored retirement programs provide retirement benefits as a result of an employment relationship. As discussed previously, a plan can also be provided by an organization where members are affiliated for an employment-related purpose. For example, a union could sponsor a plan for its members where the companies employing the union members are typically the ones making the contributions.

Employer-sponsored retirement plans can be categorized as defined contribution or defined benefit. A defined contribution plan provides a promised level of contributions and the benefit ultimately received will depend on the investment earnings on those contributions.

A defined benefit plan provides a promised level of benefit. The benefit is typically related to years of service with the employer with a larger benefit provided to longer-service employees. The benefit may also be related to the employee's earnings while working for the employer sponsoring the plan. A defined benefit plan sponsored by a union bases benefits on service, salary or both, while the member worked for employers with whom the union bargained for pension coverage.

22.3.2 Public Policy Underlying Employer-Sponsored Plans

Employer-sponsored plans reduce the need for government-provided retirement income and also reduce the risk of public welfare payments being needed to support retired citizens. As a result, the population as a whole receives a public benefit from employer-sponsored plans even though the coverage is limited, for example, to employees who work for an employer or are members of a union.

Aside from this direct public benefit, society also benefits when workers have a dignified way to leave the workforce when they can no longer perform the essential functions of their job. The retirement of older workers can provide promotional opportunities for younger workers.

22.3.3 Introduction to the Design of Employer-Sponsored Plans

Employers may sponsor a defined benefit plan, a defined contribution plan, or both. However, there are some designs that combine features of both defined benefit and defined contribution designs into a single plan. These are called hybrid plans because they are a cross between the two primary plan types.

Employers use several criteria to decide the type of plan to sponsor. The following are some of the objectives an employer has for a establishing a retirement program and related factors the employer may consider when designing the plan.

- The employer needs to be competitive in the labor market in order to hire qualified workers because the employer needs workers with characteristics similar to those of individuals employed by competing companies.
  - The types of plans offered by competing companies.
  - The level of benefit or contribution provided by employers in the same industry.
  - Input from employees or bargaining units on the preferred plan design.
  - The type of labor force desired by the employer.
- A retirement program must have expected costs that are acceptable to the employer, considering the employer's long-range financial projections.
  - Financial resources available to fund the program.
  - Long-term financial projections and available financial resources over the long-term.
  - Acceptable year-to-year fluctuation in plan funding.
- The best way to allocate various plan risks between the sponsor and plan participants.

The employer will balance the above factors and select the retirement program that is best for the organization.

22.3.4 EXERCISES

22.14 Why would an employer provide a retirement plan for its employees?

22.15 What factors would an employer consider to determine whether the expected cost of a retirement plan is acceptable?

22.16 What public policy considerations favor encouraging an employer-sponsored retirement system?

22.4 Tax Structure of U.S. Employer-Sponsored Pensions

When it is good for the public to have a certain private program, it makes sense to offer encouragement for that program to be established. One of the most effective ways to encourage an employer to provide retirement benefits for its employees is to provide a tax incentive.

U.S. private pensions receive a tax advantage designed to encourage companies to establish pensions for workers. This tax advantage to businesses and employees is called a *tax expenditure.* "Tax expenditures are revenue losses—the amount of revenue that the government forgoes—resulting from federal tax provisions that grant special tax relief for certain kinds of behavior by taxpayers or for taxpayers in special circumstances."[29]

In the United States, the tax advantages for private pensions include: (1) employers receive a tax deduction for contributions into the plan; (2) assets held in the pension fund accumulate tax-free; and (3) workers aren't taxed on the money contributed until they receive a distribution from the plan sometime in the future. This mismatch of the timing of the employer's tax deduction for contributions made and the worker's tax payment on benefits received is a tax advantage for the retirement system.

Only benefits derived from not taxing employer health insurance contributions and the deduction for interest paid on home mortgages are larger tax expenditures (Government Accountability Office, 2005, p. 34). As a result, U.S. taxpayers have a personal interest in ensuring that the public receive some sort of benefit from private pensions. Government regulation of private pensions is the means of ensuring this public benefit.

In 1974, Congress passed the Congressional Budget and Impoundment Control Act (CBA) that made changes in the Congressional budget process. It created the Congressional Budget Office as a nonpartisan source of budgetary analysis and economic information. The CBA created a focus on tax preferences, including those afforded pension plans. This focus may be at least partly responsible for the careful scrutiny given to the employer-sponsored pension system by Congress.

22.4.1 ERISA Shaped U.S. Pension Legislation and Regulation

In exchange for the tax benefit provided to the employer-sponsored retirement system, governments will establish limitations on and set expectations of the system. Government regulation can ensure that the tax advantage provided to the system doesn't result in benefits concentrated on business owners or highly-paid workers. It can also restrict the amount of the tax benefit received in any year to protect the government's tax revenue stream.

Pensions are one of the most highly regulated sectors of the U.S. economy. Laws and regulations are complex and can be categorized in many ways. We will look at them from a historical perspective.

The Revenue Act of 1921 exempted interest income earned by trusts holding stock bonus or profit sharing plan assets from current taxation and the Revenue Act of 1926 extended the tax exemption for earnings from pension trusts (McDonnell, 2005, p. 6). Neither Act permitted a deduction for benefits earned in prior years, which would have been helpful to defined benefit pension plans.

A limitation to ensure that the tax-free earnings on plan assets benefited participants in general rather than just the owner is the requirement to place the plan's assets in an irrevocable trust. This trust is separate from the company's general assets. An irrevocable trust can only be used for its intended purpose. As a result, a company can't change its mind and use the

29 Government Accountability Office (2005, p. 7).

pension assets for general operations or any purpose other than to provide retirement benefits to plan participants.[30]

The Revenue Act of 1928 finally permitted a tax deduction for contributions to fund prior benefit accruals (McDonnell, 2005, p. 6). Plans had to meet certain requirements to be entitled to the tax deduction. Plans meeting these requirements are referred to as *tax-qualified,* i.e. qualified to receive the tax advantage.

Restrictions on tax-qualified plans increased with the Revenue Act of 1942, which provided stricter standards for qualified retirement plans, capped tax deductions, and allowed benefits in qualified plan to be coordinated (integrated) with social security benefits (McDonnell, 2005, p. 6). The major focus of early regulation was to prevent discrimination in favor of officers, managers, and highly-compensated employees (McGill, et. al., 2010, p. 27).

The biggest leap in government oversight came about when the Employee Retirement Income Security Act of 1974 (ERISA) was enacted. Prior to ERISA, the major safeguards with respect to the financial soundness of private pension plans related to funding the current benefit promise rather than the entire accrued benefit, which includes benefits earned in prior years. There were also no requirements to allow participants to vest in their benefit prior to retirement and fiduciary standards for plan administrators and trustees were lax (McGill, et. al., 2010, p. 27).

ERISA created a framework for U.S. pensions to improve

- Plan funding;
- Access to pensions through vesting requirements;
- Reporting to government agencies to facilitate government oversight;
- Disclosure to plan participants;
- Security of pension benefits in the event of financial failure of the sponsoring organization; and
- Fiduciary standards for those with discretionary authority over retirement plans.

ERISA also introduced plan termination insurance for defined benefit plans to pay benefits lost when an employer-sponsored plan was terminated without sufficient assets to pay promised benefits. Workers close to retirement did not have enough time to accumulate personal savings to compensate for the loss in expected retirement income from the employer-sponsored plan. ERISA's plan termination insurance was in response to highly-publicized plan failures that left those nearing retirement with no employer-sponsored pension.

ERISA established an elaborate structure of government oversight, with multiple agencies sharing responsibility. The Department of Treasury through its Internal Revenue Service (IRS) and the Department of Labor through its Employee Benefit Security Administration (EBSA) have primary oversight responsibilities. The Pension Benefit Guaranty Corporation (PBGC) provides defined benefit plan termination insurance.

Each of the agencies issues regulations that fill in the details of legislation passed by Congress and signed into law by the President. The agencies also have enforcement authority to ensure

30 The plan sponsor can terminate the plan and recover any excess assets in the plan after all benefits have been paid. As will be discussed later, the surplus assets will be taxable.

plan sponsors comply with its regulations. The enforcement is carried out through required filings by plan sponsors and also by agency audits of the plan's written documents and ongoing operation.

EBSA is responsible for the reporting and disclosure aspects of ERISA. Plans must file an annual report with the EBSA. The filings are done electronically and are posted on the EBSA's website shortly after being filed. These filings allow EBSA to watch for possible ERISA violations, which can trigger an EBSA audit of the plan. EBSA auditors have the authority to impose civil (monetary) and criminal penalties, so plan sponsors try to avoid these audits. EBSA also oversees fiduciary compliance, and these violations can result in criminal penalties.

The IRS focuses on the tax aspects of plans. They oversee the tax qualification of plans, including plan document, nondiscrimination, and funding requirements. Each tax-qualified retirement plan must have a plan document that satisfies a long list of requirements. From the actuary's perspective, the plan document is important because it sets out the benefits the plan will provide, the eligibility and vesting requirements, distributions available to participants, and the actuarial assumptions used to convert from the normal distribution form to other forms of distribution. Even though the document contains legal terminology and can be hard to read, it is important for the actuary to study the document in order to be aware of all the details that affect the actuary's calculations.

22.4.2 Post-ERISA Pension Laws

U.S. pension legislation did not stop with ERISA. Although the framework of ERISA remains unchanged, most sessions of Congress have made adjustments to the law. We will only present the major changes that have occurred. Some plans are not subject to ERISA (church plans, unless the plan elects to be covered by ERISA, and governmental plans), but they are still required to comply with some of these laws. We will focus on laws affecting plans subject to ERISA.

Although ERISA had addressed the unexpected loss of retirement benefits by requiring vesting and adequate funding, surviving spouses could still be left with no pension protection when the worker died prior to receiving a distribution from the plan. Congress was especially concerned about death occurring shortly before the worker would be eligible to receive retirement benefits. In 1984, Congress passed the Retirement Equity Act (REA) providing spousal death benefit protection.

REA requires all plans that are subject to minimum funding requirements (defined benefit and a special, and small, subset of defined contribution plans) to provide a minimum spousal death benefit. This death benefit equals the death benefit the surviving spouse would have received if the participant had lived to qualify for a retirement benefit (early retirement or normal retirement), retired, started receiving a joint and 50 percent surviving spouse annuity, and then died the next day. The spouse essentially receives 50 percent of the benefit the participant would have received if the benefit had been paid out in a joint and 50 percent survivor annuity with the spouse as the beneficiary. If the participant was already eligible for a retirement benefit, the spouse could begin receiving the survivor annuity right away. Otherwise, the plan could delay commencement of the spousal death benefit until the participant would have been eligible to begin receiving benefits from the plan. Defined contribution plans not subject to minimum funding can avoid the requirement by paying 100 percent of the vested benefit as a death benefit. Otherwise, they are also required to provide this spousal death benefit.

Even before ERISA, plan assets were required to be placed in an irrevocable trust, so the employer establishing the trust couldn't decide later to use the assets for another purpose. Trust assets set aside to fund pension benefits are protected against the employer's and a participant's creditors. The IRC requires that a qualified trust "provides that benefits provided under the plan may not be assigned or alienated."[31] ERISA refers to this plan asset protection as an "anti-alienation" protection.

The retirement benefit is often a married couple's most valuable asset, especially young couples. REA facilitated the division of marital property by allowing a portion of the participant's benefit to be given to the spouse in a marital dissolution. In this way, REA maintained ERISA's anti-alienation provisions while allowing property division upon marital dissolution. There are strict requirements that must be met to be able to divide a retirement benefit and the court order making the division must satisfy these requirements to be a "qualified domestic relations order."

REA also protects spouses by requiring spousal consent in certain situations for plans required to provide the spousal death benefit described above. The spouse must consent before the participant can receive a distribution in an optional form that doesn't provide a survivor benefit of at least 50 percent to the surviving spouse. The spouse must also consent if anyone else is named as beneficiary under the plan.

REA lowered the minimum age that plan sponsors can require for plan participation from age 25 to age 21. Another REA provision simplifies plan administration by letting the plan sponsor pay a lump sum distribution automatically if the account balance is $3,500 or less, raising the cash-out limit from the prior level of $1,750.[32] A major advantage to being able to cash out small benefits is that the plan sponsor does not need to locate the participant many years later when a distribution from the plan is payable. For example, a terminated participant who has become entitled to a vested (nonforfeitable) benefit from the plan could be in his 20s with a deferred benefit payable more than 40 years later at normal retirement. As you can see, it is burdensome for the plan sponsor to track former employees over a long period of time.

ERISA provided protection for the accrued benefit by preventing a plan amendment from reducing what the participant has already earned. REA expanded the definition of accrued benefit to include early retirement subsidies and optional forms of distribution.

The Age Discrimination in Employment Act of 1967 protects older workers from discrimination based on their age and prohibits mandatory retirement in most situations.[33]

31 Internal Revenue Code Section 401(a)(13) located at 26 USC §401(a)(13). In this context, alienated refers to any action that results in someone other than the participant receiving the plan benefit. For example, if an employee embezzles money from the employer, the employer cannot take the money from the plan to compensate for the embezzlement.

32 This limit was subsequently raised to $5,000 by the Taxpayer Relief Act of 1997.

33 McGill, et. al. (2010, p. 6). Although this law protects older workers from forced retirement, it has had little impact on the average retirement age.

The Omnibus Budget Reconciliation Act of 1986 (OBRA '86) added more protection for older participants in retirement plans. It lowered the maximum years of participation that can be required to qualify for a normal retirement benefit from 10 years to 5 years. It also prohibits plans from excluding employees hired within 5 years of the normal retirement age from participating in the plan.

The Tax Reform Act of 1986 (TRA '86) replaced the prior IRC with a new one. This sweeping legislation made major changes to retirement plans, including adding several numerical tests to demonstrate that the plan doesn't discriminate in favor of highly compensated employees.

One numerical test looks at the participants in the plan to be sure the plan doesn't disproportionately benefit highly compensated employees. Another test looks at the benefits earned each year to ensure non highly-compensated employees receive a meaningful benefit compared to what is earned by highly compensated employees.

TRA '86 added elaborate distribution restrictions that can be summarizes as "not too early and not too late; not too little and not too much."

- "Not too early" refers to an additional income tax imposed on distributions prior to age 59½ or the plan's early retirement age if earlier. The policy reason for this restriction is to encourage plan participants to use money in a retirement plan for retirement rather than some other purpose.
- "Not too late" refers to the requirement for most participants to begin receiving distributions no later than age 70½ if the participant is no longer employed by the plan sponsor. The tax policy reason for this rule is to require a person to receive distributions from the plan rather than leaving them to someone else as a death benefit.
- "Not too little" refers to the minimum benefit that must be distributed at age 70½, or termination of employment if later. The policy reason for this rule is to ensure that the money is withdrawn and subject to income tax without unreasonable deferral of the tax.
- "Not too much" refers to limits on the amount that can be provided to a participant in a tax-qualified retirement plan. The policy reason for this limitation is that the general tax system provides a benefit for retirement plans. The largest benefits are paid to wealthy individuals and, as a matter of tax policy, there is a limit to the amount that is reasonable to allow someone to receive on a tax-preferred basis.

The Pension Protection Act of 2006 (PPA) completely changed the funding requirements for defined benefit plans. There was concern about the erosion of funding, in part because of the restrictions that were imposed by earlier legislation on how much the sponsor could contribute and deduct in good years. PPA focuses on the funding of currently accrued benefits, using a mark-to-market concept. Although some smoothing of market fluctuations in the asset value is allowed, it is less than was previously allowed.

Prior to the passage of PPA, the plan sponsor could choose the desired funding method from several allowable methods. In this way, the sponsor could determine the rate at which benefits would be funded. PPA mandates a funding method that must be used by most plans. The mandated cost method looks at benefits that accrue in the current year as well as the funded status of prior accruals. If the plan isn't sufficiently funded, additional contributions are required. There are also distribution and benefit accrual restrictions on plans with a funded status below a certain level.

Unfortunately, these increased funding requirements became effective at a time when the economy was struggling. Employers were strapped for cash and investments suffered large losses, which pushed up funding requirements. Some funding relief was provided in 2010 to avoid massive plan failures.

22.4.3 EXERCISES

22.17 How can the income tax system encourage an employer to establish a retirement plan for its employees?

22.18 List the primary objectives of the U.S. Congress when they passed the ERISA of 1974.

22.19 What is the primary responsibility of the IRS under ERISA? The Department of Labor's EBSA?

22.20 How does ERISA protect the participant's spouse?

22.21 Describe how the Tax Reform Act of 1986 accomplished the following objectives:

- **a.** Preventing wealthy plan participants from leaving assets in the plan indefinitely where they are not taxed.
- **b.** Ensuring that lower-paid participants receive a meaningful benefit compared to higher-paid participants.

22.22 How did the Pension Protection Act of 2006 change the funding of defined benefit plans?

22.5 The Role of the Courts in Retirement Plans

Courts do not create laws. Their role is to ensure that laws are followed and that they are applied consistently. In the United States, ERISA made retirement plans subject to federal law. As a result, a company operating in more than one state has only one set of laws to be concerned with in operating a retirement plan.

Courts become involved with retirement plans when someone brings legal action against the plan or the plan sponsor with respect to the plan. The legal action typically does not charge anyone with a crime. Instead, the legal action is usually about money. The person bringing the suit wants the plan or the plan sponsor to pay more than the person has received from the plan.

Legal action can also be brought by the government agency with oversight authority over the plan. This action typically begins after something has been discovered during an agency audit of the plan.

In some circumstances, criminal action may be brought by the government. The most common criminal action involves the illegal handling of plan assets. Someone might take assets from the plan and use them for business or personal purposes. If the plan requires employees to make contributions and the government audits the plan, the auditor will make sure the money withheld from an employees pay has actually gone into the plan within a few days after it was withheld from the employee's paycheck. If not, criminal action might be taken against the sponsor.

22.5.1 EXERCISES

22.23 How do courts become involved in retirement plan issues?
22.24 What is most apt to lead to criminal action against a retirement plan official?

22.6 Canadian Employer-Sponsored Pensions

22.6.1 Current State of Canadian Pension System

As in the United States, private (employer-sponsored) pensions are not required but if they are offered, they are highly regulated. Most businesses are regulated at the provincial level, including pension regulation. However, the banking, transportation, and telecommunications industries are federally regulated.

All provinces except for Prince Edward Island have existing pension legislation. There are significant differences in regulations, which can cause problems for businesses operating in multiple provinces. Pension plans are registered with the provincial pension authority in the province that has the plurality of members or, if the plurality of members is in a business that is federally regulated, with the federal pension authority. Under a reciprocal arrangement, the federal pension authority and the provincial pension authorities apply the other authorities' regulations as appropriate.

Regulations include minimum participation requirements, minimum vesting requirements, minimum interest credits on employee contributions in contributory defined benefit plans, funding requirements, entitlement locking-in, spousal benefits, marriage breakdown benefits, etc. In order to ensure that employers are providing meaningful benefits to employees, when a plan requires employee contributions, at least 50percent of any vested benefit must be provided by employer funding.

The Canadian federal government enacted the Modernization of Benefits and Obligations Act in 2000. It extends benefits and obligations to all couples (same sex and opposite sex) who are cohabitating in a conjugal relationship. The act amends both the federal Pension Benefits Standards Act and the Income Tax Act. Denial of spousal benefits to same-sex couples in a pension plan is discriminatory.

Pension regulation also imposes minimum vesting requirements. Benefits generally must vest after no more than two years of plan participation. Vesting protects against the loss of benefits by employees who do not remain with the employer until becoming eligible to receive a retirement distribution. Recent pension reform in Canada is moving toward immediate vesting.

Several provinces require a special committee to be set up when requested by a majority of pension plan members. The committee must have participant representation. Committees generally are limited to monitoring plan activity, promoting awareness and understanding of the plans and providing advice.

Provincial and federal laws impose minimum funding requirements. The funding rules in the province where the plan is registered or with the largest number of participants apply to the entire plan since it would be nearly impossible to have different requirements apply to various subparts of a defined benefit plan. The plan is generally permitted to amortize unfunded liabilities over a period of up to 15 years, although faster amortization is required for poorly funded plans or for plans that do not have sufficient funds to pay current benefit promises. This plan termination, or solvency basis is discussed in later sections.

22.6.2 Canadian Pension Reform under Consideration in 2010

In 2008, private pensions in OECD countries lost US$5.4 trillion in value, causing a widespread financial crisis for the employer-sponsored pension system. The primary source of those investment losses was equities, which represented approximately 50 percent of Canadian employer-sponsored pension assets prior to the 2008 market drop (OECD, 2009b). Table 22.10 shows 2008 real rates of return on employer-sponsored pension fund assets.

TABLE 22.10 Employer-Sponsored Pension Fund Real Investment Returns in 2008[34]

Australia	−26.7%
Canada	−21.4%
Germany	−8.5%
Japan	−20.1%
United Kingdom	−17.4%
United States	−26.2%

Not surprisingly, these large asset losses is causing a pension funding crisis as was discussed previously with respect to the United States. During 2008 and 2009, regulations became effective in Canada providing temporary solvency funding relief.

The government of Canada has been studying the security of the pension system for several years and began taking action to shore up the system in 2006. Beginning in 2006, the Canadian government introduced various measures to ease the tax burden of seniors (Canada Department of Finance, 2010).

On the provincial level, Ontario is studying pension reforms, with initial reform legislation passed in 2010. The Pension Benefits Amendment Act, 2010:[35,36]

- Provides participant protections, including immediate vesting and increased access to information about the plan, including its funded status;
- Allows plan sponsors to access pension surplus prior to a full plan termination by entering into a surplus sharing agreement with participants if the plan does not give the sponsor legal entitlement to the surplus;
- Facilitates asset transfers and plan mergers; and
- Permits plan to offer phased retirement.

34 OECD (2009b).

35 (Van Der Bij, 2010). At the time of this writing, the legislation has been proclaimed, but not enacted.

36 Laporte & Seller (2010). At the time of this writing, the legislation has been proclaimed, but not enacted.

Additional pension reform legislation was introduced in Ontario later in 2010. Alberta, British Columbia, New Brunswick, Nova Scotia, Ontario, and the federal government continue to study pension reforms (Van Der Bij, 2010a).

22.6.3 EXERCISES

22.25 Are Canadian employers required to offer retirement benefits to their employees?

22.26 Are pensions regulated at the provincial or national level?

22.27 What changes to the Canadian pension system have been instituted in recent years?

22.7 U.K. Pension System

Employer-sponsored pensions initially were limited to civil service, military or white-collar workers. In 1921, the United Kingdom provided tax relief for pension contributions, expanding coverage of the plans. By 1967, 50percent of employees were covered by an employer-sponsored plan (Mayhew, 2001, p. 19).

Employer-sponsored pensions in the United Kingdom are a combination of defined benefit and defined contribution plans, with new plans tending to be defined contribution arrangements. Approximately 70 percent of employers with 20 or more employees have a pension plan compared to only 36 percent of employers with fewer than 20 employees (Mayhew, 2001, p. 13).

The U.K. pension system has numerous components (Mayhew, 2001, p. 8).

- Basic state pension and earnings related pensions discussed above in the section on U.K. social security benefits.
- Employer-based pensions.
- Individual-funded pensions, which were first introduced in 1988.
- Income support provided by the state in the form of a means-tested social security benefit.
- Benefits in kind provided by the state such as free health care, television licenses, winter fuel payments and transportation concessions.
- Investment income, which includes income from various sources including investing home equity when an individual trades down into a smaller house or a cheaper location.
- Income from employment.

Recent evolution in U.K. pensions has the state providing a smaller portion of the retirement income and assuming a larger role as regulator of the overall system (Mayhew, 2001, p. 14). As employer-sponsored pensions shift from defined benefit to defined contribution and individual-funded pensions increase in importance, the individual is taking on more responsibility for ensuring adequate retirement income.

22.7.1 EXERCISES

22.28 What components of the U.K. pension system are similar to the United States and Canadian systems?

22.29 What components are different?

22.8 Mexican Pension System

In 1994, Mexico experienced an economic crisis caused, at least in part, by a combination of poor banking supervision, growing public debt, and fluctuating foreign interest rates. This economic crisis caused great concerns about the Mexican pension system (Desaulniers, et. al., 2006). Mexico responded by undertaking pension reform measures.

In 1997, Mexico created a three-pillar pension system based on recommendations from the World Bank. One pillar is a minimum guaranteed pension that is means-tested so the benefits are provided to those who lack sufficient retirement savings. The second pillar is a defined contribution plan funded jointly by the state, the employer, and the employee. The third pillar is voluntary individual savings (Aegon Global Pensions, 2008).

Like many other countries, Mexico is aging. In 2006, the average age in Mexico was 28, but by 2050, the average age is expected to rise to 43 as a result of lower fertility and higher life expectancy. This shift in demographics will create challenges for the reformed pension system (Desaulniers, et. al., 2006).

Mexican companies are required to provide a lump sum termination benefit to most workers and this benefit can be worth nearly two years of full compensation to a worker with 30 years of service. This lump sum termination benefit can replace 10 percent to 20 percent of the worker's pay on a lifetime basis (Desaulniers, et. al., 2006).

About 70 percent of Mexico's employer-sponsored pension plans are defined benefit plans. Nearly half of new employer-sponsored plans are defined contribution or hybrid designs, reflecting a shift in plan design (Desaulniers, et. al., 2006).

22.8.1 EXERCISES

22.30 What changes did Mexico make to its retirement system in 1997?

22.31 What termination benefit is mandatory in Mexico? How much income can that benefit replace for a 30-year employee?

22.32 Are Mexican employer-sponsored pensions primarily defined benefit or defined contribution plans?

22.9 The Actuary's Role in Employer-Sponsored Defined Benefit Pensions

The actuary's primary role with a defined benefit plan is to determine the plan's funding requirements. The annual valuation of a defined benefit plan requires the actuary to determine expected distributions over the life of the plan and value those distributions using multiple decrements.

In the United States, an actuary must be an enrolled actuary in order to sign actuarial statements filed with the government or required actuarial certifications of the plan's funded status. The Joint Board for the Enrollment of Actuaries oversees the enrollment process and the triennial renewal of enrolled actuary status. The actuary must complete both an education (examination) requirement and an experience requirement. The public policy behind the enrollment process is to ensure that the actuary overseeing the plan's funding is qualified to do so.

In addition, the actuary also assists with plan design evaluations by determining the cost, or savings, of contemplated plan changes. These calculations may involve a relatively simple actuarial spreadsheet, but they can be much more involved including complex modeling of the future impact of these changes.

Although we will look at plan funding in more detail in a later section, we will look at the basic framework in this section. To determine the funding requirements of a retirement plan, the actuary must know the future benefits promised by the plan. The value of these future benefits depends on who can receive them and how much the benefits will be. Eligibility for future benefits depends on being a plan participant and also being in the plan long enough to qualify for a benefit.

If benefits paid prior to normal retirement are not actuarially reduced, then those receiving early distributions will create an extra plan cost. Likewise, any form of distribution that is more valuable than the normal distribution form creates an additional cost.

22.9.1 EXERCISES

22.33 Why does an employer-sponsored retirement plan need an actuary's expertise?

22.34 What is an enrolled actuary in the United States?

22.10 Advantages of Having Retirement Income from Multiple Sources

Different types of plans provide different types of retirement income protection. Multiple types of retirement plans in a single retirement system avoid all of the retirement income risk being concentrated with a single party. This concept can be visualized by thinking of the retirement system as a roof and the types of plans as the pillars holding up the roof.

A roof can be supported by a single pillar, but it is not as secure as one supported by two pillars. Three or four pillars are even better. In the retirement world, the pillars most commonly represent a public plan such as social security in the United States, an employer-sponsored or other occupational plan, and personal savings (an individual plan). The fourth pillar could come from income earned during retirement or income from family members.

Table 22.11 provides some characteristics of the various types of retirement income arrangements. As you can see, each plan type has unique characteristics and having more than one source of retirement income can spread the risks inherent in any one type of arrangement. We will discuss allocation of risks in a later section.

TABLE 22.11 Common Financing and Managerial Arrangements[37]

	Formal			Informal
Characteristic	**Social Security**	**Employer-Sponsored Plans**	**Personal Savings**	**Extended Family**
Voluntary or mandatory	Mandatory	Voluntary or Mandatory	Voluntary or Mandatory	Social Sanctions
Redistribution	Yes	Yes	Minor	Family
Benefits closely linked to contributions	No	Mixed	Yes	Within family
Defined benefit or defined contribution	Defined benefit	Mixed	Defined contribution	NA
Type of risk	Political	Job mobility, company insolvency	Investment	Joint family risk
Pay-as-you-go or fully funded	Pay-as-you-go	Mixed	Fully funded	Mixed
Public or private management	Public	Private	Public or private	Private

A study in the United States shows the sources of retirement income by the source of the income. Sources include social security, public assistance such as welfare, private (employer-sponsored for non-governmental employees) pensions, government pensions (employer-sponsored pensions for governmental employees), income from personal assets, and all other sources. The results for selected years from 1975 to 2009 are shown in Table 22.12.

TABLE 22.12 Retirement Income by Source Over Time[38]

	Source of Income					
Year	**Social Security**	**Public Assistance**	**Private Pensions**	**Government Pensions**	**Investment Income**	**All Other**
1975	54%	3%	8%	11%	19%	4%
1980	53	3	8	11	23	3
1985	49	2	8	11	28	2
1990	49	1	11	11	26	2
1995	55	1	11	11	18	3
2000	55	1	12	11	17	3
2005	55	1	14	13	14	3
2009	58	1	13	13	12	3

Although social security provided the largest share of retirement income in this survey, employer-provided pensions and investment income are important sources as well. This table is a good example of how a four-pillar system operates.

22.10.1 EXERCISES

22.35 What is the advantage of receiving retirement income from more than one source?

22.36 What are the possible sources of retirement income?

37 World Bank (1994, p. 97).

38 Brady & Bogdan (2010, p. 25).

CHAPTER 23

Retirement Plan Design

23.1 Defined Benefit and Defined Contribution Plans

Retirement plans can be divided into defined benefit and defined contribution plans. As their names suggest, the benefit is defined in a defined benefit plan, and the contribution is defined in a defined contribution plan. In a defined benefit plan, the funding is intended to ensure that sufficient funds will be available to pay promised benefits. In a defined contribution, the benefit received equals the contributions to the plan adjusted for investment gains or losses.

23.1.1 Introduction to Retirement Plan Funding

In a defined contribution plan, the funding is easy to determine. The plan document will set out the details of the contribution. It might be a flat dollar amount per participant or a percentage of compensation. A defined contribution plan might base contributions on the amount employees contribute to the plan. Alternatively, a defined contribution plan might only state how the contribution will be allocated among plan participants and leave the amount of the contribution entirely to the discretion of the plan sponsor.

A defined benefit plan promises a benefit amount and the sponsor funds whatever is needed to be able to provide the promised benefit. The plan sponsor is generally not able to determine the funding requirements from year to year without the assistance of an actuary. The funding often varies a lot from year to year, making it hard for the sponsor to plan ahead without the help of actuarial projections.

23.1.2 Plan Features Common to Both Defined Benefit and Defined Contribution Plans

Both defined benefit and defined contribution plans must have a plan document containing basic provisions. We will only discuss the provisions that affect the determination of the ultimate benefit because these are important to plan funding.

The plan will have details on who is eligible to participate in the plan. There may be categories of employees who are not eligible to participate, such as union employees if the employer bargains with a union and has separate plans for union and nonunion employees. The document will also state any age and service requirements eligible employees must satisfy in order to become a plan participant. Common requirements are age 21 and the completion of one year of service.

After we know who is in the plan, we need information to determine how much they are eligible to receive from the plan, how the benefit will be paid, and when they can receive a distribution. We will discuss the contribution and benefit formulas later, so we won't go into those here. Compensation and service are common factors in determining contributions and benefits. They will be defined in the plan document.

Plans must include a definition of a normal retirement age. In the United States, the participant must have a 100 percent vested, or nonforfeitable, right to the benefit earned as of the normal retirement age. In a defined benefit plan, the benefit will be fully accrued, or earned, at the normal retirement age. This age is not necessarily the age at which any individual must or is expected to retire. It is simply a term defined in the plan document.

Participants who leave employment with the plan sponsor prior to normal retirement may still be entitled to a benefit from the plan.[1] This type of benefit is referred to as a vested benefit. The plan document will give the plan's vesting schedule to determine whether a person is entitled to a benefit and, if so, how much has been earned. One common vesting schedule doesn't provide any vesting until the participant has completed three years of service. After three years of service, the participant is 100 percent vested. The vesting schedule can also provide for gradual vesting, such as 20 percent per year of service. In this case, the participant has a vested right to 20 percent of the accrued benefit after a year of service with the percentage gradually increasing until the benefit is 100 percent vested after five years of service.

Employees can make contributions to both defined contribution and defined benefit plans, although they are much more common in defined contribution plans. In the United States, employee contributions to a defined benefit plan must generally be made on an after-tax basis so the employee does not get the tax advantage received for pre-tax contributions that are common in a defined contribution plan. As a result, employee contributions are not often used in U.S. defined benefit plans.[2]

23.1.3 Defined Contribution Plan Design

A defined contribution plan document will provide details to determine the annual contribution made by the employer on behalf of each participant as well as any required or permitted participant contributions. The investments can be managed for the participants by the trustee or investment manager or participants can be permitted to direct the investment of their account balances and future contributions.

The defined contribution formula determines how much a participant receives from each contribution to the plan by the plan sponsor. If participants make contributions to the plan, all of those contributions will be placed in the participant's account and they will not be allocated to any other participant.

Common defined contribution plan formulas are:

- Flat dollar amount per participant;
- Stated percentage of compensation per participant;
- Discretionary contribution with the manner of allocating the contribution among participants specified in the plan document, but the amount of the contribution left to the discretion of the plan sponsor;
- Matching contribution; or
- A combination of the above.

---

1 United States pension law requires benefits to be 100 percent vested once a participant satisfies the plan's normal retirement age. It is common for a plan to fully vest benefits when a participant is entitled to an early retirement, disability, or death benefit.

2 Beginning in 2010, employers with no more than 500 employees are able to establish a defined benefit plan with pre-tax employee contributions.

If the formula is a specific dollar amount, the plan sponsor can gather the necessary details about the plan population and calculate the contribution. For example, if the plan says the contribution will be $1,000 per person per year and the sponsor has 25 employees, the contribution is $25,000.

If the formula is a certain percentage of compensation, once the employer knows the payroll, the contribution is easily determined. If the annual payroll for plan participants is $500,000 and the plan states the contribution will be 5percent of payroll, the contribution for the year would be $25,000.

Even though these two formulas produce the same contribution, it will be allocated differently among participants. With a flat dollar formula, all participants will receive the same contribution allocation. In the level percentage of pay formula, those with higher pay will receive more.

If the formula is a matching formula, contributions depend on the amount employees contribute to the plan. For example, the sponsor might contribute 50 percent of the amount the participant contributes. A participant who contributes 3 percent of pay to the plan will receive 1.5 percent of pay as an employer matching contribution. A participant who contributes 6 percent of pay will receive 3 percent of pay as a matching contribution. By using a matching contribution, the plan sponsor is encouraging employees to save for their own retirement.

If the plan lets the employer determine the contribution amount each year, called a discretionary contribution, the plan will specify how the contribution will be allocated among plan participants. For example, the plan could allocate the contribution as a flat dollar amount or a percentage of pay.

There are also more complex allocation formulas available that are designed to provide maximum benefits to higher-paid participants, but we won't go into the details of those plan designs.

In the United States, the plan may be subject to nondiscrimination testing to show that the contribution allocation doesn't unfairly favor highly compensated participants. There are some safe harbor designs that don't need to be tested because the regulations say they aren't discriminatory. Some plan sponsors don't want to bother with nondiscrimination testing so they will make sure their plans stay within the safe harbor structure. The examples above are safe harbor designs.

On the other hand, some plan sponsors want to skew benefits toward highly compensated employees. In this case, annual testing will be required to ensure that the plan stays within the prescribed limits allowed in the law and regulations. Nondiscrimination testing adds a layer of complexity, and cost, to the plan's annual administration, but a business owner may feel it is worth the hassle in order to receive a larger contribution.

23.1.4 Defined Benefit Plan Design

In a defined benefit plan, the plan document contains a benefit formula specifying the benefit a participant will receive at retirement. The benefit formula is the primary focus of defined benefit plan design. It determines how generous the plan will be overall and how much each participant will receive. We will now discuss some common types of defined benefit formulas.

If the formula is a flat dollar amount, the participant will receive that amount at retirement. For example, the plan could provide $1,000 per month beginning at normal retirement. Rather than providing this benefit regardless of how long the participant was an employee, the plan might reduce the benefit if a person has worked for the employer fewer than a certain number of years, for example 1/20th for each year of service less than 20.

If the formula is a dollar amount multiplied by years of service, the benefit will increase each additional year the participant works for the plan sponsor. For example, the formula might be $25 per month for each year of service. A participant with 25 years of service will receive $625 per month beginning at normal retirement. A participant with only 15 years of service will receive $375 per month.

Non-pay-related formulas are most common in plans covering only employees paid on an hourly basis or collectively bargained employees.[3]

Pay-related plans are the most common for plans covering salaried employees. The plan document will state what pay will be used in the benefit formula. The plan might use the average of the highest five annual compensation amounts. Alternatively, it could use pay over the employee's entire career or just the last year's pay. There are some limitations on how pay and average pay can be defined, but we won't go into those details. Just be aware that all of the plan terms must fit within the legislative and regulatory framework.

If the formula is a flat percentage of average salary, the applicable salary is needed to calculate the benefit. It is common for a plan to use the average of the highest five annual salaries. If average salary is $5,000 per month and the formula provides 50 percent of average salary at normal retirement, the participant will receive $2,500 per month as the benefit from the plan. As with the flat dollar formula, it might reduce the benefit if the participant has earned less than a certain number of years of service.

If the formula is a percentage of salary times years of service, a participant with more service will receive a larger benefit. If the formula is 2 percent of average salary times years of service, a participant with 25 years of service and average salary equal to $5,000 per month will receive a monthly benefit of

$$0.02 \times \$5{,}000 \times 25 = \$2{,}500.$$

A person who only has 15 years of service will receive a monthly benefit of

$$0.02 \times \$5{,}000 \times 15 = \$1{,}500.$$

A benefit crediting a percentage of salary each year, rather than using the final average or final salary in the formula, is called a career average plan because salaries are effectively averaged over the participant's entire career. If the formula is 2 percent of pay each year and the participant earns $2,000 per month in his first year of employment and $2,100 the next year, his accrued benefit after those two years will be

$$(0.02 \times \$2{,}000) + (0.02 \times \$2{,}100) = \$82.$$

Benefits in a career average formula are typically smaller than in a final average pay plan because salaries generally increase throughout the participant's career.

3 A union involved in collective bargaining over pension benefits will communicate the impact of the bargaining on pension benefits. If the benefits are not related to pay, the impact is the same for all union members. If not, some members will have a larger benefit increase than others.

The benefit can also be coordinated with social security. This type of design is referred to as an integrated benefit formula. An example of this type of formula is one providing 1percent of average monthly pay up to $2,000 multiplied by service plus 2 percent of average monthly pay over $2,000 multiplied by service. For a participant whose average monthly pay is equal to $5,000 and who has 20 years of service, the annual benefit based on this formula is:

$$(0.01 \times \$2{,}000 \times 20) + [0.02 \times (\$5{,}000 - \$2{,}000) \times 20] = \$400 + \$1{,}200 = \$1{,}600.$$

For this person, the benefit equals 32 percent of pay ($1,600 ÷ $5,000). If the person had monthly pay of $2,000 or less, the formula would have been 20 percent of compensation. You can see that integrating the retirement plan benefit with social security provides a larger benefit as a percentage of pay as the participant's pay goes up. This type of discrimination in favor of higher-paid participants is permitted to reflect the fact that the social security benefit is heavily weighted toward lower-paid workers. The plan, however, is not required to reflect the same weighting used by social security. There are limits on how much skewing of the benefit toward high-paid workers is allowed.

23.1.5 EXERCISES

Data to use for the following exercises:

Date of hire:	January 1st
Age at hire:	50th birthday
Normal retirement age:	65th birthday
Service earned each year:	1 year
Annual investment return:	5 percent

Salary History

Age on January 1	Salary Earned During Following Year
50	$50,000
51	$52,500
52	$55,000
53	$55,500
54	$58,000
55	$57,000
56	$60,000
57	$62,500
58	$65,000
59	$68,000
60	$69,000
61	$70,000
62	$71,500
63	$68,000
64	$66,000

23.1 The employer sponsors a defined contribution plan. The employer contributes 3 percent per year to all participants and matches 50 percent of the first 4 percent contributed to the plan by participants. Assume that the participant contributes 4 percent each year and all contributions are made at the end of the year.

- **a)** What is the participant's account balance at age 55?
- **b)** At age 60?
- **c)** At age 65?

23.2 The employer sponsors a defined benefit plan with the following benefit formula: 50 percent of career average compensation.

- **a)** What is the career average compensation at normal retirement age?
- **b)** What annual benefit has the participant earned at normal retirement age?
- **c)** What is the career average compensation at age 60?
- **d)** What annual benefit has the participant earned at age 60?
- **e)** If the benefit begins prior to normal retirement, it is reduced 4 percent for each year it begins prior to normal retirement. How much can the participant receive each year beginning at age 60?

23.3 The employer sponsors a defined benefit plan with the following benefit formula: 1.5 percent of average compensation multiplied by years of service at the date the benefit is calculated. Average compensation is the highest average using five consecutive salaries.

- **a)** What is average compensation at normal retirement age?
- **b)** What annual benefit has the participant earned at normal retirement age?
- **c)** What is average compensation at age 60?
- **d)** What annual benefit has the participant earned at age 60?
- **e)** If the benefit begins prior to normal retirement, it is reduced 4 percent for each year it begins prior to normal retirement. How much can the participant receive each year beginning at age 60?

23.4 The employer sponsors a defined benefit plan with the following benefit formula that is coordinated with social security: 1.5 percent of average compensation up to $25,000 multiplied by years of service at the date the benefit is calculated plus 2 percent of average compensation in excess of $25,000 multiplied by years of service at the date the benefit is calculated. Average compensation is the average five consecutive salaries prior to the date the benefit is calculated.

- **a)** What is the average compensation at normal retirement age?
- **b)** What annual benefit has the participant earned at normal retirement age?
- **c)** What is the average compensation at age 60?
- **d)** What annual benefit has the participant earned at age 60?
- **e)** If the benefit begins prior to normal retirement, it is reduced 4 percent for each year it begins prior to normal retirement. How much can the participant receive each year beginning at age 60?

23.2 Hybrid Plan Design

As you read the descriptions of defined contribution and defined benefit plans, you can see that a defined contribution plan is easier for the average plan participant to understand. It works like a bank account. The more that goes in, the more you have. The higher the investment earnings, the more you have.

A defined benefit plan requires a mathematical calculation, which can be confusing to participants. The value of the benefit is stated in terms of a monthly or annual benefit payment, which is a lot smaller than the present value of the benefit or the equivalent account balance in a defined contribution plan. Even a generous benefit from a defined benefit plan can seem negligible when you are comparing a lifetime monthly benefit to an account balance in a defined contribution plan. For example, which might a 61-year-old prefer? One million dollars in a defined contribution account or a monthly benefit of $6,000 starting at age 65 with the first 10 years guaranteed? They are essentially equivalent, but the million dollars seems like so much more.

Participants tend to prefer defined contribution plans because they are easier to understand and seem to provide more valuable benefits even when that is not the case. Plan sponsors don't like providing benefits that aren't appreciated by employees. To overcome this obstacle but continue to have the funding flexibility provided by a defined benefit plan, some plan sponsors have used a hybrid type of plan design.

The cash balance plan design is currently the most common type of hybrid plan. In a cash balance plan, the benefit formula looks like a defined contribution plan, but the plan is really a defined benefit plan. For example, the benefit formula might credit 2 percent of pay per year into the participant's account. Recent changes in U.S. pension law permits a cash balance plan to pay a lump sum benefit equal to the hypothetical account.

Unlike a defined contribution plan, the cash balance plan account is just a hypothetical paper account. The actuary or plan administrator keeps track of the hypothetical contributions into the account and the hypothetical earnings credited to the account each year. But the funding is determined by the actuary just like any other defined benefit plan. If assets earn more than the hypothetical crediting rate, the sponsor keeps the extra earnings. If they earn less, the sponsor must fund the shortfall.

Assuming, at the end of each year, the plan provides 10 percent of pay per year as a hypothetical allocation and credits 4 percent annual interest to the account balance, Table 23.1 shows the benefit accumulation after five years if the participant earns $50,000 each year.

TABLE 23.1 Cash Balance Plan Accumulation

Year	Balance at Beginning of Year	Hypothetical Allocation	Interest Credit	Balance at End of Year
1	$0	$5,000	$200	$5,200
2	$5,200	$5,000	$408	$10,608
3	$10,608	$5,000	$624	$16,232
4	$16,232	$5,000	$849	$22,081
5	$22,081	$5,000	$1,083	$28,164

If the participant were to retire after 5 years, the balance could be converted into an annuity. From the employer's perspective this is a defined benefit plan because the annuity payments depend in a fixed manner on the salary paid each year. In addition, as in a defined benefit plan, the employer bears the investment risk. In the United States, a traditional defined benefit plan must always offer a lifetime annuity to participants, but the plan can also offer a lump sum distribution or installment payments without life contingency. A hybrid plan is not required to offer the account balance payable in a lump sum as a distribution option when a participant becomes entitled to a benefit, but it is common to do so.

23.2.1 EXERCISES

23.5 Use the participant data from the Section 23.1.5 exercises for this exercise. Use the following interest credits:

Year	Interest Credit
1–5	4%
6–10	3%
11–15	5%

The employer sponsors a cash balance plan that credits 10 percent of compensation each year as the hypothetical allocation with contributions and annual interest credited on the account balance at the end of the year.

a. What is the participant's account balance at the end of year 5?
b. At the end of year 10?
c. At normal retirement age?

23.3 Allocation of Risks in Retirement Plans

Actuaries help clients manage financial risks. Retirement plans present several risks and the plan design determines how the risks are divided between participants and the plan sponsor. In this section we will look at the major risks and how they are allocated based on plan design.

One obvious risk is investment return. If assets earn more than expected, the person bearing the risk is happy. If they earn less, the person isn't happy. In a defined contribution plan the investment risk resides with the participant. The ultimate benefit depends, in part, on investment earnings. If investments under-perform expectations, the benefit is less. If they over-perform, the benefit is more. In a defined benefit plan, the plan sponsor bears the investment risk because investment return is a component of plan funding. Investment earnings help provide for promised benefits and offset the amount that needs to be contributed by the plan sponsor.

Another risk is longevity. A defined benefit plan is designed to provide benefits over the participant's lifetime, so the plan sponsor bears the longevity risk. A defined contribution plan is designed to provide an account balance the participant must manage throughout retirement so the participant bears the longevity risk. If a person takes the benefit from the defined benefit plan as a single sum (lump sum) distribution rather than a guaranteed annuity, the participant is taking back the longevity risk. Likewise, if the participant uses the distribution from a defined contribution plan to buy an annuity, the participant is transferring the longevity risk to the annuity provider. Regardless of these opportunities to shift the risk, it is traditionally considered that a defined benefit plan puts longevity risk on the plan sponsor and a defined contribution plan puts it on the participant.

Inflation is another risk present in retirement plans. In a defined contribution plan, the participant bears the inflation risk, but the investment return should provide some protection because inflation is one component of investment return. It won't be a perfect match, though, so the participant still has some risk.

If a participant converts the defined contribution account balance to an annuity at retirement, the allocation of risk depends on the type of annuity purchased. The annuity can provide a fixed monthly benefit just like a defined benefit plan. In the United States, many educational institutions provide defined contribution plans through TIAA that was introduced previously in the discussion of the history of retirement plans. TIAA, along with its sister company College

Retirement Equities Fund (CREF), offer a product called a variable annuity. With this type of annuity, the account balance remains invested by the individual rather than being used at the outset to purchase a fixed annuity. As a result, the monthly benefits vary with the earnings on the underlying investments, giving inflation protection in the annuity. Insurance companies offering a variable annuity retain the longevity risk, but the individual bears the investment risk. Today, many insurance companies offer such annuities.

Inflation risk is more complex in a defined benefit plan. While the participant is working and earning benefits, the allocation of inflation risk depends on the type of benefit formula. If the formula is based on a dollar multiplier and not on compensation, the buying power of the benefit will decrease as inflation rises. Of course, the plan sponsor can adjust the multipliers in this type of plan to help offset the erosion caused by inflation but those adjustments are not required. In a plan that bases benefits on the highest average or final average compensation, pre-retirement inflation is at least partially reflected in salary increases. As a result, benefits rise as compensation rises in response to inflation. As with investment return in a defined contribution plan, it won't be a perfect match but it provides at least partial inflation protection as benefits are being earned. In recent years, there has been a trend toward stopping benefit accruals in defined benefit plans as a cost-cutting measure for the plan sponsor. In this case, salary increases near retirement are not included in the benefit and any inflation protection is lost.

When benefits are paid out as an annuity from a defined benefit plan, the participant bears the inflation risk unless the plan provides periodic cost of living adjustments, or COLAs. COLAs are uncommon except in collectively bargained and governmental plans. In most plans, the participant will receive the same monthly benefit for his lifetime and the benefit becomes less valuable due to inflation.

Table 23.2 shows the erosion in purchasing power of $1,000 per month if the inflation rate is 3 percent. As you can see, after 15 years, the benefit can only buy $662 worth of goods and services compared to the $1,000 it could purchase in year one. If the benefit was coming from an account balance that earned income equal to the inflation rate each year, there would be no erosion in purchasing power.

TABLE 23.2 Erosion of Purchasing Power

Year	Income	Purchasing Power
1	$1,000	$1,000
2	$1,000	$971
3	$1,000	$943
4	$1,000	$916
5	$1,000	$889
6	$1,000	$863
7	$1,000	$838
8	$1,000	$814
9	$1,000	$790
10	$1,000	$767
11	$1,000	$745
12	$1,000	$723
13	$1,000	$702
14	$1,000	$682
15	$1,000	$662

Mobility risk with respect to retirement income occurs when a person changes jobs rather than spending the entire career with one employer. In an economy in which companies are downsizing by laying off employees, there is a risk of involuntary termination of employment. Additionally, employees have become increasingly mobile, and the typical employee will have several employers during his working career. Benefits in both a defined benefit and defined contribution plan will be less if the employee does not continue working for the sponsoring employer.

The impact is more severe in a defined benefit plan because the value of the benefit accrual increases with age. Because a defined benefit plan is designed to provide a benefit at retirement, the plan may not allow the participant to take a distribution from the plan at termination of employment prior to retirement age. Defined contribution plans commonly allow the participant to receive the entire account balance at termination of employment regardless of age. They also allow the participant to leave the balance in the plan and continue to receive investment earnings until the balance is withdrawn. As a result, the mobility risk is much less in a defined contribution plan than in a defined benefit plan.

The below demonstrates the impact of mobility on an individual participating in a defined benefit plan.

EXAMPLE 23.1

Assume a person is hired at age 45 and works for an employer for 10 years. The individual then goes to work for another company for 10 years. At age 65, the person retires. The person began earning $50,000 per year and received a 3 percent salary increase each year.

Each employer has an identical defined benefit plan that provides 2 percent of final 5-year average salary multiplied by service with the employer. For simplicity, we will look at the annual, rather than monthly, benefit received.

Table 23.3 shows salary over the 20-year period and the 5-year final average salary after 10 and 20 years. After 10 years, the final average salary uses salary earned in years 6 through 10. After 20 years, it uses salary for years 16 through 20.

TABLE 23.3

Year	Salary	Final Average	Year	Salary	Final Average
1	$50,000		11	$67,195	
2	$51,500		12	$69,211	
3	$53,045		13	$71,287	
4	$54,636		14	$73,426	
5	$56,275		15	$75,629	
6	$57,963		16	$77,898	
7	$59,702		17	$80,235	
8	$61,493		18	$82,642	
9	$63,338		19	$85,121	
10	$65,238	$61,547	20	$87,675	$82,714

If the person changes employers after 10 years, the benefit will be received in two pieces: one from the first employer and one from the second employer. The two pieces of the benefit are calculated as follows:

$$(0.02 \times \$61{,}547 \times 10) + (0.02 \times \$82{,}714 \times 10) = \$28{,}852.$$

If the person only works for one employer throughout the entire 20-year period, the benefit is calculated as follows:

$$0.02 \times \$82{,}714 \times 20 = \$33{,}086.$$

With an identical salary history, the person loses more than $4,000 per year in retirement income by changing employers after 10 years rather than remaining with the same employer for all 20 years.

A participant in a defined benefit plan has some risk if the employer is not financially strong. If the employer cannot adequately fund the plan, there may not be sufficient assets when the participant wants a distribution from the plan. In the United States, a plan with a funded ratio[4] below 60 percent cannot pay lump sum distributions even if that payment option is in the plan document. Other payment options may also be restricted until the funded ratio improves.

Another risk is that the employer will stop benefit accruals in the plan, which has a big negative impact on participants if benefits are based on final average salaries. Once benefit accruals cease, no further salary increases will be reflected in the benefit ultimately received.

A defined contribution plan can be designed to invest most of the plan's assets in the plan sponsor's stock, which concentrates significant economic risk in a single entity. The employee depends on the financial solvency of the employer for his livelihood. If the retirement plan invests in the plan sponsor's stock, his retirement income is also dependent on the financial solvency of the plan sponsor and the strength of the plan sponsor's stock.

One highly publicized example of this type of risk concentration is Enron. Even when company executives knew the stock was a bad investment, they continued to encourage employees to invest their defined contribution plan assets in the company's stock and many employees followed that advice. In addition, the company match was invested entirely in Enron stock. When the company failed, nearly 58 percent of plan assets were invested in Enron stock, so not only did employees lose their jobs, many also lost their retirement savings (Costello, 2002).

23.3.1 EXERCISES

23.6 How are the following risks allocated in a defined contribution arrangement?

a) Pre-retirement inflation risk
b) Longevity risk
c) Investment risk

23.7 How are the following risks allocated in a defined benefit arrangement?

a. Pre-retirement inflation risk
b. Longevity risk
c. Investment risk
d. Post-retirement inflation risk

4 This funded ratio has a specific definition, but the details are beyond the scope of this material.

23.8 How does mobility affect a participant whose employer sponsors a final-average-pay defined benefit plan?

23.9 How can a participant in a defined contribution plan insure against the risk of outliving the benefit received from the plan?

23.4 U.S. Pension Plan Design

23.4.1 U.S. Retirement Plan Coverage

In 2009, 67 percent of United States workers in private, non-governmental, employment had access to a retirement plan, although only 51 percent of workers actually participated in the plan.[5] Table 23.4 compares access and participation in defined benefit and defined contribution plans based on selected worker characteristics. Because some workers have access to both types of plans, the total access and participation rates are not the sum of those for defined benefit and defined contribution plans separately.

TABLE 23.4 Private Sector Retirement Plan Access and Participation, March 2009[6]

	Defined Benefit		Defined Contribution	
Worker Characteristics	**Access**	**Participation**	**Access**	**Participation**
Management and professional	30%	28%	75%	60%
Production	27%	26%	63%	45%
Full-time	25%	24%	70%	51%
Part-time	11%	9%	34%	16%
Union	68%	66%	54%	44%
Non-union	16%	15%	62%	43%
Highest 25% paid	39%	38%	77%	62%
Lowest 25% paid	8%	6%	39%	19%

In March, 2009, only 4 percent of defined benefit plans required employee contribution, with no difference between union and non-union plans. By contrast, 66 percent of defined contribution plans required employee contribution.[7]

23.4.2 U.S. Employer-Sponsored Retirement Plan Shifts from Defined Benefit to Defined Contribution

The earliest retirement plans were defined benefit. Throughout the first half of the 20th century, defined benefit plans were the most prevalent, especially for large employers.

In the mid-1980s, U.S. companies saw overfunded retirement plans as a source of operating capital. There was a trend toward terminating an overfunded plan and having the surplus assets revert to the plan sponsor. The excess assets were taxed when they reverted to the company since the company had received a prior tax deduction for contributions that led to

5 U.S. Bureau of Labor Statistics (2009, Table 2 of data for private industry workers).
6 U.S. Bureau of Labor Statistics (2009, Table 2 of data for private industry workers).
7 U.S. Bureau of Labor Statistics (2009, Table 3 and Table 8 of data for private industry workers).

the asset surplus. In spite of the tax liability, some large companies found the transaction to be financially beneficial.

Table 23.5 shows plan participation and the number of plans in 1985, 1999, and 2003.

TABLE 23.5 Employer-Sponsored Retirement Plans: Number of Plans and Active Participants[8]

	1985	1999	2003	Change between 1985 and 2003
Defined Benefit				
Number of Plans	170,172	49,895	47,036	−123,136
Active Participants	28.9 million	22.6 million	21.3 million	-7.6 million
Defined Contribution				
Number of Plans	461,963	683,100	652,976	191,013
Active Participants	33.2 million	50.4 million	51.8 million	18.6 million

Another way to see the shift in plan type is to look at the type of retirement plan that provides the primary benefit to participants. As mentioned, an employer can sponsor both a defined benefit and a defined contribution plan, but one will be the plan providing the primary retirement benefit. Table 23.6 shows the plan considered the primary retirement plan for selected years from 1976 to 1998.

TABLE 23.6 Primary Source of Private Sector Retirement Income[9]

Year	Defined Benefit	Defined Contribution
1976	85.5%	14.5%
1980	82.7%	17.3%
1983	75.9%	24.1%
1988	66.4%	33.6%
1993	55.9%	44.1%
1998	44.1%	55.9%

Defined benefit plan terminations show the trend to completely move away from a defined benefit plan. Not all sponsors will offer a defined contribution plan after the defined benefit plan is terminated, but many do.

Table 23.7 shows the number of U.S. defined benefit plans covered by ERISA's plan termination insurance that were terminated from 1976 to 2008. The data shows the large number of terminations in the late 1980s. In the early 2000s, the percentage of plans terminating without sufficient assets to pay promised benefits increased sharply.

8 Government Accountability Office (2007).
9 Brady & Bogdan (2010, p. 5).

TABLE 23.7 U.S. Plan Termination Data (1976–2008)

Year	Number of Plan Terminations[10]	Percentage with Insufficient Assets
1976	9,103	1.9%
1977	7,332	1.8%
1978	5,261	2.0%
1979	4,892	1.7%
1980	4,037	2.6%
1981	5,086	2.8%
1982	6,134	2.2%
1983	6,879	2.2%
1984	7,720	1.3%
1985	8,750	1.3%
1986	6,961	1.9%
1987	10,970	1.0%
1988	10,889	0.9%
1989	11,484	0.7%
1990	11,900	0.8%
1991	8,768	2.0%
1992	6,820	2.2%
1993	5,437	2.2%
1994	4,073	3.1%
1995	3,977	2.8%
1996	3,885	2.0%
1997	3,547	1.4%
1998	2,498	0.9%
1999	2,156	9.5%
2000	1,954	3.8%
2001	1,682	7.5%
2002	1,398	15.2%
2003	1,285	14.8%
2004	1,349	13.5%
2005	1,388	9.6%
2006	1,321	5.8%
2007	1,638	3.5%
2008	1,609	1.2%

In some cases, pension surplus was used in corporate takeovers. Either a company would purchase another company that had a pension surplus and then terminate the plan in order to capture the surplus to fund future operations, or it would terminate an overfunded plan to free up assets to use to acquire another company.

In order to slow the termination of overfunded plans, Congress imposed an additional income tax of up to 40 percent over the ordinary income tax liability. As a result, in some

10 Pension Benefit Guarantee Corporation (1999, for years 1975-1998). Pension Benefit Guarantee Corporation (2009, for years 1999-2008).

cases, a company paid 90 percent of the surplus assets in taxes. Consequently the plan termination was not a worthwhile means of capturing assets to use for other business purposes.

Although defined benefit plan terminations slowed, companies continued to be interested in moving to a defined contribution plan. Some factors driving the trend toward defined contribution plans include

- Frustration over the increased funding regulation and loss of control by the company over how much to contribute to the plan;
- High administrative expenses, including steep plan termination insurance premiums even for adequately funded plans;
- Worker dissatisfaction with seemingly small benefits paid from defined benefit plans compared to the apparent rapid build-up of account balances in defined contribution plans, especially during strong investment markets;
- Worker willingness to pay part of the cost of the plan through pre-tax salary deferrals into a defined contribution plan;
- The ability to shift the investment risk to the employee;
- The desire for predictable employer contributions; and
- Provide desired benefits for mobile workforce.

23.4.3 EXERCISES

23.10 Are defined benefit or defined contribution plans more prevalent in the United States today?

23.11 What is a reason for the increase in defined benefit plan terminations in the mid-1980s?

23.12 What steps did the U.S. government take to slow these plan terminations?

23.13 List reasons plan sponsors terminate defined benefit plans.

23.5 Canadian Pension Plan Design

Nearly half of employed Canadians participate in an employer-sponsored group pension plan, although in the private sector fewer than one in four workers is covered. As in the United States, benefits for collectively bargained employees tend to be different from those provided to non-bargained employees.

Full-time employees who have satisfied a minimum period of service are required to be eligible to participate in the plan under provincial regulation. There is also a participation standard for part-time employees. Plans requiring employees to make contributions to the plan generally require those contributions as a condition of plan participation.

Generally speaking, defined benefit plans are the most common type of plan among larger employers, and smaller employers tend to have defined contribution plans. As in the United States, there is a trend toward more defined contribution plans.

Contributory plans (those requiring employee contributions) are more common in Canada than in the United States, due to the ability of participants to make tax deductible contributions to registered pension plans, although there is a trend away from contributory defined benefit plans in Canada. About half of the private-sector plans covering salaried employees are contributory, but nearly all public sector plans require employees to make contributions. Collectively bargained plans are less likely to be contributory.

Normal retirement benefits are commonly provided at age 65, with later retirement permitted. Some provinces prohibit mandatory retirement through human rights legislation. Most provinces require early retirement benefits be provided to anyone within 10 years of normal retirement. Several provinces and the federal government permit, but do not require, plans to offer phased retirement so employees can receive benefits from the plan while continuing to work reduced hours for the employer sponsoring the plan.

Automatic cost of living adjustments are unusual except in public sector and educational institution plans. Ad hoc adjustments, which provide some inflation protection without creating an unsustainable obligation on the employer, are offered in some plans. Ad hoc adjustments typically are about one-third to two-thirds of the increase in the CPI.

Plans are required to provide a spousal death benefit based on the benefit earned (accrued) after the effective date of the legislation requiring the death benefit. The death benefit must be 60 percent to 100 percent of the actuarial value of the applicable portion of the accrued benefit.

After retirement, it is common to have a normal form of distribution that pays benefits for the participant's lifetime with a guarantee of five years of payments, especially if the plan requires member contributions. This type of distribution provides at least some protection against an early death of the employee. Of course, the employee could elect an optional form of distribution providing a greater death benefit, although the benefit received during the employee's lifetime would likely be lower to reflect the additional value of the death benefit protection provided by the form of annuity selected for the distribution.

23.5.1 EXERCISES

23.14 Are plans requiring employee contributions more common in the United States or Canada?

23.15 What type of death benefit must be provided in a Canadian retirement plan?

23.16 What types of plan is the most common in Canada - defined contribution or defined benefit?

23.6 Using Retirement Plans to Manage an Employer's Workforce

Benefits can help attract employees. In a strong economy, employees have a choice when they are looking for a job and the benefits offered by the employer will factor into the employment decision. Younger workers are most apt to be attracted by a defined contribution plan because of the even contributions across all age groups. They are probably not planning to make a career of working for their current employer so they want to build up retirement savings that can be taken to the next employer.

Older workers generally gain more from a defined benefit plan. Because of the shorter period of time to fund benefits for older workers, those benefits are generally more expensive to the employer and more valuable to the older worker. However, defined benefit plans are harder for workers to understand than defined contribution plans, so older workers may not appreciate the benefit even though it is valuable to them.

Defined benefit plans offer workforce management opportunities not available to the plan sponsor in a defined contribution plan. Defined benefit plans encourage employees to remain with the employer because each year's benefit accrual is more valuable than the prior year's accrual. For example, a plan using a formula based on pay and service rewards an employee for staying with the employer, especially when benefits are based on final or, more commonly, final average compensation because pay tends to increase over time.

Both defined benefit and defined contribution plans reward workers who stay at least for a few years and become vested in the benefit. While a plan can offer 100 percent immediate vesting, currently it is not common. It is more common to require the employee to earn three to five years of service to be fully vested, although partial vesting may occur sooner. As employees near full vesting, they will be aware of the financial incentive to stay another year or two to become fully vested.

The plan can encourage employees to stay until early retirement but not all the way to normal retirement by providing subsidized early retirement benefits where the reduction for early commencement of benefits is less than a full actuarial reduction. In this case, ignoring the value of continued benefit accruals, the benefits are more valuable when they start at an earlier retirement age.

The employer can also offer an early retirement incentive program through the retirement plan, often called an early retirement window program. The program offers subsidized or enhanced retirement benefits during a limited period of time for older employees. A subsidized benefit is one that is not reduced for early commencement. For example, the early retirement benefit could provide unreduced benefits as early as age 60 compared to the plan's normal reduction of 25 percent. An example of an enhanced benefit is one where the participants taking the early retirement window are credited with an extra five years of service, increasing the benefit amount.

The window must be carefully designed to ensure that it isn't discriminatory in favor of highly compensated employees. A window program can be very effective for an employer that needs to reduce the workforce and that has older employees. This type of arrangement can benefit both the employer and the employee by providing extra benefits to the employee and reducing the workforce without layoffs.

Generous benefits can also help fend off unions if that is a priority for the employer. If the employees are already getting good pay and good benefits, the union is less able to convince workers they need someone to negotiate on their behalf with the employer.

23.6.1 EXERCISES

23.17 Do defined benefit or defined contribution plans offer the plan sponsor more opportunities for workforce management?

23.18 How can a retirement plan be used to attract workers?

23.19 How can a retirement plan be used to discourage workers from terminating their employment with the plan sponsor?

23.20 How is an early retirement window used to manage the workforce?

CHAPTER 24
Funding for Employer-Sponsored Retirement Plans

Employer-sponsored defined benefit and defined contribution plans are typically funded in advance. For these types of retirement plans, advance funding is required in both the United States and Canada.

For a defined contribution plan, the funding is merely the contribution promised by the plan for the current year. If the plan is a profit sharing plan, the sponsor often has discretion to choose the amount to fund; however, once that amount is selected, it must be funded. The present value of future benefits in a defined contribution plan equals the sum of the participant account balances. As a result, generally, no unfunded liability exists under a defined contribution plan.

For a defined benefit plan, the funding is determined by the actuary each year. The goal of funding is to accumulate sufficient assets to provide benefits over time as participants retire or terminate and take a benefit distribution from the plan. The future benefits considered in the funding calculation can span many years. If a participant in the plan is age 20 and lives to age 100, the total of the benefit accumulation and benefit payout periods will be 80 years. It's easy to see why an actuary is needed to perform the required calculations.

24.1 Overview of Employer-Sponsored Defined Benefit Plan Funding

The plan sponsor, typically the employer, has the responsibility to fund enough to provide the promised benefits and do so in keeping with laws and regulations. Of course, the promised benefits aren't all due in the current year so the funding is spread over many years. A pension actuarial valuation estimates the long-term cost of the plan.

The ultimate cost of a defined benefit plan equals the cost of benefits provided plus the cost of administering the plan. Because benefits are funded in advance, there will be investment income on the plan's assets that will help provide for the payment of future benefits.

There are many steps in completing an actuarial valuation, including the following:

- Participant census data and plan asset information must be collected, and the actuary will review the information for reasonableness.
- The actuary must estimate the amount and timing of future benefit payments.
- A set of actuarial assumptions, discussed below, is selected along with an actuarial cost method to determine the funding stream.
- The plan document must be reviewed and plays an important role in the valuation as well because it provides the details of the promised benefits. The plan document will specify:
  - Plan participation requirements;
  - Service and salary, if any, to use in the benefit calculation;
  - The benefit formula to use to determine benefits;

- The form in which the benefits will be paid;
- The plan's vesting schedule;
- The age at which benefits will be paid from the plan;
- The reduction to apply to benefits that begin prior to normal retirement; and
- Any increase to apply to benefits that begin after normal retirement.

24.1.1 Uses of Actuarial Valuations

The most common, and perhaps most important, use of an actuarial valuation is to determine annual funding requirements. The actuary must be knowledgeable about the plan itself, the plan sponsor, economic trends, plan demographics and the applicable laws and regulations to be able to prepare a useful funding valuation.

The pattern of future benefit distributions and contributions is also an important business planning consideration. An actuarial valuation is also used by the plan sponsor to make plan design decisions by providing information about the cost of possible plan changes. Generally the cost of plan changes is hard to predict without preparing actuarial calculations.

If a company is considering merging with another company or spinning off a portion of the company to form a new entity, the funded status of the retirement plan is a factor in determining the value of the company. If the plan has surplus assets, it can be considered an asset in the business transaction. If current liabilities are larger than plan assets, the plan will be a liability.

In the United States, if the plan is subject to ERISA, the plan sponsor must file an annual disclosure report with the Department of Labor. One of the schedules in this filing for a defined benefit plan is an actuarial schedule. As a result, an annual actuarial valuation is required so the actuary will have the necessary information to complete the disclosure schedule.

Companies prepare annual financial statements. If the company has its financial statements audited, the company's annual report must include information about the assets and liabilities of any defined benefit and defined contribution plans sponsored by the employer. Even if the company doesn't have audited financial statements, it still may need to prepare the same sort of information if it borrows money from a commercial bank.

If the plan is a multi-employer collectively-bargained plan, a valuation determines the liability an employer must pay if it no longer participates in the plan. This withdrawal liability payment is required to avoid employers withdrawing from an underfunded plan and leaving other employers to bear the financial burden.

If a pension plan is terminated and assets are not sufficient to fund all plan benefits, an actuarial valuation is needed to determine what benefits the plan can provide and what ones must be forfeited. Not surprisingly, it is difficult for an underfunded plan to be terminated without the sponsor contributing whatever is needed to provide all benefits.

24.1.2 Allowable Funding Range

Pension laws and regulations establish the minimum amount that must be contributed in a particular year. The minimum required contribution is intended to be enough to provide for benefits earned in the current year and a reasonable amortization of benefits earned in the past that are not yet fully funded.

Laws and regulations also establish the maximum amount that can be contributed and taken as a tax deduction in the current year by the plan sponsor. The maximum deductible contribution ensures sponsors don't use a pension plan as a tax avoidance vehicle in years when the sponsor is particularly profitable. In the United States, the maximum deductible contribution decreased significantly as a result of the Tax Reform Act of 1986, beginning an underfunding crisis when investment markets weakened in 2001. Lower funding when the investment markets were strong led to underfunded plans when the investment markets weakened, creating the need to raise minimum funding requirements enacted with the Pension Protection Act of 2006.

The plan sponsor is free to contribute any amount between the minimum required and the maximum deductible amounts. As a result, the employer can contribute extra in good years to help build up the plan's assets and hopefully have more investment return to offset future funding requirements.

24.1.3 Two Types of Actuarial Valuations

Actuarial valuations may be open group and closed group. The difference between the two is whether the valuation anticipates new participants entering the plan after the current year.

An open group, or dynamic, valuation anticipates future new participants and considers events that will happen in the future with respect to the current and future membership. It cannot be used as the basis of determining the minimum required or maximum deductible contribution in the United States or Canada. The maximum deductible contribution is used to determine current tax deductions, which in turn affects the plan sponsor's current tax liability. Allowing a tax deduction based on assumed future new participants is unacceptable from a tax policy perspective because it allows the plan sponsor to manipulate the tax deduction by adjusting the new entrant assumption to produce a desired tax deduction.

An open-group valuation is particularly helpful when the plan sponsor wants to see the expected contribution pattern year by year in order to make a business decision or decide on plan changes.

A closed group, or static, valuation only considers current plan participants, and sometimes includes those who are expected to enter the plan during the current year. However, it considers events that will happen in the future with respect to current participants. Future employment patterns, compensation, and rates of death and disability are all incorporated into the valuation through the actuarial assumptions.

24.1.4 EXERCISES

24.1 What role does the actuary play in defined benefit plan funding?

24.2 What determines the ultimate cost of a defined benefit plan? A defined contribution plan?

24.3 Why is the plan document important to the actuary in preparing a defined benefit plan valuation?

24.4 What is the primary purpose of an annual actuarial valuation?

24.5 Compare open and closed group valuations and describe common uses of each.

24.2 Actuarial Assumptions Used in Defined Benefit Plan Valuations

Some assumptions are used in all valuations and others are used if they are applicable to the plan being valued. In the United States, assumptions used to determine the plan's funding range are selected by the actuary. For a plan covered by ERISA, the choice of some of the assumptions used for the minimum required contribution has been limited by laws and regulations.

If the valuation will be used for the company's financial statement, the company is responsible for selecting the assumptions, although the actuary will provide valuable advice. Assumptions used for the company's accounting purposes will be discussed in a later chapter.

A rate of interest must be selected to discount future benefit payouts to the date of the valuation and is dependent on the purpose of the actuarial valuation. Depending on the funding method, the rate may also be used to discount expected future contributions. The rate can reflect the rates currently available in the annuity purchase market if the valuation is an estimate of the plan termination funded status and liabilities. Otherwise, the rate will reflect annuity purchase rates over a long period of time.

U.S. plans determine minimum funding requirements using rates on high-quality corporate bonds, which are widely available and approximate annuity purchase rates. Interest rates used for minimum funding vary by the duration of the liability being valued. A benefit expected to be paid in the next year will be valued at a different rate from the one used to value a benefit expected to be paid 20, 30, or 40 years in the future. The rates also change from one valuation to the next. In this way, the liabilities are valued on a basis consistent with securities that can be used to immunize the liabilities against future interest rate fluctuations.

Unless the plan has just been established, it will have already accumulated some assets, so an investment return must be selected. This rate will reflect the mix of investments in the plan's asset portfolio. As with all actuarial assumptions, although the goal is to estimate the future investment return, the only data available to the actuary are past investment returns. In selecting the investment returns, the actuary will usually include an estimate of inflation and the expected investment earnings in excess of inflation for each asset class held in the plan's asset portfolio.

If the plan uses the participant's compensation in the benefit formula, the actuary will need to estimate future salary increases. The salary increase assumption includes several components: cost of living increase, productivity increase, and merit increase. The plan sponsor will provide advice on projected salary increases in the short-term because that information would be included in the company's budgeting process. The actuary will consider current economic conditions, the salary history of the plan sponsor's industry if that data is available, information about prior salary increases of plan participants and the plan sponsor's financial projections.

Several actuarial decrements are also used in the valuation. Rates of retirement, mortality, disability, and turnover (termination of employment prior to retirement) may be used depending on the plan provisions and the size of the population being valued. Simplified assumptions are typically used for plans with a small number of participants. Not all plans provide disability benefits, so termination on account of disability may be rolled into the turnover assumption. Mortality, disability, and turnover will likely be based on published tables, although very large plans will have statistically reliable data and may use their own experience to develop rates of decrement. Retirement rates are generally selected based on the experience of the plan sponsor's workforce and/or industry. Tables published by the Society of Actuaries and other actuarial bodies are an important resource for the pension actuary.

If the plan allows participants to select optional forms of benefit distribution more valuable than the normal form of benefit, the actuary may include an assumption about the distribution option participants will select. If the plan sponsor pays administrative expenses from plan assets rather than from the company's assets, the assumptions must include a provision for those expenses.

24.2.1 EXERCISES

24.6 Describe how the inflation rate assumption is used in a defined benefit valuation.

24.7 How is the interest rate assumption different from the expected return on plan assets?

24.8 What decrement rates may be used in a valuation?

24.3 Terminology Commonly Used in Pension Funding

The method used to determine the plan's funding is referred to as the funding method or the actuarial cost method. We will use these terms interchangeably. The funding method consists of the underlying formulas applied to the assumptions, data, and plan provisions to determine how the plan's liabilities are allocated to the past, current, and future years.

The normal cost is a liability allocated to the current year by the funding method. There may also be prior year's costs that need to be amortized, so the normal cost may not be the only funding component for the current year.

Actuarial accrued liability refers to the liability attributed to prior years by the funding method. It is also called the actuarial liability or the past service liability. If a new plan credits service prior to the effective date of the plan, an actuarial accrued liability will exist at the plan's inception. An additional actuarial accrued liability is created when a plan is amended to increase benefits attributable to service earned prior to the effective date of the amendment. The portion of the plan's actuarial liability that is already funded by existing plan assets is referred to as the funded actuarial liability.

Actuarial assumptions are used in the funding calculations, but they will never exactly reflect the plan's experience in any year. The difference between actual and assumed experience creates actuarial gains and losses. An actuarial gain means the actual experience was more favorable, and less costly, than the assumed experience. An actuarial loss means the opposite was the case.

24.3.1 EXERCISES

24.9 What creates actuarial gains?

24.10 How is the actuarial accrued liability different from the normal cost?

24.4 Funding Methods

24.4.1 Overview of Funding Methods

The funding method determines how plan costs are allocated over prior and future years. Many funding methods used today have been used for many years and reflect various philosophies of how quickly assets should accumulate to provide future benefits. Because of legislative, regulatory, and accounting changes, fewer funding methods are in wide use today.

Single-employer plans in the United States that are subject to ERISA are limited to a single method for calculating the minimum required contribution. The maximum deductible contribution usually only depends on the plan's unfunded current accrued liabilities determined according to specific rules. However, there are other funding methods that can be used by governmental and church plans that are not subject to ERISA as well as by multi-employer plans in the United States and plans outside the United States.

We will divide our discussion of funding methods into two major categories. One category is referred to as group methods, which means the costs are determined for the plan population as a group. The other category is referred to as individual methods, and the costs for this category are determined for each individual and then totaled to get the cost for the entire plan.

In addition to being either a group or individual method, an actuarial funding method will either allocate benefits or costs to various periods of time.

24.4.2 Benefit Allocation Methods

A benefit allocation method determines plan costs on an individual basis. It allocates the benefit over the participant's service and then applies actuarial formulas to determine the funding for a particular year. If the benefit formula uses compensation, the accrued benefit allocation method can use the current salary in the calculation. Alternatively, it could use the current salary increased to retirement using a salary increase assumption. If salary increases are anticipated when determining the benefit allocated to the current year, the plan will fund more in early years. This approach is a way of keeping the annual funding from increasing too much from year to year.

The normal cost equals the present value of the benefit allocated to the current year by the funding method. Note that this is not necessarily the same as the benefit actually accrued in the current year.

Funding for plans using a benefit allocation method typically increases each year. If future salary increases aren't included in the normal cost, funding will increase as salaries increase. Another reason for the funding increase is that the cost of each benefit accrual increases with age as the discount factor becomes smaller. Although mortality and disability rates increase over time, they are not large enough to offset the effect of the shorter discounting period.

Benefit allocation cost methods are referred to either traditional unit credit or projected unit credit. If salaries are not projected to retirement, the benefit allocation method is called the traditional unit credit (TUC) method. If they are projected to retirement, the method is called the projected unit credit (PUC) method. The following example compares the normal cost calculation in the two unit credit funding methods.

EXAMPLE 24.1

We will use the benefit formula from Example 23.1. This benefit formula is 2 percent multiplied by final five-year average salary multiplied by years of service.

The normal cost equals the benefit allocated to the current year, B_x, times an interest discount, I_{r-x}, multiplied by the probability of reaching retirement, ${}_{r-x}p_x$, multiplied by a single-premium annuity factor at retirement age, $\ddot{a}_r$. The TUC and PUC methods differ with respect to the calculation of B_x.

If the individual receives a 3 percent salary increase from age 45 to age 65, using Example 23.1, a salary of \$50,000 at age 45 when the person was hired will grow to \$87,675 at age 65. If the person is age 50, the current five-year average salary will be \$53,391. At age 65, the five-year average salary grows to \$82,714.

Applying the benefit formula, the person earns another 2 percent each year. Both TUC and PUC will use this 2 percent multiplier, but PUC will use projected average salary (\$82,714), whereas TUC merely uses current average salary (\$53,391).

The calculations are

$$B_{50}^{TUC} = 0.02(53{,}391) = 1{,}068 \quad B_{50}^{PUC} = 0.02(82{,}714) = 1{,}654$$

At 5% interest, $I_{15} = 1.05^{-15} = 0.481$

Assume ${}_{15}p_{50} = 0.75$ and $\ddot{a}_{65} = 12$

TUC normal cost is $1{,}068 \times 12 \times 0.75 \times 0.481 = \$4{,}623$

PUC normal cost is $1{,}654 \times 12 \times 0.75 \times 0.481 = \$7{,}160$.

As discussed, the normal cost increases as the participant ages because the participant is more likely to survive in service to the age of decrement and the interest discount is less. However, the impact on the overall cost of the plan depends on the relative number and age of new participants compared to participants who leave during the year.

The actuarial accrued liability is the present value of benefits attributable to prior years. The calculation is like the calculation for the normal cost, but the benefits attributable to prior years is used in the formula rather than the benefit allocated to the current year.

EXAMPLE 24.2

Continuing with the information from Example 24.1, the participant has five years of service. The actuarial accrued liability is determined as follows:

TUC accrued liability: $\$1{,}068 \times 12 \times 0.75 \times 0.481 \times 5 = \$23{,}117$

PUC accrued liability: $\$1{,}654 \times 12 \times 0.75 \times 0.481 \times 5 = \$35{,}801$

24.4.3 Cost Allocation Methods

Cost allocation methods allocate the plan's cost over the life of the plan. They provide funding flexibility for the plan sponsor because there is a generally a wide range between the minimum required and maximum deductible funding levels.

Cost allocation methods begin with the present value of projected benefits and then allocate the present value to each year either as a dollar amount or a percentage of payroll. Cost allocation methods can determine the contribution for the plan as a whole (group method) or for individual participants (totaling all of the contributions to get the overall plan cost).

The following formula is the normal cost formula for a commonly used individual cost allocation method called entry age normal (EAN). EAN allocates the cost of a person's benefit from the age when the person enters the plan until the person leaves the plan.

$$\text{EAN normal cost: } \frac{\textit{Present Value of Benefits at Entry Age}}{\textit{Temporary Annuity Factor from Entry Age to Retirement}}$$

The EAN normal cost for a person will stay the same each year as long as the person's salary increases by the assumed amount. The normal cost for the plan is the sum of the normal cost amounts for each individual. The normal cost of the plan will vary from year to year depending on the impact of participants entering and leaving the plan.

The accrued liability under the EAN cost method is the present value of the benefit projected to normal retirement minus the present value of future normal costs. Example 24.3 shows the calculation of the normal cost and accrued liability using the EAN cost method.

EAN is no longer permitted for determining minimum funding requirements in the United States for plans subject to ERISA.

EXAMPLE 24.3

We will use the benefit formula from Example 23.1 and the assumptions from Example 24.1.

The EAN normal cost and actuarial accrued liability need the following additional factors:

Temporary annuity factor at entry age: $\ddot{a}_{45:\overline{20|}} = 13.462210$

Temporary annuity factor at attained age: $\ddot{a}_{50:\overline{15|}} = 11.379658$

Benefit at entry age using salaries at normal retirement age: $0.02 \times 82{,}714 \times 20 = \$33{,}086$

Present value factor at entry age: $1.05^{-20} = 0.377$

Survival factor at entry age: ${}_{20}p_{45} = 0.66667$

$$\text{EAN normal cost: } \frac{\$33{,}086 \times 12 \times 0.66667 \times 0.377}{13.462210} = \$7{,}412$$

EAN accrued liability at age 50:

$$(\$33{,}086 \times 12 \times 0.75 \times .481) - (\$7{,}412 \times 11.379658) = \$58{,}883$$

Most cost allocation methods have separate components that are amortized, including:

- The cost allocated to all prior years of service (or years prior to the plan's effective date);
- The change (increase or decrease) in actuarial accrued liability resulting from differences between actual and assumed experience (actuarial gains and losses);
- The change (increase or decrease) in actuarial accrued liability resulting from a change in actuarial assumptions used for the funding calculations; and
- Changes in actuarial accrued liability attributable to changes in the benefit promised by the plan.

24.4.4 EXERCISES

The following information will be used for the following exercises:

Age at entry into plan	25
Normal retirement age	65
Current age	30
Projected annual benefit at normal retirement	\$116,928
Annual accrued benefit at age 30	
• with salary increase to normal retirement	\$14,616
• with no salary increase after current year	\$3,704
Benefit accrual allocated to age 30	
• with salary increase to normal retirement	\$2,923
• with no salary increase after current year	\$741
Temporary annuity factor	
• at age 25	16.224543
• at age 30	15.736780
$\ddot{a}_{65}$	12
Interest discount rate	6%
${}_{35}p_{30}$	100%

24.11 Calculate the traditional unit credit normal cost at age 30.
24.12 Calculate the projected unit credit normal cost at age 30.
24.13 Calculate the projected unit credit actuarial accrued liability at age 30.
24.14 Calculate normal cost at age 30 using the entry age normal cost method.

24.5 Asset and Participant Data Needed for the Actuarial Valuation

After all of the applicable assumptions have been selected and the funding method determined, the actuary also needs participant census data and plan asset information. This information is used to update the actuary's records from the prior valuation date to the current valuation date. Any difference between the expected data changes and the actual data changes will contribute to actuarial gains and losses.

24.5.1 Plan Asset Information

The plan's trustee or the custodian, such as a bank or insurance company, holding the plan's assets will prepare asset statements for the plan. These statements will have a balance sheet of the various investments and the value of the assets in each investment. It will also have a transaction statement showing information on what came into the plan's asset account and what went out.

Amounts coming into the account will include investment income and any contributions from the plan sponsor, and employees if the plan allows or requires employee contributions. Because the asset statement will reflect the market value of assets, amounts coming into the account will include realized and unrealized investment gains. Realized gains are gains the plan has received because an investment has been sold or liquidated at a gain. Unrealized gains are those gains that have accumulated in the investment but have not yet been realized by the plan.

Amounts going out of the plan will include benefit distributions and plan expenses. Plan expenses can include various administrative expenses such as actuarial valuation fees and audit fees, although some plan sponsors pay these expenses from the company's assets rather than from the plan. Depending on the plan's demographics, the plan may pay benefit distributions. A new plan generally won't have any benefit distributions for a few years. A mature plan may have significant benefit distributions because participants will have reached the age and have earned sufficient service to receive a benefit from the plan.

As discussed, because the asset statement will reflect the market value of assets, amounts going out of the account will include realized and unrealized investment losses. Realized losses are amounts lost because an investment has been sold or liquidated at a loss. Unrealized losses have not yet been realized by the plan through an investment sale or liquidation.

24.5.2 Participant Census Information

To perform an actuarial valuation, the actuary needs basic information on all plan participants, including date of birth, gender if sex-distinct mortality is used in the valuation, date of hire, and date and type of decrement if the participant is no longer actively employed by the plan sponsor. As discussed previously, decrements can include mortality, disability, retirement, and termination of employment.

If the plan is a pay-related plan, salary information will also be needed. If the plan determines service on the basis of hours of service (e.g., one year might be credited if the participant has 1,000 hours of service in a calendar year) rather than using elapsed time (one year of service is credited for each 12 months worked in a calendar year), the actuary also needs information on hours of service worked during the prior year.

Complete census data is also needed for new employees who entered the plan between the last valuation date and the current valuation date. For participants who were included in the last valuation, only updated service information and salary information, if applicable, is needed.

If a participant dies and the death benefit is paid to a beneficiary as an annuity over the beneficiary's lifetime, the actuary will need census data on the beneficiary.

24.5.3 EXERCISES

24.15 What participant census data is needed?

24.16 Who provides asset information?

24.17 What asset information is needed?

24.6 Selecting the Amount to Fund

The actuarial valuation is the means by which the actuary determines the plan sponsor's range of minimum required and maximum deductible contributions. The plan sponsor then uses this information to determine the actual funding level within this range. Some plan sponsors routinely contribute only the minimum required amount or the maximum deductible amount. However, other plan sponsors will have a contribution amount that fits with the company's other financial obligations to produce a desired cash flow or a desired result on the financial statements. They will contribute that amount as long as it falls between the minimum required and the maximum deductible amounts.

The plan sponsor often has a funding philosophy or policy. For example, the sponsor may want fairly level contributions from year to year. If the company is growing and a lot of new participants are entering the plan each year, the overall cost will rise because there are more participants in the plan, but the cost as a percentage of payroll may not increase. If the company has a mature (relatively stable) workforce, the sponsor will have more difficulty avoiding increasing pension costs. Participants are aging and the population is relatively static so there may not be a significant number of younger participants entering the plan. The plan sponsor is the only one who knows the expected growth of the company and the hiring philosophy, and this information is helpful in anticipating short-term future funding requirements.

The actuary can assist the sponsor with the annual funding decision by explaining the implications of a particular contribution. For example, contributing only the minimum required amount does not build up a funding cushion that can provide funding flexibility in later years. Lack of funding flexibility can lead to rising minimum required contributions in soft investment markets. Contributing a higher amount provides funding flexibility in future years and will also provide the opportunity for additional investment return because of the additional assets in the plan.

The extremes of the permitted funding range provide a form of protection, although the purpose of the protection is different for the minimum and maximum contribution levels. The minimum required contribution protects plan participants by requiring ongoing plan funding at a meaningful level. From a public policy perspective, it helps protect any pension insurance system, such as the Pension Benefits Guaranty Corporation in the United States, against the transfer of unfunded liabilities from severely underfunded plans to the entity providing the insurance guarantee. The maximum deductible contribution protects other taxpayers against excessive tax deductions by profitable companies.

24.6.1 EXERCISE

24.18 How does a plan sponsor decide how much to contribute to a defined benefit plan for a particular year?

24.7 Actuarial Valuation—Stakeholders and Their Views

An actuarial valuation affects numerous stakeholders who may have conflicting views. The actuary, although not the plan sponsor or a participant, is still a stakeholder because of the actuary's professional responsibilities. For example, the actuary needs to be willing to set limits on the actuarial assumptions the plan sponsor might want the actuary to use to ensure that the actuary is comfortable with each individual assumption and also the set of assumptions when considered together. Although the actuary isn't required to audit the participant census data and asset information, questions must be raised if things don't look reasonable.

The plan sponsor is a stakeholder because the sponsor is the one who will fund the plan each year. The sponsor will have a philosophy about the desired pattern of funding. For example, should the contributions start out small and gradually increase as the company becomes more profitable or should they be fairly level through the life of the plan. Regardless of the desired funding pattern, the sponsor will want the contributions to be as predictable as possible. Contributions are most predictable when the actuarial assumptions most closely reflect actual plan experience, making it important for the actuary and plan sponsor to work together to select the most accurate assumptions to use in the valuation model.

Participants are stakeholders in the valuation because the plan's funded status affects the likelihood that promised benefits will actually be paid. While participants typically do not participate in the decision-making process concerning plan funding, they are affected by the results of that process.

Any investors in the plan sponsor are also stakeholders because the funding decisions affect the cash flow and profitability of the sponsor. As with participants, the investors typically do not exercise discretion over the plan's funding even though they are affected by it.

CHAPTER 25
Pension Accounting in the United States

25.1 Policy Reason for U.S. Pension Accounting Requirements

The Securities and Exchange Commission (SEC) has authority over financial reporting of publicly traded companies. Their mission is to "protect investors, maintain fair, orderly, and efficient markets, and facilitate capital formation."[1]

Until the mid-1980s, it was common for a company to use results from its funding valuation in preparing its financial statements. Companies had different philosophies with respect to pension funding, so two companies with identical pension plans and employee populations might have very different pension information reported in their financial statements.

When a potential investor is making a decision between two investments, part of that decision-making process will involve comparing financial information on the companies. The Financial Accounting Standards Board (FASB) is an independent organization that publishes rules for companies to use when preparing financial statements and for accountants to use in auditing those statements. These rules are recognized as authoritative by the SEC.

One reason for the rules is to have some commonality in the preparation of financial statements to allow more reliable comparison by potential investors. As stated on the FASB web site, "decisions about the allocation of [financial] resources rely heavily on credible, concise, and understandable financial information."[2]

Pension differences created an area of unreliability in financial statements. The FASB issued a Statement of Financial Accounting Standards (SFAS) that brought much more standardization to the calculations. As a result, investors can more easily compare companies and be confident that all pertinent information about a pension plan has been recorded and disclosed.

The International Accounting Standards Board (IASB) establishes standards that apply in all countries who adopt its standards. The ultimate objective is to have consistent financial accounting standards on a global basis. At some point, the IASB's standard governing pension accounting will become effective in the United States, making it easier to evaluate global investments. The International Accounting Standards became effective for the European Union countries in 2005 and was adopted in Canada in 2010.

25.1.1 EXERCISES

25.1 What role does the U.S. SEC play?

25.2 What rules apply to a company's financial statements?

25.3 What is the role of the IASB?

---

1 http://www.sec.gov/about/whatwedo.shtml. Accessed November 24, 2010.

2 http://www.fasb.org/facts/index.shtml#structure. Accessed November 24, 2010.

25.2 Pension Accounting Requirements

The accounting standards contain details on the calculation of the pension expense that is reported in the company's income statement. Rather than showing the cash contribution for the year calculated using regulations published by the IRS, the company reports the pension expense calculated using the applicable SFAS promulgated by the FASB.

A principle of corporate accounting is that income recognized in a particular year should be offset in the same year by the expense of generating the income. Employees of a company work to generate income for the company. A company treats employees well, including appropriate pay and benefits, in hopes of receiving employee loyalty and appreciation.

Expenses associated with employees, including compensation and benefits paid, are recorded as an expense in the financial statements. Pensions are a form of deferred compensation that can either be recorded when benefits accrue or when they are paid out of the plan.

Pension accounting is based on the philosophy that employees view benefit accruals as part of their current compensation even though benefits aren't received until a later year. As a result, the company must recognize the value of the benefit attributable to the current year as the pension expense in its income statement and the value of benefits attributable to prior years as the pension liability must be disclosed in a financial statement footnote.

It is important to separate the assets set aside in a trust for pension benefits from other assets vailable to the organization because it cannot access the pension assets for ordinary operating purposes. In the United States and Canada, legislation and trust law have strong protections for assets set aside to fund pension benefits.

25.2.1 EXERCISES

25.4 How is the cost of a retirement plan recognized for company accounting purposes?

25.5 Where does pension information appear in a company's financial statements?

25.3 Inputs into Pension Accounting Calculations

As with funding calculations, the actuary needs participant census data, asset information, and assumptions to enter into the actuarial model in order to calculate information needed for pension accounting and financial statement disclosure. The elements of pension census data needed for the pension accounting calculations are the same as those needed for pension funding. However, it may not be possible to obtain updated data for the calculations as of the valuation date because of timing constraints for issuing the company's financial statements. The pension expense for the year will typically be calculated based on readily available participant census data available at the time the valuation is to be completed.

The company's fiscal year used for financial statements is most commonly the calendar year, as is the plan year used for funding calculations. It is not unusual for a company to want the information for its financial statements within a month of the end of the fiscal year. The company cannot generally provide updated participant census data quickly enough to be included in the year-end calculations, although asset information will generally be available within a few days after the end of the year. As a result, the actuary will estimate updated participant census information using assumptions provided by the company for the year-end pension accounting calculations.

The actuarial assumptions used in pension accounting calculations are set by the company, and the company's management is responsible for their reasonableness. Actuaries provide valuable assistance in setting the assumptions because of the actuary's familiarity with the model that is used to perform the calculations and an understanding of the impact of sets of assumptions. For example, the salary increase assumption has less impact on a plan population where employees only stay for a few years than it does with a plan population with significant longevity.

25.3.1 EXERCISES

25.6 How are inputs used by the actuary for accounting calculations different from similar inputs used for retirement plan funding calculations?

25.7 Who selects the assumptions used for pension accounting calculations? What role does the actuary play?

25.4 Responsibility for Company Financial Statements

Company management has ultimate responsibility for its financial statements. If those statements are audited, as is the case for all publicly traded companies, a qualified accountant will review the details of the financial statements as well as the footnotes.

The pension expense and the disclosure information will be included in the audit. The accountant may question the data or assumptions used by the actuary in order to be comfortable with the information subject to audit. The actuary must comply with Actuarial Standards of Practice with respect to accounting calculations even though the actuary does not have ultimate responsibility for the information in the company's financial statements.

25.4.1 EXERCISES

25.8 Who has ultimate responsibility for information in a company's financial statements?

25.9 What is the actuary's responsibility with respect to a company's financial statements?

25.5 Pension Expense

Benefits under the plan's benefit formula may be earned at the same rate each year or the accrual rates may vary. Pension accounting recognizes the benefit proportionately over the employee's working career regardless of any accrual variations in the benefit formula. The expected benefit includes a provision for future salary increases beyond the current year, so the actuarial method used for pension accounting is a projected benefit allocation method.

The service cost is the actuarial present value of the projected benefit, including future salary increases if applicable, attributable in the current year. The service cost is analogous to the normal cost in funding calculations using projected unit credit.

The plan's liability determined including future salary increases, if applicable, is called the projected benefit obligation (PBO). The liability determined without salary increase, is called the accumulated benefit obligation (ABO). If the benefit does not use salaries in the benefit formula, the PBO will equal the ABO. The interest cost is the interest that accrues on the PBO.

The amortization components in a pension expense calculation include:

- The value of any plan changes attributable to prior years of service (called prior service cost);
- The value of benefits attributable to years prior to the plan's inception or, if later, the date the plan first complied with pension accounting rules currently in effect (referred as the transition asset or obligation);
- Actuarial gains and losses, including the effect of changes in actuarial assumptions; and
- The effect of a change in the actuarial assumptions used to determine the pension expense.

Plan assets are measured using fair (market) value and also a market-related value that allows some smoothing of investment gains and losses. The plan's assets are expected to have earnings that offset, in part, what the company needs to expense for the plan. This expense component is called the expected long-term return on plan assets. The expected investment earnings is based on the market-related (smoothed) value of plan assets held by the plan.

Annuity contracts are typically excluded from assets and the associated liabilities represented by the contracts are excluded from the liabilities. If the contracts are participating contracts, the value of the future dividends is reflected in the accounting calculations. Accounting rules provide details on how to value participating contracts for pension purposes.

The formula below shows the components of the pension expense where SC is service cost, IC is interest cost, AC is the amortization cost and ROI is the expected return on plan assets.

$$SC + IC \pm AC - ROI = Expense$$

If future benefit increases have been promised in a collective bargaining agreement, they are treated like future salary increases and reflected in the service cost and PBO, but not in the ABO. A history of increasing prior benefit accruals in a non-pay-related plan or in a plan that averages pay over the employee's career will require the plan sponsor to anticipate benefit increases in the service cost and PBO because of an implied commitment to make adjustments in the future.

25.5.1 EXERCISES

25.10 What are the components of pension expense?

25.11 Compare the ABO and the PBO.

25.12 Does the ABO ever equal the PBO?

25.6 Pension Disclosure

Although the pension expense is shown in the company's income statement, it does not give the full picture of the company's pension obligations. The accounting standards require one pension item to be included on the company's balance sheet and additional information disclosed in a footnote to the financial statements.

Defined benefit plans are difficult for investors to analyze. The financial obligation is not merely a particular dollar amount or percentage of compensation each year. As a result, accounting standards require financial statement footnote disclosures to provide investors with sufficient information about the pension plan to make an informed investment decision.

There is a timing difference in the cash funding and accounting expense of the plan because the pension expense generally is different from the amount funded for a year. If the cumulative contributions to the plan exceed the cumulative pension expense included in the income statements, an accounting liability is recognized on the company's balance sheet. If the cumulative pension expense is larger, an asset is shown on the balance sheet. The pension asset or liability is not a separate balance sheet entry. It is shown with all other timing differences and is not separately identified.

Footnote disclosure includes, separately for each plan sponsored by the employer, the following:

- Components of the pension expense;
- Reconciliation from the prior year end to the current year end of;
  - PBO;
  - Fair (market) value of plan assets;
  - Accrued or prepaid pension expense;
  - Unrecognized transition asset/obligation;
  - Unrecognized prior service cost;
  - Unrecognized net gain/loss;
- Expected contributions to fund the plan for the year;
- Estimated future benefit payments;
- ABO; and
- Actuarial assumptions used for the year-end calculations.

25.6.1 EXERCISE

25.13 What is the objective of financial statement footnote disclosures?

CHAPTER 26

Modeling Actuarial Costs and Expense

26.1 Actuarial Forecast Modeling System

The computer program used to perform the calculations needed for a retirement plan valuation is an actuarial model. An actuarial model applies standard actuarial formulas to project the participant census data, including years of service and salaries, year by year into the future using assumed decrement rates. Modeling typically uses the open group method, so new entrants will be assumed in future years.

The actuarial modeling system will determine the value of the benefit for each year's decrement at the assumed benefit commencement date depending on the plan's provisions.

26.2 Uses of Actuarial Forecast Modeling for Retirement Plans

The plan sponsor may want to understand the expected cash or accounting requirements of the pension plan over a period of time. An actuarial modeling study can also show the likelihood that the plan will not have sufficient assets to pay promised benefits at some point. Actuarial valuation software typically has the capability of producing the desired information.

If a static actuarial model is used, the actuary develops a set of assumptions for each year in the future. For example, the investment return will be set for the current year, the next year, and so on. The assumption does not need to be the same year by year. The actuary also develops another set of assumptions that are used as if it was the actual experience which the model will use to update asset and participant data, and calculate actuarial gains and losses.

The static actuarial model will provide the plan sponsor with information on the pattern of the cash and accounting requirements going forward. The sponsor can use this information in budgeting, but the information is also helpful in making decisions about the plan. The sponsor may find the plan is too expensive, requiring future benefit reductions or even plan termination. Alternatively, the sponsor may find that the plan can be enhanced and still remain within budget.

Dynamic, or stochastic, modeling differs from static modeling through its use of a Monte Carlo simulation approach. The assumptions are input year by year as with a static model. However, the actual future experience is allowed to fluctuate around these values based on the probability of various outcomes. The results of dynamic modeling will provide the plan sponsor with information about the probability of certain outcomes. For example, the actuary could tell the sponsor that 90 percent of the time the plan's contributions for the first five years will be $100,000 or less. Or, alternatively, in only 10 percent of the trials were the contributions at the end of the first five years more than $100,000.

In either static or dynamic modeling, the actuary will build in an assumption of new entrants into the plan. As discussed previously, this assumption cannot be used to determine the plan's funding obligations, but it is an important assumption in modeling.

The pension expense and other accounting information can be modeled along with funding requirements. This additional component helps the plan sponsor with financial planning.

The actuary cannot predict the future, but static and dynamic modeling allows the actuary to provide valuable information about the financial future of the retirement plan.

26.2.1 EXERCISES

26.1 Why would a plan sponsor want to see the results from modeling actuarial costs?

26.2 How is dynamic modeling different from static modeling?

26.3 What assumptions are needed for modeling that are not needed to determine the funding range in the actuarial valuation?

CHAPTER 27
Retirement Plan Solvency

A plan is considered solvent on an ongoing basis if it has sufficient assets to pay its current benefit obligations. Annual benefit payouts will generally be a fraction of the obligation for all accrued benefits because most plan participants are still earning additional benefits. A mature plan that has a significant percentage of retired participants must be concerned with the liquidity of investments to ensure that the plan doesn't have to sell investments at a loss in order to meet its distribution requirements.

All funding methods consider both benefits accrued in the past as well as benefits accruing in the current year in the determination of the plan's funding requirements. However, the pattern of actual funding and the pattern of cost allocation by the funding method will produce different results with respect to the adequacy of funding for current accrued benefits.

The U.S. Pension Protection Act of 2006 restricts benefit accruals and benefit distributions from a severely underfunded plan in order to protect remaining participants. No benefit accruals will be allowed if the plan is severely underfunded (less than 60 percent) until the funded percentage of accrued benefits (funded status) improves to at least 60 percent. Plans that are moderately underfunded (between 60 percent and 80 percent) cannot allow participants to receive their entire benefit in an accelerated form of distributions such as a lump sum distribution until the funded status improves to at least 80 percent.

Future solvency is one of the items that can be studied through actuarial modeling. The plan sponsor may want to know the plan's funded status under a variety of economic scenarios. These projected results can help the company determine whether the current funded status is a concern in light of its own future financial projections.

A plan is considered solvent on a plan termination (wind-up) basis at any point in time if current assets are sufficient to pay current benefit promises. It is not unusual for a plan to be insolvent on this basis. As long as the sponsor intends to continue the plan's operation and has the financial strength to fund the plan in the future, insolvency on a plan termination basis should not be a concern.

If the plan is not sufficiently funded and the sponsor encounters financial difficulty, the plan may not be able to meet its future obligations. In the United States, the Pension Benefit Guaranty Corporation (PBGC) is concerned with the current funded status of the plan since it provides plan termination insurance for defined benefit plans subject to ERISA. The insurance premium plans pay to the PBGC includes a component that is based on the plan's funded status. This variable premium component is larger for poorly funded plans and is $0 for plans considered adequately funded.

When a U.S. plan terminates with more assets than needed to satisfy the plan's obligations, the extra assets are either returned to the plan sponsor or allocated to participants according to the plan document. In the United States, an employer who terminates a plan with excess assets may be required to pay a very high excise tax on the extra assets that are returned to the company when the plan terminates. This large excise tax has caused plan sponsors to monitor the funded status to be sure the plan's assets are not too high, especially if the company is considering terminating the plan. Unfortunately, this motivation to reduce pension surplus has made plans less able to weather a downturn in financial markets without creating an underfunded situation.

When a plan terminates and has enough assets to pay all accrued benefits, those benefits will become fully vested. The plan can then settle its obligations through the purchase of annuities and lump sum distributions depending on the option selected by the participant. There are also circumstances where a plan is determined to have a partial termination, requiring affected participants to become fully vested.

If a plan is terminated, but it does not have sufficient assets to pay all of the promised benefits, the plan document will specify how assets are to be allocated among participants. If the plan is covered by the PBGC, the allocation is specified in the law. This allocation is akin to the allocation of assets of a bankrupt organization among its creditors. This type of termination in the United States is called a distress termination. The highest priority is given to any contributions made to the plan by employees and also to retirees who have been receiving benefits from the plan for a few years. The lowest priority is given to accrued benefits that have not yet become vested under the plan's vesting schedule.

27.1.1 EXERCISES

27.1 Is it important for a defined benefit plan to always have assets at least equal to the present value of accrued benefits?

27.2 What restrictions apply to a U.S. plan with assets less than 60 percent of the value for current accrued benefits?

27.3 What restrictions apply to a U.S. plan with assets at least 60 percent but less than 80 percent of the value for current accrued benefits?

27.4 Why would a plan sponsor not want to build up as much as it can afford in plan assets?

PART 5
GROUP AND HEALTH INSURANCE

Matthew C. Varitek

CHAPTER 28
Introduction to Group Insurance

28.1 Principles of Insurable Groups

Insurable groups consist of individuals connected to each other through common characteristics. The connection may be through an employer, a professional organization, a union or trade association, a government program or a creditor. The key principles of insurance—the existence of an insurable interest and protection against individual financial risk through pooling—apply to group products in the same manner as to products sold to individuals.

Group insurance products evaluate the relevant risks of the group as a whole, rather than separately considering each individual member's risk. Group products allow for more efficient distribution than individual products because they are marketed, billed, and otherwise administered through plan sponsors. This allows the offering entity to reach a greater volume of people as quickly and cheaply as possible. Groups may buy products to cover health care costs, protect against short-term or long-term disability, provide for long-term care and insure the lives of the members where an insurable interest exists. These products may be sold directly to individuals—though certain key components of the products' design (e.g., eligibility to receive benefits, processes for obtaining covered services) generally do not vary by whether they are sold to individuals or groups. The per-person cost of the products may differ substantially between individual purchasers and group purchasers due to different risk characteristics in addition to the relative efficiency of administration. For example, members of an employee group are likely to exhibit at least a minimum level of health that allows them to work. In addition, depending on their occupation, they may be subject to physical fitness requirements on an ongoing basis.

28.2 Buyers of Group Insurance Products

This section describes various purchasers of group insurance products. In the United States the National Association of Insurance Commissioners (NAIC) model law, adopted by all states, defines groups that are eligible to purchase group insurance. Members of eligible groups generally share a common characteristic or trait aside from their desire to purchase insurance. In order to be eligible to purchase insurance, the group must not have been formed for that explicit purpose.

28.2.1 Single Employers

Plans offered to single employers cover the employees and may cover their dependents. The employer holds the insurance policy and pays the premium, but may limit eligibility to certain classes of employees, or may require an employee contribution to offset part of the cost. Smaller employers typically purchase full insurance coverage; larger employers may choose to self-insure against some or all of the relevant financial risk. Employers who self-insure often pay an insurer or other third party to administer the benefits.

28.2.2 Multiple-Employer Trusts

Some small employers are not able to access or afford insurance by themselves due to the aggregate risk characteristics of their employee group. Other employers may seek to share administrative expenses or protect against the aggregate risk of their employee group by joining a trust with other employers.

28.2.3 Associations

Associations include individuals that share common professions, activities, interests, or goals. Professional organizations, trade organizations, alumni organizations, or affiliation groups like the American Automobile Association (AAA) may offer group insurance products to their members. Like employer plans, the association holds the policy. Unlike employer plans, the association member typically bears the entire cost of the product, either through membership dues, remittance of premium to the association, or direct payment to the insurer.

28.2.4 Labor Unions

Labor unions may hold a group insurance policy or may participate in a Taft-Hartley multiple employer trust. The policy benefits and member premium contributions are typically defined in a collective bargaining agreement. Premium payments may also be required from the employers of the union members.

28.2.5 Government Employee Groups

Public employers at the federal, state and local levels may provide employee benefits in the same manner as private employers. The Federal Employees' Health Benefit Association (FEHBA) and Federal Employees' Group Life Insurance (FEGLI) plans are the most prominent plans offered to employees of the United States government. TRICARE offers coverage for services rendered outside military treatment facilities and covers retired military members, their dependents, and dependents of active military personnel.

28.2.6 Government Social Insurance Programs

These programs may be available to the entire population or to segments of the population that may have difficulty accessing private insurance programs. In the United States, the best-known programs that offer health care services or funding are Medicare, Medicaid, and Social Security disability. These programs reach people that might otherwise be unacceptably exposed to risks of high costs and insufficient access to care.

The U.S. Medicare program is available to everyone age 65 or older and to those under age 65 who have received Social Security Disability Insurance (SSDI) benefits for at least 24 months (though the 24-month requirement is waived for people diagnosed with ALS or end-stage renal disease). Different types of health care services are covered under different parts of the program. Part A is mandatory and covers inpatient hospital admissions, residence at skilled nursing facilities, and home health services. Part B is optional and covers outpatient hospital and physician services, ambulance transports, durable medical equipment, and other non-physician providers (e.g., therapists). Part D is voluntary and provides coverage for prescription drugs. These programs are funded on a pay-as-you-go basis. Payroll taxes are the primary source of funding, though some member cost-sharing applies, and member premiums are collected for optional types of coverage. Part C coverages, also known as Medicare Advantage plans, include all services covered under Parts A and B and may add benefits for vision, hearing, dental, and health and wellness programs. Further, some Medicare Advantage plans include Part D coverage for prescriptions. Medicare Advantage plans are offered through private insurers and typically encourage—or require—use of a preferred provider network.

Medicaid is available in the United States for the financially indigent, though states may set different levels of eligibility that are generally described in terms of proportion of income to the federal poverty level. Medicaid also covers blind and disabled recipients of care. Its coverage is generally comprehensive, and member cost-sharing very low. Provider reimbursements represent deep discounts from billed charges, and as such, physicians are not mandated to participate in Medicaid, though most hospitals are required to do so. State government agencies administer Medicaid, though the majority of the program funding comes from the federal government. States have stepped up efforts to move away from a *fee-for-service* provider reimbursement model—which defines a payment amount for each physician procedure, piece of equipment, or other relevant component of a patient's treatment and then pays providers for the volume of each service that they provide—toward a *capitated* rate schedule, which reimburses a flat amount per member enrolled in the plan. Since utilization rates for some subsets of the Medicaid population are much higher than those for commercially insured populations (e.g., elderly whose long-term care services are provided through Medicaid), the change in payment model offers greater opportunities for cost control. Expansion of Medicaid is a central component of the Patient Protection and Affordable Care Act (PPACA), which will be discussed further in the next chapter.

In Canada, most people receive health care coverage through provincial-sponsored plans, also known collectively as Medicare. Canadian Medicare is funded primarily through the provinces' general revenues and federal transfer payments. Providers generally receive reimbursements on a fee-for-service basis and bill directly to the government without collecting payments from patients. Canadian citizens can receive all care deemed essential and necessary—including inpatient hospital care, primary physician care, X-rays and lab tests, immunizations, and most surgeries and specialty physician care—by showing a provincial health card. Some types of services, such as prescription drugs, dental care, vision care, and ambulance transportation, are not covered through Medicare.

28.2.7 Creditor Groups

Banks and other lenders may purchase group insurance—typically life insurance or disability-income insurance—on people to whom they have lent money or extended credit. The creditors hold the policy, may charge premium to the debtors through fees or interest rates and receive benefits if the debtors die or become disabled.

28.2.8 Discretionary Alliances

Purchasing alliances and similar groups may form primarily to provide insurance or self-funded benefits. Insurers or third-party administrators sometimes sponsor these groups to improve efficiency of administration.

28.3 Sellers of Group Insurance Products

Group insurance products are offered by different entities that serve sometimes-disparate populations by a variety of methods, assume various levels of risk, are subject to different regulatory principles and possess different organizational motivations. This section describes sellers of group insurance products.

28.3.1 Insurance Companies

Insurance companies offer a full range of group products that offer benefits for any or all of the following: medical services, dental services, prescription drugs, life insurance, disability-income insurance and long-term care. The most prominent medical plans include indemnity plans, preferred provider organization (PPO) plans, capitated or subcapitated plans and point-of-service (POS) plans. The insurer may offer full insurance coverage to its policyholders, or may offer administrative-services-only (ASO) contracts to groups preferring to self-fund their benefits. The most prominent insurance companies possess a national marketing presence and an extensive provider network, and are licensed to do business in most states. Hence they can offer potential customers a wide range of products that reach a vast area but originate from a single source.

Insurance companies may be structured for stock ownership or operated as a mutual company. Stock companies have greater access to capital in the financial marketplace than do mutual companies and not-for-profit organizations, but are subject to greater pressure to earn a satisfactory return on shareholder investments. Industry trends in recent decades include a shift away from mutual ownership toward stock ownership. Within the health insurance industry, even the largest national insurers often hold a smaller market share in any particular area than do the local Blue Cross/Blue Shield plans and managed care organizations. Thus, the operational efficiencies of scale that the largest insurers can achieve must be weighed against the less substantial provider discounts and other cost management procedures that they can negotiate and implement.

28.3.2 Health Care Service Corporations (HCSC)

Most Blue Cross/Blue Shield plans or Delta Dental plans are HCSCs, which are not-for-profit organizations that are often exempt from state premium or income tax. These plans typically focus on one state or small region and as such maintain longer-term relationships with providers and relatively high penetration levels in that particular market. These conditions may therefore allow the HCSC to negotiate deeper discounts on provider charges or more restrictive standards on practice efficiency. HCSCs generally offer medical and dental products, and like insurance companies, may offer full insurance coverage or contract on an ASO basis with groups. Should a group seek to offer ancillary products such as life or disability insurance to its members, the group must often seek out another carrier. The products offered by HCSCs are popular among collectively bargained plans such as those offered to government employee groups and unions.

28.3.3 Health Maintenance Organizations (HMO)

These organizations are generally licensed as separate entities from insurance companies or HCSCs, and in some cases may be publicly owned. HMOs may contract with providers to provide services, often paying a per-member capitation rate, or may own hospitals and directly employ physicians. They are directly involved in care management to a greater extent than insurers and HCSCs. They generally provide comprehensive medical benefits to members, often with lower member cost-sharing than most plans offered by insurers. However, they generally reimburse only for services provided by doctors or facilities within the approved network, and they may impose greater restrictions on care, such as requiring pre-certification for hospital admissions and other high-cost services, or requiring that members seek care from a specialist physician only after being referred by a *gatekeeper* primary-care physician. HMOs grew more influential during the 1980s as care management offered cost savings, but have declined in popularity during recent years as members weighed the cost savings against the restrictions on provider choice and care patterns.

28.3.4 Provider-Owned Organizations

In the 1990s, providers sought to reclaim control of care delivery and reimbursement for services. They established physician-hospital organizations (PHOs), provider-sponsored organizations (PSOs), and provider-sponsored networks (PSNs) as provider-owned organizations that would contract directly with employers, government, insurance companies or other managed care organizations to provide care. These organizations are locally focused and may offer marketing advantages when compared with provider networks developed by national insurers. However, these organizations may not be as skilled or efficient in administrative services or organizational management, or may not be as well prepared to assess and accept risks associated with medical costs (e.g., utilization and cost trends, changing demographics, etc.)

28.3.5 Other Funding Arrangements

28.3.5.1 Fully insured plans

The classic insurance agreement is known as a fully insured plan. Under fully insured contracts, the premiums represent the entire financial responsibility of the policyholder; the insurer guarantees payment for all the claims incurred by the covered members and thus assumes the entire risk of adverse claims experience, but gains the potential to profit from favorable experience. The insurer will further be responsible for premium taxes and will be subject to the insurance laws and regulations of the state where the contract is delivered.

Certain types of funding arrangements contain special financial provisions that fall outside the regular insurance function. These arrangements affect timing of cash flows or the level of risk transfer between the insurer and the group. These arrangements may exist as complete contracts, or as riders that modify existing contracts.

28.3.5.2 Self-insured plans

Some employers prefer to create self-insured plans, which retain the claims risk associated with covering the members of the group and do not guarantee payment of benefits in the manner of an insurance company. These plans allow the employer to retain funds that would otherwise be paid as premiums, and earn investment income on the funds. These plans also allow the employer to avoid premium taxes and government mandates to cover certain services. The decision to self-fund, however, must carefully consider the plan sponsor's ability to absorb the associated risks, the level of expertise needed to administer the benefits, and the cost-effectiveness of the funding mechanism and the method of administration. Often, self-insured employers will contract with insurers or third-party administrators (TPAs) to perform the functions of administering benefits without assuming insurance risks (and therefore charging an extra premium for risk protection). Commonly known as ASO contracts, these agreements cover the following services:

- Enrollment;
- Eligibility;
- Claim administration;
- Consultation on benefit plan design; and
- Actuarial and financial services.

The ASO contract may be further modified to provide individual conversion contracts as needed through the insurer. Some employers seek to insure themselves against the most extreme deviations in claims costs through stop-loss coverage that covers claims in excess of defined limits. The limits may refer to claims incurred by individuals (specific stop-loss), by the entire group (aggregate stop-loss), or both.

28.3.5.3 Reserveless plans

Insurers prefer to include a charge in the premiums for the purpose of building up reserves. However, employers have exerted greater pressure on insurers to find ways to allow the policyholders to maintain more of the funds that would be used to build those reserves. In a reserveless agreement, the employer agrees to a terminal premium payment upon cancellation in return for a reduction of the premium that would be directed toward reserve accumulation.

Since the terminal premium payment may be substantial, the insurer must monitor the policyholder and underwrite on an ongoing basis in order to be certain that the premium can be collected. The policyholder may establish its own reserve for the terminal premium; the funds held in that reserve are often subject to fewer restrictions on investment practices than are the reserves held by an insurer. Reserveless plans are sometimes designed to defer premium, often creating a 90- to 120-day grace period for each premium payment—though all unpaid premiums would come due immediately upon termination.

28.3.5.4 Minimum premium contracts

A minimum premium contract is essentially a combination of a fully insured plan and a self-insured plan. Under this arrangement, the policyholder deposits most or all of the portion of the total premium that represents expected claims into a trust or separate account. The insurer will draw directly from the account to pay claims, while assuming the risk for claims in excess of the account funds. The funds in the trust do not constitute premiums and as such are generally not subject to premium taxes. The premium therefore equals the fully insured premium, minus the account contributions and the premium tax on the self-insured portion. This arrangement is similar to stop-loss coverage, which has become more prevalent than the minimum-premium plan in recent years due in part to a California court decision that considers the account contributions subject to premium tax.

28.3.5.5 Stop-loss contracts

Stop-loss coverage is often attached to an ASO contract as a method of allowing the policyholder to insure against the risk of excessive claims costs. The level of costs that must be reached before the stop-loss coverage pays benefits is called the attachment point. The attachment point may refer to claims for one individual (specific stop-loss) or for the group in total (aggregate stop-loss). Both forms of stop-loss coverage may be combined; in those instances, the specific limits apply first and may thus reduce the cost of aggregate coverage. Both forms may accumulate claims toward the limit on an incurred basis or on a paid basis.

28.3.5.6 Retrospective premium arrangements

This arrangement allows the policyholder to pay a lower premium upfront—usually around 90 percent of the regular premium—but requires the policyholder to pay additional premium in the event of adverse experience. Favorable experience may result in a refund payable directly to the policyholder or to the rate stabilization reserve. This arrangement most commonly exists as a rider attached to a standard group plan, and negatively impacts the insurer's ability to accumulate a rate stabilization reserve.

28.4 Overview of Health Economics

Health insurance differs from other forms of insurance—like life, homeowners, or automobile coverages—by engaging into extensive relationships beyond that between the insurer and the covered member. Generally, the member is not responsible for submitting claims against the policy or collecting the benefits of the policy; the providers of covered services submit claims on behalf of their patients and are reimbursed by the insurer for the services and goods provided. Health insurance policies may ensure access to providers of health care services (medical, dental, or pharmaceutical) and are most often built around networks of preferred providers, who agree to a schedule of reimbursements, a per-member capitation payment or discounts on charges for services. Some products cover only the services received from providers within a specified network.

Health insurance policies typically provide coverage for routine events of care in addition to relatively infrequent and often unexpected events. As such, health insurance is partially prepaid medical care and partially catastrophic risk protection. Most plans require *cost sharing*, that is, partial payments that members make toward the cost of the care they receive. The most common forms are a *deductible*, or an amount that a member must pay out of pocket before the insurer pays any costs; *coinsurance*, or a percentage of the cost that the member pays after meeting the deductible; and a *copayment*—or *copay*—that is, generally a fixed dollar amount required from a member for a specified service (such as an office visit or a prescription). Often, the services that involve member copays are not subject to the deductible and coinsurance; that is, the insurer will reimburse the entire amount reimbursed to the provider less the copay, even when the member has not yet met the deductible. The deductible helps the insurer avoid the costs and administrative efforts of paying some of the claims.

Additionally, as plan deductibles and copays increase, members are less likely to utilize services, which will lead to lower premiums. The increased member cost-sharing may discourage unnecessary utilization, but may have undesirable health consequences. For example, consider a physician office visit for a sore throat or other mild symptoms that may be easily treated without professional intervention. A member who is responsible for little or no cost sharing is more likely to see the doctor than is a member who would need to pay a larger copay or has yet to reach the deductible amount.

In contrast, consider a physician office visit for a bone scan that could identify tumors or risks for osteoporosis. Early detection of such conditions may prevent high-cost illnesses or fractures. The member responsible for more of the cost of the office visit is more likely to forgo it—and the missed opportunity to detect the precursor of the condition may ultimately lead to higher total costs. The challenge for the plan sponsor is therefore to design a plan that maximizes value by ensuring appropriate levels of different forms of care.

28.4.1 Health vs. Health Care

In the context of health insurance and benefit plans, the term *health care* commonly refers to a basket of services such as those provided by hospitals and physicians, medications prescribed, facilities that provide forms of specialized care (such as inpatient rehabilitation facilities or skilled nursing facilities), transportation via ambulance, and durable medical equipment—in short, services that are offered by professionals for purchase to improve or maintain health. Maintaining one's health involves lifestyle choices and activities that are not necessarily under the jurisdiction of a benefit plan. However, benefit plans may seek to encourage personal health maintenance by providing wellness programs, giving discounts for healthy new members, or applying higher rates for smokers and other policyholders who exhibit potentially costly health conditions.

28.4.2 Stakeholders in the Health Care Benefits Environment

There are five major groups of stakeholders in the environment of health care benefits. These stakeholders influence the health care and benefits environment to a differing extent in every country in the world.

- Individuals—the end users of health care services and the benefit plans that fund them;

- Providers—the hospitals, physicians, and other medical, dental, and pharmaceutical professionals that offer health care services;
- Employers—broadly defined to include private businesses, government employee groups, associations, and other plan sponsors;
- Insurers—broadly defined to include insurance companies, HCSCs, and HMOs; and
- Governments—federal, state, and local agencies that monitor and regulate other stakeholders to varying degrees.

28.4.3 Various Models of Health Care Funding Systems

Each country has developed its own health care delivery and funding methods. These methodologies can be categorized into four general models.[1]

28.4.3.1 The Bismarck model

In France, Germany, Japan, and Switzerland, among others, health care services are provided and funded through a model that can be traced to the Prussian chancellor Otto von Bismarck's Health Insurance Bill of 1883. In these countries, health care providers and payers are private entities. Individuals generally are required to participate in one of the available insurance plans. Insurance plans are funded through payroll deduction, are not-for-profit, and do not decline enrollment to potential members. Providers are subject to tight regulation of medical services and fees but are consequently protected against liability for malpractice if they can show that treatment followed accepted procedures. Patients may be responsible for payment upon receipt of services, though most or all of the payment is returned to the patient through the insurance program.

28.4.3.2 The Beveridge model

In Great Britain, Italy, Spain, Hong Kong, and much of Scandinavia, a model associated with 1940s British social reformer William Beveridge empowers the government to provide and finance most health care services. Most, if not all, hospitals and clinics are government-owned; the majority of physicians are government employees; and the government dictates provider fee schedules for reimbursement. Some physicians operate private practices or supplement their income by providing services outside the confines of the national health system. Insurance companies may therefore sell policies that cover such supplemental services or arrange for preferential treatment in the distribution of care (known as *queue jumping*).

28.4.3.3 The national health insurance model

In Canada, Taiwan, and South Korea, elements of the Bismarck and Beveridge models create a system wherein health care is provided by private doctors and hospitals, but the government pays for the care through a single-payer insurance plan funded by some combination of taxes and premiums. It should be noted that the Canadian Medicare system is administered through the provinces, and not all health care services are delivered through Medicare. The

1 These categories are taken from Reid (2009).

principles laid out in the Canada Health Act of 1984 and reaffirmed by the First Ministers' Accord in 2003 require the provincial health care plans to be universal, accessible, portable, comprehensive, and publicly managed on a not-for-profit basis.

28.4.3.4 The out-of-pocket model

In most countries in the world, where incomes are too low and provider access too scattered to organize a national plan funded at an appropriate level, people receive the medical care that they can afford, purchased out-of-pocket without an insurance plan of any kind. These populations may therefore be more susceptible to disease epidemics, since medical care is spotty and uncertain. The out-of-pocket model also represents a portion of expenditures in economically advanced countries. Insurance plans, whether public or private, may exclude coverage for elective procedures, alternative medicinal treatments, or other services based on economic benefit analysis or potential for abuse. Thus, even in countries that have implemented national health plans, some costs of health care are paid directly by the patient.

28.4.3.5 All four systems at work in the United States

The funding models described above all apply to different populations; indeed, millions of people experience each of the models at some point in their lifetimes. For most working people under age 65 who receive employer benefits, their coverage is akin to the Bismarck funding model. For military members receiving government-funded care at government-owned facilities through the Department of Veterans Affairs, their coverage mimics the Beveridge model. For Medicare and Medicaid recipients, their coverage is like the national health insurance model. Finally, for the uninsured—most of whom are working-class people who earn too much to qualify for public insurance programs, but do not have employer-provided coverage available to them—their care is largely funded out-of-pocket.

28.4.4 Characteristics of the Current Health Care Environment

There are several issues that affect the economic environment for the provision and funding of health care services. Policy debates center around the consequences of these issues, and the extent to which public efforts can influence these forces. Since the various stakeholders have competing agendas on some issues, the effectiveness or desirability of any given proposal is often a matter of perspective—or put simply, one person's health care expenditure is another's health care income.

28.4.4.1 Annual increases in per-capita health expenditure

In most advanced economies around the world, the health care expenditure per capita has increased faster than overall inflation in recent years. Table 28.1 shows the annualized percentage rate of growth between 2000 and 2007 in several OECD countries.[2]

2 OECD Health Data 2010, available at http://stats.oecd.org/index.aspx?DataSetCode=HEALTH, accessed April 17, 2011.

TABLE 28.1 Health Care Expenditure per Capita in the United States, 2000–2007

Country	2000	2002	2005	2007	Avg % Growth
Australia	$2,266	$2,559	$2,980	$3,353	5.8%
Canada	$2,519	$2,875	$3,456	$3,867	6.3%
France	$2,553	$2,931	$3,306	$3,593	5.0%
Germany	$2,669	$2,934	$3,353	$3,619	4.4%
Japan	$1,969	$2,137	$2,474	$2,729	4.8%
Mexico	$508	$584	$731	$824	7.2%
United Kingdom	$1,837	$2,192	$2,701	$2,990	7.2%
United States	$4,703	$5,453	$6,563	$7,285	6.5%

These annual increases, or *trends* as they are commonly known, may occur at different rates for different categories of service.

28.4.4.2 Rising share of GDP for health expenditures

In most advanced economies around the world, the percentage of GDP directed toward health expenditures has grown in recent years. This phenomenon is especially evident in the United States and has been a major driver of the urgency behind efforts to reform or overhaul the U.S. health care system. Table 28.2 illustrates the growth in health care costs as a percentage of GDP in several OECD countries.[3]

TABLE 28.2 Health Care as Percentage of GDP, 2000–2007

Country	2000	2002	2005	2007
Australia	8.0%	8.4%	8.4%	8.5%
Canada	8.8%	9.6%	9.9%	10.1%
France	10.1%	10.5%	11.1%	11.0%
Germany	10.3%	10.6%	10.7%	10.4%
Japan	7.7%	8.0%	8.2%	8.1%
Mexico	5.1%	5.6%	5.9%	5.8%
United Kingdom	7.0%	7.6%	8.3%	8.4%
United States	13.4%	14.8%	15.4%	15.7%

28.4.4.3 Growth in the number of uninsured and underinsured

In the United States, these cost trends have contributed to steady growth in the number of people who go without health insurance or are underinsured—that is, whose benefits are often inadequate to cover expenses associated with catastrophic events. Table 28.3 contains annual estimates of U.S. population and number of uninsured between 2000 and 2009 (U.S. Census Bureau, 2011, Table HIA-1).

3 OECD Health Data 2010.

TABLE 28.3 Percentage of Uninsured in United States, 2000–2009

Year	U.S. Population Estimate (000s)	Number of Uninsured Estimate (000s)	Percentage of Uninsured Estimate
2009	304,280	50,674	16.7%
2008	301,483	46,340	15.4%
2007	299,106	45,657	15.3%
2006	296,824	46,995	15.8%
2005	293,834	44,815	15.3%
2004	291,166	43,498	14.9%
2003	288,280	43,404	15.1%
2002	285,933	42,019	14.7%
2001	282,082	39,760	14.1%
2000	279,517	38,426	13.7%

Generally, the uninsured receive lower levels of health care than the insured; further ripple effects of growth in uninsured numbers are observed through increased financial pressures on public programs, and on health care providers, who may provide more uncompensated care.

28.4.4.4 Erosion of retiree benefits

Plan sponsors' reactions to economic pressures include reduction of benefits provided to retirees. Health benefits for retired employees not yet eligible for Medicare (or supplemental benefits for those eligible for Medicare), and other ancillary benefits are less prevalent or less generous than in previous times. Employers offering retiree health coverage have increased member premium contribution and cost-sharing requirements in recent years. The Medicare Modernization Act of 2003 included a provision to subsidize this coverage—but the subsidies are only available for retirees who are eligible for Medicare.

28.4.4.5 Tax treatment of employer-provided health insurance

In the United States, employer contributions to health insurance are tax deductible as a business expense, and employer-paid premiums for health benefits are not considered taxable income to the employees. Tax exemptions for employee group benefits date to the 1940s, developed in reaction to wage and price controls implemented during World War II. More recently, tax advantages for employer contributions to employee health savings accounts, and tax credits to assist in the purchase of insurance by small employers that might not otherwise be able to afford it, have helped stem the tide against expansion of the segment of uninsured and reduced pressures of health care cost inflation for workers who are more vulnerable to cost increases. However, concerns exist regarding the share of the market that consists of benefit-rich plans—for which fewer financial controls on service utilization are in place—and the suboptimal targeting of tax subsidies, which result in greater value for higher-income households.

28.4.4.6 Shift to less stringent managed care in the United States

Member satisfaction with the requirements of managed care has decreased, thus HMO products are less popular than in previous years. Employers and other plan sponsors find that PPO products are best received among their members, as public backlash developed in recent years against procedural controls and restrictions on utilization. Financial incentives that steer consumers toward lower-cost choices and reduced demand for services have been more broadly accepted by the members.

28.4.4.7 Insurance industry consolidation and competition

Mergers and acquisitions among private insurance companies, and conversion of not-for-profit Blue Cross/Blue Shield plans to for-profit, stockholder-owned insurance companies, have impacted the competitive landscape, the regulatory environment, and the policymaking sphere. Within most states and metropolitan areas, the market concentration of the largest health insurers has grown in recent years.[4] The report observed that in 2008, the five largest carriers held a combined market share of 75 percent or more in 34 of 39 states, while that level of concentration existed in just 19 of 34 states in 2002.

28.5 Key Influences on Health Care Funding Models

The various funding models and designs of insurance products, social programs, and self-funded plans all represent efforts to make improvements in three key areas of influence: cost, access, and quality. Natural trade-offs exist between these areas. Increased access commonly increases costs, and similar exchanges between each pair of issues do not necessarily represent a net improvement to the system. However, it is possible—and some would argue that it is critical—to focus on solutions that strengthen one or more areas without offsetting detractions. Within each of these areas, the interdependence between stakeholders may complicate efforts to control costs, expand access, and improve quality, but the interdependence highlights the importance of shared solutions.

28.5.1 Issues of Cost

Individuals seek to control costs for health care services and insurance coverage through methods such as engaging in healthy lifestyle choices; comparison shopping for insurance plans and choosing benefit designs most consistent with their personal budgets; or choosing facilities for care based in part on insurance benefit designs (e.g., lower copayments for visits to urgent care facilities than to emergency rooms).

Providers seek to control their costs through measures that improve efficiency in administration with insurers, by negotiating for reimbursement levels that fit with their investments in new technology, and may go farther to form provider-owned organizations. They may seek to influence legislation regarding medical malpractice awards.

Employers seek to control their costs through restrictions on eligibility for employee benefits; fixing dollar contributions to employee benefits or requiring greater employee contributions; leveraging competition among insurers; and self-funding benefits in a manner consistent with their financial capability and risk appetite.

4 Government Accountability Office (2009).

Insurers seek to control their costs through selection and underwriting of potential enrolled groups and retention of existing inforce groups; coverage exclusions for health conditions that new members already exhibit prior to commencement of coverage (known as *pre-existing conditions*); network development and fee schedule negotiations with providers; improvements in administrative efficiency; and analysis and influence on federal and state regulations that may ultimately increase service costs.

Governments fill dual roles as plan sponsors for their employees and the members of the programs they administer and as regulators of conditions in the private-sector environment. Thus, they may restrict eligibility for benefits, shift costs for certain services, authorize lower reimbursements to providers that offer services to program members, or set restrictions on insurer and provider practices.

28.5.2 Issues of Access

Individuals seek to ensure or expand their access to health care (and funding for health care) through favoring employers that provide insurance benefits; collective bargaining to preserve or expand existing employer benefits; and directly or indirectly encouraging providers to join their insurer's preferred network.

Employers assist in these efforts for reasons such as employee recruitment and retention, improved employee productivity and tax advantages. Similarly, providers have an interest in ensuring that their services are available and affordable. Hospitals and physicians alike direct a portion of their efforts toward charity care or uncompensated care, the costs of which are not directly charged to the patients that receive it.

Insurers may seek to expand access through development of provider networks and insurance products that fit the varying risk appetites and purchasing power of potential customers. Recent years observe an expansion in the use of consumer-driven health plans (CDHPs) that cause a greater portion of health care costs to be paid out-of-pocket by the members that receive the services, and thus provide incentives for members to seek more cost-effective forms of care. The members can accumulate funds to use as needed for their out-of-pocket costs, often with the help of their employers. Thus the most common design of a CDHP pairs a high-deductible health plan (HDHP) with a health savings account (HSA) in which members may save money that can be used for the high plan deductible or for other eligible expenditures.

Governments help to expand access most directly through public programs, usually targeted first toward people in need of the most care (such as the elderly) or toward the people who are least able to afford the services that they need. Other governmental efforts to ensure access to health care funding include insurance market reforms and restrictions on rating, tax deductions and credits for health insurance premiums and HSA contributions, and any-willing-provider laws that require insurers to include all providers willing to accept the reimbursement schedule developed for network providers.

28.5.3 Issues of Quality

Quality health care is defined differently by each of the stakeholders, and by each individual participant involved in the provision of care. Thus, patients seek improved health outcomes and attentive providers; providers work to maintain freedom to make their best professional judgment of optimal treatment patterns within the confines of insurance network contracts; and insurers strive for cost efficiency in the services covered. While these concepts are intuitive, it is a complicated problem to reach consensus on the terms by which high quality could be defined and measured. Even where systemic disagreements and disconnects between the stakeholders can be resolved, standardization of quality is difficult to achieve, due to the personal characteristics of each patient that dictate the forms and levels of customized treatment needed.

Considerations of quality in health care delivery include necessary care delivered by qualified facilities and professionals; medical practice consistent with professional standards of practice or accepted community norms; and health outcomes that meet or exceed expectations and goals. URAC, the organization formerly known as the Utilization Review Accreditation Commission, accredits health care organizations for their adherence to standards for network management, utilization management, quality improvement, credentialing, and member protection. The National Committee for Quality Assurance (NCQA) likewise accredits managed care plans, with the help of the Health Plan Employer Data and Information Set (HEDIS) that collects quantitative performance data in a format that can be used for meaningful statistical analysis. NCQA certification is mandated in some states. The Joint Commission, formerly known as the Joint Commission on Accreditation of Healthcare Organizations (JCAHO), similarly accredits health care providers that meet standards for patient safety.

The ability to measure quality on a consistent basis is enhanced by innovations in health information technology, and efforts to increase its use among providers and insurers. Electronic transmission of health information can improve coordination of care among the various providers who treat a patient, and can reduce the frequency of medical errors by storing accurate medical history and warn against mixing medications that interact in a harmful manner. However, privacy concerns must be addressed, especially when written into law.

Insurers seek further guarantees of quality through the use of pay-for-performance (PFP) reimbursement agreements and evidence-based treatment protocols. In order to find the level of treatment that is most effective and most cost-efficient, PFP seeks to strike a balance between fee-for-service reimbursements, which may encourage excessive utilization, and capitated payment rates, which may encourage insufficient utilization. Similarly, evidence-based medicine attempts to improve cost efficiency by encouraging the treatment patterns found most effective by clinical studies or otherwise certified by the best available objective evidence.

28.6 Overview of Disability Insurance

Disability insurance plans provide a level of income replacement for people who lose some or all of their ability to perform work functions or other daily activities. The events that trigger benefits under disability insurance plans are infrequent; therefore, the insurance function is well suited to disability policies. Products exist to respond to disability for a short term (typically less than one year) or for a long term (most often after the short-term disability benefits expire, and may pay benefits until normal retirement age). These products are not intended to replace employment income entirely, as that could create a disincentive to return to work—or even a moral hazard that encourages disablement—but they allow disabled workers to meet basic financial obligations while they recover or rehabilitate.

The most important feature of a disability insurance contract is the definition of disability. The definition speaks to the insured's capability to perform material and substantial occupational duties, and the loss of earnings that the insured suffers as a result. The policy benefits apply first for a specified period of time during which the insured is limited in performing their *own occupation*. The policy benefits may be extended if the disability persists beyond that time, though some policies restrict these extended benefits to only those less capable of performing the duties of *any gainful occupation* for which their education, training, or experience suits them. Some policies further reduce frequency of payout by basing eligibility on the inability of the insured to feed, bathe, or dress themselves—to perform basic *activities of daily living* (ADLs).

Long-term disability (LTD) benefits are commonly paid out on a monthly basis after an elimination period, which serves the same function as a deductible on a health insurance policy. The benefits are paid to each recipient for either a specified period of time (most commonly two years or five years) or until *normal retirement age* as determined by Social Security. The benefit amount paid each month is usually a function of earnings prior to the disability and is offset by income received through other avenues such as Social Security disability income or workers compensation benefits. The offset is important to ensure that total post-disability income and benefits do not exceed pre-disability earnings, which would create a disincentive to return to work.

Benefits are subject to certain limitations and exclusions based on the subjective nature of the evaluation of disablement or the potential for abuse (such as for mental and nervous conditions), self-inflicted injuries, acts of war, or criminal acts. Optional features of disability insurance contracts include cost of living adjustments to benefits, spousal or survivor benefits, and extra payments for day-care expenses, lost pension contributions, or for catastrophic disablements such as total paralysis.

In comparison to LTD benefits, short-term disability (STD) benefits are generally payable after a shorter elimination period, in smaller amounts and for a shorter period of time. While STD claims are much more frequent than LTD claims, overall costs for STD tend to be much more predictable than LTD due to the reduced severity and reduced variance among claims. It should be noted that the presence of STD benefits may ultimately increase LTD claims, since STD benefits make it easier for one who is disabled to stay out of work through the LTD elimination period.

28.7 Overview of Long-Term Care Insurance

Group long-term care (LTC) insurance provides coverage for costs associated with custodial care. As aging trends help create demand for services that assist the disabled and the chronically ill—and programs that provide public funding for those services face pressure to keep up—insurance-based solutions become more attractive. Employers who recognize the growing demand may thus sponsor voluntary group LTC plans, typically requiring the employees that select it to pay the entire cost, but some employers subsidize the cost of coverage. An aggressive enrollment campaign is crucial to generating the level of employee participation that covers marketing and acquisition costs while helping to ensure that the plan is not joined only by the people who perceive the greatest need for it. Thus, the sale of LTC products involves a first sale effort to market the products to plan sponsors and a second sale effort to encourage group members to sign up for the coverage offered to the group.

LTC insurance most commonly reimburses the costs of custodial care, either paying the provider directly or paying to the insured, with claims subject to review that the providers are appropriately qualified per the policy certificate. Similar to disability insurance, a waiting period and a specific benefit trigger typically apply. Other coverage models reimburse a fixed amount per day or per week.

The benefit trigger is defined within the Health Insurance Portability and Accountability Act (HIPAA). The trigger must be either a severe cognitive impairment that requires substantial supervision or an inability to perform at least two of a prescribed list of ADLs. The list includes bathing, maintaining continence, dressing, eating, toileting, and transferring from bed to chair. Generally, care is covered as provided by nursing homes, assisted living facilities, hospices, home health services, independence support services, and care management services. Training for caregivers and respite care is included in the coverage.

28.8 Overview of Group Life Insurance

Group life insurance products provide payments to a group member's designated beneficiaries upon the death of the member. They are sold on a short-term basis, rather than the permanent whole life or longer term coverage often found on policies sold to individuals. The contract defines the benefit amount payable and generally does not allow members to choose different benefit amounts. Some products define the benefit payable as a multiple of earnings or may develop a table of different amounts payable based on job titles. Group members do not undergo the same extent of medical underwriting that individual life insurance requires. An *individual health statement,* which is a questionnaire that asks for information about a member's medical history, will usually suffice at a member level. The insurer achieves additional control of risk by enforcing rules of eligibility for enrollment and *participation requirements,* which define a minimum percentage of eligible employees that must enroll in coverage in order for the group policy to take effect. Members may be allowed to purchase additional benefits, but at their own cost and possibly with additional underwriting.

Premiums are generally expressed in terms of a monthly rate per *unit of coverage*—in the United States, typically $1,000—that will be payable as a benefit. The total premium charged to the group will account for the demographic composition of the group, but the average monthly rate will be applied to each unit of coverage received by a member, regardless of the age or gender of the member. Similarly, it is often the case that when employee contributions are required to pay a portion of the premium (or the entire premium), the amount required cannot be different for males and females.

In many cases, the benefit payable for one member's death is greater than the entire group's annual premium. Such an event poses a substantial risk to the financial stability of a small- or moderate-sized group carrier. As such, these carriers will seek to reduce their exposure through *reinsurance* on some or all of the value of their inforce policies. Reinsurance allows the insurer to receive a payment after paying out the benefits of the sold group policy. This gives the insurer the ability to write policies of a higher total value without taking on all the risk associated with the higher value.

A group plan may contain one or more optional ancillary coverages that provide different benefits than the standard death benefit. The premium for the basic group life coverage offered to employees will often be paid entirely by the employer, but the ancillary coverages may require the employee to pay part—or all—of the premium. Members may be able to purchase *dependent life* coverage that pay benefits upon the death of their spouse or children. Dependent life premiums are almost always paid entirely by the employee. The benefit levels of dependent life coverage are generally relatively small compared to the employee coverage amount. *Accidental death and dismemberment* (AD&D) coverage pays benefits when deaths or injuries occur due to accidents. The injuries typically covered under AD&D plans include loss of limbs, loss of fingers, paralysis, or loss of sight. The benefit amount paid for these injuries are lower than the death benefit amount. Members may be able to purchase coverage that pays a *survivor income benefit*, which pays an ongoing benefit—usually a percentage of the deceased member's salary—to a surviving eligible beneficiary. Another optional coverage pays *living benefits* (also known as accelerated death benefits), which are paid to members upon diagnosis with a terminal illness, incidence of a catastrophic illness (e.g., heart attack, stroke, or renal failure), or development of health conditions that require long-term care in a nursing home or permanent home health care. Precise definitions of the events that trigger payments are a necessary component of product development for living benefits.

When a group terminates its coverage, the insurer typically offers the members a chance to *convert* their basic life coverage to individually owned permanent policies at regular rates. On average, the members who exercise the opportunity to convert are less healthy than the members who do not convert. Thus, an insurer must generally include a margin in the premiums to mitigate risk. In addition to the conversion option, some insurers offer a *portability* provision, which permits the members to keep their group life coverage in force even after terminating employment through the plan sponsor.

CHAPTER 29

External Factors

29.1 Forces Driving the Need for Benefit Plans

As noted in Chapter 28, benefit plans allow their enrollees to pool financial risk and to assure themselves greater accessibility to services, whether those plans are sold on a group basis or an individual basis. From the carrier's perspective, group products improve risk selection and allow for more efficient marketing and administration. Other forces influence the demand for group benefit plans, the design of the available plans, and the primary objectives in establishing funding for the plans.

Employer liability laws hold employers responsible to various degrees for employment-related deaths, injuries or illnesses. Employers may therefore protect themselves against lawsuits by providing workers compensation insurance, health insurance to facilitate prompt treatment for medical conditions and disability-income insurance to help protect against longer-term financial hardships. Additionally, governments or other entities may require their contractors to demonstrate acceptable levels of liability insurance.

Benefit plans help employers differentiate themselves when competing for potential employees. The existence of an employee health plan may encourage interviewees to select an employer. The value of a health or disability plan may entice an existing employee to remain with the current employer rather than to retire, seek a job change or make an entrepreneurial effort that might result in a new competitor for the employer. Large majorities of employees consider health insurance to be their most valuable employer-provided benefit and would prefer to receive health benefits through their employer rather than to receive additional salary to purchase health insurance on their own. Additionally, consider that younger employees who do not expect to incur high health costs may choose to participate in an insurance program simply because the premiums are largely (or completely) paid by the employer. If left completely to their own devices with respect to the decision to purchase insurance, these healthy people would be less likely to buy coverage; the insured block would increasingly consist only of less healthy members and average per-member claims costs would increase. Other chapters will examine this skewing of the risk pool, which is known as *anti-selection*, in different contexts.

Employers lose productivity when their employees are sick, injured, disabled or concerned about the risks of these maladies. In recent years, growing numbers of employers have instituted wellness programs in an effort to keep employees healthier—and more productive—while lowering insurance costs. Even when benefits are not provided directly by an employer, as is the case for some forms of voluntary LTC insurance, the employer may find it advantageous to provide a platform for a sales agent or broker to advertise directly to the employees.

Tax policy over several decades has encouraged employer-provided benefits. In the United States, employee benefits were exempt from World War II-era wage and price controls, which gave incentive to employers to use more generous benefits to attract talent. Generally, employer-paid health benefits are tax deductible to the employer, and do not constitute taxable income from the employee's perspective. Favorable tax treatment allows the employer to purchase coverage for the group of employees that is more comprehensive than the individual employees could purchase on their own. In addition, employee contributions to insurance premiums can be made with pre-tax dollars.

The Revenue Act of 1978 established Section 125 of the IRC. Benefit plans established in response to this regulation allowed employers to provide funds or credits to cafeteria plans that an employee could use to purchase coverage. Pre-tax dollars could also be contributed to flexible spending accounts (FSAs) used to purchase section 213(d) expenses not covered in a medical benefit plan. In more recent years, health savings accounts (HSAs) and health reimbursement accounts (HRAs) have gained attention as a method by which employers can increase control medical expense, while employees can gain control and flexibility in the use of the account.

29.2 Cultural and Social Values

29.2.1 Ethics and Religion

Societal ethics influence the demand to establish a national health plan or a program that provides benefits for a segment of the population (e.g., Medicare for the elderly in the United States) and affect the design of the plan or program. Ethical questions spark debate on issues of cost and accessibility when resources are limited. For example, medical ethicists consider the appropriate allocation of resources toward expensive therapies for advanced diseases or toward broadening availability of basic care.

Religious beliefs may impact the nature or timing of medical care services that a patient seeks, such as treatment received—or declined—at the end of life, refusal of medications that contain prohibited ingredients or the preference of an expectant mother to give birth at home. Some care providers may cite their beliefs in refusing to perform certain procedures (e.g., abortions) or prescribing contraceptives. Similarly, some policymakers and taxpayers oppose public funding for such services on religious grounds, while others cite spiritual compassion for the sick and destitute in support of efforts to expand public programs that ensure funding for health care services.

29.2.2 Objectives of Health Care Systems in Different Cultures

Within each country around the world, the sense of urgency by which various concerns must be faced can be quite different. In Third World countries where access to care is spotty, epidemics can spread relatively unchecked through vast numbers of people. Public efforts may therefore be geared toward prevention of sexually transmitted diseases, contraception, or improving access to clean water and proper nutrition.

In OECD countries where the basics of good health are more widely available, public efforts may be focused on segments of the population that lack sufficient access to care in the absence of those efforts. Principles of national solidarity and social justice serve as primary motivators for those nations where a guarantee of universal coverage exists.

29.2.3 Entities that Provide Funding for Health Care

Consider the various stakeholders in the benefits environment as referenced in Chapter 28 and these examples of how each stakeholder provides funding for health care benefits.

- Individuals—primarily through insurance premiums, employee contributions to group-sponsored plans, tax payments and directly out of pocket;
- Employers—primarily through insurance premiums, employer direct payment of claims for ASO plans and tax payments;
- Providers—reduced reimbursements for services provided to recipients of public aid, discounts on charges for members of insurance programs or managed care organizations and charity care;
- Government—financing of public programs of varying size and scope; and
- Insurers—the role of the insurer in the group benefits environment is often seen as intermediary between the other stakeholders, with considerations for risk protection and influence on service cost levels. Governments and employers can also be considered to be intermediaries, though of a different form. Federal and state or provincial governments direct tax payments toward programs like Medicare and Medicaid and employers seek to recover the costs of their employee benefit programs through the prices they charge for their products.

29.3 Demographics

Various demographic forces affect availability of services, whether through provider supply or patient demand, utilization and cost levels and trends, and funding mechanisms for coverage of service costs.

- Aging Population and Increased Life Expectancy—Per-capita health expenditures are highest on the elderly (generally used to refer to people age 65 or older). Thus, as life expectancy increases and a population ages, cost pressures are most clearly evident on plans that cover the elderly. In the United States, the oldest of the baby boomers (generally referring to people born between 1946 and 1964) are eligible for Medicare. The aging of this cohort supports a Census Bureau projection[1] that the number of elderly will double between 2010 and 2050. The cost increases may be more properly attributable to the costs of care at the end of life, as the most intense and expensive forms of care are provided in life-saving efforts.
- Fertility Rates—In recent years, economic pressures have contributed to a decline in birth rates. The overall decline is not observed among women in their 40s, as advances in medical technology and personal tradeoffs lead to greater numbers of women choosing to postpone child-bearing or to extend periods of fertility. Additionally, the highest per-capita expenditures among children are incurred during the first year of lif. (Sutton, Hamilton & Mathews, 2011).
- Geographic Issues—Urban population centers, and their suburban surroundings, generally see higher incomes (U.S. Department of Agriculture, 2011) and greater

1 U.S. Census Bureau. Interim Projections by Age, Sex, Race, and Hispanic Origin, Table 2a. http://www.census.gov/population/www/projections/usinterimproj/. Based on Census 2000 data. Accessed April 17, 2011.

access to providers (Government Accountability Office, 2003) than do rural areas. In recent decades, the percentage of the populace that resides in rural areas has declined.[2]

- Income and Education—Higher incomes and advanced education generally correlate with good health. Thus the World Health Organization rankings of nations' health care systems adjust the measures of population health for relative levels of income and education (World Health Organization, 2000).
- The Role of DI and LTC—Disability insurance benefits alleviate the ongoing pressures of earning income, which helps those who are temporarily disabled or diseased focus their time and energy on recovery. Expected life spans follow, as they do when LTC insurance assists the elderly whose living situations and personal health may make them more susceptible to falls, improper medication, or other potentially fatal risks.

29.4 Impact of Policy and Regulation

29.4.1 Key Contributors to Health Care Policymaking

Elected officials formally introduce legislation and provide publicly accountable faces for policy discourse. The making of policy—and the supporting regulations from the agencies that implement and enforce principles of legislation—includes input from other contributors. Trade and industry organizations like America's Health Insurance Plans, the Blue Cross Blue Shield Association and the National Association of Insurance Commissioners (NAIC) provide data and analysis on policy proposals. Further, they may advance their own proposals, offer public comment to assist (or resist) specific efforts, or make financial contributions to support lawmakers and candidates friendly to their perspectives.

Private research organizations such as the Kaiser Family Foundation, the Urban Institute and the RAND Corporation—colloquially known as think tanks—similarly provide analysis on proposals at various stages of debate and their impacts to existing conditions. Their reports supplement information available from government agencies like the Congressional Budget Office. Advocacy groups such as AARP analyze and comment on the impact of proposals to the specific group of people, or political perspective, that they represent.

The input of actuaries, often channeled through research performed or coordinated by the SOA and the American Academy of Actuaries (AAA), adds special value to policy debate. The SOA and the AAA take care to present nonpartisan support and scenario analysis that thinks through potential consequences, intended or unintended, of policy proposals. Actuaries have offered testimony, issue briefs, cost-benefit analysis and informal comments to presidential administrations, congressional committees and public media.

29.4.2 Role of Policy

Public policies legislated by federal or state lawmakers seek to address the issues of cost, access, and quality, as well as to ensure the solvency of public and private health plans. Given

2 Census Bureau data for 1790–1990 available at http://www.census.gov/population/www/censusdata/files/table-4.pdf. Accessed April 17, 2011.

the growth in health care expenditure as a percentage of GDP and the rapid inflation in health insurance premiums—far outstripping overall inflation and wage growth—a broad agreement that health care costs must be controlled is easily reached. Of greater difficulty is finding consensus on acceptable ways to achieve cost control. Policies may be targeted toward expanding public programs like Medicaid or the State Children's Health Insurance Program (SCHIP), or toward expanding private insurance coverage.

Methods that regulatory agencies may use to address issues of access or affordability of insurance include:

- Restricting insurer practices, such as excluding certain rating variables such as gender or age from premium calculations, or limiting the percentage by which a group's premium can increase at renewal;
- Limiting the allowable proportion between premiums charged to different age groups;
- Mandating coverage for specific services, such as mammograms or behavioral health treatment;
- Prohibiting insurers from declining applications for insurance (*guaranteed issue*); and
- Requiring insurers to offer renewal to the groups they cover (*guaranteed renewal*) subject to certain conditions.

These methods have met with mixed success. Insurance premiums typically decrease for some people but increase for others as a result, and the overall costs of health care are not directly impacted.

Other methods such as the creation of consumer-directed plans, the use of tax credits to subsidize premiums, and restrictions on liability for medical malpractice may result in one-time decreases to health costs or insurance premiums but do not reduce inflationary trends.

The solvency of insurance plans is monitored by state insurance departments with guidance from the NAIC. Ensuring solvency provides consumer protection by validating that a plan possesses the financial capability of paying its members' costs of health care. Additionally, solvency regulations protect care providers and other entities that enter into agreements with health plans. Relevant standards are typically enforced by state regulators, and include requirements on capital holdings and management policies, statutory financial reporting, reserving, and licensing.

29.4.3 The Patient Protection and Affordable Care Act

In 2010, President Barack Obama signed the Patient Protection and Affordable Care Act (PPACA) into law. Certain provisions in the law became effective immediately or in a very near term, while other provisions are scheduled to be implemented in coming years. Broadly, its objectives include improving accessibility of insurance, improving quality and efficiency of care, and reducing long-term cost trends for businesses and government plans. Its principles therefore require behavioral changes from all of the stakeholders in the health care environment (as identified in Chapter 28). The Secretary of the Department of Health and Human Services (HHS) retains primary responsibility for development and enforcement of the supporting regulations, though other existing agencies and entities will assume new responsibilities, and new agencies will be created to advise and create regulations or to enforce practices.

The components of PPACA that are most visible to the public are scheduled to take effect on January 1, 2014. The legislation included some notable items for implementation prior to 2014, such as:

- Insurance companies may not place lifetime limits on benefits; must extend adult dependent coverage to age 26; may not rescind policies except in cases of fraud or intentional misrepresentation; may not apply pre-existing condition exclusions to child policies; and must cover preventive services without requiring member cost-sharing and no annual limits on essential benefits;
- Rebates for Medicare Part D beneficiaries whose out-of-pocket spending for prescriptions reaches the *donut hole*, or the differential between the initial coverage limit and the catastrophic coverage threshold;
- Minimum loss ratio requirements—Generally, the *loss ratio* refers to the percentage of premiums that is spent on clinical services. PPACA requires insurers to report their loss ratios, allowing inclusion of amounts spent on quality-of-care measures. The insurer must provide rebates to policyholders if the loss ratio is below 80 percent for individuals and small groups, or below 85 percent for large groups. The reporting requirement became effective in 2010, and the rebate requirement begins in 2011;
- HHS may review reasonableness of premium increases filed with state departments of insurance;
- Accountable care organizations (ACOs) that meet thresholds for high quality of care may share in the cost savings that they produce for Medicare and Medicaid.

Prominent components scheduled to be implemented in 2014 include:

- Guaranteed issue and renewability of insurance, regardless of health status;
- Individual mandate to carry health insurance or pay a tax penalty (with exceptions for income, religious conscience or other conditions as prescribed by HHS);
- Mandate on employers of more than 50 employees to offer health insurance benefits or pay a penalty;
- Expansion of Medicaid plans to cover households with income up to 133 percent of the federal poverty level (FPL);
- Premium subsidies for purchase of private insurance through the exchanges when household income is between 133 percent and 400 percent of FPL;
- Development of health insurance exchanges to facilitate comparison among insurers' plan offerings;
- Rating for individual and small group products may only vary for age, geographic area, family composition and tobacco use;
- Plans sold through the exchanges must cover a package of essential health benefits and limits required member cost-sharing;
- Plans must have a minimum Actuarial Value (AV) of 60 percent. For this purpose, the actuarial value is roughly defined as the *paid-to-allowed ratio,* which will be explored further in Section 3, for essential benefits. This limit is most significant on the individual market, where many plans are below that level;

These lists of components are not exhaustive, and several components contain exceptions or exemptions for certain entities or conditions. The specific terms of these and other components of PPACA are subject to ongoing review and comment. Actuaries therefore possess an opportunity to speak out in a credible manner on the details of proposed rules and regulations and the unintended consequences of proposed changes.

29.4.4 Regulation of Health Care Providers, Goods, and Services

Health care providers are subject to regulation concerning their licensure to practice medicine, which is normally evaluated at the state level in the United States, and their accreditation by a relevant professional organization. Further, providers are subject to privacy requirements found within HIPAA. Strict prohibitions exist against use of protected health information (PHI) for purposes not clearly specified as acceptable or disclosure to parties not authorized in writing by the patient. The development and enhancement of electronic health records (EHRs) and other uses of information technology related to health care delivery and administration can add security to health records, though requirements of privacy still apply. Accordingly, regulatory standards exist to measure the security and confidentiality of health IT systems, and to ensure their ability to perform a defined set of functions. Health IT systems are certified at the federal level through the Office of the National Coordinator for Health Information Technology, a division of HHS.

Provider quality is monitored by the Agency for Healthcare Research and Quality (AHRQ) division within HHS. Various state agencies license practitioners of medicine in accordance with their state's standards of qualification, and conduct further monitoring of hospital and professional facilities, emergency care centers, medical homes, and other service-specific outlets for treatment. The Food and Drug Administration (FDA) monitors the safety and efficacy of medications, medical devices, biologics, and the supply of blood available for transfusions.

CHAPTER 30

Pricing for Group Benefit Plans

For fully insured products, the insurer retains the risk associated with claims costs. The product premiums are intended to cover the expected claims costs incurred by the insured members, the expenses associated with administering the product, the premium tax paid by the insurer on the product, and a charge for risk and profit. Save for limited cost-sharing for services included in the plan benefit design, the premium payments represent cost certainty for the insured, regardless of the total costs incurred for services received. It is therefore paramount that the products are priced as accurately as possible. The financial viability of the insurer depends on it.

An insurer seeks to gather data on previous experience that will be sufficiently predictive of future experience and thus be useful for determining the premium that should be charged for the product. It is important to understand the ways in which the characteristics of the members and the services and benefits they received during the past time period being studied (the *experience period*) can vary from the future time period for which the product will be priced (the *rating period*).

30.1 Data and Assumptions

Actuaries rely on data in order to perform analyses and make recommendations. Processes such as developing premium rates, analyzing trends, calculating reserves, managing provider networks and reimbursement schedules, or developing new products all benefit from decisions made using high quality data. Quality data should be accurate, appropriate, reasonable and comprehensive, given time constraints and cost/benefit concerns. Data may be collected from external or internal sources, but must be selected, reviewed and disclosed in accordance with actuarial standards of practice. In the United States the standards of practice are published by the Actuarial Standards Board. Their Actuarial Standard of Practice (ASOP) No. 23, "Data Quality," speaks extensively to data quality and applies to all branches of actuarial practice. Additionally, ASOP No. 5, "Incurred Health and Disability Claims," states that actuaries must make appropriate efforts to obtain accurate data.

It is not sufficient, however, strictly to look backward—to use past experience from internal or external sources—when setting premium rates. Proper rates require assumptions about expected future results, since the premiums are intended to cover costs that will be incurred during some future time period. Changing enrollment and demographics, trends in service costs and utilization, evolving market conditions, and new or revised regulations and tax policy all affect the rates that should be charged for a benefit plan.

External data is used most often for projects that develop new products, reach new geographic markets or create new benefits. External data may also supplement internal data deemed insufficiently credible or serve as a reasonableness check for internal data. Data from external sources may have been collected by observing a population with characteristics that differ from the members covered by the product, or may be collected in a manner inconsistent with internal records for existing members. Thus, it is important to consider carefully the appropriateness and accuracy of data from external sources.

The U.S. federal government supports several sources of data on mortality, morbidity, demographics, cost, utilization levels and trends. Institutes and agencies such as the Census Bureau, the Bureau of Labor and Statistics and the Centers for Medicare and Medicaid Services produce useful studies and statistics. Reports may be published online or available through the Technical Information Service of the Department of Commerce.

Several actuarial publications provide data, usually relating to insured populations and often relevant to specific products (e.g., the Group Long-Term Disability Valuation Tables); illnesses (e.g., HIV/AIDS); or group characteristics (e.g., duration of coverage[1]). The SOA offers periodical publications and special research activities and projects relating to all the lines of business in which its members practice. The SOA's Group Life Insurance Experience Committee develops an intercompany study using data submitted from several large carriers. The most recent study was published in 2006 and contains experience that can be tabulated using member demographics (age, sex, location); group characteristics (industry, group size); and coverage types (benefit provisions, case size). A previous version of the intercompany study provided the basis for the 1960 Commissioners Standard Group (CSG) Mortality Table. This table, known as 1960 CSG, was adopted by the NAIC as a standard for minimum group life premium rates and subsequently used for regulatory purposes in some states.

Actuarial consulting firms produce guidelines, pricing models, and volumes of data on utilization and costs of services. Other external sources of data include state health data organizations, which report on hospital discharges and ambulatory care; organizations like America's Health Insurance Plans and the American Association of Preferred Provider Organizations that analyze data from HMOs and PPOs; medical publications like the *Journal of the American Medical Association* and the *New England Journal of Medicine;* and the NCQA, which produces the HEDIS, a set of standardized quality measures that consumers and employers can use to compare health plans' performance on a consistent basis.

Internal data sources tend to be most critical for actuarial analytics. The actuary can best ensure the relevance of the data to the project at hand, and can most easily demonstrate the experience that supports the recommendations made. Internal data best reflects the insurer's risk selection and administrative efficiency. Analysis of group medical product lines may be performed by studying various functions within the premium billing and collection processes or the claims payment processes.

The actuary may study the internal data for demographic or underwriting risk characteristics of the insurer's members, distributions of the providers used and services incurred by the members, or patterns of the lag times of provider reimbursement payments made by the insurer, to name just a few concepts for exploration.

1 Brink et al. (1991–92).

30.2 Network Management and Plan Design

A network of approved providers is a central component of health insurance benefit plan design. Providers who contract with an insurer agree to the terms of reimbursement for services. The provider may be reimbursed on a fee-for-service basis, at a capitated rate per patient or member, or at a percentage discount from billed charges. The insurer must therefore recruit providers to join the preferred provider network and reimburse at an acceptable rate—but will then use claim data to analyze each contracted provider's cost efficiency and treatment patterns. Most benefit plan designs offer incentives to the member to seek out preferred providers for the care needed. For example, a regular office visit to an in-network physician may require only a low fixed dollar copayment from the member, where the same office visit to a non-network provider would be subject to deductible and coinsurance. Some plan designs go as far as to require use of in-network providers and do not provide any benefits when non-network providers are used. The provider gains access to a block of potential customers by contracting with an insurer, since the insurer's members will be more likely to choose that provider for their care. Some insurers compete for members by offering a broad network of contracted providers, maximizing availability and choice of doctors and facilities; others compete by offering a select network of providers that may agree to deeper discounts on services or more stringent restrictions on treatment patterns, thus reducing expected claims costs. Insurers may develop different product lines that follow either strategy.

Provider networks that support HMO plans take greater control over health care utilization and assume a greater share of the risk of excess utilization. Under these plans, providers are usually reimbursed on a capitated basis, receiving a fixed amount per enrolled member regardless of the volume of services each member receives. Primary care physicians (PCPs) may be responsible for a gatekeeping role, wherein a member must seek a PCP's referral to a specialist. In order to receive the maximum level of benefits, insured members may be required to obtain pre-certification, or authorization for care, before seeking admission to a hospital or receiving certain kinds of services. However, in exchange for following these guidelines of care, members typically are responsible for lower copayments and other forms of cost sharing for the services they receive. The most common HMO plan designs do not include member deductibles or coinsurance.

Networks that support PPO plans generally include more providers than HMO networks and impose fewer procedures and restrictions on the members. Member cost sharing for services covered by PPO plans is typically higher than on HMO plans, with most or all services subject to a deductible and coinsurance.

30.3 Estimating Claims Costs

The expected claims costs for benefits received and services incurred by covered members comprise the largest portion of the premium that an insurer will charge. For life and disability insurance products, the insurer estimates the frequency of benefit payments and the severity of each payment. Since benefits for these coverages are typically paid directly to the members and their beneficiaries, claims cost estimates do not require considerations other than the expected payments.

30.3.1 Anatomy of a Claim, from Billed to Paid

Claims costs for health insurance products can be examined from multiple perspectives. Generally, the contracted providers submit claims to the insurer for services delivered to the members; the insurer processes the claim, adjudicating its eligibility for reimbursement, calculating the total reimbursement due to the provider per the financial terms of the contract, and allocating the reimbursed amount between the insurer and the member per the benefit plan design. The insurer will then pay its share of the reimbursement to the provider and inform the provider of the level of cost-sharing for which the member is responsible; the provider should then only bill the member for the copayment or other cost-sharing due. Depending on the member's plan design and the provider's familiarity with the insurer, the provider may collect some of the member cost-sharing upfront (e.g., copays for office visits or emergency-room visits).

Dollar totals for health insurance claims costs may thus refer to the amount *billed* by the providers for their services; the amount *allowed* or reimbursed to the providers; or the amount *paid* by the insurer after member cost-sharing is applied to the allowed amount. While the overall financial outcome of a product may be impacted by reinsurance recoveries or coordination of benefits (COB) when a member receives benefits through multiple payers, these considerations are often ignored when analyzing claims costs. Table 30.1 distinguishes the key types of claim amounts determined within the processing of a claim for a physician office visit.

TABLE 30.1 Amounts Determined in Claim Processing

Amount Billed by Provider for Office Visit	200.00
Prevailing Fee for Office Visit	165.00
Negotiated Provider Discount	−20%
Amount Allowed to Provider	132.00
Member Copay per Benefit Plan—Paid by Member	25.00
Amount Paid by Insurer	107.00

In this example, the amount billed represents the charges that the provider submits to the insurer. The *prevailing fee* refers to a base level of reimbursement for each particular service delivered by the provider. The prevailing fee is typically lower than the amount billed, as it represents a cutback to the *reasonable and customary (R&C)* amount that a provider would bill for the service in question. The allowed amount then reflects the discount level that the insurer negotiates with the provider. The provider will accept a lower reimbursement in order to improve access to potential customers and to streamline the payments for service. At many companies, there is not an initial R&C cutback; there is merely a negotiated fee schedule which is the allowed amount.

An insured member who needs medical services will typically refer to the insurer's *provider directory*, which lists the providers that have contracted with the insurer, in order to choose a provider whose services will be available to the member and will generally require the lowest possible amount to be paid by the member. The insurer guarantees payment to the provider for covered services in accordance with the contract, and providers receive reimbursement within 30 days of submission to the insurer for most of the claims they submit. Providers who seek direct payment from patients must often seek upfront payment and thus lose some customers, may ultimately wait much longer to receive payment for the patients they treat without upfront payment, or, may not receive payment at all.

The insurer's *prevailing fee schedule* typically contains a different reimbursement amount for each procedure code. The procedure code for each service is supplied by the provider. Depending on the nature of the service, the procedure code may be taken from the DRG published by the CMS, the Current Procedural Terminology (CPT) code set published by the American Medical Association, or from the Healthcare Common Procedure Coding System (HCPCS) published by the CMS. The insurer will then seek providers who will agree to accept the amounts from the fee schedule—or possibly an amount discounted further, as shown in Table 30.1. Thus, the allowed amount reimbursed to the provider may be substantially less than the billed amount, and the paid amount—which is net of member cost-sharing and represents the insurer's financial responsibility for the service provided—will be less than or equal to the allowed amount.

The total dollars are most meaningfully expressed on a basis of exposure units. The exposure units considered in the analysis may be the number of employees, contracts, subscribers or members insured during the experience period. Note that changes in family composition, new enrollment, and termination of enrollment may occur throughout the policy period and distort analyses that do not account for these forces. It is most common to examine the number of members covered and the number of months throughout the experience period for which each member is covered. Thus premium and claims costs can be compared on a per-member-per-month (PMPM) basis. In disability coverages this may be expressed per 100 of monthly benefit and in life insurance coverages it may be in terms of amount inforce.

30.3.2 Manual Rates and Common Rating Variables

The *manual rate* for a group represents an average claims cost that can then be modified for a specific group in consideration of different types of risk characteristics. These characteristics, called *rating variables*, are associated with substantial variations in claims costs between groups or across different population segments. Insurers generally begin by developing a *manual base rate* that reflects average expected costs for a group whose demographics and risk profile are representative of those for the entire experience block and account for group-specific variations through a series of multiplicative factors that apply to the manual base rate. When using historical claims experience to produce projections for a block that is expected to differ substantially in terms of demographics or other rating considerations, it is helpful to adjust or *normalize* the experience by dividing out the component members' aggregated factors for different rating variables.

EXAMPLE 30.1 CASE STUDY INTRODUCTION

Pricing concepts will be illustrated with a comprehensive case study. In addition to displaying tables with relevant calculations throughout the text, the Excel file "Health Case Study.xlsx" contains all the tables and calculations. It is available with the book's online resources.

The case study uses hypothetical membership, claims, and premium experience observed for a block of business. The case study includes claims incurred between January 2009 and March 2011, paid through March 2011. The base rate and factor analysis uses the 2009 incurred claims, since all claims incurred during that period are assumed to be paid as of March 2011.

30.3.2.1 Age and gender

The members included in the analysis are typically grouped by gender and into five-year age bands. Insurers may observe claim costs per member age 60–64 that are five times the costs per member under age 25. Insurers also observe that the proportional costs between older and younger members are different for men and women. Factors thus typically vary by gender and age band. They may be set so that the average age/gender factor equals 1.0 for the members included in the experience used to set the factors—or they may be set using 1.0 for a certain gender and age band (e.g., the male age 40–44 band). Additionally, insurers often find it appropriate to develop separate factors for medical costs and prescription drug costs, since the distribution of costs across age/gender bands can differ for those types of services.

EXAMPLE 30.2 CASE STUDY CLAIMS DATA

The table, "Claims Experience by Age and Gender," from the Excel file summarizes the hypothetical block's claims experience by gender and age band and shows the age/gender factors (AGF) applicable to the premium collected during the experience period. Note that these factors are the ones assumed to be in use during the experience period, not the factors that are implied by the claims data. The only calculated item is the Allowed Claims PMPM which is equal to (Allowed Claims/ Members)/12.

30.3.2.2 Geographic area

Local variations exist for utilization frequency levels and provider reimbursement rates. In states, counties or ZIP codes where care is more easily accessible, members may be more likely to seek care—but in areas where care is less accessible, providers often have greater influence over reimbursement rates. Factors most commonly vary by county, metropolitan statistical area (MSA) or three-digit ZIP code. Many insurers lack sufficient volume in any particular area—especially when refined to smaller areas—to study geographical variations in claims costs. It is often useful in this context to supplement claims experience with data from consultants or analysis of competitors' rates or to set area factors independently of localized claims experience (e.g., to use the area factor to represent variations in provider reimbursement levels).

EXAMPLE 30.3 CASE STUDY AREA FACTORS

The table, "Rating Factors by Area," available in the Excel file, summarizes the claims experience by geographic area as defined by the insurer and shows the area factors applicable to the premium collected during the experience period. As before, the Allowed Claims PMPM is a calculated value and the rating factors are those in use during the experience period.

EXAMPLE 30.4 CASE STUDY MANUAL BASE RATE CALCULATION

Table 30.2 illustrates how the average allowed claims PMPM can be normalized by dividing out the member-weighted age/gender factor and area factor for the block. The normalization process allows analysis of claims costs independently of demographic risks and facilitates adjustment of the manual base rates to account for known or anticipated changes in the demographics of the block going forward. The demographic characteristics of the experience that drives the manual base rate calculation may be noticeably different from those of the experience that was used previously to set the factors. Under this method, the manual base rate equals the expected claim costs for a member whose age/gender and area factors equal 1.0.

TABLE 30.2 Manual Base Rate Calculation with Current Age/Gender and Area Factors

Total Allowed Claims (1)	38,634,068	
Allowed Claims PMPM (2)	401.18	
Total AGF (3)	1.6520	
Total Area (4)	0.9543	
Normalized Allowed PMPM	**254.48**	**= (2)/(3)/(4)**

EXAMPLE 30.5 CASE STUDY SMOOTHED AND NORMALIZED AGE/GENDER FACTORS

From the tables in the Excel file, the insurer observes that the age/gender and area factors in force during the experience period do not accurately reflect the proportions of allowed claims PMPM between the different age bands and areas. The premium rates by member for each *cell* (combination of gender, age band and geographic area) will be determined in part by the age/gender factors and area factors. Thus the insurer will rebalance these factors in an attempt to align the premiums by cell with the expected claims by cell. The member-weighted average age/gender factor and area factor will both equal 1.0. The manual base rate will then equal the overall allowed claims PMPM (401.18), as illustrated in the table "Rebalancing and Smoothing Age/Gender Factors" in the Excel file.

In the table, "Rebalancing and Smoothing Age/Gender Factors," the Allowed Claims PMPM by gender and age band, as found in the table "Claims Experience by Age and Gender," are averaged separately for females (465.65 PMPM) and males (328.28 PMPM). Then the Relativity to Gender Average represents the Allowed Claims PMPM for each age band divided by the overall Allowed Claims PMPM for the gender. The Curve Fit Factor fits the relativities to an exponential curve using the GROWTH function in Excel, with the midpoint of each age band (e.g., 32 for the 30–34 age band) as the x values and the relativities as the known y values. Fitting separate curves for females and males will allow the final factors to follow separate patterns of increase with age for each gender. Finally, since the member-weighted average of the Curve Fit Factor equals 1.0038 for females and 0.9277 for males (using the member counts by gender and age band in "Claim Experience by

Age and Gender"), each Curve Fit Factor is divided by the member-weighted average and multiplied by the ratio of (the gender total PMPM to the overall PMPM) so that the overall member-weighted average of the Final Fitted Factor equals 1.0 for the block. For purposes of this example, the Final Fitted Factors will represent the age/gender factors that the insurer will use for the rating period. It is not necessary to rebalance males and females separately; it may be preferable to combine all members especially if the insurer desires to set one cell at a prescribed factor (e.g., the insurer may want to use a factor of 1.0 for males age 40–44) or if concerns exist about the credibility of the experience for either gender by itself.

The decision to smooth factors is often based on external knowledge and market forces. For example, the experience data indicates a lower cost for females age 40–44 than for females age 35–39, followed by a sharp increase at ages 45–49. Unless there is a sound explanation for this pattern, using these factors will likely lead to unprofitable business at ages 40–44 followed by lapses at ages 45–49. While exponential smoothing was selected for this example, there are many ways a company may choose to smooth the experience data.

EXAMPLE 30.6 CASE STUDY NORMALIZED AREA FACTORS

Similarly, in the table "Rebalancing Area Factors," the relativities of the Allowed PMPM by area to the overall PMPM represent the area factors that the insurer will use for the rating period, for purposes of this example. Note that no smoothing was done for the area factors. This company has no *a priori* reason to believe there is a pattern of relativities from one area to another and thus there is no guidance regarding smoothing to be done.

In practice, the insurer often seeks to minimize the *disruption* (percentage change caused) to the premium rates by cell that results from rebalancing the factors. Substantial premium increases for one or more cells could lead to rates that are uncompetitive in the marketplace. Large increases can lead to selection risks among existing plan members—the subset of members who are relatively healthier would be more likely to terminate their coverage. Additionally, the experience data may be anomalous in some way when compared with historical patterns. The actuary should make a reasonable and justifiable judgment regarding the maximum level of change that would occur in any cell and choose the proposed final factors accordingly.

If the company has no expenses, wishes to make no profit, there are no cost-sharing provisions and there are no cost changes due to inflation or new coverage provisions, premiums are determined by multiplying the base rate by the appropriate factors. Thus, the premium for a 48-year-old female living in area Bravo is $401.18 \times 1.4122 \times 1.0162 = 575.72$. Note that if the age/gender factor and area factor had not been rebalanced, the calculated premium for the same member would be $254.48 \times 1.8000 \times 1.0000 = 458.06$. Rebalancing of demographic factors is generally designed to be *revenue-neutral*; that is, the total premium collected for the entire membership should be equal using either the existing base rates and factors or the proposed rebalanced ones to calculate the premium for each member. Generally, it is preferable that the insurer use factors that represent the proportional claims costs expected for each cell, as closely as is feasible. Otherwise, the insurer will be exposed to risks of anti-selection. If the premium is too low in relation to expected claims costs for some cells and is too high for other cells, the insurer is likely to observe over time that its enrollment will include a growing share of its members in the cells where the premium is too low, and ultimately, the block will lose money because the premium will be insufficient.

30.3.2.3 Benefit plans

Even when all other demographic conditions and risk characteristics are equal between collections of members, different benefit plans will lead to differences in claims costs. Recall the different network types discussed earlier; the products supported by different levels of care management and breadth of provider availability appeal to different market segments. To some extent, benefit plans influence member utilization. That is, groups that buy plans with high deductibles and other member cost-sharing typically observe lower utilization than the groups that buy plans with lower member cost-sharing. Higher copayments and deductibles can deter people from seeking care. Additionally, expected utilization influences the benefit plan that some groups seek. Groups comprising relatively healthy members who expect lower utilization may prefer a higher-deductible plan in order to reduce premiums. Factors are typically developed for each available benefit plan with the help of a claim probability distribution (CPD, which will be explored in greater detail in Section 30.5). Experience studies most accurately normalize data collected on all plans to reflect in context of one benefit plan—most commonly the richest benefit plan or the plan selected by the greatest number of members.

30.3.2.4 Adjustments for benefit exclusions

Internal data is often less available for specific services that may not be covered by some or all of an insurer's plans (e.g., chiropractic care). Similarly, coverage for prescription drugs, vision benefits, and other ancillary benefits may not have been in force for all the groups included in the experience study. The experience data should be adjusted as appropriate for the product being priced and the groups to which it is targeted.

30.3.2.5 Other group characteristics

The industry, size, and duration of the groups included should be considered and normalized within experience data. Industries that involve physical labor (like construction) or relatively hazardous surroundings (like mining) typically observe above-average claims costs, as are industries where the employees are generally better aware of the services available and more likely to take full advantage of their benefits. The manual rate typically includes an *industry load* factor determined by the group's code defined within the NAICS. Similarly, the manual rate includes a *size load* factor that is derived from the size of the group, normally defined by the number of employees covered. The per-member costs of small groups are more volatile since the effects of including individual members with very high costs are more evident when fewer total members are involved. The duration of a group refers to the length of time that has passed since the group first enrolled with the insurer. Since coverage limitations for pre-existing conditions are most evident in the first year of coverage—and group members' health quite often deteriorates during the ensuing time frame—a durational factor that reflects *underwriting wear-off* should also be included in the manual rate.

30.3.2.6 Adjustments for changes to utilization management and provider reimbursement

Experience data should be normalized for the impact of revisions to programs that monitor necessity of treatment, appropriateness of setting for care and ongoing patient progress. Data should also be adjusted for the impact of changes to the method of provider reimbursement. If a capitation schedule applied during the experience period but will not apply during the rating period, detailed claim information may not be available for services received while the capitation schedule was in effect.

30.3.3 EXERCISES

30.1 Which gender/age/area cell would observe the largest absolute percentage of disruption as a result of rebalancing the age/gender and area factors as shown in Example 30.5 and Example 30.6?

30.2 The state in which the given claim experience occurred recently passed new rating restrictions, requiring unisex rates (which means the insurer cannot use different age/gender factors for males and females) and a 3:1 age band (which means that the rate charged to members of any age cannot be more than three times that amount charged to members of any other age). Use the method illustrated in Example 30.5 to calculate new age/gender factors that meet both restrictions and are revenue-neutral in total to the existing ones.

30.4 Projecting Costs to the Rating Period

After developing a summary of experience data and normalizing as appropriate, it is then necessary to trend the experience forward to the rating period. Trend estimation is a critical step in rate development, because the premiums charged for the rating period represent projected expected costs incurred over a future time frame. The trend estimate contains several components that reflect various influences on average claim costs. These influences include changes in the

- Unit costs per service;
- Volume of services and the distribution between types of service;
- Benefit design;
- Practice patterns;
- Cost shifting between payers;
- Spread of new technologies, devices, and medications; and
- Revisions to provider reimbursement methods or rates.

Trends in premiums, expenses, enrollment, or other business conditions must be frequently examined to facilitate quick responses to changes in the business environment. These components should be analyzed to distinguish *secular trends*, which are long-term impacts to a static population independent of benefit changes or other temporary effects, from other short-term influences.

Review of secular trends may include analysis of data from internal and external sources. Especially where experience data represents a non-credible sample or is otherwise limited, trend review may incorporate econometric models, health care market surveys and studies, or other outside sources for useful assumptions. Trends may be expressed in total for all services covered, or may be refined to greater detail as desired. It is often beneficial to observe that some trends operate in opposing directions; for example, accelerating trends for prescription drug utilization tend to correlate with decelerating trends for utilization of medical services.

Trend analyses commonly involve historical average rates of change, possibly examined with the help of a regression model and adjusted for judgment related to current and future conditions. Trends can be evaluated over any period of time desired. It is most common to consider trends over rolling periods of twelve months and of three months. Annual trends correspond with the most common frequency of policy renewal and the most common length of provider contracts at given levels of reimbursement. The three-month trend is often a leading indicator of future trends. As with claim experience, historical trend increases are not necessarily predictive of future trends. New sales, lapses, and changes in claim processing systems impact the rates at which costs will increase.

EXAMPLE 30.7 CASE STUDY TREND

The table, "Types of Year-Over-Year Trend," in the Excel file illustrates *year-over-year* trend rates for different totals of claims incurred by the block in the case study. Year-over-year trend rates fit into the frame of reference most easily understood by a broader internal audience. Trend is generally expressed as the change in rates per member or per unit. The Billed PMPM trend can be split out into component trends of utilization and cost per service, using the year-over-year ratios. Expressed numerically, $(1 + 10.19\%) = (1 + 5.96\%) \times (1 + 3.99\%)$. Similarly, the Allowed PMPM trend can be broken out into utilization and cost components.

It is helpful to split out the components in order to better understand the forces that drive the trend increases and to respond properly to those forces. Utilization trends may illustrate changes in the demographic mix of the block being studied, changes in the availability of providers, changes in practice patterns, or underlying influences on the demand for services (e.g., a flu outbreak). Utilization trends are also affected by changes in plan designs. Leaner plans that feature higher member cost-sharing typically observe lower utilization rates. Trends are therefore impacted by shifts toward leaner plans as more groups *buy down* their benefits by increasing the deductible, coinsurance, or copay amounts for which the member will be responsible. Programs that manage care by requiring utilization review or other protocols control trend increases, but have been become less popular in the marketplace.

Review of billed and allowed trends in unit costs per service should consider changes in provider reimbursement schedules and rates, including shifts between procedure fee schedules, case rates, and per diem rates. Trend review should also account for cost shifting between payers. Providers exert greater leverage over reimbursement rates charged to commercial plans, where Medicare and Medicaid programs have greater influence on reimbursements for services received by their members. Paid trends accelerate through *leveraging* on existing cost-sharing amounts. As costs inflate over time, a given deductible amount or fixed-dollar copayment covers fewer services and becomes less effective as a financial deterrent.

Trend analyses are often more thorough than calculating the year-over-year trend rate. Typically, the actuary can access historical claim data for more than two years; additionally, it may be useful to examine trend rates using claim amounts measured for each month of an experience period. When using monthly claim amounts, it is often advisable to adjust them for *seasonality*, which is a cyclical influence on the distribution of claims throughout the year. For example, allowed and paid PMPM claim amounts for the months in the fourth quarter of the calendar year are generally higher than the allowed and paid PMPM averages for the year. This happens because as greater numbers of members reach their deductibles and out-of-pocket maximums, the financial disincentive to use services is reduced.

The effects of leveraging and seasonality are more pronounced on high-deductible health plans and HSA plans. The table, "Illustration of Deductible Leveraging," in the Excel file, illustrates leveraging by showing how a 10 percent year-over-year increase in a member's incurred claims may result in a much larger percentage increase in the claims paid by the insurer. With respect to the impact of plan deductibles on seasonality factors, note that generally, members considering elective care prefer to receive those services after they've met their deductible, which is usually later in the calendar year. That is, when the choice exists between having a non-emergency procedure performed in December for which the insurer will pay most or all of the cost, or having it in January when the member could be responsible for the entire cost because the next year's deductible will apply, most members will rush to have such procedures done in December. As plan deductibles get larger, that emphasis becomes greater, because a wider range of procedures and surgeries could be affected (and the member dollars at stake are greater).

EXAMPLE 30.8 CASE STUDY TREND BASED ON MONTHLY DATA

The table, "Allowed Trends on Three Years Data, with Seasonal Adjustments," in the Excel file, shows the allowed PMPM for each month for which claim data is available for the hypothetical block used in the case study. The insurer can develop a trend assumption based on a longer claim history, and can use monthly claim data to examine seasonal variations. The seasonality factors are calculated by determining the average allowed PMPM for each calendar month in the three-year period (ignoring the Dec-07 figures for this purpose), and dividing by the average allowed PMPM for the entire 36 months. Thus the average January PMPM equals

$$(2{,}875{,}432 + 3{,}000{,}000 + 3{,}298{,}654)/(8186 + 8025 + 7877) = 380.86$$

and the seasonality factor for January equals

$$(380.86/398.24) = 0.9563.$$

The seasonally adjusted allowed PMPM for each month equals the actual allowed PMPM divided by the seasonality factor. In practice, the seasonality factors for each month may be adjusted for the number of work days that occurred during the month. The incurred claim volume in a given month is impacted by the number of days that certain facilities (e.g., physicians' offices) are open, which are typically weekdays that aren't holidays. Note that in June 2008, there were 21 such days, while in June 2009 there were 22 such days. For purposes of this example, this distinction is not considered.

Then, using the GROWTH function in Excel, the seasonally adjusted allowed PMPMs are fit to an exponential curve—thus determining a constant monthly trend rate that can be found by dividing any month's Fitted Seasonally Adjusted PMPM by the previous month's fitted PMPM and subtracting one. In this example, the average monthly trend equals (438.56/436.16 − 1) = 0.55%. Since trends are most commonly expressed on an annual basis, the annual trend equals (1.0 plus the monthly trend) ^ 12 − 1.0 = 6.82%. While other functions may be used, exponential trend is most common.

Identifying the causes of accelerated trend rates helps the insurer react appropriately. For example, if unit cost trends are consistent with known increases in provider reimbursement, but utilization trends suggest that the members are encountering providers more frequently, changing the plan benefit design (e.g., applying a limit on the number of covered visits to a certain type of provider) may be preferable to increasing the premiums.

30.5 Calculating Benefit Factors

The impact of deductibles, coinsurance, out-of-pocket maximums, and annual benefit maximums on claims costs can be evaluated with the help of a claim probability distribution (CPD). CPDs may be developed for a specific type of service—such as physician office visits—in order to properly evaluate the value of a fixed-dollar copayment. A CPD often contains experience collected on a block of groups that are similar in size and benefit design, such as the range of PPO plans available to small groups. This method is most useful for valuing cost-sharing that applies to comprehensive or major medical coverage plans and can be accumulated over a number of provider encounters, such as a deductible or an out-of-pocket maximum.

EXAMPLE 30.9 CASE STUDY CLAIM PROBABILITY DISTRIBUTION

Table 30.3 illustrates a common CPD layout. The first column of the CPD defines different ranges of allowed dollars. The second column shows the frequency of members whose incurred claims for the year fall within each range. The third column is the average incurred claims per member by the members who fall within each range. The values in the fourth column—the annual cost for each range—are the products of the values in the second and third columns for each range. The cumulative frequency in the fifth column shows the frequency of members whose incurred claims for the year are not less than the minimum dollar amount for each range. The sixth column in each row sums the annual costs for that row and all rows below it. This column is used to calculate the value of member cost-sharing that accumulates over the course of the policy period (deductible and coinsurance). The CPDs most commonly used will contain many more rows, with smaller ranges of allowed dollars and lower frequencies for each row. The table in this example is condensed for illustrative purposes.

TABLE 30.3 Claim Probability Distribution, Allowed Dollars per Member

Range	Frequency	Average Annual Claims	Annual Cost	Cumulative Frequency	Cumulative Annual Cost
0.00	0.114891	—	—	1.000000	4,814.21
0.01–500.00	0.246978	234.39	57.89	0.885109	4,814.21
500.01–2,500.00	0.328847	1,242.06	408.45	0.638131	4,756.33
2,500.01–5,500.00	0.132835	3,701.55	491.69	0.309283	4,347.88
5,500.01–10,500.00	0.079875	7,609.55	607.82	0.176449	3,856.18
10,500.01–100,000.00	0.091838	24,799.74	2,277.56	0.096573	3,248.37
Above 100,000.01	0.004735	205,019.41	970.81	0.004735	970.81

EXAMPLE 30.10 CASE STUDY BENEFIT PLAN VALUE

The table, "Value of Benefit Plans," in the Excel file, illustrates how two different benefit plans can be valued using the CPD. Recall from Section 30.3 that the allowed claims refer to the amount reimbursed to the providers for services, while the paid claims refer to the portion of the allowed claims for which the insurer is ultimately responsible, net of member cost-sharing. In this example, all claims are subject to the deductible and coinsurance as determined by the plan—but the member's responsibility cannot exceed the sum of the deductible and the coinsurance maximum. This sum is thus known as the *out-of-pocket maximum.* For the "High" plan the out-of-pocket maximum is 1,500 (500 + 1,000). The *threshold* refers to the amount of allowed claims that would result in a member reaching the out-of-pocket maximum. This maximum occurs for the "High" plan when claims hit 5,500. At this point the member has paid a deductible of 500 and coinsurance of 0.2(5,500 – 500) = 1,000.

In the table, the value of the deductible equals the allowed claims per member minus the cumulative annual cost of claims above the deductible; the value of member coinsurance equals the member coinsurance percentage times the difference between the cumulative annual cost of claims above the threshold and the cumulative annual cost of claims above the deductible; and the insurer's paid claims per member equals the allowed claims per member minus the sum of the value of deductible. The relative value of each benefit plan is then easily and consistently expressed by the *paid-to-allowed ratio* for each plan.

For pricing PPO, HMO, POS, and other benefit plans that apply copayments for various services, it is useful to develop an *actuarial cost model* that builds up total costs for each specific service covered. This method requires tracking the frequency, or annual utilization, of each type of service and the cost per service within each type. A cost model allows for more precise calculation of the value of copayments and other forms of cost-sharing that vary by service. Consider that among physicians, specialists typically charge more per office visit than do primary care physicians. Thus, when a PPO benefit plan design includes a lower copayment for a visit to a primary care physician and a higher copayment for a visit to a specialist, each copayment can be properly valued in the context of the total provider reimbursement per encounter. The cost model by type of service includes calculation of the allowed cost, or the frequency of encounters times the allowed charges per encounter, and the paid cost, which reduces the allowed cost by the value of applicable cost-sharing. This method is most commonly expressed on a PMPM basis.

EXAMPLE 30.11 CASE STUDY COST MODEL

The table, "Using a Cost Model to Evaluate Paid Claims," in the Excel file, breaks out the allowed claims by type of service (inpatient, outpatient, professional, and prescription drugs). The benefit plan used in this example does not include deductibles or coinsurance maximums; it applies a flat 20 percent member coinsurance to all medical services and requires a member copayment of 10 for each prescription. The allowed claims PMPM is (utilization per 1000 members) × (allowed cost per service)/12,000. For the first three services, the value of cost sharing is 20 percent of the allowed claims. For prescription drugs, it is 10 × utilization per 1,000/12,000.

Within an employer group, some employees will decline to be covered under the employer's plan, either because they have coverage available from another source (e.g., a spouse) or because their perceived need for coverage does not justify the required premium contribution (e.g., young, healthy employees who do not expect to need health care services). Some groups design plans that allow their members to choose from multiple benefit options, such as the two plans shown in the table "Value of Benefit Plans." Typically, the members who select richer benefits would then be responsible for a larger contribution to the premium. When these choices are available to a group, the insurer is exposed to selection risk. Each member has the opportunity to select the plan that would result in the lowest possible out-of-pocket cost to the member. Thus, the members who perceive themselves relatively healthy will more likely choose the Low plan—if they opt to be covered at all—since their premium contributions would be lower, and the unhealthier members would more likely choose the High plan, since they would receive plan benefits faster than they would under the Low plan. The insurer may seek to protect against selection risk in these ways:

- Instituting minimum levels of participation (e.g., requiring that at least 75 percent of the employees enroll in the coverage);
- Adding a margin to the premium charged to the group;
- Limiting the difference in employee contributions to premium;
- Limiting the difference between the benefit design options available;
- Designing benefit options such that the cost-sharing requirements for different types of services are not always greater on one of the options; and

- Designing benefit options that do not clearly create antiselection (e.g., if one option included mental health services and the other option excluded them, the members who anticipated needing mental health services would only select the first option).

The premium development for a group with multiple-option coverage therefore requires calculating the relative actuarial value of each benefit option (as shown in the table "Value of Benefit Plans"); estimating the mix of enrollment and the relative health status of the enrollees for each option; calculating the average premium per exposure unit, weighted by the estimated enrollment mix and health status; and applying a loading factor for selection as determined to be appropriate. Over time, the insurer must monitor the relative experience of each plan option to ensure that the estimates of enrollment distribution and health status are valid and the selection risk is adequately mitigated.

30.5.1 EXERCISES

30.3 Using the CPD in Example 30.9 (Table 30.3) and the method shown in Example 30.10, calculate the paid-to-allowed ratio for a plan that features a 1,000 deductible and 30% member coinsurance up to a 4,000 out-of-pocket maximum.

30.4 In what ways should the tables in Example 30.9 and Example 30.11 be revised or expanded in order to calculate an expected paid-to-allowed ratio for a plan with the following features:

- Inpatient—services always subject to deductible and coinsurance
- Outpatient—surgeries and high-tech radiology subject to copays, but all other services subject to deductible and coinsurance
- Professional—physician office visits subject to copays that differ between primary care physicians and specialists, but all other services subject to deductible and coinsurance
- Prescriptions—all prescriptions subject to copays that differ between generic drugs and brand-name drugs

30.6 Impact of Benefit Changes

As discussed previously, changes in benefit design may impact utilization in addition to reallocating the total reimbursed amount between the insurer and the member. For example, an increase to the copayment for an office visit generally acts as a deterrent for some members and for some instances of elective care. That increase, however, will be most evident to the members simply in terms of their outlay for services. A cost model can be developed to demonstrate the savings both to allowed dollars and paid dollars net of member cost-sharing. The cost model should consider services covered under capitation arrangements; changes to member copayments for those services will not impact rates unless the capitation rate is revised, since the amount paid out by the insurer would be unaffected.

EXAMPLE 30.12 CASE STUDY IMPACT OF BENEFIT CHANGES

The table, "Using a Cost Model to Evaluate the Impact of a Benefit Change," in the Excel file, illustrates the impact of changing the member coinsurance to 25% on medical services and increasing the copayment per prescription to 15. In this example, assume that the change in coinsurance has no effect on utilization but the increase in Rx copay decreases scripts by 2%. The calculations are identical to those used in that table. The impact is (309.72 − 329.52)/329.52 = −6.01%.

In some contexts, it is useful to consider how benefit changes for one specific service may impact utilization of multiple service categories. For example, consider the previous observation that prescription drug utilization trends often act counter to trends for medical services. An increase to the copayment for prescriptions may discourage some members from continuing needed maintenance of chronic health conditions—which could lead to more acute hospitalizations; thus, ultimate costs to the insurer may go up in spite of an effort to shift costs to the members.

30.7 Calculating Manual Gross Premiums

Manual rates that show average expected paid claims per exposure unit can be *grossed up* by adding a load per unit to reach the gross premium. In order to calculate gross premiums, it is necessary to develop assumptions for expenses—including administrative expenses, commissions and other sales expenses, taxes, and contributions to surplus—and investment income on assets and cash flow. The gross premium thus equals the manual rate plus expenses minus investment income credits and represents the expected cost of the insurance coverage to the plan member.

30.7.1 Non-Claim Pricing Assumptions

Administrative expenses include the costs of product design and development, sales and marketing, underwriting, benefit processing, and other functions associated with delivering the product to its covered members. These expenses are commonly classified as either *direct*, which means that they can be clearly attributed to the product, or *indirect*, which refers to overhead expenses typically associated with multiple products or with the overall operation of the insurer. The long-term viability of a product—indeed, of an insurer as a whole—necessitates proper evaluation of product expenses and consideration within the premium charged. In the short term, however, certain expenses may be partially or completely excluded from product premiums for competitive reasons, or the timing of expense recoveries may vary from the timing of expense outlays.

Expenses of administering a group policy are highest in the first year that the policy is in effect. Costs for sales and marketing, including commissions (which are often higher for new sales than for renewals of existing groups), for enrollment and billing systems processing, and for issuance of member ID cards all apply disproportionately to new groups. Costs associated with product development and establishment on the company's IT infrastructure are similarly front-loaded. Thus, an insurer may choose to amortize the first-year expenses over a longer period of time, such as the average duration of all policies sold within the product, in order to improve the attractiveness of the initial offering. The insurer must strike the right balance between keeping introductory premiums competitive, spreading expenses into the future and ensuring that a sufficient share of the membership will be retained in future years so that all the product expenses can ultimately be recovered.

Indirect expenses must be allocated between the products that an insurer offers. The method by which these expenses are charged to each product may unintentionally distort the relative profitability of different products, or may skew performance comparisons across different time periods. It is thus desirable to develop an allocation model that is transparent to a broad internal audience—easily explained to senior management, clearly defined for those responsible for classifying and tracking expenses, and useful for forecasting purposes—and applied on a consistent basis. The most common allocation methods assign expenses on an activity basis or on a functional basis. An activity-based allocation establishes a charge for each piece of mail, marketing brochure, or other functional unit associated with the product. A functional expense allocation shares the total expense between products based on the time spent on each product—measured either through real-time internal reporting or through retrospective estimation—and can be refined to classes of group sizes, new or renewal business, or other business details as desired.

Expenses are typically expressed on a per-member, per-policy, or per-claim basis, or as a percentage of premiums or claims. Ideally, the expenses are charged in accordance with the activities undertaken for each product, so that competitive considerations and the varied customer demands by product for service and reporting are properly allocated. As before, misallocation of expenses between products can distort measures of their relative profitability and may lead to suboptimal financial results.

Data for determining expenses may be acquired from internal or external sources. The most common internal sources are the company's finance department and accounting systems, which track expenses by type (e.g., salaries and benefits, travel), by department, or by other functional description. The level of detail to which expenses are tracked is usually consistent with the company's annual statement or tax filing. External sources include industry studies, special surveys, and analyses of competitors' published annual statements, premium quotes or rate filings. However, since competitors may allocate expenses differently and the accuracy of the data collected cannot be validated to the same extent as internal data, external data is often most useful as a reasonableness check.

Commissions are paid to agents or brokers who market an insurer's products. The commission structure established by the insurer should reflect the costs of services provided during the sales and bid processes, and may include incentives to reward high sales, low lapse rates or other performance indicators deemed desirable by the insurer. Commissions are typically determined as a percentage of premiums for small groups, but may be calculated as a flat dollar amount per member for large groups. Some insurers prefer to employ salaried salespeople rather than pay commissions to independent brokers. Salaried salespeople may be eligible for performance bonuses that are targeted to company goals in the same manner as the commission-based incentives. Other sales expenses include advertising and promotional expenses, and may be split into direct expenses to reflect costs for services specific to a product, and indirect expenses for broader-based efforts to promote the company name.

Taxes paid by an insurer include a state-based premium tax, which may be reflected in multistate insurers' pricing by state, and federal and state income taxes. Premium tax rates vary among states, and certain types of insurers (e.g., nonprofit health care service corporations) or premiums received for certain types of groups may be exempted from premium tax calculations as determined by state laws.

Risk charges theoretically vary by product type, benefit design, administrative resources required, and group size, in order to reflect the types and degrees of risk that an insurer faces when enrolling each new group. Insurers face risks of estimation of expected claims; fluctuation of experience or catastrophic single claims; regulations that may prevent insurers from increasing premiums at the rates necessitated by a group's experience; growth in expenses that cannot be sufficiently recouped through pricing; lapse rates that vary from expectations involved in building expenses into the premiums charged for each product; investment returns below expectations applied to pricing; and financial risks that may vary by the type of funding arrangement established by a group. For example, self-insured groups present less risk to the insurer than fully insured groups. Additionally, competitive considerations often influence the level of charges passed along into the marketplace.

Insurers commonly pool the risk charges for small groups, just as the claims experience for those groups is usually pooled for pricing purposes. For large groups, risk charges are more easily applied separately to each group. Premiums are generally set to overall targets of risk and profit margins to be realized after claims and expenses are covered, and a portion of the premiums contributed to the insurer's surplus or reserves.

Investment income is most commonly earned by the insurer on the reserves held or on cash flows. This income may be reflected explicitly in pricing as a rate component, used as an offset to expenses or the risk/profit provision, or applied an as adjustment to pricing targets for loss ratio or profit margin. For products with long-term liabilities, investment income is allocated directly to each product as earned by portfolios of assets dedicated specifically to each product. For short-term liabilities, return rates may be calculated for an insurer's total investment portfolio and credited to each product based on cash flows, or may be credited equally to each product.

30.7.2 Group Specific Manual Premium

Manual premium rates represent the premiums that would be charged to a group given no credible claims experience or special considerations in the underwriting of the group. When experience is available, it is usually weighted in some way to adjust the manual premium calculation. The manual rates include all the rating variables that the insurer applies to premiums, and further account for market conditions and regulatory restrictions.

As examined in Section 30.3.1, the most common rating variables include plan design characteristics, composite member demographics, group industry and size considerations, and cost trends. These variables are typically applied through a series of multiplicative factors on top of a base rate that represents the average expected costs that will be incurred by an average member, employee or other exposure unit. In general, the rating variables used on each group are the same normalized for in Section 30.3 when analyzing historical data. The base rate and rating factors must therefore be frequently monitored to ensure that the manual rate calculations—and thus final premiums—are kept current and sufficiently reflect future expectations for claims and expenses. While the premium calculations are generally built up using information about each member to be covered, the final rates quoted to a group will average out some or all of these elements across all members of the group. They are almost always quoted per subscriber or employee of the group. Thus, the exact age and gender mix of the members will apply in the premium calculation, but the rates quoted to the group would be broken into a structure of rating tiers that seeks to distinguish the family status of each employee and allocate the premium accordingly. The most common rating tier choices are as follows:

- One Tier—composite; same rate charged for each employee regardless of the number of dependents covered
- Two Tier—classifies employees as employee-only (no dependents) or family (one or more dependents); rates differ for each class
- Three Tier—classifies employees as employee-only, employee plus one dependent or family (more than one dependent)
- Four Tier—classifies employees as employee-only, employee plus spouse, employee plus one or more children, or family
- Five Tier—same as four-tier, with the employees-plus-children tier split into employees with one child and employees with more than one child

Note that in some states, certain tier structures may not be permitted for use in rating small groups (typically defined to cover 50 or fewer employees, though that limit can vary by state), and that large groups are often allowed to choose which tier structure they prefer to apply. The choice of tier structure does not affect the total premium charged to the group; it simply determines how the total premium is allocated to each member, which is helpful to the plan sponsor in setting employee contribution rates.

When group premiums are determined for a one-year term—such as for most health care plans—it is usually necessary only to project the claims and expenses costs, investment earnings and other components of premium over the twelve months following issuance or renewal. Some of the risks of errant projections are therefore reduced when compared to the projections needed for long-term care or other coverages that calculate premium rates that are in effect for longer periods of time.

On the whole, manual premium rates are intended to reflect expected costs paid by the insurer, with differences between products or plan designs that relate to the levels of benefits available. Premium rates are further adjusted to account for rating restrictions, such as those that limit the use of age bands or the level that rates can increase from one year to the next; competitive standing of the products; and rational considerations such as small variations in relatively larger group sizes that ought not result in substantial premium differences. For example, many insurers identify the groups with fewer than 100 employees as a separate block from the groups with 100 or more employees. These blocks may observe noticeably different claims experience. However, most insurers prefer to set their premiums such that a group with 98 employees will pay a per-member premium similar to a group with 103 employees, all other group characteristics equal.

EXAMPLE 30.13 CASE STUDY LOSS RATIO METHOD

The table, "Census for Potential New Group," in the Excel file, contains a census of five members in a potential new group whose coverage goes into effect as of 1/1/2011, and whose benefits will be as illustrated in the table "Value of Benefit Plans." The census includes the gender, age, and geographic location of each member.

The insurer uses the census to calculate the average age/gender factor and area factor for the group, applying the new factors developed in the tables, "Rebalancing and Smoothing Age/Gender Factors" and "Rebalancing Area Factors," in the Excel file. The table, "Loss Ratio Method for Premium," in the Excel file, illustrates the manner in which the premium rate would be built up using the loss ratio method.

In this example, the insurer seeks to set the premium such that the loss ratio equals 75%. Note that when the loss ratio is not greater than 75%, the premium will be sufficient to pay the administrative expenses, commissions, taxes, risk charges and profit—expressed as a percentage of premium in this example—in addition to the insurer's paid claims. The premium will be based on the calculated base rate, trend assumption, group-specific demographic factors and expense assumptions.

Thus the manual base rate PMPM—the expected claims cost in allowed dollars from tables "Rebalancing and Smoothing Age/Gender Factors" calculated from calendar year 2009 (CY 2009) data—is trended forward two years using the annualized trend factor developed from the table "Allowed Trends on Three Years' Data, with Seasonal Adjustments." Then, the trended allowed PMPM is multiplied by the group-specific demographic factors from the census. This means that the expected allowed PMPM for this group in 2011 equals $(401.18 \times 1.0682^2 \times 1.0418 \times 1.0195) = 486.17$. Then, multiplying the group's expected allowed PMPM by the benefit factor for the low plan selected by the group equals $(486.17 \times 0.7889) = 383.56$. This figure represents the expected claims cost PMPM that will be paid by the insurer. Finally, since the paid claims PMPM is targeted to be 75% of the premium, the premium PMPM charged to the group will be $(383.56/0.75) = 511.41$ PMPM. These calculations are performed in the table "Loss Ratio Method for Premium."

30.8 Experience Rating

Experience rating allows groups to receive premium concessions for claims history that is better than average, and allows insurers to charge premiums more reflective of expectations for groups whose history suggests that their costs will be higher or lower than average. Experience rating may be performed on a prospective basis, projecting probable claims experience for an upcoming policy period—or on a retrospective basis, either collecting a limited amount of additional premium for unfavorable experience relative to projections or refunding a limited amount for favorable experience.

The claims experience of large groups is considered fully credible; thus those groups' premiums are most often based entirely on their own experience. Insurers set their own thresholds for full credibility of a group's experience. A commonly used threshold is 12,000 member months—a number which is easily communicated and fits with standard utilization measures (e.g., cost models that reflect utilization per 1,000 annualized members, or 12,000 member months). The very largest groups may receive additional concessions, since their enrollment boosts an insurer's perception in the marketplace, improves efficiencies of scale in marketing and administration and can help the insurer gain leverage in provider negotiations. These concessions may take the form of premium discounts or of special considerations in reporting or claims processing.

30.8.1 Considerations in Experience Rating

Experience rating methods reflect the insurer's differing ability to rate for favorable and unfavorable experience. Insurers have greater latitude in giving discounts, refunds, and other considerations to groups with favorable experience than they have in seeking charges or extra premium from groups with unfavorable experience. A careful balance must therefore be struck, taking into account considerations both theoretical and practical.

Lines of business can be drastically different in the extent to which past experience is predictive of future experience. For example, consider products that offer non-occupational accidental death benefits. The number of accidental deaths to members of a given group that will occur in the next year is often assumed to be essentially independent of the number that occurred last year within the same group. As such, it is improper to give credit to the groups with fewer deaths than average and charge extra to the groups with more deaths. The insurer would most likely lose the groups that would be charged more, since they could shop for a better rate—and it would likely collect insufficient premium in the next year from the groups that remained, because the probability of accidental deaths is unchanged, regardless of their relatively few deaths last year. Then consider products that offer health care coverage. A significant portion of health care costs are incurred by people with chronic conditions. Thus a group's experience in the past year is more predictive of claims costs for the rating period.

The phenomenon of antiselection occurs when pricing patterns unintentionally encourage coverage lapse among groups with favorable experience, or attract a subset of groups with higher costs than the existing block. Antiselection can be caused by rating based on non-predictive experience, as described in the accidental death benefit example. Similarly, pooling of groups with credible experience fails to give full credit for favorable experience to the groups with lower costs, and assigns a portion of unfavorable experience to the other groups in the pool. Thus the inclusion of credible groups in the pooling process causes some of the groups with favorable experience to cancel coverage. It is important to draw a line that states as clearly as possible which groups' experience should be considered fully or partially credible.

Insurers draw this line by developing credibility models that determine the predictive ability of a given group's experience. The insurer will give weight in pricing to the group's experience according to the results of the credibility model, and use the manual rates to complement the weight given to the experience. The credibility model returns the percentage weight to give to the experience.

Experience is considered more credible as the exposure base grows. Larger exposure bases dampen the volatility of claims costs, whether that volatility is based on variance between individual members in claims costs, or on variance of costs for a single claim. Low frequency/high severity claims are especially volatile. The exposure unit should consider the number of members covered by the group and the length of time for which the members were covered. Thus the credibility model usually uses the member-month, or the life-year, as the base unit to assign credibility weighting. In this manner, experience may be considered fully credible above some volume of membership, and partially credible above a lower volume. The model is further affected by the level of statistical confidence desired by the insurer. As risk tolerance decreases, the model must increase the volume required for full credibility.

These theoretical concerns of experience rating must be weighed against practical concerns. A cost/benefit analysis should be performed to ensure that the value of added new sales and improved retention is sufficient for the costs of applying experience rating. The business areas (e.g., the underwriting department) must be able to administer experience rating appropriately, and the rating practices should preserve consistency between different lines of business and avoid adverse effects on existing business. Management philosophy and competitive pressures also affect the nature and depth of acceptable experience rating practices.

30.8.2 Prospective Experience Rating

Prospective claim rating involves using historical claims costs for a group or block of business to predict future claims costs. The prediction applies to the claims that will be incurred during the rating period, and is based on the costs of claims incurred during the experience period, including an estimate of claims incurred that haven't been paid yet. Insurers who maintain a claims processing data warehouse can generally pull data on claims already processed—that is, *incurred and paid*—based on criteria for the incurred dates of claims.

From there, the completion factors used in the reserving process (which will be examined in greater detail in the next chapter) can be applied to estimate the claims amounts that are *incurred but not reported* (IBNR). An estimate of ultimate amount of claims incurred, or the *completed incurred claims*, during the experience period is thus produced by adding the IBNR amount to the incurred and paid amount. Where the exact incurred date is not available, financial reporting may provide the information necessary to determine claims incurred; the claims incurred by a block of business for a given time period equal the claims paid for that block plus the change in the IBNR for that block during that time period. It is often preferable to improve the accuracy of the completed incurred estimate by pulling data for an incurred period that is at least a few months past. As processing continues over time or *runs out* for incurred claims, the picture of the ultimate claims incurred during the experience period becomes clearer, and the portion of IBNR included in the completed incurred estimate becomes smaller.

Historical analysis observes among groups a high level of fluctuation in claims costs that is effectively random, even after adjusting for demographics and other risk characteristics. The insurer can apply several different *pooling methods*, or techniques that smooth out these random fluctuations by spreading a portion of the claims of one or more highly adverse groups across all the groups included in the study. These practices are intended to improve the attractiveness of the rates by reducing the largest rate increases that the insurer would seek, while limiting the risk of antiselection that can follow from assigning the same percentage increase to each group. Pooling does not involve ignoring or excluding any of the claims costs from the total. In addition, pooling methods do not affect the contractual relationship between the insurer and the group.

30.8.2.1 Pooling methods

Catastrophic claims, or *shock claims*, refer to single claims that exceed a dollar limit selected by the insurer. The insurer pools catastrophic claims by removing the amounts in excess of the limit from the experience for the specific groups that contain them, and dividing the sum of the excess amounts across all the groups in the study. This pooling helps distribute the rate increase in a manner that balances premium sufficiency with selection risk, though as before, it does not affect the total claims cost or total premium needed.

EXAMPLE 30.14

Consider this example of the premium and claims experience for a block of five groups. Assume that the experience period is 12 months, and that all members were active for the entire period. The experience for group #3 includes one member who underwent an expensive hospital stay and incurred a catastrophic claim amount of 200,000. Table 30.4 summarizes the premium and claims by group.

TABLE 30.4 Premium and Claims Experience by Group

Group#	Members	Total Premium	Premium PMPM	Total Claims	Claims PMPM	Loss Ratio
1	20	48,000	200.00	28,800	120.00	60.0%
2	30	79,200	220.00	48,600	135.00	61.4%
3	40	120,000	250.00	240,000	500.00	200.0%
4	50	168,000	280.00	126,000	210.00	75.0%
5	60	216,000	300.00	158,400	220.00	73.3%
Total	**200**	**631,200**	**263.00**	**601,800**	**250.75**	**95.3%**

For demonstration purposes, assume that no increase in overall claims costs is expected for the rating period, and that the insurer targets an 80 percent loss ratio in pricing the block—thus, the future premium should be such that the ratio of claims to premium is 0.80. The insurer therefore needs to collect premium equal to

$$(250.75 \text{ claims PMPM})/0.80 = 313.44 \text{ premium PMPM},$$

which represents a rate increase of

$$(313.44 \text{ future premium})/(263.00 \text{ experience premium}) - 1 = 19.18\%.$$

Should the insurer apply that rate increase to each group, the future premium and projected loss ratio by group would be calculated as shown in Table 30.5.

TABLE 30.5 Applying Constant Rate Increase

Group#	Members	Current Premium PMPM	Future Premium PMPM	Future Claims PMPM	Future Loss Ratio
1	20	200.00	238.36	120.00	50.3%
2	30	220.00	262.19	135.00	51.5%
3	40	250.00	297.94	500.00	167.8%
4	50	280.00	333.70	210.00	62.9%
5	60	300.00	357.53	220.00	61.5%
Total	**200**	**263.00**	**313.44**	**250.75**	**80.0%**

Note that four of the five groups observed experience lower than the target loss ratio. Were they to receive a 19.2 percent rate increase, they would be more likely to cancel their coverage—and the future premium for group #3 would still be insufficient to cover its expected claims. However, it is not optimal simply to calculate varying rate increases such that each group's projected loss ratio would be 80 percent, as seen in Table 30.6.

TABLE 30.6 Applying Group-Specific Rate Increases

Group#	Members	Current Premium PMPM	Future Claims PMPM	Future Premium PMPM	Calculated Rate Increase
1	20	200.00	120.00	150.00	−25.00%
2	30	220.00	135.00	168.75	−23.30%
3	40	250.00	500.00	625.00	150.00%
4	50	280.00	210.00	262.50	−6.25%
5	60	300.00	220.00	275.00	−8.33%
Total	**200**	**263.00**	**250.75**	**313.44**	**19.18%**

The catastrophic claim incurred by the member in group #3 is likely not predictive of the total claims that the group will incur in the rating period. Further, a rate increase of that size is often prohibited by rating restrictions (as discussed in Section 29.4.2), and would likely prompt a negative response in the marketplace. The group would be expected to lapse, and the other groups more likely to renew given the lower rates—but the random event that happened to that particular member could happen to a member of one of the other groups in the future, and the insurer would have received less premium to prepare for it.

Suppose the insurer were to set a catastrophic claims threshold of 50,000, and pool the excess claims above that amount across all groups on a PMPM basis. The excess amount would be 150,000, which can be expressed as

$$(150{,}000 \text{ excess claims})/(12 \text{ months} \times 200 \text{ members}) = 62.50 \text{ PMPM}$$

This amount is known as a *pooling charge* and will be added to the claims experience for all members in the block. By subtracting the excess claims from the total for group #3, adding 62.50 PMPM to each group's claims (including group #3), and calculating group-specific increases that produce a projected loss ratio of 80 percent for each group, the necessary rate increases change as shown in Table 30.7.

TABLE 30.7 Rate Increase with Pooled Catastrophic Claims

Group#	Members	Pooled Total Claims	Pooled Claims PMPM	Necessary Premium PMPM	Necessary Rate Increase
1	20	43,800	182.50	228.13	14.06%
2	30	71,100	197.50	246.88	12.22%
3	40	120,000	250.00	312.50	25.00%
4	50	163,500	272.50	340.63	21.65%
5	60	203,400	282.50	353.13	17.71%
Total	**200**	**601,800**	**250.75**	**313.44**	**19.18%**

Note that the overall premium PMPM for the rating period is the same; but three of the five groups receive a lower increase than they would have in Table 30.5, and the increases for each group fall within a much narrower range than in Table 30.6.

The same purpose is achieved by setting an upper limit on the loss ratios observed by the groups in the study, or by setting a limit on the rate increase that would be charged to any group included in the pooling. As in the catastrophic claims pooling example, the amounts deemed to be in excess of the pooling limit are charged to all the groups, whether or not they incurred excessive claims.

Credibility weighting assigns a factor between zero and one to the experience of a group, depending on the extent to which the experience can be considered predictive of its future experience. The complement of the factor is then applied to the pooled experience of all groups in the block being studied. Thus, a commonly used formula states that

$$\text{Group Incurred Claims after Pooling} = (Z)(\text{Group Incurred Claims Before Pooling}) + (1\text{-}Z)(\text{All Groups' Average Incurred Claims})$$

where Z is the credibility factor, usually determined for each group by the number of members or other exposure units. The factor is generally the result of a credibility model, which may be developed using principles of limited-fluctuation or greatest-accuracy credibility theory. The formula thus combines the group-specific experience with the overall average for the block. This formula can be modified to use loss ratios in place of incurred claims.

Multi-year averaging can be used in place of pooling between groups where multiple years of experience can be observed for a group. This method can also be used to average out annual fluctuations of an entire block of business; usually, this method involves a weighted average with more weight given to recent years. For example, a "1-2-3" weighting of loss ratios over three years can be expressed as

$$\text{Pooled Loss Ratio in Year } N = ((3 \times LR_N) + (2 \times LR_{N\text{-}1}) + (1 \times LR_{N\text{-}2}))/6$$

These different methods of pooling need not be applied exclusively of each other. Combinations of methods allow analysis and projections that both reduce variance among groups and smooth out spikes in experience over time.

30.8.2.2 Monitoring experience of pooled blocks of business

Prospective experience rating requires frequent monitoring of claims and rating assumptions. Most insurers cover groups with renewal dates that occur throughout the year. This complicates analysis of a pool of experience-rated groups at any given point in time.

As noted previously, the application of a pooling formula should not change the calculated total of all incurred claims. Since the result produced by the formula for a particular group will vary from the actual incurred claims observed for the group, it is common to refer to the estimate produced by the pooling process as the *charged claims* for the group in question. The term is most appropriate in the context of retrospective experience rating, where an actual charge to a dividend or refund takes place.

It is important to maintain consistency between the units of measurement for the exposure base and the per-unit claims costs. The exposure base can be either the earned premium or the number of people covered. Different insurers use different terminology to describe the people included in the block of experience; they may refer to employees, subscribers, or members, where members may include subscribers and their dependents. If rates are charged on a per-employee basis, then an analysis of claims on a per-member basis is not directly applicable.

Analysis often includes groups with different benefit plans, based in different geographic areas, or otherwise misaligned in terms of their expected claims costs. The analysis should normalize for the different risk factors, as discussed previously, and the mix of conditions in the experience should be representative of future expectations for the block. Conditions that may change from the experience time period to the rating time period, and thus affect expected costs for the rating period, are generally referred to as *trends* and include:

- Mortality trends;
- Utilization trends in medical care;
- Trends in rates of disablement or length of disability;
- Cost trends, including impacts of changes to provider agreements;
- Changes in benefit designs;
- Changes in group demographics;
- Changes in government programs that affect costs of benefits intended to supplement the programs (e.g. Medicare supplemental insurance);
- Antiselection that follows from rate actions or changes in the competitive environment; and
- Other changes in the insured, economic, or financial environment.

Typically, trends are applied for the length of time between the midpoint of the experience period and the midpoint of the rating period, although conditions exist that discourage use of the midpoints as the determinant of the trend length (e.g., rapidly growing blocks of business; if significantly more members were covered in the later months of the experience period, then the average exposure date will be later than the midpoint). The expected costs per exposure unit for the rating period—known variously as *net rates* or *claim cost PMPM* are thus estimated by trending the claims experience forward to the rating period.

30.8.2.3 Calculating gross premium from net rates

The premiums actually charged to groups, or *gross premiums*, reflect net premiums plus several types of added costs associated with the insurer's ability to retain the group. Some of the additions, or *loads*, will be the same as for manual premium. There are other loads that are unique to the experience rating funding methodology. Additionally, the insurer may find it desirable to set group-specific loads for experience-rated groups that differ from the standard amounts applied to small groups. The most common types of loads include:

- Expense loads (admin expenses, commissions if applicable, and taxes)—usually expressed as a percentage of gross premium, per contract or per member, per unit of coverage, or per claim processed; follow from the method of allocation between lines of business;

- Contingent risk and profit charge—the margin that an insurer will explicitly build into the premiums; for protection against unexpectedly high claims cost experience or high lapse/cancellation rates, and for expected profit; some insurers may create potential profit margins by padding assumptions of trend or other influences on expected costs;
- Investment income—most often used as an offset to other expenses, reducing premiums charged; the investment credit can be negative if a group carries a negative fund balance, or if the insurer loses investment income due to late collections of premiums;
- Adjustments for factors unrelated to adequacy of premiums (e.g., considerations for groups with high public-relations value).

Less frequently, the gross premiums may include a deficit recovery charge to help the insurer recoup losses from prior years, or pooling charges that aren't built into the development of experience. These charges must be applied with caution in order to preserve competitiveness of rates and resist antiselection.

30.8.3 Retrospective Experience Rating

In recent years, insurers have more frequently sought arrangements that allow groups to receive credit for incurring costs lower than expected—or to be held accountable for costs above expectations—in the year that the experience materializes. Credit for favorable experience may be refunded to the group, through an experience rating refund or dividend—or accumulated in an account held by the insurer, called a premium stabilization reserve, claim fluctuation reserve, or contingency reserve.

Retrospective experience rating processes do not apply to all group policyholders. Typically, the retrospective rating provisions apply to groups above a certain size, where smaller groups can only be priced on a prospective basis. For mutual insurers, each group's participation in a refund program may be guaranteed by a contract provision. For other types of carriers, the availability of retrospective rating considerations may be restricted by senior management philosophy, or limited by the financial capability of the insurer. Retrospective arrangements are offered less frequently by insurers that cannot build up substantial reserves and are thus more vulnerable to rapid increases in claim costs.

The components of the retrospective refund calculation are described in the following subsections. The general calculation for the formula balance is as follows:

$$
\begin{aligned}
\text{Formula Balance} = {} & \text{Prior formula balance carried forward} \\
& + \text{premiums} \\
& + \text{investment earnings on funds held} \\
& - \text{claims charged} \\
& - \text{expenses charged} \\
& - \text{risk charge} \\
& - \text{rate stabilization reserve addition} \\
& - \text{profit.}
\end{aligned}
$$

30.8.3.1 Account credits

Positive account balances from prior years may be eliminated through a payout or through moving the balance out of a group's individual account and into the general company surplus. Likewise, negative account balances may be eliminated by a retrospective premium payment or by funding from company surplus (thus writing off the group's negative balance). If the accumulated balance is not eliminated in one of these ways, it will generally be carried forward into the next year's formula.

The premium used in this formula will usually just be the premium paid by the group for the contract year, but may contain adjustments for interest charges or credits for timing of premium payments. Investment earnings on claim reserves or other significant funds held by the insurer are typically credited to the group's account and may be a substantial source of income for groups that carry larger balances.

The amount of the investment income credit usually involves applying an assumed rate of return to the average balance of the existing account for a given period of time. The rate of return may be calculated before taxes or after taxes paid by the insurer.

30.8.3.2 Account charges

Several steps are needed to develop the component for claims charged. As with prospective rating, it is preferable to evaluate claims experience on an incurred basis, including a calculation for claim reserves. Unlike prospective rating, it is not necessary to measure claims on a per-exposure unit basis, since the bottom line of aggregate dollars of gain or loss represents the primary interest of both the insurer and the group. Retrospective reserves typically include larger margins than prospective reserves because competitive pressures are weaker; groups offer less resistance to higher reserves because funds held in excess of claim costs will ultimately be refunded to the groups; and conservatism in reserving creates greater comfort for insurers when groups terminate coverage.

Claims experience must be modified to account for contractual or administrative guarantees. Incurred claims in excess of the specific stop-loss level for individual claims, or the aggregate stop-loss level for the group's total claim amount, are removed from the experience. This removal is then offset with a pooling charge. Further adjustments take place to account for conversion privileges, where a member leaving a group may retain the same benefits on an individual basis. In the United States, these privileges typically exist on life and health coverage; in Canada, they are typically limited to life coverage. Finally, the insurer should consider all other policy provisions or administrative practices that affect the ability to hold a group financially accountable for incurred claims, and adjust as appropriate.

Thus, a general formula to determine charged claims is as follows:

$$\begin{aligned}\text{Claims Charged} = {} & \text{Claims paid} \\ & + \text{increase in claim reserves} \\ & - \text{pooled claims} \\ & + \text{pooling charges} \\ & + \text{conversion charges} \\ & + \text{claim margins, if any}\end{aligned}$$

Expense charges applied to specific groups are often impacted by the group's size and the competitive leverage maintained, and the administrative capabilities of the insurer. The expenses charged to each product depend in part on the allocation methods used by the insurer, and in part on the duration of the groups. As discussed previously, expenses are typically highest in the first year that a group is active, due to the costs of acquisition (including commissions and marketing costs) and new enrollment processing. The basis unit can differ among the products that the insurer offers. Internal reporting on expenses may break out to levels of detail that distinguish claim administration, commissions and sales expenses, premium taxes, conversion charges, corporate overhead, risk and pooling charges, and other expenses that are not large enough to justify a separate line on the experience report.

Risk charges account for uncertainty in the rate of cancellations or nonrenewals of groups, especially those that do not remain in force long enough for the insurer to recover the acquisition expenses, and statistically expected variance in claims costs given the size of the groups. The risk to the insurer of being in a deficit position is reflected through a separate risk charge to aid accumulation of a rate stabilization reserve. Additional risk protection is offered through conditions on release of the reserve, and depending on the contract with the group, the reserve may not even be payable to the group upon termination. The reserve can help to stabilize rate increases, but if the reserve is exhausted, rate increases may be higher in order to rebuild the reserve.

The inclusion of an explicit profit margin is less desirable when experience exhibits must be shown to a group policyholder. Thus, insurers will be more likely to build margins into assumptions for other rating variables in order to earn a profit (or an acceptable contribution to surplus, for mutual insurance companies or not-for-profit organizations).

CHAPTER 31
Reserving

The claims data available at any given point in time does not necessarily represent the ultimate financial responsibility for which the insurer or plan sponsor will be liable. Policyholders and members often do not immediately file claims as soon as a claim event occurs. There may be delays in submitting claims for processing from providers. On the insurer's end, determination of eligibility, backlogs in processing, and changes to claim processing systems result in further delays between the date of the claim event and the date that the applicable payment is made. For certain lines of insurance products, such as long-term disability (LTD) or long-term care (LTC) insurance, benefits are payable over months or years into the future. This creates uncertainty even when all of the relevant claims have been filed and processed.

Plan sponsors will therefore prepare for the outstanding financial liability by developing estimates of claim reserves, or funds to be held for payouts on claims that are believed to have been incurred but not yet paid. The proper estimation of reserves ensures solvency and provides the most accurate picture of profitability—either for a particular product, or for the entire operation of a carrier. This chapter will distinguish between short-term reserves for products that reimburse for services already provided or pay benefits that can be more precisely measured in advance (e.g., health or life policies) and long-term reserves for products that pay benefits over a period of time (e.g., LTD or LTC).

31.1 Definitions of Terms

The following terms help clarify aspects of the reserving process:

- Valuation date—the date at which reserves are estimated;
- Incurred date or loss date—the date on which an event occurs that causes a liability. This could be the date of death, disability, encounter with a medical provider, or filling of a prescription;
- Service date—the date that a service is actually performed or delivered. Each service date must be assigned an incurred date;
- Reporting date—the date that a claim is reported or submitted for processing;
- Paid date—the date that a claim is paid or reimbursed to the provider and moved from reserve status to paid status;
- Lag—refers to the length of time between two dates. Types of lag include
  - Reporting lag, between incurred date and reporting date;
  - Service lag, between incurred date and service date;
  - Payment lag, between incurred date and paid date; and
  - Accrual lag, between service date and paid date;
- Claims incurred and paid to date—the amount of claims that have been paid up to a specific point in time that were incurred during a given time period (e.g., the year and month in which services were provided);
- Runout—a term used to describe the ongoing process of payments for claims that were incurred at a given point in time and paid during subsequent months or years;

- Ultimate incurred claims—the total amount of claims that were incurred during a given time period, usually estimated until a substantial amount of time has passed; and
- Completion factors—estimated ratios of claims incurred and paid to date to ultimate incurred claims for a specified time period; developed by analyzing historical percentages of claims paid after various lag periods.

The timeline in Figure 31.1 tracks the order of dates most relevant to health reserving. Other dates identified above carry importance to different lines of business. For example, on LTD claims, multiple service dates are assigned to one incurred date.

FIGURE 31.1 Claim processing timeline

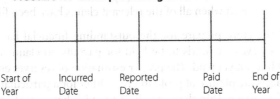

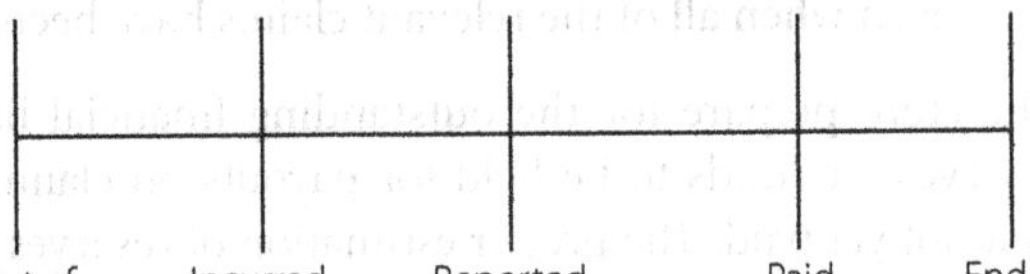

When speaking of claim reserves, it is common to include both *reserves* and *liabilities*, though these terms do not strictly refer to the same concept. As defined by statutory accounting principles, liabilities represent payments for services that have already been delivered, while reserves are established for future rendering of services related to claim events that have occurred. The plan sponsor will hold funds in reserve for these categories of claims:

- Due and unpaid—for claims have been submitted and processed, and an amount calculated to be paid or reimbursed, but payment has not yet been made;
- In course of settlement—for claims that have been submitted but not yet processed, as further information or investigation may be needed, and the amount due has not been determined;
- Incurred and reported—for claims submitted that are unpaid, or the sum of the due and unpaid amount and the in course of settlement amount;
- Incurred but not reported (IBNR)—for claims that result from events or services that occurred prior to the valuation date, but have not been submitted as of the valuation date; these amounts are thus unknown to the insurer and are typically estimated by examining patterns of claim runout;
- Unaccrued—for services that are after the valuation date but tied to events that occurred on or before the valuation date; most common for LTD and LTC coverage;
- Deferred maternity or other extended benefits—for benefits triggered by events prior to the valuation date, where contractual provisions allow for payments into the future; and
- Other special reserves—for premium waivers on disability coverage or similar commitments that are not necessarily related to claim events

Estimation of reserves is a critical component of premium development. As such, premiums and reserves should be calculated on a consistent basis of timing. That is, if rates are set by examining claims experience that covers a range of incurred dates, then the reserve calculation should likewise measure claims paid and outstanding over a range of incurred dates.

Several different spheres of influence impact the level of reserves to be established. These influences are all connected by a common thread; namely, they all relate to the anticipated financial obligation of the insurer that results from the policies issued. Reserves can be calculated under different accounting standards (e.g., statutory, GAAP and tax) that feature varying regulations and required assumptions. For example, statutory reserves include more conservative margins for adverse experience than do GAAP reserves, which are based on best-estimate assumptions of future claims.

31.1.1 Other Health Reserves

Carriers may set up other reserves during the course of operations for liabilities that they may have incurred. These reserves are set for certain contractual obligations of the carrier with third parties. The techniques described in this note may be used to fully account for the total liability to these third parties.

- Premium Deficiency Reserves—Carriers may be required to set aside reserves for non-performing lines of business or contracts to reflect losses that will not be able to be required until a future renewal period.
- Unearned Premium Reserves—Reserves are required for premiums that have paid to the carrier for periods that span across a valuation date and thus have not been earned by the carrier. Accounting periods generally are set assuming premiums are due on the first of the month with the valuation date as of the last date of the month. This assumes that the premium paid has been fully earned by the carrier. There may be situations where the premium is for a longer period of time or is paid in the middle of the month and therefore has not been fully earned by the carrier. In these cases an unearned premium needs to be set aside that is a pro-rate portion of the premium paid. If commissions or other obligations have already been paid these may be removed from the premium.
- Provider Liabilities—Reserves for contracts with providers for risk sharing arrangements. In certain instance carriers have risk sharing arrangements with providers. The carrier may only pay a certain percentage of the claims payable with the rest held as a deposit. If claims experience is good the carrier will settle with the provider at an agreed upon date. These contracts are created so that the provider is rewarded if certain utilization and claim payment targets are met. That is, they share in the risk of the claims experience.
- Refund Liabilities—Reserves for policyholders where risk sharing arrangements have been made for favorable experience that can be used to offset future premiums. Carriers may enter agreements with contract holders to share in positive experience of the policy holder. These agreements are usually sought by larger clients who do not want to self-insure, but do want to benefit from positive experience. The group may not have a tolerance for adverse results but may be large enough to negotiate participation in their positive experience. Refund liabilities, premium stabilization reserves or other forms of participating reserves are created by the carrier for

the policyholder's benefit. Rather than a lump sum payment to the contract holder, positive results may be used to offset future premiums.

- Expense Adjustment Reserve—Reserve set aside for the cost of adjudicating claims in the future. In addition to reserves for adverse deviations, carriers are required to set aside reserves for the administration of claims past the valuation date. These reserves are usually stated as a percent of the reserves already being held. They represent the expense of administering claim payments beyond the valuation date.

31.2 Short-Term Reserves

31.2.1 Influences on Claim Reserve Calculations for Short-Term Products

Reserve calculations are influenced by:

- Whether reserves are set up for services that have already occurred, or for services that will be delivered in the future
- Accounting basis—Statutory, GAAP, and tax reserves often use different assumptions of trends, interest rates, or allowable margins;
- Application of a discount rate—Discounts to future payments do not usually apply for products where payouts are generally expected to occur soon after the claims are incurred (e.g., major medical), but may be used if payouts are projected far into the future;
- Reconciliation—Reporting practices, claim inventory counts, reported hospital admissions and other data should reconcile to accounting department;
- Internal company practices—Claim payment patterns slow down or speed up due to personnel events, changes in processing systems or other company-specific practices such as the method of dating claims;
- External forces—New laws, regulations or governmental mandates impact lags in claim payments. Providers may affect the payment pattern by catching up on claim submittal at the end of each year;
- Policy provisions—Claim sizes, benefit designs, and plan provisions that affect utilization (either pre-certification requirements or other efforts to dampen utilization, or cost-sharing reductions or waivers that encourage utilization) affect claim runout patterns. Further, different runout patterns exist for various lines of insurance coverage. For example, the vast majority of claims are paid within a few months of incurral for life and health products. However, disability claims observe a much longer runout, since disability products pay continuing benefits contingent on disablement;
- Insurance characteristics—New plans initially observe longer lags, as members and insurers alike may be relatively unfamiliar with the benefit design, claim filing and processing procedures, or impact of pre-existing condition exclusions. Additionally, since larger claims generally require greater investigation efforts, lags tend to increase as inflationary trends increase severity of claims;
- Reserve cells—Different product lines or categories of plan designs often carry different reserves. This allows the insurer to reflect each product's claim payment pattern, utilization trend and cost trend. The reserving process for a particular product may calculate separate completion factors for different types of services. For

example, claims for inpatient admissions, for which hospitals often delay submission of claims while billing, coding and other internal processes are followed and insurer administration efforts are relatively greater, run out—or *complete*—at a slower pace than claims for prescriptions, which usually include only one claim line per prescription and can be electronically submitted and efficiently processed;

- Care management—Precertification requirements, referral procedures, utilization review and other care management practices all affect lag distributions, and may result in reduced frequency of high-cost claims that tend to have longer lag periods. Provider discounts and risk-sharing arrangements like *withholds* (delayed payments that are conditional on certain performance requirements), *settlements* (retroactive payments or refunds between the insurer and the provider that bring total payments into a negotiated range), or incentive payments also affect claim cost levels and therefore levels of necessary reserves;
- Trends—Reserves do not typically depend directly on trend rates. However, the trends that result from the reserve calculation may be tracked and analyzed over time;
- Seasonality—Claim levels typically vary by noticeable amounts over the course of a year. Benefit designs, certain types of services and the incurral dating method chosen by the insurer may all produce claim incurral patterns that should be considered in developing ultimate estimates. For example, medical plans with annual deductibles and out-of-pocket limits tend to observe higher claim levels at the end of the year, as members who have reached their plan limits elect to receive more services before the new policy year begins and the cost-sharing accumulations reset;
- Economic influences—Recessions reduce demand for elective care but may result in increased utilization and greater average duration of enrollment; and
- Administrative expenses—Expense liabilities must be related to incurred claims, rather than paid claims, per the Actuarial Standards of Practice.

31.2.2 Reserve Methods

Besides the various influences on the reserve calculation, claim liability reserves can be calculated using a method that most appropriately reflects the pattern of claim runout, efficiency in claims processing, the method of incurral dating, or the manner by which the component assumptions are developed. This section describes the most common methods used in reserve calculations, and the case study illustrates the application of a few of these methods. The IBNR estimate is the basis for the reserve calculation in the given examples. Reserves commonly include a margin, or *PAD*, on top of the IBNR estimate in order to improve the likelihood that the total financial liability for claims will be met.

EXAMPLE 31.1 CASE STUDY CLAIMS TRIANGLE

The table, "Incurred/Paid Claims Triangle," in the Excel file, shows the case study *claims triangle*, which cross-tabulates the claim dollars that the insurer paid by the months in which claims are incurred and paid. Each row represents a month in which claims are incurred, and each column represents a month in which claims are paid. For example, in May 2009, there was 372,318 paid in respect of claims incurred in March 2009. Note that for this block, most of the claims incurred in each month are paid within the first three months following incurral. All claims are paid within 15 months of the incurred date. The reserves will be calculated for a valuation date of 3/31/2011 for all claims incurred prior to that date.

31.2.2.1 Factor method

This method establishes a reserve as a percentage of premiums. Analysis of reserves from prior valuations will recommend the percentage to use. The analysis observes the claims incurred before the valuation date but paid after the valuation date, and compares those claim amounts to the premiums in force on the valuation date. This method is most commonly used for products with relatively short runout periods, such as group life insurance.

EXAMPLE 31.2 CASE STUDY RESERVE BY FACTOR METHOD

Table 31.1 demonstrates the reserve calculated by the factor method as of 3/31/2011 for all claims incurred prior to that date. Note that separate factors are calculated for each incurred year, since claims incurred for each year are run out to different points in time (e.g., claims incurred during 2010 are much closer to completion of payments than are claims incurred during 2011).

TABLE 31.1 Reserve Using Factor Method

Year	**2009**	**2010**	**2011**
Member Months	96,300	94,524	24,813
Premium PMPM	400.00	440.00	484.00
Total Premium	38,520,000	41,590,560	12,009,492
Incurred in CY2009			
Paid thru EOY	29,373,796		
Paid after EOY (Runout)	1,533,458		
Runout as % of Premium	3.981%		
Reserve for CY 2010		**1,655,695**	
Incurred in 1Q2010			
Paid thru 3/31		6,424,797	
Paid after 3/31 (Runout)		1,473,435	
Runout as % of Premium		3.543%	
Reserve for YTD 2011			**1,701,848**
Reserve at Valuation Date 3/31/2011			**3,357,543**

The "Paid thru EOY" value is the sum of all entries in the claim triangle that were incurred in 2009 (rows 2 through 13 in the spreadsheet) and paid that same year (columns B through M). The runout comes from the same rows, but columns N through AB. It is assumed that there will be no payments after March 2011 for claims incurred in 2009. The reserve for claims incurred in 2010 is then taken as the runout percent multiplied by the 2010 premium (41,590,560 × 0.03981) = 1,655,695. A similar calculation is used to determine the reserve for claims incurred in the first three months of 2011, though note that the reserve for 2011 equals the 1Q 2010 runout factor times the annualized 2011 premium (4 × 12,009,492 × 0.03543) = 1,701,848.

31.2.2.2 Lag/development method

Development methods analyze historical progression of claim payments over time in relation to their incurral dates. The key assumption behind these methods is that a future runout pattern can be assumed, and known amounts of claims incurred and paid to date can therefore be extrapolated into an estimate of ultimate claims. The data set used should be sufficiently large to credibly illustrate the runout pattern of the claims included. Credibility can be enhanced by combining products or blocks if their runout patterns are similar—but blocks with dissimilar patterns should not be combined, as neither block's pattern would be accurately represented.

EXAMPLE 31.3 CASE STUDY RESERVE USING LAG METHOD

To calculate an IBNR estimate using this method, first create a claims triangle as used for the factor method. Preferably, the rows of the claims triangle represent short incurred periods—typically months or quarters. In the table "Claim Payment Runout, for Reserve Using Lag Method," in the Excel file, the "Incurred and Paid to Date" column is the total of all claims paid in respect of the given incurral month. For each lag, the entry is the cumulative paid claims through that time. Thus for claims incurred January 2009, which total 2,334,988 incurred and paid to date, the lag-zero paid amount (paid in January 2009) is 1,482,716; the lag-one paid amount (paid in February 2009) is 613,644, which means that a total of 2,096,360 was incurred in January 2009 and paid through February; and so on.

Then, express each lag-month's cumulative paid total as a percentage of the total incurred and paid to date, as shown in the table "Claim Payment Ratios by Lag Month, for Reserve Using Lag Method," in the Excel file. For example, the first Lag0 factor is 1,482,988/2,334,988 = 0.634999. The *completion factor* for each lag month, shown in the Average row at the bottom of the table, is the arithmetic average of the percentages in each column. The Lag0 value is interpreted as 58.36 percent of the ultimate payments in respect of a given month are paid that same month. Similarly, 87.29 percent of ultimate payments are paid by the end of the following month. The actuary has latitude in determining the number of months over which the average can be calculated, the weighting used to calculate the average, and the subset of the incurred months to use in setting the completion factors.

The final calculation is in Table 31.2. Calculate the ultimate incurred claims estimate for each incurred month which is not assumed to be completely run out, and subtract the amounts paid to date for each of those incurred months from the ultimate estimate. The remainder for each month is the IBNR estimate, and the reserve is the sum of the IBNR estimates for all the uncompleted months. The ultimate incurred estimates are obtained by dividing the incurred and paid to date value by the lag factor from the previous table.

TABLE 31.2 Lag Method IBNR

Incurred Yr/Mo	Incurred and Paid to Date	Lag Factor	Ultimate Incurred Estimate	Estimated IBNR
2010/01	2,751,933	1.000000	2,751,933	–
2010/02	2,277,418	0.999110	2,279,446	2,028
2010/03	2,868,881	0.998771	2,872,412	3,531
2010/04	2,456,518	0.997936	2,461,598	5,080
2010/05	2,479,960	0.996982	2,487,466	7,506
2010/06	2,791,607	0.996451	2,801,549	9,942
2010/07	2,567,085	0.995786	2,577,947	10,863
2010/08	3,241,420	0.994936	3,257,918	16,498
2010/09	2,481,387	0.993832	2,496,787	15,400
2010/10	2,421,387	0.991614	2,441,865	20,478
2010/11	2,389,325	0.988243	2,417,750	28,425
2010/12	2,885,882	0.980563	2,943,087	57,205
2011/01	2,778,713	0.943487	2,945,152	166,439
2011/02	2,197,649	0.872885	2,517,686	320,037
2011/03	1,822,806	0.583605	3,123,355	1,300,549
Total	**38,411,972**		**40,375,951**	**1,963,979**

The estimates by month are generally given less credence if incurred claims for recent months are used in setting the factors. Inconsistency in claim submission and short-term processing rates often leads to a relatively wide range of completion factors observed in the months of lag zero through two, as shown in the first three factor columns in the table "Claim Payment Ratios by Lag Month, for Reserve Using Lag Method." Note that the lag-zero completion factor ranges between 0.461846 and 0.653507, and the lag-one factor varies between 0.798052 and 0.926002. Thus, if completion factors were to be based on claims observed for recent months, they should be used with caution. Typically, another method such as a trended claim PMPM amount, a percentage of earned premiums, or an assumed loss ratio would be applied to estimate claims for 2011 incurred months in that scenario.

The calculated completion factors may need to be adjusted for seasonality concerns. If the block of business included in this example generally observes higher claims at the end of the year, then factors determined by analyzing the runout pattern of claims incurred in January through June may not be representative of the expected pattern for months where claim volumes are higher and submissions or processing may be delayed. Thus the completion factor calculation may be improved by using data from previous years for the same calendar months. Additionally, development methods can be unreliable when longer payout periods are involved, claim amounts fluctuate less predictably, or large settlements may be paid out that create spikes in the runout pattern.

31.2.2.3 Loss ratio method

This method is most commonly used for new blocks of business, where sufficient experience to evaluate claim volumes and runout patterns does not exist, or to estimate claims for the most recent incurred months in conjunction with a lag/development method. As in other methods, the reserve equals the estimate of ultimate incurred claims minus the claims paid to date. The ultimate incurred claims estimate multiplies the earned premium by an estimated loss ratio, often the target loss ratio used in pricing.

EXAMPLE 31.4 CASE STUDY LOSS RATIO METHOD

Table 31.3 demonstrates the calculation of IBNR estimates using this method, assuming the premiums in force were set using a 75 percent target loss ratio. The incurred claim estimate is the premium multiplied by the pricing loss ratio. Note that the claims paid to date were already in excess of 75 percent of premiums for 2010. Thus, the IBNR estimate for 2010 is negative in the example, which is unrealistic in practice. For lines of business that typically observe short runout periods, it isn't useful to use the loss ratio method for claim periods that are nearly complete. The IBNR estimate for 2011 is far more likely to be valid. The 2010 estimate would likely be set at a relatively small positive number to reflect the likely condition that some claims incurred during 2010 are still outstanding, and more payments will therefore occur.

TABLE 31.3 Loss ratio method

Year	2010	2011
Total Premium	41,590,560	12,009,492
Pricing Loss Ratio	75.0%	75.0%
Incurred Claims Estimate	31,192,920	9,007,119
Incurred and Paid to Date	31,612,804	6,799,168
IBNR	(419,884)	2,207,951
Reserve at Valuation Date		**1,788,067**

Note that the reserve estimates calculated using different methods do not equal each other. This does not imply by itself that one method is preferable to the others; there is no unique and correct answer to the question "How much should the plan hold in reserve for incurred claims?" Combinations of these methods, or modifications to the results of any of these methods, may be applied in order to reach the final amount established as the reserve. The actuary is responsible for making reasonable choices that are consistent with known business conditions, regulatory considerations and internal claim processing capabilities. Company financial objectives may mean that the final amount booked as reserves will be different from the actuarial estimate. The reserve should help the plan prepare adequately for expected claims and scenarios of adverse deviation without needlessly overstating expectations for ultimate claims, which could distort profitability measures and cause the insurer to raise premiums beyond the necessary amount.

31.2.2.4 Examiners method

This method is most commonly used to set *case reserves*, which are calculated on an individual basis for specific known claims. It relies on qualified personnel to estimate the remaining claim payments based on characteristics of each claim. Doctors' statements and historical experience on similar claims may be used to make the estimates. These claims are often subject to lawsuits, and as such, the legal department should be involved in the process. Like the average size claim method, this method establishes separate estimates for reported claims and unreported claims.

31.2.2.5 Stochastic approaches

The various reserve methods described in this section are all deterministic in nature. That is, they suggest that future runout patterns and incurred claim estimates can be precisely predicted from past experience and known conditions (e.g., enrollment). Each of these methods, however, can incorporate a stochastic approach, which lends itself to statements about the probability that the level and adequacy of reserves are sufficient, or about probabilities related to specific components (e.g., trend assumptions) of the claims estimates. The reserve can then be calculated as a function of one or more of these components, and the potential variability in the reserve estimate properly examined.

Several advantages follow from using a stochastic approach in the development of reserves. Explicit guidance is provided in establishing a PAD. Similarly, company decision-makers receive explicit illustration of potential variability in reserve levels and reported earnings. Reserves for separate lines of business can be better evaluated in the proper context. Finally, the variability found within different internal and external influences on claim runout can be quantified, and the potential error in the financial entry for reserves becomes clearer.

However, other issues complicate the use of stochastic methods, and the cost/benefit analysis of implementing processes based on these methods must be considered. The audience for the results of the stochastic modeling may be less aware or less accepting of advanced statistical methods that are difficult to understand. They may also become surprised or confused when past reserve estimates are adjusted to reflect current probability expectations. These methods are often time- and labor-intensive, and as such, issues of feasibility of implementation must be considered, as must the relevance of a method for which few people in a given audience would appreciate the complexity.

31.2.2.6 Modeling techniques and considerations

As discussed in the previous subsection, stochastic approaches involve modeling separate components of the reserve and combining the results of the component models to build up the reserve estimate. For example, when using an average size claim method to estimate incurred claims, consider the claim size as an independent random variable with an observed mean and variance. The probability function associated with the claim size can then be used to compute a likelihood interval, which is a concept that is statistically rigorous but can be grasped by people without a strong mathematics background.

Techniques available for use in stochastic modeling include:

- Parametric distribution fitting—This technique involves directly fitting a distribution to a data set. It works best for stationary processes, where the distribution fitted to experience data is expected to be valid for future experience. Other techniques are preferable when trends, cyclical patterns, or other influences exist that impact the mean and variance of the variable being modeled.
- Ordinary least-squares regression—This technique allows for simple forecasting models of projected loss ratios or trends. It can be used in conjunction with the fitted distribution to capture cyclical patterns (e.g. seasonality) or inflationary trends.
- Generalized linear models—These models account for boundaries on the variable being modeled, such as a requirement that the variable be greater than zero at all times, or skewing effects to the distribution of the variable when those boundaries exist.
- Stochastic time series models—These models are useful when values are correlated across time.
- Monte Carlo sampling/simulation—Sampling techniques are useful in combining results of different models.

Stochastic model development requires consideration of several conditions that affect the choice of modeling techniques, the level of sophistication built into the model, and the degree of actuarial judgment needed to interpret the results. Changes in these conditions, as well as the forces that contribute to the levels of reserves needed, require that the model structure and results be continuously monitored and evaluated.

- Availability of data—The amount of data available affects the ability to perform historical validation, confirm model assumptions, create valid results, and communicate them in a manner that is meaningful to decision-makers.
- Appropriateness of data—Within the model development process, the extent to which the historical data is predictive of future experience should be considered. As discussed previously, data for relatively new or growing blocks of business may not be sufficiently credible to represent future expectations. Similarly, projections for closed blocks that are no longer adding new members and are caught in an antiselective death spiral should adjust the data analysis to reflect the changing expectations. Changes in payment processes and systems should also be considered, whether the changes are one-time or permanent.
- Appropriateness of model—It is critical to choose a model that is proper to apply to the data at hand. Use of a model or technique published in a paper or textbook may be appealing, but if the model is not developed for the purpose at hand, its results can be misleading. Additionally, since the results of the model directly depend on the component assumptions, validation of the assumptions is necessary.
- Access to statistical software—A lack of access, or a lack of understanding of its proper application, may limit the choices available. Programs available through commercial vendors may not be designed with the appropriate consideration for company-specific or product-specific conditions.

31.2.3 EXERCISE

31.1 Given the premium and claims figures in Table 31.3, recalculate the Estimated IBNR for CY 2011 incurred months using the loss ratio method, based on an 80% loss ratio assumption.

31.3 Long-Term Reserves

31.3.1 Aspects of Long-Term Insurance Products

LTD insurance and LTC insurance are the most prevalent forms of long-term health benefits. The risks associated with each of these product lines differ, but setting reserves for long-term benefits must consider several characteristics shared by these products. These characteristics affect the amount and timing of benefit payments, which determine the value of the benefits and therefore must be explicitly included in the calculation of reserves.

- Elimination Periods—Both types of products include a feature that requires a short length of time to pass after a claimant becomes eligible for benefits before any benefits will actually be paid. Thus the function of the elimination period is similar in some ways to a deductible on a health insurance policy; and just as many health insurers offer several deductible options for their products, several different elimination periods are available for LTD and LTC plans. The most common elimination periods are 90 days or longer.
- Periodic Benefits—LTD and LTC plans typically pay a defined benefit amount per time period. LTD plans will usually specify an amount to be paid each month, where LTC plans will usually reimburse actual expenses up to a daily limit.
- Long-Term Benefit Periods—While LTD and LTC plans pay a specified benefit per month or day, the length of time over which the benefit is to be paid can vary by claimant, but is generally much longer than other health benefits. Both products set a maximum benefit so that the benefit period is not completely open-ended. LTD plans often pay benefits from the date of disability until age 65 (sometimes specifying a different "normal retirement age" at which point benefits are no longer payable), where LTC plans set a maximum lifetime dollar amount that indirectly creates a maximum benefit period.
- Optional Riders—Both types of products offer plan options, also known as *riders*, that can be added on to a standard policy and impact the amount and timing of benefits payable. Common riders include cost-of-living adjustments that increase benefit payments in step with inflation rates, and partial disability benefits that pay a reduced amount if the claimant, though disabled, is able to work part-time.
- Integration of Benefits—Both types of products usually provide for reductions in the benefit amount by coordinating with public programs that pay benefits to their recipients. Thus LTC plans often integrate with Medicare long-term care programs, while LTD plans coordinate with Social Security and Workers Compensation to ensure that total disability benefits do not exceed a percentage of pre-disability earnings.
- Limitations and Exclusions—Both products may feature shortened benefit periods for specific types of claims (e.g., mental or nervous conditions, which are often limited to a two-year maximum payable period) or exclude coverage for other types of claims that produce a moral hazard (e.g., intentionally self-inflicted injuries).

31.3.2 Types of Claims and Reserve Methodologies

Long-term claims are usually classified into three types that are treated separately for reserve calculations due to the different amounts of information available for each type. Each claim can be defined either as an *open claim* if benefits are already being paid, as a *pending claim* if it has been reported to the insurer but benefit payments have not begun, or as an *IBNR claim* if the claim event has already occurred but has not been reported to the insurer.

31.3.2.1 Open claims

Open claims represent the largest portion of the total claim reserve for LTD and LTC plans. The reserve calculation for open claims uses tables of expected claim termination rates. Thus, the term *tabular reserves* is commonly used to refer to reserves for open claims. The open claim reserve calculation represents the probability that each scheduled benefit will be paid and the value of each scheduled benefit payable, discounted for interest. The reserve at claim duration n (where n is measured from the claim incurral date) is expressed as

$$_{n}V = \sum_{t=0}^{BP-n-1} \text{Benefit}_{n+t} \times \text{Continuance}_{n+t} \times \text{InterestDiscount}_{t}$$

The first term represents the benefit to be paid t periods from now, the second term represents the probability that the benefit will be paid and the third term represents a discount factor for a payment to be made t periods from now. BP is the number of payment periods from incurral to the end of the benefit period. The benefit amount depends on the design of the plan; some plans provide for a constant monthly benefit while others include benefits adjusted for inflation or other considerations as described in Section 31.3.1. The formula should therefore reflect known changes to the benefit amount at each time payable during the benefit period.

The continuance factor typically is developed from data in a continuance table, which tracks experience history on the number of claimants that reached different benchmarks of claim duration. A sample continuance table is provided in Table 31.4.

TABLE 31.4 Sample Continuance Table

Claim Duration	Number of Claimants, Age At Claim x		
in months	30	40	50
0	500	500	500
1	490	480	460
2	480	460	420
3	470	440	380
4	460	420	340
5	450	400	300
6	440	380	260
7	430	360	220

The values for each month represent the number of the initial claimants that remain disabled at the end of each month. Thus, the table illustrates the probability that a person who becomes disabled at a given age will remain disabled for a given number of months.

The reserve formula can be restated in notation commonly used by actuaries, which breaks out the component assumptions, as follows

$$_{n}V = \sum_{t=0}^{BP-n-1} b_{n+t} \frac{l_{[x]+n+t+0.5}}{l_{[x]+n}} (1 + i)^{-(t+0.5)/12}.$$

The formula assumes monthly payments and it is assumed that benefits are paid in the middle of the month. Using a uniform distribution of decrements within the month,

$$l_{[x]+n+t+0.5} = \frac{l_{[x]+n+t} + l_{[x]+n+t+1}}{2}.$$

Note that select table notation is used to reflect the fact that, as illustrated in Table 31.4, continuance probabilities depend on the age at claim incurral.

EXAMPLE 31.5 TABULAR RESERVE CALCULATION

The following demonstrates the calculation (using Table 31.4) of the tabular reserve at time three months for a 40-year-old claimant whose plan contains a three-month elimination period, a three-month benefit period, and a 1,000 monthly benefit, with a 6% annual interest rate assumption.

$$_{3}V = 1000\frac{430}{440}1.06^{-1/24} + 1000\frac{410}{440}1.06^{-3/24} + 1000\frac{390}{440}1.06^{-5/24}$$

$$= 974.90 + 925.06 + 875.67 = 2{,}775.63.$$

31.3.2.2 Pending claims

The reserve calculation for pending claims is similar to that for open claims, but includes an additional factor that represents the likelihood that a claimant will reach eligibility for benefits. Recall that pending claims refer to people who have reported claims to the insurer but are not yet receiving benefits. The *pending factor* reflects the probability that the claimant will remain disabled throughout the elimination period and will be approved for benefits when the elimination period ends.

Thus, the claim reserve for pending claims still in the elimination period equals the tabular reserve at the end of the elimination period multiplied by the pending factor. The formula is

$$_{n}V' = \text{Pend} \times {_{n}V}.$$

Similarly, the claim reserve for pending claims that have completed the elimination period but are not yet approved for benefits equals the sum of two terms (1) the tabular reserve at the current claim duration and (2) the value of benefit payments already due contingent on approval, with interest accrued to the valuation date. This sum is multiplied by the pending factor. The pending claim reserve formula at claim duration n, where EP is the length of the elimination period and n is greater than the number of months in the elimination period, is

$$_{n}V' = \text{Pend} \times \left\{ {_{n}V} + \sum_{t=EP+1}^{n} [Benefit_t \times (1 + i)^{(n-t)/12}] \right\}.$$

Pending factors are developed from internal experience and may be established as separate factors for pending claims in the elimination period and pending claims that have completed the elimination period, but most often a single factor is used that combines both concepts. Some companies add the pending claims to the IBNR claims in order to develop an IBNR reserve.

31.3.2.3 IBNR claims

IBNR claims are unknown at the valuation date and must therefore be estimated. The most common methods to develop the IBNR claim estimate are the lag method and the loss ratio method. These methods are applied to long-term benefits in much the same manner as for short-term benefits.

The lag method is preferred when credible experience is available. The steps of calculating the IBNR estimate are similar to those of the factor method described for short-term reserves. The lag periods between the incurred date and the paid date are often much longer for long-term products than for health or other short-term products. Hence, calculating the completion factor in the same manner described in the short-term section may be less reliable. It requires examining historical data on incurred claims that were not reported as of a prior valuation date and calculating a tabular reserve for each of those claims as of that prior valuation date. The sum of those tabular reserves represents the amount that would have been held for those claims if they had been reported, and is usually expressed as a percentage of premiums earned during the year of the valuation date and known as the *IBNR reserve factor*. This factor can then be multiplied by the premium earned during the year of the current valuation date to reflect the IBNR reserve as of the valuation date. In this way, the reserve established is a function of the size of the block, which makes intuitive sense.

The loss ratio method applies when certain conditions are met, such as for newer or smaller blocks of business that have not developed sufficiently credible experience. The method determines the IBNR reserve factor by subtracting the actual loss ratio—incurred claims (or paid claims plus change in reserves) for the year divided by the earned premium—from the target loss ratio used in pricing. As in the lag method, the IBNR reserve factor is multiplied by the earned premium to compute the IBNR reserve. This method should only be used when the lag method does not produce a realistic result, and must be applied with caution because in some instances the actual loss ratio already exceeds the target loss ratio—which would result in a negative value in the calculation, but since unreported claims likely exist, an IBNR reserve should still be established.

The tabular method is typically used for long-term disability claims. The tables that support this method, such as the 1964 Commissioners Disability Table (CDT) or the 1987 Commissioners Group Disability Table (CGDT), contain factors that represent the present value of expected remaining claim payments, as determined by continuance probabilities or values of annuities. The factors generally vary by age of disablement, gender, and length of disability as of the valuation date. Regulatory standards establish minimum reserves for such claims. As such, the interest rate used to discount the expected payments may be prescribed by law.

31.3.3 Influences on Claim Reserve Calculations for Long-Term Products

This section identifies the components and conditions that influence the level of reserves that should be established for long-term benefits.

31.3.3.1 Continuance table

The continuance table used depends on the type of benefit for which reserves are to be calculated, and on the type of financial reporting being performed. Thus, continuance tables are different for LTD or LTC products, and may vary for statutory, GAAP or tax reporting, or for management reporting and experience analysis. Continuance tables for LTD benefits often consider gender, age at disability, claim duration, and length of elimination period.

In the United States, the NAIC model law provides that statutory reserves for LTD claims with less than two years' duration may be based on company experience if credible, but that reserves for claims older than two years should generally be based on the 1987 Commissioner's Group Disability Table (1987 CGDT). Continuance tables for LTC reserves are not specified by law because experience varies widely among insurers.

31.3.3.2 Interest rate assumption

Interest rates to be used in statutory reserves are normally specified by law as the maximum interest rate permitted for valuation of whole life insurance contracts. Similarly, interest rates for tax reserves are given by the IRS. For GAAP reserves, which represent companies' best estimates of financial performance and are therefore less conservative than statutory and tax reserves, the assumed rate generally equals the expected rate of return on the investments of the assets backing the reserves.

31.3.3.3 Policy provisions

Certain policy provisions, such as those examined in Section 31.3.1, must be explicitly considered within reserving. These provisions result in adjustments to the benefit amount payable or variations in the amount paid on each day. For example, an in-home therapist may provide services on three days each week. In this scenario, the reserve calculation should reflect actual payment patterns, either by calculating a per-diem average or by exact calculation of benefits payable on each day.

31.3.3.4 Claim expenses

Claim expenses are often expressed as a percentage of claim payments, and thus claim expense reserves are calculated in proportion to the tabular reserves for those claims. Statutory reserving must include claim expense reserves per the NAIC, and GAAP reserves normally include them. However, since these reserves are not tax deductible, the IRS does not require their calculation for tax filing purposes.

31.3.3.5 Diagnosis-based tabular reserves

Conceptually, different disabling conditions exhibit continuance probabilities based on their varying expectations of recovery. For example, a disability claimant with a debilitating chronic condition is less likely to recover than one who suffers a limb fracture or a muscle tear that is expected to heal completely. Though industry standard practice generally computes a reserve based on an aggregate morbidity basis, it is possible to develop different continuance tables that more accurately reflect the likelihood of recovery for various maladies. However, credibility concerns discourage the effort, as does the added complexity, which may not be justified by the gain in accuracy (if that gain exists) and the fact that either the diagnosis-based approach must be used for all claims, or for none of them.

31.3.3.6 Case reserves

Case reserves may be used by LTC insurers for small blocks not considered credible, or for claimants with specific ailments that have a sufficiently large expected payout associated with them. This labor-intensive method involves evaluating individual claimant's medical reports and plan for care, rather than using an aggregate morbidity table.

31.3.3.7 Data validation

Errors in claim data or failure to recognize certain benefit provisions, such as a limited benefit period, can cause far greater errors of scale for long-term benefits than similar errors in data for short-term benefits. Claim data should therefore be regularly audited to ensure that all data is present, member demographics properly identified, all policy provisions correctly captured, and cause of disability and claim status accurately stated.

31.3.4 EXERCISE

31.2 A long-term product includes a cost-of-living adjustment that increases the monthly benefit at a compound rate of 0.25% per month. How would the adjustment be reflected in the calculation shown in Example 31.5?

31.4 Evaluating Claim Reserve Adequacy

Claim reserves must be tested frequently to ensure that they are adequate. This testing is performed by comparing claims payment experience to the reserves established to support those claims. This section describes the two most prevalent methods.

Runoff studies test previous reserve balances—usually by incurral year for beginning and ending reserve dates—against claim payments between the reserve dates. The runoff for each incurral year represents the present value of the payments made between the reserve dates for claims from the given incurral year plus the present value of the ending reserve balance for the given incurral year. The margin for each incurral year then equals the beginning reserve minus the runoff. The results of these studies evaluate the relative strength of reserves for various durations, and allow the insurer to adjust morbidity assumptions as desirable. These studies must be interpreted carefully, however, as positive margins may disguise reserves that become weaker as duration increases.

For long-term disability products, actual to expected (A/E) claim termination rate studies provide additional support for changes to the assumed morbidity basis by claim duration. In this study, the actual claim terminations observed in the exposure base are compared to the expected claim terminations as given by the continuance table used in setting reserves. If the ratio of actual terminations to expected terminations is greater than one, then the reserves are adequate, because the number of claimants continuing on disability would be fewer than the number assumed in the reserve calculation. Similarly, an A/E ratio less than one shows that reserves are inadequate. Preparation of an A/E claim termination rate study should consider the credibility of available data, the types of terminations included (normally, only terminations due to recovery and death are included, because those due to benefit limitation or expiration of the benefit period are not reflected in most morbidity tables), and characteristics of the exposure base that might hint at anomalies within the rates of termination (e.g. a large number of claims for maternity or other short-term disabilities).

31.5 Guidelines and Practice Standards for Reserves

Several of the ASOPs apply to methods and considerations in calculating claim reserves, as do other guidelines produced by professional organizations or trade groups. The following sources offer guidance:

- ASOP 5, "Incurred Health and Disability Claims"
- ASOP 18, "Long-Term Care Insurance"
- ASOP 22, "Statements of Opinion Based on Asset Adequacy Analysis by Actuaries for Life or Health Insurers"
- ASOP 23, "Data Quality"
- ASOP 28, "Compliance with Statutory Statement of Actuarial Opinion Requirements for Hospital, Medical, and Dental Service or Indemnity Corporation, and for Health Maintenance Organizations"
- ASOP 42, "Determining Health and Disability Liabilities Other Than Liabilities for Incurred Claims"
- American Academy of Actuaries Guides to Professional Conduct and Health Practice Notes
- NAIC Health Reserves Guidance Manual, Accounting Practices and Procedures Manual, and other guidelines and model regulations relevant to reserve standards and opinion statements
- NAIC Statements of Statutory Accounting Principles No. 54, "Individual and Group Accident and Health Contracts," and No. 55, "Unpaid Claims, Losses, and Loss Adjustment Expenses"

Textbooks and professional periodicals and literature offer additional topical knowledge. These guidelines require that the methods and assumptions used in the reserve calculation are properly reviewed for appropriateness. Further, the guidelines advise that it is not sufficient to blindly apply calculation results without actuarial analysis and judgment and that proper analysis must be performed to determine the reasonableness and adequacy of reserves calculated by published tables or commercial software. Setting reserves demands informed subjective input in addition to objective claim data.

Bibliography

The Actuarial Profession. (2010). What Does an Actuary Do? http://www.actuaries.org.uk/becoming-actuary/pages/what-does-actuary-do. Accessed December 12, 2010.

Aegon Global Pensions. (2008). Mexico's Pension System: A Work in Progress. http://www.aegonglobalpensions.com/Documents/aegon-global-pensions-com/Publications/Newsletter-archive/2008-Q4/2008-Mexicos-pension-system-a-work-in-progress.pdf. Accessed October 27, 2011.

Allaben, M., Diamantoukos, C., Dicke, A., Gutterman, S., Klugman, S. Lord, R., Luckner, W., Miccolis, R., & Tan, J. (2008). Principles Underlying Actuarial Science., *Actuarial Practice Forum*. July 2008. Available at www.soa.org/library/journals/actuarial-practice-forum/2008/august/apf-2008-08-allaben.pdf, accessed April 7, 2011.

American Council of Life Insurers. (2010). *Life Insurers Fact Book*. Washington, DC.

Anderson, J. (1959). Gross Premium Calculations and Profit Measurement for Nonparticipating Life Insurance. *Transactions of the Society of Actuaries*, XI, 357–394.

Bellis, C. (2004). Actuarial Control Cycle. In Tuegels, J. & Sundt, B., eds. *Encyclopedia of Actuarial Science* (pp. 14–16). Chichester: John Wiley and Sons.

Bellis, C., Lyon, R., Klugman, S. & Shepherd. J., eds. (2010). *Understanding Actuarial Management: The Actuarial Control Cycle*, 2nd ed. Sydney: Institute of Actuaries of Australia.

Bellis, C., Shepherd, J., & Lyon, R., eds. (2003). *Understanding Actuarial Management: The Actuarial Control Cycle*. Sydney: Institute of Actuaries of Australia.

Bernstein, P. (1996). *Against the Gods: The Remarkable Story about Risk*. New York: John Wiley & Sons.

Bozio, A., Crawford, R. & Tetlow, G. (2010). The History of State Pensions in the UK: 1948 to 2010. Economic and Social Research Council Institute for Fiscal Studies Briefing Note BN105. http://www.ifs.org.uk/bns/bn105.pdf. Accessed November 13, 2010.

Brady, P. & Bogdan, M. (2010). Research Perspective: A Look at Private-Sector Retirement Plan Income after ERISA. *Investment Company Institute*, November 2010, Vol. 16, No. 2. http://www.ici.org/pdf/per16-02.pdf. Accessed November 29, 2010.

Brink, S., Modaff, J., & Sherman, S. (1991–92). Variation by Duration in Small Group Medical Insurance Claims. *Transactions of Society of Actuaries Reports*, 1991–92. pp. 333–380.

Callahan, R., Donnelly, V., & McCrossan, W. (2000). *The Purpose of Regulation*, Study Note 5-22-00. Chicago: Society of Actuaries.

Canadian Institute of Actuaries. (2011). Standards of Practice. http://www.asb-cna.ca/. Accessed July 28, 2011.

Canada Department of Finance. (2010). Ensuring the Ongoing Strength of Canada's Retirement Income System. http://www.fin.gc.ca/activty/consult/retirement-eng.asp. Accessed November 16, 2010.

Canadian Life and Health Insurance Association. (2010). *Canadian Life and Health Insurance Facts*, Toronto: Canadian Life and Health Insurance Association.

Carpenter, J. (2000). *Introduction to Financial Security Systems*. Study Note 5-24-00. Chicago: Society of Actuaries.

Casualty Actuarial Society. (2010). About CAS. http://www.casact.org/about. Accessed December 12, 2010.

Chalke, S. (1991). Macro Pricing. *Transactions of the Society of Actuaries*, XLIII, 137–230.

Congressional Budget Office. (2010). Legislative History of IRAs. http://www.cbo.gov/OnlineTaxGuide?Page_2A.htm. Accessed November 24, 2010.

Costello, M. (2002). The Enron Problem. *CNN Money*. http://money.cnn.com/2002/01/29/401k/401k_stock/. Accessed November 7, 2010.

Desaulniers, P., Marin, E., & Maxnuk, A. (2006). Pension plans in Mexico. http://www.mercer.com/print.htm?indContentType=100&idContent=1244510&indBodyType=D&reference=true. Accessed November 16, 2010.

Eadie, S., Hall, D., & Powills, J. (2009). Road to SUCCESS, *The Actuary*, Vol. 6, Issue 3. Also available at http://www.soa.org/library/newsletters/the-actuary-magazine/2009/june/act-2009-vol6-iss3-eadie.aspx, accessed December 15, 2010.

Financial Accounting Standards Board. (2008). Statement of Financial Accounting Standards No. 60. http://www.gasb.org/pdf/aop_FAS60.pdf. Accessed August 20, 2011.

Financial Accounting Standards Board. (2008a). Statement of Financial Accounting Standards No. 97. http://www.gasb.org/pdf/aop_FAS97.pdf. Accessed August 20, 2011.

Goford, J. (1985). The Control Cycle: Financial Control of a Life Assurance Company. *Journal of the Institute of Actuaries Students*' Society, Vol. 28, 99–114.

Graham, B. (2011). 'Strong' Whole, Universal Life Sales Spur Overall Growth, IFAwebnews.com. http://ifawebnews.com/2011/03/01/strong-whole-universal-life-insurance-sales-spur-overall-growth/. Posted March 1, 2011, Accessed May 27, 2011.

Gribble, J. (2006). Unit Pricing, Governance and Control Cycle. *Actuary Australia*, Issue 116, December 2006.

Government Accountability Office. (2003). Physician Workforce: Physician Supply Increased in Metropolitan and Nonmetropolitan Areas but Geographic Disparities Persisted. GAO-04-124. http://www.gao.gov/new.items/d04124.pdf. Accessed April 17, 2011.

Government Accountability Office. (2005). Government Performance and Accountability: Tax Expenditures Represent a Substantial Federal Commitment and Need to be Examined. GAO 05-690. http://www.gao.gov/new.items/d05690.pdf. Accessed December 4, 2010.

Government Accountability Office. (2007). Employer-Sponsored Health and Retirement Benefits; Efforts to Control Employer Costs and the Implications for Workers, GAO-07-35. http://www.gao.gov/new.items/d07355.pdf. Accessed November 14, 2010.

Government Accountability Office. (2009). Private Health Insurance: 2008 Survey Results on Number and Market Share of Carriers in the Small Group Health Insurance Market. http://www.gao.gov/new.items/d09363r.pdf. Accessed April 17, 2011.

Hald, A. (1990). *A History of Probability & Statistics and their Applications before 1750*. New York: John Wiley & Sons.

Hickman, J. (2004). History of Actuarial Profession. In Tuegles, J. & Sundt, B., eds. *Encyclopedia of Actuarial Science* (pp. 838–848.). Chichester: John Wiley and Sons.

Institute of Actuaries of Australia. (2010). Frequently Asked Questions. http://www.actuaries.asn.au/Sitefunctions/faq.aspx. Accessed December 12, 2010.

Insurance Bureau of Canada. (2009). Facts of the General Insurance Industry in Canada. http://www.ibc.ca/en/Need_More_Info/documents/Facts%20book%202009_ENG.pdf. Accessed August 9, 2011.

Insurance Information Institute. (2011). Industry Overview. www.iii.org/media/facts/statsbyissye/industry. Accessed August 3, 2011.

Jennings, R. & Trout, A. (1982). *The Tontine: From the Reign of Louis XIV to the French Revolutionary Era*. Philadelphia: S.S. Huebner Foundation.

Jones, J. (2010). Americans Shift Expectations About Retirement Funding. http://www.gallup.com/poll/127592/americans-shift-expectations-retirement-funding.aspx. Accessed October 1, 2011.

Kellison, S. (2008). *Theory of Interest*, 3rd ed. Boston: McGraw-Hill/Irwin.

Klugman, S., Panjer, H., & Willmot, G. (2008). *Loss Models: From Data to Decisions*, 3rd ed. New York: John Wiley and Sons.

Knox, D. & Lyon, R. (1995). Australians Make Changes in Actuarial Education. *The Actuary*, Vol. 29, No. 8, 6–7.

Kollmann, G. (2000). Social Security: Summary of Major Changes in the Cash Benefits Program. Social Security Administration. http://www.ssa.gov/history/reports/crsleghist2.html. Accessed November 5, 2010.

Laporte, J-P. & Seller, S. (2010). Canada: Pension Reform: Ontario's Bill 236 and Canada's Bill C-9 Are Now Law – Are You Ready? http://www.mondaq.com/canada/article.asp?articleid=114380, Accessed November 16, 2010.

Maruska, D. (2004). *How Great Decisions Get Made: 10 Easy Steps for Reaching Agreement on Even the Toughest Issues*. New York: AMACOM.

McDonnell, K. (2005). Facts from EBRI: The U.S. Retirement Income System. *EBRI Notes*, Vol. 26 No. 4, April 2005.

McGill, D., Brown, K., Haley, J., & Schieber, S. (2010). *Fundamentals of Private Pensions*, 9th edition. New York: Oxford University Press.

Medicine Encyclopedia. (2010). Population Aging—Age Distribution Of A Population. http://medicine.jrank.org/pages/1377/Population-Aging-Age-distribution-population.htm. Accessed September 6, 2010.

Leonhardt, D. (2010). The Social Security Deficit. http://economix.blogs.nytimes.com/2010/11/26/the-social-security-deficit/. Accessed October 1, 2011.

Luenberger, D. (1998). *Investment Science*. New York: Oxford University Press.

Mayhew, L. (2001). A Comparative Analysis of the UK Pension System Including the Views of Ten Pension Experts. http://www.iccr-international.org/pen-ref/docs/penref-d2-uk.pdf. Accessed November 13, 2010.

Mitchell, R. (1974). *From Actuarius to Actuary: The Growth of a Dynamic Profession in Canada and the United States*. Chicago: Society of Actuaries.

Moo, D. (2009). Retirement and Savings Plans in China. Hewitt Associates. http://www.jscpa.or.jp/aniv/pbss/pdf/program/MOO_DavidP.pdf. Accessed October 26, 2011.

OECD. (1998). Working Paper AWP 3.8 Retirement Income Systems for Different economic, Demographic and Political Environments published by the Organization for Economic Co-operation and Development. http://www.oecd.org/dataoecd/21/22/2429016.pdf. Accessed on November 10, 2010.

OECD. (2009). Pensions at a Glance 2009: Retirement Income Systems in OECD Countries: United States. http://www.oecd.org/dataoecd/18/35/43021725.pdf. Accessed November 11, 2010.

OECD. (2009a). Pensions at a Glance 2009: Retirement Income Systems in OECD Countries: France. http://www.oecd.org/dataoecd/27/28/43126248.pdf. Accessed November 11, 2010.

OECD. (2009b). Pensions at a Glance 2009: Retirement Income Systems in OECD Countries: Canada. http://www.oecd.org/dataoecd/41/3/44008042.pdf. Accessed November 11, 2010.

OECD. (2010). OECD Pensions Indicators. http://www.oecd.org/document/16/0,3343,en_2649_34757_45558288_1_1_1_1,00.html. Accessed November 11, 2010.

OECD. (2011). Society at a Glance 2011—OECD Social Indicators. www.oecd.org/els/social/indicators/SAG. Accessed November 30, 2010.

Pension Benefit Guarantee Corporation. (1999). Pension Insurance Data Book 1998. http://www.pbgc.gov/docs/1998databook.pdf. Accessed November 14, 2010.

Pension Benefit Guarantee Corporation. (2009). Pension Insurance Data Book 2008. http://www.pbgc.gov/docs/2008databook.pdf. Accessed November 14, 2010.

Rankin, J. (2003). Should You Go Global? *Resource Magazine*, LOMA, October 2003.

Reid, Terry. (2009). *The Healing of America: A Global Quest for Better, Cheaper and Fairer Health Care*. New York: Penguin.

Scahill, P. & McKay, S. (2002). Introduction to Retirement Income Security Systems. Society of Actuaries Study Note 5-21-02. Chicago: Society of Actuaries.

Service Canada (2010). Canadian Pension Plan Contribution Rates. http://www.servicecanada.gc.ca/eng/isp/cpp/contribrates.shtml. Accessed November 6, 2010.

Service Canada. (2011). Old Age Security (OAS) Payment Rates: April–June 2011. http://www.servicecanada.gc.ca/eng/isp/oas/oasrates.shtml. Accessed April 4, 2011.

Shimek, L. & Wen, Y. (2008). Why Do Chinese Households Save So Much? *International Economic Trends*, August 2008, Federal Reserve Bank of St. Louis.

Society of Actuaries. (2003). Control Cycle Provides Framework for Actuarial Education Redesign. *The Actuary*, Vol. 37, No. 8, 7–8.

Society of Actuaries. (2010). What is an Actuary? http://www.soa.org/about/about-what-is-an-actuary.aspx. Accessed December 12, 2010.

Society of Actuaries. (2010a). Lapse and Mortality Experience of Post-Level Premium Period Term Plans. http://www.soa.org/research/research-projects/life-insurance/research-shock-lapse-report.aspx. Accessed August 17, 2011.

Society of Actuaries. (2011). Competency Framework. http://www.soa.org/professional-development/competency-framework/default.aspx. Accessed August 1, 2011.

Society of Actuaries and LIMRA. (2009). U.S. Individual Life Insurance Persistency. http://www.soa.org/research/experience-study/ind-life/persistency/2004-2005-ind-life-persistency.aspx. Accessed August 17, 2011.

Summerfield, A. (2007). The Control Cycle. *The Actuary*, July, 2000, 28–29.

Sutton, P., Hamilton, B., & Mathews, T. (2011). Recent Decline in Births in the United States, 2007–2009. U.S. Department of Health and Human Services, National Center for Health Statistics, NCHS Data Brief No. 60, March 2011. http://www.cdc.gov/nchs/data/databriefs/db60.pdf. Accessed April 17, 2011.

United Nations Secretariat. (2005). The Diversity of Changing Population Age Structures in the World, Population Division, Department of Economic and Social Affairs. http://www.un.org/esa/population/meetings/EGMPopAge/1_UNPD_Trends.pdf. Accessed November 30, 2010.

U.S. Bureau of Labor Statistics. (2009). National Compensation Survey: Employee Benefits in the United States, Bulletin 2731. http://www.bls.gov/ncs/ebs/benefits/2009/ebbl0044.pdf. Accessed November 14, 2010.

U.S. Census Bureau. (2011). Health Insurance Historical Tables. http://www.census.gov/hhes/www/hlthins/data/historical/index.html. Accessed April 17, 2011.

U.S. Department of Agriculture. (2011). State Fact Sheets: United States. http://www.ers.usda.gov/statefacts/us.htm. Accessed April 17, 2011.

U.S. Department of Health and Human Services. (2007). Growing Older in America: The Health & Retirement Study. http://hrsonline.isr.umich.edu/sitedocs/databook/HRS_Text_WEB.pdf. Accessed November 10, 2010.

U.S. Department of Health and Human Services. (2010). United States Life Tables 2006. National Vital Statistics Reports, Vol. 58, No. 21. http://www.cdc.gov/nchs/data/nvsr/nvsr58/nvsr58_21.pdf. Accessed November 12, 2010.

U.S. Department of Labor, Bureau of Labor Statistics. (2011). Career Guide to Industries 2010–11 Edition. www.bls.gov/oco/cg/cgs028.htm. Accessed April 6, 2011.

U.S. Department of Labor. (1997). Working Group on the Merits of Defined Contribution vs Defined Benefit Plans with an Emphasis on Small Business Concerns. http://www.dol.gov/ebsa/publications/dbvsdc.htm. Accessed November 13, 2010.

U.S. Department of the Treasury. (2011). Daily Treasury Yield Curve Rates. http://www.treasury.gov/resource-center/data-chart-center/interest-rates/Pages/TextView.aspx?data=yield. Accessed March 14, 2011.

Van Der Bij, L. (2010). Bill 236—First Stage of Ontario Pension Reform—Receives Royal Assent. http://www.pensionsbenefitslaw.com/2010/05/articles/another-category/bill-236-first-stage-of-ontario-pension-reform-receives-royal-assent/. Accessed November 16, 2010.

Van Der Bij, L. (2010a). New Brunswick to Study Pension Reform. http://www.pensionsbenefitslaw.com/2010/11/articles/another-category/new-brunswick-to-study-pension-reform/. Accessed November 16, 2010.

Wang, D. (2005). China's Urban and Rural Old Age Security System: Challenges and Options. Institute of Population and Labor Economics, Chinese Academy of Social Sciences, Working Paper Series No. 53. http://iple.cass.cn/file/53.pdf. Accessed December 4, 2010.

Wentworth, S. & Pattison, D. (2002). Income Growth and Future Poverty Rates of the Aged. Social Security Bulletin, Vol. 64, No. 3. http://www.ssa.gov/policy/docs/ssb/v64n3p23.html. Accessed November 9, 2010.

World Bank. (1994). Averting the Old Age Crisis, A World Bank Policy Research Report. New York: Oxford University Press.

World Heath Organization. (2000). Health Systems: Improving Performance, The World Health Report 2000. http://www.who.int/whr/2000/en/whr00_en.pdf. Accessed April 17, 2011.

Index